CAD COMPANION WORKBOOK FOR 2D and 3D CAD and Intro to Civil Engineering for MicroStation® and AutoCAD®

Second Edition

Michael D. Jue, P.E.

Previously Titled: **CAD Companion Workbook for Civil Engineering CAD I for MicroStation®**

Images on pages cover, 1, 3, 20, 24, , 25, 29-36, 39-40, 42-48, 50, 53-62, 73-77, 80, 88–96, 100-106, 108–110, 115, 116–125, 128, 131- 133, 145–151, 154–164, 169, 171-177, 181-182, 185, 189, 193–200, 212–213, 222, © Bentley Systems, Inc.

Images on pages cover, 1, 3, 118, 130, 167, 216-217, 219, 303, 305-311, 314, 327-331, 339-341 AutoCAD® is a registered trademark of Autodesk, Inc. Autodesk screen shots reprinted courtesy of Autodesk, Inc.

Cover images © Shutterstock.com

www.kendallhunt.com
Send all inquiries to:
4050 Westmark Drive
Dubuque, IA 52004-1840

PAK ISBN 978-1-7924-8556-5
Text ISBN: 978-1-7924-8557-2

Published in the United States of America

TRADEMARKS

MicroStation® is a registered trademark of Bentley Systems, Inc. Intergraph is a registered trademark and IGDS is a trademark of Intergraph Corporation. AutoCAD® is a registered trademark of Autodesk, Inc. Additional products and services mentioned in this book are the trademarks or registered trademarks of their respective owners. The author does not make any claims to these marks.

ACKNOWLEDGEMENTS

I would like to thank Vicki for all the great help and her great patience and Gina and David for putting up with the time away from them. I would like to thank Dr. Xudong Jia, Chair, Civil Engineering Department and everyone in the CE department at Cal Poly Pomona for their tireless efforts.

WARNING AND DISCLAIMER

The author has made every effort to make the information provided accurate for the versions of the software covered; however, no warranty with respect to accuracy or completeness is implied. The information is provided on an "as-is" basis. In no event shall the publisher or author be liable to anyone for special, collateral, incidental, or consequential damages in connection with or arising out of the use of this material.

INTENDED USE

This material is intended to be presented by an instructor to students enrolled in an Engineering curriculum needing an introduction to Civil Engineering and training in CAD software usage.

About the Author

Michael Jue has been involved with CAD since 1985. He received many Intergraph training classes covering basic IGDS graphics through VAX 11-751 system management up to UNIX and MicroStation PC usage. He also received AutoDesk's AutoCAD, Inventor and SDRC's Pro-Engineer and SolidWorks training. He has used and taught all of these products over the years.

> *Mr. Jue's first actual involvement with a computer "plotted" drawing was in 1976 (nearly 45 years ago). He had to produce punch cards that were run through a mainframe computer that was connected to a "drum" plotter that plotted out a circle. The activity was completed after 7 days!*

In Rockwell International's, Facilities and Industrial Engineering group in Anaheim, he quickly became known as the one who could take the training classes and be able to redeliver the training to the rest of the troops while maintaining the highest level of patience. As application manager and CAD system administrator he implemented and developed many of the standards for use in production and maintenance of the many drawings required. He created many short-cut menus and UNIX programs to automate drawing production and assist users.

His duties as CAD administrator were only part-time with most of his time spent as a Mechanical design engineer and actual CAD user. This is where he gained his most extensive experience with the workings of CAD. He learned AutoCAD along the way and began developing a CAD study program for students at California State University at Fullerton in 1994. By 1995 he was the instructor for most of the CAD classes in their CAD/CAM certificate program. He has also been teaching MicroStation for Cal Poly Pomona's Civil Engineering department and AutoCAD for Mt SAC's Physics and Engineering department since 2002.

Mr. Jue continues to work in a top-tier semiconductor manufacturing firm in California and has taught over four thousand students in both AutoCAD and MicroStation and other Autodesk and Bentley Systems products at the college level. His duties as a Mechanical Engineer and Energy Management specialist still require use of CAD on a nearly daily basis.

Mr. Jue received his Bachelor of Science in Engineering (major in Mechanical) from the University of California at Irvine and is a registered Professional Engineer in the state of California for both Control System Engineering and Mechanical Engineering. He can be contacted via e-mail at mdjue@cpp.edu.

Future plans call for more revisions to the CAD course books and a continued interest in his favorite diversions which include filmmaking, screenwriting and comedy.

How to Use This Material

The student will benefit by understanding the following about this material:

This material is ***not*** intended as a replacement to the software manuals. It is ***not*** intended as a reference guide for all the options of all commands.

It is intended to be presented in a classroom situation for Engineering students or practicing Engineers by an instructor experienced in using the products. It may be suitable for those intending to become full-time draftsmen, but that is not the intended audience. Note, this class is not titled, CAD for Draftsmen.

> *Some courses may not provide face-to-face instruction in a classroom situation, ie. a course taught via distance learning. Please note: There are many video lessons accessible, provided with this text (see back of the front cover) and within the MicroStation CONNECT Edition product, itself. All students are encouraged to view these additional materials.*

Becoming skillful enough at CAD to make it useful to you will require ***"on the job practice"*** beyond the time limitations of the class in which you are enrolled. In the short duration of this class, the ***most important features*** of CAD will be taught to you. You should be able to come away from this class with the ability to perform most of the basic functions, ***easily***. And, hopefully, to be able to perform some of the more moderately difficult functions with a little practice.

This class will attempt to give you the ***best possible footing for advancing in CAD***. It will identify the areas in which to concentrate for the fastest possible learning. It will show you how practicing engineers and operators ***really use*** the products. The examples and exercises that the instructor will show and have you practice are ones specifically designed to provide training in the areas considered ***essential. DO THE EXERCISES AND PRACTICE LABS!***

It is very highly recommended that you get as much <u>additional</u> practice as is possible with your employer or at your own computer. It is further encouraged that you complete the advanced CAD courses following this introductory course. ***Enrolling in this class will allow you to purchase some educational versions of the software at discounted prices. Having your own software at home to practice on is the best way to practice!***

One of the biggest advantages of this class over many others is that the ***methods shown are the ones actually being used.*** CAD is used throughout the industry today because it provides tremendous efficiencies and is very cost effective versus manual drafting when used by **"*trained*"** operators. The majority of ***Engineering students become gainfully employed performing very satisfying work***, requiring the very CAD skills you are about to be receive training in. Getting CAD skills is both fun ***and*** rewarding!

With this said, Ladies and Gentlemen, ***"Start your Computers!"***

Special Notes: Software

In this text, **MicroStation V8*i*** will be on the **left** or **top**. **CONNECT Edition** will be shown on right or bottom. A Lime Green outline may denote **CONNECT Edition**.

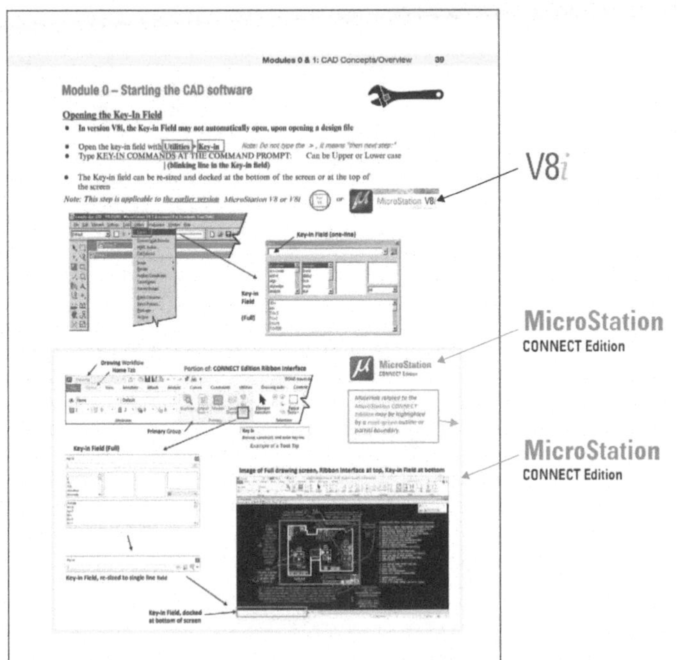

Figure 1. Example V8i top, CONNECT Ed. bottom

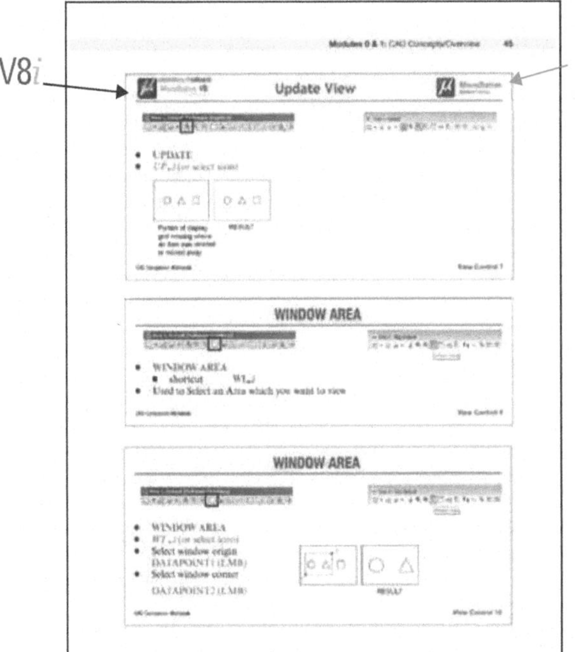

Figure 2. Example V8i left, CONNECT Ed. right

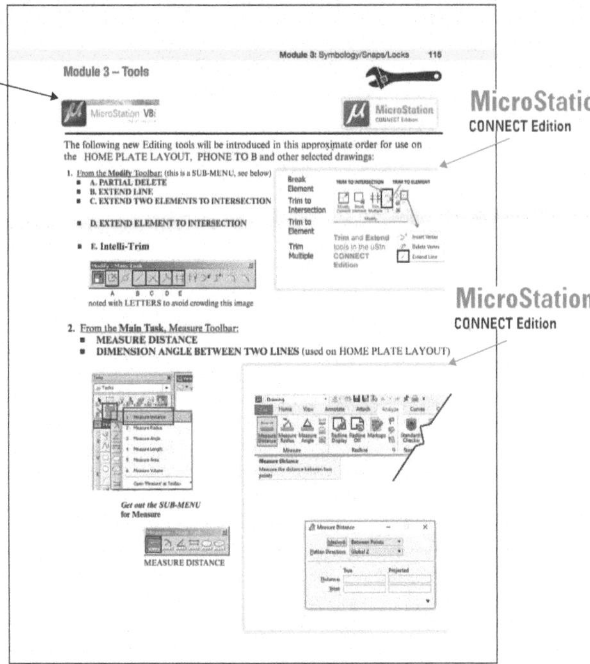

Figure 3. Example CONNECT Ed. in Lime Green

In this text, **AutoCAD** may be noted by the **AutoCAD logo**. This will mainly be in **Appendix B** and **C**. See Figure 4, below.

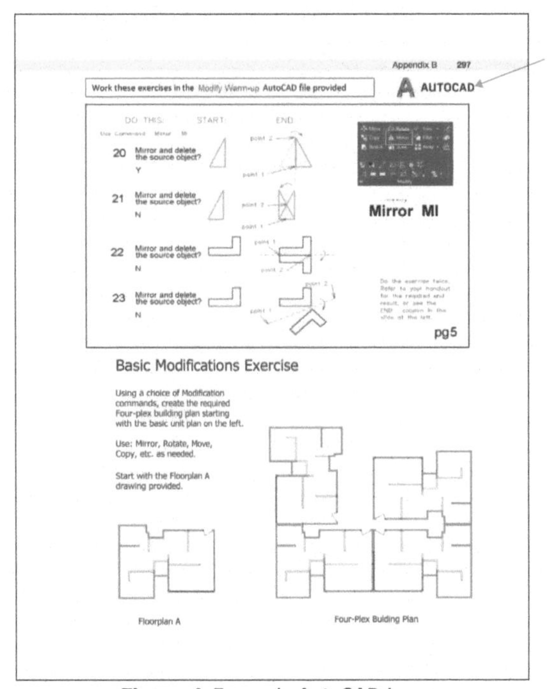

Figure 4. Example AutoCAD logo

Concept – Discussion on Learning CAD Skills

CAD Knowledge vs. CAD Skills

Learning CAD can be divided into two categories of education: **gaining knowledge** and **gaining skills**. The more important part of learning CAD is the gaining of skills by the new CAD user.

- **The knowledge part** of learning CAD can be accomplished by reading a text, listening to the instructor and watching the presentations in a classroom. *Most students are usually very well acquainted with this type of learning by this stage in their education.*
- **The skills part** is entirely gained by the student when he or she **actually operates the CAD system**, spends time pushing the mouse around, keys in commands, watches the screen and becomes familiar with the way the CAD reacts to the users inputs. This takes actual **practice time**, working on drawing exercises, making mistakes and recognizing how to correct them. *Some students may find this active involvement in learning new skills to be challenging. Please note, the skills portion CANNOT be easily gained from reading a text or listening to a lecture!*

How can one best understand the difference between these two types of learning activities? Let's illustrate by talking about two other activities that are also heavily biased toward gaining skills as opposed to gaining knowledge.

Student Discussion:

1. What mostly influences the ability to **Parallel Park** a car? **Knowledge or Skills?**
   Think about this. **Did you learn to parallel park by reading a book?** Or, did you learn to parallel park by actually taking the car out onto the road, out to the curb and learn to turn the wheel on your own and moving forwards and backwards as needed to fit into the space without crunching the cars ahead of and behind you? What good is *knowing* about parallel parking while not knowing how to do it?
2. What mostly influences the ability to **Snowboard** down a slope skillfully? **Knowledge or Skills?**
   Think about this. **Does someone learn to snowboard by reading a book?** Or, did the learning take place by actually strapping on the board, going down the slope, experiencing the wind in the face, falling down more times than you can count and then doing it all again?

CAD Skills are to be learned by the student

So it is with CAD … to gain the skills part of CAD, one must actually push the mouse around, hit the right and left mouse buttons, see what happens on the screen when the wrong command is selected, make the mistakes and learn from them. This takes time! There is no substitute for this and cramming for CAD practice time makes as much sense as cramming to learn parallel parking or snowboarding. The CAD concepts are not complicated when compared to Chemistry or Math.

Conclusion/Practical application:

Work thru the CAD exercises or homework assignments. Become familiar with each new concept, command or tool being utilized. Work it again, if you are unfamiliar with the commands. Get help if you need more assistance. Spend time on the computer or in the lab doing CAD work. Also take advantage of the video lessons and intro materials discussed below!

On-line Video Lessons included with this Text

On the inside of the front cover, see info for logging onto the khpcontent.com website to access this text's included **On-line content**.

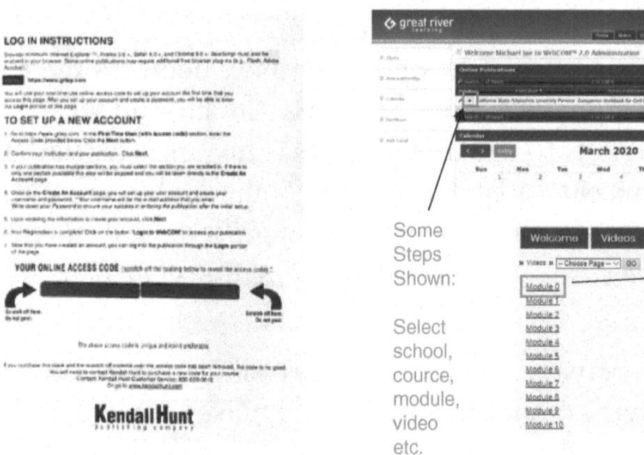

Inside of the front cover

Modules

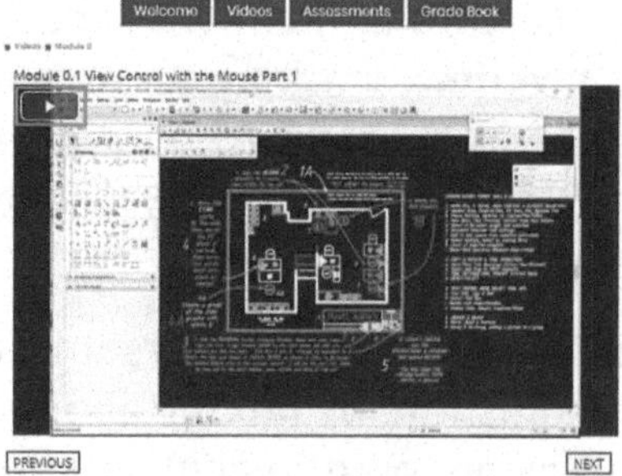

Beginning of Video Lesson sample

Intro to MicroStation CONNECT Edition Videos (in the product)

Note: In CONNECT Edition Update 13 and on, the sample drawings and videos are in the Help function.

The Welcome Page has some very informative **Videos** introducing the MicroStation CONNECT Edition.

The first one introduces itself and the Ribbon Interface.

Start with it!

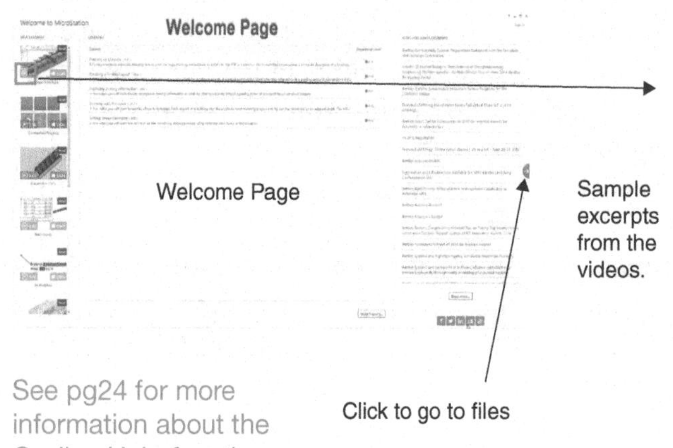

See pg24 for more information about the On-line Help function.

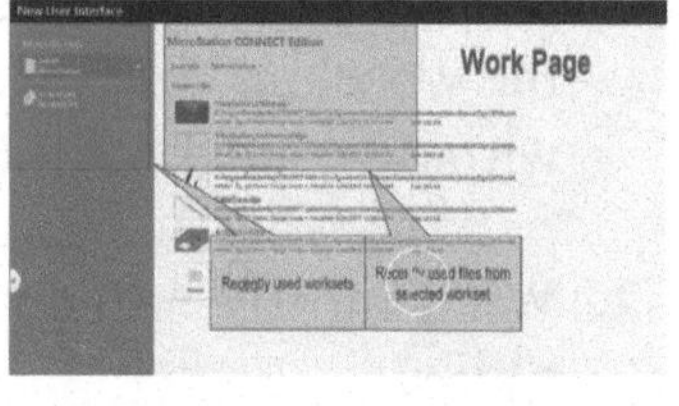

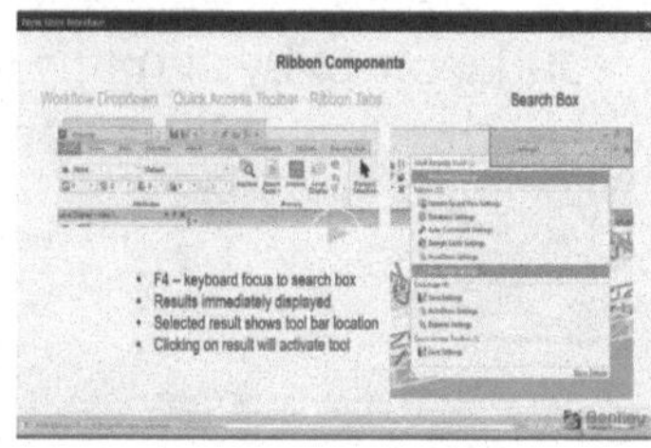

Generic Syllabus *mm/dd/yy* – CE nnn/L, Section nn

Civil Engineering CAD I / II, Design and Lab

MEETING TIMES: DD: hh:mm pm - hh:mm pm (Lecture), Room 17-nnnn

DD: hh:mm pm - hh:mm pm. (Lab), Room 17-nnnn

Course: CE nnn /L, section n, CRN nnnnn & nnnnn INSTRUCTOR: Mr. Michael D. Jue, P.E. OFFICE HOURS: DD hh:mm pm-hh:mm pm *Office xx-xxx /(also check Lab room)* **Attendance will be taken each class*	EVALUATION Attendance 10% & Quizzes 15% — 25% 1 midterm (written & drawing) exam — 25% Project & HW Assignments — 20% Final (written & drawing) exam — 30% TOTAL — **100%**

CPP wk#	MTG #	Date	Module#	Description
1	1	3-Apr	0	Intro to CAD. Student computer accounts--Basic tools and view control. Element Selection, element attributes and display control. Getting help.
1L		3-Apr	1	University Academic Integrity policy, Exercises, Intro HW1 & written assign't
2	2	10-Apr	2	Place Line, Basic edits, Precision Input, Working units,
2L		10-Apr	2	Placing linear elements. **written assignment due**
3	3	17-Apr	2	The manipulate toolbox, the modify toolbox. **HW 1 due**
3L		17-Apr	3	Locks, Snaps, Attributes, Levels. Intro HW 2.
4	4	24-Apr	3	Change symbology of elements, Fences
4L		24-Apr	3	Intro to Text, AccuDraw,
5	5	1-May	4	Place and Manipulate Text, **HW 2 due**
5L		1-May	0-4	Measurement tools, Coordinate Read-out. Intro HW 3
6	6	8-May	4	Grouping/Complex Elements, More Text Tools,
6L		8-May	4/5	**MID-TERM TEST**
7	7	15-May	5/6	Dimensioning, Bearing Angular Expression,
7L		15-May	6	Exercises, Intro HW 4 **HW 3 due**
8	8	22-May	6	Misc. Addl' Topics
8L		22-May	6/7	Cells, Introduction to Final Project
9	9	29-May	7	Cont' Cells, Patterning, Reference Files.
9L		29-May	8	Final project -- begin drawings, Intro to 3D **HW 4 due**
10	10	5-Jun	9	3D Exercises, Raster Images
10L		5-Jun	9	Final Project
Finals Wk		13-Jun	0-10	**Final Exam and Student Final Project 100% due**

ACADEMIC INTEGRITY POLICY:
Cheating on any aspect of this course is not tolerated. The use of any previous quarter's (or other class section's) drawings, quizzes, exams or other materials is expressly NOT permitted. See the University and College of Engineering's policy at: http://www.csupomona.edu/~engineering/current/integrity.htm and at http://www.dsa.csupomona.edu/judicialaffairs/academicintegrity.asp

FINAL Exam & Final Project Submission:
Final Exam covers the entire course material, scheduled on Month DD, YYYY, h:mm pm-h:mm pm, Bldg/Rm nn/nnnn The Student's Final Project 100% submission (assigned since week 8) is also due at the end of the Final Exam period.

COURSE MATERIALS:
Required: **CAD Companion Workbook**
Additional references: "Help" documentation within the CAD software, MicroStation User's Manual

INSTRUCTOR'S CONTACTS: Email: mdjue@cpp.edu
Office nn-nnn/(also check Lab room). Phone (909) 869-2488 campus

Contents by Study Topic

Table of Contents

Introduction

2D and 3D CAD and Intro to Civil Engineering

MicroStation® V8*i*

MicroStation
CONNECT Edition

AUTOCAD®

and
Introduction to Civil Engineering

Michael D. Jue, P.E.

1.1

© Monstar/Shutterstock.com. Adapted by Michael D. Jue.

Typical Session 1 & Lab

- 20 min Preliminaries/Prerequisites
- 30 min **Overview/Basic Concepts**
  - The Look and Feel of MicroStation
  - Graphical User Interface, Operations, View Control
- End Lecture/break
- 80 min Intro Basic Elements & Manipulations, Exercises
- 10 min Break
- 80 min Continue Lab/HW exercises
- End Lab

1.2

© Gorodenkoff/Shutterstock.com

© Gorodenkoff/Shutterstock.com

Course Outline – Modules

- Mod 0 – Introduction, Basic Concepts, Starting Off, View Control
- Mod 1 – Basic Element Placement, Editing & Precision Graphics
- Mod 2 – Manipulation & Modification
- Mod 3 – Locks, Snaps, Symbology & Grouping
- Mod 4 – Element Selection, Fences, Text Placement and Manipulation

1.3

Course Outline – Modules

- Mod 5 – Data Fields, Measurements & Dimensions
- Mod 6 – Bearing Angles, Multi-lines, AccuDraw
- Mod 7 – Reference Files, Cells & Patterning & 3D

The above may differ from term to term.

1.4

Session 1 Objectives

1. **Receive Preliminary Information and an Introduction to the Class.** ***(What this class is all about)***
2. **Receive an Overview of CAD & General Concepts.**
3. **Get training and practice with MicroStation's Graphical User Interface (GUI) and basic operations.**
4. **Open files and learn Viewing commands and mouse and keyboard usage to activate commands.**
5. **Work on lab assignments, get reading assignment**

1.5

Preliminaries

Please refer to the course material provided by your instructor for the following:

- Course: ______________________________
- Course Numbers: ______________________________
- Location: ______________________________
- Attendance: ______________________________
- In-Class: ______________________________
- Grades: ______________________________

1.6

Some Icons you may see

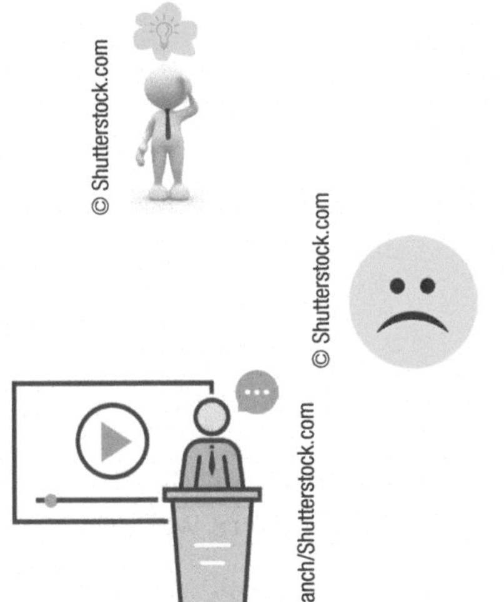

An Important Note: This information is important for you to consider and remember. Generally worth some extra thought or effort to think about.

Unfortunate: Some type of bad news. Used to indicate a feature hard to use, something rarely used but necessary or some other concept or matter that the author may have low opinion of.

Video Lesson: Indicates that an instructor guided video lesson may be available that provides expanded or detailed coverage of a topic or drawing exercise. Please see page xii and the inside front cover for more information.

For V8: This indicates that the procedure or concept shown applies specifically to MicroStation *V8* (an earlier version of *V8i*)

For V8*i*: Applies to MicroStation V8*i*, the version preceding MicroStation CONNECT Edition. V8*i* may still be widely used by employers and at educational institutions.

For CONNECT Edition: Applies to MicroStation CONNECT Edition, the most current version of MicroStation as of this text's printing. V8*i* users may be in the process of converting over to the CONNECT Edition version.

For AutoCAD: Applies to commands and concepts using AutoCAD software.

1.7

Some Icons you may see

© Shutterstock.com

Useful Tip: This symbol indicates information especially useful to the CAD student regarding concepts, commands or procedures.

© Shutterstock.com

Warning! This symbol indicates Dangerous commands or Powerful commands. Best to think about what you are doing here. Not necessarily discouraging their use, however.

© Shutterstock.com

For Advanced Users: This fellow usually indicates extra credit exercises for those students advancing along ahead of the pack.

1.8

Prerequisites

Please refer to your institution's requirements for the course you are taking.
You may also refer to your class syllabus for more information.

- Previous CAD experience is not required
- PC or MAC/Other and **Mouse** usage needed
- Familiarity with Drafting is advantageous
- What to do if you lack PC/MAC/Computer skills ... Get outside help & practice
- A **minimum level of proficiency** will be required ... we will not make others wait

1.9

Notes Regarding Computer & OS

- Engineering offices and engineering schools operating professional or academic versions of either **MicroStation** or **AutoCAD** software, typically utilize the "**Win-tel**" configuration of computers and OS (**Windows** and **Intel**-based computing).

  Apple MAC users may wish to run the Windows-only based **MicroStation** software using **"Bootcamp"** software. It allows both **Window 10** and your native **MAC OS** to run on: *MacBook, MacBook Air, MacBook Pro, Mac mini, iMac, iMac Pro, Mac Pro* and possibly other newer Apple products.

  See more details in the following link (or Google **"Bootcamp for MAC"**)
  https://support.apple.com/en-us/HT201468

  Please see the following link if you wish to load **AutoCAD** on your MAC:
  https://www.autodesk.com/education/edu-software/overview

1.10

About This Class

- Basic exercises required for all
- Advanced students can work on **additional advanced exercises**
- **Practice outside of class is encouraged**
- A PC lab may be available or other facility. Please check with your instructor.
- **Educational Copies** may be available and are **HIGHLY RECOMMENDED!**
  https://education.bentley.com/ for MicroStation software
  https://www.autodesk.com/education/home for AutoCAD software

1.11

About Exercises & HW

- There will be two types of exercises
- Type 1: **Sample exercises**
  - Show how a concept works – single TOOL
  - These are very simple and brief
- Type 2: **Homework exercises**
  - Show their application in a real drawing
  - Require MULTIPLE TOOLS
  - More Realistic and taken from real-life projects
- Sample Exercises are not turned in, but homework (HW) assignments *are* turned in

1.12

HW summary List

Note: Potential HW drawings. The instructor will provide up-to-date assignments in class. This is just an "example" listing

HW 1	Travel, Orgchart, Warm-ups
HW 2	Precision, Tub, Shower, Tank Farm,
HW 3	Layout/Jet Port, Home Plate Layout, Phone to B
HW 4	Theater, Phone to E, TBD
HW 5	Phone to F, Dimensioned HW2 & 3
HW 6	Traverse/Cul-de-Sac, TBD
Project	Final Project drawings 25% & 100%

1.13

Various Add'l Drawings

- The Instructor may choose from many additional drawings for the HW assignments, depending on the emphasis of the particular course.
- Many Extra Credit drawing assignments will also be available.
- Sample Exam problems may be shown during the course.

1.14

About Session 1

- This session #1 is unlike the following ones since we are covering some preliminaries and other introductions, prerequisites and the like which cannot be skipped.
- The latter part of this session and all of the following sessions will concentrate on "HANDS-ON" CAD usage!

1.15

How the Class will Go

- Review of last week's material, if req'd / Q & A
- Intro to Concepts/Commands/Tools using these slides and demonstration on the PC
- At times, follow along material in the text
- Students follow along on their PCs
- Work on Lab Exercises, instructor assists
- Complete review quiz by the next session
- Complete assigned reading by next session

☺ Get Practice!

1.16

Goals of this Course

- Understanding CAD Fundamentals
  - Make CAD Work for You, Easier
- Proper Usage of the CAD program
  - Specific Topics, Basic Skills to Advanced Tricks
- Show you the Basics of MicroStation 2D & 3D
- Provide the Prerequisites for CE courses
  - Provide the foundations to build on

1.17

Goals of this Course

- Learn how to Get Your Work Done Faster
- Shortening Your Learning Curve
- Give you "Hands On" experience
- Emphasis on what's Most Useful to users
- Provide information for further learning such as other texts, best methods to advance, etc..
- Guidance for access to on-line video lessons included with this text and to the ones included within the CONNECT Edition product.

1.18

NOT Covered in this Class

- Basic PC Skills
- **ALL** Commands in **V8*i*** and CONNECT Edition **are NOT covered**
- Every Option of every Command
- Hardware considerations & configurations
- Customization and programming
- Third-party add-on products

1.19

Student Survey

- What Experience do You have?
- New to PC's & Computers?
- Will you be using a Desktop PC, Laptop, Tablet (w/Touch-screen)?
- Using Windows / DOS / UNIX / MAC?
- Other CAD products? **(AutoCAD, VersaCad, CADAM)**
- Other graphic software? **(Paintbrush, Visio, Photoshop)**

1.20

Survey of Attendants

- How Long using any CAD? **# of Yrs/Mo**
- How many CAD Drawing hours?
  - 0–80, 80–200, 200+? **Your Skill Level is ?**
- Had **Formal MicroStation/ACAD Classes?**

1.21

Example Drawing Images

On the following pages:

1. **LAYOUT FOR A TRAVEL AGENCY**
2. **DEVELOPMENT OF A CORDLESS PHONE**
3. **HOTEL, THEATER AND SHOPPING COMPLEX**
4. **INDUSTRIAL SEMICONDUCTOR PLAN**
5. **WIRE FRAME IMAGES - Samples**
6. **Three-Building Complex in "2D"**
7. **3D Buildings Exercise seen in V8i**
8. **3D Buildings sample finished image**
9. **CULDESAC seen in MicroStation CONNECT Edition**
10. **3D Rendering of a Small Airport**

1.22

Example Drawing Notes

- We will be modifying the TRAVEL AGENCY drawing in an upcoming exercise.
- We will be drawing all the PHONE series drawings.
- We will be modifying and adding to portions of the THEATER drawing.
- We will examine drawings when we introduce 3-D, time allowing.
- Many ADDITIONAL exercises, not shown here, will be available for practice on, also.

1.23

1. LAYOUT FOR A TRAVEL AGENCY

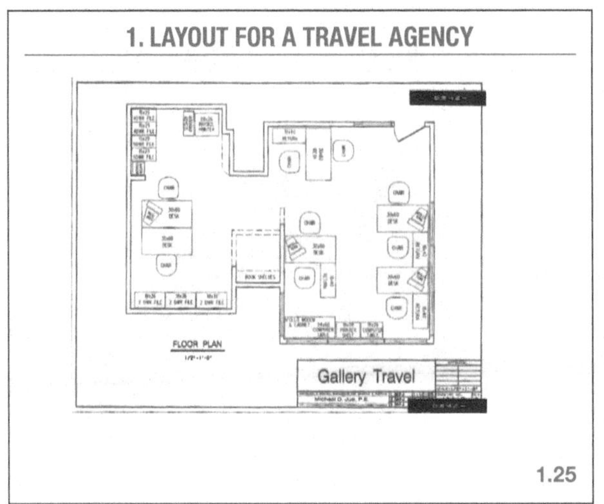

1.25

2. DEVELOPMENT OF A CORDLESS PHONE

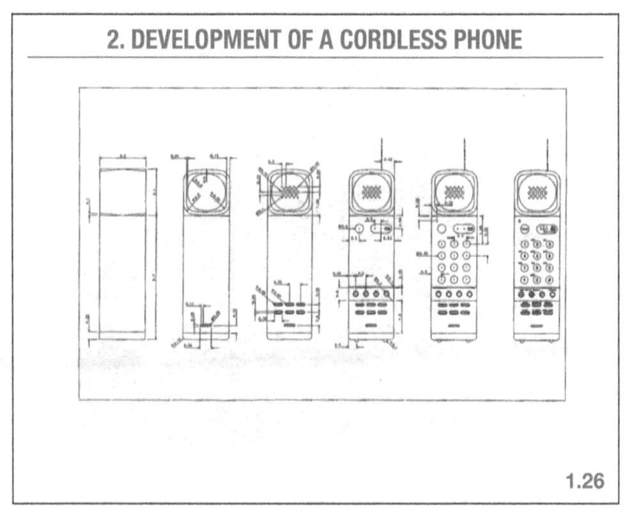

1.26

3. HOTEL, THEATER AND SHOPPING COMPLEX

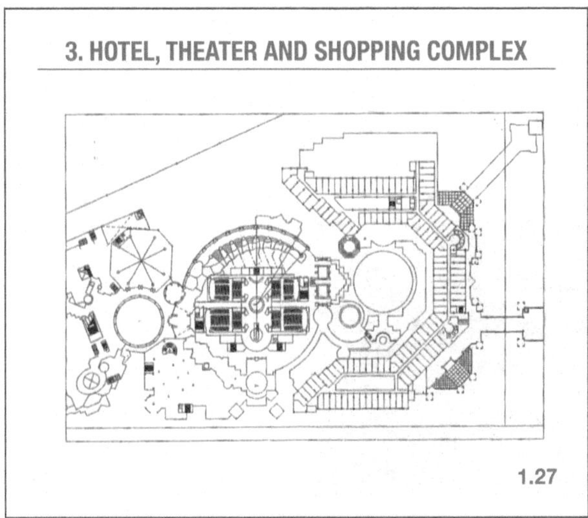

1.27

4. INDUSTRIAL SEMICONDUCTOR FACTORY PLAN

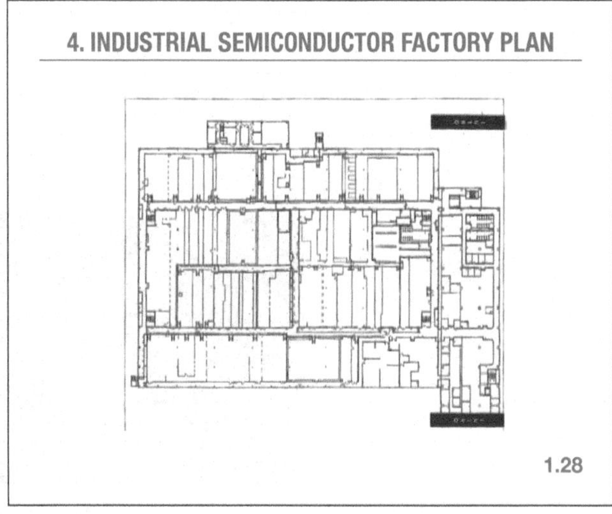

1.28

5. WIRE FRAME IMAGES - Samples

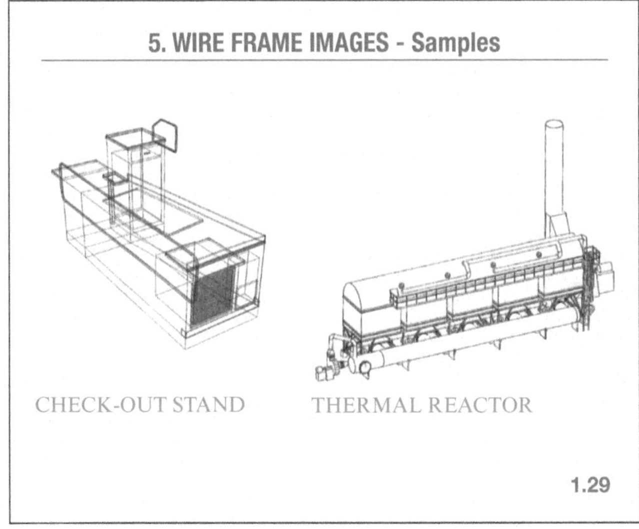

1.29

6. 3-Building Complex in "2D"

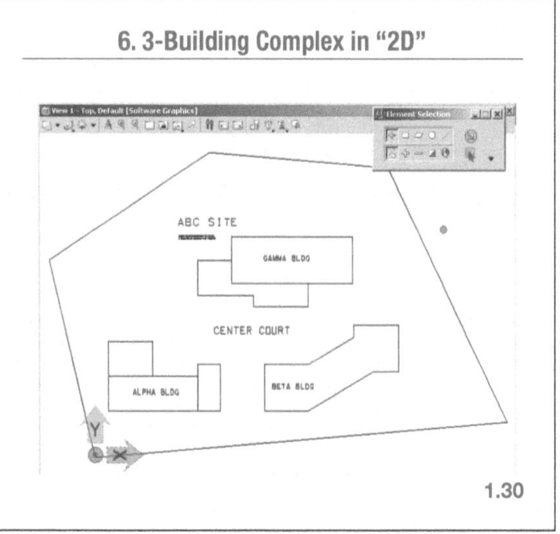

1.30

7. 3D Buildings Exercise seen in V8i

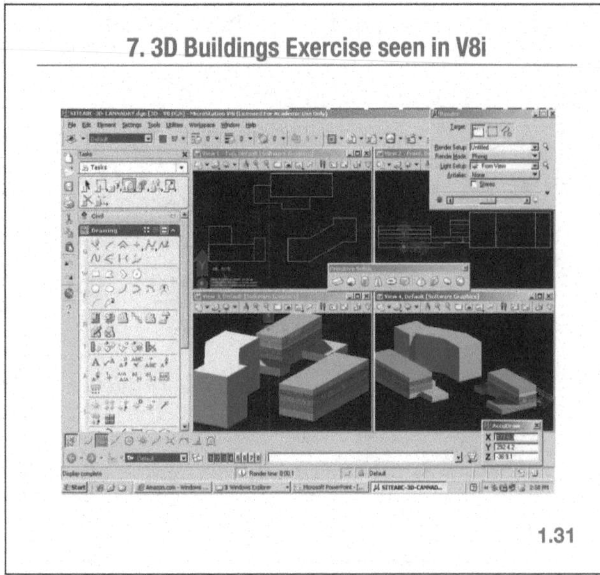

1.31

8. 3D Buildings sample finished image

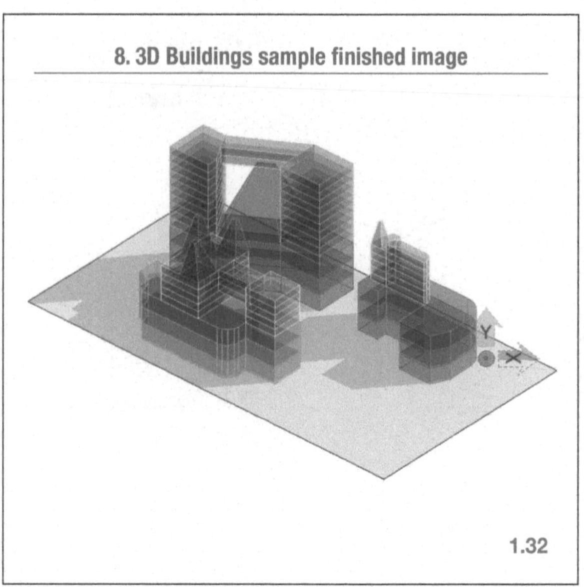

1.32

9. CULDESAC seen in MicroStation CONNECT Edition

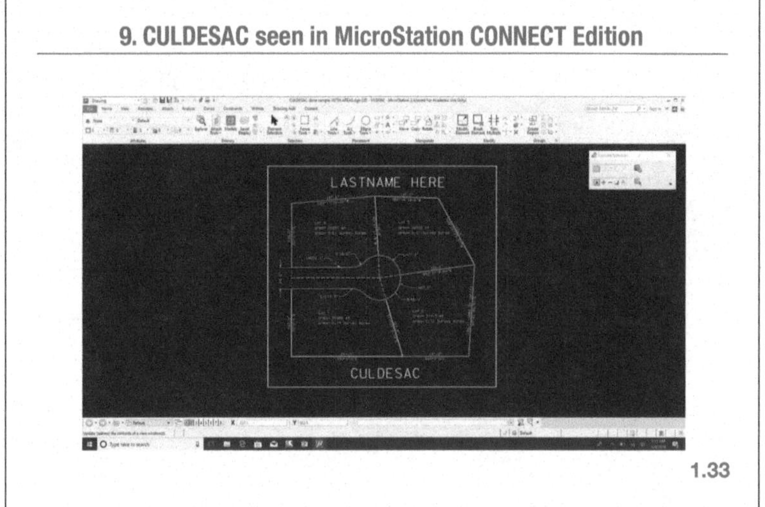

1.33

10. 3D Rendering of a Proposed Small Airport

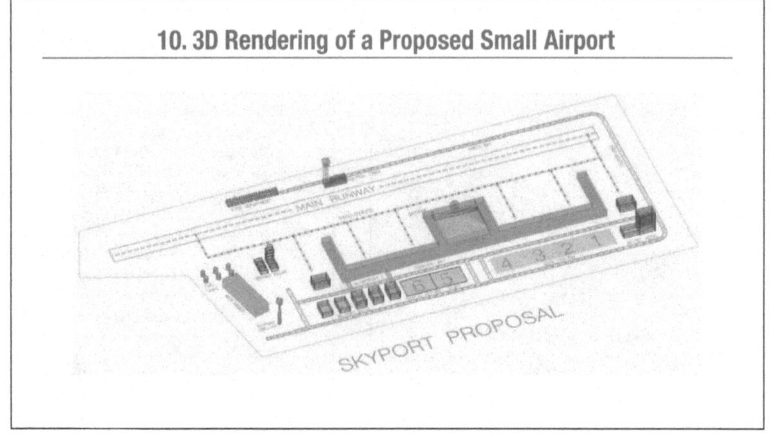

Intro to Civil Engineering

Engineering Drawings Basics 1

Drawing Sheet Basics
Common Sheet sizes:

English – ANSI std
A 8.5x11"
B 11x17" or alt. 12x18"
C 17x22" or alt. 18x24"
D 22x34" or alt. 24x36"
E 34x44" or alt. 36x48"
(alt. or custom sizes may exist in CAD plotting software)

Metric - ISO 216 std
A4 210x297mm 8.3x11.7"
A3 297x420mm 11.7x16.5"
A2 420x594mm 16.5x23.4"
A1 594x841mm 23.4x33.1"
A0 841x1189mm 33.1x46.8"

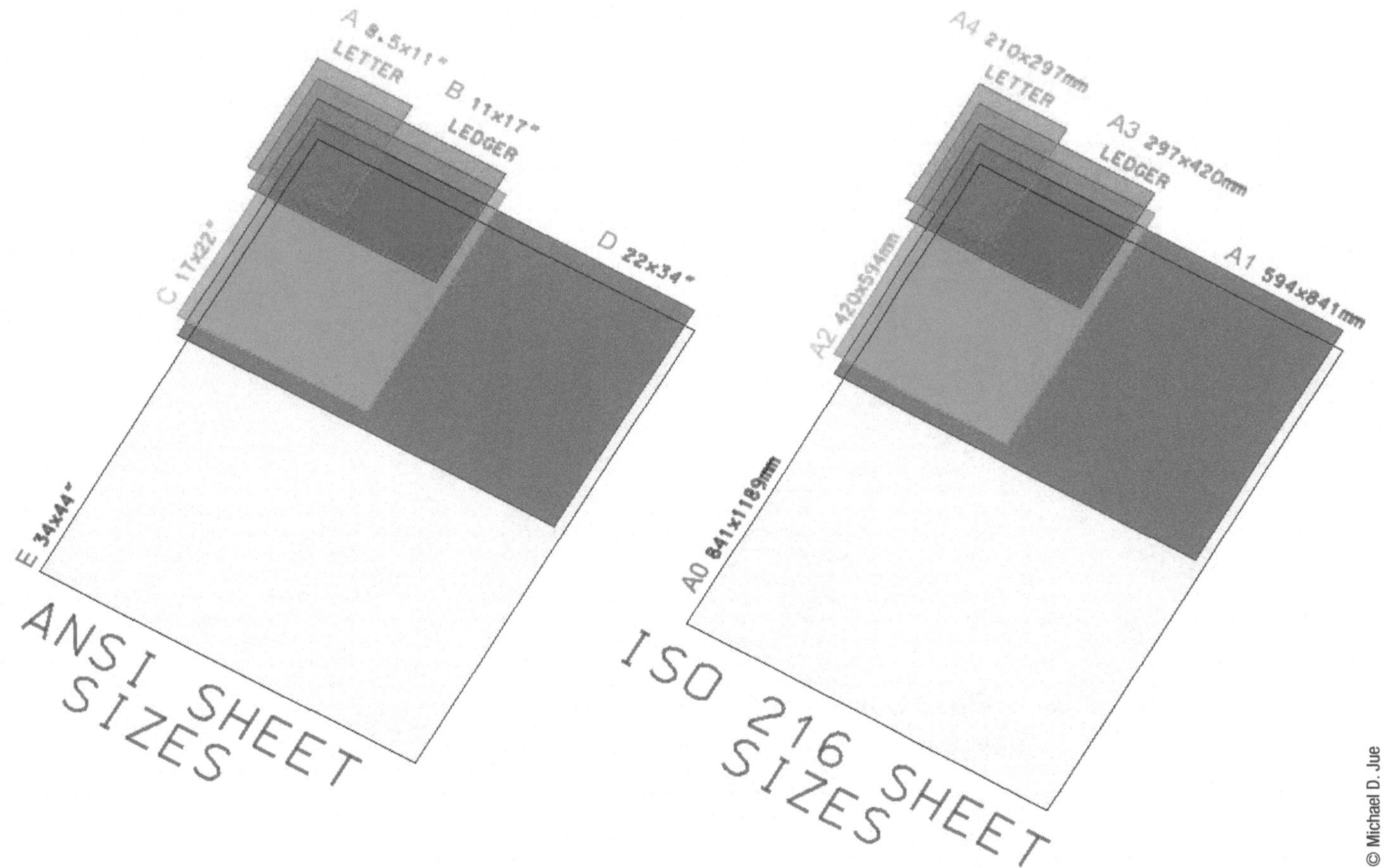

Intro to Civil Engineering

Types of drawings Civil/Architectural field:

Cover Sheets / Title Sheets (fig. 3)
Siteplans
Land Survey
Topographic Map
Landscape Plans
Building Plans
Floor Plans

Reflected Ceiling Plan
Elevations (fig. 6)
Details (fig. 7)
Sections (fig. 7)
Partial Plans(fig. 8)
Structural

Rendering / Artists Conceptual
General Notes/Abbreviations (fig. 5)
Equipment Schedules

Specialized Civil Drawings

Common components:

Title/Revision Block: (fig. 3)
Project Name
Company Name(s) / Logo
Client Name(s)
Contact Name(s)

Engineer Name(s)
Addresses
Drawing / Sheet Number
Revision / Release Number
& Dates (fig 4)

CAD Specific:
CAD Directory / Filename
Timestamp/ Print date

Reviews/Approvals (fig. 4)
Submittal / Plan Check

Drawings List
As-Built Stamps
Disclaimers / Copyright
Licensing Stamp: P.E. / S.E.
other (fig. 3 & 5-8)

Common Drawing Contents:

Vicinity Map (fig. 3)
Work Area (fig. 3)
Keyplan

Graphic Scale
Drawing Scale

North Arrow
General Notes

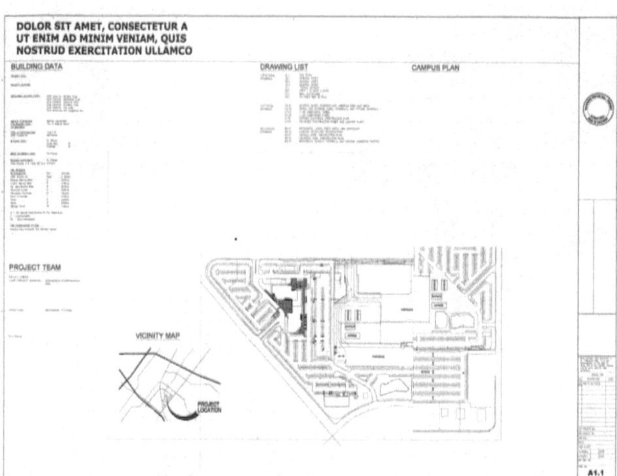

Fig. 3 Cover Sheet

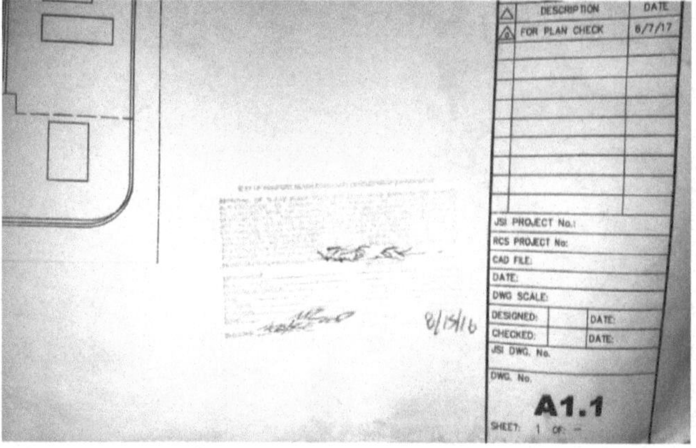

Fig. 4 City Approval stamps & Signatures

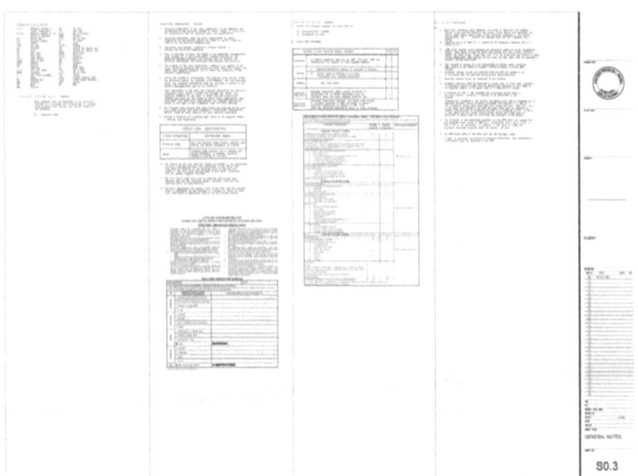

Fig. 5 General Notes (with Abbreviations)

Fig. 6 Wall Elevations

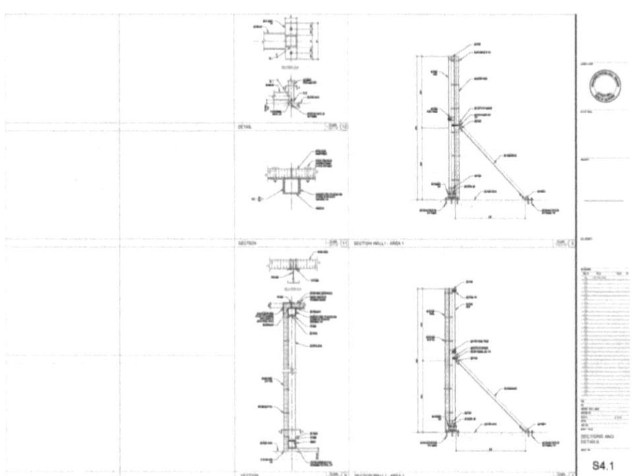

Fig. 7 Sections & Details

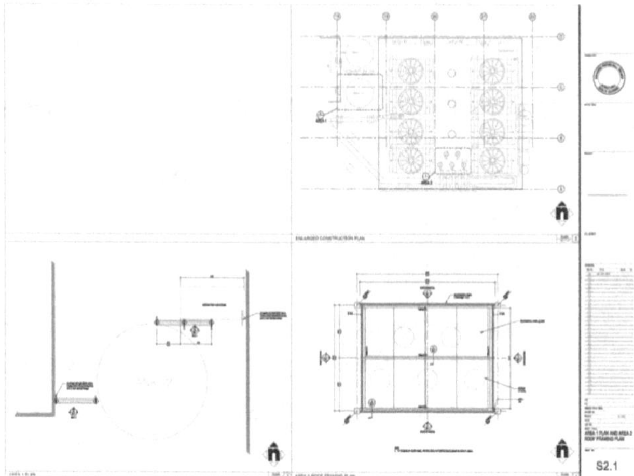

Fig. 8 Area Plans

Please see Module 7, pages 207-210 and the links below for skills regarding understanding and creating Plans, Elevations, Details and Sections. Additional concepts for working in 3D are covered in pages 211-220. (Your instructor will provide guidance on these materials for the course you are taking)

On-line References and Resources

Intro to Trimble SketchUp — Free version — Web based 3D sketching software:
https://www.sketchup.com/products/sketchup-free

Engineering Graphics Essentials - Orthographic Projection and Exercises:
https://static.sdcpublications.com/pdfsample/978-1-58503-610-3-1.pdf

Spatial Vis Engineering / Spacial Vis 3D:

Spatial Vis Engineering is a training tool for engineering and pre-engineering students. The app teaches freehand sketching of 2D and 3D views, which is an important skill for technical communication and improving one's ability to visualize shapes in 3D. These skills have been shown to increase GPAs and graduation rates in STEM. (Your instructor should be providing information regarding acquiring this software at a discount arranged for students)

https://egrove.education/

Intro to Civil Engineering

On-line References and Resources cont' (many with videos)

Bentley Infrastucture Yearbooks:
https://www.bentley.com/en/infrastructure-yearbook

Links to Traffic Engineering Videos by WSDOT:
WSDOT 1-90 Snoqualmie Pass East Design Concept Animation (4:00 CAD Animation)
https://www.youtube.com/watch?v=N24V_8YMLu0

The roadway design software used is Bentley InRoads (now called Bentley OpenRoads)
All of the 3D modeling and animation was done with Bentley MicroStation SS3 CAD software.

WSDOT Marvin Road DDI-Diverging Diamond Interchange (4:07 Video & CAD Animation)

https://youtu.be/5gLxlXamhgY

https://www.youtube.com/results?search_query=wsdot+marvin+road+ddi

Bentley Reality Modeling -- ContextCapture - Ultimate 3D model of Paris:
Paris in 3D from aerial and ground imagery automatically generated with Bentley ContextCapture (1:32)

https://youtu.be/2mXftejS9zl

ContextCapture CONNECT Edition Overview:
ContextCapture is Bentley's reality modeling software that can quickly produce 3D models of existing conditions for infrastructure projects of all types, derived from simple photographs and/or point cloud (5:13)

https://youtu.be/y5qoqHIl3fY

ContextCapture Tutorial: ContextCapture Overview:
A short video reviewing ContextCapture workflow. (2:36)

https://youtu.be/dtYQhjl_Oxw

- Information in the public domain from Bureau of Labor Statistics:
About Civil Engineers
https://www.bls.gov/ooh/architecture-and-engineering/print/civil-engineers.htm

About Environmental Engineers
https://www.bls.gov/ooh/architecture-and-engineering/environmental-engineers.htm

About Architects
https://www.bls.gov/ooh/architecture-and-engineering/architects.htm#tab-2

Resume Tips for College Students:
https://www.thebalancecareers.com/college-student-resume-example-2063202

https://theundercoverrecruiter.com/top-resume-tips-college-students/

https://www.monster.com/career-advice/article/resume-tips-for-college-students

https://www.monster.com/career-advice/article/how-to-write-first-resume-0518

Tips for formatting:
http://rossiercareers101.usc.edu/uploads/3/1/2/2/31223567/5b_-_resume_formatting_guidelines.pdf
https://resumegenius.com/how-to-write-a-resume/resume-fonts-margins-paper-guidelines

Module 0

CAD Concepts/Overview

CAD Overview

- Why cover Basic Concepts?
- For a Beginner this is obvious
- For Intermediates, this **cements** the Foundation upon which to build
- If you **misunderstand** a Foundational Concept, problems will arise, when you attempt to Build!

© Fedor Selivanov/Shutterstock.com

1.31

CAD Overview

- The Definition of CAD
  - What do you think CAD is?
  - Equipment? Software?
- The Goals of Using CAD
  - Why do companies have CAD?
- Your CAD Mind-set
  - Is it Equipment or a Tool? Do you USE it?
  - Does it do ALL the work?

© Shutterstock.com

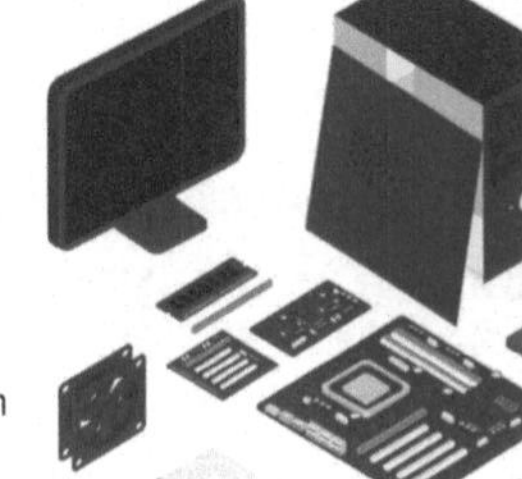

CAD?

© ClassicVector/Shutterstock.com

1.32

Example Misconceptions

- CAD is a Thing for Status < **WRONG!**
  - An Architect got CAD and put it **in the corner of his office** like his competitor did
  - He would point over to **The CAD** and proudly announce to his clients, **"Yes, WE HAVE CAD**, and **There IT IS**, it cost me alot and **It's the very BEST one!"**
  - His firm closed up about 5 years ago
  - He thought of CAD as a shiny toy for show!

© Shutterstock.com

- CAD does it all for you, just push a button & tap the screen! < **WRONG!**
  - There's no need to learn!
    A student once told me, he had no need to learn CAD, since he saw the salesman just hit a button, tap the screen and a WHOLE BUILDING just drew itself! Ah Ha!, **BUT**, that was actually a **pre-made** demo, being run by an engineer that had many 100's or 1000's of hours of training!

© JJFarq/Shutterstock.com

create a whole building icon??
Sorry, guy, no such thing!

1.33

The Definition of CAD

- **C**omputer - Most know what this is
  - Hardware
  - Software
- **A**ided - This is the **most Forgotten** part
  - **The Human Element is the KEY to CAD**
  - **CAD without the Human does NOTHING!**
- **D**rafting - But CAD is MORE!
  - The Activity / The Product / Organized Results!
  - "Drafting" is NOT "Drawing"

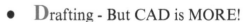

© Shutterstock.com

© PR Image Factory/Shutterstock.com

CAD requires YOU!

Without YOU, CAD does NOTHING!

* The acronym is Not C.D. That would be Computer Drafting.

1.34

What is a CAD System?

- A CAD System is **People using automation**, equipment & software
- A CAD system does NOTHING by itself, except use power if left on!
- **Trained personnel** operate the CAD system Equipment, **use** the software
- The CAD System is flexible enough to **produce the desired results**

© Shutterstock.com

1.35

The Goals of Using CAD

- **Greater Efficiency and Productivity**
- Create Drawings **More Accurately & Faster**
- Faster **Copying and Revising** of Drawings
- Make Drawings Available to Others by creating a **Sharable** database of drawings
- Ability to do **Complex Drawings**
- Easily **Manage** many Drawings
- Adhere to your **Client's Requirements**

© Shutterstock.com

1.36

CAD is a Tool

- CAD is the "**Wordprocessor**" of Drawings - discussion
- The Woodshop/Carpenter/Mechanic Analogy and "cutting logs"
- Rule #1 in ALL of these activities UNDERSTAND WHAT YOU ARE ATTEMPTING TO DO!!!!!
- Analogies …

1.37

Analogy to CAD #1

- CAD can be analogous to a woodshop or machine shop with all of its tools. Really you can **MAKE** most anything! If you have the right tools and **SKILLS**.
- Also, different software can be thought of as tools from different manufacturers. Certain basic tools will work exactly the same. More complex ones will differ.
- Skil saws and Makita saws have variations

1.38

Analogy to CAD #2

- A bakery or a kitchen with all of its appliances and implements is also similar to CAD. Really you can **COOK** most anything, if you have the right appliances and **SKILLS**.
- Different software can be thought of as *appliances* from different manufacturers. Certain *basic* appliances will work exactly the same. More complex ones will differ.
- Waring blenders and Osterizers are different.

1.39

CAD is a Tool

- So, with CAD, really you can **DRAW** most anything, if you have the right software, hardware and SKILLS.
- In CAD software of different brands, certain basic commands will work exactly the same. More complex ones will differ.

1.40

CAD Overview

- Aptitude in which activity is best for CAD:
  - a. Drafting b. Math c. Computers d. Typing
- Producing a drawing with CAD is most like:
  - a. Pushing a couple of buttons
  - b. Pounding a few nails
  - c. Building a kitchen cabinet
- What are the most likely causes of failing at CAD:
  - a. No previous CAD or computer experience
  - b. Not given enough training or opportunity to train
  - c. Not given enough real assignments or practice
  - d. Not enthusiastic about learning CAD

1.41

CAD Overview

- Aptitude in which activity is best for CAD:
  - (a.) Drafting b. Math c. Computers d. Typing
- Producing a drawing with CAD is most like:
  - a. Pushing a couple of buttons
  - b. Pounding a few nails
  - (c.) Building a kitchen cabinet
- What are the most likely causes of failing at CAD:
  - a. No previous CAD or computer experience
  - b. Not given enough training or opportunity to train
  - (c.) Not given enough real assignments or practice
  - (d.) Not enthusiastic about learning CAD

1.42

The CAD Learning Curve

- The Goal, Get past the Beginning!
- Time, Effort & **Assignments** are Key
- **Most Fail to Progress Due to Lack of Spending Time, Effort or Getting Real Assignments to use the CAD on. And they don't care about it.**
- If you **want to learn** you **WILL** spend Time
  - even away from class lecture
- Large, Long Term Projects are the Best
- It's Hard to Learn on Short, Rush Jobs

1.43

The CAD Learning Curve

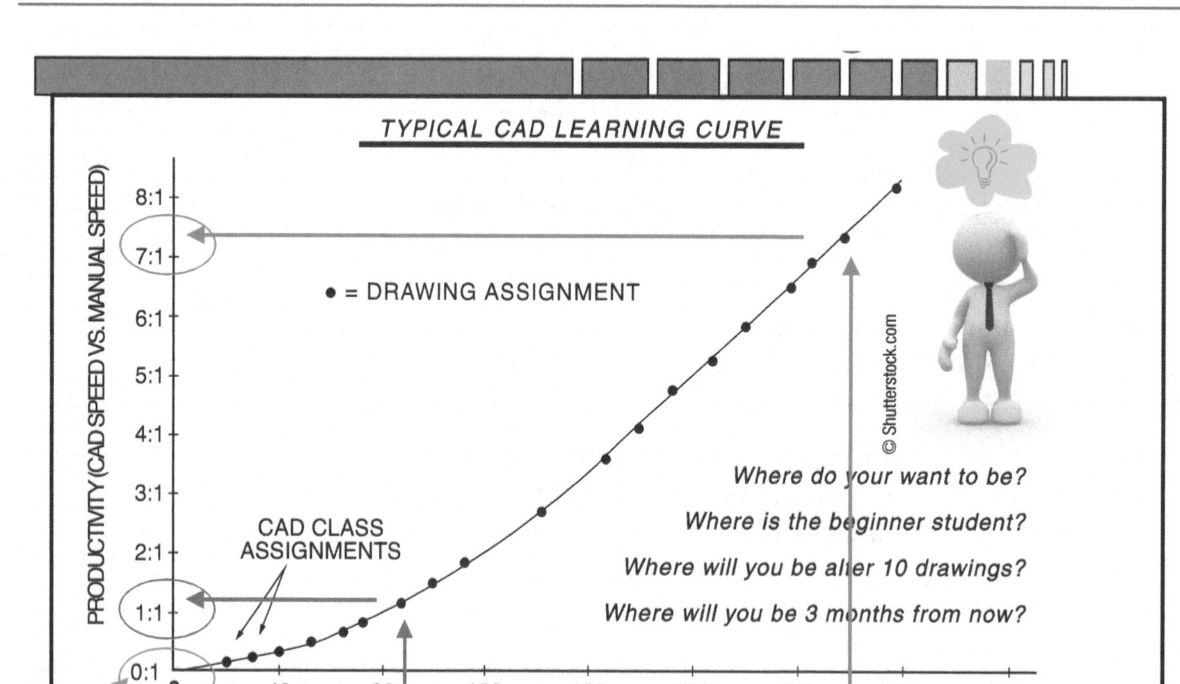

1.44

The CAD Learning Curve

- The Typical CAD Learning Curve Chart shows that even after a typical CAD class, most students will not be able to draft faster by CAD than by Hand. In others words, give the student something to draw, and they will complete it faster with pencil and paper than with the CAD. This is perfectly natural and to be expected.

© Shutterstock.com

- However, notice that the curve rises quite quickly after **a few hundred hours** are put in by the student.

1.45

Learning Curve Concepts

- The primary factor that increases "productivity" (the y-axis value) is increasing CAD drawing hours (the x-axis value). That is the TIME spent practicing on CAD drawings

© Shutterstock.com

- This is NOT the same as "time spent studying" or "time listening to lecture" or "time spent reading". These actions are not Drawing time.
- The primary factor is NOT the speed of the PC or the speed that you move the mouse.
- The Main Factor for CAD efficiency increase is increasing the "Practice time on CAD"

1.46

Key CAD exercise concepts for initial sessions (Week 1):

The student should be exposed to the following during the initial sessions with MicroStation and should become *initially* familiar with these concepts *from hands-on exercises.*

Suggested files/exercises and commands/concepts: This should be the first exposure, many repetitions of the following are also planned.

General/All

- Starting CAD software
  - Student Accounts
- Opening existing files
- Directory Structure
  - Location of Student and class folders
- Creating New CAD files
- Mouse operation, Tablets, Laptops
- Keyboard entry/Key-in Field
- Terminology of CAD screen items
- Appearance of the cursor
- Pull-down menus, Floating menus (V8*i*)
- The Ribbon Interface (CONNECT Edition)
- Selecting a tool from a toolbar or from a Ribbon Group
- Entering Datapoints
- HELP function (Differences from V8*i* to CONNECT Edition)

Travel.dgn

- Opening an existing file
  - Basic Viewing techniques on PC, laptop & tablet
  - Zoom-in/out
  - Window Area
  - Fit View
  - Window/view open/close
  - Window resizing/repositioning
  - Window/view Tile and Cascade
- Activating Tools
  - Basic Edits with Element Selection Tool
  - Selections, delete, move, and rotate
  - Copy Element
  - Mirror Element about a vertical
  - Text Edit
  - Change Attributes
  - Modify/Stretch

Orgchart.dgn

- Creating a new file
- Basic Tool Operation
- Docking and Undocking toolbars (V8*i*)
- Using tools from various toolbars and Ribbon Groups (CONNECT Edition)

- Introduction to the following tools:
  - Place Line
  - Place Block
  - Place Circle
  - Copy
  - Mirror Element about a vertical
- Use of Grid
- Intro to Grid Lock
- Tool Settings Dialog Box

Review List: Key Words/Phrases/Concepts/Terminology/Syntax

1. Window / View Related
    a. Window title area
    b. Window frame
    c. View
    d. Tile
    e. Cascade
    f. Arrange *
    g. Re-size
    h. Reposition / move views
    i. Pop-to-the-top / Sink
    j. Open / Activate / Turn-on views
    k. Close / De-activate / Turn-off views
    l. Update View
    m. Window Area
    n. Zoom In / Out
    o. Fit View
    p. Pan
    q. View Control
    r. View Attributes *
    s. Grid display / Grid lock
    t. Grid points / Grid reference
2. Design file / .dgn
    a. Working Units *
        i. Settings > Design File > Working units
        ii. Master units
        iii. Sub-units
3. Design plane / Drawing plane *
4. Global origin *
5. Menu Related/Ribbon Interface
    a. Floating menus/Tabs / Groups
    b. Docking / slamming menus
    c. Tools / Toolbars
    d. Tearing out menus
    e. Child menus
    f. Check-box / toggle
    g. Pull-down menu
    h. Icon / menu item
    i. Tool settings window
6. Commands
7. Elements / Placing Elements
8. Element Manipulations *
9. Element Attributes
    a. Level *
    b. Color
    c. Style
    d. Weight
10. Key-in field
    a. Focus *
    b. Escape key *
11. Enter key / Hit
12. Status field
13. Prompt field
14. Error field
15. Accelerator key-ins / key stroke
16. Mouse Related
    a. Datapoint / Data / "D" / Accept button (LMB)
    b. Reset / Reject / "R" button (RMB)
    c. Tentative snap / "T" Snap button (MMB)
    d. LMB – Left Mouse Button
    e. RMB – Right Mouse Button
    f. MMB – Middle Mouse button (wheel)
    g. Click / Tap
    h. Double Click
    i. Drag
    j. Scroll (with wheel)
    k. Digitize
17. Cursor
18. Pointer
19. Select
20. High-light *

21. Dynamic preview *
22. Rubber-banding *
23. Jaggies / Pixelated *
24. GUI – Graphical User Interface
25. Feedback
26. Learning Curve
27. Efficiency
28. Getting Help *
    a. Help > Contents >
        i. QuickStart Guide
            1. Getting Started
                a. Fundamentals
                b. Viewing Designs
            2. Tutorial
                a. Your First Session
                b. Workflow Basics
            3. Glossary
        ii. User Guide (week 1-2)
            1. The Level System
            2. Placing Elements in 2D
            3. Drawing Technique
29. CONNECT Edition On-line Help
    a. Help Contents
    b. CONNECT Advisor
    c. Example & videos in CONNECT
    d. CAD COMPANION WORKBOOK Videos
30. Tool Tips
31. Saving your work *
    a. (2 Different Saving Options)
        i. Save as you work
        ii. Save only on Exit or Save command
    b. File > Save Settings <Ctrl> b

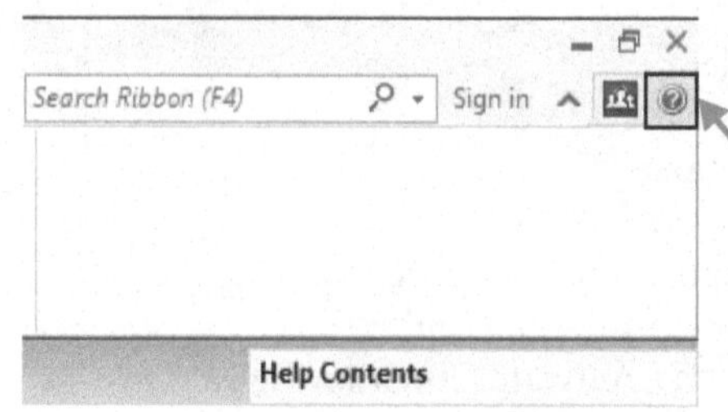

Applicable to **CONNECT Edition** for Update 12 and earlier

Help Contents in the MicroStation CONNECT Edition is available at this icon at the far upper right part of your screen.

The MicroStation CONNECT Edition On-Line Help will be started up.

It will look similar to the screen image shown on pg 25.

The Help function was revised for Update 13 and beyond (see below)

One method to open Help Contents, another is below.

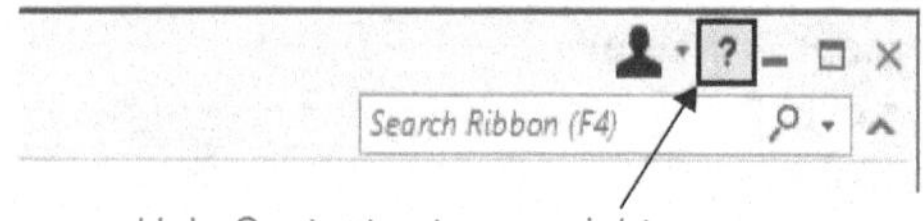

a. Help Contents at upper right on screen

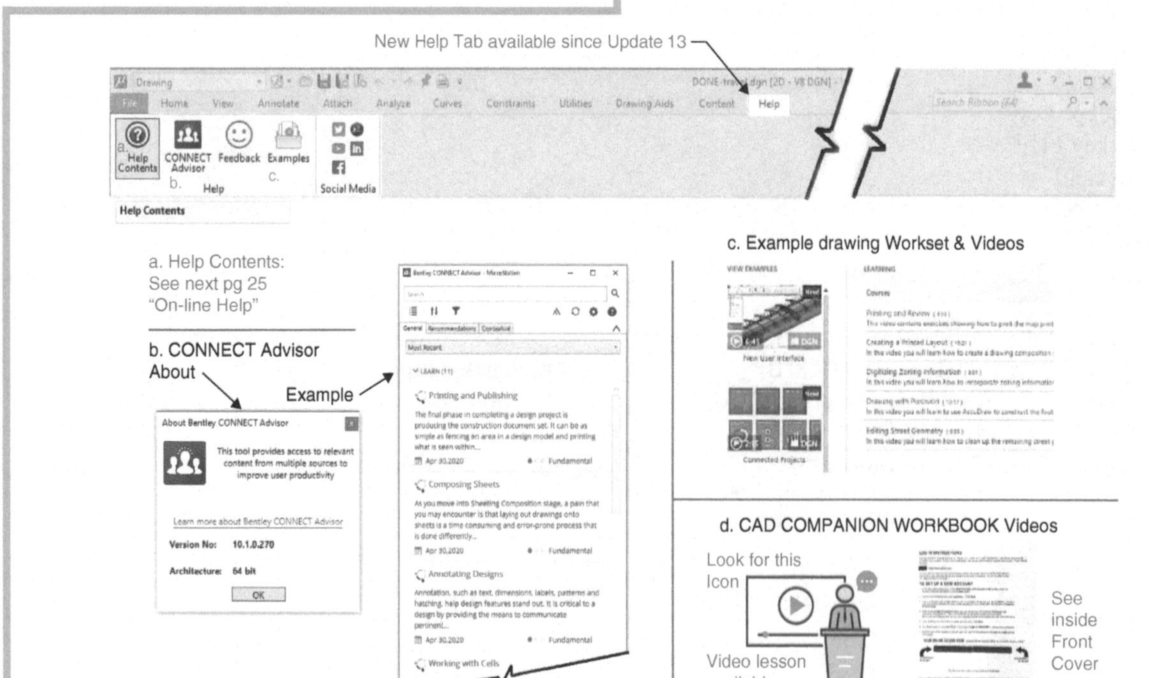

MicroStation CONNECT Edition On-line Help activated by either method shown on pg 24.

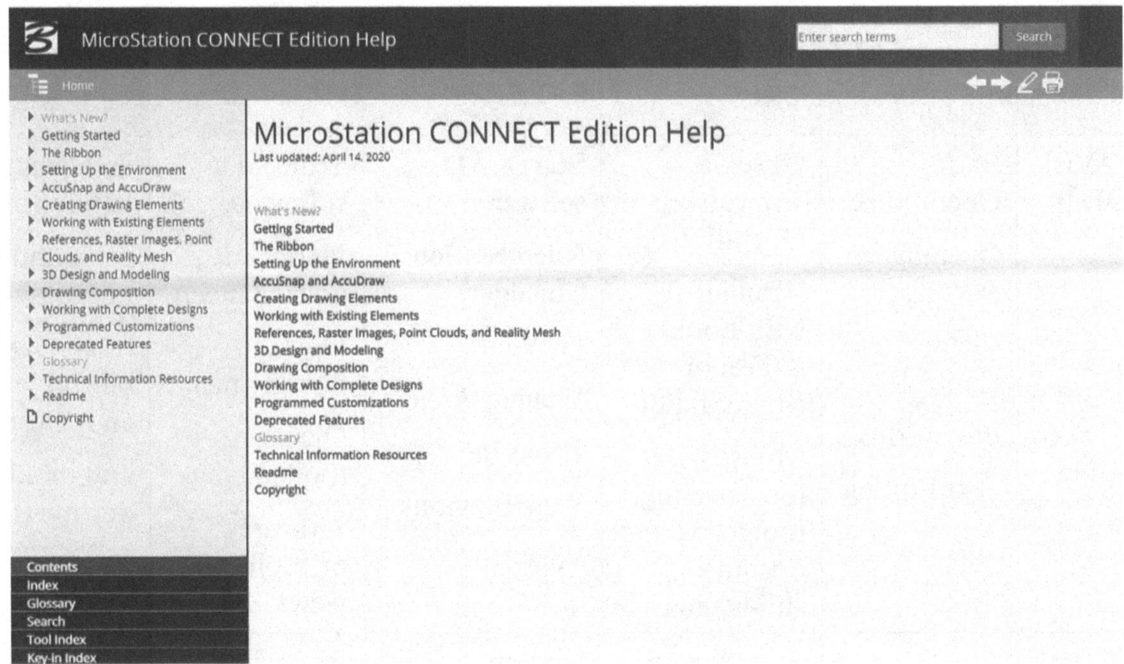

Example of On-line Help article accessed from: Getting Started > The Ribbon > Ribbon Interface

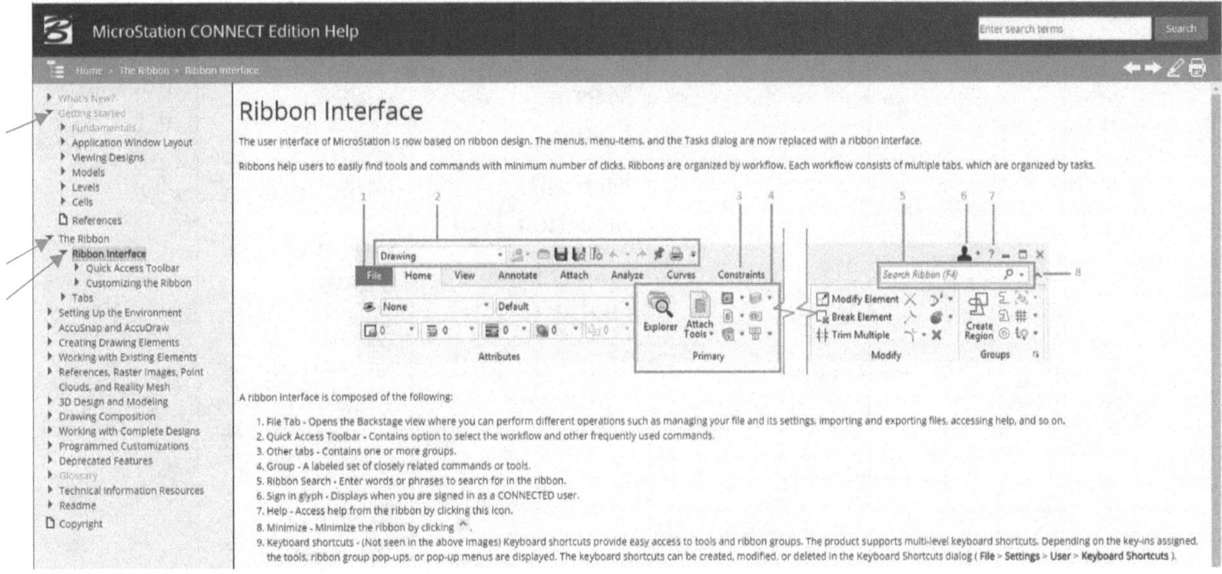

MODULE 0 and 1 OUTLINES

Filename	General Concepts	Learning Goals	New Tools (first time) used before = *	Toolbar/ Window/View operations	Mouse usage
TRAVEL MOD 0 & 1	Basic Operations. Opening existing files. View Control. Basic Edits. Text Editing	Observe Typical Operations. Familiarity with Look & Feel of MicroStation. Mouse usage for: selecting tool icons opening sub-menus.	**Start CAD software** **MicroStation Manager.** **Fit View** **Window Area** **Zoom In** View Previous View Next	Tear out a submenu Undock a docked menu Dock a floating menu Dismiss a toolbar. Title area of toolbars/ views	**data point**—left button press and release. **reset**—right button press and release. **drag**-hold down left
		Exposure to basic edits. non-precision editing techniques	Update. **Move Element** **Delete Element** **Rotate Element** **Mirror Element** **Element Selection Tool** **Tool Settings Dialog box** Text Edit tool	Restoring Primary toolbar Restoring Attributes toolbar Restoring Standard toolbar Restoring Main toolbar. Opening Views Minimize/ Maximize View Close Views Resize Windows Pop to the top Cascade/Tile	button and reposition while holding down the left button. **double-click**—two quick taps of the left button

Filename	General Concepts	Learning Goals	New Tools (first time) used before = *	Toolbar/ Window/View operations	Mouse usage
ORG-CHART MOD 1	Creating a new file. Precision placement and editing of elements by grid usage. Multiple element selection	Using the Grid, by snapping to it with grid lock on. Using Copy and Mirror with copy option on. Using Element Selection Tool to select single and multiple elements. Save Settings	**New or File > New** **View Controls *.** **Grid Display on/off** **Grid Lock on/ off.** **Place Block Shape** **Place Line** **Copy Element**	same as above	same as above
			Delete Element * Place Circle Place Text **Mirror Element (copy on)** **Element Selection Tool.** Tool Settings Dialog box * File > Save Settings <Ctrl> F		

Note: the Travel drawing is used in Module 0, just to familiarize the student with Opening Files and View Control. It is used again in Module 1, when the student will learn basic editing techniques

< REVIEW

Immediately Preceding Material Highlights:

Page

15 CAD Concepts / Overview Why Cover Basic Concepts Definition of CAD Example Misconceptions Goals of using CAD

20 The Learning Curve Time, Effort & Assignments

22 Key Exercise Concepts and Keywords General operations Opening an existing file Viewing Techniques Activating Tools

25 Module 0 & 1 Outline

15 16 17 18 19

20 21 22 23 24

25 26 27

PREVIEW >

Immediately Following Material Highlights:

Page

29 Basic Operations V8i and CONNECT Edition Registration Interface Screen

37 Mouse Button Usage Terminology

39 Key-in Commands Key-in Field

42 View Control View Attributes

51 Engineering Symbols Primer

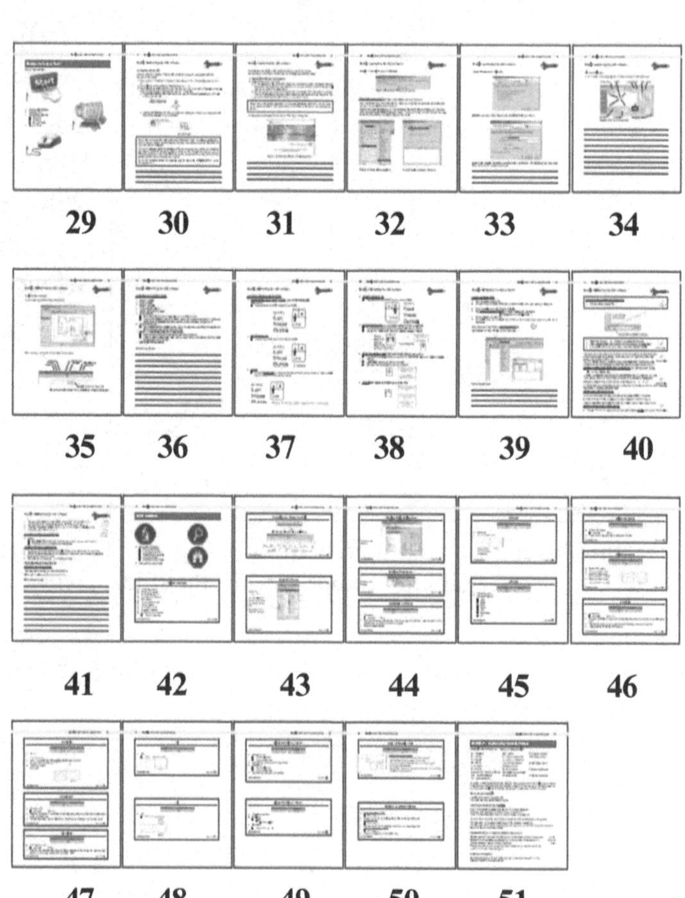

Module 0 –Tools – Part 1

Basic Operations

Viewing MicroStation CONNECT Edition selection of drawing exercises

- Starting the Software
- Opening Files
- The Interface Screen
  - Windows
  - Toolbars
  - Prompt Fields
- Mouse Usage

Viewing CONNECT Edition Video Lessons

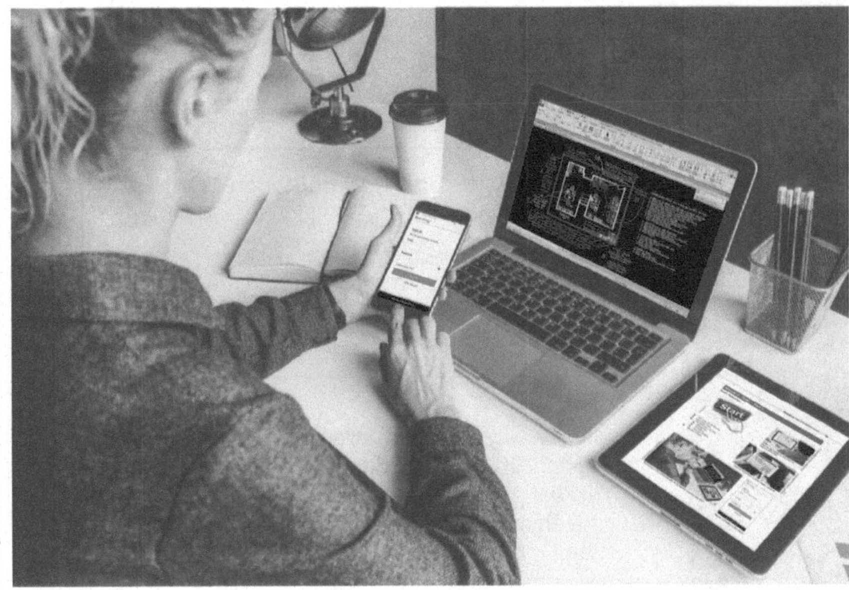

Reviewing a CAD COMPANION WORKBOOK drawing exercise

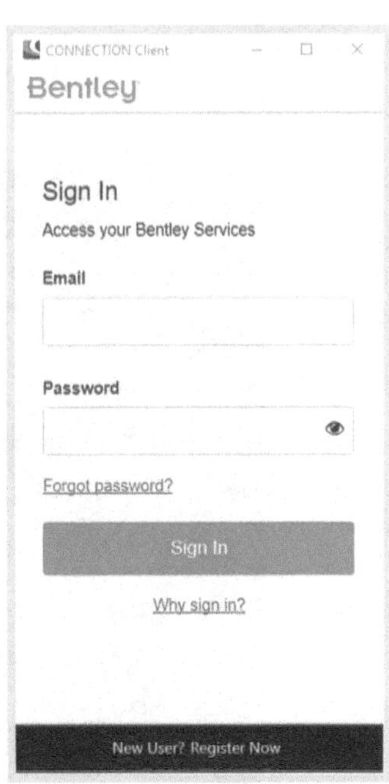

Bently CONNECTION Client

Module 0 – Starting the CAD software

Starting MicroStation V8i

Possible options, or similar to that shown below, for starting or opening MicroStation : (use one of the below):

1. Start button > Programs > Bentley > MicroStation V8i > Bentley MicroStation V8i … or …
2. Double-click on MicroStation V8i Desktop icon … or …
3. Double-click on a MicroStation type dgn file icon, tile, thumbnail or filename in a directory or folder listing of existing files (dgn file = design file)
   a. Typical MicroStation file icons (small and big) and filename appearance in Windows 10 OS

   b. Typical MicroStation file tile and thumbnail appearance (Thumbnail appearance will vary by the contents of the DGN file!)

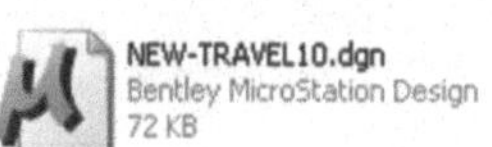

> Note: The "file extension" of MicroStation DGN files is ".dgn". This 3-character extension may or *may not* appear on your filename displays, depending on how your Windows OS (or other OS) is configured.
>
> The above examples show the filenames with the extension (.dgn) visible. The Windows procedure to show file extensions may be covered in lab, but since that skill is a part of Windows software, it and other Windows specific procedures will not be included in this packet, for the sake of preservation of space!
>
> ie. for the examples above, the filename may be shown as: NEW-TRAVEL10 (note: no .dgn shown!)

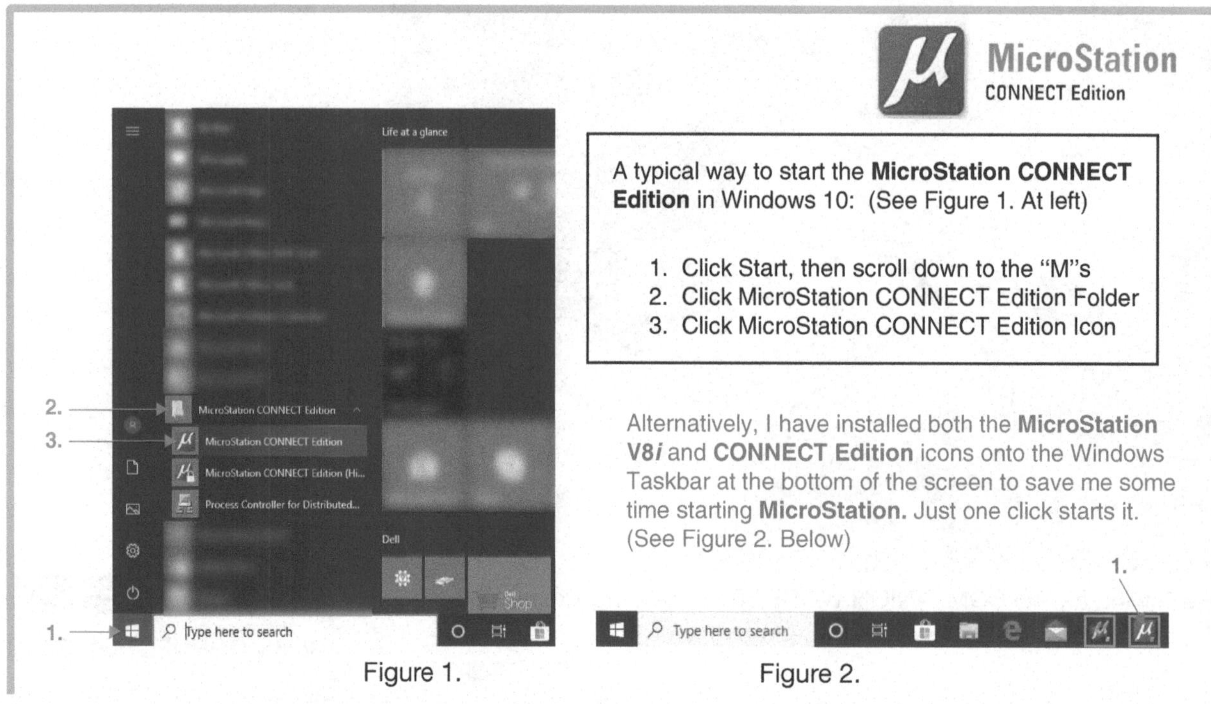

MicroStation
CONNECT Edition
A typical way to start the **MicroStation CONNECT Edition** in Windows 10: (See Figure 1. At left)
1. Click Start, then scroll down to the "M"s
2. Click MicroStation CONNECT Edition Folder
3. Click MicroStation CONNECT Edition Icon
Alternatively, I have installed both the **MicroStation V8*i*** and **CONNECT Edition** icons onto the Windows Taskbar at the bottom of the screen to save me some time starting **MicroStation.** Just one click starts it. (See Figure 2. Below)
Life at a glance
2.
3.
MicroStation CONNECT Edition
MicroStation CONNECT Edition
Process Controller for Distributed...
Dell
1.
Type here to search
1.
Type here to search

Figure 1.

Figure 2.

Module 0 – Starting the CAD software

Depending on the status of the installation used, ie. school lab or your own laptop/pc or workplace installation, the following may initially appear:

1. Bentley/MicroStation "splash screen"

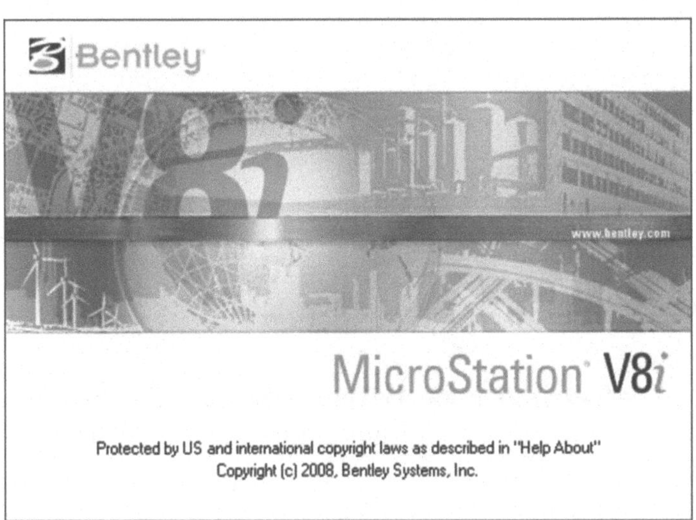

Figure 1. Bentley MicroStation V8i Splash Screen

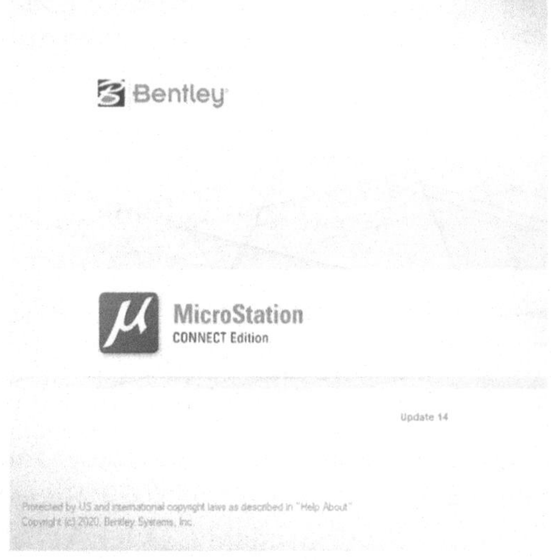

Figure 2. MicroStation CONNECT Edition Splash Screen

2. Registration screen or messages
   a. If this appears in the school lab, bypass any registration request. Normally, students should not need to perform any registration of the lab software, as this is usually handled by the school's tech department.
   b. See later section (or handout) for registration or licensing of your personal or academic copy of the software, if starting up the software on your laptop or home computer. The procedure may vary from year to year or from term to term.

> Please take notes on any registration or licensing procedures provided in lab that may be an update or different from instructions noted within at the time of the printing this packet.

3. MicroStation Manager Dialog box or "File Open" Dialog box

Module 0 – Starting the CAD software

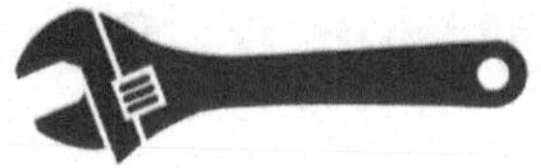

Sample of Possible Registration Message

Note: At the time of this text printing, Bentley Systems, no longer offers the Academic version of **MicroStation V8*i*** through their Student Server Website. If a free Student version of the **V8*i*** is desired, please contact your instructor or local Bentley Systems representative. The **MicroStation CONNECT Edition** is currently freely downloadable. Please see the next page.

This page 32 and top of page 33 cover MicroStation V8i legacy registration procedures. Please check with your instrutor or system administrator for any updated procedures, if you are using MicroStation V8i.

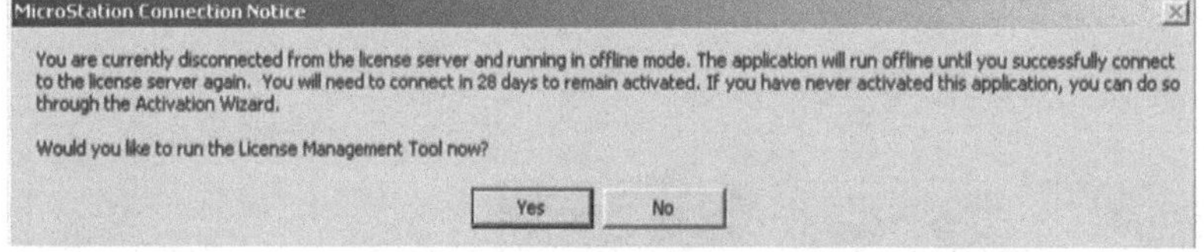

Figure 2. Running in Offline mode message

<u>License Management Tool</u> (for use on the student's personal computer)

Can be activated from the dialog box that comes up, or can also be activated by the user with the menu bar (pull-down tools) sequence:

Utilities > License Management > Tools > Product Activation Wizard > SELECT subscriber with a deployed (local) SELECT Server > Next > then paste in the required information provided from your Student CD README file. See below.

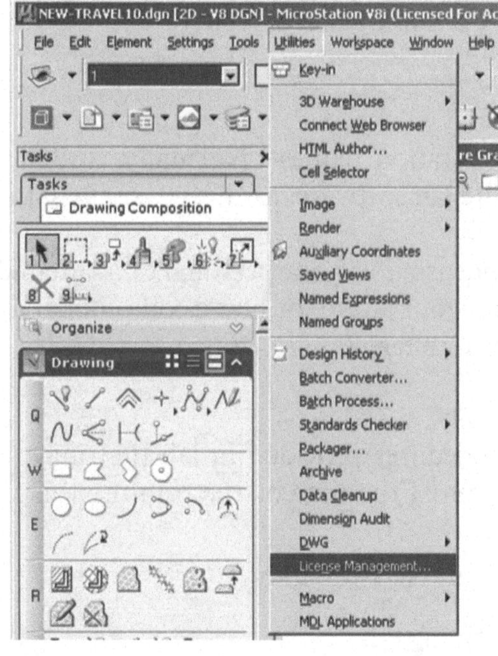

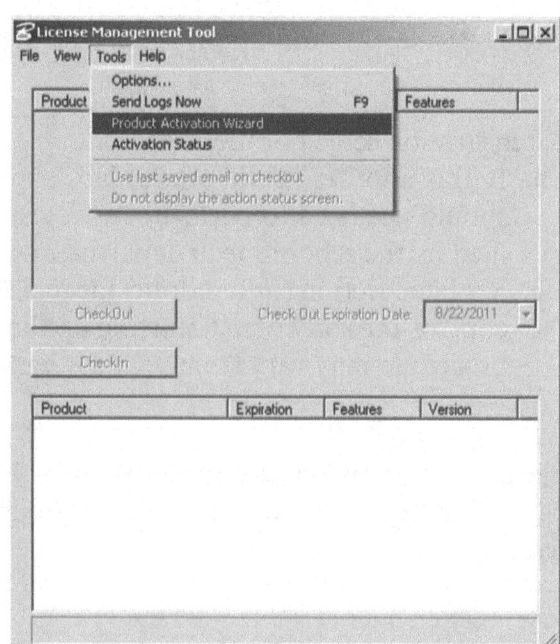

Utilities > License Management > **Tools > Product Activation Wizard >**

Module 0 – Starting the CAD software

License Management Tool (cont')

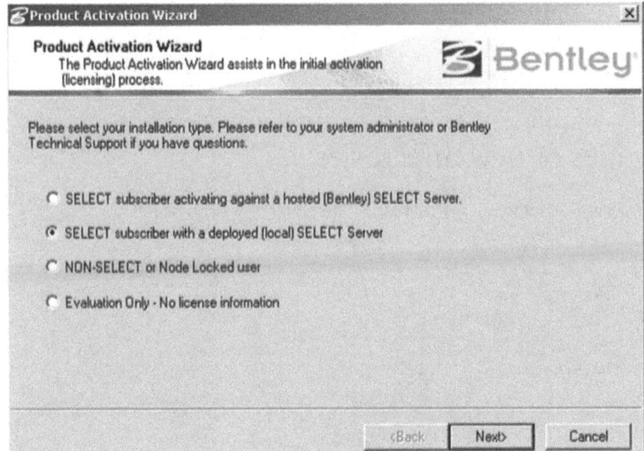

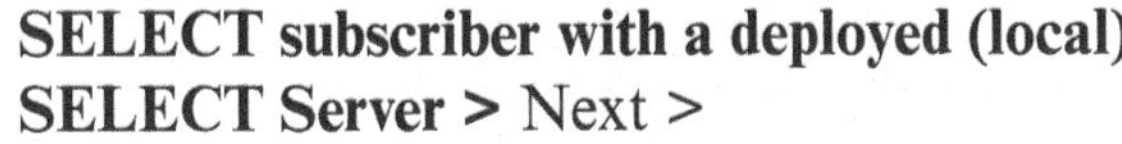

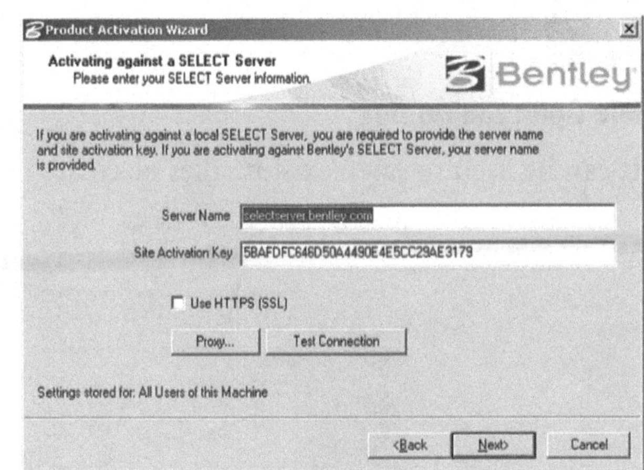

SELECT subscriber with a deployed (local) SELECT Server > Next >

paste in the required information provided from your Student CD README file, then select Next, which should complete the process.

Students can download the **MicroStation CONNECT Edition** from this link to the Bentley Student Server. Additional log-in information may be required from your school or institution for registration.

http://apps.bentley.com/studentserver/

Once you have registered on the Student Server, downloading software is one of the many options.

After you have downloaded the Bentley software desired, the **CONNECTION Client** will be available which is utilized to validate your license and allow continued software use.

Your school may provide a "Virtual Software Lab", for using MicroStation without needing to download it. VSL information is provided separately

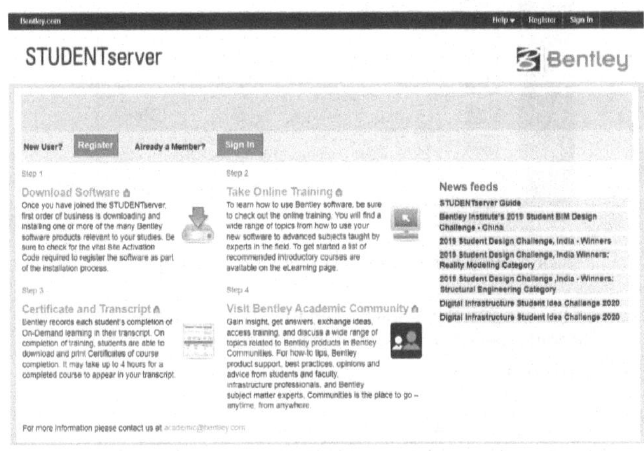

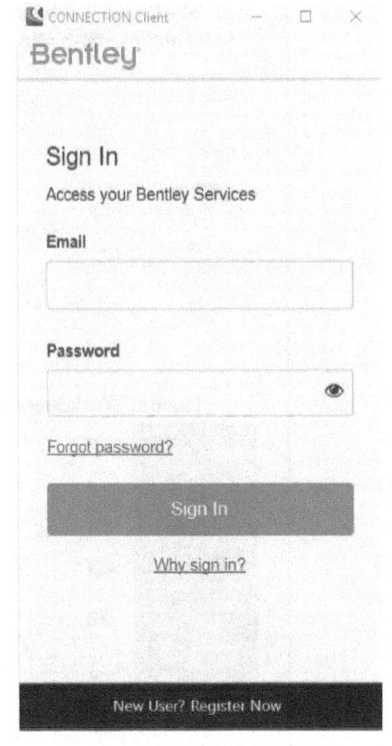

Bentley CONNECTION Client

Module 0 – Starting the CAD software

File Open Dialog box

It can be used to open existing files or create new files or new directories.

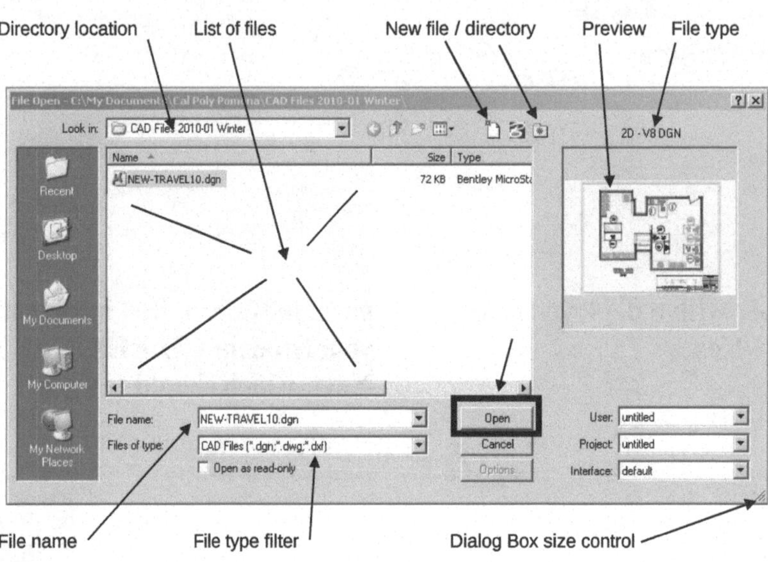

Figure 3. File Open Dialog Box

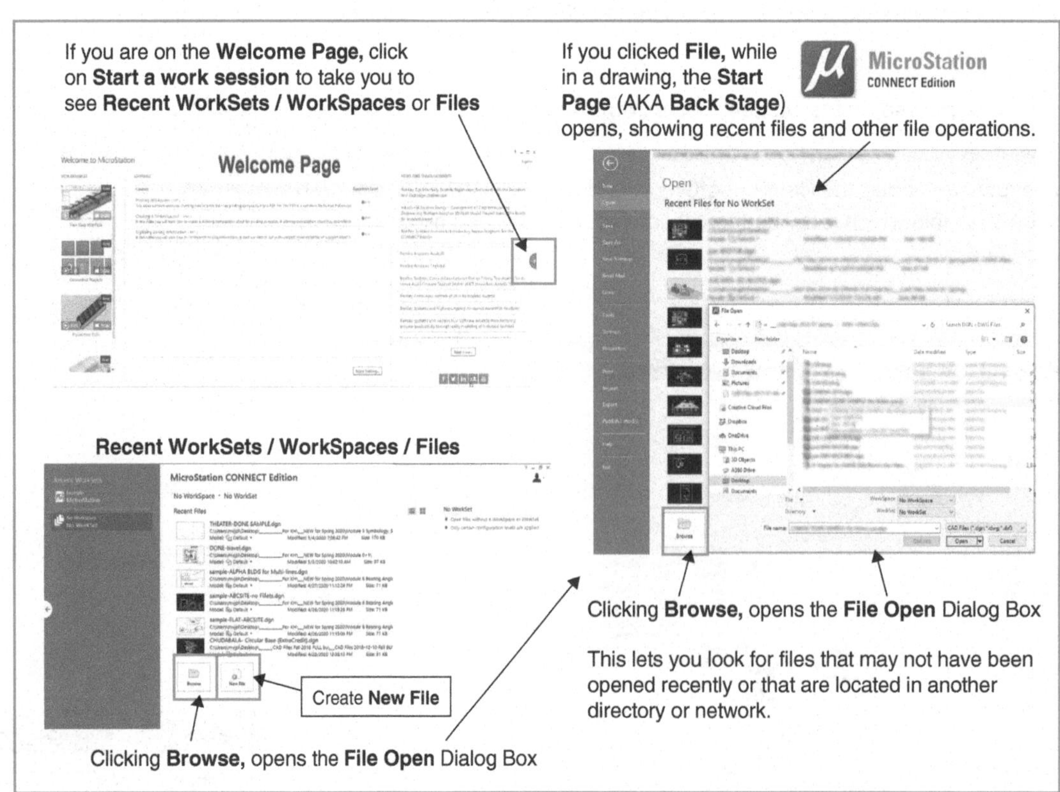

Module 0 – Starting the CAD software

The INTERFACE SCREEN

It has many components (more detail later)

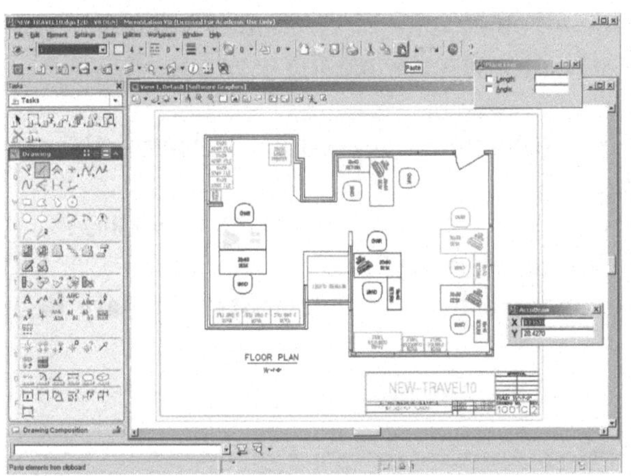

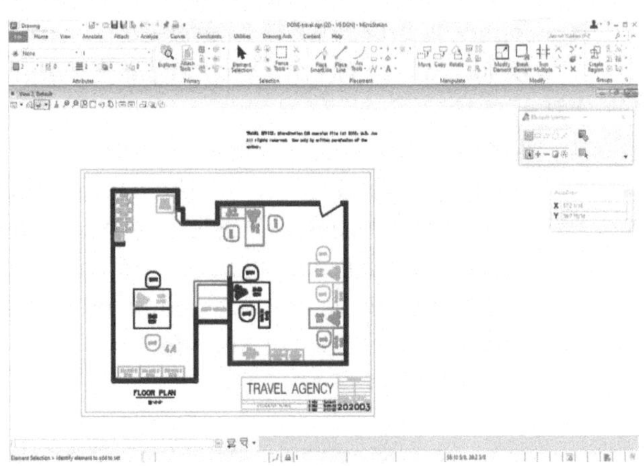

View Controls: (at top left of each view on the screen)

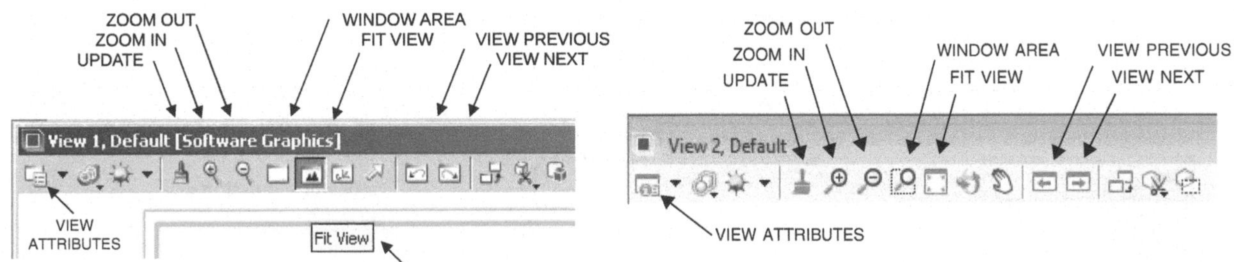

EXAMPLE OF A TOOL TIP

(FLOAT MOUSE OVER TOOL DESIRED, NAME APPEARS)

Module 0 – Starting the CAD software

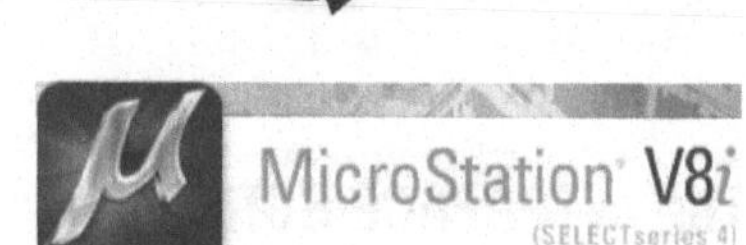

OPENING & CLOSING FILES

- FILE > OPEN
- FILE > NEW
- FILE > CLOSE
- FILE > EXIT (EXIT)
- QUIT *note: work is saved
- FILE > SAVE
  - **Note: MicroStation saves "As-you-draw" in its default mode.**
  - **There is NO NEED to ever do a "Save", unless you change "Preferences" to a different mode, where the drawing and editing activity is only saved when the user does it.**
- FILE > SAVE AS
  - **Very common action to make another copy of the currently opened file and name the new file an alternate name of the user's choosing.**
- FILE > COMPRESS DESIGN (COMPRESS) **Key-in Field (one-line)**
  - **Removes deleted elements from the file and "buffer memory".**
  - **Once the file is compressed, Undo actions cannot bring back elements that have been "compressed" out of the file.**
- SAVE SETTINGS (FILE)

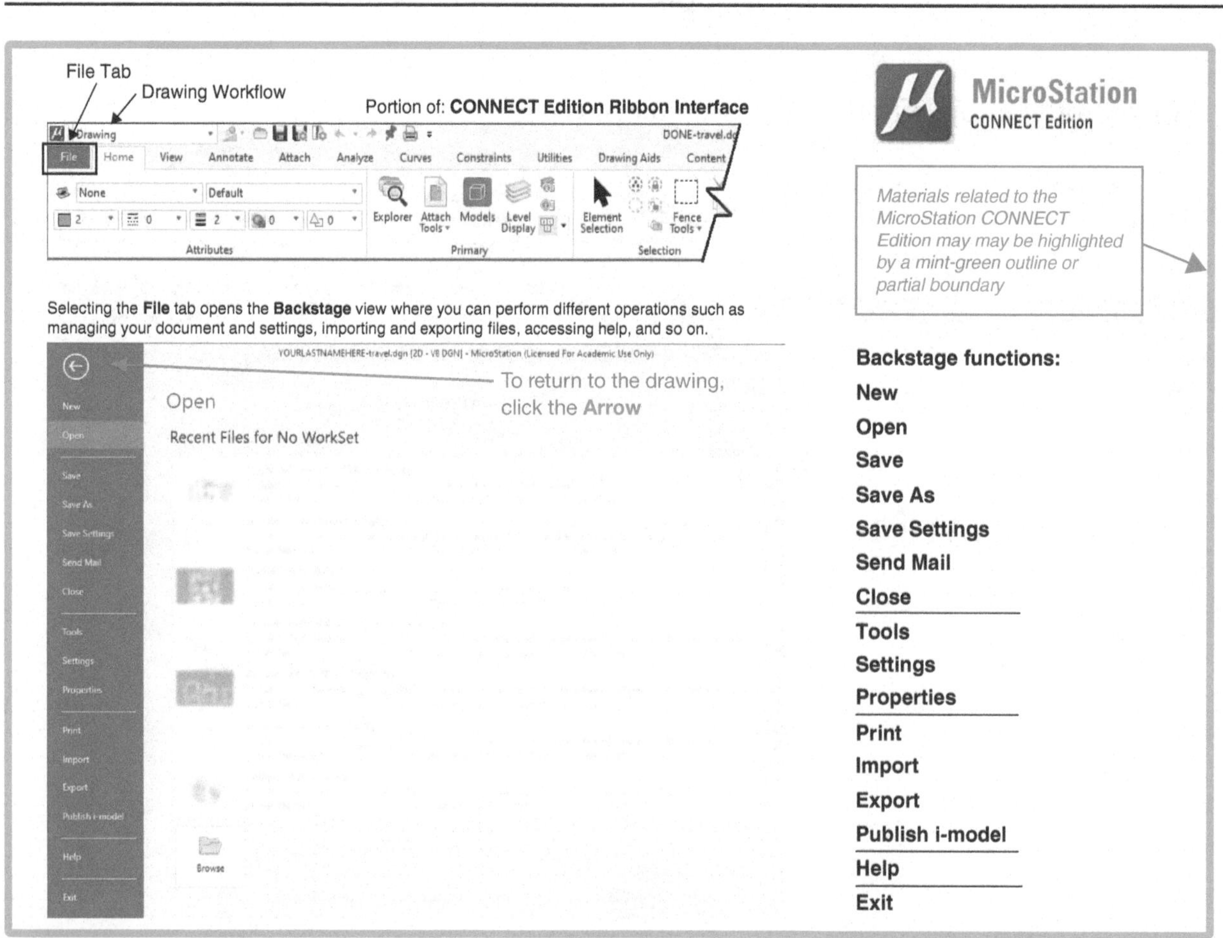

Module 0 – Starting the CAD software

MOUSE OPERATIONS / SYNTAX

- DATAPOINT, DP, D, DATA, CLICK (ALL HAVE THE SAME MEANING)
  - **Tap and release the LEFT mouse button (LMB)**

(LMB):
LEFT
MOUSE
BUTTON

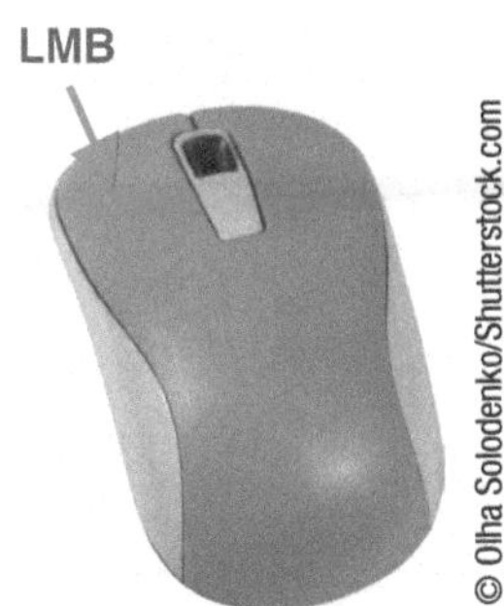

© Olha Solodenko/Shutterstock.com

- DOUBLE-CLICK
  - **2 Quick Taps of the LEFT mouse button (LMB)**

(LMB):
LEFT
MOUSE
BUTTON

2 times

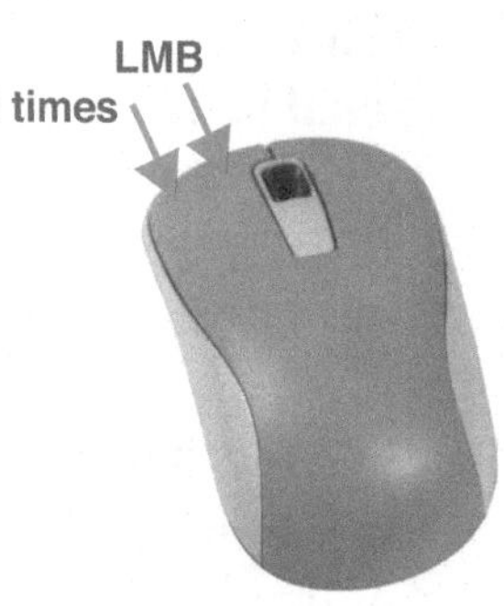

- DRAG
  - **Press and Hold down** the left mouse button, and while holding down the LMB, reposition the pointer as req'd and then release

(LMB):
LEFT
MOUSE
BUTTON

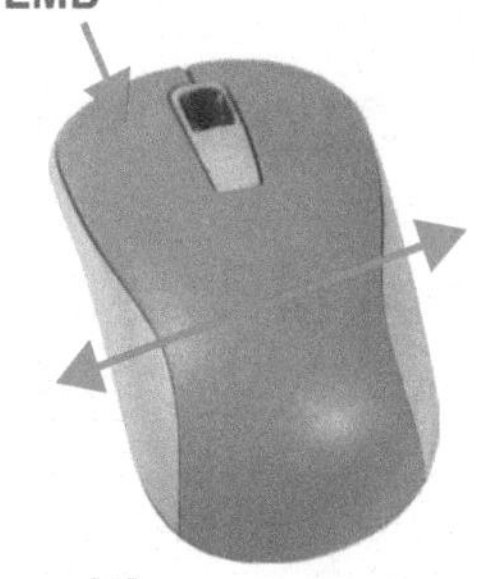

Press & Hold, then reposition mouse then release

- RESET / REJECT / R
  - **Tap and release** the RIGHT mouse button (RMB)

3 Ways you can right click (RMB) on a Mac Computer:

1. Get a mouse with a right mouse button.
2. Hold the "control" button as you click.
(Note this is different than the Ctrl key on PCs)
3. Use two fingers on the trackpad

https://www.businessinsider.com/how-to-right-click-on-a-mac

(RMB):
RIGHT
MOUSE
BUTTON

Module 0 – Starting the CAD software

- <u>ZOOM</u> — **Changes the Magnification of the View**

Zoom In
or
Zoom Out

use the
Roller Wheel
(Do not move
the Mouse)

<u>Zoom</u>: with MIDDLE "wheel":

Put the mouse into the zoom in/out, location as desired, then

Roll the wheel, "up" or "down"
to zoom <u>in</u> or <u>out</u>

- <u>PAN and/or SCROLL</u> — **"REPOSITIONS / SCROLLS the View"**
  - **Press & Hold & reposition** the mouse with the **"MIDDLE" button of a 3-button mouse: "Wheel"**
  - **"small hand"** may appear when operating
  - **This may vary by installation on your computer**

Pan / Scroll

Press and Hold Down the Roller Wheel and then REPOSITION the MOUSE

<u>Pan or Scroll</u>: with MIDDLE "wheel":

Press & Hold & Reposition the mouse

- <u>TENTATIVE POINT</u>, **or called SNAP, SNAP POINT or T-SNAP**

  Not a view control, but a special type of Data Point, covered later
  - **Press BOTH** mouse buttons, simultaneously and then release
  - Can use the **"MIDDLE" button of a 3-button mouse: "Wheel"**

Press
BOTH
MOUSE
BUTTONS
SIMULTANEOUSLY

Then Release

OR..

<u>Tentative Point</u>: with MIDDLE "wheel":

Press & Release

Module 0 – Starting the CAD software

Opening the Key-In Field

- **In version V8i, the Key-in Field may not automatically open, upon opening a design file**

- Open the key-in field with **Utilities** > **Key-in** *Note: Do not type the >, it means "the next step:"*
- Type <u>KEY-IN COMMANDS</u> AT THE COMMAND PROMPT: Can be Upper or Lower case

  | (blinking line in the Key-in field)
- The Key-in field can be re-sized and docked at the bottom of the screen or at the top of the screen

Note: This step is applicableto <u>the earlier version</u> MicroStation V8 or V8i. For V8 or MicroStation V8i (SELECTseries 4)

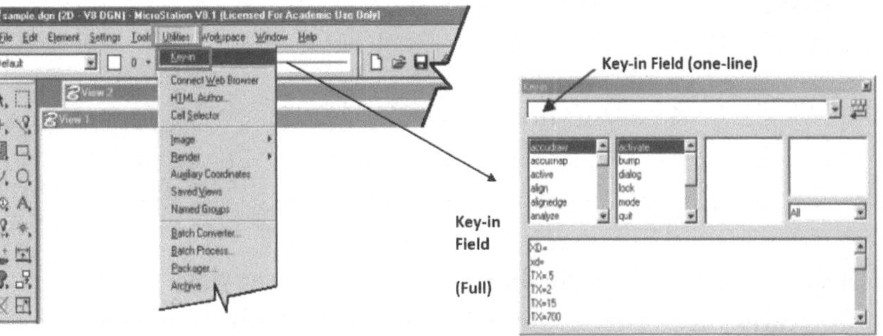

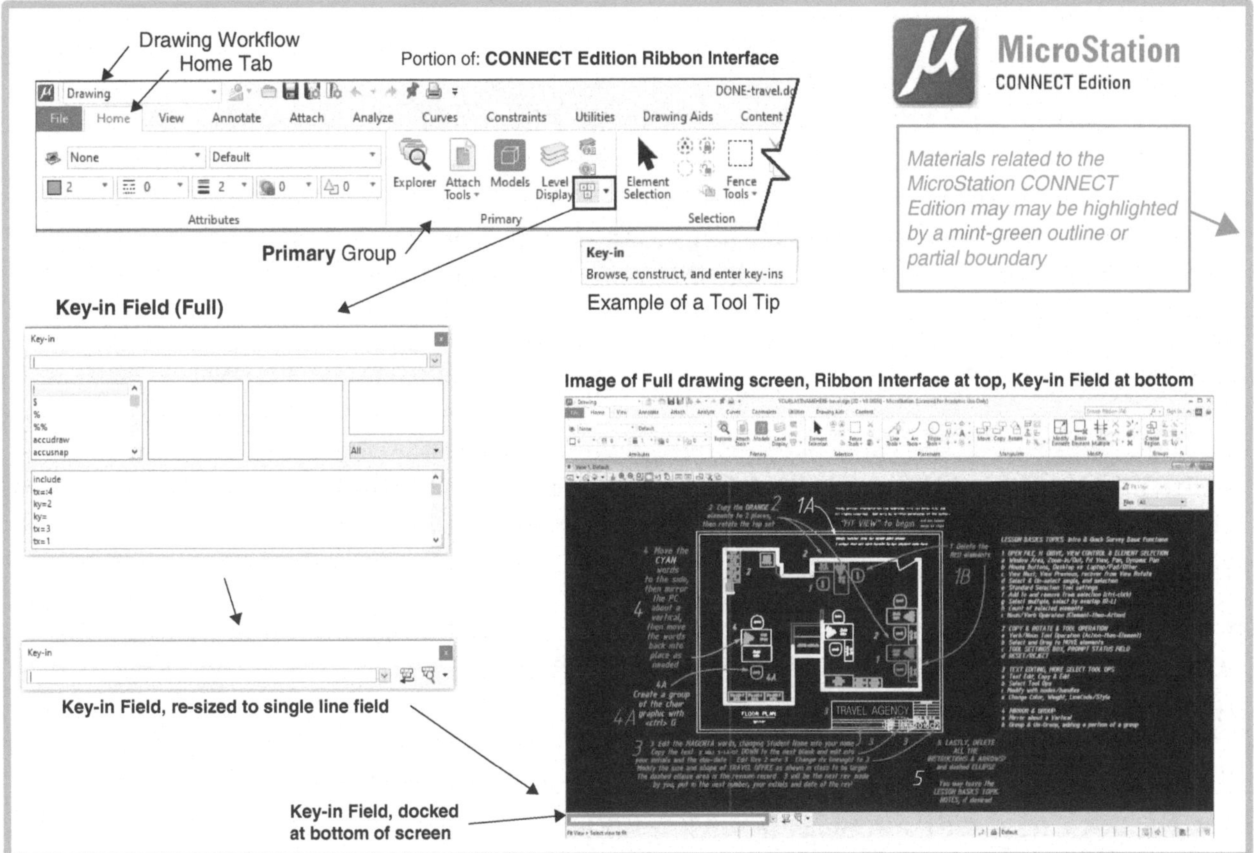

Module 0 – Starting the CAD software

ACTIVATING COMMAND PROMPTS

- *(For the earlier version V8)*

Please note the change from V8 (an earlier version) to the newer V8*i* and CONNECT.

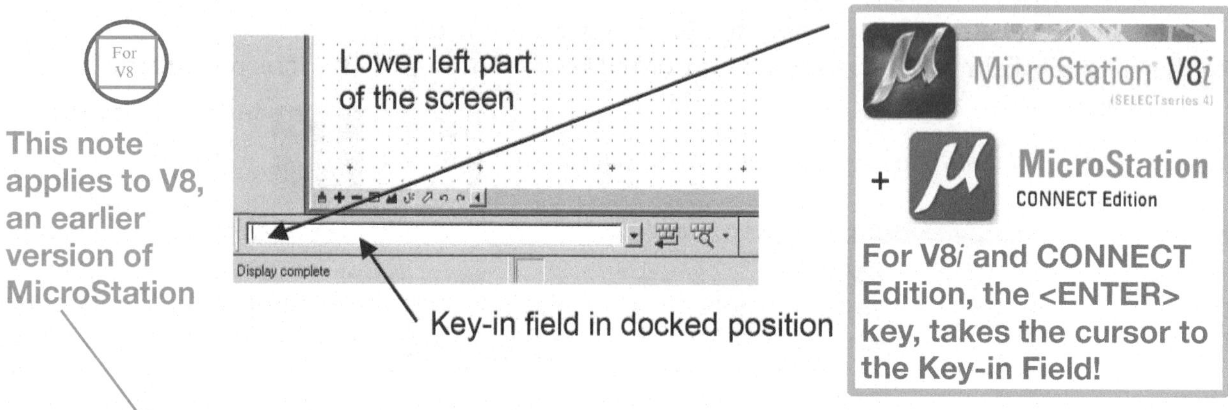
For V8
This note applies to V8, an earlier version of MicroStation
Lower left part of the screen
Display complete
Key-in field in docked position
MicroStation V8i
(SELECTseries 4)
+
MicroStation
CONNECT Edition
For V8i and CONNECT Edition, the <ENTER> key, takes the cursor to the Key-in Field!

- **<Esc> key (better!!)** .. or .. **"Click" in the key-in browser field**
- **<Esc> automatically takes the keyboard input focus to the key-in field**
- If the key-in field is not open, open it first with **Utilities > Key-in**

© Shutterstock.com

This method is better, since you don't have to reposition the mouse away from your active drawing area on the screen. <Esc> with your left hand leaves your right hand on the mouse, ready to roll!

© Shutterstock.com

For *V8i*, Use the <Enter> to take the focus to the Key-in field. This is better than rolling the mouse and clicking in the field. See why that is, same reason as above.

KEY-IN COMMANDS MUST BE COMPLETED BY "ENTERING" THEM

- Use the **<Enter>** key

A VERY COMMON MISTAKE BY BEGINNERS IS TO FORGET TO USE THE **<Enter>** KEY AT THE CONCLUSION OF A KEY-IN COMMAND!

Hitting the **<Enter>** key is often shown as this symbol: ↵... or ... **< ↵ >**

In old manuals and sometimes by older instructors, it is shown as <R> or <CR> meaning: RETURN or CARRIAGE RETURN

© Shutterstock.com

KEYBOARD KEY NOTATION:

In General, keyboard keys can be shown as their **name within < > brackets.**

ie. < Esc > < Ctrl > < F1 > < Space > < Alt > < Shift > < Tab > < Caps >

They are sometimes shortened, as shown in **< Caps >**, rather than < Caps Lock >

Module 0 – Starting the CAD software

REPEAT PREVIOUS COMMAND(S)

© Shutterstock.com

- Use the "UP Arrow" key to recall almost ***ANY*** previous Key-in Commands
- Go more steps **back** into the "stack", with more "UP Arrow's" < ↑ >
- Go **forward** in the "stack" by using the "DOWN Arrow" **key** < ↓ >
- Can Edit the recalled key-in, use **< ← >, < → >, < Del >, < Backsp >,** etc.
- Complete with <Enter>, < ↵ >

(C) Michael D.Jue

CANCEL PREVIOUS COMMAND

- UNDO
  - **SHORT-CUT: <** Ctrl **>** Z, ^Z **Note: the < Ctrl >** can be symbolized as ^
  - CANCELS THE PREVIOUS COMMAND

ABBREVIATING COMMANDS

- In general, most MicroStation keyed-in words can be shortened to 3 characters
- Where the shortened name is still unique at 2 characters, the abbreviation may work
- Some words can go to 1 char
- MicroStation is forgiving: ie. all these are valid,

UPDATE,UPDAT,UPDA,UPD,UP

OTHER ABBREVIATIONS

The name MicroStation, is often abbreviated as:

μ-Stn, μS, or **m-Stn, ms.** Greek **μ,** means micro

Notes/Questions:

___

___

___

___

VIEW CONTROL

- Seeing your Drawing
  - Fitting everything
  - Zooming In & Out
  - Windowing to an Area
  - Panning Around
  - Previous & Next Views
- Saving & Recalling Views

VIEW CONTROL

- **UPDATE (option)**
- **WINDOW AREA**
- **ZOOM IN (factor)**
- **ZOOM OUT (factor)**
- **FIT VIEW**
- **VIEW PREVIOUS**
- **VIEW NEXT**
- **DYNAMIC PAN**
- **NAMED VIEWS**
- **OPEN/CLOSE VIEWS**
  - **Tiling & Resizing**

CAD Companion Workbook View Control 1

View Attributes

<Ctrl > b is a keyboard short-cut to open the View Attributes dialog box.
* Lazy software programmers and teachers may write this as ***^b***, which still means **<Ctrl>b**. When written as ***^b***, do NOT use a keystroke of ^ then ***b***. A handwritten ***^b***, still means **<Ctrl>b**, which is to: hold down the **<Ctrl>** key, the depress the **b** key

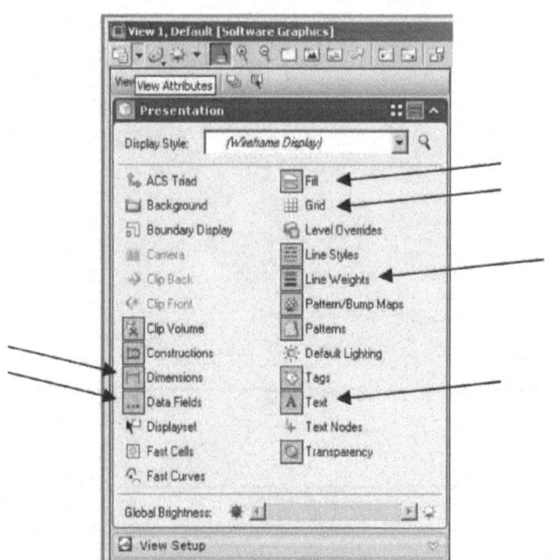

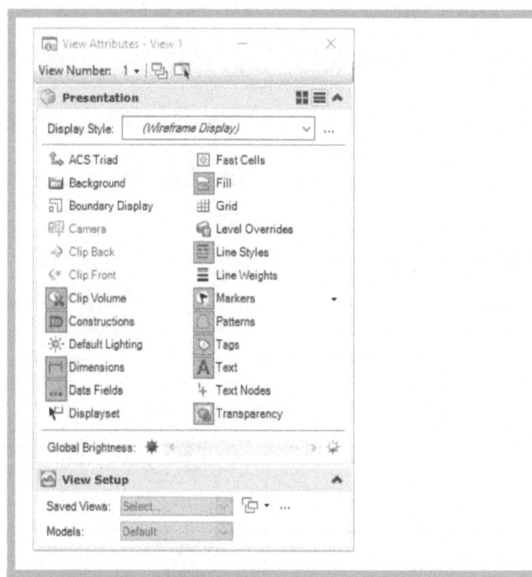

<Ctrl>b can be remembered as "**B**etter Viewing".

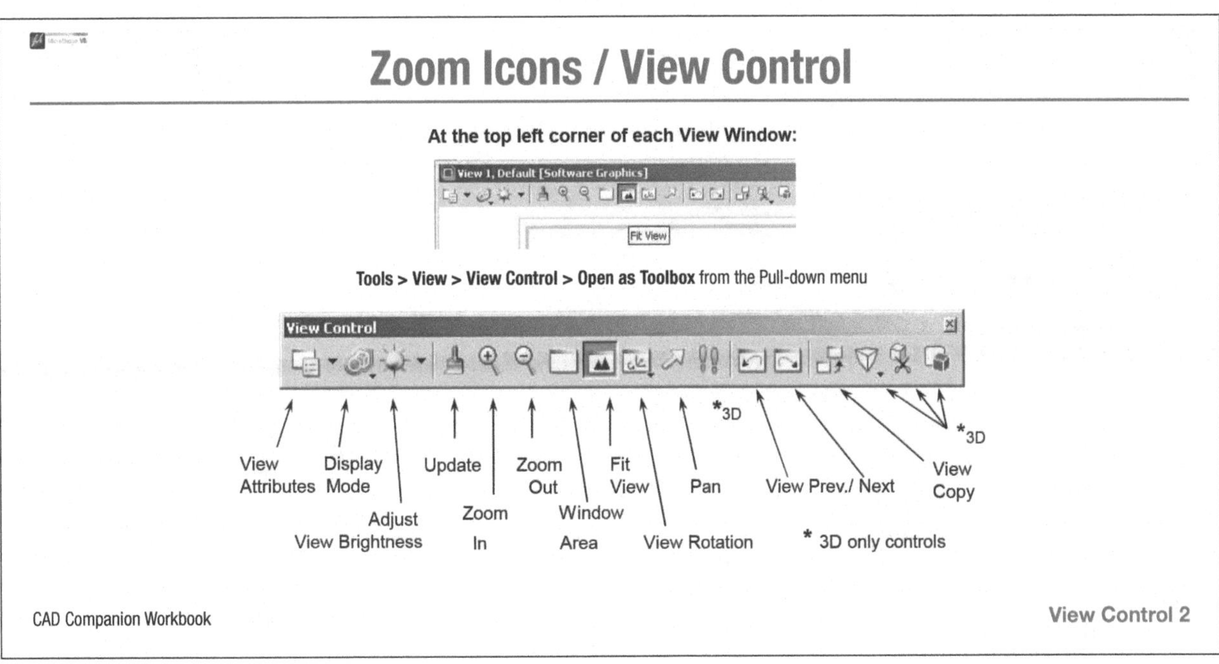

Zoom Icons / View Control

MicroStation CONNECT Edition

Pan can be done by press and hold center mouse button and then re-position.

At the top left corner of each View Window:

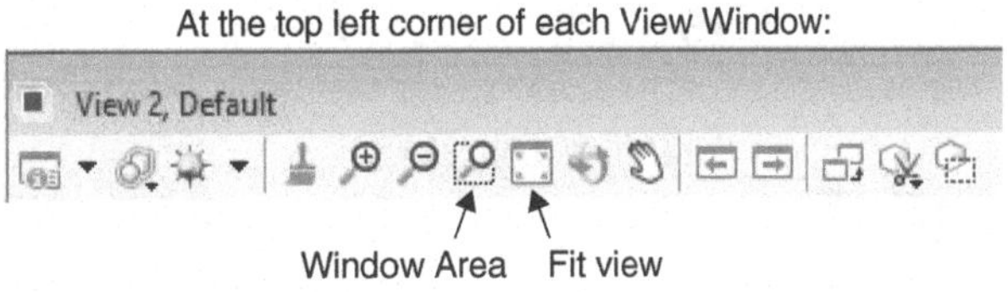

View 2, Default

Window Area   Fit view

Fit View can also be done by a double-click of the center mouse button!

The View Tab of the Ribbon interface at the top of the screen

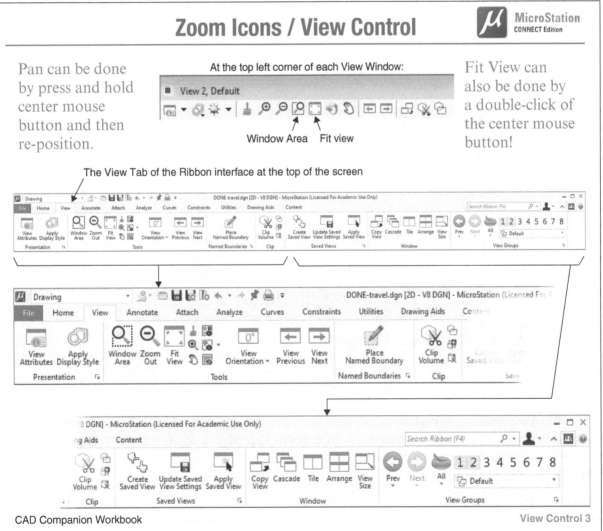

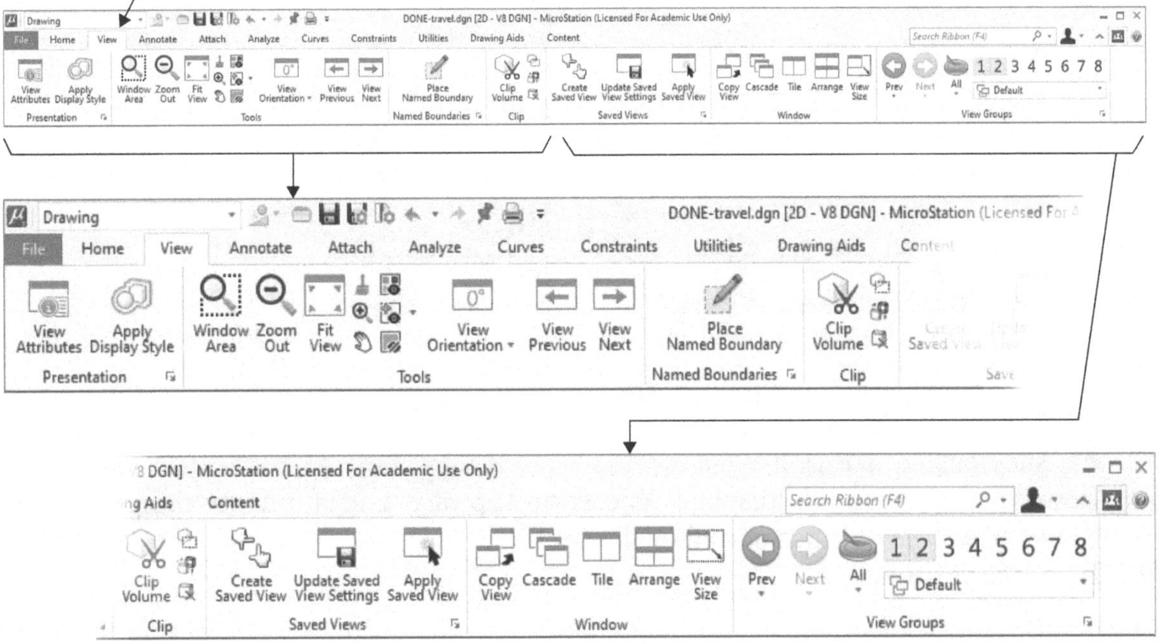

Drawing | DONE-travel.dgn [2D - V8 DGN] - MicroStation (Licensed For Academic Use Only)

File | Home | View | Annotate | Attach | Analyze | Curves | Constraints | Utilities | Drawing Aids | Content

View Attributes | Apply Display Style | Presentation | Window Area | Zoom Out | Fit View | View Orientation | View Previous | View Next | Tools | Place Named Boundary | Named Boundaries | Clip Volume | Clip | Create Saved View | Update Saved View Settings | Apply Saved View | Saved Views | Copy View | Cascade | Tile | Arrange | View Size | Window | Prev | Next | All | 1 2 3 4 5 6 7 8 | Default | View Groups

Display Style Dialog box

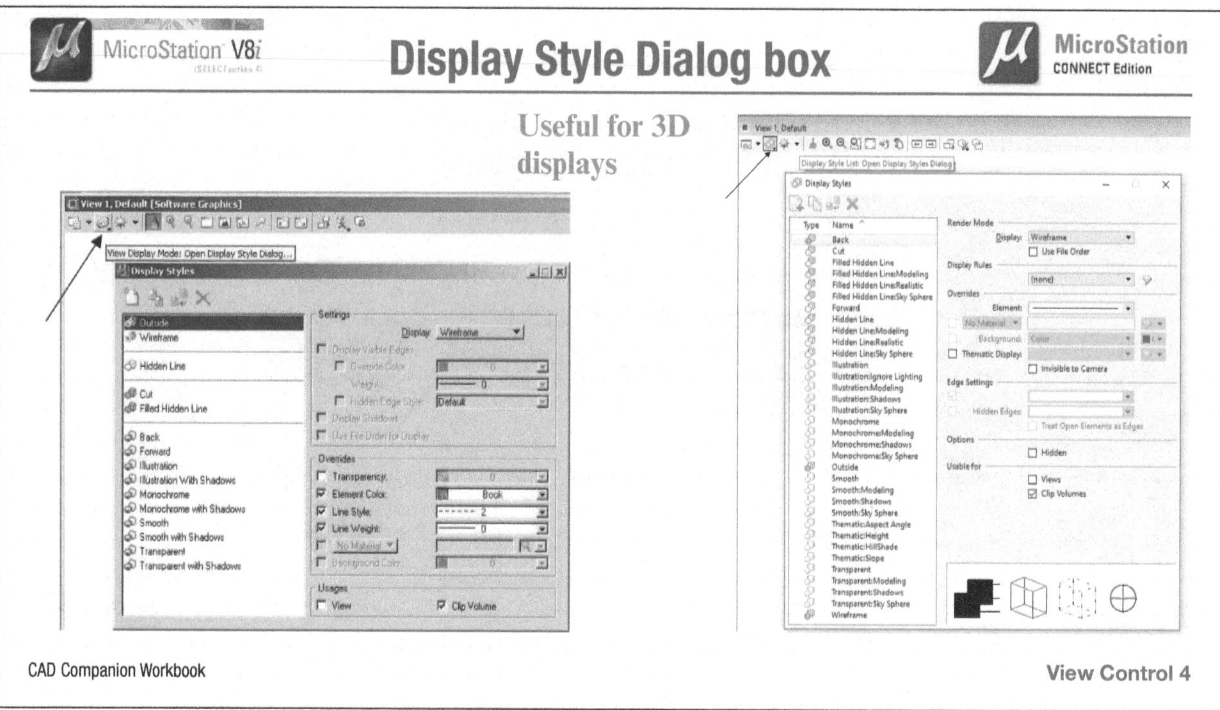

CAD Companion Workbook

View Control 4

Display Brightness

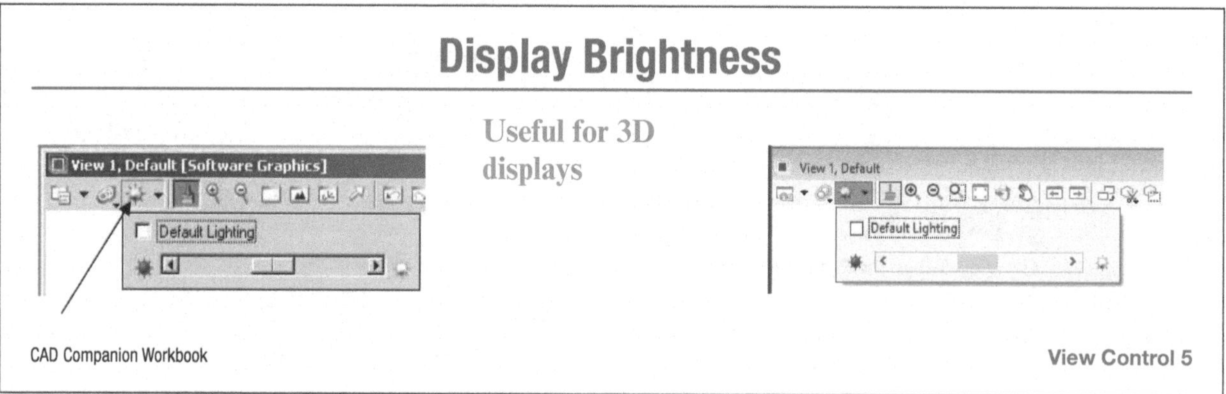

CAD Companion Workbook

View Control 5

Update View

- UPDATE
  - shortcut UP↵
- Restores the screen grid display. Objects on top of a grid dot cause the grid dot to vanish when the object is moved or deleted.
- Removes ghost images

CAD Companion Workbook

View Control 6

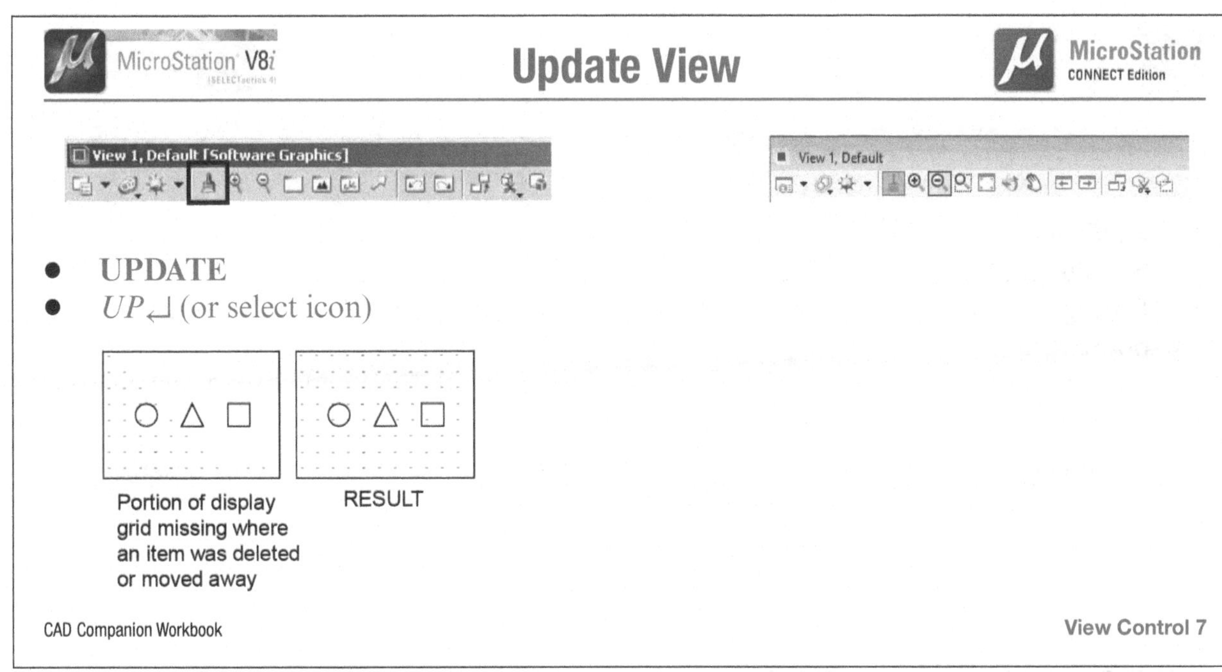
MicroStation V8i
Update View
MicroStation CONNECT Edition
View 1, Default [Software Graphics]
View 1, Default
UPDATE
UP↵ (or select icon)
Portion of display grid missing where an item was deleted or moved away
RESULT
CAD Companion Workbook
View Control 7

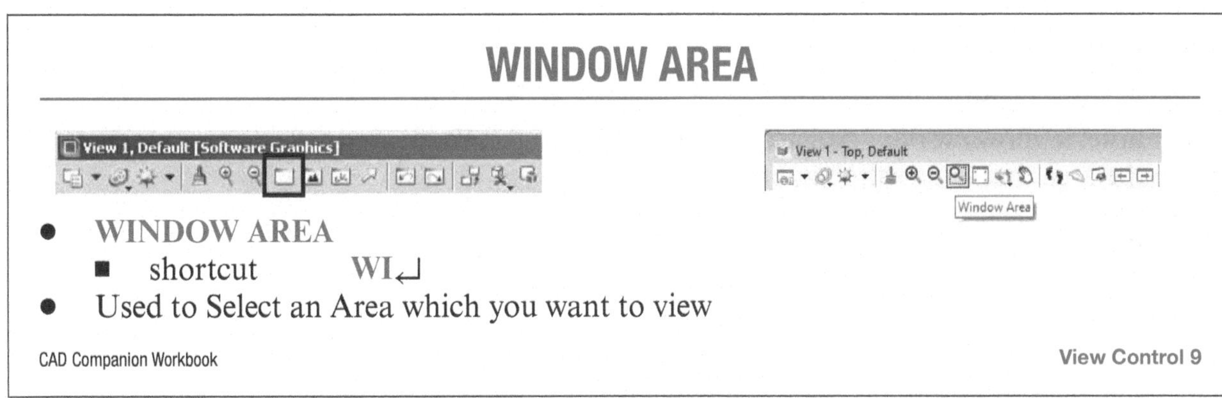
WINDOW AREA
View 1, Default [Software Graphics]
View 1 - Top, Default
Window Area
WINDOW AREA
shortcut WI↵
Used to Select an Area which you want to view
CAD Companion Workbook
View Control 9

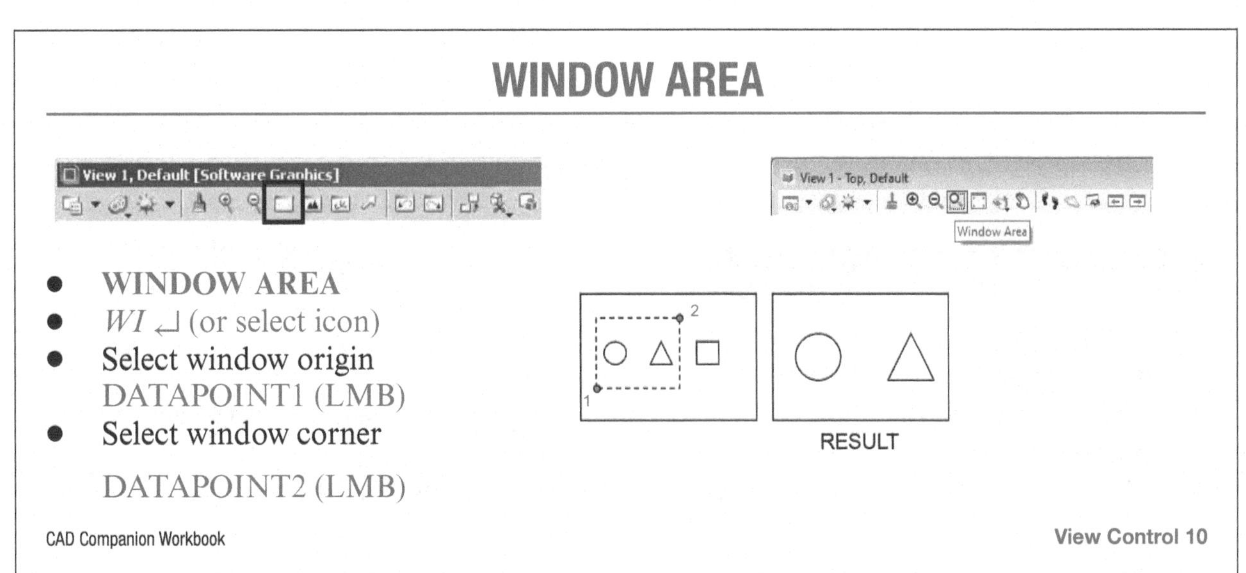
WINDOW AREA
View 1, Default [Software Graphics]
View 1 - Top, Default
Window Area
WINDOW AREA
WI ↵ (or select icon)
Select window origin
DATAPOINT1 (LMB)
Select window corner
DATAPOINT2 (LMB)
2
1
RESULT
CAD Companion Workbook
View Control 10

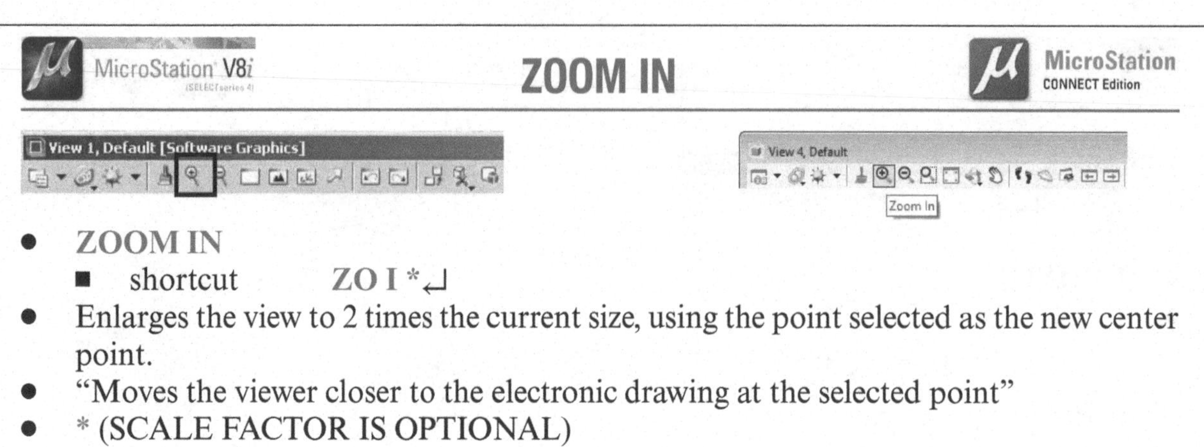
MicroStation V8i
ZOOM IN
MicroStation
CONNECT Edition
View 1, Default [Software Graphics]
View 4, Default
Zoom In
● ZOOM IN
■ shortcut ZO I *↵
● Enlarges the view to 2 times the current size, using the point selected as the new center point.
● "Moves the viewer closer to the electronic drawing at the selected point"
● * (SCALE FACTOR IS OPTIONAL)
CAD Companion Workbook
View Control 11

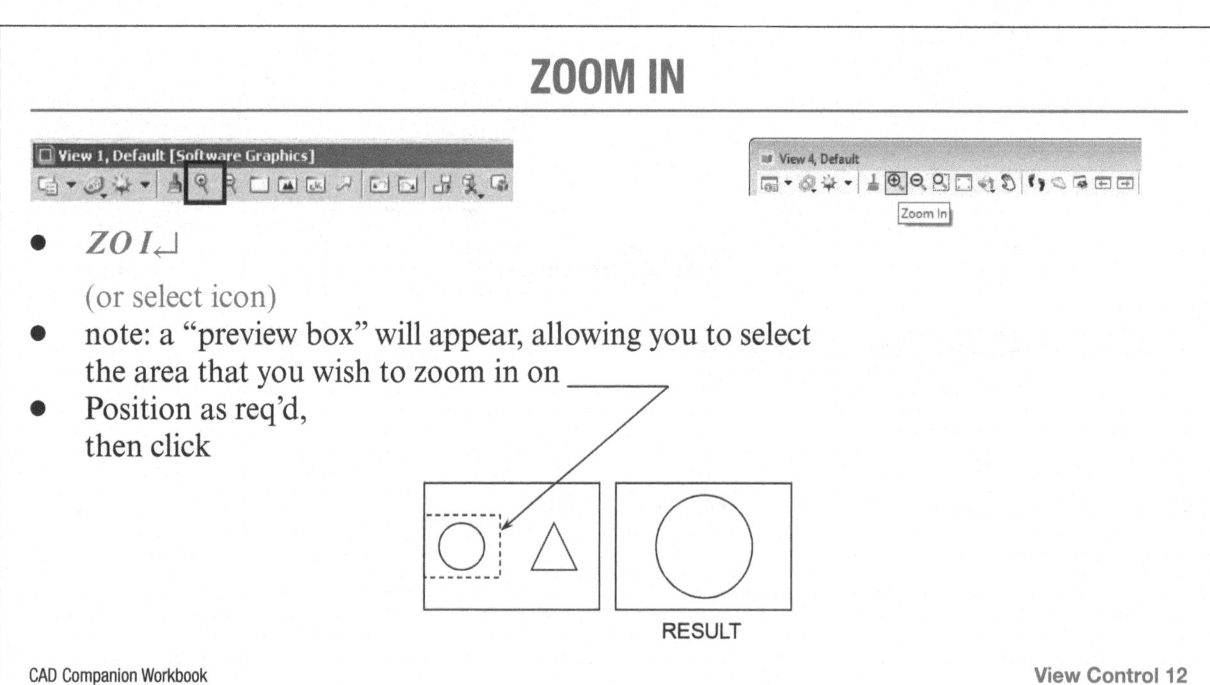
ZOOM IN
View 1, Default [Software Graphics]
View 4, Default
Zoom In
● ZO I↵
(or select icon)
● note: a "preview box" will appear, allowing you to select the area that you wish to zoom in on
● Position as req'd, then click
RESULT
CAD Companion Workbook
View Control 12

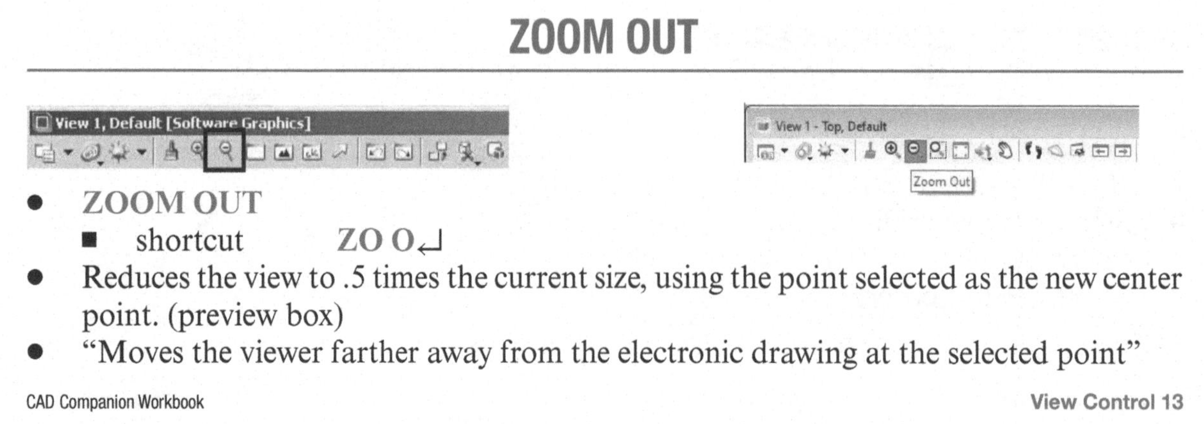
ZOOM OUT
View 1, Default [Software Graphics]
View 1 - Top, Default
Zoom Out
● ZOOM OUT
■ shortcut ZO O↵
● Reduces the view to .5 times the current size, using the point selected as the new center point. (preview box)
● "Moves the viewer farther away from the electronic drawing at the selected point"
CAD Companion Workbook
View Control 13

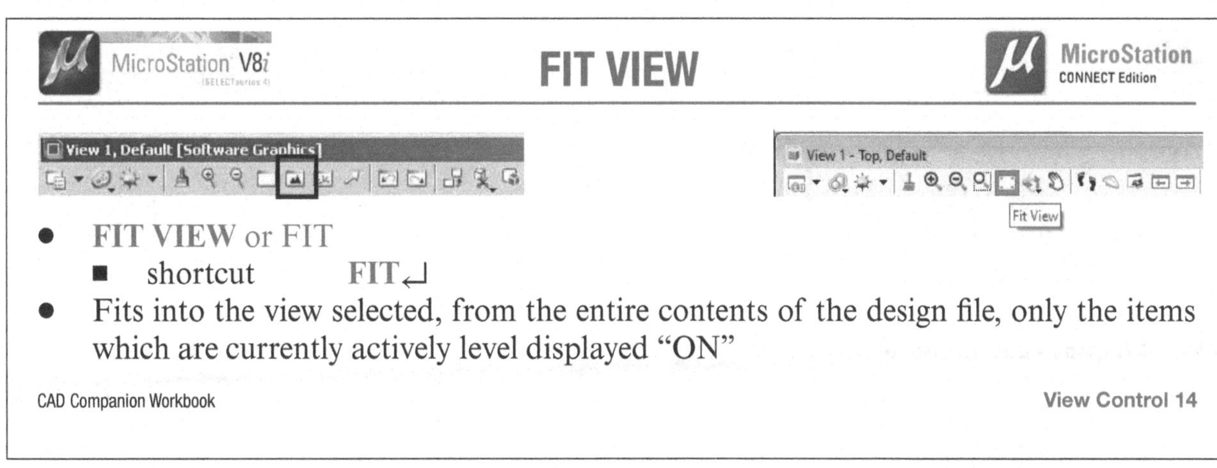

- FIT VIEW or FIT
  - shortcut FIT↵
- Fits into the view selected, from the entire contents of the design file, only the items which are currently actively level displayed "ON"

CAD Companion Workbook View Control 14

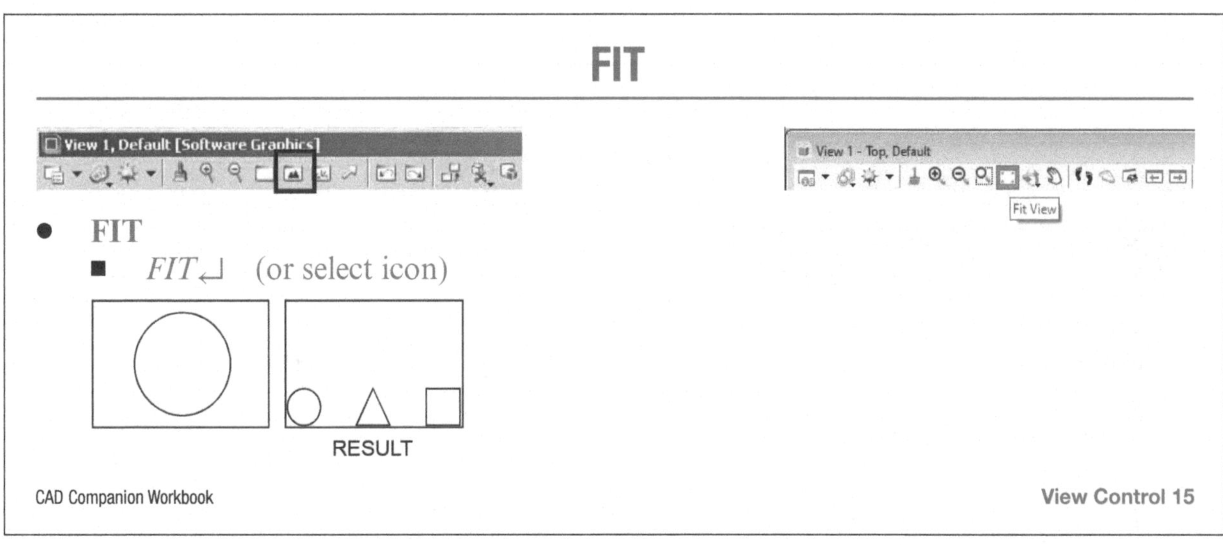

- FIT
  - *FIT*↵ (or select icon)

RESULT

CAD Companion Workbook View Control 15

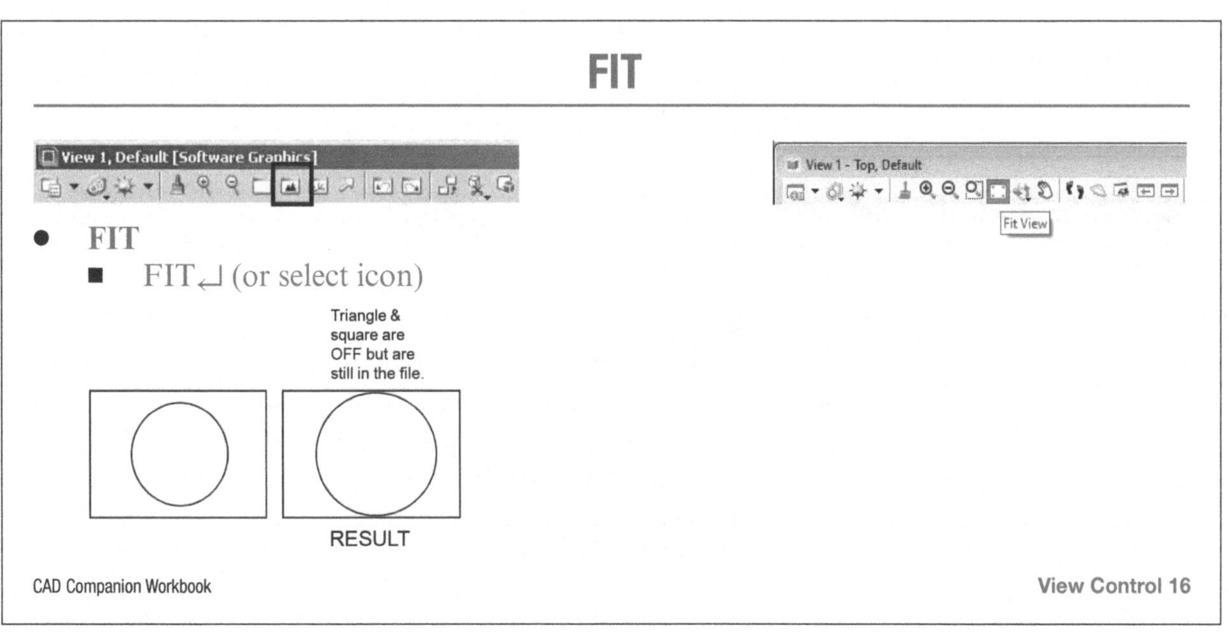

- FIT
  - FIT↵ (or select icon)

Triangle & square are OFF but are still in the file.

RESULT

CAD Companion Workbook View Control 16

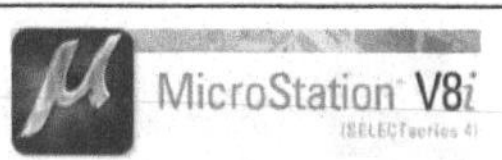

VIEW PREVIOUS / NEXT

- View-Previous
  - (Use Pull-down)
  - can go many steps
- Displays the previous area being viewed
- View-Next
  - (Use Pull-down)
  - can go many steps
- Displays the next area being viewed

VIEW PREVIOUS / NEXT

- View-Previous/Next
- **Pull-down**
  - View
    - Previous / Next
- Short-cut:
  - <Alt> V P .. or .. N

PAN / DYNAMIC PAN

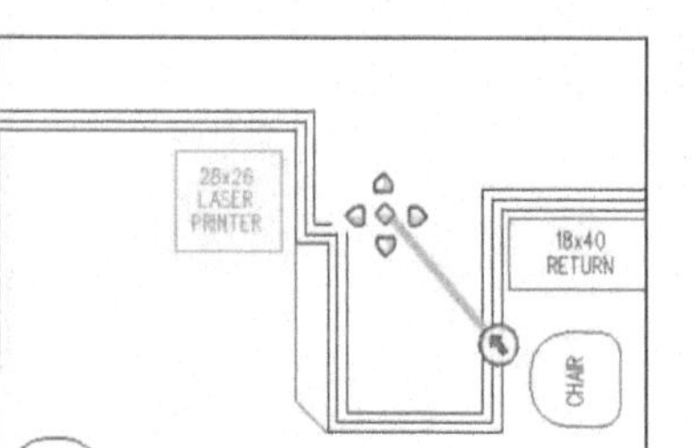

- <u><Shift> drag (left button)</u>
- Observe the Instructor perform the manuever
- Best to Start from the center of the view
- Then move cursor in the direction you wish to move
- Image pans dynamically
- The farther you move your mouse from the start location, the faster the Pan action

TOUCH SCREEN OPTIONS

Additional View Control options exist for tablet and touch screen-enabled laptops, monitors and smart phones. (Procedures may vary for your device.)

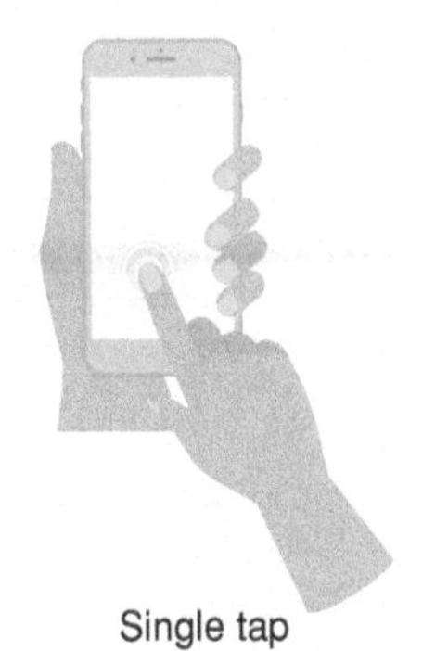

Single tap
= **Click** or **Date Point**

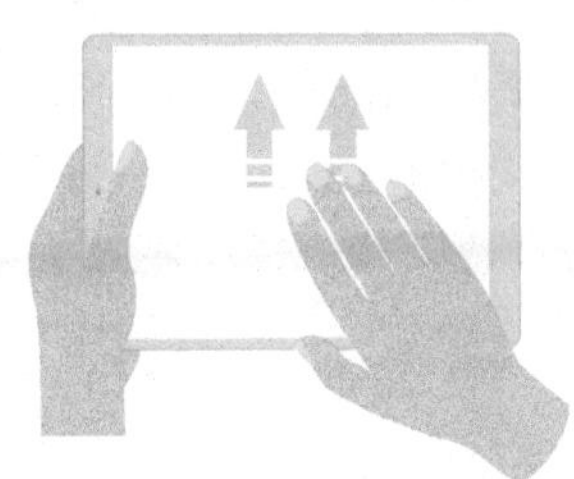

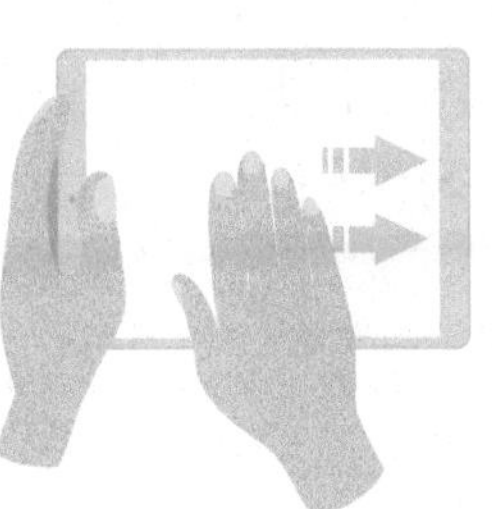

Two-Finger Drag or Swipe
= **Pan View / Scroll**

Touch and drag
= **Drag**
(Typically, NOT Scroll)

Expand or Anti-Pinch
= **Zoom In**
(enlarge the image)

Pinch
= **Zoom Out**
(shrink the image)

NAMED or SAVED VIEWS

- SAVE NAMED VIEW
  - SV= *name* ↵
- Define an area of the drawing which you are using frequently
- SAVED VIEW
  - VI= name ↵
- Display an area of the drawing which you are using frequently
- DELETE NAMED VIEW
  - DV= *name* ↵
- Delete the definition of the saved area

(Technology Preview) V8i Task Theme

New feature in CONNECT Edition 

(Technology Preview) V8i Task Theme in MicroStation CONNECT Edition (From CONNECT Edition On-line Help)

The V8i Task Theme is now provided in MicroStation CONNECT Edition to provide a familiar user interface for users who have recently migrated from MicroStation V8i. As a new user it may take you some time to get acquainted with the new Ribbon Interface in MicroStation CONNECT Edition. While you explore the benefits of using the ribbon, you can use the familiar V8i Task Theme to access your frequently used tools and finish-up your project.

You can now easily turn on the V8i Task Theme from the **Select V8i Mode** drop-down in the Quick Access toolbar. From the drop-down menu you can choose the Ribbon, Dialog, Toolbox or Combobox style to display the V8i tools. You can also access the V8i Task theme by selecting the **Task Navigation** workflow and picking the desired task form the **Select Task** drop-down in the Quick Access toolbar.

Setting	Description
Ribbon	Displays the legacy **V8i** tools in the Ribbon.
Dialog	Displays the V8i tools in the **Tasks** dialog on the left-hand side.
Toolbox	Displays the **Tasks** toolbox.
Combobox	Displays the Tasks combobox.

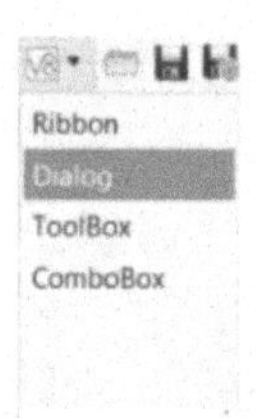

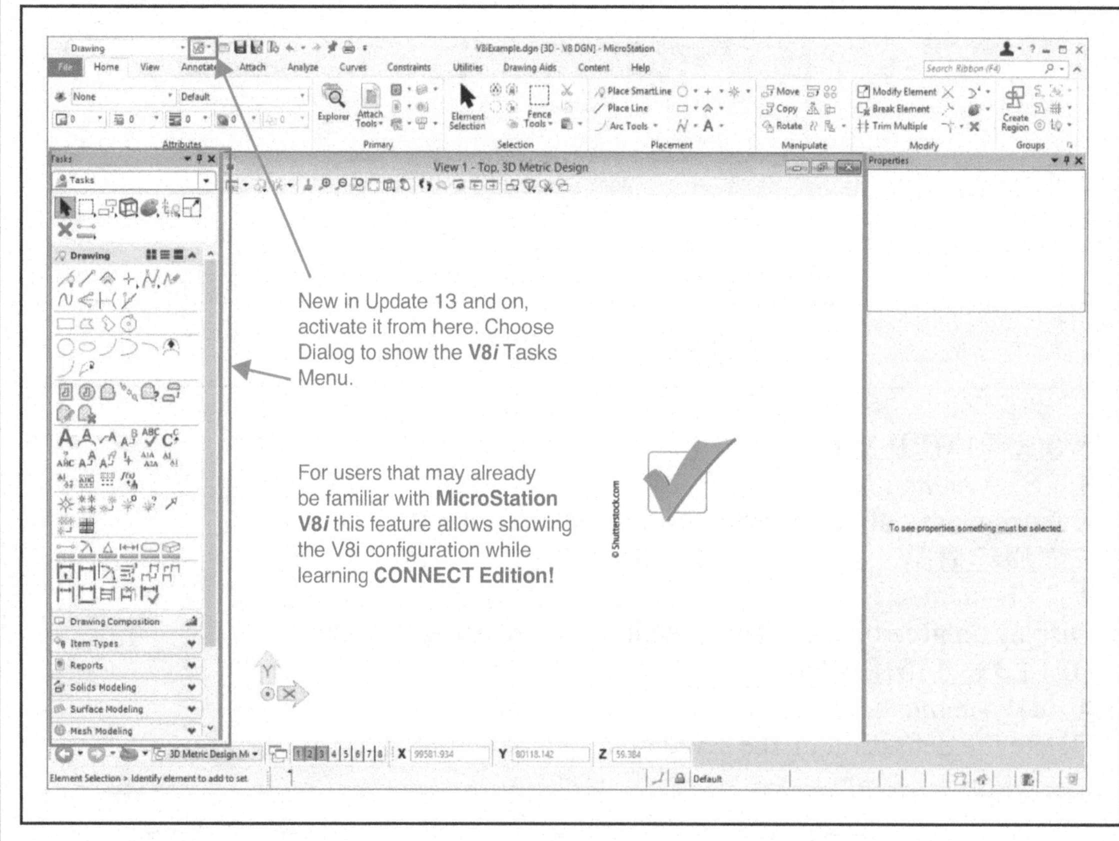

Module 0 – Engineering Symbols Primer

Symbol/ Abbreviations: (this is not exhaustive list)

Ø = diameter
R = radius
H = Height
W = Width
L = Length
D = Depth
× means "by", used: L × W × H
OD = outside diameter
ID = inside diameter

EQ = equal
Σ = sum or summation
Δ = delta , or difference
~ means approximate
# means pounds
lb also is pounds
NA means not applicable
W/ means with

W/O means without
TYP means typical
℄ Centerline symbol
⍁ means square area
s.f. means square feet

K prefix or suffix means thousands, example: $10k means $10,000 (or ten-thousand dollars)
k can also stand for kilometers (1000 meters), example: 100 kph means 100 kilometers per hour
m prefix means milli- (one thousands of), example: 1 millimeter =1/1000 of a meter

More Greek symbols:

μ prefix means micro (one millionth)
α β, alpha and beta, usually denote angles

European conventions vs. U.S.

Use of the comma can mean same as the U.S. period, Examples:
in Europe they may write 1,0 which means *one **point** zero*
in the U.S, we would write this as 1.0 which means *one **point** zero*

(note: in ALL of sessions that I teach, we follow the U.S., normal usage of the period)

U.S. Example: **1,000** means **one-thousand** (U.S. standard convention)
U.S. Example: **1.000** means **one point zero zero zero,** same as **1.0** (U.S. standard convention)
Metric vs. English units (discussion)

Hand-written or computer printed characters:

Written numeral **7** can have a horizontal bar to distinguish it from a number one
Written letter **Z** can have a horizontal bar to distinguish it from a number **2**
Written number **1** can be written as shown
Numeral zero Ø can have a slash through it (common on computer printouts)
Letter **O** *never* has a slash through it

7 is a 7
Z is a Z
1 is a 1

Drafting standards:

Repeating dimensions are not shown but can be called out "typical" or " typ.
Unneeded detail is preferably left out

< REVIEW

Immediately Preceding Material Highlights:

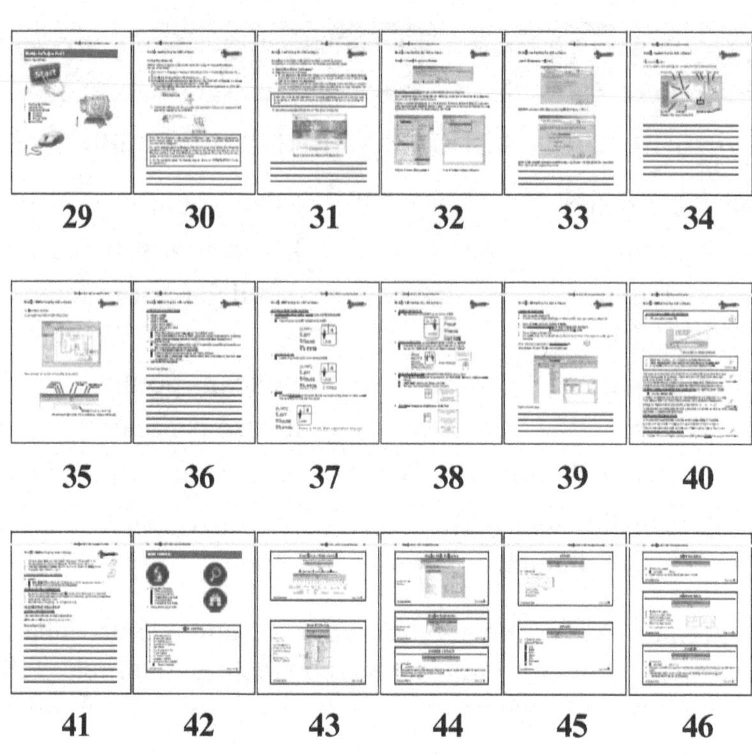

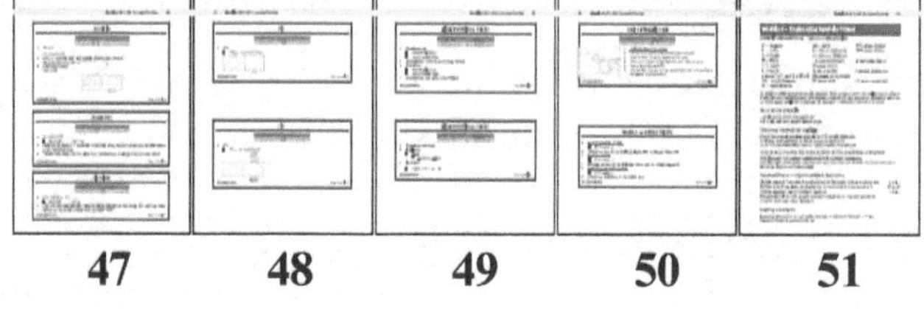

PREVIEW >

Immediately Following Material Highlights:

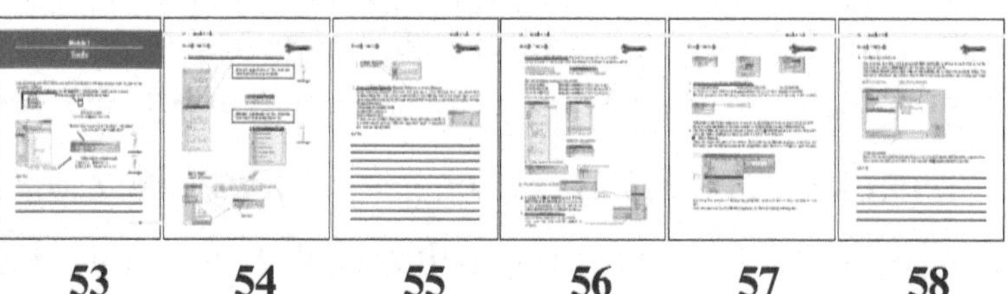

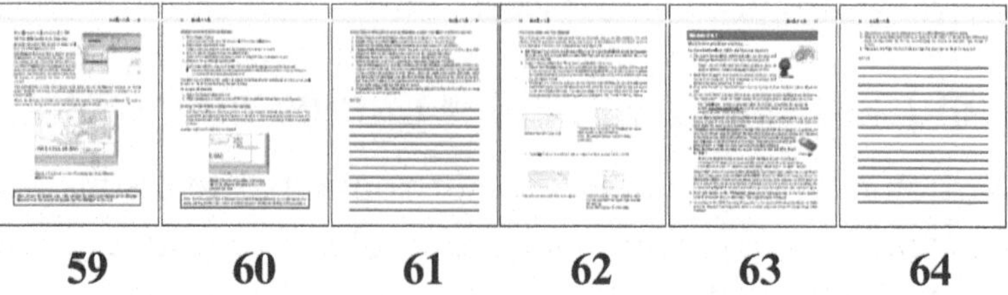

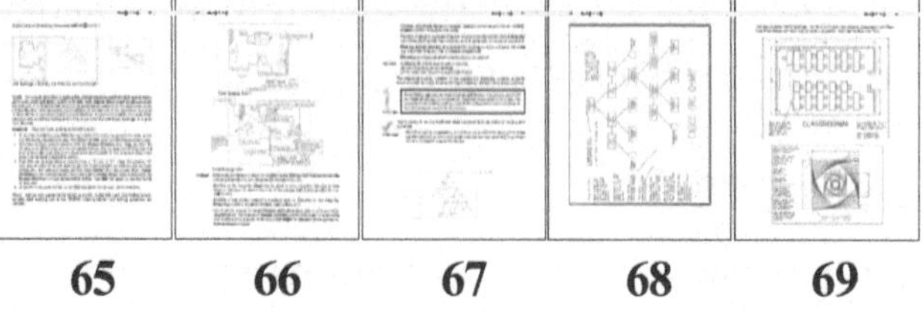

Module 1

Tools

<<<< The top half of this page introduces **V8*i*** Tools

The following new EDITING tools will be introduced in this approximate order for use on the TRAVEL drawing:

1. <u>From the **Main Tasks #3**:</u> (the SUB-MENU "Manipulate" Task can be opened)
   - **COPY**
   - **MOVE**
   - **ROTATE**
   - **MIRROR**

bold boxes point out the new tools to learn

Alternate names: toolbox, sub-menu and task.

© Shutterstock.com

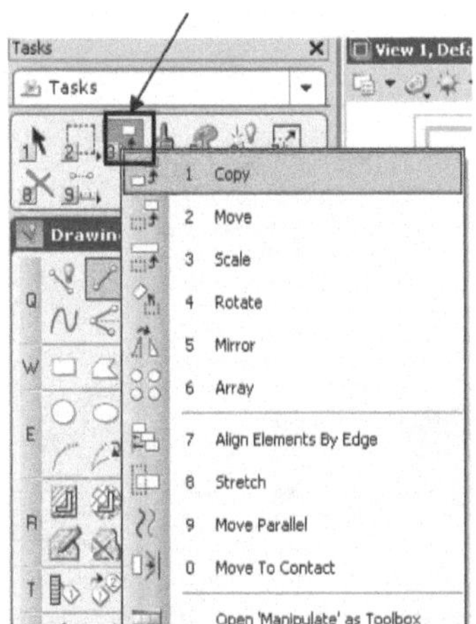

"Manipulate" opened as a "Toolbar". "Floating" Also referred to as "un-docked"

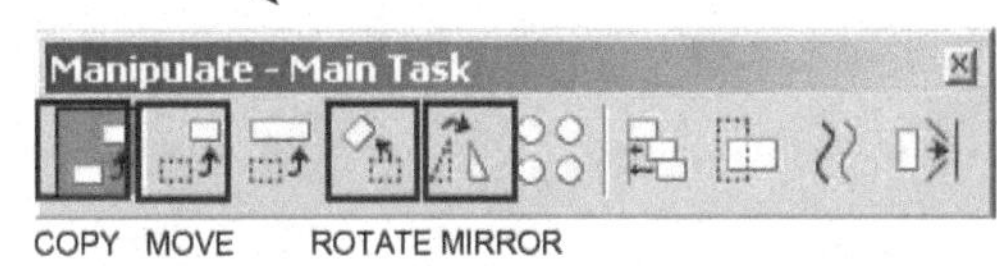

COPY MOVE ROTATE MIRROR

© Shutterstock.com

POSITIONAL KEYBOARD NAVIGATION can also be llsed to activate tools:

Copy is 3 1 Move is 3 2
Rotate is 3 4 Mirror is 3 5, etc

< POSITIONAL KEYBOARD NAVIGATION short-cuts are discontinued in the CONNECT Edition.

The bottom half of this page introduces **CONNECT Edition** Tools > >

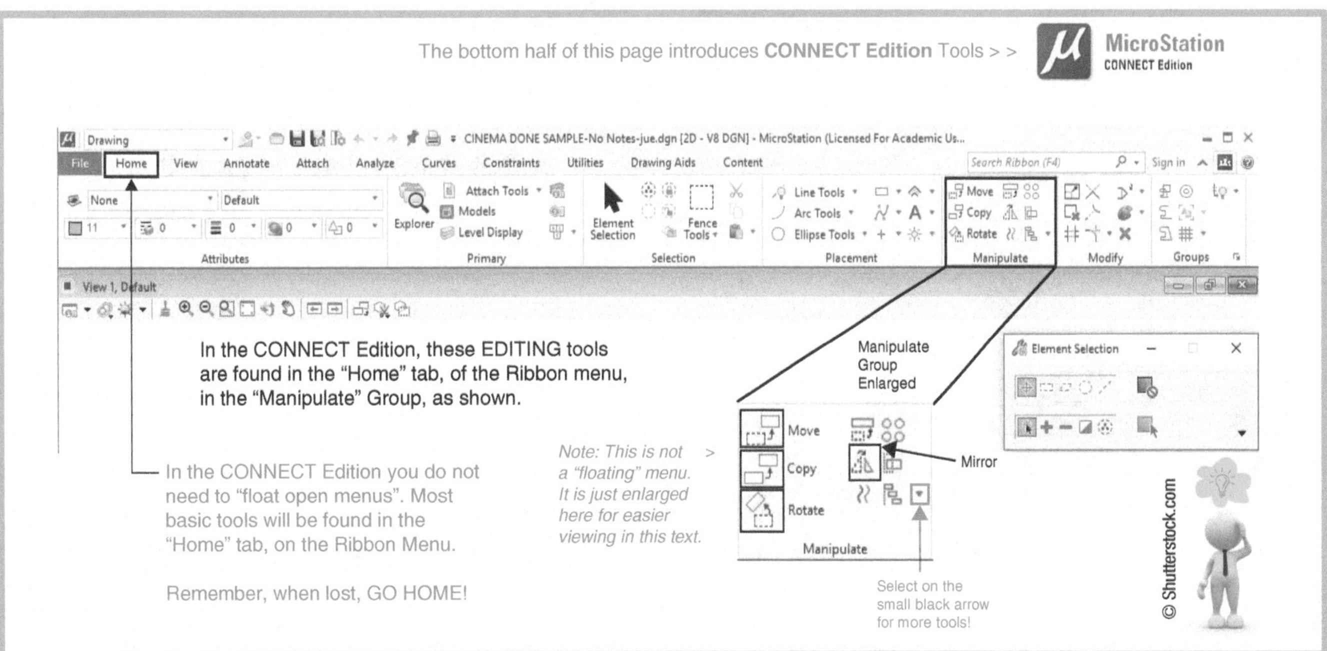

In the CONNECT Edition, these EDITING tools are found in the "Home" tab, of the Ribbon menu, in the "Manipulate" Group, as shown.

In the CONNECT Edition you do not need to "float open menus". Most basic tools will be found in the "Home" tab, on the Ribbon Menu.

Remember, when lost, GO HOME!

Note: This is not a "floating" menu. It is just enlarged here for easier viewing in this text. >

Select on the small black arrow for more tools!

© Shutterstock.com

Module 1 – Tools

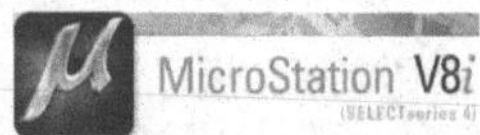

< < < < The top half of this page introduces **V8*i*** Tools

2. EDIT TEXT From the **Drawing** or **Annotate** Task Panel Layout mode:

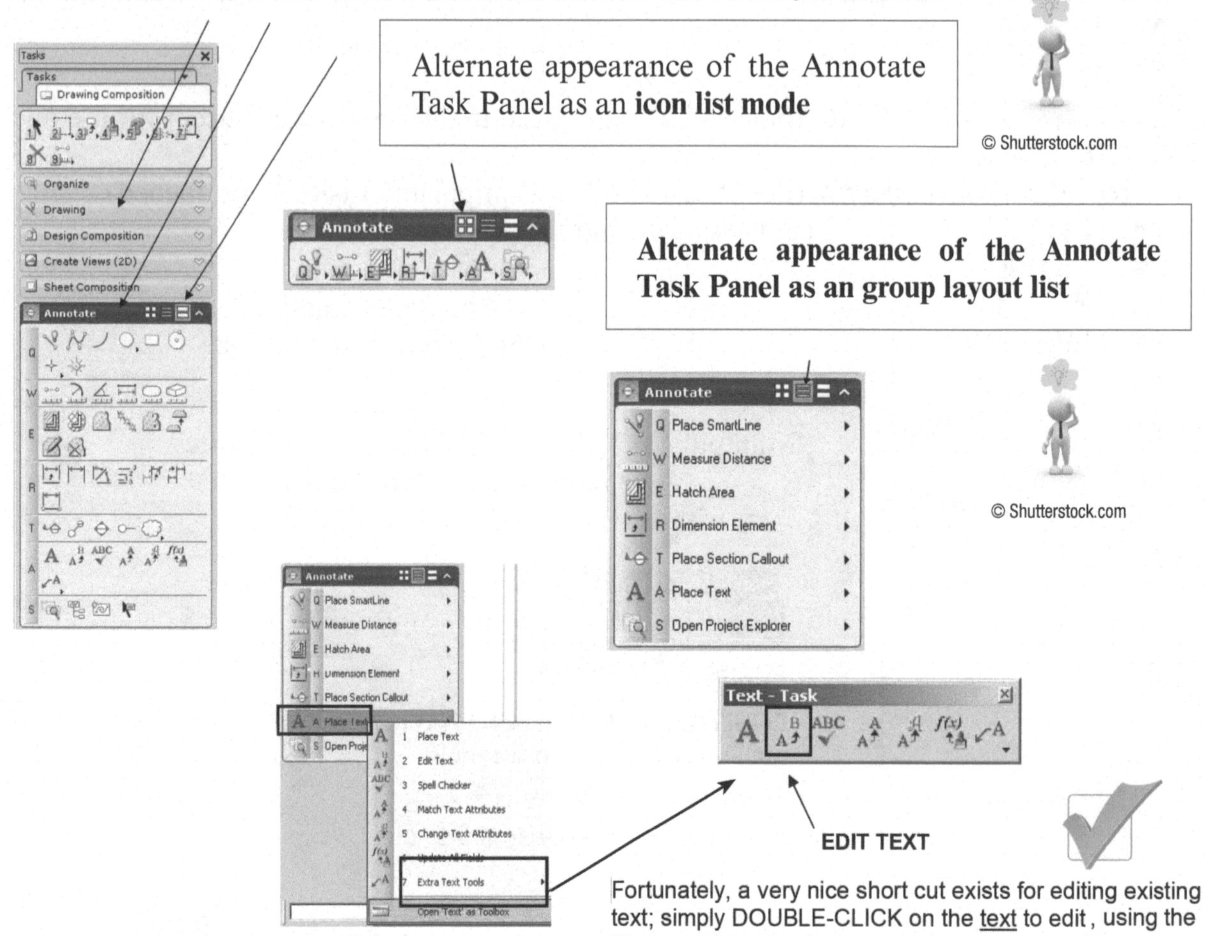

Fortunately, a very nice short cut exists for editing existing text; simply DOUBLE-CLICK on the text to edit, using the Element Selection tool.

The bottom half of this page introduces **CONNECT Edition** Tools > >

Explore the **"Annotate" Tab.**

While in the "**Drawing**" **Workflow,** the "**Annotate**" **Tab** in the Ribbon menu is shown.

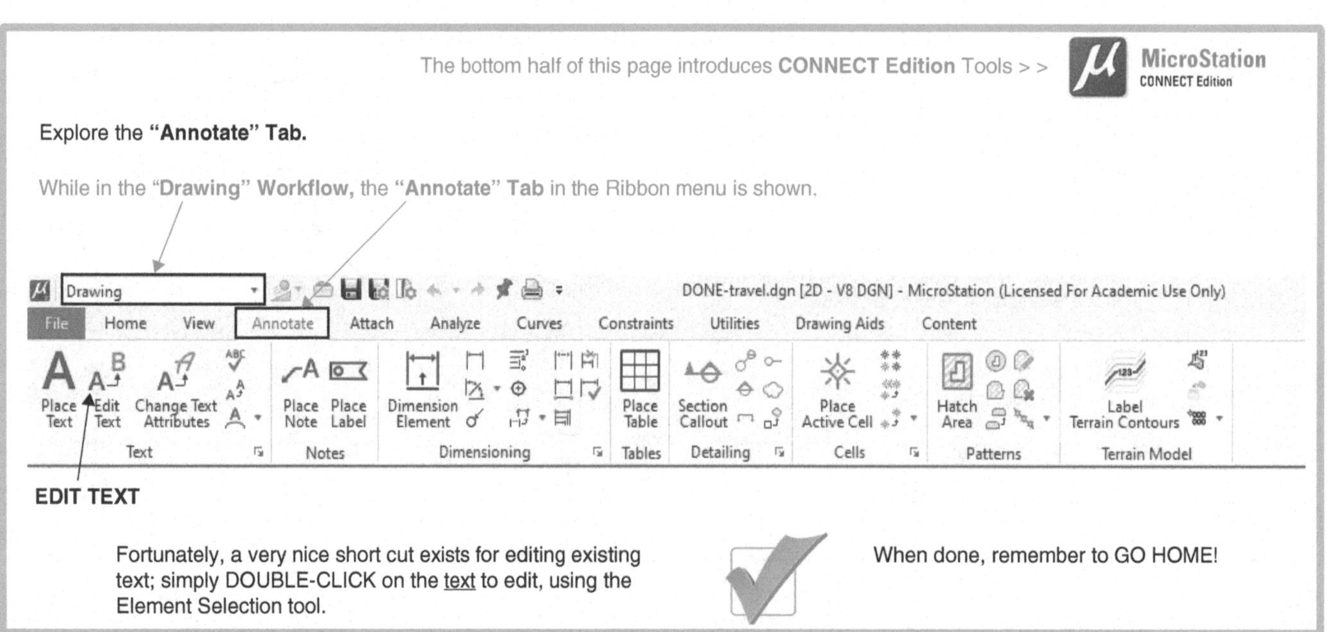

Fortunately, a very nice short cut exists for editing existing text; simply DOUBLE-CLICK on the text to edit, using the Element Selection tool.

When done, remember to GO HOME!

Module 1 – Tools

< < < < The top half of this page introduces **V8*i*** Tools

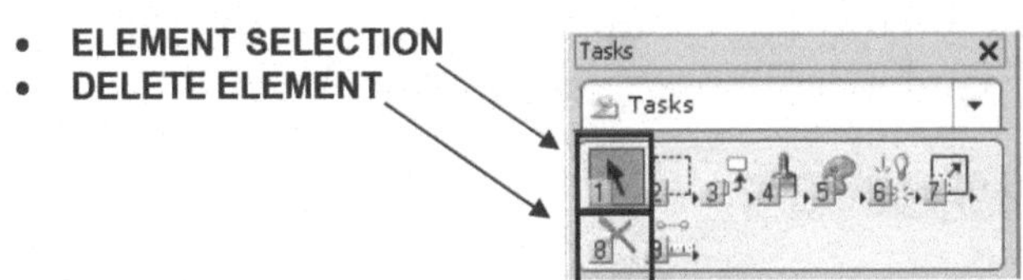

3. <u>From the **Main Tasks #1**:</u> **Element Selection & Delete Element**
   Once activated, Element Selection will pop up a "Tool Settings Window" associated with Element Selection. The proper location for a Tool Setting Box is the upper right part of the screen. More info on the settings available will be shown in the detailed section covering Element Selection.
   Other ways to activate tools:
   Element Selection is 1
   Delete Element is 8
   if these do not activate when you type them, you may already be in a view control tool, hit <Enter> then type "null" to deactivate any tool (no parentheses)

Tool Setting Window

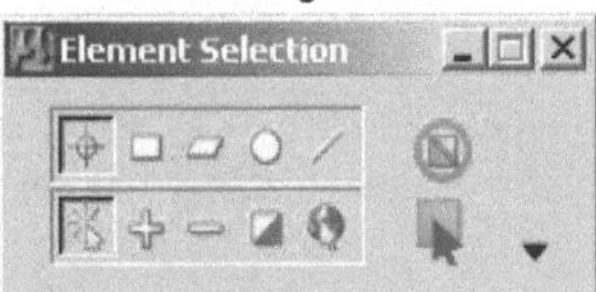

The bottom half of this page introduces **CONNECT Edition** Tools > >

MicroStation CONNECT Edition

Locating the **Element Selection Tool, Tool Settings Window** and **Delete Element.**

While in the "**Drawing**" **Workflow,** the "**Home**" **Tab** in the Ribbon interface is shown.

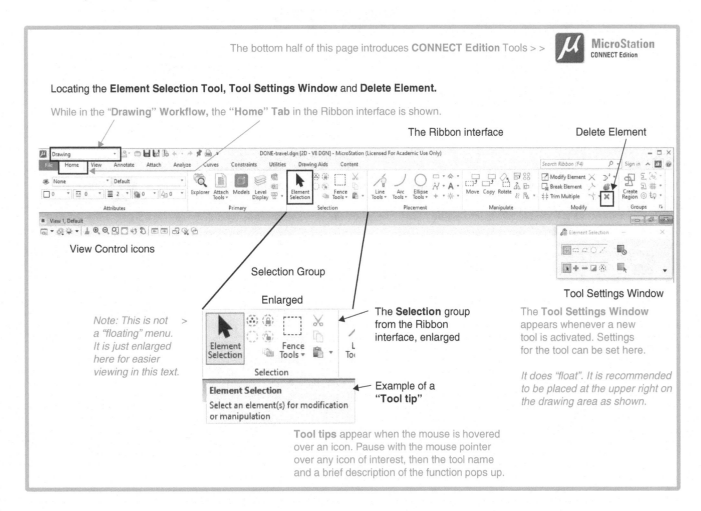

The Ribbon interface

Delete Element

View Control icons

Selection Group

Enlarged

Note: This is not a "floating" menu. It is just enlarged here for easier viewing in this text. >

The **Selection** group from the Ribbon interface, enlarged

Element Selection
Select an element(s) for modification or manipulation

Example of a **"Tool tip"**

Tool tips appear when the mouse is hovered over an icon. Pause with the mouse pointer over any icon of interest, then the tool name and a brief description of the function pops up.

Tool Settings Window

The **Tool Settings Window** appears whenever a new tool is activated. Settings for the tool can be set here.

It does "float". It is recommended to be placed at the upper right on the drawing area as shown.

Module 1 – Tools

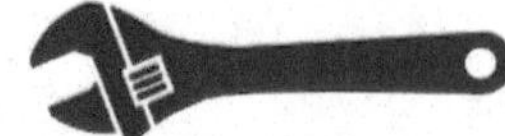

<<<< The top half of this page introduces **V8*i*** Tools

__On the **Draw Main Task Panel**:__ Expand the **Drawing** group if it is not visible on the left side of the screen. One can expand or collapse it as shown below.

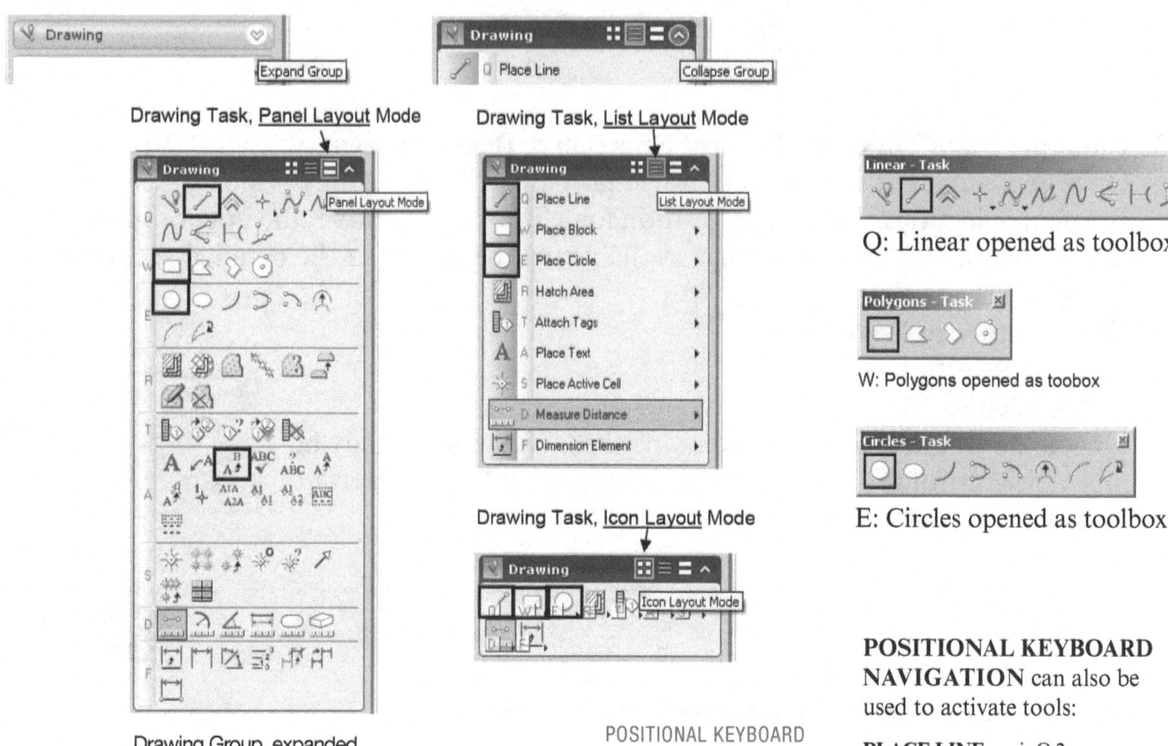

POSITIONAL KEYBOARD NAVIGATION short-cuts are discontinued in the CONNECT Edition.

POSITIONAL KEYBOARD NAVIGATION can also be used to activate tools:

PLACE LINE is Q 2
PLACE BLOCK is W 1
PLACE CIRCLE is E 1

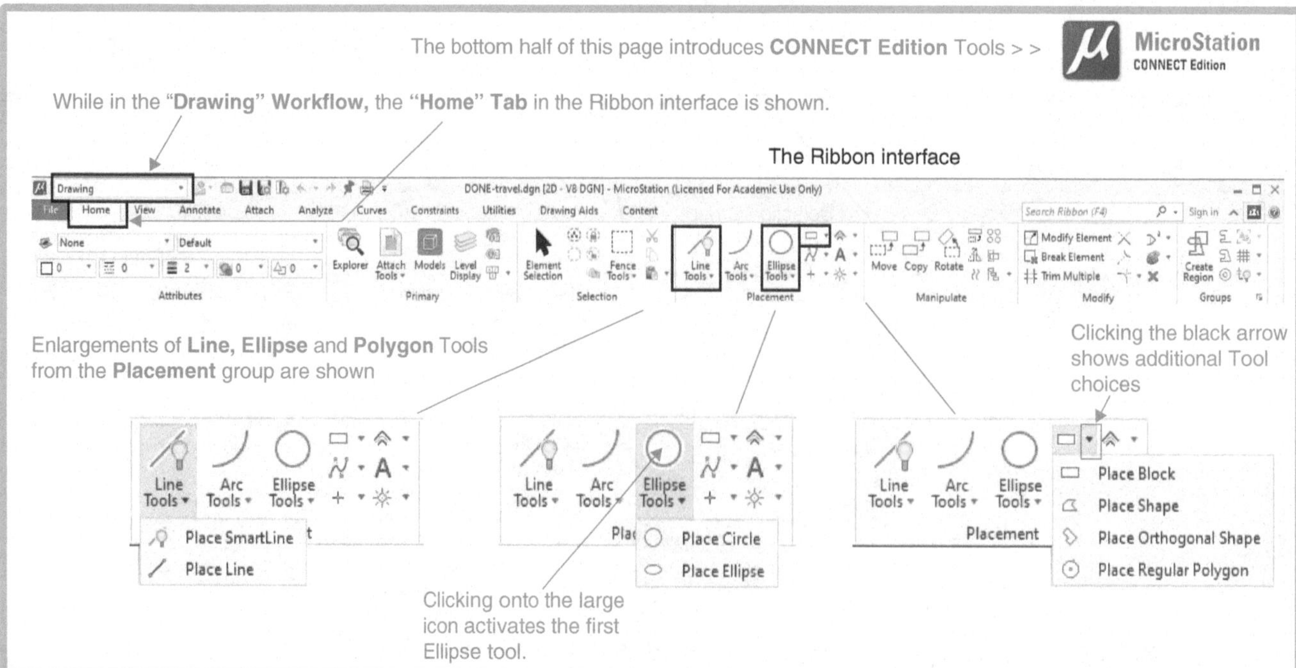

Module 1 – Tools

<<<< The top half of this page introduces V8*i* Tools

4. **LOCKS POP-UP MENU** and **6. TOOL SETTINGS WINDOW** will be introduced in this approximate order for use on the **ORGCHART and FLOCHART** drawings:
5. On the **Locks** Pop-up Menu:
   (on the lower right part of the screen click onto the little LOCK **symbol** to activate)

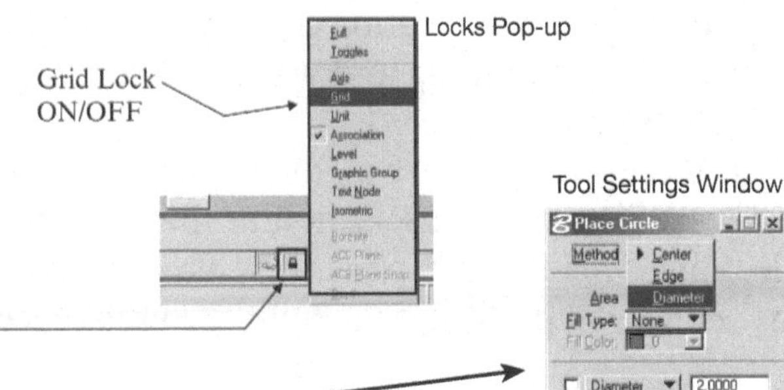

6. Appearance of TOOL SETTINGS for PLACE CIRCLE:

Tool Settings Window

7. A Toolbar to turn OFF for now – **AccuDraw:** (do not dock it, dismiss it entirely) We will introduce **AccuDraw** in a later session and will not use it for now. It is a bit more advanced tool and can conflict with some tools we are using in a basic fashion for now.

AccuDraw

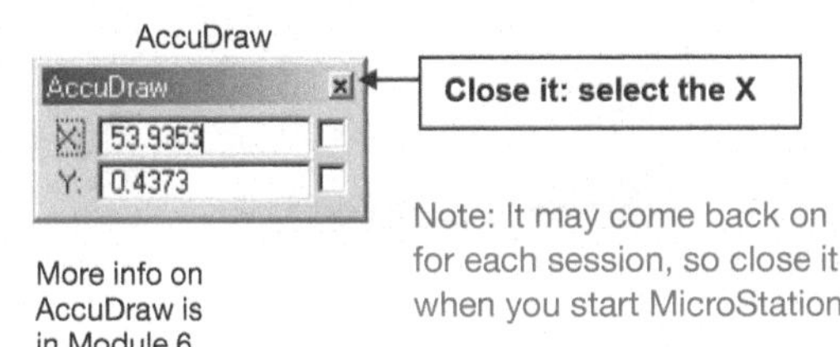

More info on AccuDraw is in Module 6

Note: It may come back on for each session, so close it when you start MicroStation.

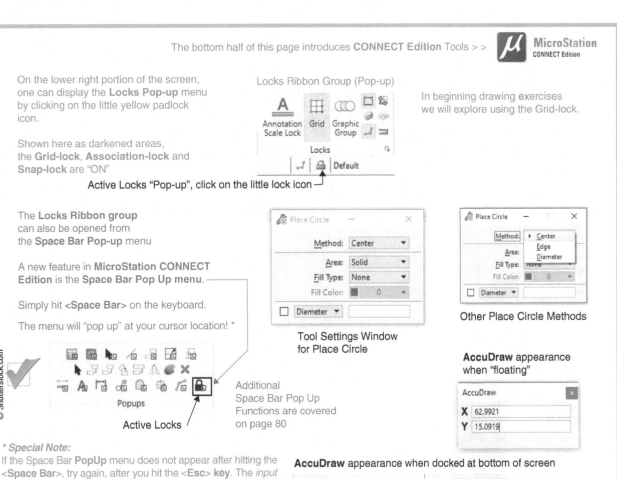

The bottom half of this page introduces **CONNECT Edition** Tools > >

MicroStation CONNECT Edition

On the lower right portion of the screen, one can display the **Locks Pop-up** menu by clicking on the little yellow padlock icon.

Shown here as darkened areas, the **Grid-lock**, **Association-lock** and **Snap-lock** are "ON"

Locks Ribbon Group (Pop-up)

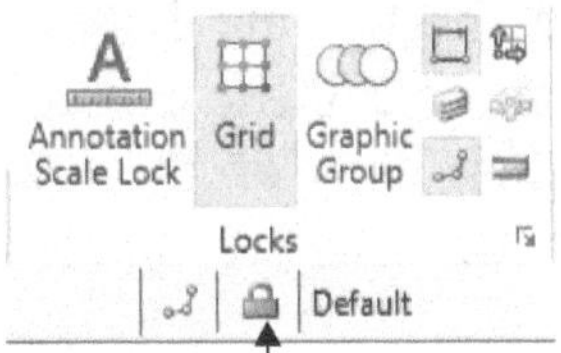

Annotation Scale Lock | Grid | Graphic Group | Locks | Default

Active Locks "Pop-up", click on the little lock icon

In beginning drawing exercises we will explore using the Grid-lock.

The **Locks Ribbon group** can also be opened from the **Space Bar Pop-up** menu

A new feature in **MicroStation CONNECT Edition** is the **Space Bar Pop Up menu**.

Simply hit **<Space Bar>** on the keyboard.

The menu will "pop up" at your cursor location! *

Place Circle
Method: Center
Area: Solid
Fill Type: None
Fill Color: 0
Diameter

Tool Settings Window for Place Circle

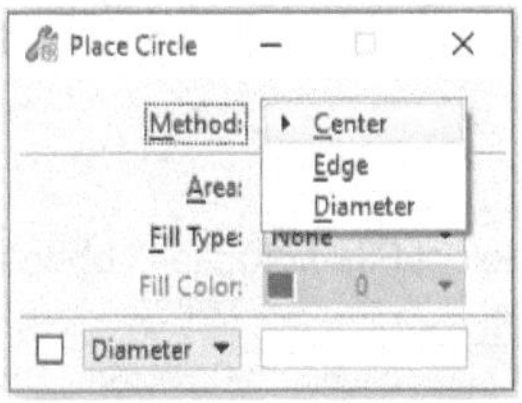

Place Circle
Method: Center / Edge / Diameter
Area:
Fill Type: None
Fill Color: 0
Diameter

Other Place Circle Methods

© Shutterstock.com

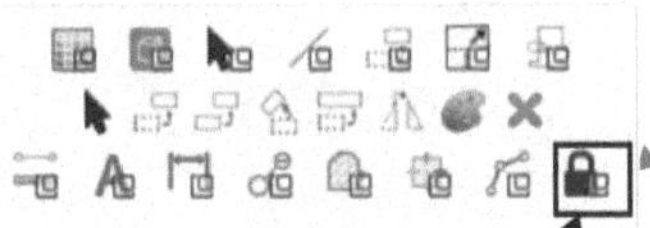

Popups

Active Locks

Additional Space Bar Pop Up Functions are covered on page 80

AccuDraw appearance when "floating"

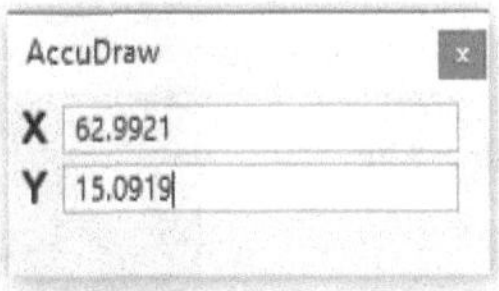

AccuDraw
X 62.9921
Y 15.0919

** Special Note:*
If the Space Bar **PopUp** menu does not appear after hitting the <**Space Bar**>, try again, after you hit the <**Esc**> **key**. The *input focus* may have been in the **Key-in Field**, the **Tool Settings Window** or in the **AccuDraw** window. Or you may need to close the **Text Editor** window in case you are in **Place Text**.

AccuDraw appearance when docked at bottom of screen

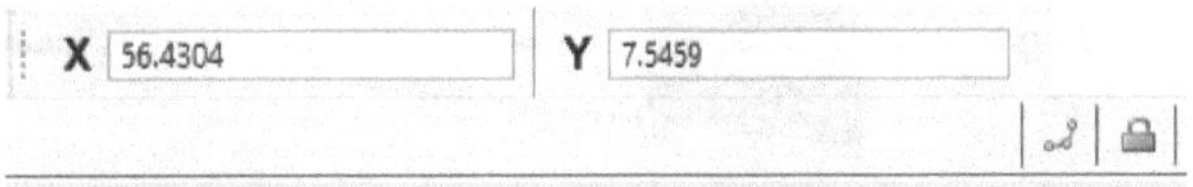

X 56.4304 Y 7.5459

Module 1 – Tools

< < < < The top half of this page introduces **V8*i*** Tools

8. The **File > Save As** operation command from the Pull-down Menu will be needed when you open the Travel drawing and want to save a copy of it for yourself.
   - **File > Save As**

   From the upper left part of the screen. Note how the pull-down sequence is written: the first word lists the first selection in the pull-down, then there is a **>** symbol, then the next selection. This method of writing the pull-down sequences will be used throughout this text. After you perform this Pull-down sequence, the **Save As** dialog box appears.

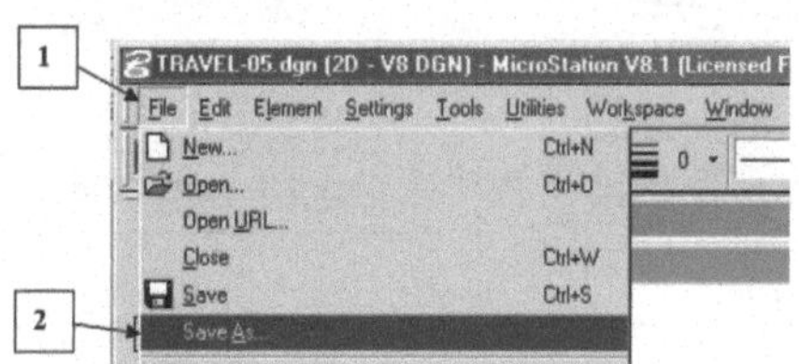

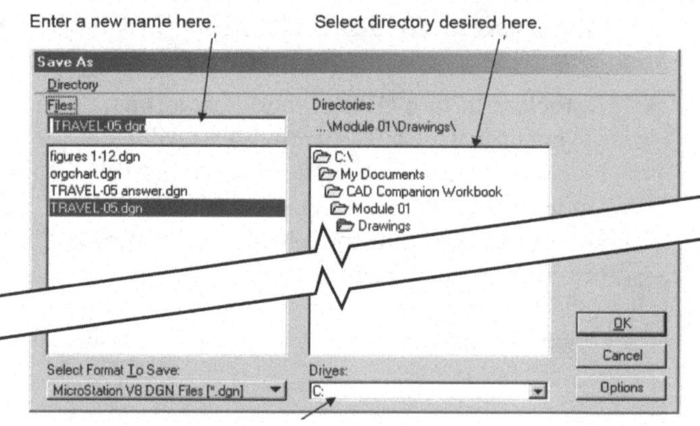

9. The **Save As** dialog box:

   The user can then select the appropriate **drive** and **folder** locations to put a copy of the file into and can enter a **file-name** to call the **new** copy of the file.

   The student should create their copy of the drawing file in their own personal folder. The Instructor will show the student where this is for each particular lab section and CAD course in session.

   Note: This location will vary depending on each facility's server and file system organization. Your instructor will inform you of the required **file-naming convention** in class.

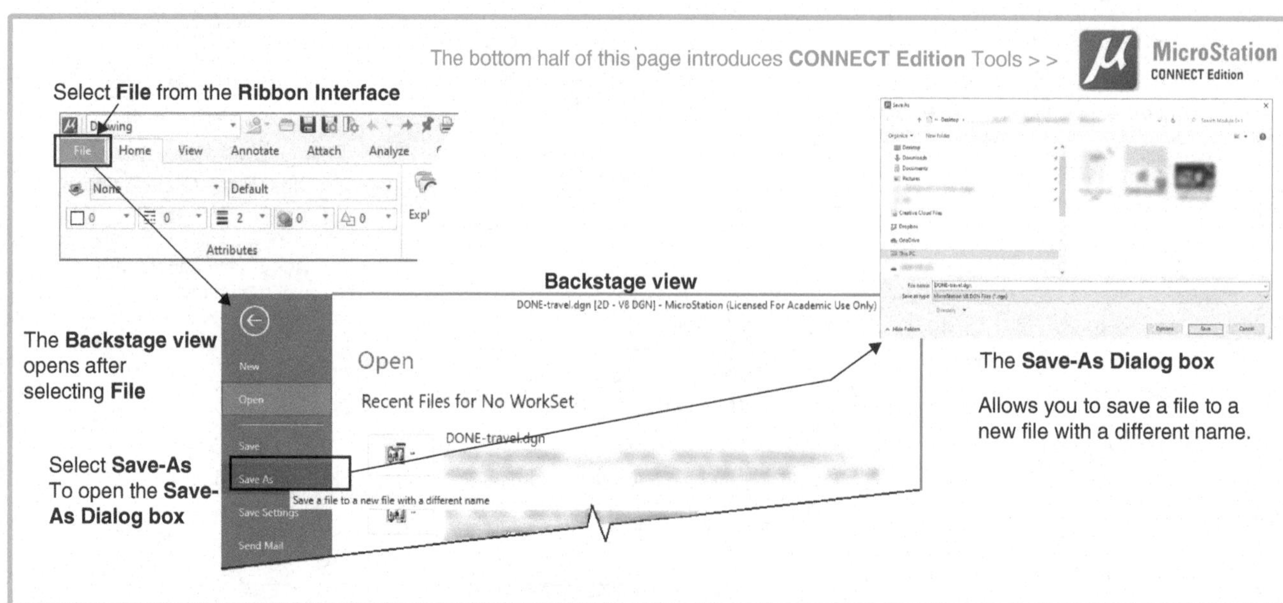

and

Element Selection (Big Arrow) It's a Multi-purpose tool!

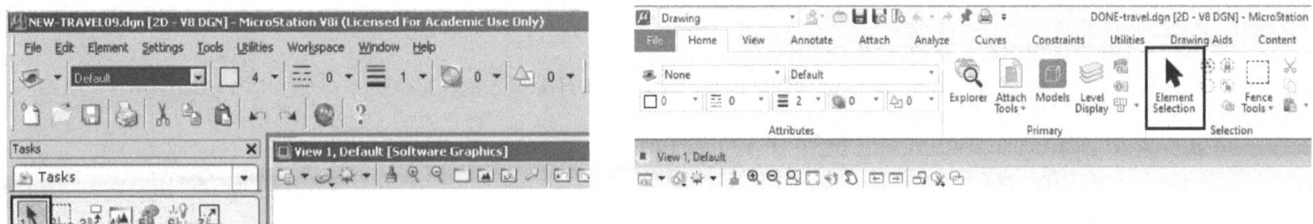

The *Element Selection* Tool is used to perform Pre-selection of element(s) for other tools or for editing of the element(s) by the selection tool itself. Pre-selection of elements to be acted upon by another tool is called the "noun-verb" method. The element(s) are selected first, then the action to perform on them is selected second.

This distinguishes it from other typical tools, which use the "verb-noun" method. In "verb-noun" method, the action to perform is selected first then the element(s) to perform it on is selected next.

When the *Element Selection* tool is selected, the pointer becomes an arrowhead with a small circle at the tip of the arrow. (see example at right & below)

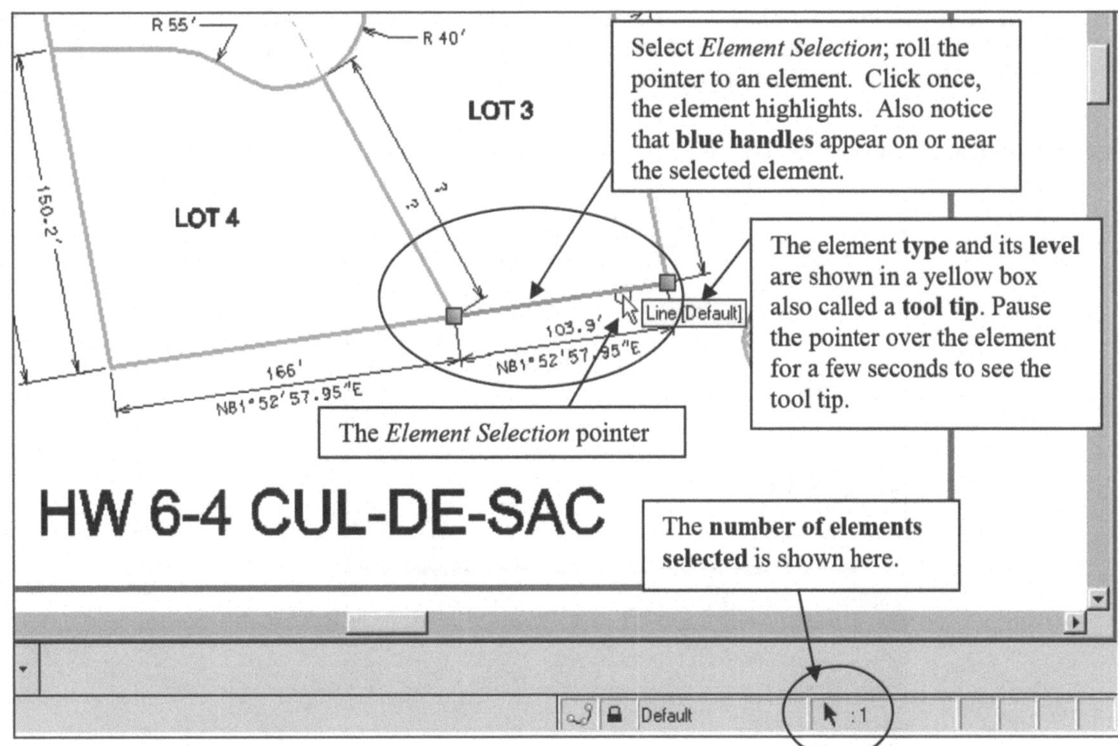

Figure. 1 Portion of a screen illustrating use of the **Element Selection tool**

and

Multiple methods of selecting elements:

1. Select single element
   (point and then click onto the element – it becomes hi-lighted)

2. Select many elements at once
   (drag a selection window from **LEFT to RIGHT** around the elements you want to select)

3. Add or remove elements from the selection set
   (hold <Ctrl> while selecting more to add or remove from the selection set)

4. Selection by an overlapping window
   (Drag a selection window from **RIGHT to LEFT**
   —elements that are inside or touching the selection window are added to the selection set … or removed if they were already selected)

The selection set stays active until it is deselected. This allows additional actions to be performed on the set as needed until the user is done.

To deselect all elements:
1. Activate the Element Selection tool
2. Click anywhere in a blank portion of the view (anywhere where there is no element)

Showing Tooltips without actually selecting anything:

Just float the *Element Selection* pointer over any element **without** any click needed. The little information box will appear to the side of the element after a second or so. No action is performed, other than the information appearing on the screen. This is very useful at times.

Another example of selecting an element:

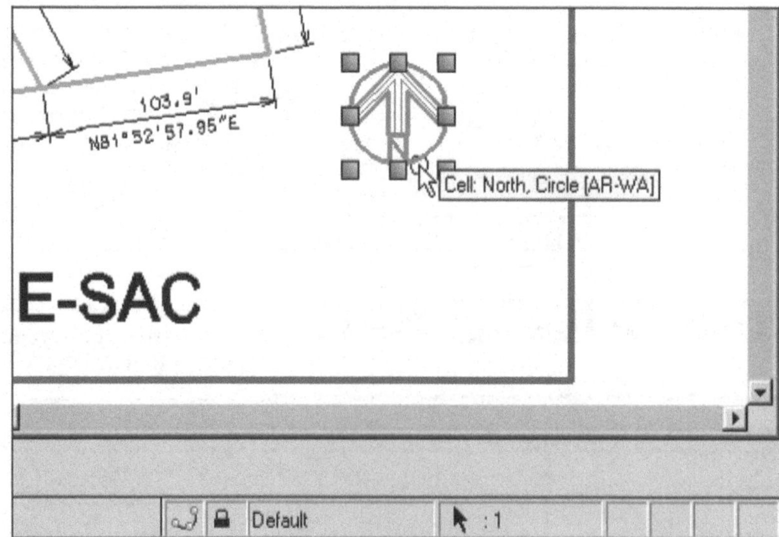

Figure. 2 Portion of a screen illustrating use of the **Element Selection tool**, a cell is selected this time.

Note: A cell is a special type of element, composed of many elements, but it acts similar to a group (see # e. below) It also counts as a single element. We will work with cells in module 6.

and

Action Choices after a selection of an element(s) is made: (note – lots of different choices!!)

a. **Move** (drag a non-handle – the element(s) is dragged to the new location)

b. **Modify (drag on a handle)** – the element(s) is modified to the new shape)

c. **Delete (hit the delete key or delete icon** – the selected element(s) are deleted)

d. **Change Symbology/Attributes** (select the new attribute on the attribute toolbar, then click within the view on the blank screen area to see the change take place)

e. **Make into Group** – turn the selection set into a **Group** with **<Ctrl> g**
Return the group back to it's ungrouped status with **Ungroup**, **<Ctrl> u**

f. **Copy & Paste – Copy or Cut the selection set to the Windows clipboard** with **<Ctrl> c for copy or <Ctrl> x for cut.** You can then **paste the selection set with <Ctrl> v.** The new copy of the selection set appears at your cursor**. *Note: the active scale factor and active angle will take effect at placement (see the Tool Settings Window).*** Reposition the cursor as needed, and then click to place. If you paste a selection set containing text elements into MicroSoft Word or Notepad, only the text will be pasted.

g. **Other – Select ANY other MicroStation tool** – the elements in the selection set will be operated on by the tool as applicable.

NOTES

and

New functionality with Text Elements

The following new actions dealing with text are available in the MicroStation V8 2004 edition (V08.05) and later versions. V8i and the CONNECT Edition also function similarly.

a. **Edit Text** – If you activate the Element Selection Tool and **double-click on any text element,** MicroStation will automatically activate **Edit Text** and will place your selected text in the text editor window. ... or ...

b. **Adjust Text Wrap or Modify** – If you activate the Element Selection Tool and **click on any text element ...**

   1. **Adjust Text Wrap** – Using the Element Selection tool, handles will display at the corners and side edges of the text element (**9 adjustment handles**) which allows the user to adjust the text window.

      Using a corner handle adjusts the text "wrap". The size of the letters is NOT adjusted. See the figures below.

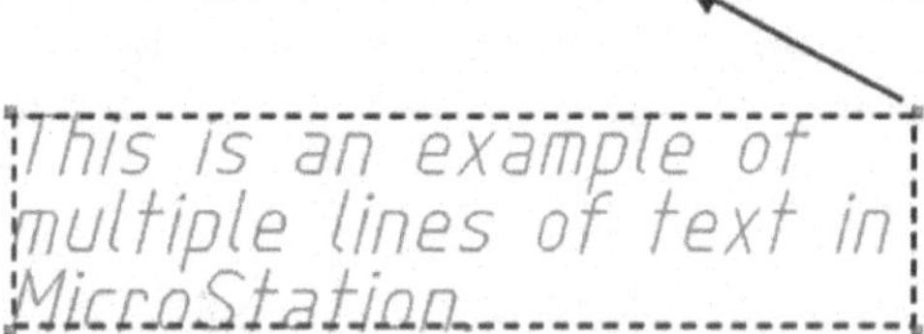

Text selected with one click

This text had the "wrap" adjusted when the user repositioned the upper right handle. Note: NO change of letter sizes.

   2. **Modify** – If you touch the multiple line text element, the typical **9 adjustment handles** will appear on the text element and will allow the user to adjust the size of the entire text element (Modify). **Use a side edge handle**! The size of the entire text element is affected (this is the standard modify action available in previous versions of V8).

Text selected once.

This text was "modified" by dragging the right edge handle to the left. Note: the re-sized text element, and NO wrap performed.

Module 0 & 1

Wait! Before you Draw anything . . .

See these Additional tips, tidbits and Challenge Questions

TIPS & TIDBITS

© Shutterstock.com

1. **The mouse buttons – left, middle and right one, are each used for different functions!** Don't use them interchangeably!

   Think! Are the brake and accelerator pedals in your car used for different, non-interchangeable purposes? Yes!

2. **Read Your Prompts!** Your instructor should show you often the value of doing this. Is there a message in the prompt field saying something important to you?
3. Deal with "alerts" or "windows" that come up on top of other windows. (Basic Windows ops)
4. **Do not "hold down" a mouse button if the action does not require holding down the button.** The "data point", "click" or "pick" action do not require you to hold down the button.

   The "data-point" action is generally done as follows: reposition the mouse as needed, then Press and Release the Left mouse button. Some of you may be familiar with the term "Point and Click"!

5. **Do not indiscriminately hit additional button presses!** Do not tap-tap-tap-tap on the mouse button. It may or may not affect how fast the elevator gets to your floor, but in CAD this most likely will mess up your drawing!
6. **Unfamiliar with the new material or a concept?** See the Review list on page 23, in general, for the topics covered. And Get HELP! See item #28 listing some helpful articles for beginners in the Help section within MicroStation. These articles provide discussions and diagrams of the Software and Concepts. Your instructor should show students how to utilize the Help function within MicroStation.
7. **Keep the items you are working on, on your screen in view and BIG! Don't be "Shy"!**

   Would you think of trying to work on CAD drawings on your Smart Phone? Of course NOT, its screen is too small! But you are doing the exact same thing, if the objects on your 21" monitor are kept small, about only 3" to 4" across!

   Being "Shy" refers to beginners who invariably, don't want their neighbors to see what's on their screen, since they are EMBARRASSED!

   Don't be "Shy"! Let them see! Don't be EMBARRASSED! If they can't see what's on your screen, then chances are YOU won't be able to either! You are more inefficient if you select incorrect points on your drawing due to items being displayed too small and have to perform the operation over and over again.

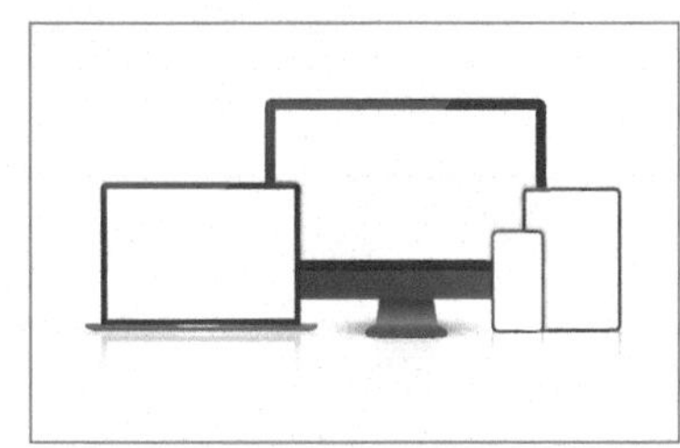

© 4zevar/Shutterstock.com

8. **Don't rely heavily on the "Pull-down" menu** entries when selecting tools. Learn specific icons & memorize them to save steps. This helps you gain efficiency.

CHALLENGE QUESTIONS

1. According to the CAD Learning Curve, what is the expected Productivity Ratio of CAD speed vs. Manual Drafting speed, after a student practices about 80 hours doing CAD drawings.
2. Name some of the major components of the MicroStation interface screen.
3. What is it called when you perform a "press & hold down" of the left mouse button and while holding down the button, repositioning the pointer as required, then release it? bottom
4. Name any two View Control tools and describe what they do. Now try them out!

NOTES

____

____

____

____

____

____

____

____

____

____

____

____

____

Summary of Drawing Exercises – Module 1

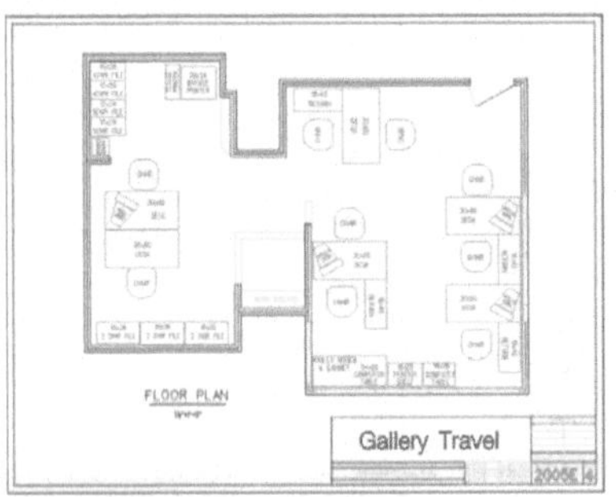

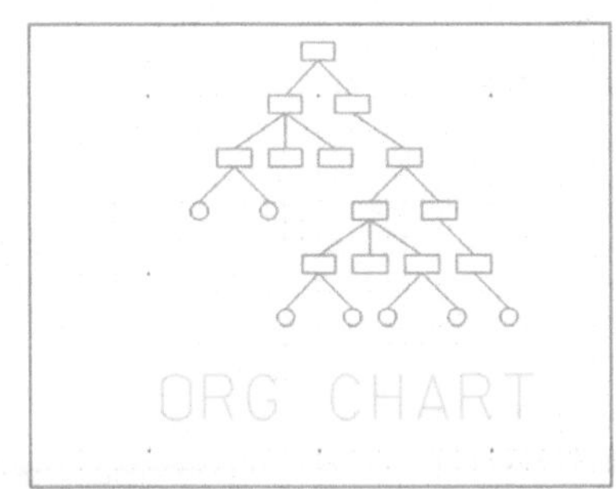

HW drawings: TRAVEL and ORGCHART

Travel

Pranch/Shutterstock.com

Introduces the student to **opening files, viewing operations and basic edits such as delete, move, copy, rotate and mirror**. Additionally, **undo, redo, element selection and mouse operations** are explored. It is suggested that the instructor performs the majority of the operations as the student watches. Later, the student can be asked to do the majority of the operations, but none of these will be to any precise locations or specifications. It is easier for a student to begin CAD exercises with an existing drawing such as this, rather than with new blank drawings, such as in later exercises.

Summary:

Open the Travel drawing as described earlier.

1. In the right hand-side room, **delete** the top cubicle of furniture composed of a desk, return and two chairs, along with the texts. Also **delete** the lower right cubicle from the same room.

2. Introduce multiple element selection with the **Element Selection** tool. **Copy** the four file cabinets from the left room into the two spaces vacated. For the upper set of four, the student needs to first copy them into a blank space in the middle of the room and then rotate them. Use the **move** command as needed.

3. **Text Edit** the drawing revision number from a "2" into a "3". **Copy** the revision "2" information down to the next space in the title block and have the student edit the three initials into their own and change the date from 02-23-05 into the current date. **Change the weight** of the drawing number 1001C rev 3 into a heavier weight (this is done with the **Element Selection** tool and the **Attributes toolbar**. **Text Edit** the name on the title block to their own.

4. In the left room, **move** the text on the desk and **mirror** the monitor about a vertical.

Notes:

See the edits marked by the ellipses and notes on the next page. The student doesn't actually draw anything new in this TRAVEL drawing exerise, only editing operations are involved.

Pranch/Shutterstock.com

TRAVEL drawing exercise

Step-by-step guidance is shown in the **On-line Video Lessons** (see inside cover)

Use MicroStation V8*i* or the CONNECT Edition for drawing the exercises.

Open the pre-drawn TRAVEL drawing.

Edits wanted:

Remove the workstations at B and E. Put 4 file cabinets each, at B and E in their place. Mirror the monitor at workstation A so that it is not near the wall, but nearer to the walk-way.

The student gets familiarity with basic operations and practice with these basic skills:

Opening files, Using the mouse, View Controls, Element Selection, Delete, Move, Copy, Mirror and Text Edit.

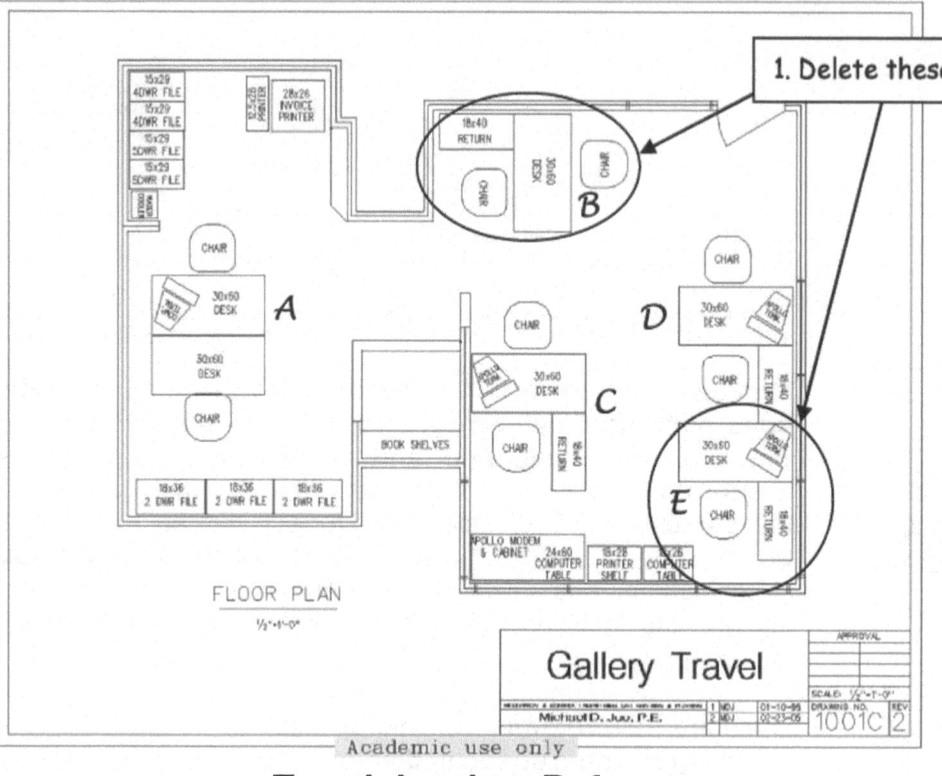
1. Delete these elements
A
B
C
D
E
FLOOR PLAN
Gallery Travel
Academic use only

Travel drawing, Before

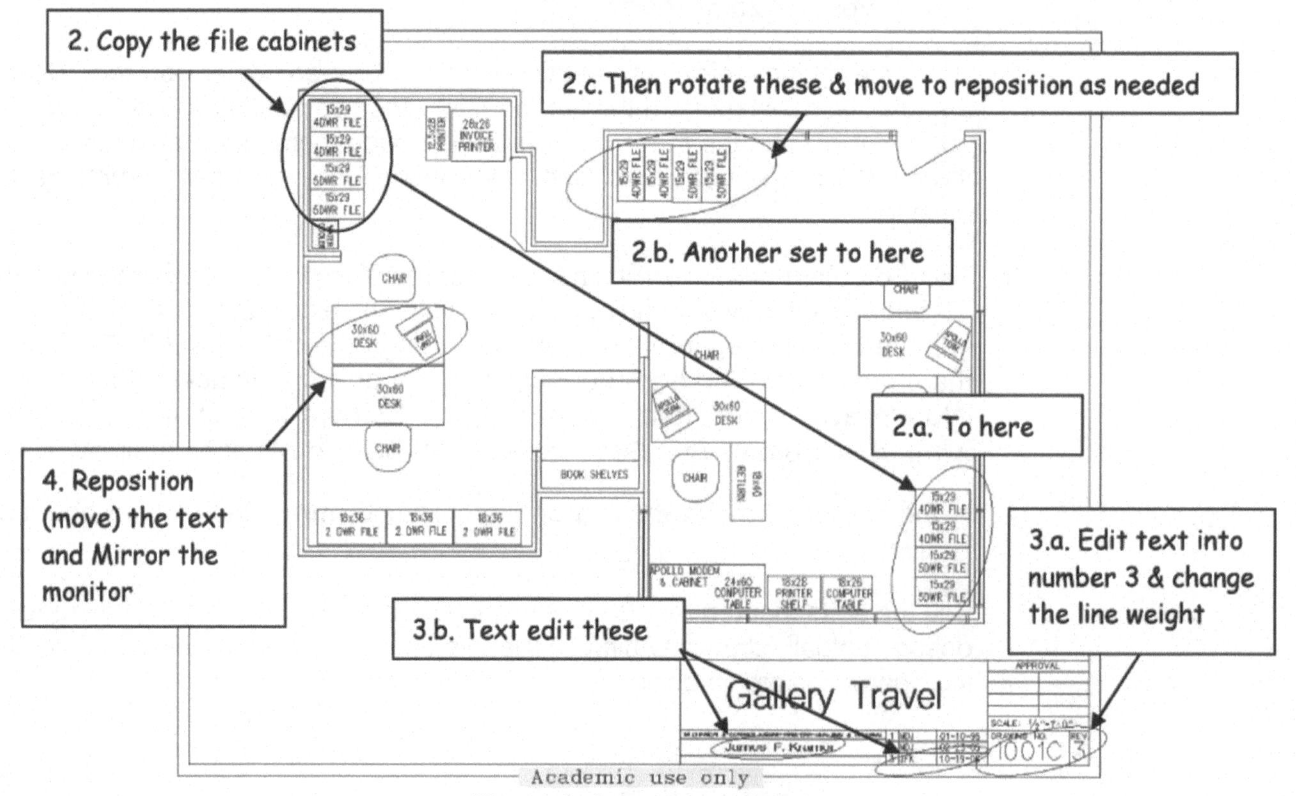
2. Copy the file cabinets
2.c. Then rotate these & move to reposition as needed
2.b. Another set to here
2.a. To here
4. Reposition (move) the text and Mirror the monitor
3.a. Edit text into number 3 & change the line weight
3.b. Text edit these
Gallery Travel
Academic use only

Travel drawing, After

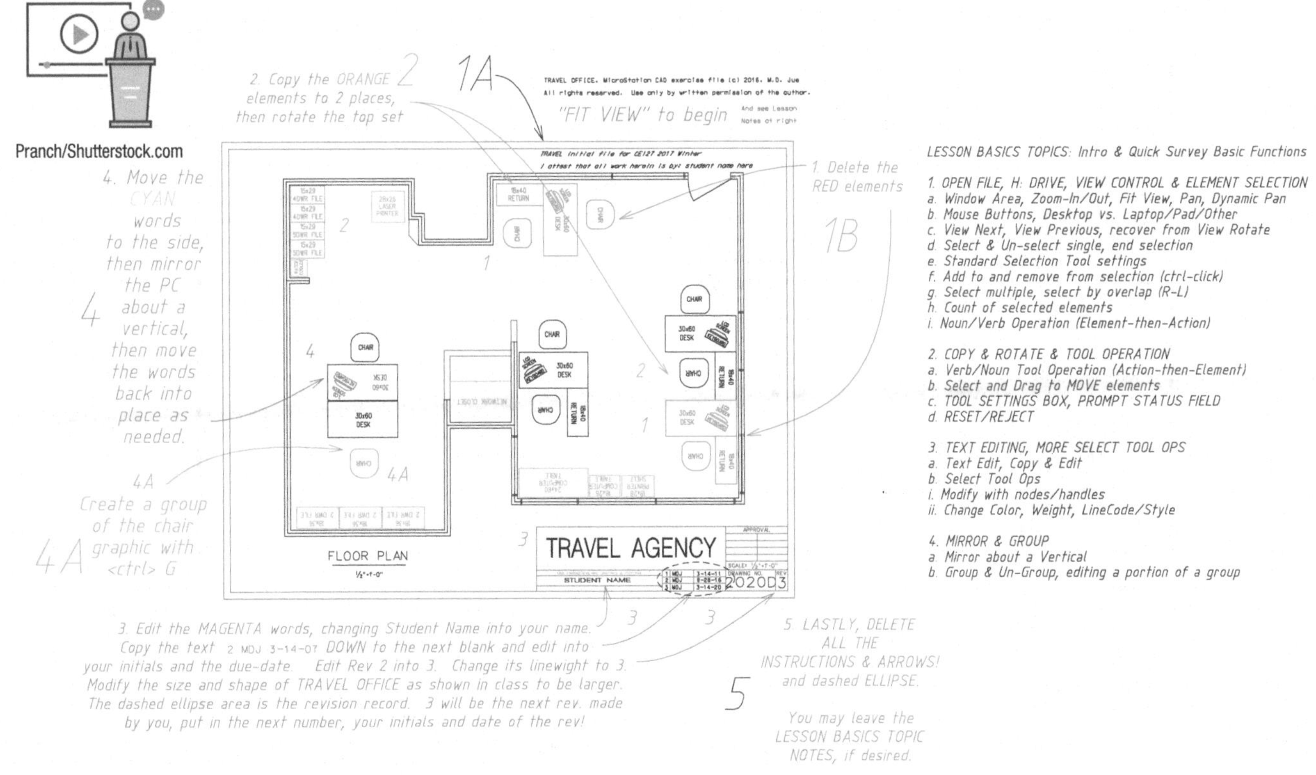

LESSON BASICS TOPICS: Intro & Quick Survey Basic Functions

1. OPEN FILE, H: DRIVE, VIEW CONTROL & ELEMENT SELECTION
a. Window Area, Zoom-In/Out, Fit View, Pan, Dynamic Pan
b. Mouse Buttons, Desktop vs. Laptop/Pad/Other
c. View Next, View Previous, recover from View Rotate
d. Select & Un-select single, end selection
e. Standard Selection Tool settings
f. Add to and remove from selection (ctrl-click)
g. Select multiple, select by overlap (R-L)
h. Count of selected elements
i. Noun/Verb Operation (Element-then-Action)

2. COPY & ROTATE & TOOL OPERATION
a. Verb/Noun Tool Operation (Action-then-Element)
b. Select and Drag to MOVE elements
c. TOOL SETTINGS BOX, PROMPT STATUS FIELD
d. RESET/REJECT

3. TEXT EDITING, MORE SELECT TOOL OPS
a. Text Edit, Copy & Edit
b. Select Tool Ops
i. Modify with nodes/handles
ii. Change Color, Weight, LineCode/Style

4. MIRROR & GROUP
a. Mirror about a Vertical
b. Group & Un-Group, editing a portion of a group

Orgchart Introduces the student to steps for creating a **new drawing** and file-naming specifications and specifics of the computer file system at the lab.

Pranch/Shutterstock.com

Specifics of the computer file-system in place at your computer lab may be discussed at this time. (ie. Server location, folder names, disk drives specified for the cad-lab, etc.)

Specifics of any student computer accounts may be discussed at this time. (ie. Saving files, location of student folders, class folders, etc.)

Introduces the concept of the **grid display and locking** input points to the grid with the **grid lock on**. The concept of **element attributes** can be introduced to show selection of **colors**, such as green or red and a **line weight or thickness** before placing or drawing elements begins.

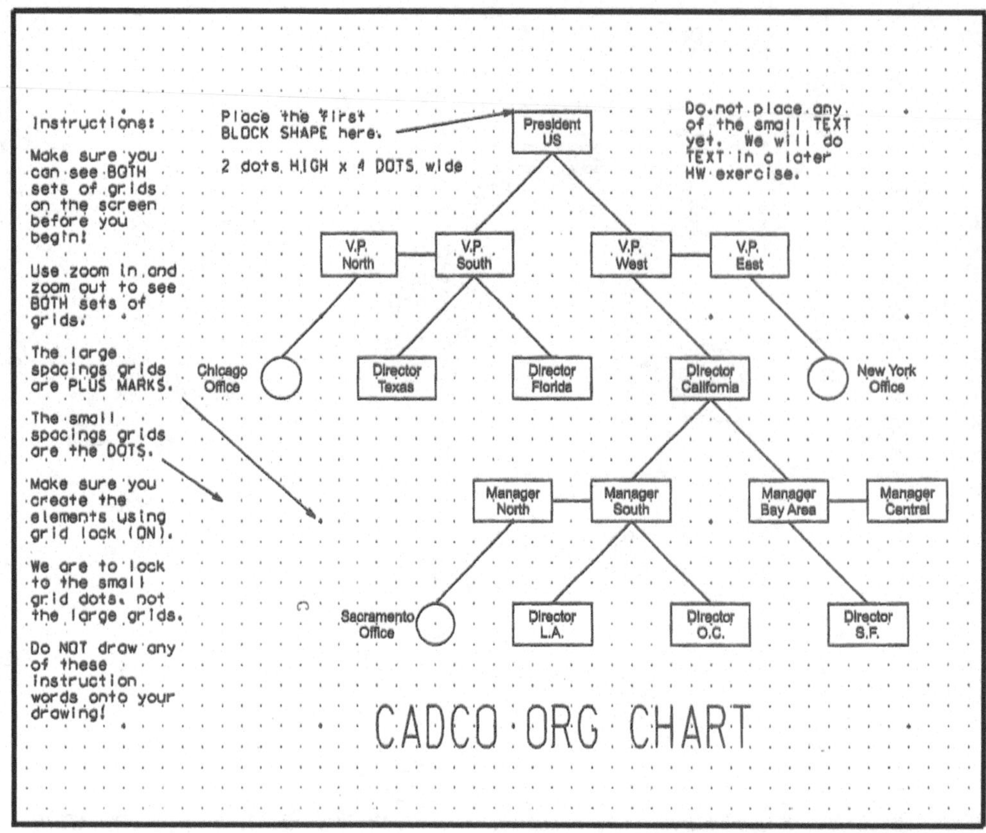

Drawn in MicroStation V8i (names in the boxes are not needed)

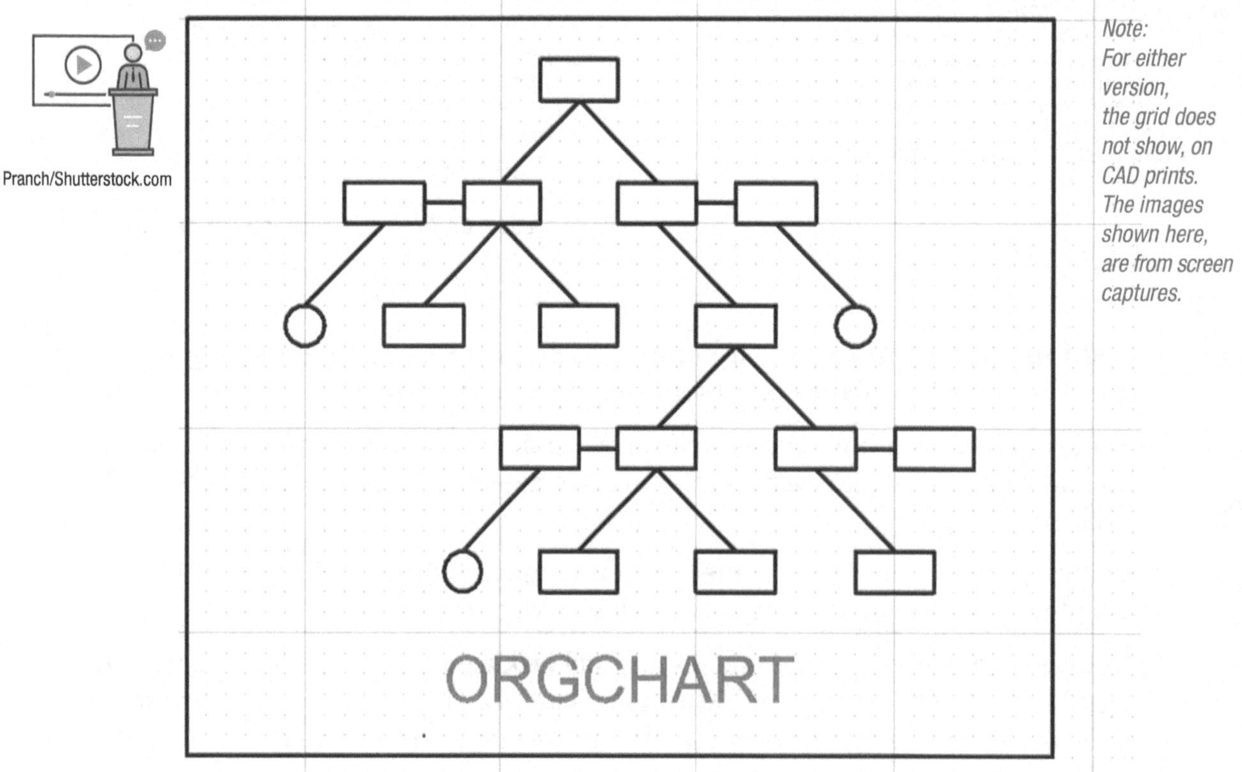

Note: For either version, the grid does not show, on CAD prints. The images shown here, are from screen captures.

Drawn in MicroStation CONNECT Edition (notice grid style differs)

Two simple Extra Credit drawings. Use Grid Lock and basic element placement tools Place Line, Place Shape and basic manipulations as needed. Also use the Selection Tool.

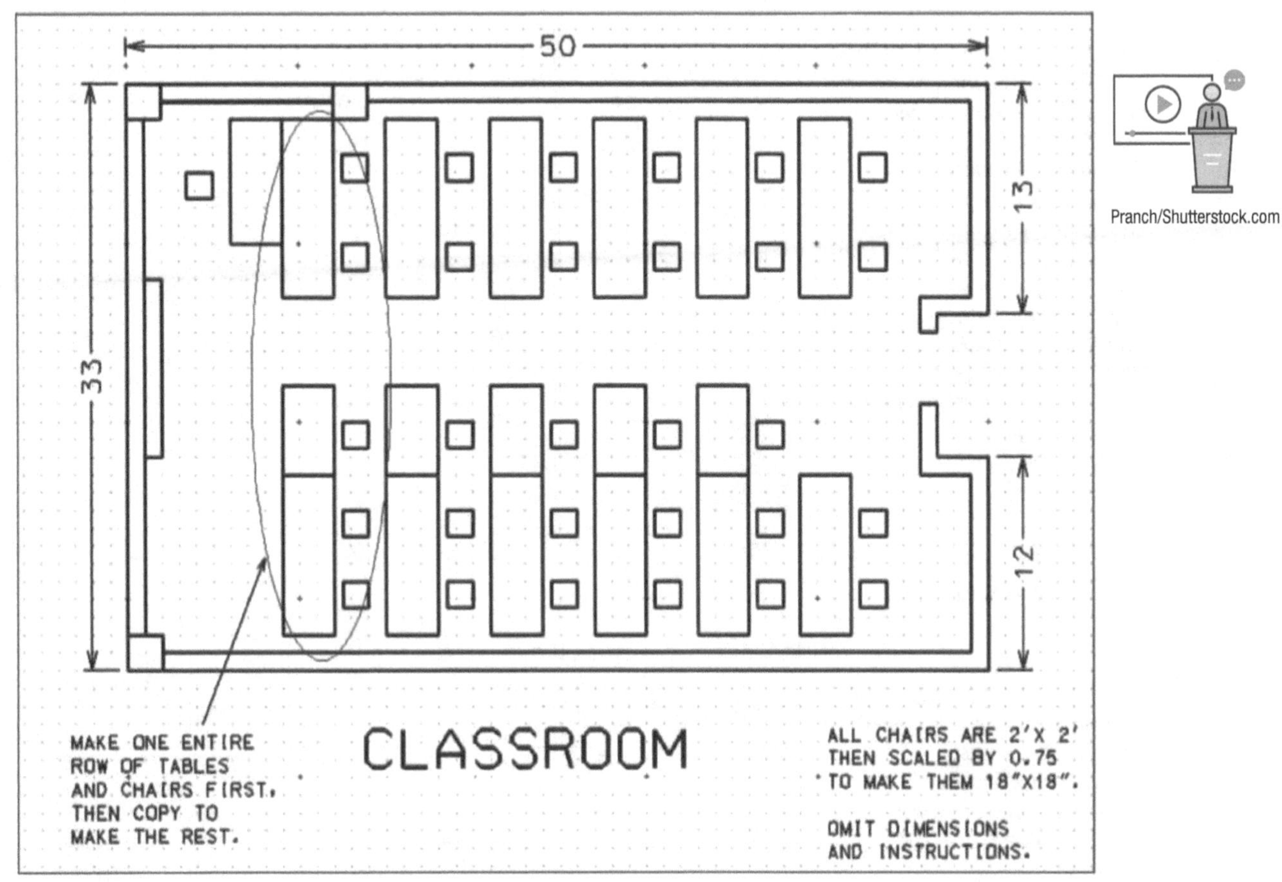

Pranch/Shutterstock.com

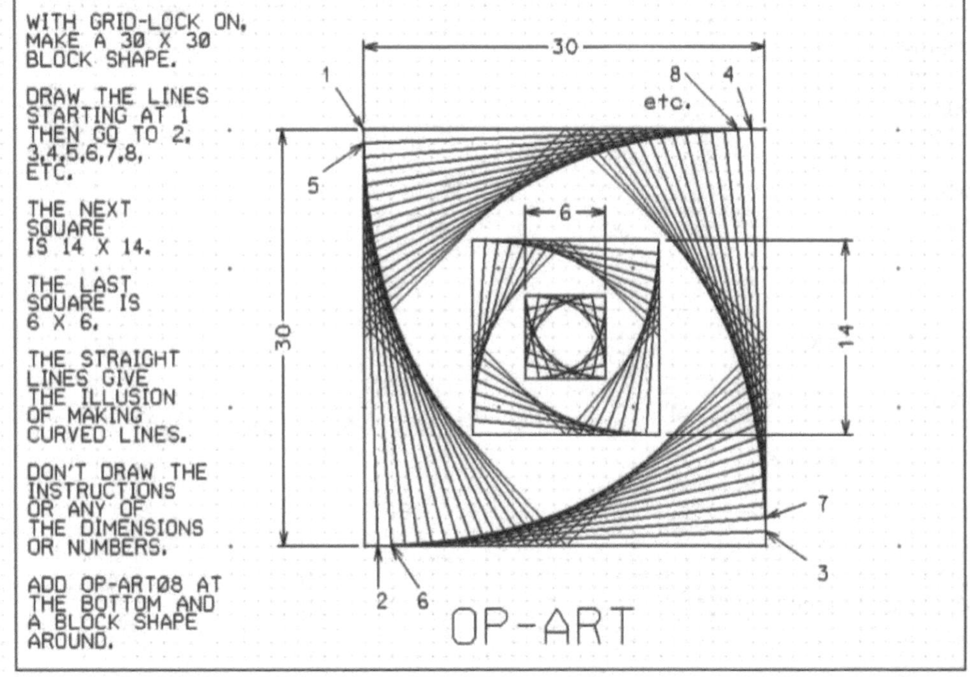

WITH GRID-LOCK ON, MAKE A 30 X 30 BLOCK SHAPE.
DRAW THE LINES STARTING AT 1 THEN GO TO 2, 3,4,5,6,7,8, ETC.
THE NEXT SQUARE IS 14 X 14.
THE LAST SQUARE IS 6 X 6.
THE STRAIGHT LINES GIVE THE ILLUSION OF MAKING CURVED LINES.
DON'T DRAW THE INSTRUCTIONS OR ANY OF THE DIMENSIONS OR NUMBERS.
ADD OP-ART08 AT THE BOTTOM AND A BLOCK SHAPE AROUND.
30
1
8
4
etc.
5
6
30
14
7
3
2
6
OP-ART

Pranch/Shutterstock.com

< REVIEW

Immediately Preceding Material Highlights:

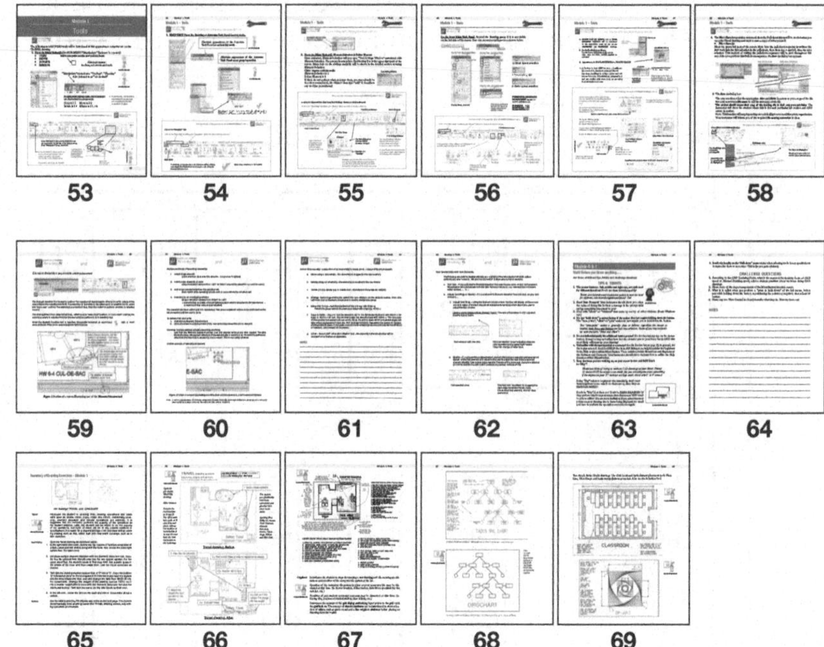

PREVIEW >

Immediately Following Material Highlights:

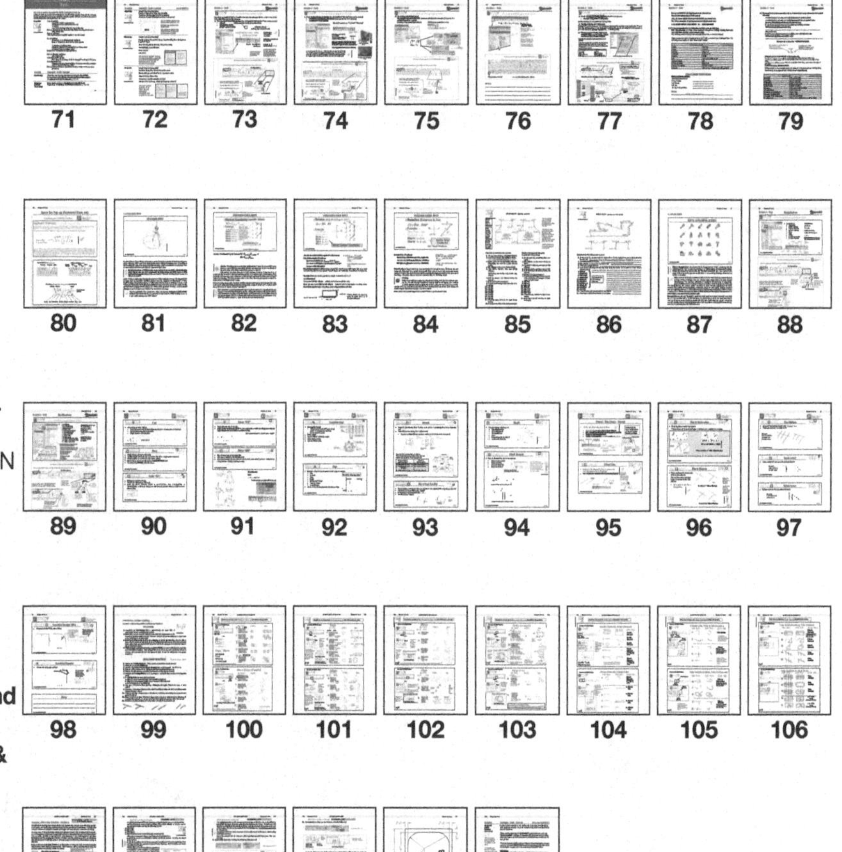

Module 2

Tools

Key CAD exercise concepts for initial sessions (Week 2):

Additional skills are required for completion of the following exercises. These are the concepts that the student will be exposed to and those that the student will use for perhaps the second and third times since the beginning of the course.

General/All

© Pranch/Shutterstock.com

Basic Operations
- Key-in Field, Recall of previous key-ins
- Tool tips (to find and verify correct tool to use)
- Undo, Redo
- Use of the Tool Settings Dialog box, Prompt field usage

Intro to Snap functions, Keypoint snap, Midpoint snap, Intersection snap, Center snap
Intro to Axis Lock
View Attributes (turning OFF display of the Grid dots)

Precision Input
- Cartesian x-y coordinate system definition
- Entry of lengths, Decimal and by working units

1. Absolute coordinate entry
2. Relative Cartesian (Rectangular) coordinate entry
3. Relative Polar coordinate entry

Definition of Conventional angle expression

Intro to Element Attributes
- Color, Weight, Style

Basic Element Placements
- Place Line, Block Shape, Circle by Center, Place Regular Polygon,

Basic Manipulations
- Construct Chamfer, Circular Fillet, Construct Array (Rectangular and Polar), Break Element, Trim

Intro to Measure Distance (between points) to verify correct precision placements

Exercise	Concepts / Tools / Lessons
Precision.dgn	Creating a new drawing, Opening and using the **Key-in Field.** Precision input with **Absolute Coordinates, Relative Rectangular Coordinates** and **Polar Coordinates.** pg 85–86
Manipulate & Modify Warm-up.dgn	More details on usage of **Manipulate** and **Modify Tools**. Begin usage of **AccuSnap** and **Element Attributes** pg 100–106

Exercise	Concepts / Tools / Lessons	For MODULE 2

Bigtub.dgn

Length input (working units)
Precision Input, Place Line, Copy Parallel,
Construct Chamfer (with 2 differing lengths)
Construct Circular Fillet (with truncate both option)

© Pranch/Shutterstock.com

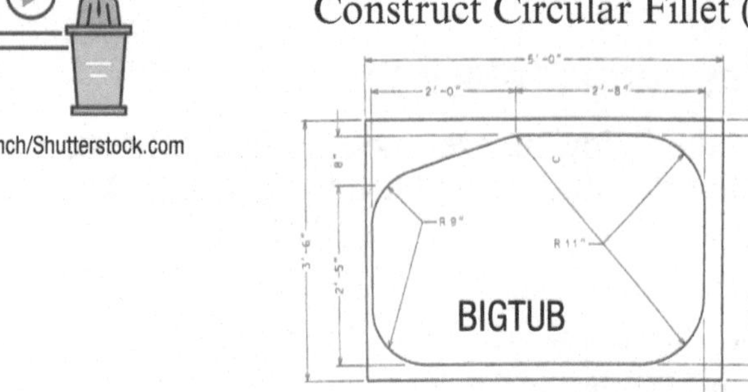

This is an instructor "guided" drawing exercise covered on pages 107–111.

Nearly every step is provided for the student to follow.

Initial exercises are "guided" for the student, and serves to introduce the use of new tools and concepts.

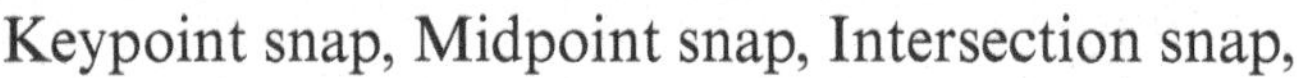

Shower.dgn

© Pranch/Shutterstock.com

Length input (working units)

Precision Input, Place Block Shape, Copy Parallel, Place Circle, Place Regular Polygon

Keypoint snap, Midpoint snap, Intersection snap,

Trim Multiple, Break Element

Undo & Redo

Axis Lock

This instructor "guided" drawing exercise in Appendix A, pages 221 and 222 has more abbreviated instructions given, but still has lots of new material.

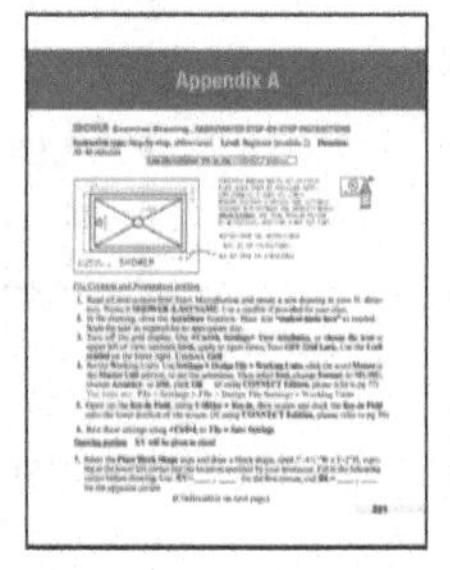

Range.dgn

© Pranch/Shutterstock.com

Length input (working units)

Precision Input, Place Block Shape, Place Line

Element Placement "offset" from a specific location

Keypoint snap, Center snap

Construct Array (Rectangular & Polar)

Selection Tool & Group <Ctrl>G, Un-group <Ctrl>U

Instructor "guided". Appendix "A" on Pages 223–225. Abbreviated instructions. New material and concepts.

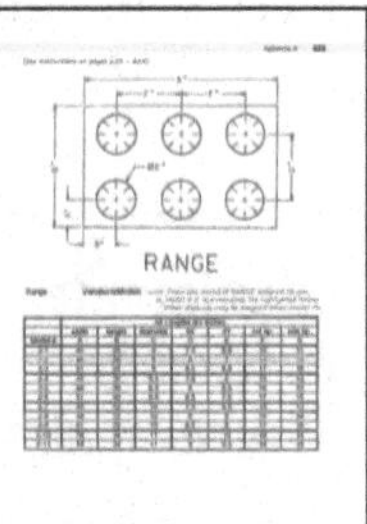

Module 2 – Tools

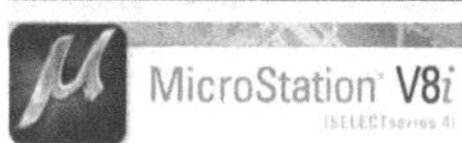

< < < < The top half of this page introduces **V8*i*** Tools

The following new EDITING tools will be introduced in this approximate order for use on the TUB, SHOWER & RANGE drawings:

1. From the **Main Tasks #3 Manipulate**: (the SUB-MENU "Manipulate" Task can be opened)
   - **ARRAY**
   - **MOVE PARALLEL (COPY option is within)**

bold boxes point out the new tools to learn

Alternate names: toolbox, sub-menu and task.

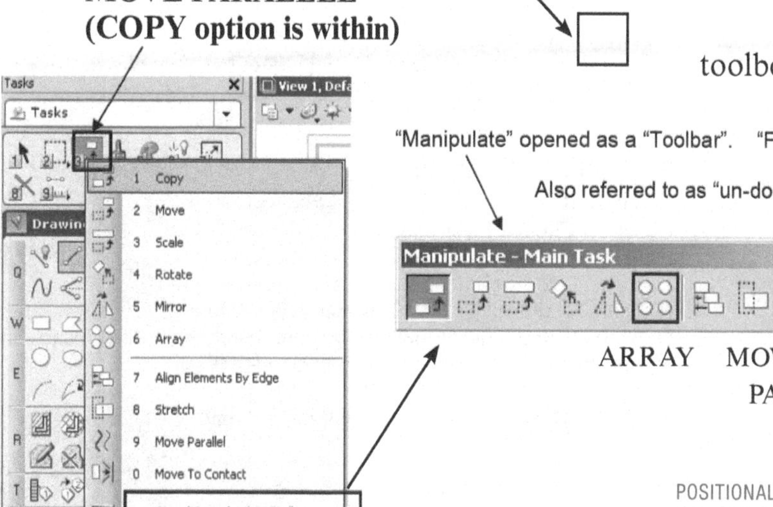

ARRAY MOVE/COPY PARALLEL

Another way to activate tools in **V8*i*** is called:

POSITIONAL KEYBOARD NAVIGATION

Array is 3 6
Move Parallel is 3 9

If the tool fails to activate, hit **<Esc>**, then re-try. You may be In **Place Text** or the **keyboard input focus** may be elsewhere.

POSITIONAL KEYBOARD NAVIGATION short-cuts are discontinued in the CONNECT Edition. >

The bottom half of this page introduces **CONNECT Edition** Tools > >

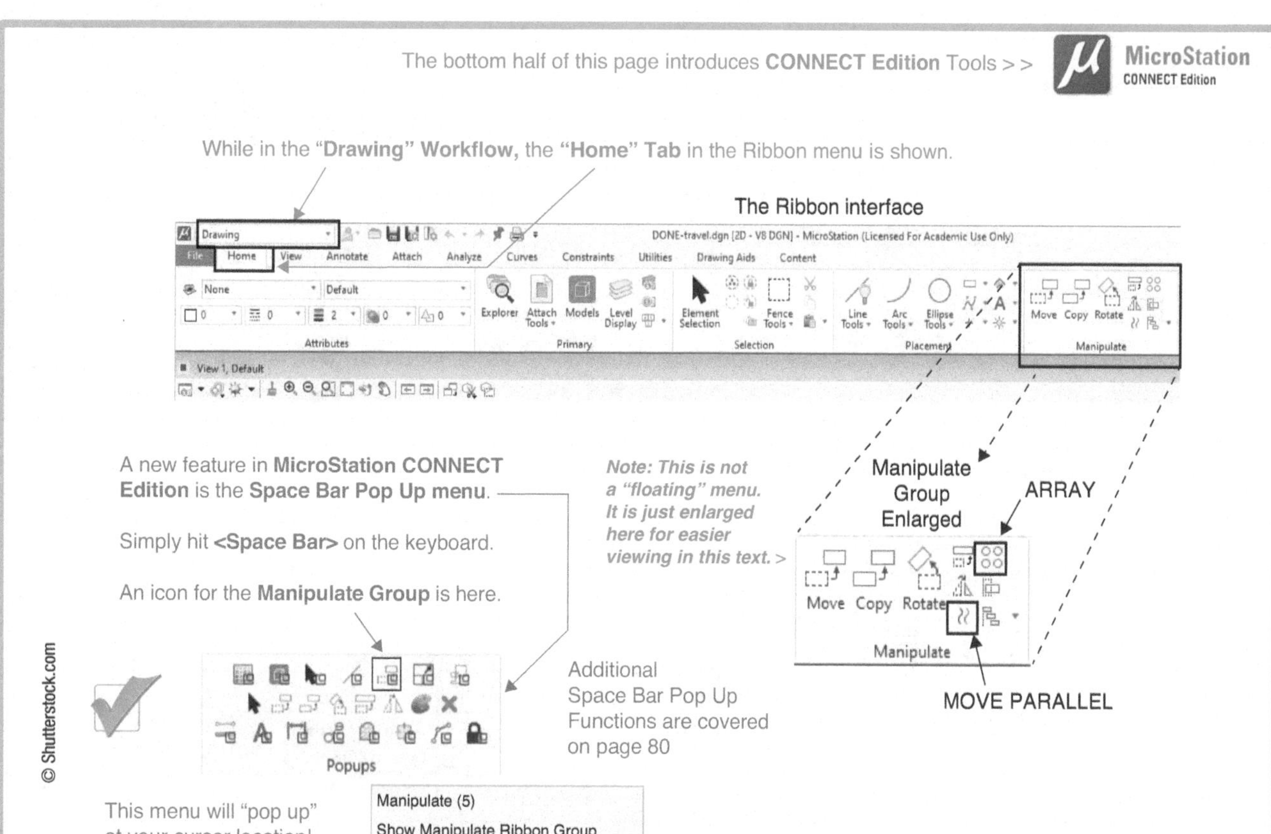

A new feature in **MicroStation CONNECT Edition** is the **Space Bar Pop Up menu**.

Simply hit **<Space Bar>** on the keyboard.

An icon for the **Manipulate Group** is here.

Note: This is not a "floating" menu. It is just enlarged here for easier viewing in this text. >

Additional Space Bar Pop Up Functions are covered on page 80

This menu will "pop up" at your cursor location!

Module 2 – Tools

< < < < The top half of this page introduces **V8*i*** Tools

2. From the **Main Tasks #7 Modify**: (the SUB-MENU "Modify" Task can be opened)
   - **CONSTRUCTCIRCULAR FILLET** (both used in the TUB drawing)
   - **CONSTRUCT CHAMFER**

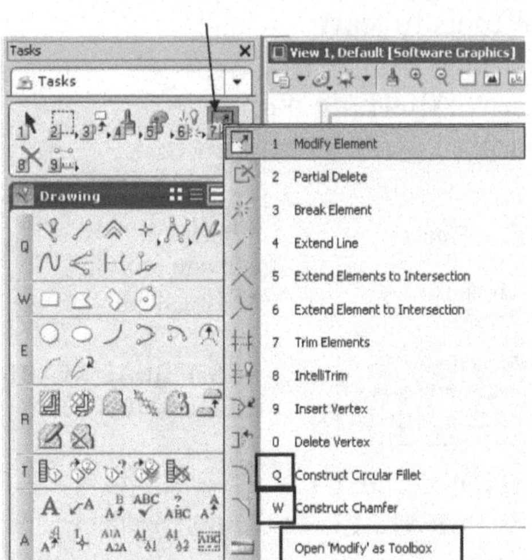

"Modify" opened as a "Toolbar". "Floating"

CONSTRUCT CIRCULAR FILLET   CONSTRUCT CHAMFER

POSITIONAL KEYBOARD NAVIGATION

	lower case is OK
Construct Circular Fillet is 7 Q	7 q
Construct Chamrer is 7 W	7 w

Note: In CAD drawings, **"Fillet"** typically relates to engineering materials or machinery: ie: to round off (an interior angle) with a fillet. pronounced: **fil** -it

They do NOT mean a boneless cut of meat: fi-**ley**

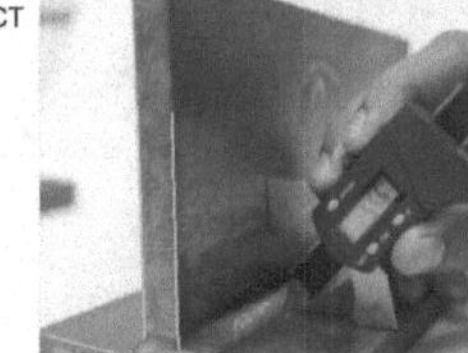

Fillet measurement
fil - it

Medium-Rare **Filet** Mignon
fi-**ley**

It is recommended for new CAD students to keep the toolboxes "un-docked", since docking them hides the name of the toolbox. The instructor will refer to the toolboxes (or toolbars) by name quite often; and beginning students are not familiar with the icons by sight, yet!

The bottom half of this page introduces **CONNECT Edition** Tools > >

MicroStation CONNECT Edition

While in the **"Drawing" Workflow,** the **"Home" Tab** in the Ribbon menu is shown.

The Ribbon interface

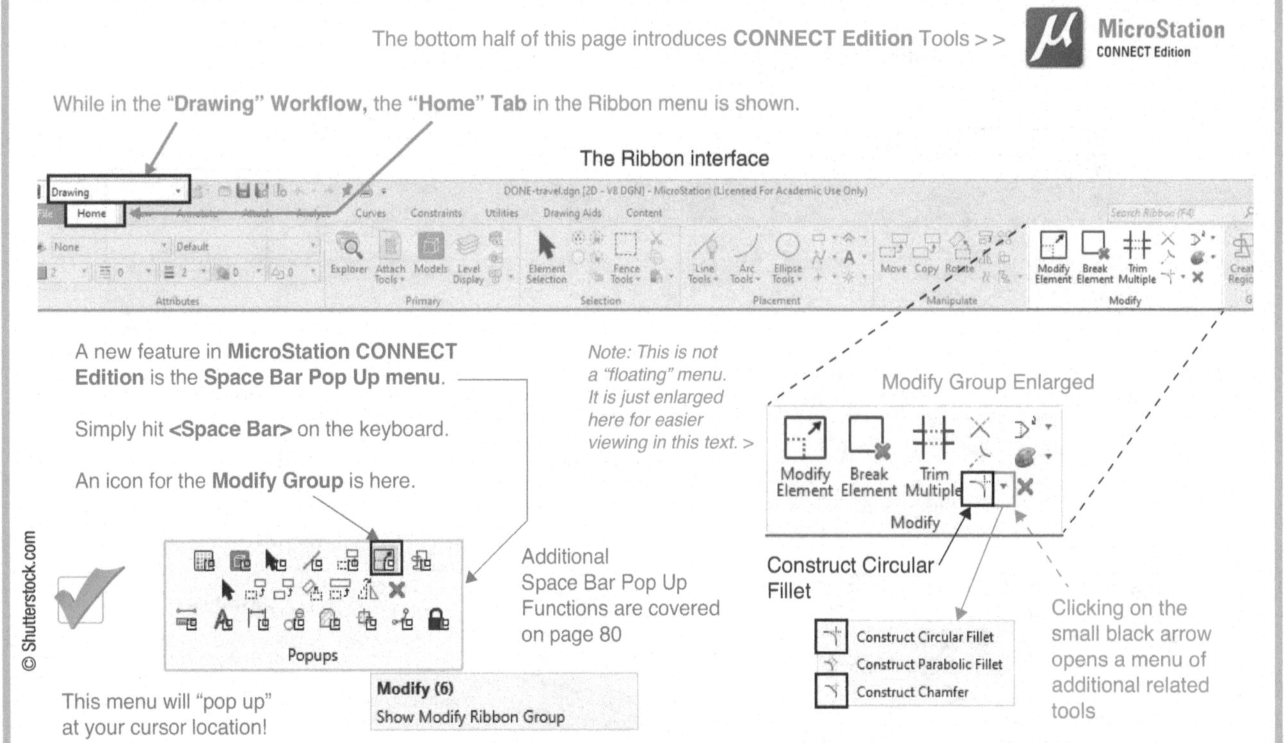

A new feature in **MicroStation CONNECT Edition** is the **Space Bar Pop Up menu**.

Simply hit **<Space Bar>** on the keyboard.

An icon for the **Modify Group** is here.

This menu will "pop up" at your cursor location!

Note: This is not a "floating" menu. It is just enlarged here for easier viewing in this text. >

Additional Space Bar Pop Up Functions are covered on page 80

Construct Circular Fillet

Clicking on the small black arrow opens a menu of additional related tools

Module 2 – Tools

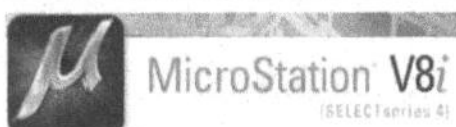

< < < < The top half of this page introduces **V8*i*** Tools

3. On the **Draw Main Task Panel**:
   PLACE REGULAR POLYGON alternate activation: Place Regular Polygon is W 4 **(within Place Block toolbox)**
   Drawing Task, Panel Layout Mode W: Polygons opened as toobox

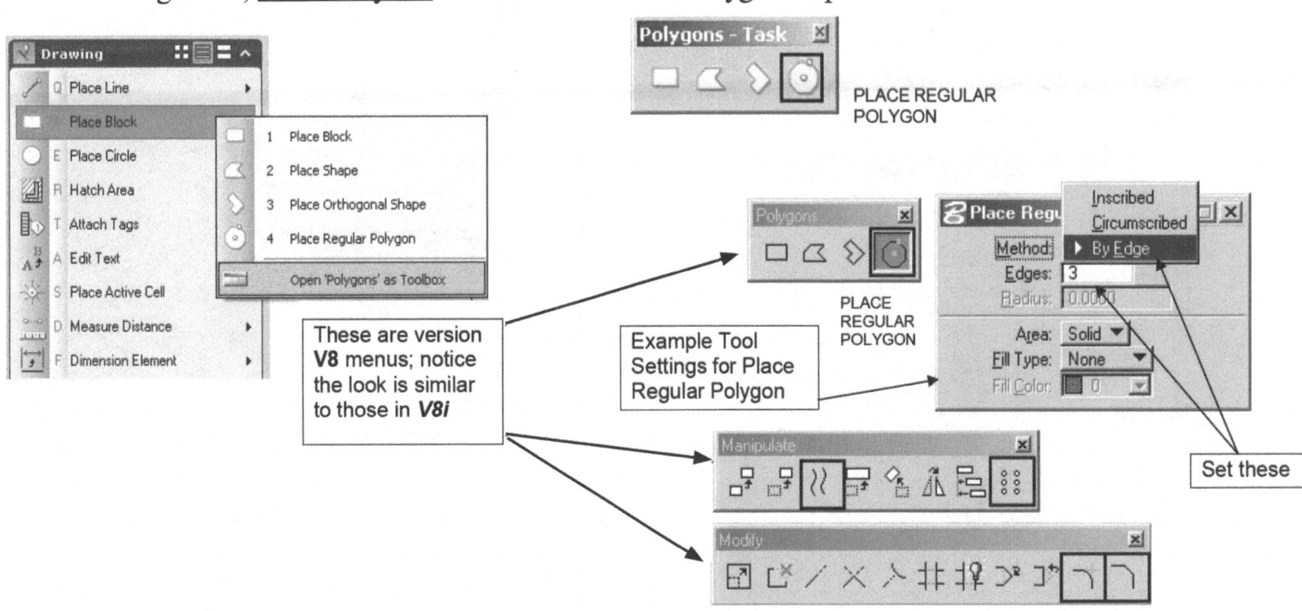

The bottom half of this page introduces **CONNECT Edition** Tools > >

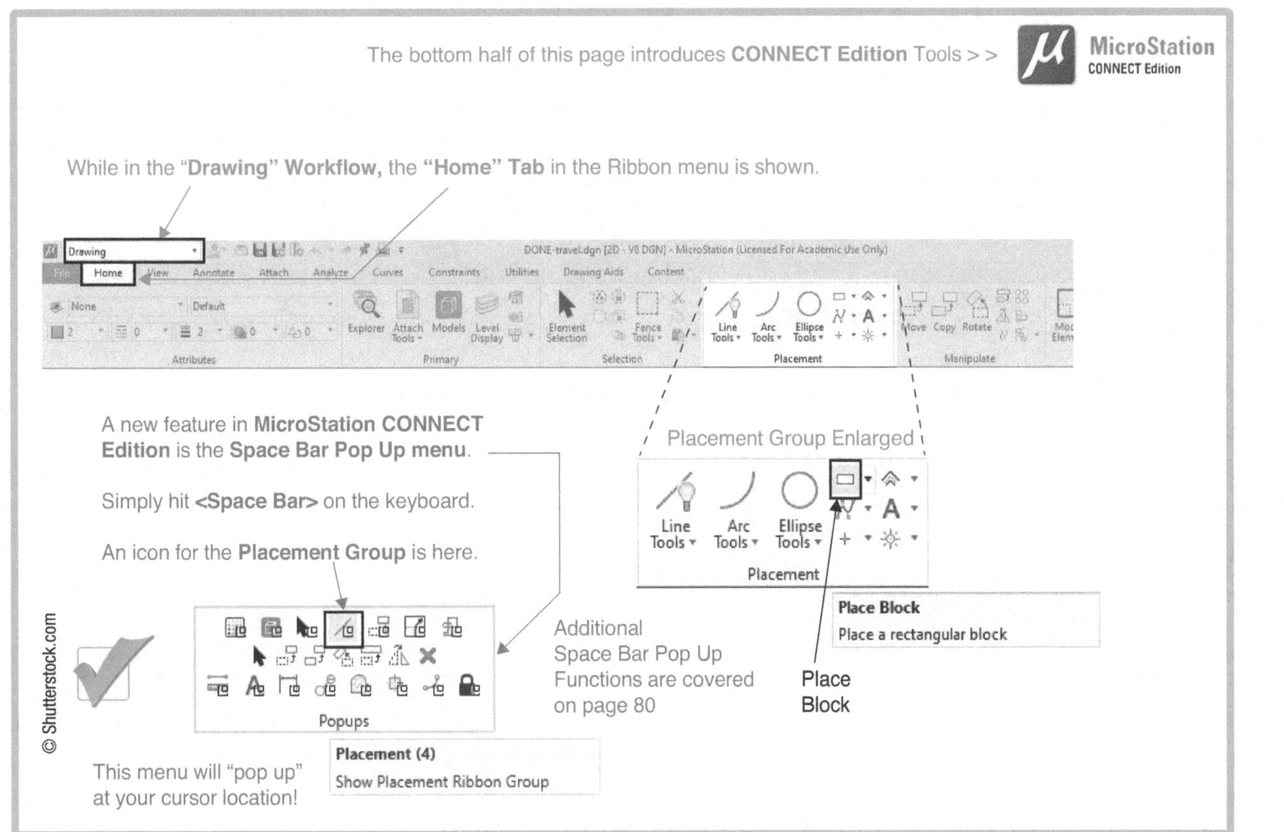

Module 2 – Tools

MicroStation V8*i* <<<< The top half of this page introduces **V8*i*** Tools

We will be using this to turn off the GRID display.

.. or .. use <Ctrl> b to bring up View Attributes.

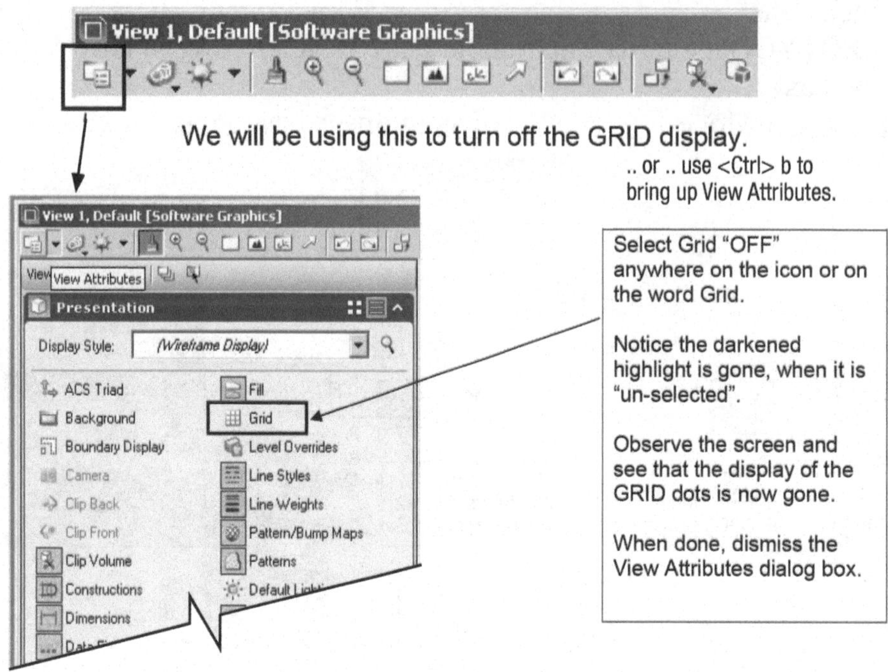

Select Grid "OFF" anywhere on the icon or on the word Grid.

Notice the darkened highlight is gone, when it is "un-selected".

Observe the screen and see that the display of the GRID dots is now gone.

When done, dismiss the View Attributes dialog box.

The bottom half of this page introduces **CONNECT Edition** Tools > > MicroStation CONNECT Edition

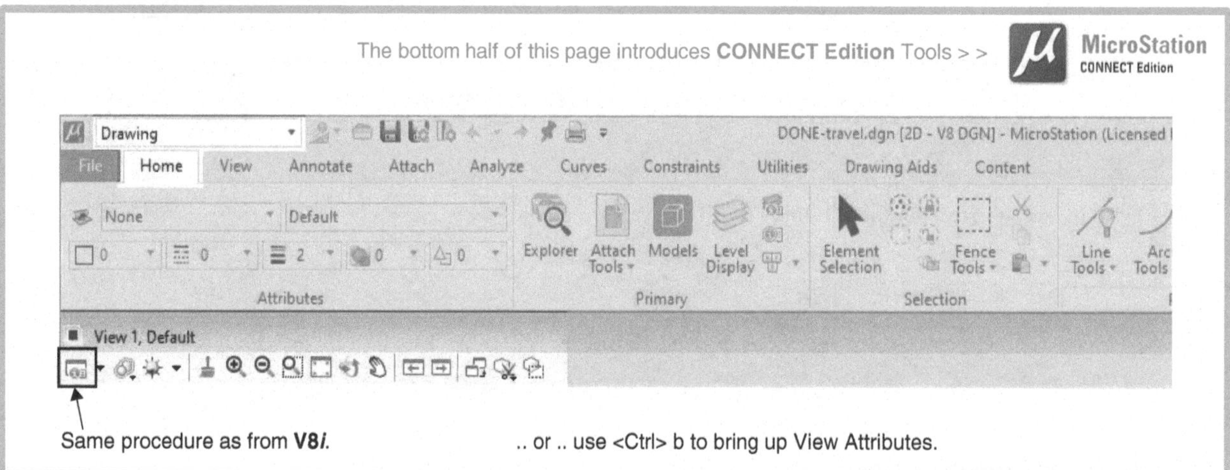

Same procedure as from **V8*i***.

.. or .. use <Ctrl> b to bring up View Attributes.

NOTES:

Module 2 – Tools

< < < < The top half of this page introduces **V8*i*** Tools

5. We will be setting the **Working Units** using this Pull-down sequence:
   - **Settings > Design File > Working Units**

See the next page for a discussion on Working Units.

1. **Checking or Setting the Working units**

Working Units define the size of your elements in the design file as related to real world units. To set or check the existing setting of your design file's working units, use the following Pull-down sequence to get to this dialog box: Settings > Design File … > Working Units

1.1 The most common Working Units error is FORGETTING to set the working units. If you don't set them, the units are mu:su.

The default mu (Master Unit) in MicroStation is Meters!

If the drawing exercise or problem requires that the elements have a size in feet and inches, then the **Master units** should be set to feet and the **Sub units** should be set to inches.

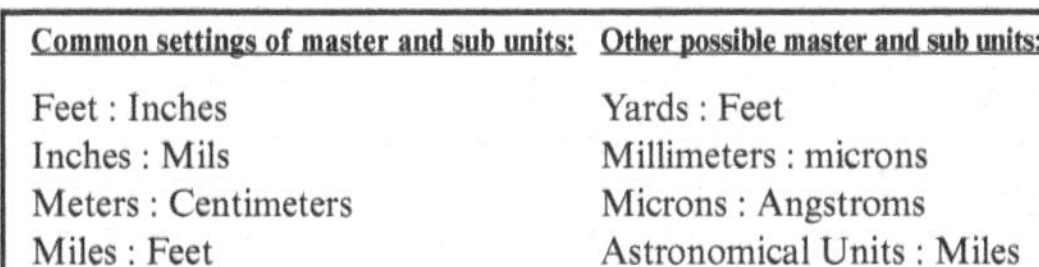

Common settings of master and sub units:	Other possible master and sub units:
Feet : Inches	Yards : Feet
Inches : Mils	Millimeters : microns
Meters : Centimeters	Microns : Angstroms
Miles : Feet	Astronomical Units : Miles

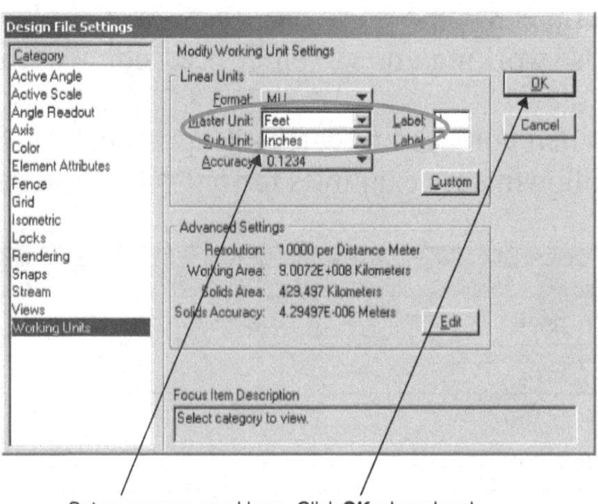

Set **mu : su** as need here, Click **OK** when done!

The bottom half of this page introduces **CONNECT Edition** Tools > >

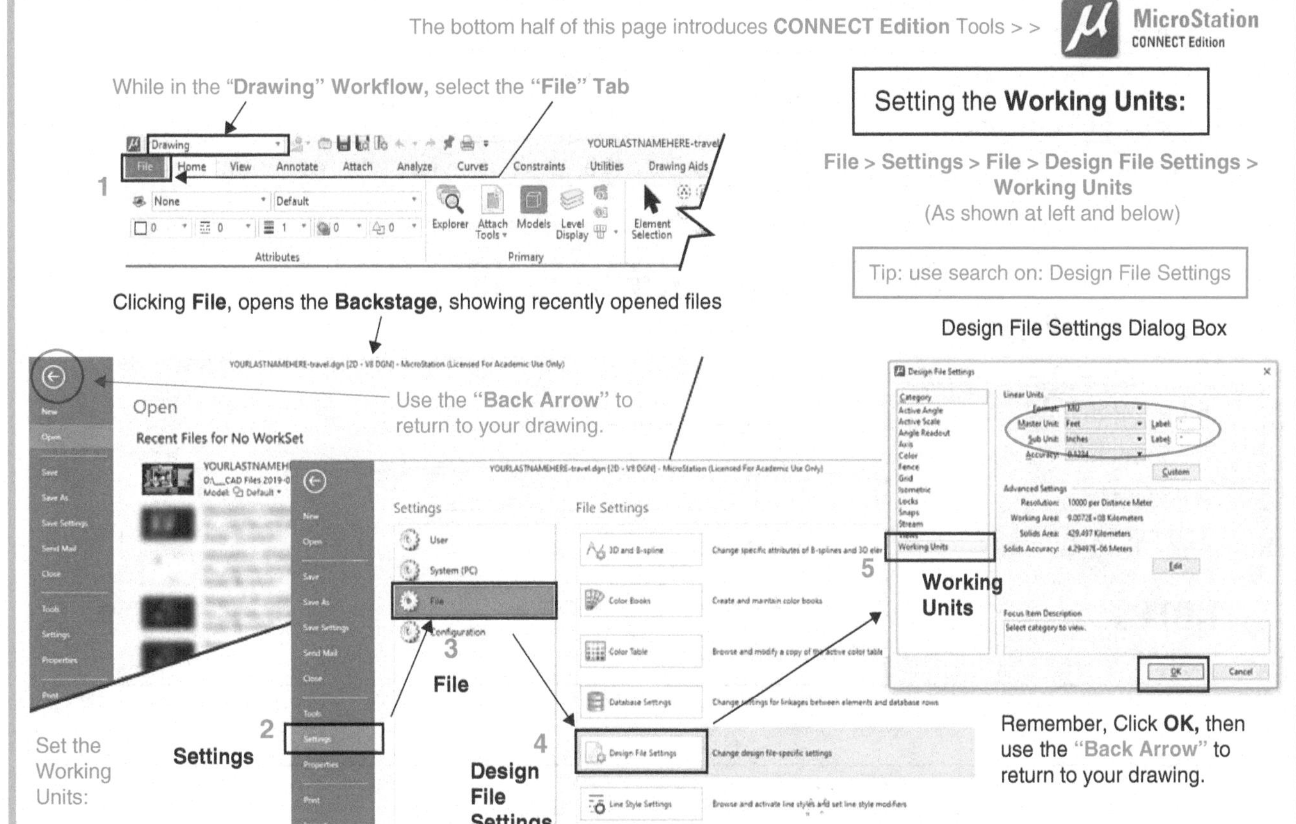

Module 2 – Tools

Note: you CANNOT mix English and metric units such as:

Meters : Feet (this setting is NOT correct!)

Also, the master unit should always be LARGER than the sub unit.

The Colon : character always separates master units from sub units

ie: **MASTER UNITS : SUB UNITS** like **FEET: INCHES**

1.2 To keep your settings for your design file, remember to do the following:
File > Save Settings, or **<Ctrl> f** after setting Working Units **2. Using Working Units (the form is MU:SU meaning: master units:sub units)**
Use working units to enter precision lengths. (Refer also to Precision Input)

When you need to enter a length, such as 4 ft, 11 ½", you should use Working Units. The following are examples for **mu = feet** and **su = inches**

Spoken English dimension:	Expressed in Working Units:
6 feet	6.0 or 6
7 feet	7.0 or 7
0.5 feet	0.5 or .5
0.75 feet	0.75 or .75
5.739 ft	5.739
3 ft	3.0 or 3 or 0:36 or :36
5 feet, 4 inches	5:4
2 foot, 3 inches	2:3 or :27
4 feet, 11 ½ inches	4:11.5 or :59.5
6 inches	0:6 or :6 or .5 (instructor will explain)

CHALLENGE QUESTIONS

Student challenge exercise:

Write the expressions for:

6 foot, 7 inches ______________

7.356 inches ______________

4.95 feet ______________

129 feet, 8 and ¾ inches ______________

NOTES

Answers in Answer Section

____

____

Module 2 – Tools

2.1 The second most common error is to mix up decimal number entry with master unit and sub unit entry:

A decimal number and units, such as **0.9 inches** means **9 tenths of an inch.**

A decimal number and units, such as **10.9 feet** means **10 feet + 9 tenths of a foot.**

However, this is different than Master unit : Sub unit entry:

If <u>*MU is set to feet*</u> and <u>*SU is set to inches*</u> **10:9** means **10 feet + 9 inches**

This is completely different than 10.9 feet

Also, ponder this:

If <u>*MU is set to **miles***</u> and <u>*SU is set to feet*</u> **10:127**, means **10 miles + 127 feet**

This is completely different than 10.127 miles

It's very easy to remember WORKING UNITS !

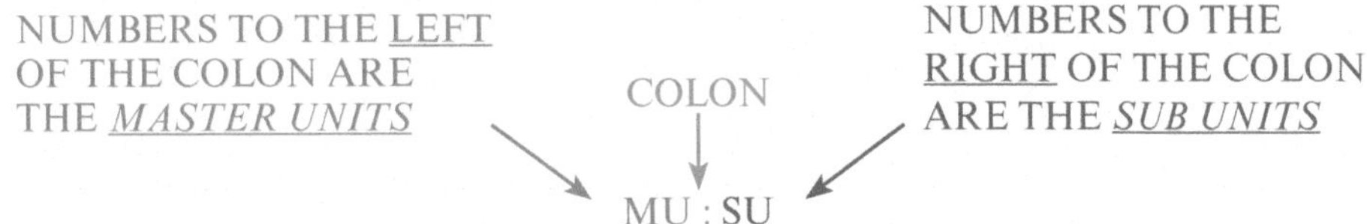
NUMBERS TO THE LEFT
OF THE COLON ARE
THE MASTER UNITS
COLON
NUMBERS TO THE
RIGHT OF THE COLON
ARE THE SUB UNITS
MU : SU

More Examples for FEET:INCHES as the working units.
12.3 is 12 + 3 tenths of a foot (12.3 feet). There is no colon, so it is a master unit.
12:3 is 12 feet **and 3 inches**. The 12 is on the left of the colon, the 3 is on the right of the colon.
0:2.7 is zero feet **and 2.7 inches**. The 0 is on the left of the colon, the 2.7 is on the right of the colon.

2.2 More examples, this time in Metric:

When you need to enter a length, such as 65 meters, 47.9 cm you should use Working Units.

The following are examples for **mu = meters** and **su = cm (centimeters)**

Spoken English dimension:	Expressed in Working Units:
6 meters	6.0 or 6 or :600
7 meters	7.0 or 7 or :700
0.5 meters	0.5 or .5 or :50
0.75 meters	0.75 or .75 or :75
5.739 meters	5.739 or 5:73.9
3 meters	3.0 or 3 or 0:300 or :300
30 centimeters	:30 or 0.3 or .3
5 meters, 40 centimeters	5:40 or 5.4
2 meters, 3 centimeters	2:3 or :203
4 meters, 11.27 centimeters	4:11.27 or :411.27
6 centimeters	0:6 or :6 or .06 (instructor will explain)

Space Bar Pop-up (Keyboard Short-cut)

New feature in CONNECT Edition

Keyboard Shortcuts (From CONNECT Edition On-line Help)

Keyboard shortcuts, are shortcuts to specific groups or tools in the ribbon. The product supports multi-level keyboard shortcuts. Depending on the key-ins assigned, the tools, ribbon group pop-ups, or pop-up menus are displayed.

The default keyboard shortcut for **<Space>** key contains tools as well as shortcuts for different ribbon groups.

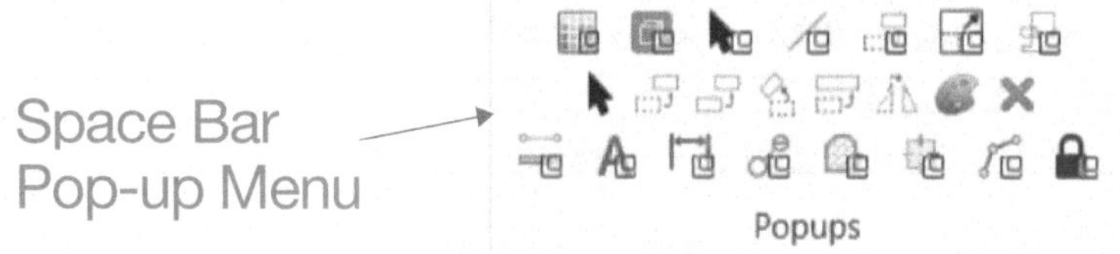

© Shutterstock.com

Simply hit <**Space Bar**> on the keyboard. This menu will "pop up" at your cursor location! Problems? See *** *Special Note***, below.

As you can see above, the first row contains ribbon group shortcuts. These are shortcuts for frequently used ribbon groups in the **Home** tab. Clicking or activating any of them opens the respective ribbon group pop-up. The second row contains frequently used tools. The third row contains shortcuts to frequently used ribbon groups. Each of the icons in the ribbon group have a shortcut key. This shortcut key is displayed when you hover the pointer over the icon. With the ribbon group pop-up displayed, if you press the shortcut key, the respective tool or group activates.

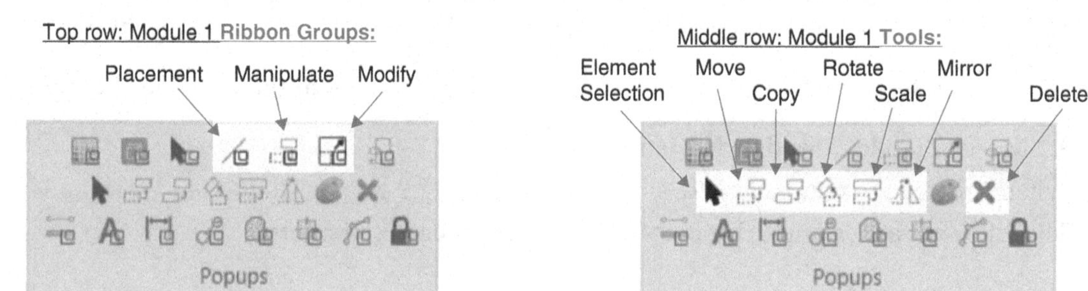

*** *Special Note:*** If the **Space Bar PopUp menu** does not appear after hitting the <**Space Bar**>, try again, after you hit the <**Esc**> **key**. The *input focus* may have been in the **Key-in Field**, in the **Tool Settings Window**, in the **AccuDraw** window, or in another window or dialog box. Or you may need to close the **Text Editor** window in case you are in **Place Text**.

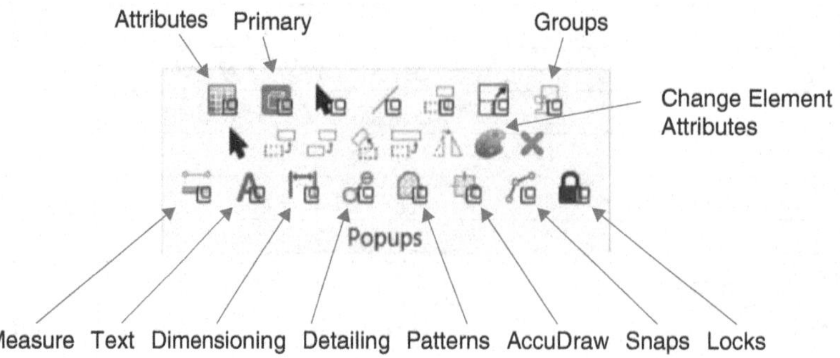

2.2 PRECISION INPUT

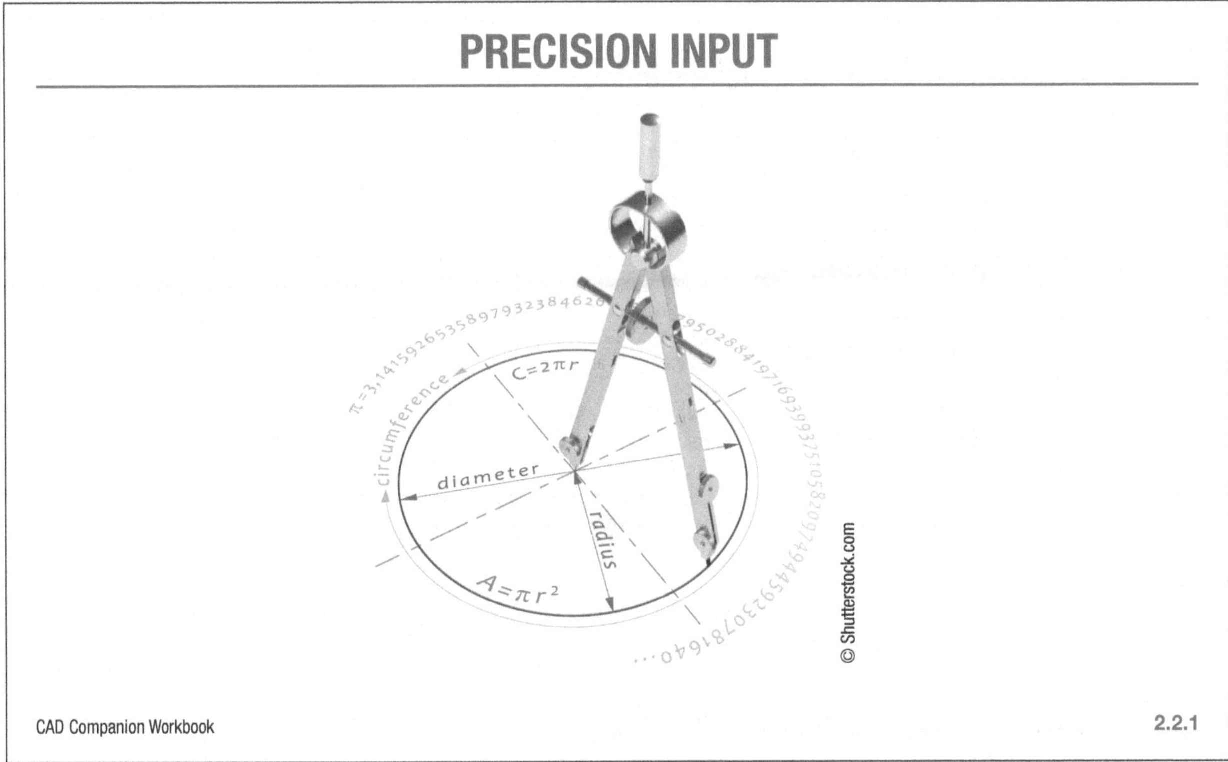

Precision Input—The ability to create exact, precise linework to specific dimensions and geometry is what sets CAD apart from drawing and photo editing capabilities such as available in the CorelDRAW suite of products, Adobe's Photoshop or Microsoft's Paint or even their Visio product which is noted as a professional diagramming product.

© Shutterstock.com

Precision input is one of THE most important aspects of both AutoCAD and MicroStation, along with all other true CAD programs. If the student learns just ONE aspect of CAD, he should learn precision input. What use would a "drafted" drawing have if it were not "Drawn-to-Scale"?

Some Architects taking this class may have some problems with this concept. Traditional CAD packages such as AutoCAD and MicroStation were not designed for "sketching" or "free-hand" drafting. The specific purpose of CAD is the creation of exact drawings. The use of the "Computer" make this much easier, but the Human has to learn the specific processes to make the "Machine" understand what needs to be drawn. CAD generated drawings can be beautiful although most would say not as "artistic" as hand drawn drawings.

© Shutterstock.com

Tip: Pay extremely close attention to what you type in, **make sure it is EXACTLY correct!** Think about this: Do you get your money from the ATM machine, if you do a typo while entering your PIN number?

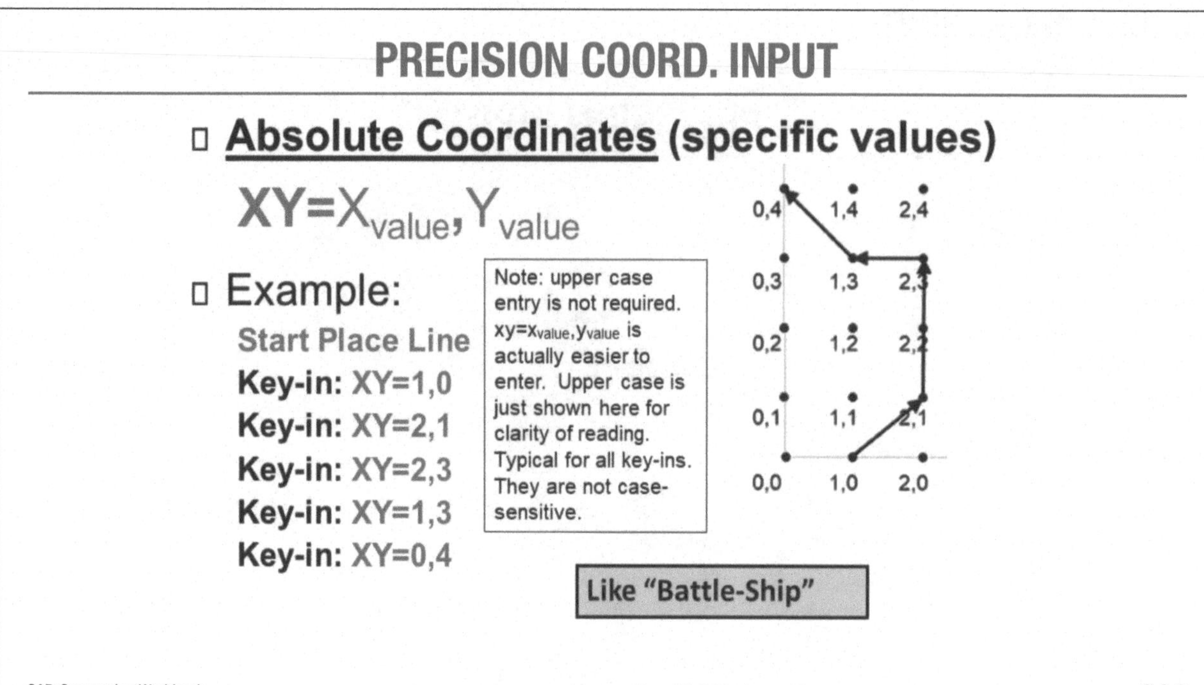

Absolute Coordinates key-in format: XY=$X_{coordinate}$,$Y_{coordinate}$ or

XY=$X_{address}$,$Y_{address}$

Absolute Coordinate input is the **least used method** of input for most CAD users, since it is quite inefficient. It requires that the user figure out all the coordinates of the end-points of the shape being drawn, ***before*** you draw it!

This method does have relevance for civil engineers, however, if they have lots of positional data stored in a database regarding terrain or a particular plot of land. Many CAD programs can be set up to take volumes of positional data and create drawings such as "topo" maps from the data. This is beyond the scope of this class. You may get exposed to this technique in later Civil Engineering courses.

Please note that, *fortunately*, AutoCAD and MicroStation perform precision input nearly identical to each other, just with slight differences in the syntax required. Syntax is a "computer-nerd" term, which sort of means computer "grammar".

MicroStation is very picky with syntax regarding key-in entries. For example, if the user intends to key-in XY=1,0 but leaves out the comma, MicroStation will see the entry as XY=10 which is completely different! When a trailing entry is left off in a MicroStation key-in, it is assumed to be 0, so the example in the previous sentence would appear to be XY=10,0 to MicroStation … quite different than the intended entry!

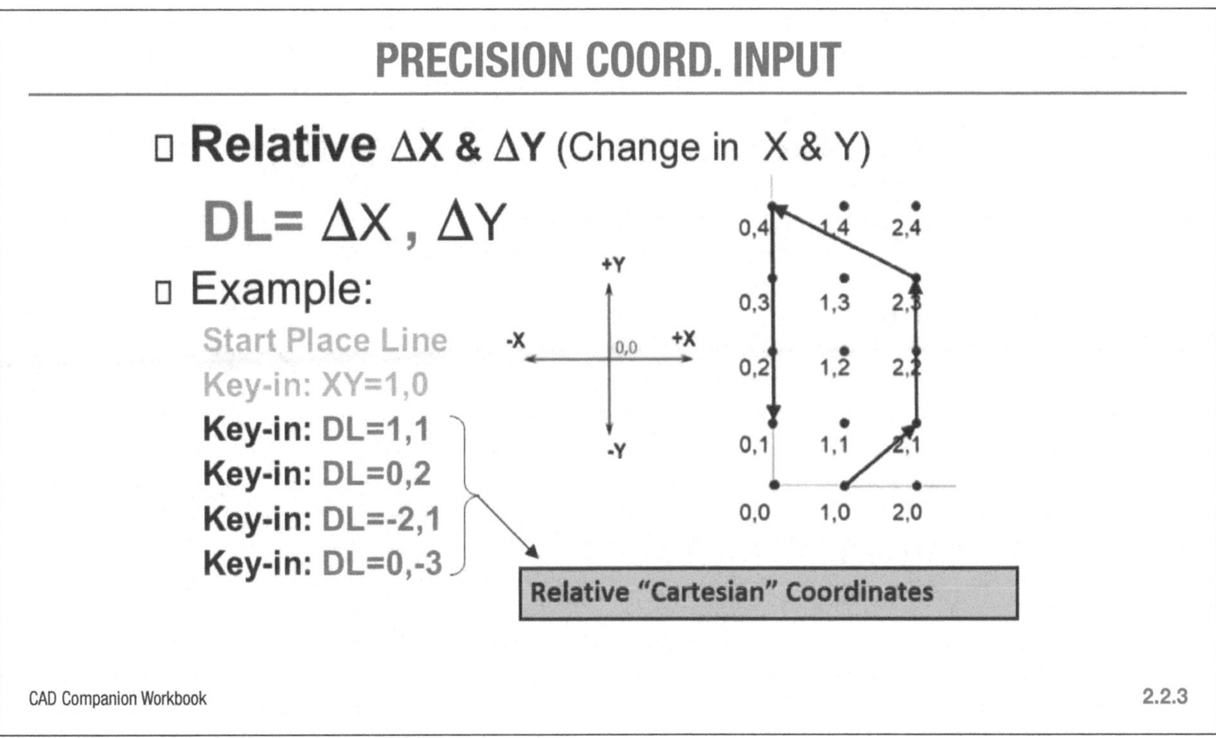

PRECISION COORD. INPUT
Relative ΔX & ΔY (Change in X & Y)
DL= ΔX , ΔY
Example:
Start Place Line
Key-in: XY=1,0
Key-in: DL=1,1
Key-in: DL=0,2
Key-in: DL=-2,1
Key-in: DL=0,-3
Relative "Cartesian" Coordinates
CAD Companion Workbook
2.2.3

Also known as: Relative Rectangular Coordinate entry

Relative Rectangular Coordinates

key-in format: DL=Delta $X_{coordinate}$, Delta $Y_{coordinate}$

also stated as **DL=Delta X** Length, **Delta Y** Length

(remember **DL=DLx,DLy**)

Note: DL = __, __ can be typed in all lower case characters: dl=__, __ which is easier to type.

Upper case is shown here only for clarity.

Relative Rectangular Coordinate input is used fairly often by most CAD users. It is most often used when the user knows a specific "offset" distance in both Delta X and Delta Y dimensions.

Example: Drawing a simple precision rectangle of dimension 4.7 x 2.1

Start **Place Block**

First point: **XY=3,2 <Enter>** ← this is an absolute coordinate entry

Enter opposite corner: **DL=4.7,2.1 <Enter>** ← this is a relative rectangular coordinate entry

Place Block requires entry of 2 points, across a diagonal from each other.

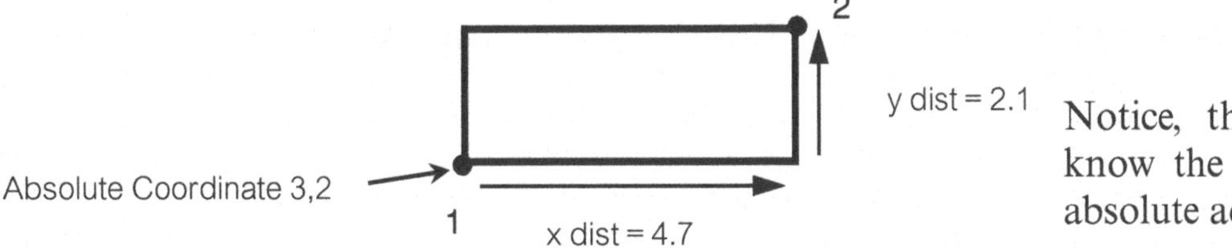

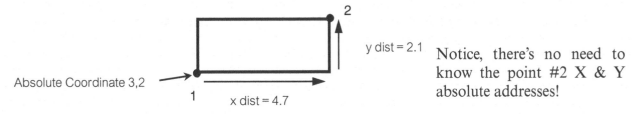

Notice, there's no need to know the point #2 X & Y absolute addresses!

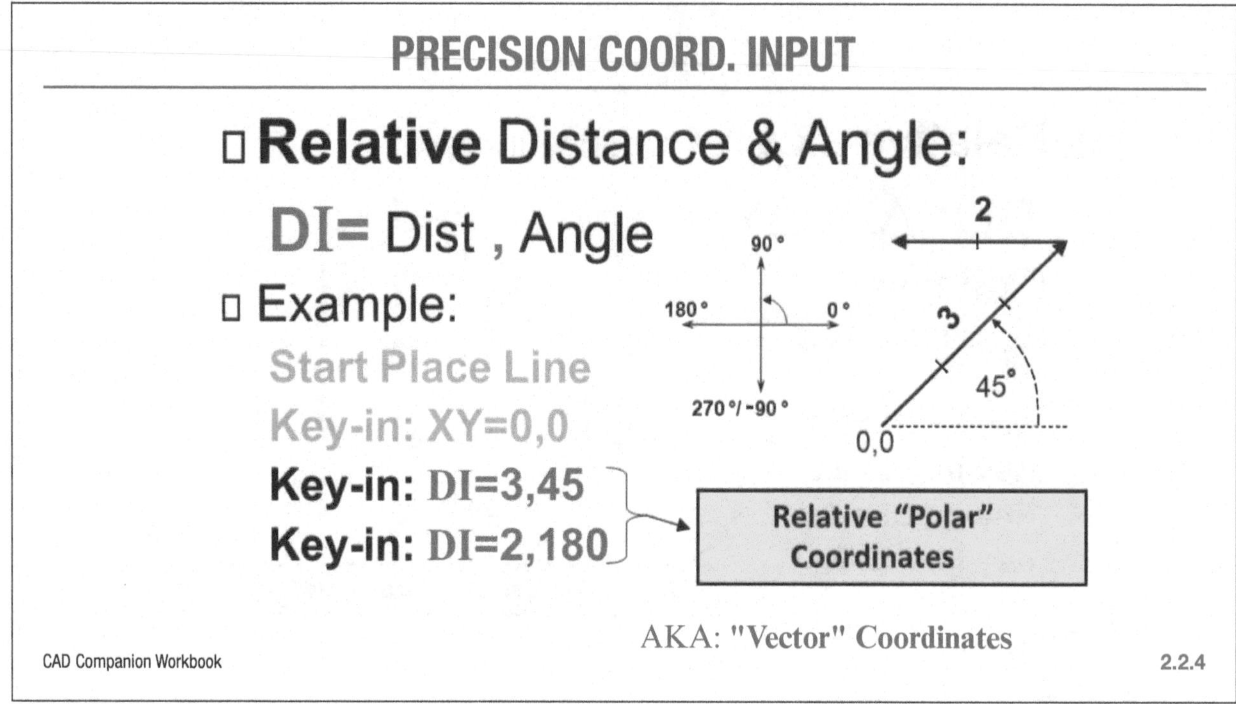

PRECISION COORD. INPUT
Relative Distance & Angle:
DI= Dist , Angle
Example:
Start Place Line
Key-in: XY=0,0
Key-in: DI=3,45
Key-in: DI=2,180
Relative "Polar" Coordinates
90°
180°
0°
270°/-90°
2
3
45°
0,0
AKA: "Vector" Coordinates
CAD Companion Workbook
2.2.4

Relative Polar Coordinates

key-in format : DI=Distance value, Angle value

also stated as **DI=Length, Direction** or **DI=L,α**

DI=Distance, Direction (remember **DI=Di,Di)**

Note: DI = __, __ can be typed in all lower case characters: di=__, __ which is easier to type.

Upper case is shown here only for clarity.

Polar Coordinate input is the most often used method of precision input. Whenever the user knows the "Distance" in a certain "Direction", Polar entry is by far the easiest and fastest method of input. This method is most similar to giving directions to someone, let's say to go to San Diego. You give a distance and then a direction like, Go 150 miles, South.

Warning:

While it is possible to *redefine* the directions by which the Polar Coordinates operate, (ie. you could change "north" to 0 degrees, "east" to 90 degrees, and continue *clockwise* with the positive angles), this would confuse the heck out of you or anyone else who ever would have to work with your drawings later!! So, please don't change the default angular directions and sense of positive angles!

Notice the bomb is much bigger than normal? There's a good reason for this!

© Pranch/Shutterstock.com

PRECISION drawing exercise

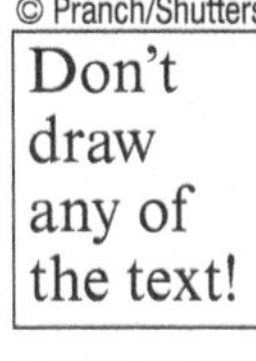

Don't draw any of the text!

You won't see the "dots" on the lines.

See pg 76 for turning off grid display

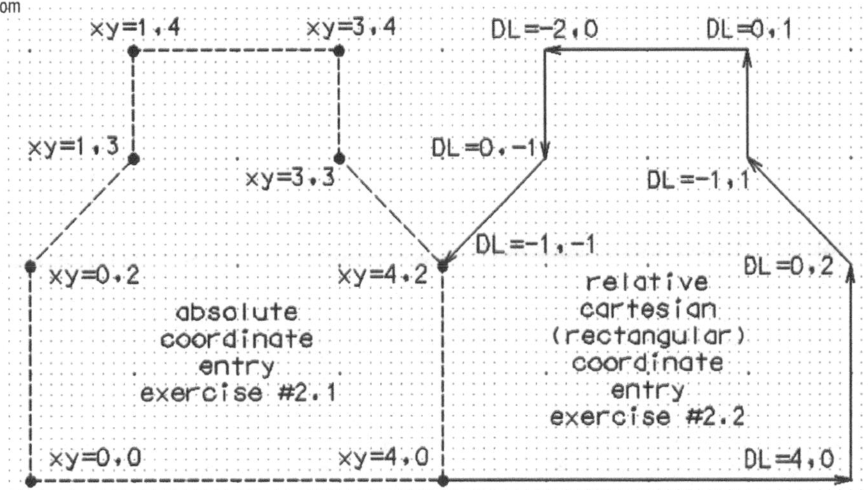

The student will gain experience creating a new drawing and making Precision Input Key-ins.

They should also gain a better understanding of the differences between Absolute, Relative Cartesian and Relative Polar entry from this exercise.

This PRECISION exercise is on pg 85 AND pg 86

Absolute Coordinate entry exercise

1. Create a new drawing, call it PRECISION.
2. Open the key-in field with **Utilities > Key-in.** (or, if using **CONNECT Edition**, see pg 39)
3. Resize and dock the key-in field, then start **Place Line**, but don't hit a point with the mouse.
4. Hit **<Enter>** to take you to the key-in field.
5. Type **LC=2** <Enter>, then type **xy=0,0** <Enter>

   (LC=value, sets the line code, in this case, dotted)
6. Roll the mouse a bit without hitting any buttons
7. Notice a line has been started.
8. Type in the following and hit enter after each:
9. **xy=4,0**
10. **xy=4,2**
11. **xy=3,3**
12. **xy=3,4**
13. **xy=1,4**
14. **xy=1,3**
15. **xy=0,2**
16. **xy=0,0**
17. Then hit reset, which is the right mouse button.
18. Your figure should look like the left side figure.

Relative Cartesian (Rectangular) **Coordinate** entry exercise

1. In the same file, start **Place Line** once again.
2. Hit **<Enter>** to take you to the key-in field
3. Type **LC=0** <Enter>, then type **xy=4,0** <Enter>
4. (this time LC=0, sets line code to solid)
5. Roll the mouse a bit without hitting any buttons
6. Notice a line has been started.
7. Type in the following and hit enter after each, the entries can be upper or lower case, it doesn't matter:
8. **DL=4,0**
9. **DL=0,2**
10. **DL=–1,1**
11. **DL=0,1**
12. **DL=–2,0**
13. **DL=0,–1**
14. **DL=–1,–1**
15. Then hit reset, which is the right mouse button.
16. Your figure should look like the right side figure.

PRECISION is continued on pg 86 >>>

PRECISION drawing exercise (cont')

© Pranch/Shutterstock.com

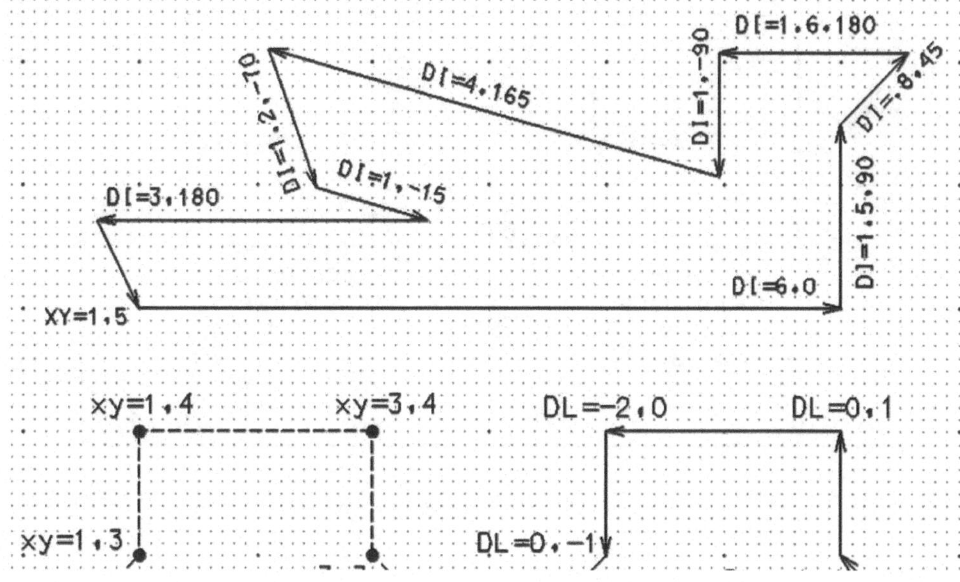

Relative Polar Coordinate entry exercise

1. In the same file, use the scroll bar and scroll to a location just above your existing drawing (see above) *(one can also "Pan" to the area above using the mouse, if desired)*
2. Start **Place Line** once again.
3. Hit **<Enter>** to take you to the key-in field *(see the cursor in the key-in field)*
4. Then type **xy=1,5** <Enter>
5. Type in the following and hit enter after each, the entries can be upper or lower case, it doesn't matter:
6. **DI=6,0**
7. **DI=1.5,90**
8. **DI=0.8,45**
9. **DI=1.6,180**
10. **DI=1,–90**
11. **DI=4,165**
12. **DI=1.2,–70**
13. **DI=1,–15**
14. **DI=3,180**
15. **XY=1,5**
16. Then hit reset, which is the right mouse button.
17. Your figure should look like the above figure.

Relative Polar Coordinate Key-ins

2.2 BASIC EDITS

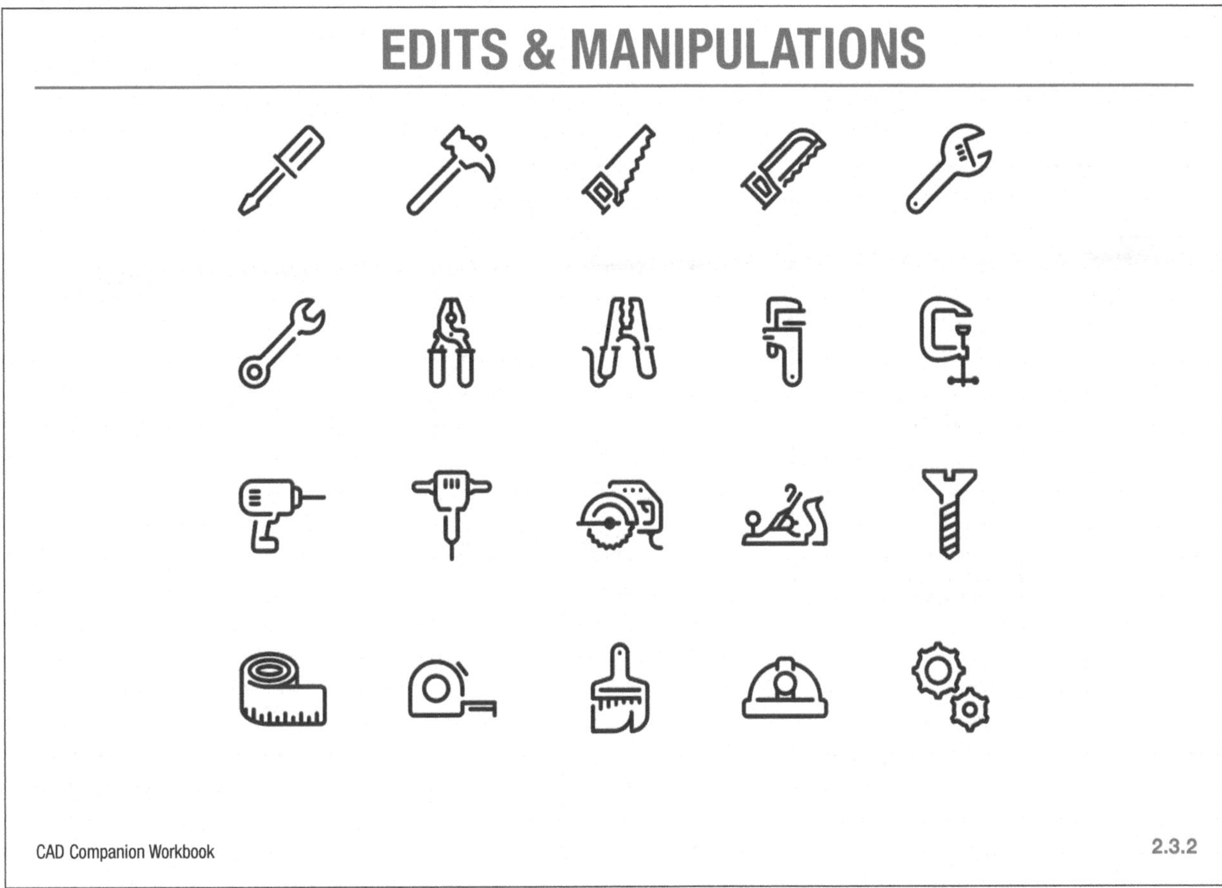

Edits & Manipulations—are another whole classification of CAD commands that the beginning CAD user is sometimes unaware of. **This category of commands is tremendously important, even more so than the "drawing" commands**. It is very common that entire CAD jobs involve just the modification of pre-existing drawings, drawn by you earlier or by others.

Most everyone is already somewhat familiar with the basic drawing commands, such as lines, circles, rectangles, arcs, etc. because we've drawn them ever since around Kindergarten. The drawing commands are usually readily picked up by most users, just by fiddling around or by just looking at examples of them in textbooks. With edits and manipulations, the common drafter may have no direct manual equivalent to the CAD method. The editing and manipulation commands, which are very useful, must be acquired into the beginning users set of CAD skills in order to build speed and efficiency. CAD provides a right tool for almost any situation. **Part of this section's goal is to start to show you how to select which tool to use for each particular task!**

Example: How would you **"re-scale"** a predrawn small detail by manual means? If you don't have a copy machine with a "scale" function, you would have to erase the detail and draw it over again! Seems pretty inefficient doesn't it?! Well, with CAD there are special commands to scale existing objects, without having to erase them first. How convenient! Now the trick is, how do you use them properly. We'll show you.

Module 2 – Tools

Manipulations

< < < < The top half of this page introduces **V8*i*** Tools

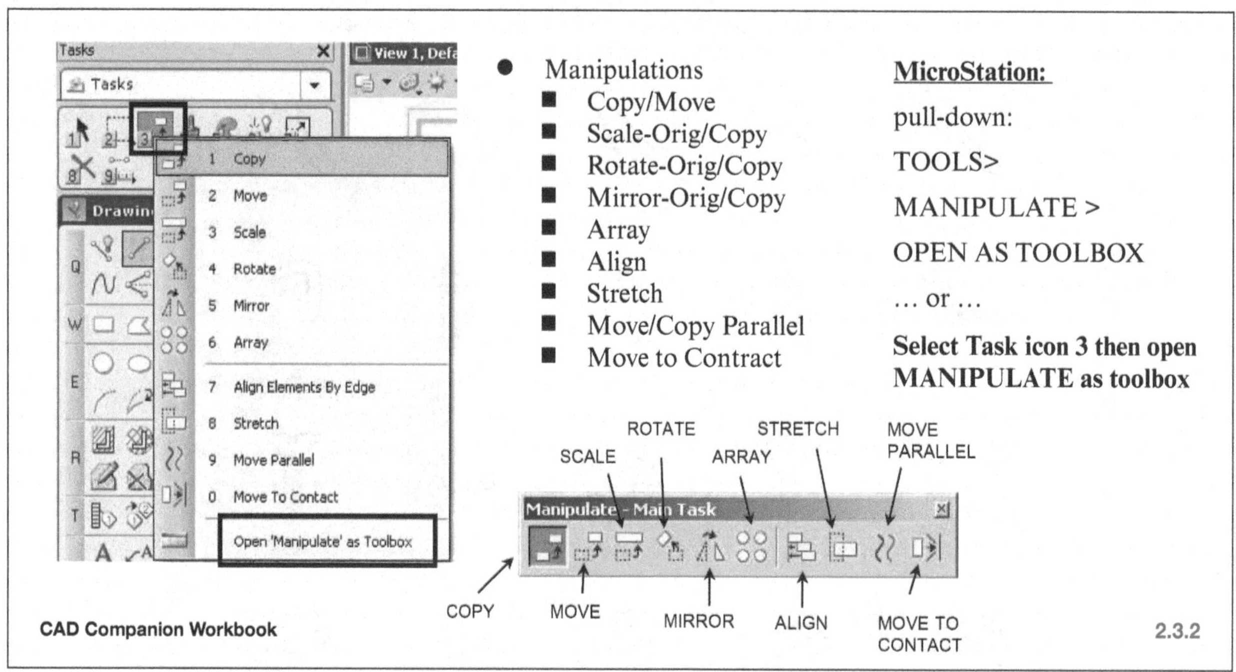

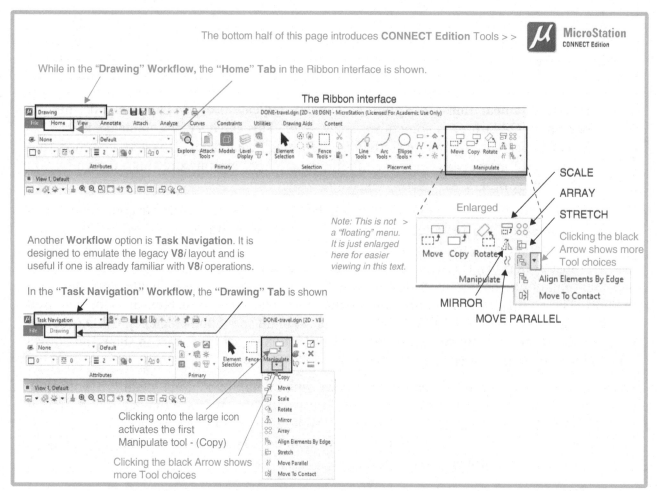

The bottom half of this page introduces **CONNECT Edition** Tools > >

MicroStation CONNECT Edition

While in the "**Drawing**" **Workflow**, the "**Home**" **Tab** in the Ribbon interface is shown.

The Ribbon interface

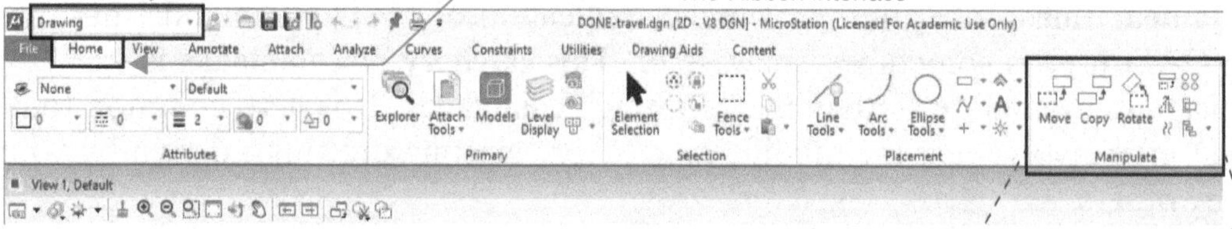

SCALE

ARRAY

STRETCH

Enlarged

Note: This is not a "floating" menu. It is just enlarged here for easier viewing in this text.

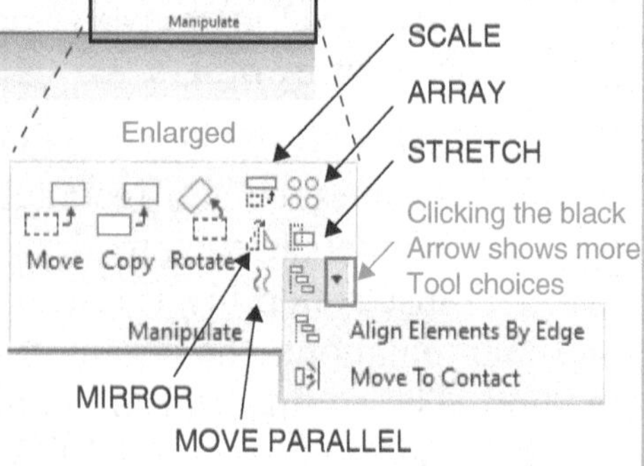

Clicking the black Arrow shows more Tool choices

Move Copy Rotate

Manipulate

Align Elements By Edge

Move To Contact

MIRROR

MOVE PARALLEL

Another **Workflow** option is **Task Navigation**. It is designed to emulate the legacy **V8*i*** layout and is useful if one is already familiar with **V8*i*** operations.

In the "**Task Navigation**" **Workflow**, the "**Drawing**" **Tab** is shown

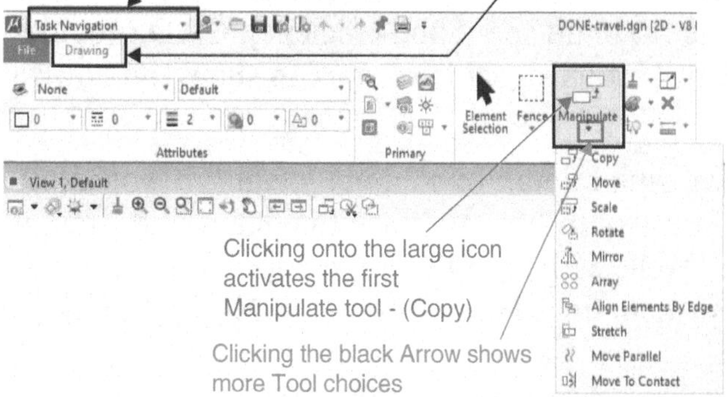

Copy
Move
Scale
Rotate
Mirror
Array
Align Elements By Edge
Stretch
Move Parallel
Move To Contact

Clicking onto the large icon activates the first Manipulate tool - (Copy)

Clicking the black Arrow shows more Tool choices

Module 2 – Tools

Modifications

< < < < The top half of this page introduces **V8*i*** Tools

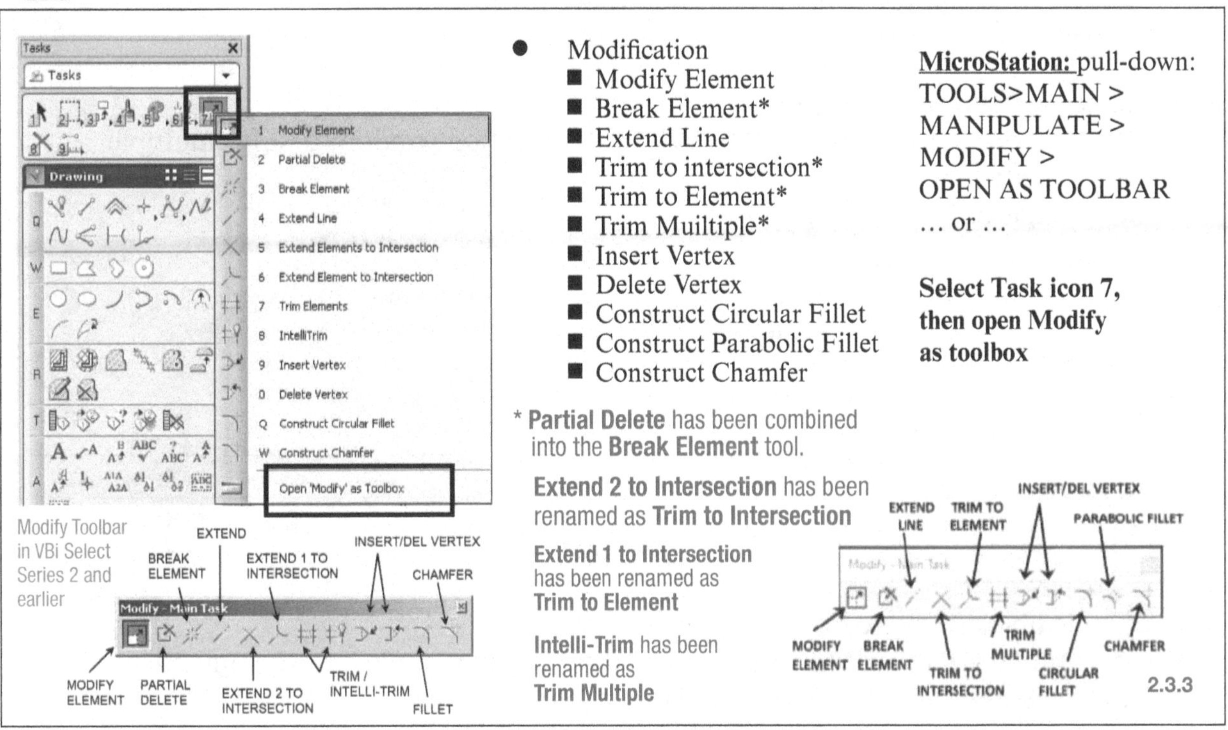

- Modification
  - Modify Element
  - Break Element*
  - Extend Line
  - Trim to intersection*
  - Trim to Element*
  - Trim Muiltiple*
  - Insert Vertex
  - Delete Vertex
  - Construct Circular Fillet
  - Construct Parabolic Fillet
  - Construct Chamfer

MicroStation: pull-down:
TOOLS>MAIN >
MANIPULATE >
MODIFY >
OPEN AS TOOLBAR
… or …

Select Task icon 7, then open Modify as toolbox

* **Partial Delete** has been combined into the **Break Element** tool.

Extend 2 to Intersection has been renamed as **Trim to Intersection**

Extend 1 to Intersection has been renamed as **Trim to Element**

Intelli-Trim has been renamed as **Trim Multiple**

2.3.3

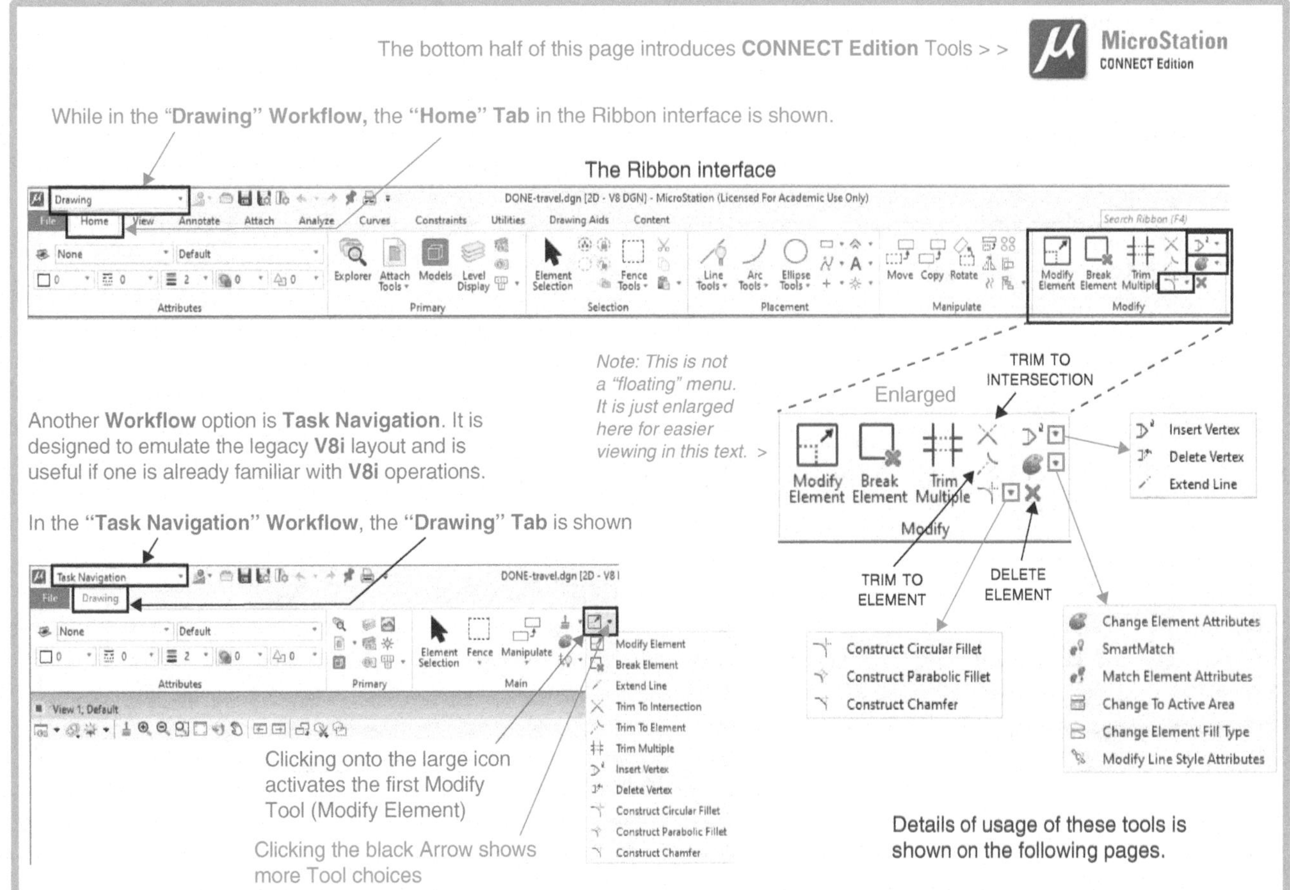

The bottom half of this page introduces **CONNECT Edition** Tools > >

MicroStation CONNECT Edition

While in the "**Drawing**" **Workflow**, the "**Home**" **Tab** in the Ribbon interface is shown.

Note: This is not a "floating" menu. It is just enlarged here for easier viewing in this text. >

Another **Workflow** option is **Task Navigation**. It is designed to emulate the legacy **V8i** layout and is useful if one is already familiar with **V8i** operations.

In the "**Task Navigation**" **Workflow**, the "**Drawing**" **Tab** is shown

Clicking onto the large icon activates the first Modify Tool (Modify Element)

Clicking the black Arrow shows more Tool choices

Details of usage of these tools is shown on the following pages.

Copy

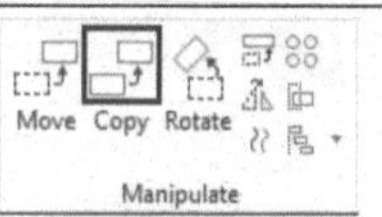

- select single or many objects
  - Surround many objects with a Element Selection window, first for multiple
  - specify first point, then destination
  - Single element copy example:

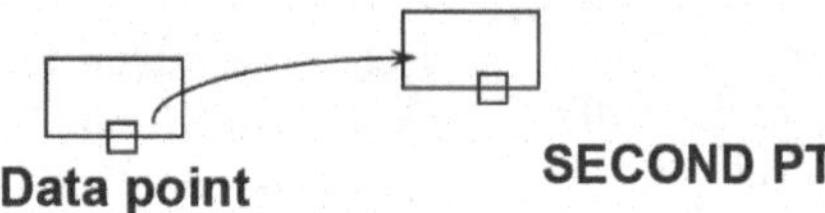

CAD Companion Workbook 2.3.4

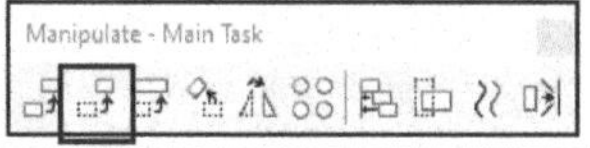

Move

- Single objects, selected by Data Pts
- Additional DP (on blank area or on next object) to complete the command
- Continue DP's for new location (or more copies)
- Many objects can be pre-selected by the **SELECTION tool**
- Or selected by **FENCE**, click ***Use Fence***

CAD Companion Workbook 2.3.5

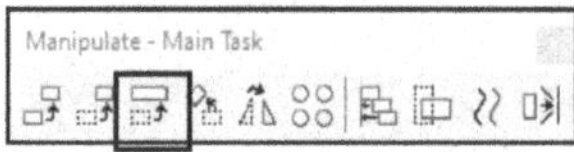

Scale "SCA"

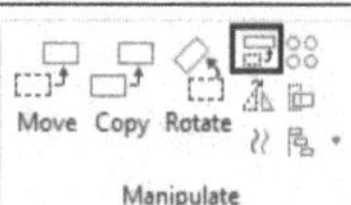

- Enlarges or Shrinks objects
- Can set the "X" scale or "Y" scale
- μ-Stn use key-in: shortcut "SCA" & AS=FACTOR, also, XS=FACTOR or YS=FACTOR or fill in the dialog box with the scale desired enter more DP's to continue scaling

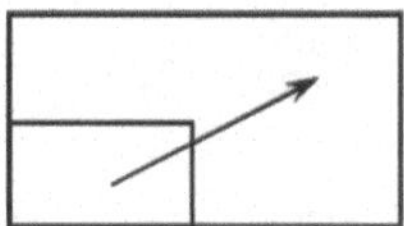

CAD Companion Workbook 2.3.6

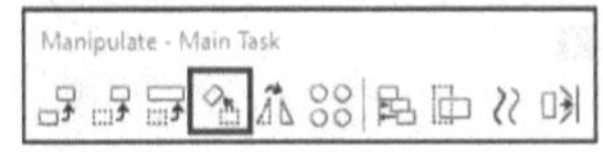

Rotate "ROT"

- Turns elements based on angle
- **μ-Stn use key-in: shortcut "ROT" & AA=angle value or fill in the dialog box with the angle desired enter more DP's to continue rotating**

MicroStation key-in: AA="Active Angle"

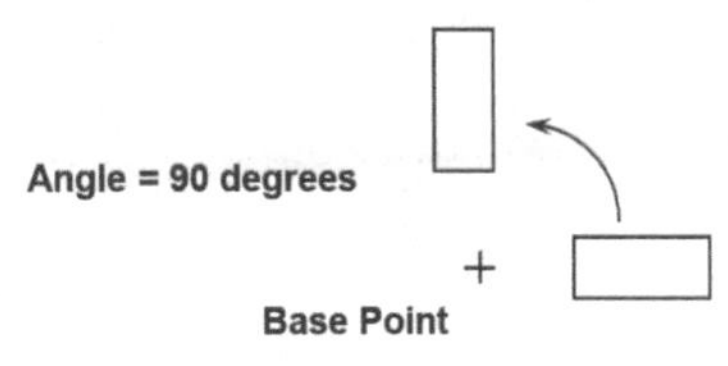

CAD Companion Workbook 2.3.7

Mirror "MIR"

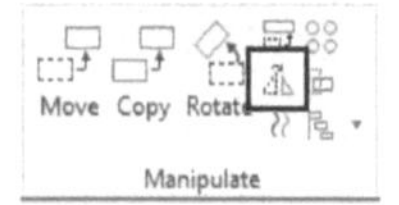

- Flip objects about an imaginary line
- Can make a COPY or flip ORIGINALS
- μ-Stn lets you select about a vertical or horizantal, then define 1 point or define about a line, just like ACAD, requiring 2 points

CAD Companion Workbook 2.3.8

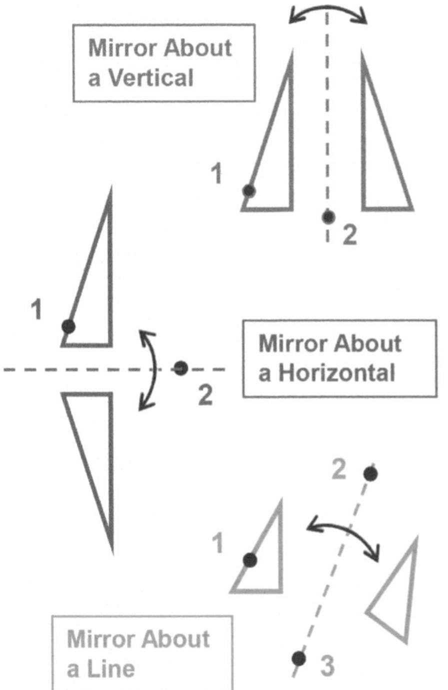

MicroStation:

MIR

… or … use icon

Tool Settings automatically pops-up

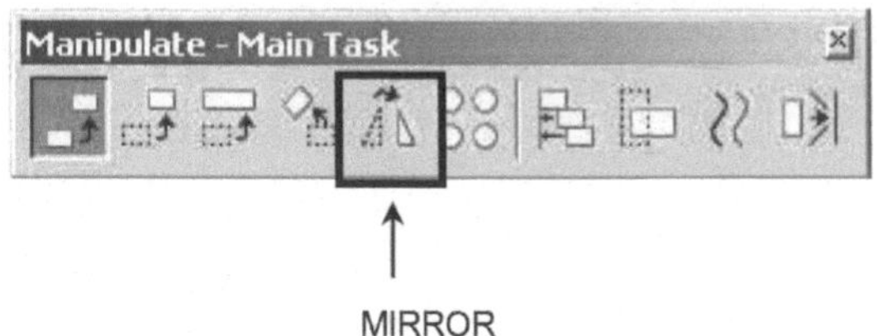

MIRROR

MicroStation V8i
(SELECTseries 4)

MicroStation
CONNECT Edition

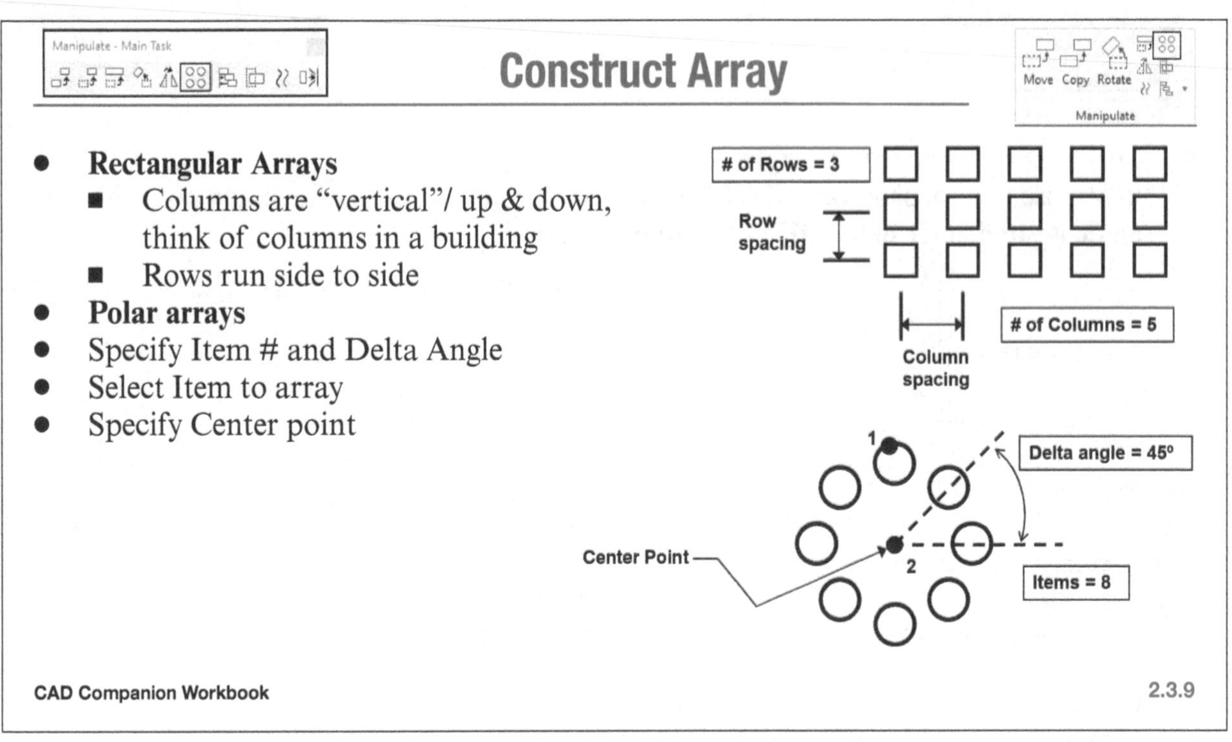
Manipulate - Main Task
Construct Array
Move
Copy
Rotate
Manipulate
- **Rectangular Arrays**
  - Columns are "vertical"/ up & down, think of columns in a building
  - Rows run side to side
- **Polar arrays**
- Specify Item # and Delta Angle
- Select Item to array
- Specify Center point
# of Rows = 3
Row spacing
# of Columns = 5
Column spacing
1
Delta angle = 45º
Center Point
2
Items = 8
CAD Companion Workbook
2.3.9

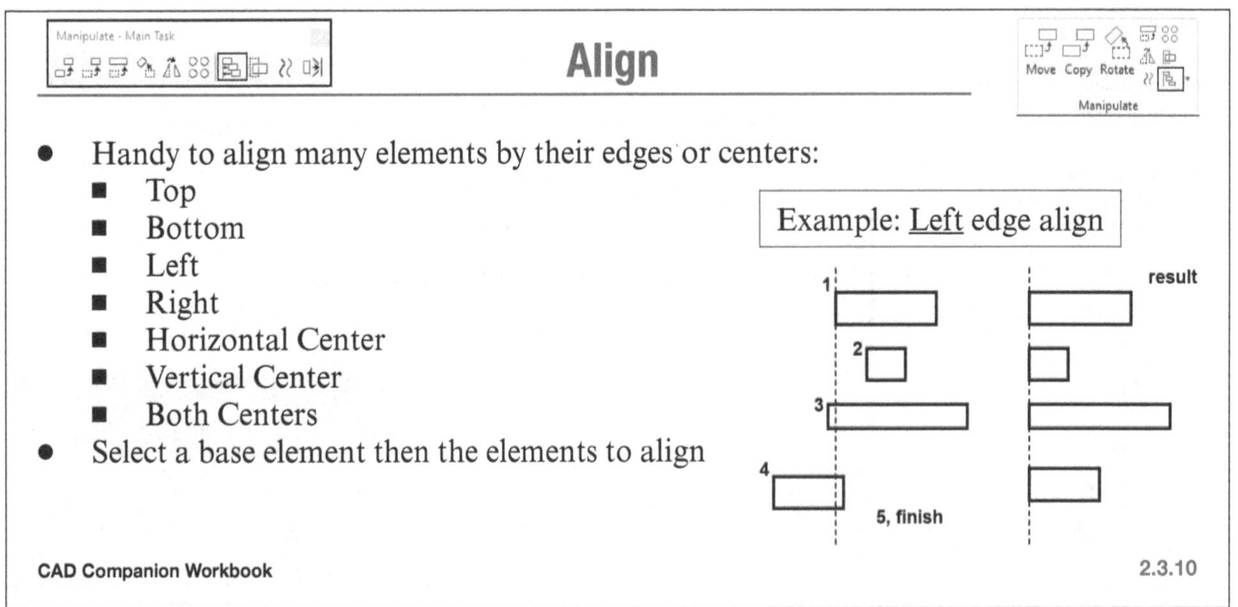
Manipulate - Main Task
Align
Move
Copy
Rotate
Manipulate
- Handy to align many elements by their edges or centers:
  - Top
  - Bottom
  - Left
  - Right
  - Horizontal Center
  - Vertical Center
  - Both Centers
- Select a base element then the elements to align
Example: Left edge align
result
1
2
3
4
5, finish
CAD Companion Workbook
2.3.10

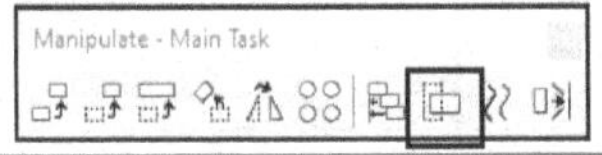

Stretch

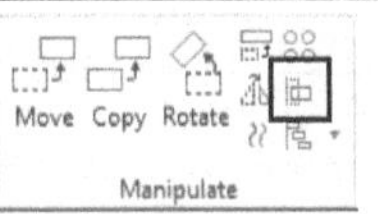

- Stretch is found in the Fence Toolbar as an option of the Manipulate Fence Contents tool
- Stretch Deforms objects, like a rubber band
  - based on a **Fence** (always assumes overlap mode for the fence operation)

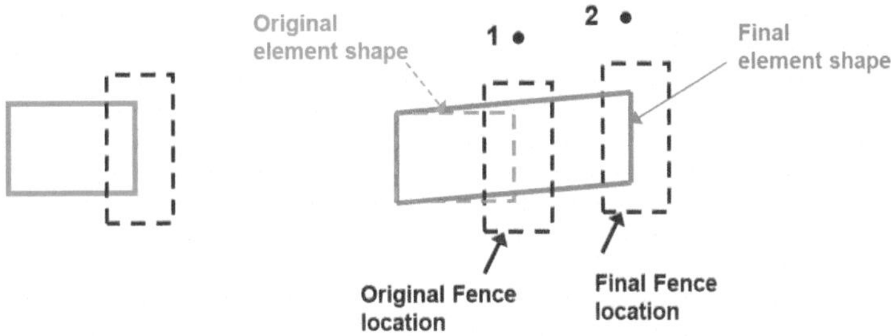

There are **Three basic Rules of Stretch.**
These are based on the position of the elements relative to the position of the fence placed.

Element Position relative to fence	Result of Stretch Action
1. Fully inside the fence ->	The elements move
2. Overlapping the fence Boundary ->	The elements stretch
3. Fully outside the fence ->	No effect to elements

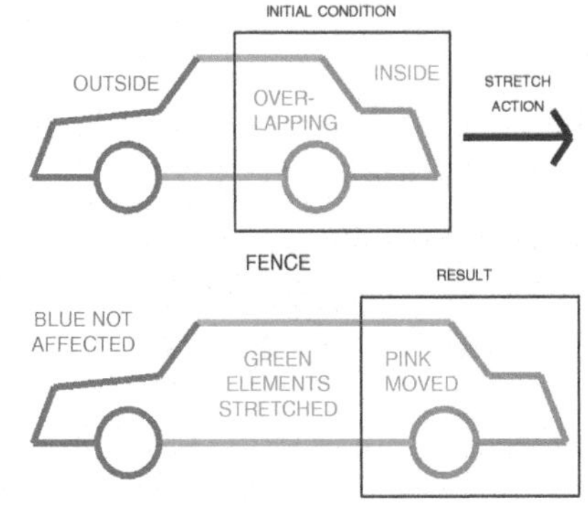

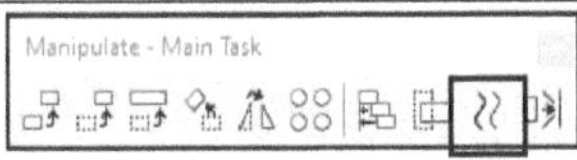

Move/Copy Parallel

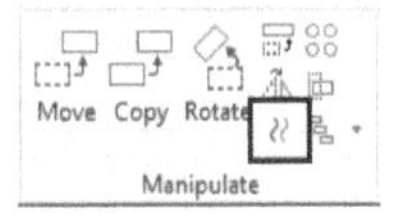

- Used to Move or Copy an object to one side of the original, Pick original, specify side
- The new copy is parallel to the original
- Datapoint to specify graphically … or …
- Specify precise distance

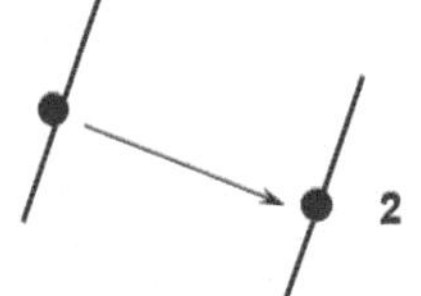

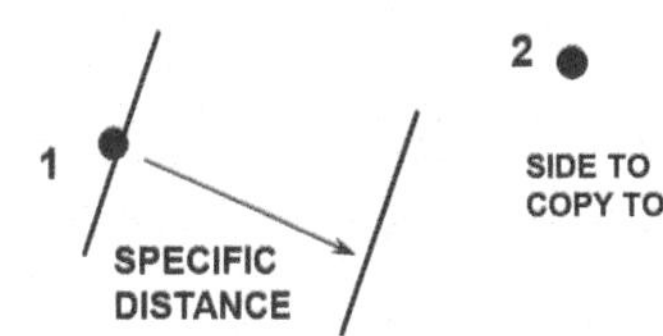

Modify

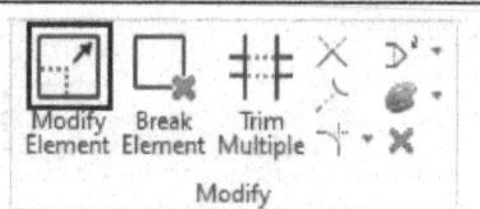

- Used to change the shape of:
  - Lines/Linestrings
  - Blocks/Polygons
  - Circles/Ellipses
  - Arcs
  - Dimensions (in module 5)
  - Additional elements

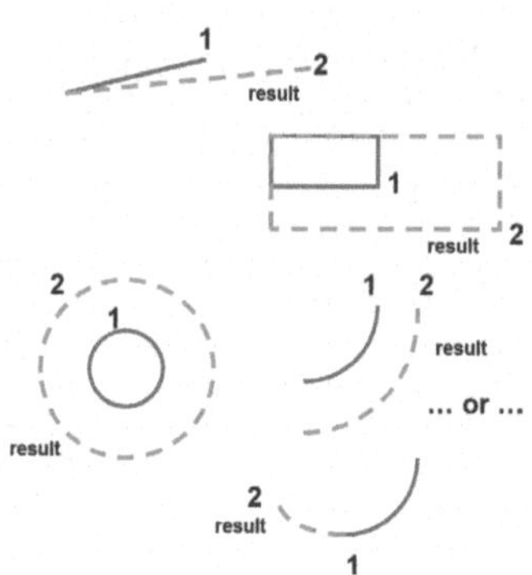

© Shutterstock.com

Break Element

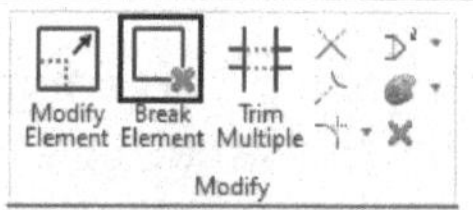

- Cuts an element into two or more pieces
  - Break by two points
  - Break by point
  - Break by drag line
  - Break by element

Tool Settings Window

BREAK BY TWO POINTS
(Previously PARTIAL DELETE)

The **Tool Settings Window** automatically appears when a tool is activated and there are various settings or modes that the user can set or alter.

© Shutterstock.com

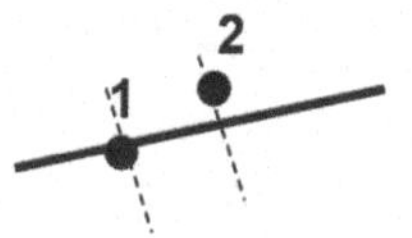

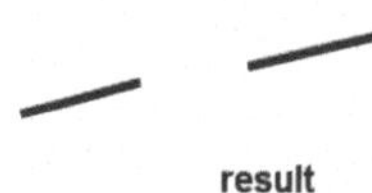

result

Example of **Break by two points**, on a line

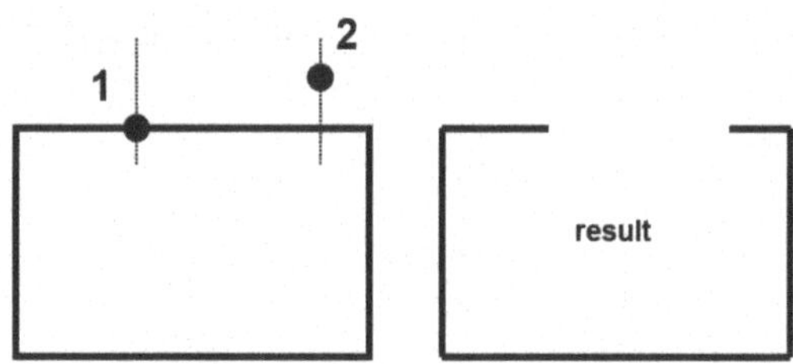

Example of **Break by two points**, on a shape

- Always select line being extended First
  - Extend Line, to a new point or by set distance
  - NO OTHER INTERSECTING LINE REQUIRED
  - TRIM TO INTERSECTION
  - TRIM TO ELEMENT ——► is similar to ACAD

© Shutterstock.com

Latest versions use a combination of the tool names **Extend** and **Trim**

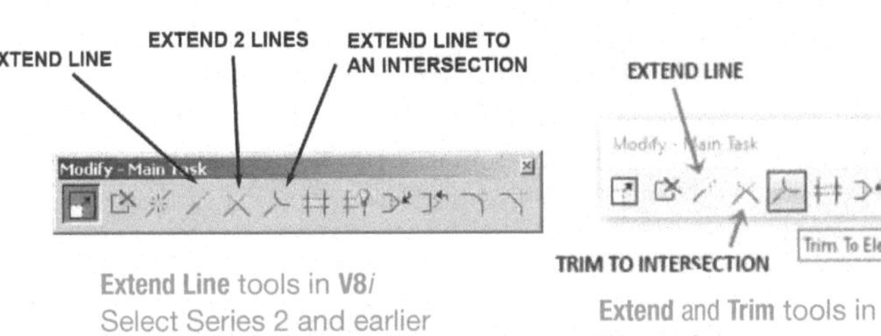

Extend Line tools in V8*i* Select Series 2 and earlier

EXTEND LINE

Modify - Main Task

TRIM TO INTERSECTION

Trim To Element

Extend and Trim tools in later V8*i* versions

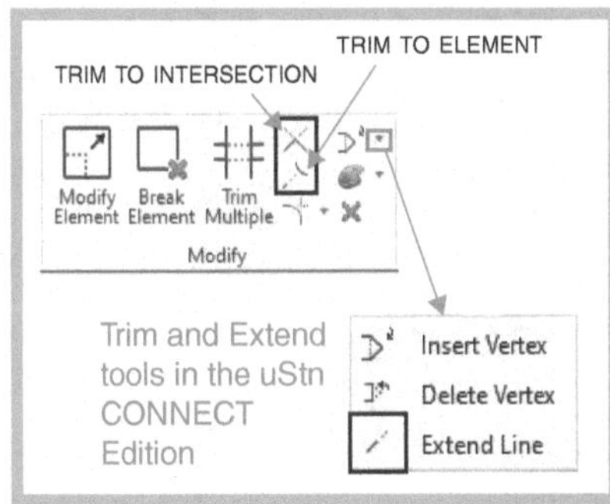

Trim and Extend tools in the uStn CONNECT Edition

CAD Companion Workbook 2.3.15

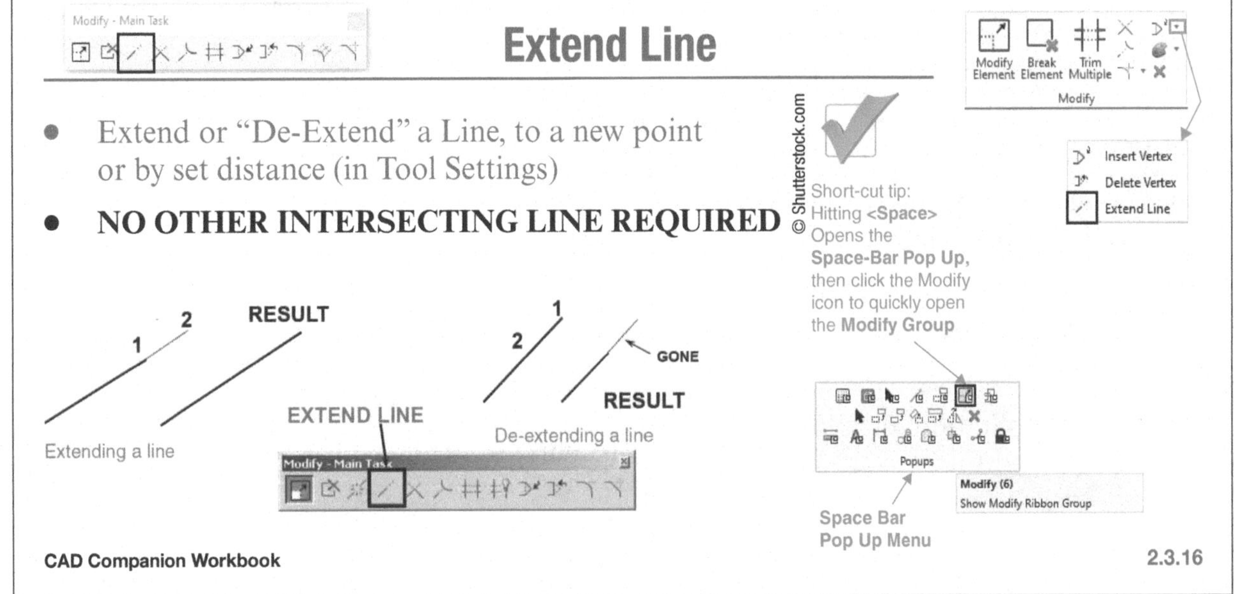

Modify - Main Task
Extend Line
Modify Element
Break Element
Trim Multiple
Modify
Insert Vertex
Delete Vertex
Extend Line
Extend or "De-Extend" a Line, to a new point or by set distance (in Tool Settings)
NO OTHER INTERSECTING LINE REQUIRED
© Shutterstock.com
Short-cut tip:
Hitting <Space> Opens the Space-Bar Pop Up, then click the Modify icon to quickly open the Modify Group
1
2
RESULT
Extending a line
EXTEND LINE
Modify - Main Task
1
2
GONE
RESULT
De-extending a line
Popups
Modify (6)
Show Modify Ribbon Group
Space Bar Pop Up Menu
CAD Companion Workbook
2.3.16

Trim to Intersection

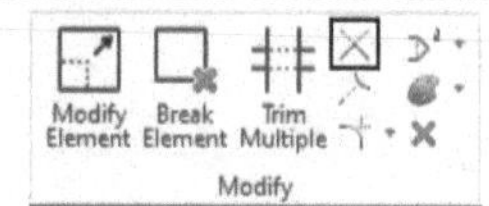

- Trims two lines to their intersection
  The two lines can be extended longer or shorter or a combination of either.

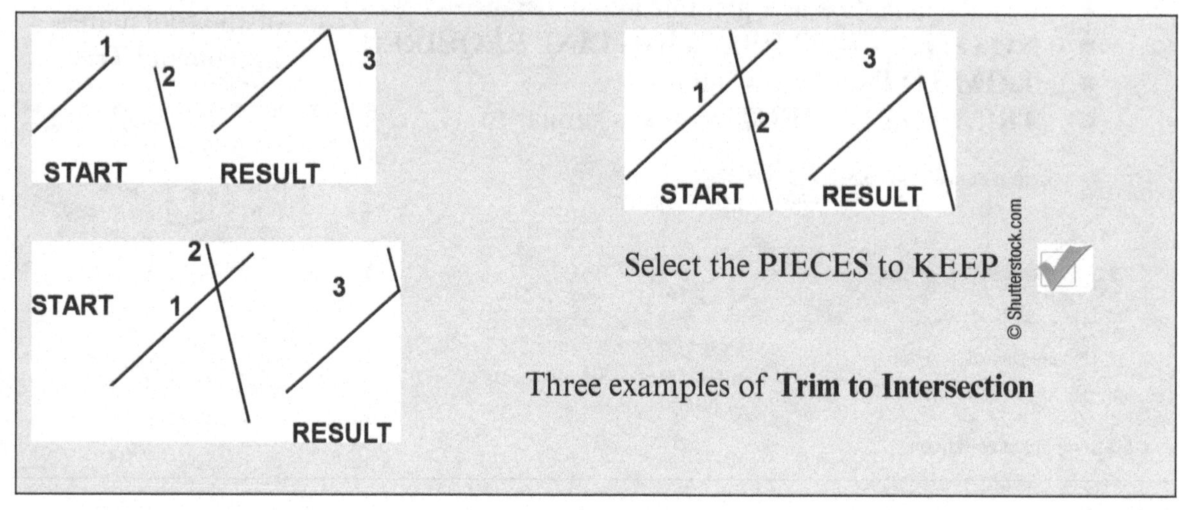

Three examples of **Trim to Intersection**

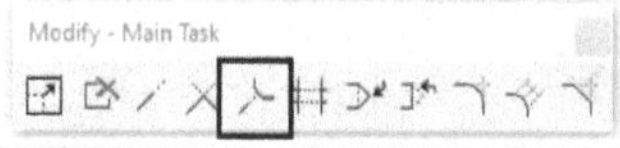

Trim to Element

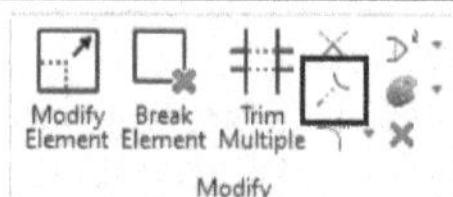

- Trims one line to its intersection with another element

  The one line can be extended longer or shorter to the other element

  - MicroStation: pick line to Extend First

© Shutterstock.com

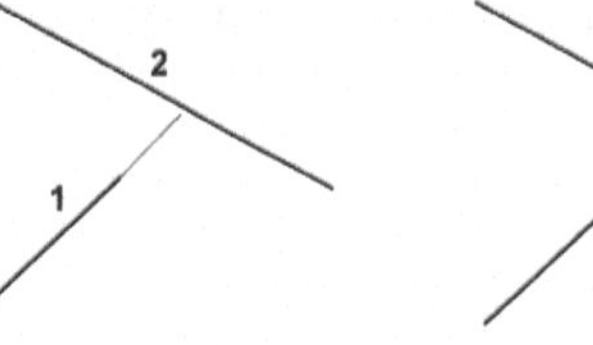

Example #1: **Trim to Element**

Notice: The second element does NOT get changed!

The user does NOT need to select the second element at the point of interection!

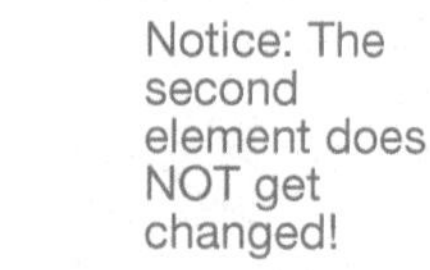

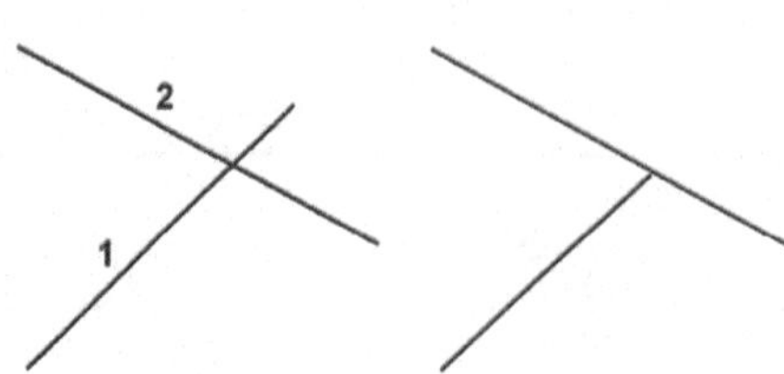

Example #2: **Trim to Element**

© Shutterstock.com

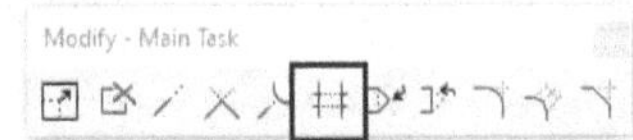

Trim Multiple

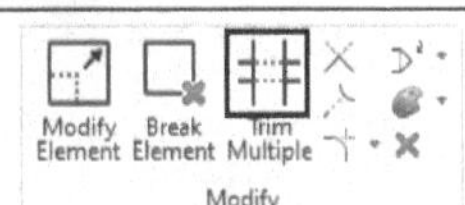

- Select an intersecting object as the "Cutting" Tool
- Then select parts to be trimmed off

Example:
Line 1 is used as the "knife" for the Trim action.

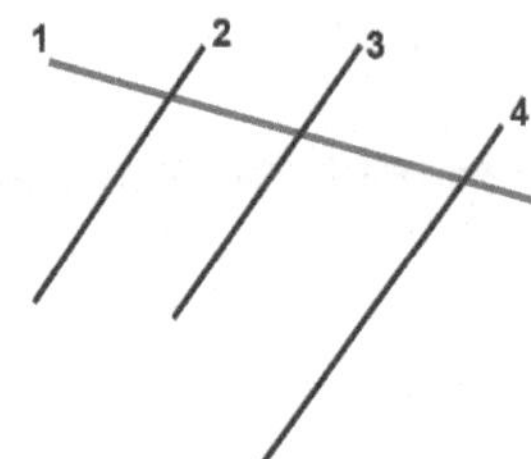

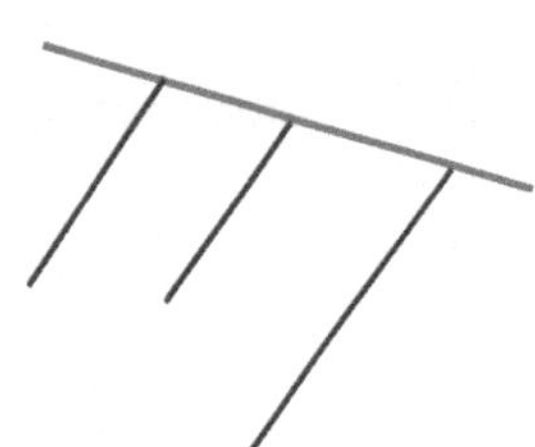

CAD Companion Workbook 2.3.19

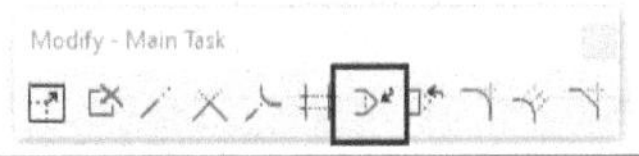

Insert Vertex

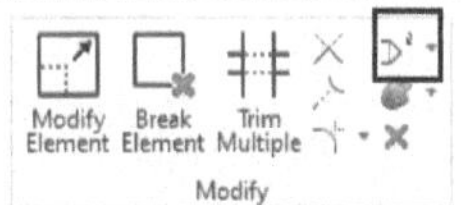

- Adds additional vertices to the selected element

Example:
Add a vertex to the right edge

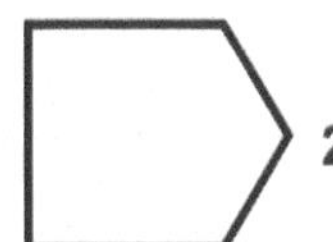

CAD Companion Workbook 2.3.20

Delete Vertex

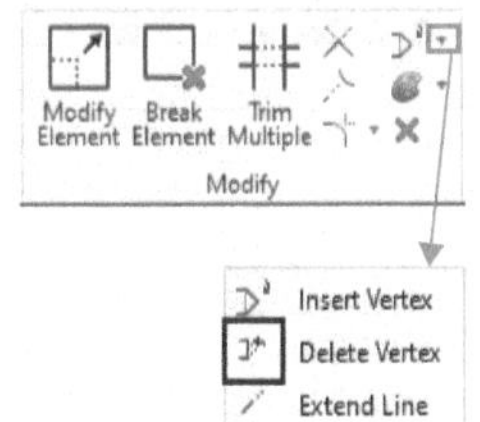

- Deletes vertices from the selected element

Example:
Delete the vertex at location 1.

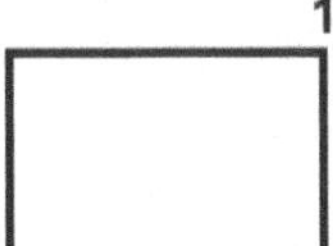

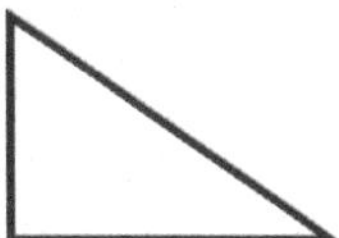

CAD Companion Workbook 2.3.21

MicroStation V8i
(SELECTseries 4)

MicroStation
CONNECT Edition

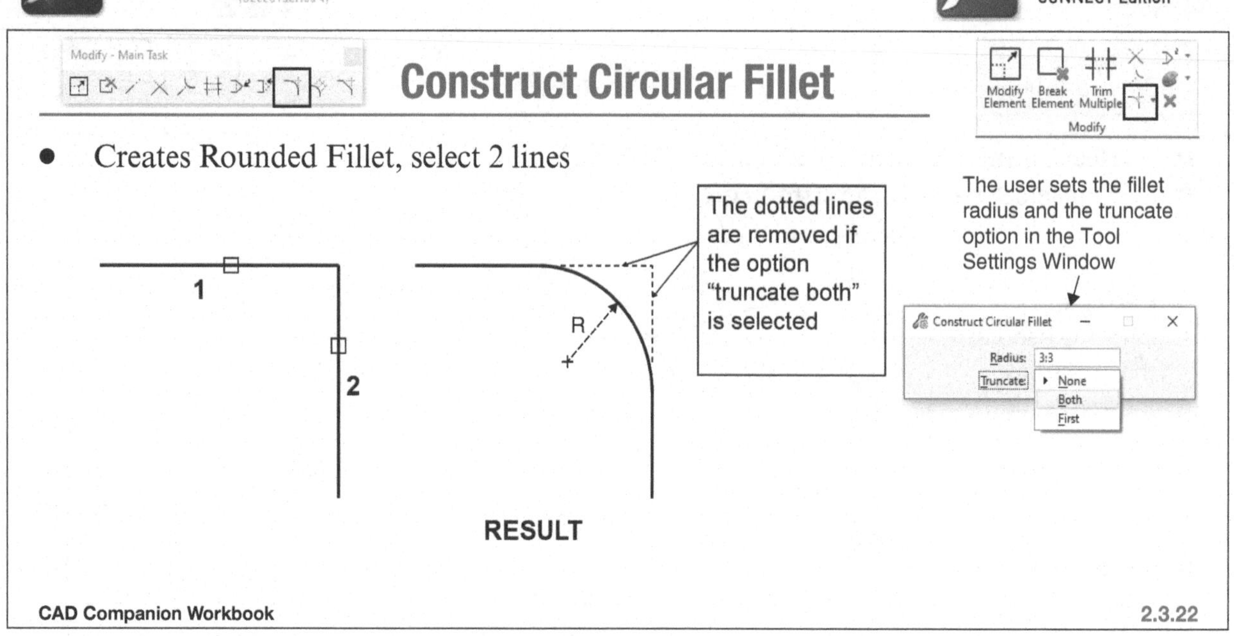
Modify - Main Task
Construct Circular Fillet
Modify Element
Break Element
Trim Multiple
Modify
• Creates Rounded Fillet, select 2 lines
1
2
R
The dotted lines are removed if the option "truncate both" is selected
The user sets the fillet radius and the truncate option in the Tool Settings Window
Construct Circular Fillet
Radius: 3:3
Truncate:
None
Both
First
RESULT
CAD Companion Workbook
2.3.22

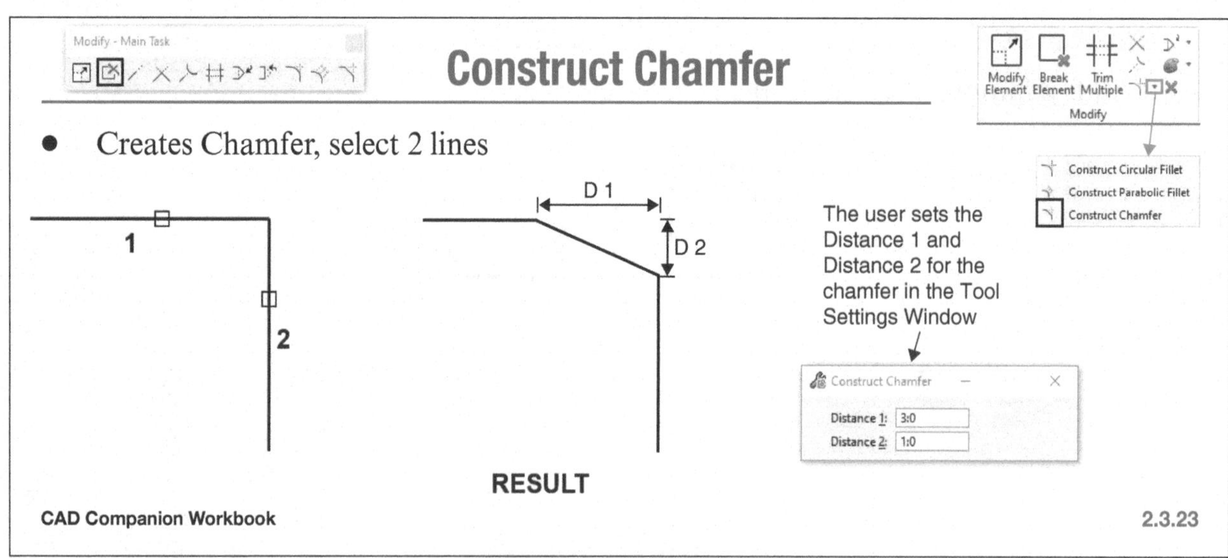
Modify - Main Task
Construct Chamfer
Modify Element
Break Element
Trim Multiple
Modify
• Creates Chamfer, select 2 lines
Construct Circular Fillet
Construct Parabolic Fillet
Construct Chamfer
1
2
D 1
D 2
The user sets the Distance 1 and Distance 2 for the chamfer in the Tool Settings Window
Construct Chamfer
Distance 1: 3:0
Distance 2: 1:0
RESULT
CAD Companion Workbook
2.3.23

Notes

CAD Companion Workbook 2.3.24

Wait! Before you Draw anything …

See these Additional tips, tidbits and Challenge Questions

TIPS & TIDBITS

© Shutterstock.com

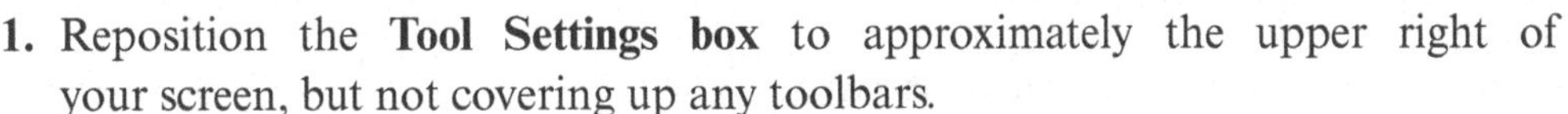

1. Reposition the **Tool Settings box** to approximately the upper right of your screen, but not covering up any toolbars.
2. Make sure you can view the entire Prompt field and Status areas on the bottom of the MicroStation screen. Why is it a bad practice to have this area or even a part of it covered up or off the screen?
3. **Don't dock all the menus that you are attempting to use for the first time**, since the title of the toolbar is not shown when it is docked. The instructor will refer to the toolbars by their name quite often, and students will have a harder time locating an icon when the name of the toolbar is not visible.
4. **Think about the action you are trying to perform FIRST**, before you blindly select tool after tool within MicroStation. After using CAD more and more, your experience will grow and you will automatically pick the right tool right off the bat with greater and greater frequency.

CHALLENGE QUESTIONS

Answers in Answer Section

1. What is the **Tool Settings box**? What does it do and when does it appear?
2. Where do you set the **Grid Lock**?
3. Should a beginning CAD user **Dock all menus** that are being used? See #3 above.
4. What is a short-cut key-in for calling up the **View Attributes** dialog box?
5. What is the quickest way to put the keyboard focus into the key-in field?
6. What are the **Working Units** set to if you forget to set them? (very common Working Unit error)
7. If **Working Units** are set to Feet and Inches:
   a. How do you express the length 5.379 ft in MicroStation?
   b. How do you express the length 5 feet 4 inches in MicroStation?
   c. Is 10:9 the same as 10.9? Explain.
8. One type of Precision Input specifies a **Distance and Angle**. What is this type of entry called?
9. One type of Precision Input specifies **the X coordinate value and the Y coordinate value**. What is this type called?
10. There is one other common type of Precision coordinate entry. What does it specify and what is it called?
11. Have you practiced these 3 Precision Input types enough to understand the difference? If you need more practice, be sure to work (or work again) the exercise called "precision"
12. Find the tools that do these and name them correctly. Now try them out!

Work these exercises in the **Manipulate Warm-Up** MicroStation file provided

Use **V8*i*** or **CONNECT** Edition

MicroStation V8i

Manipulate - Main Task

Copy Move

... or ...

MicroStation CONNECT Edition

Move Copy Rotate

Manipulate

Copy Move

Manipulate Tools Warm-up exercises pg1

*Your instructor will also introduce AccuSnap

DO THIS:	START:	END:
Use Tool Copy		
1 Make 3 more copies of the square as shown		
2 Make 3 more copies of the square as shown		
Use Tool Move		
3 Move the last square to the position shown		
4 Move the middle square to the position shown		
Use Tools Move / Copy		
5 Move & Copy as needed to change Start to End		

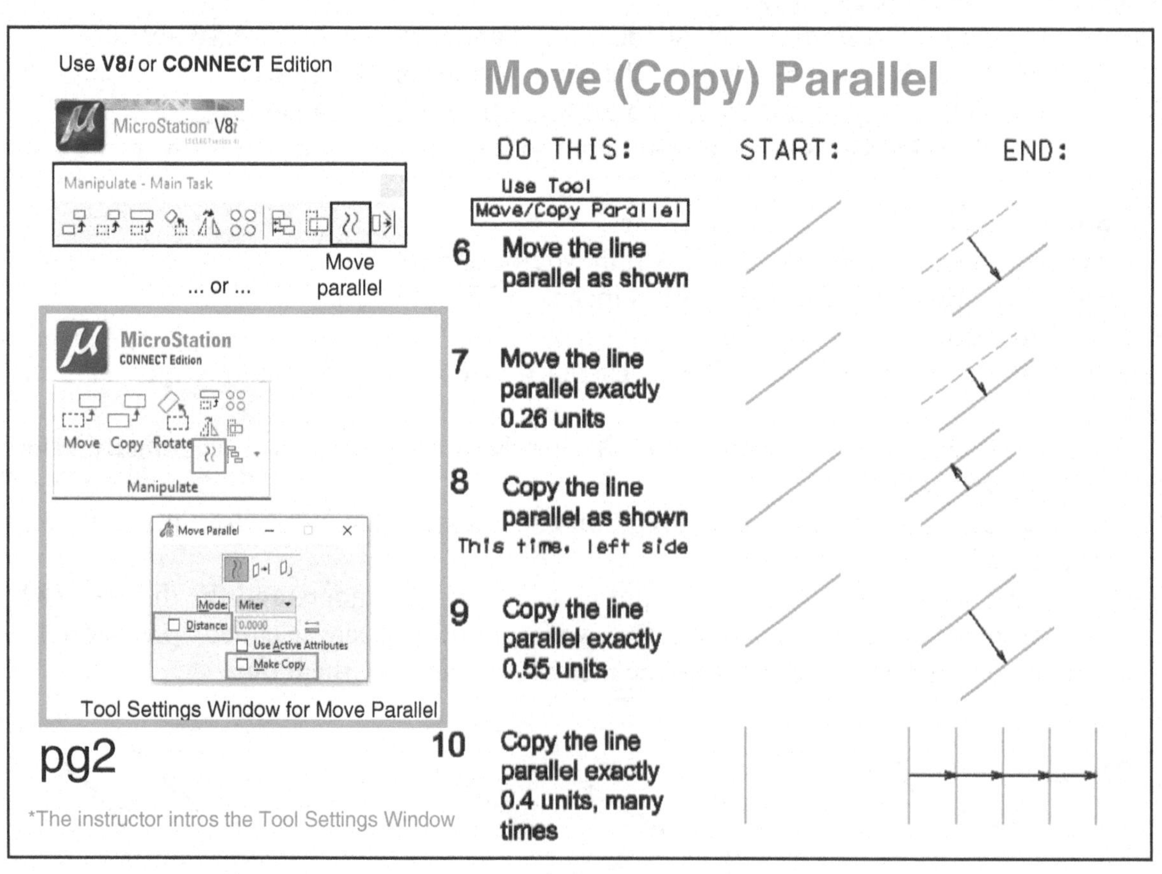

Work these exercises in the **Manipulate Warm-Up** MicroStation file provided

Use **V8*i*** or **CONNECT** Edition

MicroStation V8*i*

Manipulate - Main Task

Scale

... or ...

MicroStation CONNECT Edition **Scale**

Move Copy Rotate

Manipulate

Remember to use **AccuSnap** to snap exactly at the points required!

More practice with **Tool Settings** and introduction to using the **Key-in Field**. Please review pg 39 for opening the **Key-in Field**

Method: Active Scale
X Scale: 1.000000
Y Scale: 1.000000
Copies: 1
Use Fence: Inside
About Element Center

Tool Settings Window

Scale Element > Identify element

Key-in Field: dock it at the bottom of the screen

pg3

Scale

DO THIS: START: END:

Use Tool Scale

11 **Scale the shape as shown. AS=2** ← Do a Key-in for this! — Point to scale about

12 **Scale the shape as shown. AS=0.55** ← Do a Key-in for this! — Point to scale about

13 **Scale the shape as shown. AS=0.55** ← Key-in with Copy "ON" — Point to scale about

14 **Scale the shape as shown. XS=2.3 YS=0.5** Two different Key-ins! — Point to scale about

15 **Scale the shape as shown. XS=1 YS=2.5** Two different Key-ins! — Point to scale about

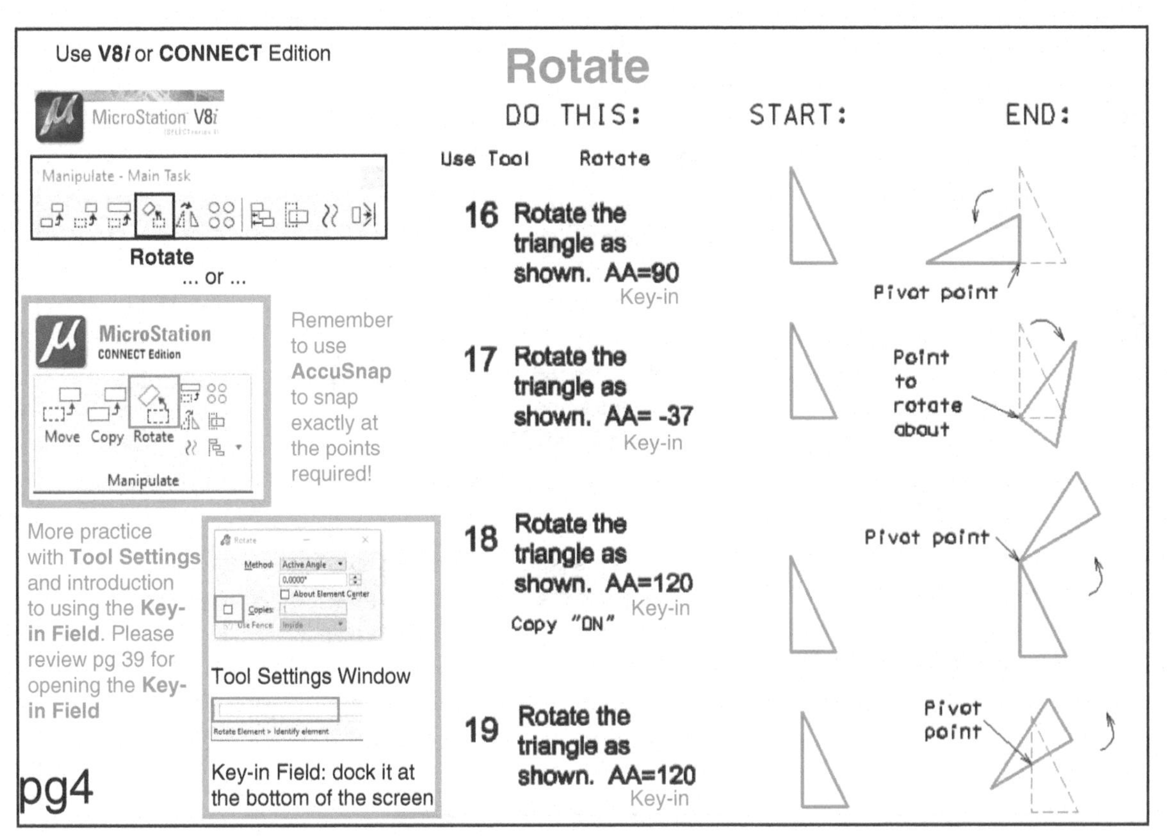

Work these exercises in the **Manipulate Warm-Up** MicroStation file provided

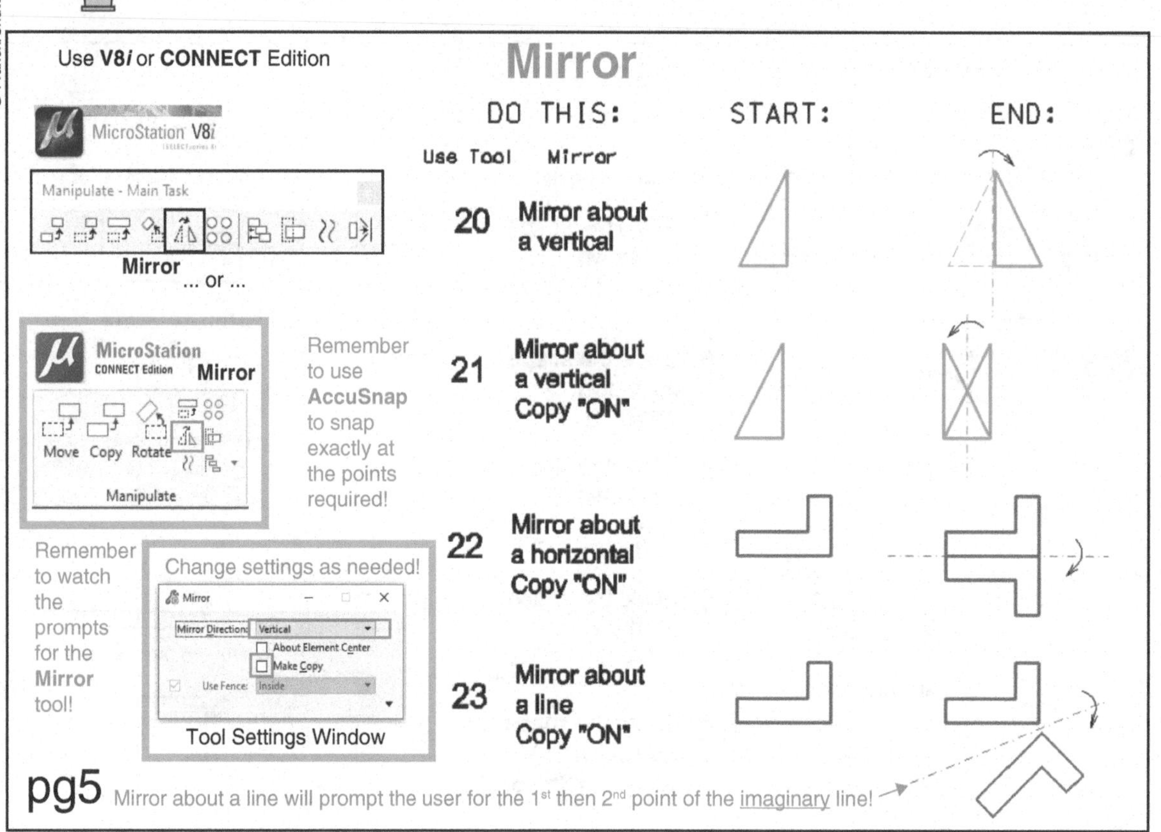

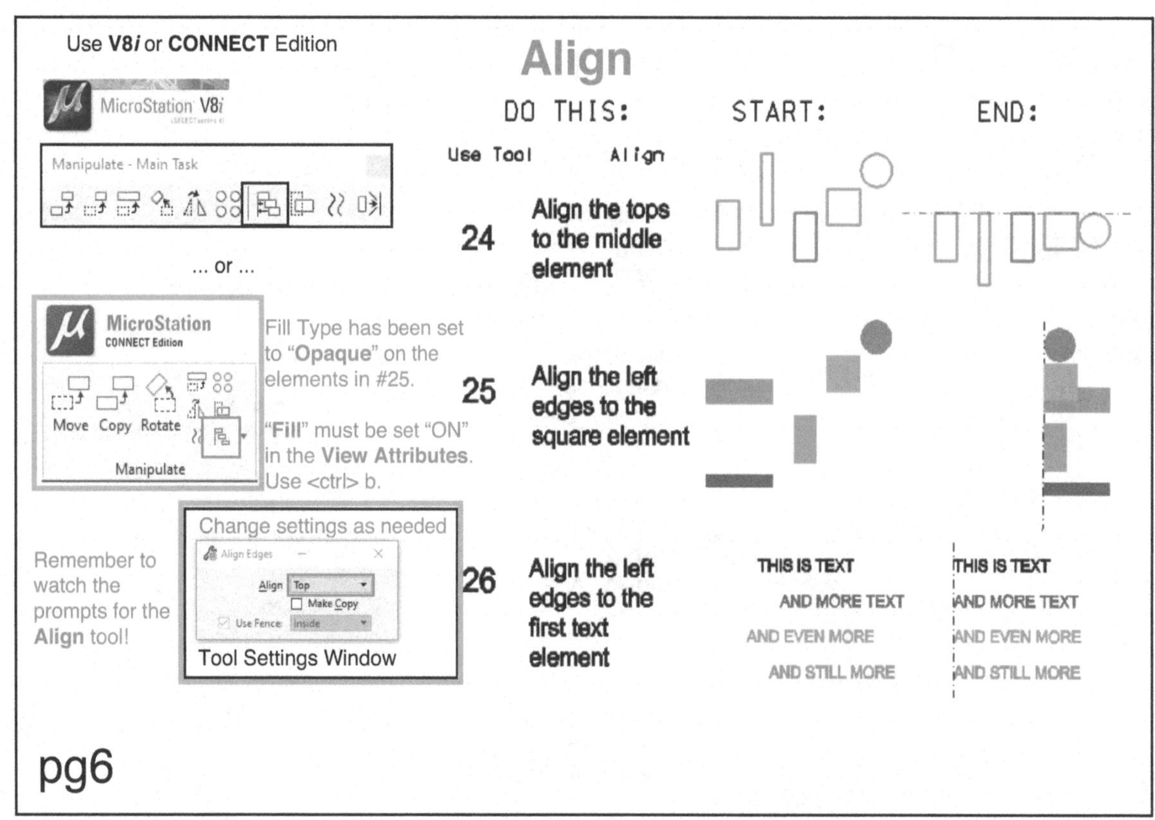

Work these exercises in the **Manipulate Warm-Up** MicroStation file provided

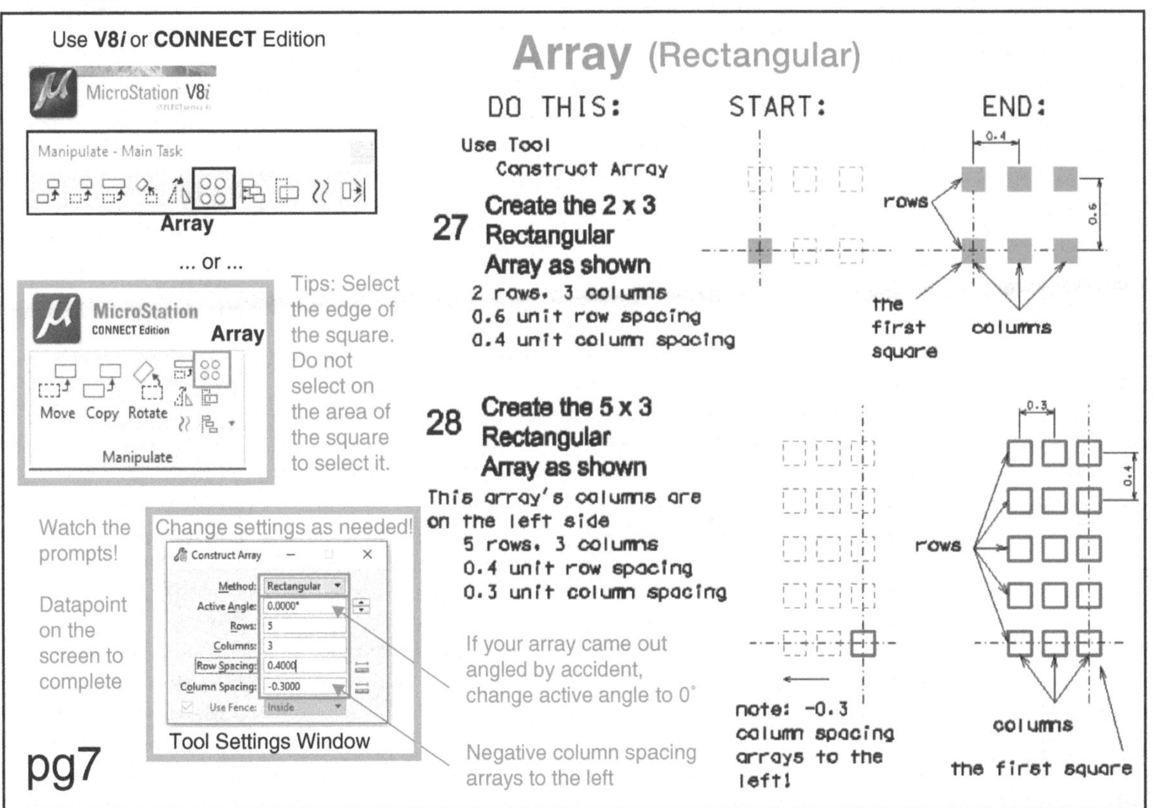

Use V8i or CONNECT Edition
MicroStation V8i
Manipulate - Main Task
Array
... or ...
MicroStation CONNECT Edition
Array
Move Copy Rotate
Manipulate
AccuSnap to the center of your array accurately!
Tips: Select the edge of the square. Do not select on the area of the square to select it.
Watch the prompts!
Datapoint on the screen to complete
Change settings as needed!
Construct Array
Method: Rectangular
Active Angle: 0.0000°
Rows: 5
Columns: 3
Row Spacing: 0.4000
Column Spacing: -0.3000
Use Fence: Inside
Tool Settings Window
pg7
Array (Rectangular)
DO THIS:
START:
END:
Use Tool
Construct Array
27
Create the 2 x 3 Rectangular Array as shown
2 rows, 3 columns
0.6 unit row spacing
0.4 unit column spacing
0.4
0.6
rows
the first square
columns
28
Create the 5 x 3 Rectangular Array as shown
This array's columns are on the left side
5 rows, 3 columns
0.4 unit row spacing
0.3 unit column spacing
0.3
0.4
rows
If your array came out angled by accident, change active angle to 0°
Negative column spacing arrays to the left
note: -0.3 column spacing arrays to the left!
columns
the first square

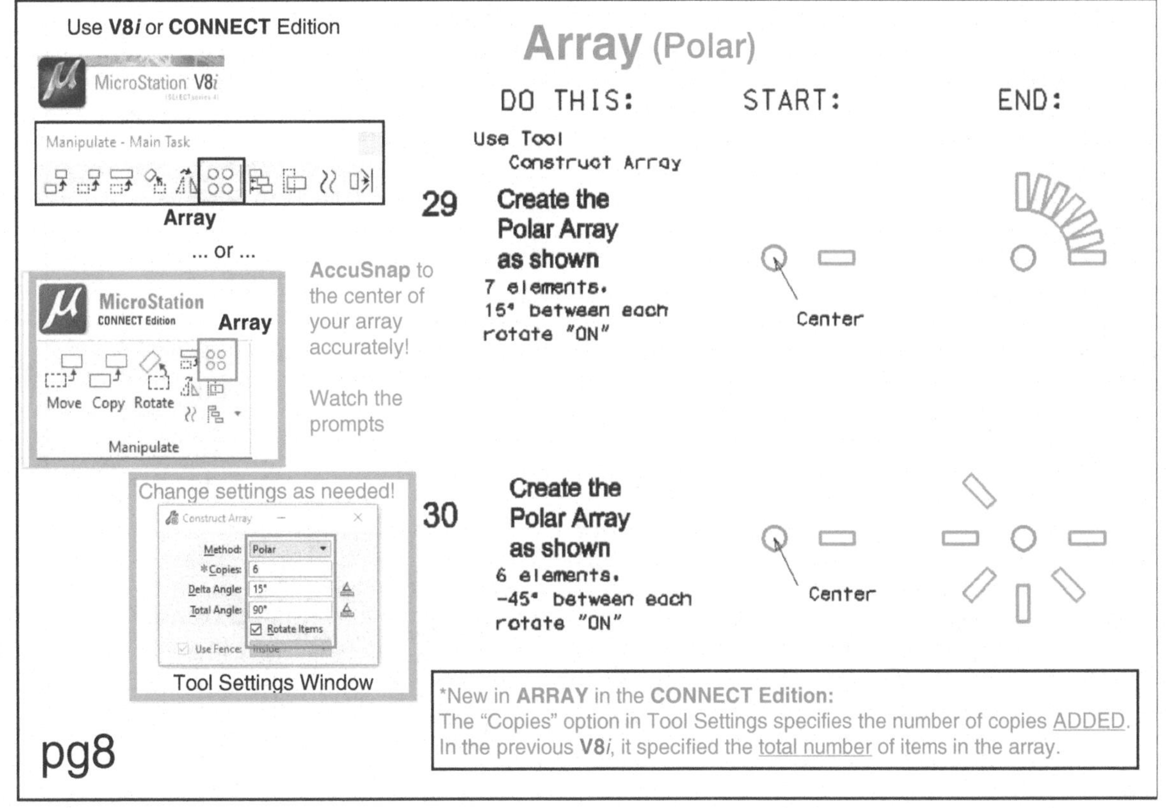

The "Copies" option in Tool Settings specifies the number of copies ADDED.
In the previous V8i, it specified the total number of items in the array.

Work these exercises in the **Modify Warm-Up** MicroStation file provided

Use **V8*i*** or **CONNECT** Edition

Modify Element, Break Element

MicroStation V8*i*

Modify - Main Task

Modify Element Break Element ... or ...

MicroStation CONNECT Edition

Modify Element Break Element Trim Multiple

Modify

Break Element

These modifications only need to be performed to the approximate locations shown.

	TURN THIS:	INTO THIS:	USING TOOL:
1			**Modify Element**
2			**Modify Element**
3			**Modify Element**
4			**Break Element** "Partial Delete" in V8*i* SS2 and earlier
5			**Break Element** "Partial Delete" in V8*i* SS2 and earlier

Use the Break by two points option for these Break Element exercises

Modify Tools Warm-up pg1

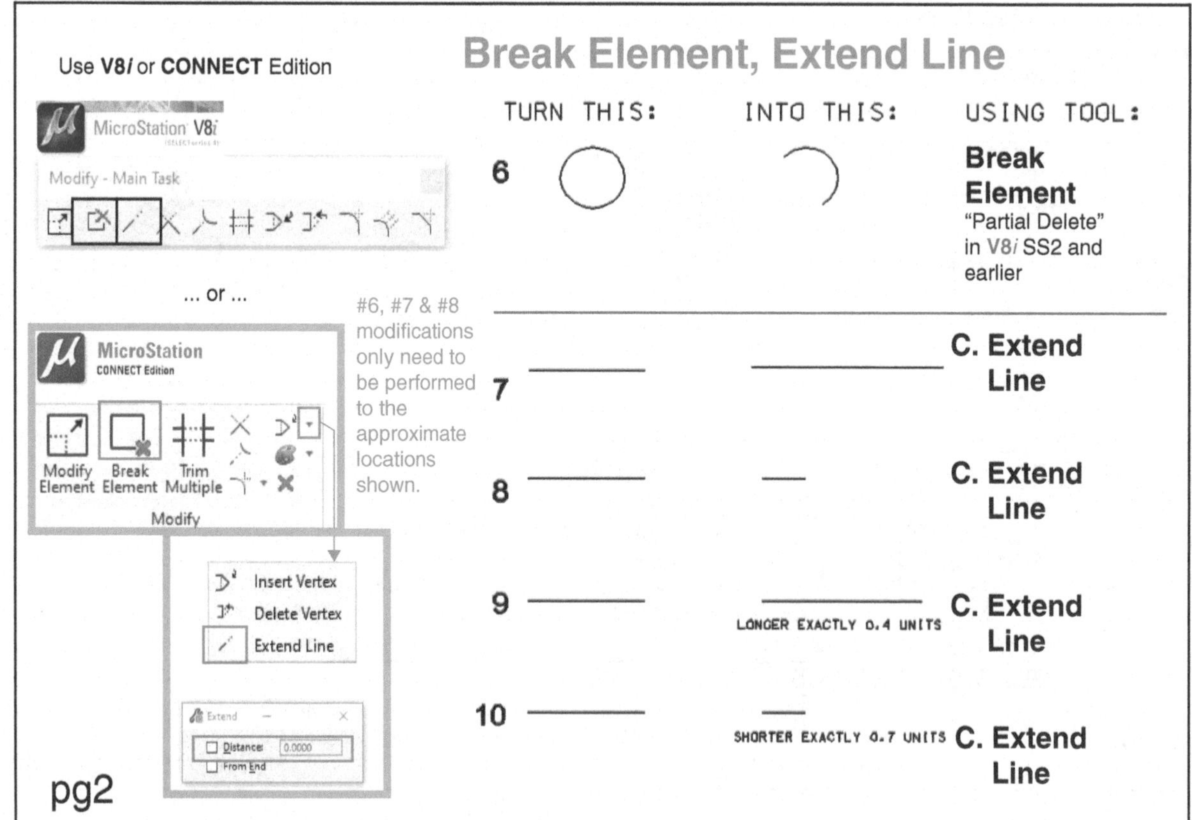

Work these exercises in the **Modify Warm-Up** MicroStation file provided

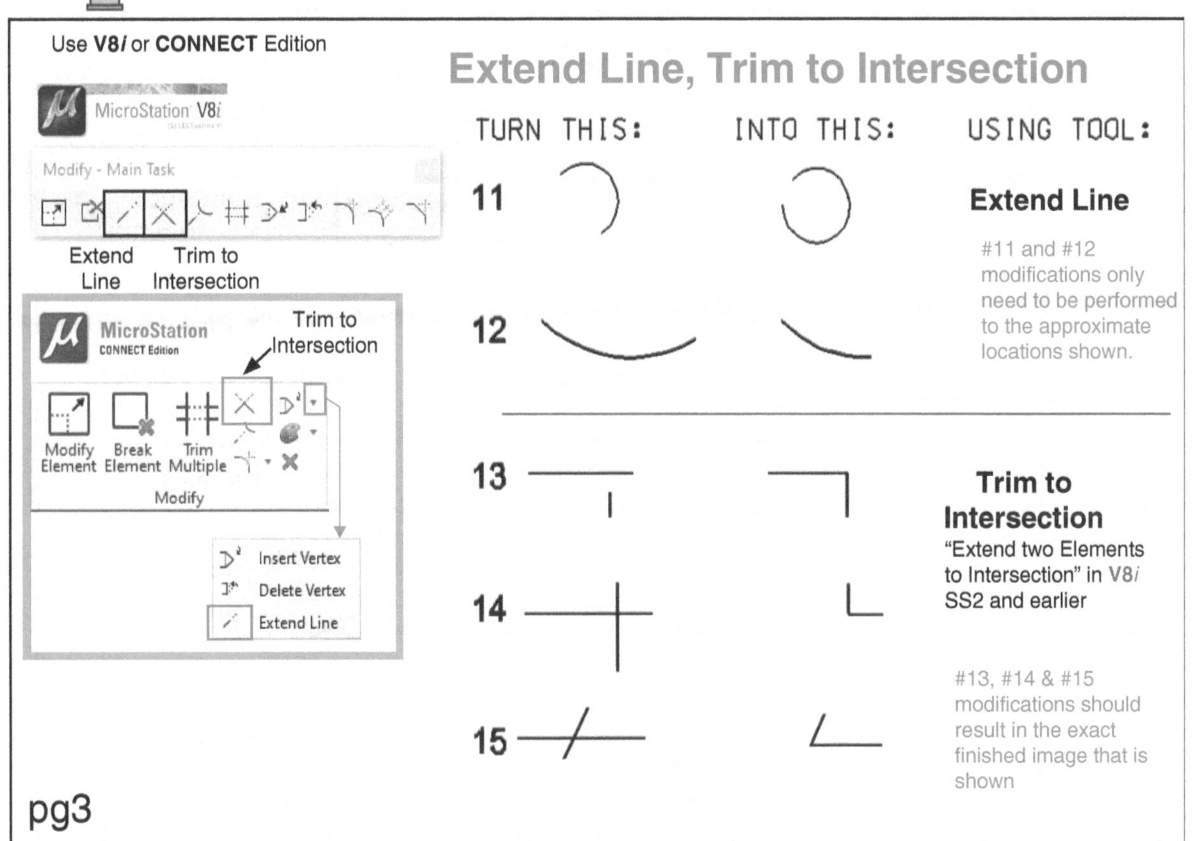

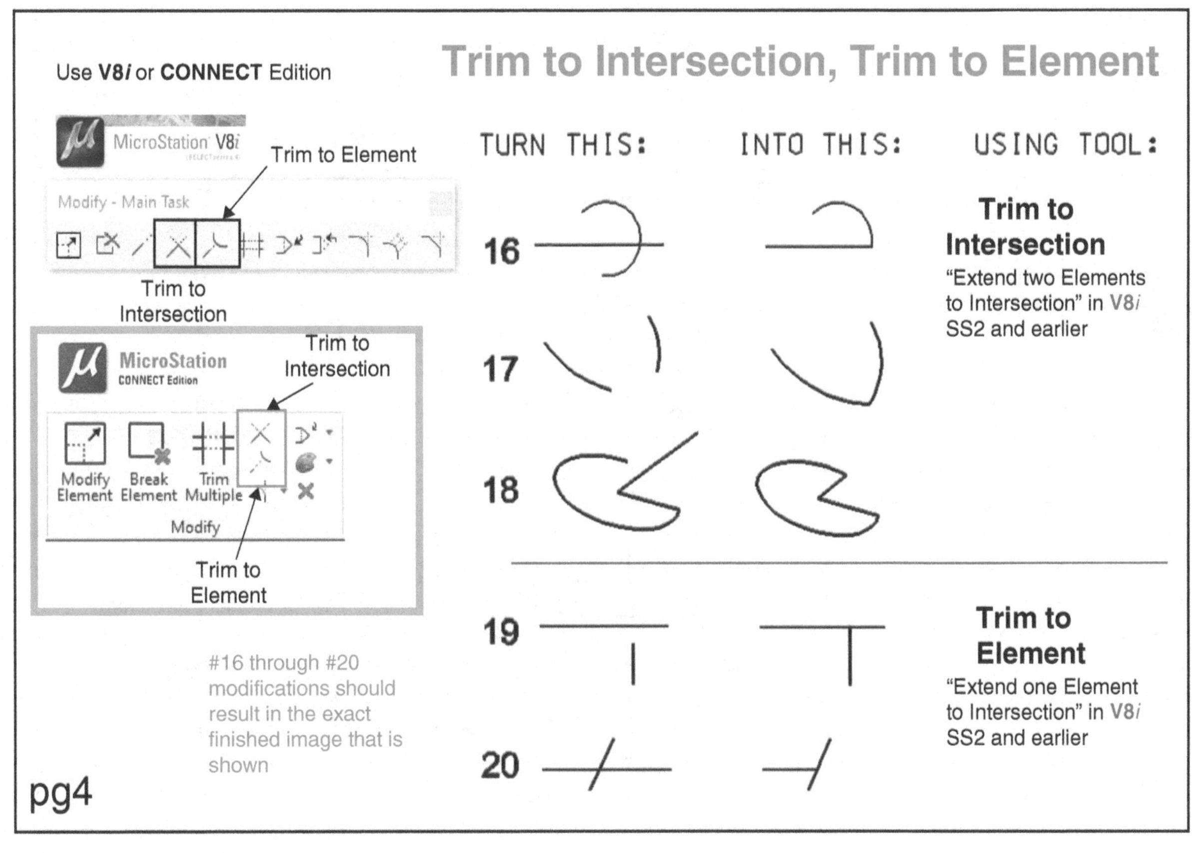

Work these exercises in the **Modify Warm-Up** MicroStation file provided

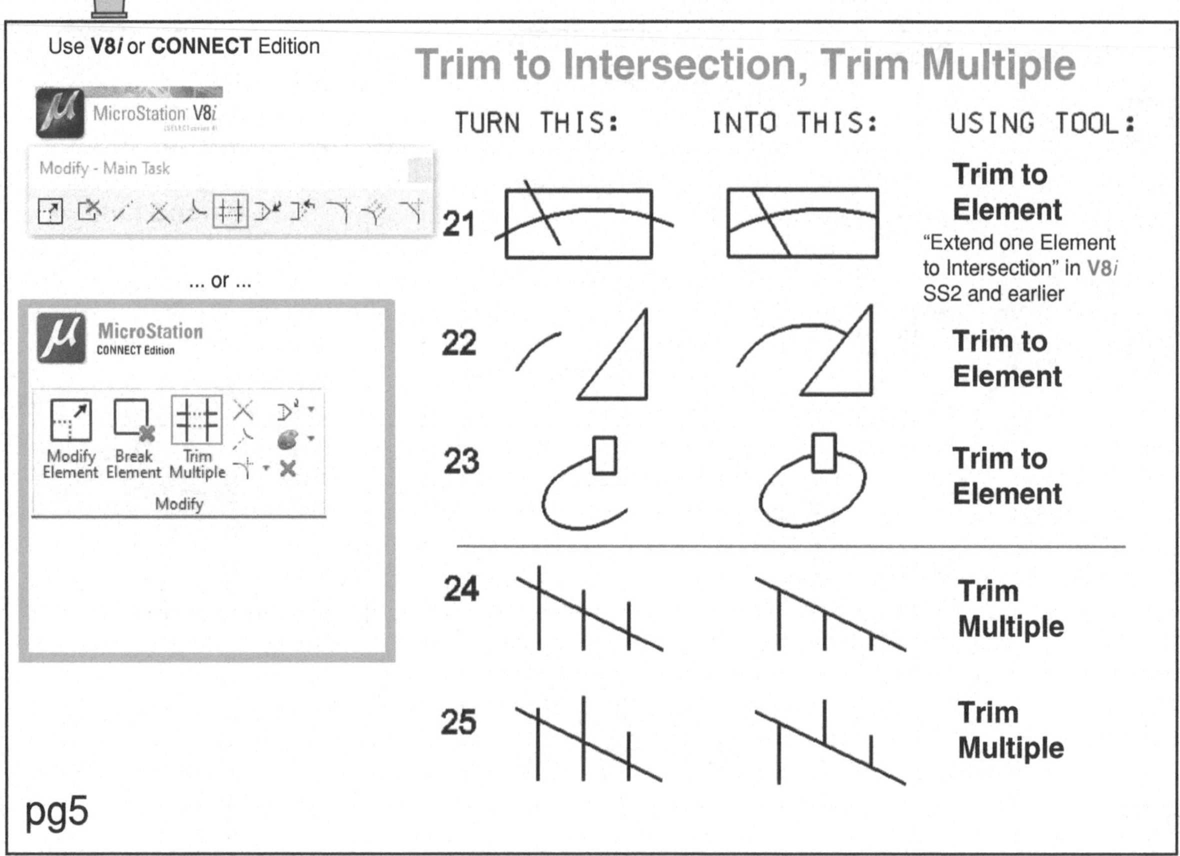

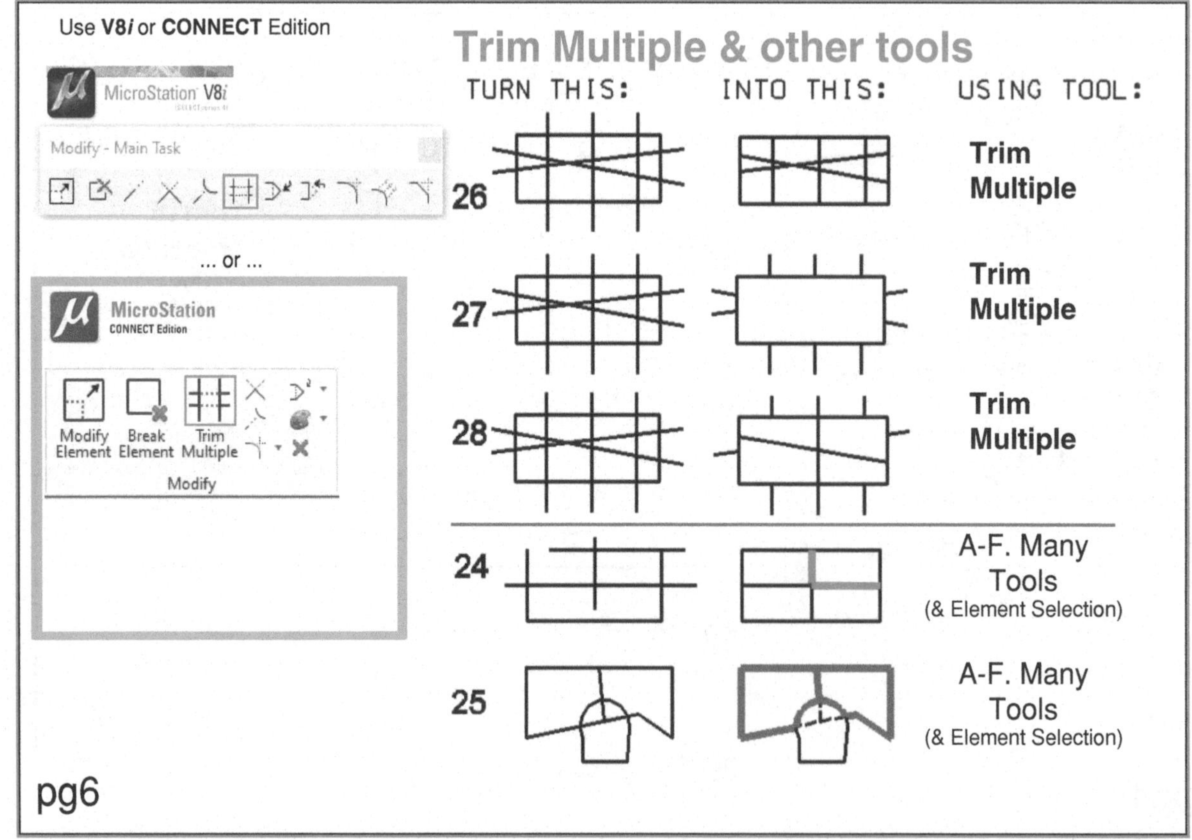

Use MicroStation **V8*i*** or the **CONNECT Edition** for drawing the exercises.

Summary of Drawing Exercises – Module 2

The Module 2 drawings show the student for the first time the concepts of precision sized graphics related to real world units, such as feet and inches or meters and centimeters. Working units are used and precision input of lengths and angles will be required to create these drawings.

By now, some of the rudimentary functions required to create a new drawing should be understood by students and the step-by-step instructions for these functions will not be listed. Refer back to earlier modules or get help from your instructor if you don't remember the steps. Examples would be: starting the software, creating a new file, opening a toolbar, etc. However, this summary section still lists most of the steps required and can be followed step-by-step at this time.

Refer to the section: **Module 2 Tools** for an illustration of where the tools are found and what they look like when deployed on the screen. Your instructor will be showing these in class, but you may want to review them in this document.

Please preview all this pages 107 - 111 before beginning the exercise

BIGTUB Exercise

Introduces the student to:

ABSOLUTE COORDINATE INPUT	(xy = xvalue, yvalue)
RELATIVE POLAR COORDINATE INPUT	(DI = length, angle)
MOVE/COPY PARALLEL	(with copy option on)
CONSTRUCT CHAMFER	(with 2 different values)
CONSTRUCT CIRCULAR FILLET	(with truncate both option on)
TOOL SETTINGS dialog box	(for each of the above tools)

Summary:

1. Create a new file called **BIGTUB** as described earlier.
2. Dismiss the **AccuDraw Toolbox**. We will use **AccuDraw** in a later module, but not now in these early modules.
3. Turn off the display of the grid using **<Ctrl> B**. Apply the setting to all views.
   *The short-cut **<Ctrl> B** can be remembered by the phrase **"Better Viewing"**. I still remember this from my first training class in this CAD products predecessor over 30 years ago!*
4. Call up the working units dialog box with **Settings > Design File > Working units**, if using V8*i* (if using **CONNECT Edition**, please refer to pg 77), Change the Format from **MU** to **MU : SU**. from pg 77: **File > Settings > File > Design File Settings > Working Units**
5. (step #5 is NOT needed in V8i, if the MU are already set to Feet!) Set the **Master-units to feet** and the **Sub-units to inches**. Note: once you select the master-units of feet, the normally corresponding sub-units of inches are selected by MicroStation automatically.
6. Perform a **<Ctrl> F**, to save settings. Open the **Key-in Field** and dock it.
7. Start **Place Line** and enter for the first point and following points: (remember to hit **<Enter>** to automatically take you to the **Key-in field** before typing and hit **<Enter>** after each entry)
   a. xy=0,0 note: You will need to have the **Key-in Field** opened for key-ins.
   b. DI=5,0 Please see pg 39 or PRECISION, pg 85 for review if required.

*Observe the screen after the first five foot line is placed and see that it is pretty small on the screen. The instructor will show you how to **Window Area** to the elements being drawn and then continue on with your drawing.*

(BIGTUB exercise continued) Use MicroStation **V8*i*** or the **CONNECT Edition**

*Do this by selecting the **Window Area** icon, doing the window area around the new line and then hit **reset** to continue with your **Place Line** activity. **<Enter>** to take you back to the key-in field before entering the following key-ins.*

c. DI=3:6,90
d. DI=5,180
e. DI=3:6,-90
f. then hit **reset** on your mouse (the right mouse button)

***Alternate procedures for step e.**, your instructor should show you:*

***e.** Hit the up arrow to recall previous key-ins and hit the <Enter> key when the display shows xy=0,0*

***e.** Use the AccuSnap and roll the mouse to the location near 0,0 at the beginning of your drawing and when the appropriate tentative snap lights up, click the left mouse button, completing the last line.*

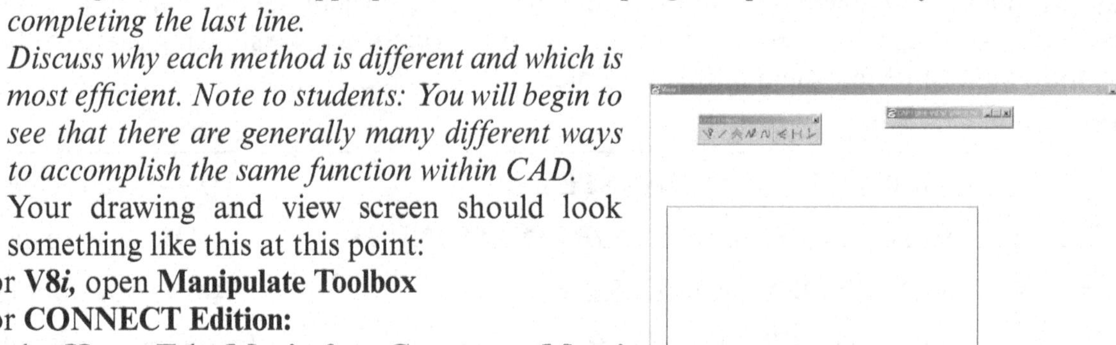

Discuss why each method is different and which is most efficient. Note to students: You will begin to see that there are generally many different ways to accomplish the same function within CAD.

Your drawing and view screen should look something like this at this point:

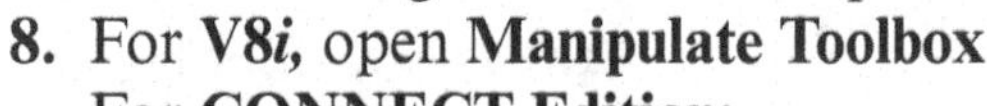

8. For **V8*i*,** open **Manipulate Toolbox**

For **CONNECT Edition:**

In the **Home** Tab, **Manipulate** Group use **Move/Parallel** with the **Distance** and **Make Copy** options **on** to copy each of the lines inward by the specified distances. Set the required distances in the **Tool Settings** box for each of these lines.

g. Right line copy inward by **:3** (click a point inward)
h. Left line copy inward by **:1** (click a point inward)
i. Top and bottom lines copy inward by **:2.5** (points clicked inward)

Manipulate toolbar & Tool Settings box for Move/Copy Parallel

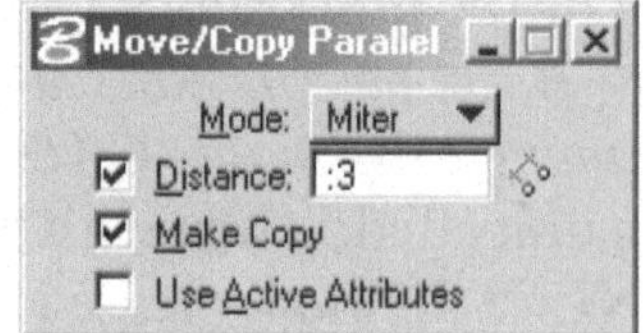

Manipulate Ribbon Group, from the **Home** Tab

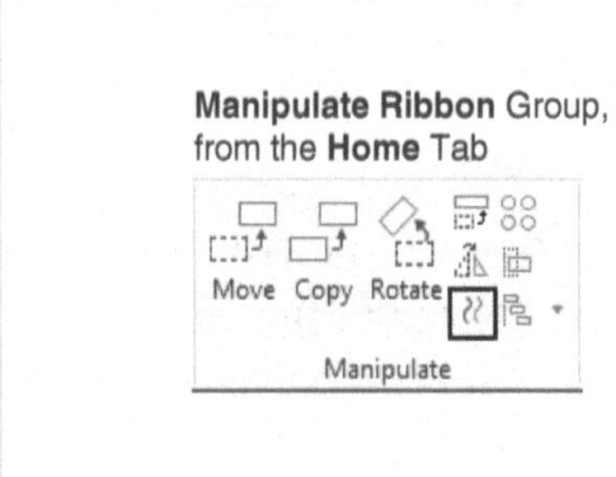

Tool Settings window (box)

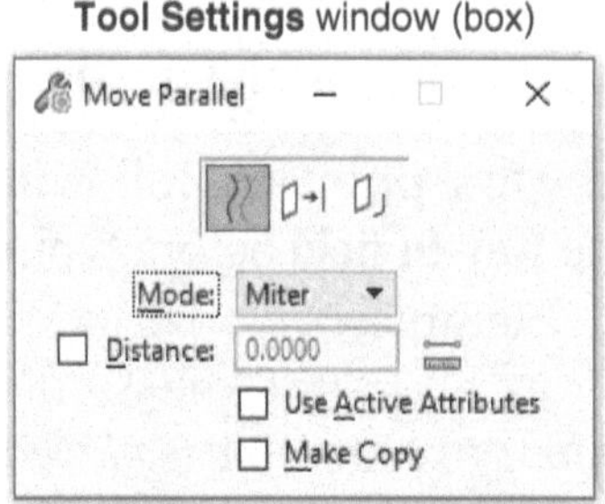

(BIGTUB exercise continued)

Use MicroStation V8*i* or the CONNECT Edition

*The beginning student usually does an **unnecessary step** at this time. He or she **will try to specify with the mouse, where the copied line should land on the screen.** The instructor will demonstrate why this is unnecessary and is just considered a wasted maneuver on the part of the student. The distance is specified in the **Tool Settings box**, not by the mouse location for this exercise.*

The efficient CAD user learns the proper way to utilize tools and learns to avoid making totally unneeded steps.

Record the example that the instructor gives regarding unneeded steps here: (the door example)

9. Open the Modify toolbar and use the Construct Chamfer tool.

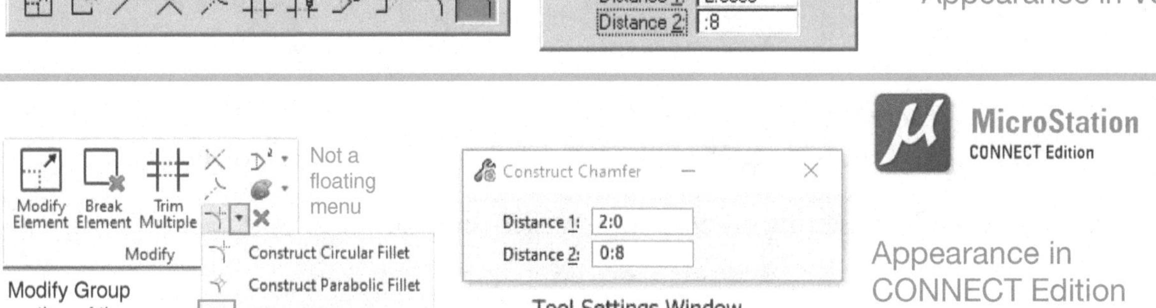

j. Set the distances to 2 feet for distance # one and 8 inches for distance # two. Note how we are using Working Unit entry:
2 feet is entered simply as **2** remember to hit <Enter>
8 inches is entered as **:8** remember to hit <Enter>

note: MicroStation will translate these into master units after the user hits <Enter> for each of the entries.

k. Select the lines in this order: to perform the chamfer. Your drawing should look like this:

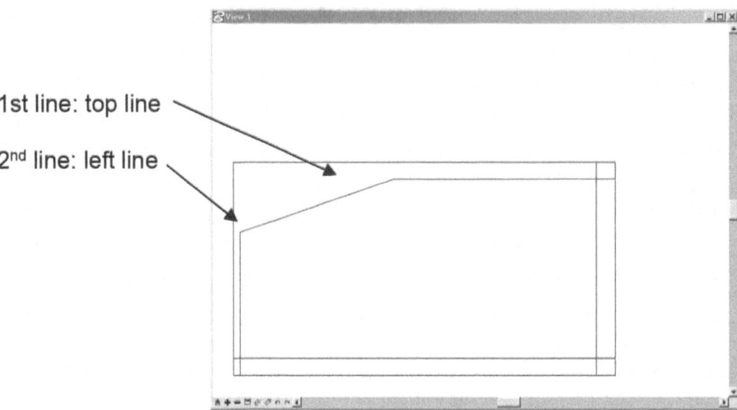

(BIGTUB exercise continued) Use MicroStation **V8*i*** or the **CONNECT Edition**

10. On the Modify toolbar, use the Construct Circular Fillet tool.

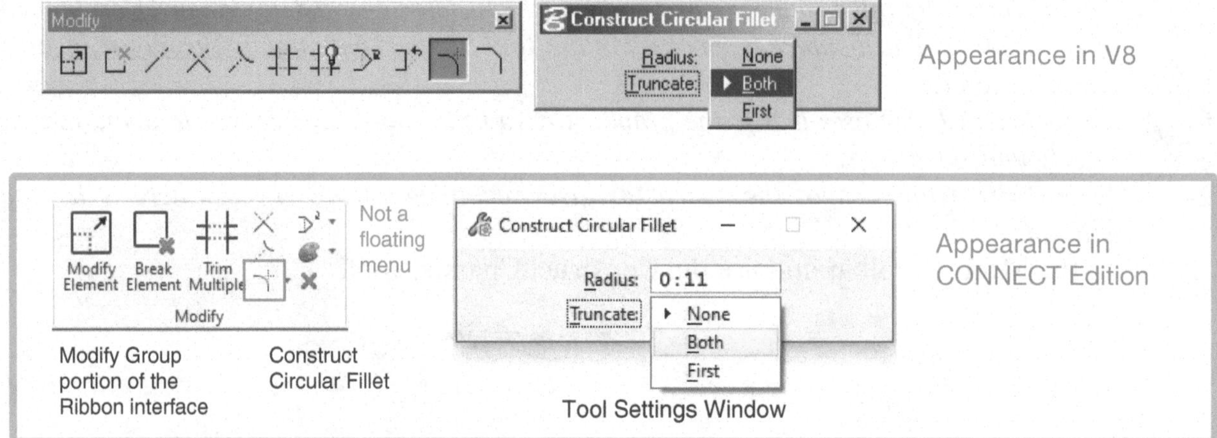

l. Set the **Truncate** to the **Both** setting and set the Radius to **:11** for the two right side corners **AND** the top vertex of the tub. Click line 1 and line 2 as shown.

m. Repeat with the setting on **:9** for the two left side corners of the tub.

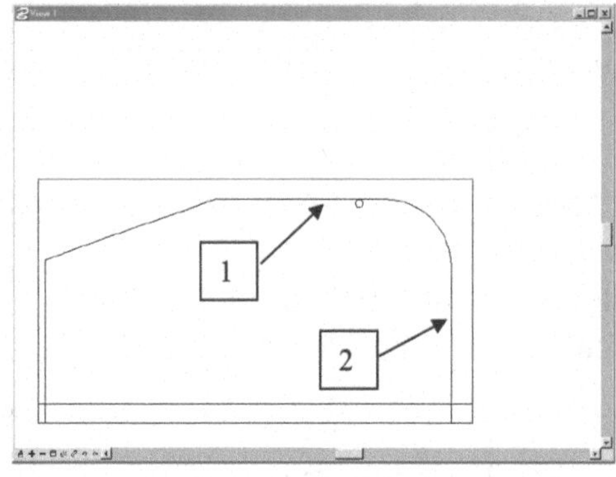

After the first fillet is done.first upper corner is filleted.

Step 11. Do **Fit View** and **<Ctrl> F**

Step 12. Add the text BIGTUB as shown on the following page.

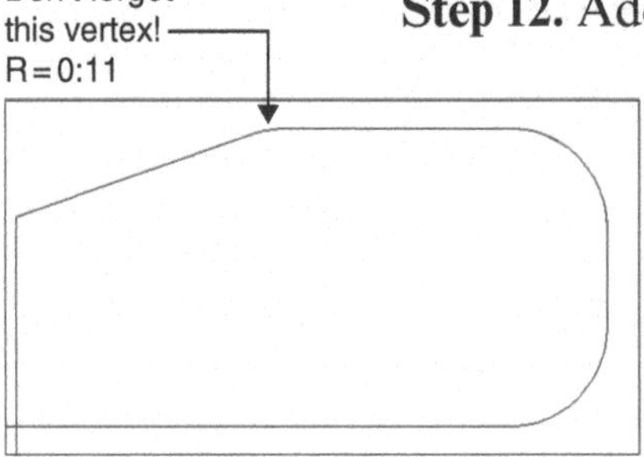

after step 10.1 — three corners filleted.

after step 10.m — The TUB is DONE!.

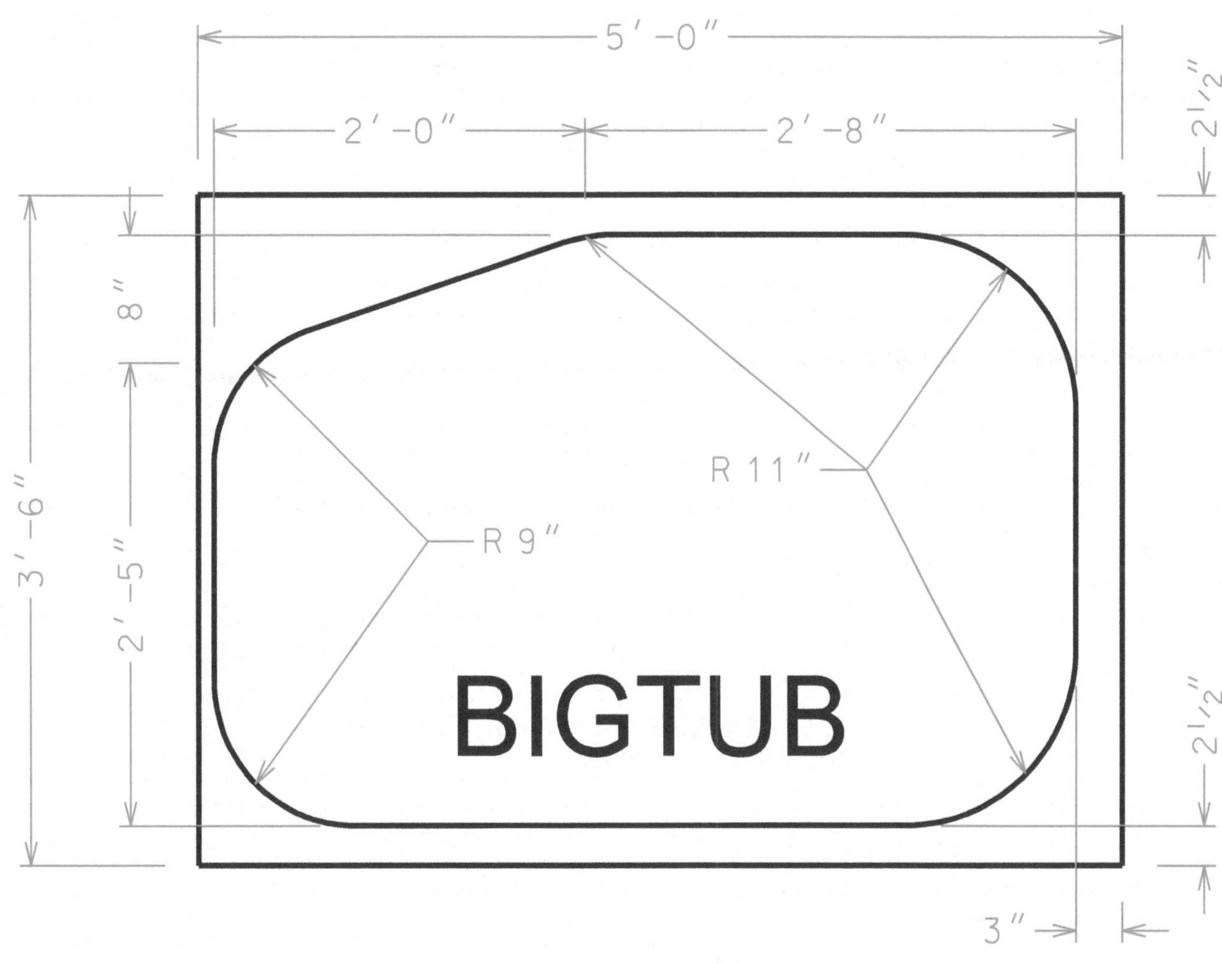

NOTES:

Dimensions are not needed, yet. They can be added after completing module 5.

Exercise	Concepts / Tools / Lessons (E.C.) For MODULE 2
Many self-guided exercises (See below)	Practice with a majority of the CAD tools covered up thru Module 2, with emphasis on usage of precision input and precision manipulations and modifications.

These exercise drawings are **"self-guided"**as opposed to the previous **"instuctor-guided"** drawings. The student will gain experience recalling the proper steps to perform many functions that were previously step-by-step guided.

These exercises may be assigned as normal credit or as Extra-Credit. **(E.C.)**

Check with your instructor for your drawing assignment.

There may be some small portions of these exercises thst require concepts yet to be covered in MODULES 3 and beyond, but the majority can be worked with concepts and tools covered up thru MODULE 2.

High-lights:
CREATING NEW DRAWINGS -- SETTING WORKING UNITS
CREATING PRECISION LINES, SHAPES, CIRCLES
PRECISION MOVEMENT TO LOCATIONS DESIRED
PRECISION USAGE OF MANIPULATION & MODIFICATION TOOLS

Note: Recommended prerequisites to working on these exercises: Completion of all exercises up thru the end of MODULE 2, including the instructor guided: **TRAVEL, ORGCHART, PRECISION, MANIPULATE WARM-UP, MODIFY WARM-UP, BIGTUB, SHOWER,** and **RANGE.** Also recommended before working these exercises: Completion of **CLASSROOM** and **OP-ART**.

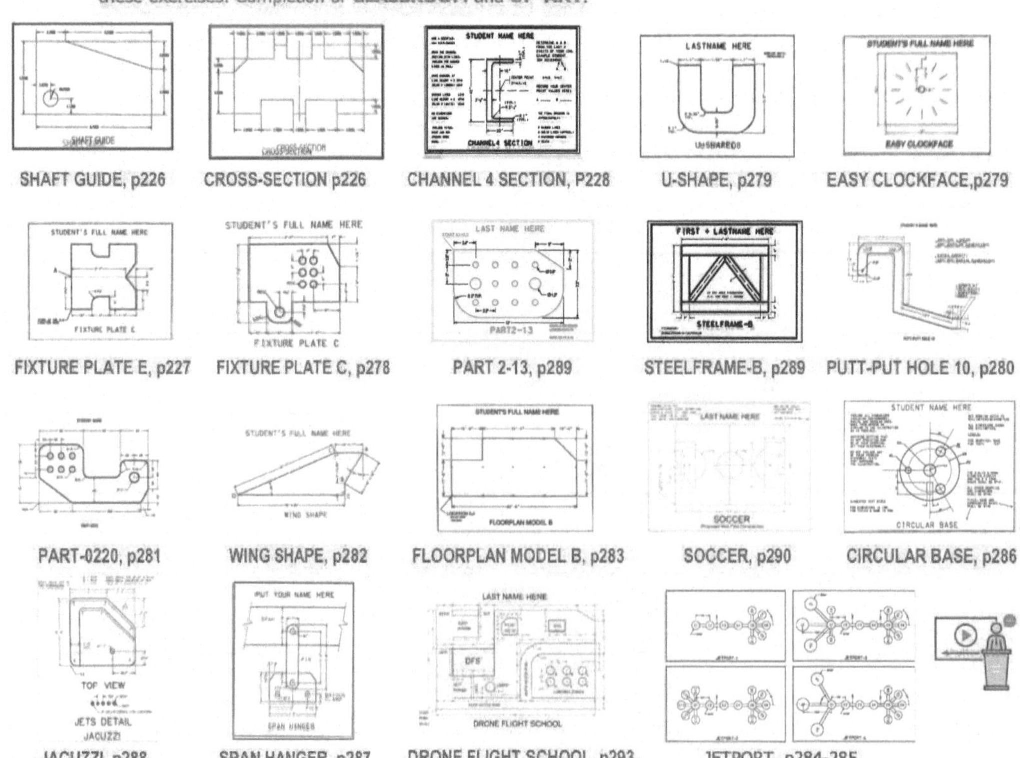

Module 3

Symbology/Snaps/Locks

Key CAD exercise concepts for Module 3

Additional skills are required for completion of the following exercises. The student will be learning to complete exercises without complete directions being provided by the instructor. The instructor will show additional techniques utilizing snaps and creating graphics from previously drawn elements.

The student will gain expertise with previously introduced tools. The student will be using some of the earlier tools for the fifth and sixth repetition by this time, although applied differently in the new exercises.

Note: **Drawings assigned may vary from term to term.**

General/All

Precision Break Element
Mirror Copy
Place Line, Break Element
Place Arc, Arc modifications

Additional practice with:
Absolute Coordinate entry

$XY = X_{value}$ (absolute), Y_{value} (absolute)

Cartesian Coordinate entry

DL = ΔX length, ΔY length (relative from last point)

Polar Coordinate entry

DI = length, angle (relative from last point)

Copy multiple elements to another location in the drawing
Place Arc (by edge, by center)
Student completes drawing without directions being provided

Exercise	Concepts / Tools / Lessons	For MODULE 3

Home Plate Layout.dgn

Completion of drawing with minimal guidance provided
Precision Coordinate entry
Place Lines (angled lines, by Polar coordinate entry)
Element Attributes: color, weight and linestyle

© Pranch/Shutterstock.com

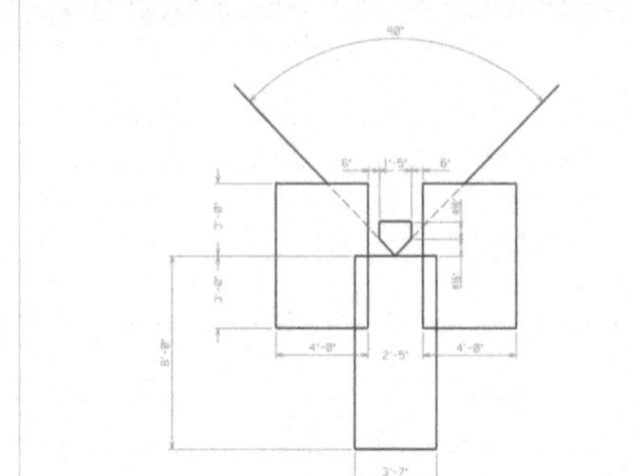

This is an instructor "guided" drawing exercise shown on page 269 of Appendix A.

The student is exposed to working out strategies on creating the drawing, but this time without all the instructions provided to them.

Phone to "B"

Additional Drawing Techniques shown by the Instructor:
Precision graphics from Placement of Elements "offset" from specific locations
Copy (of multiple elements) by a precision distance

Practice of Placement and Manipulation tools by the student

Construct Circular Fillet
Construct Array
Move (moving multiple elements by precision snap points)
Copy Parallel
Place Arc
Modify Arc Angle (sweep)

© Pranch/Shutterstock.com

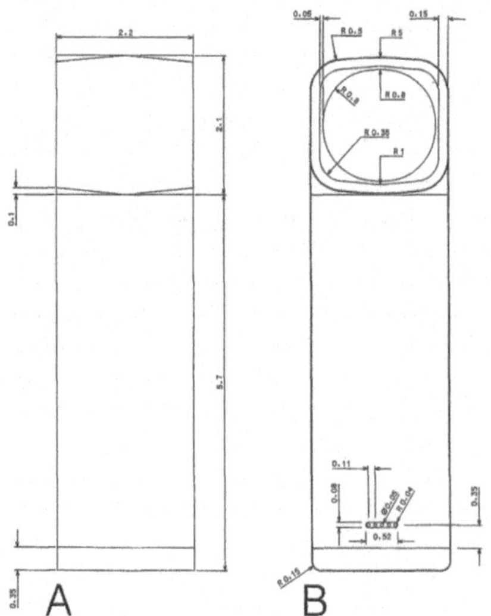

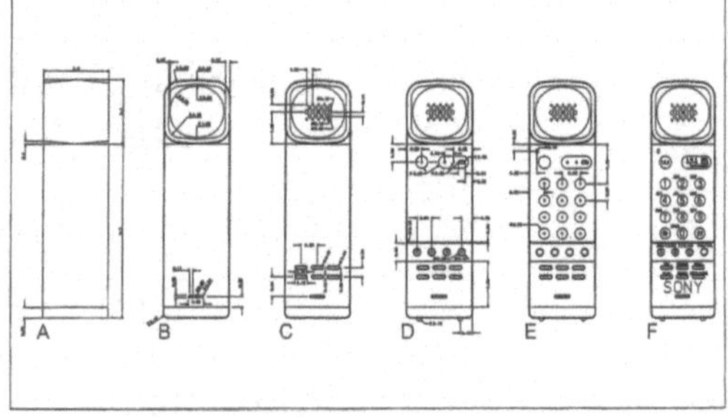

The PHONE to B is an instructor guided drawing exercise shown on pages 270-273 of Appendix A. This is a multi-week exercise. C - F are on pages 274-277.

After completing A and B, the student continues with PHONE C - F without all the instructions provided. They learn how to develop strategies to complete the drawing.

Module 3 – Tools

The following new Editing tools will be introduced in this approximate order for use on the HOME PLATE LAYOUT, PHONE TO B and other selected drawings:

1. From the **Modify** Toolbar: (this is a SUB-MENU, see below)
   - **A. PARTIAL DELETE***
   - **B. EXTEND LINE**
   - **C. EXTEND TWO ELEMENTS TO INTERSECTION***
   - **D. EXTEND ELEMENT TO INTERSECTION***
   - **E. Intelli-Trim***

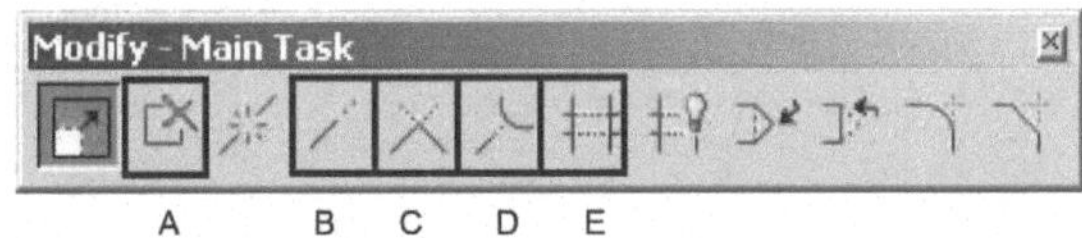

noted with LETTERS to avoid crowding this image

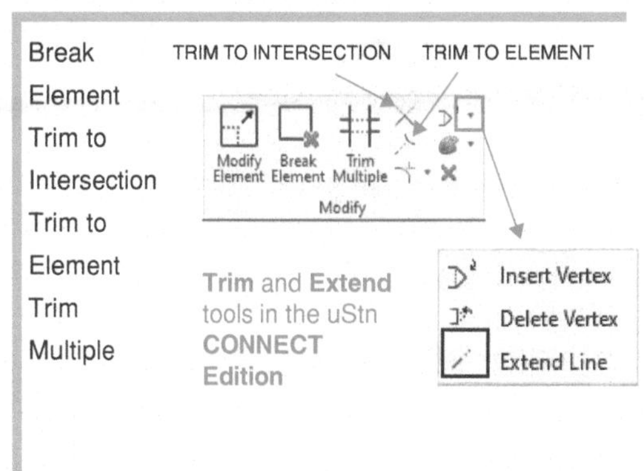

* **Partial Delete** has been combined into the **Break Element** tool.

Extend 2 to Intersection has been renamed as **Trim to Intersection**

Extend 1 to Intersection has been renamed as **Trim to Element**

Intelli-Trim has been renamed as **Trim Multiple**

2. From the **Main Task**, Measure Toolbar:
   - **MEASURE DISTANCE**
   - **DIMENSION ANGLE BETWEEN TWO LINES** (used on HOME PLATE LAYOUT)

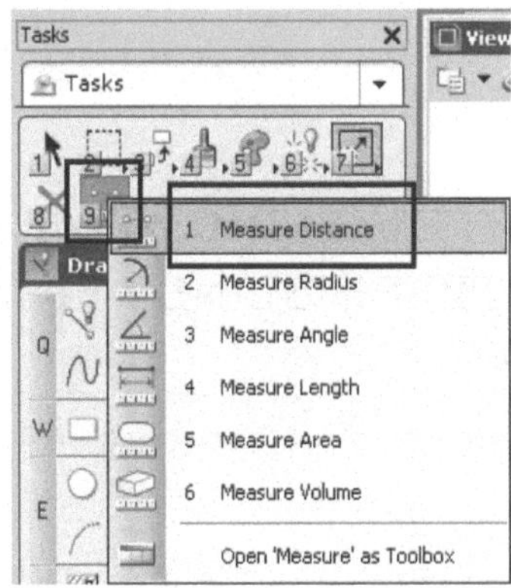

Get out the SUB-MENU **for Measure**

MEASURE DISTANCE

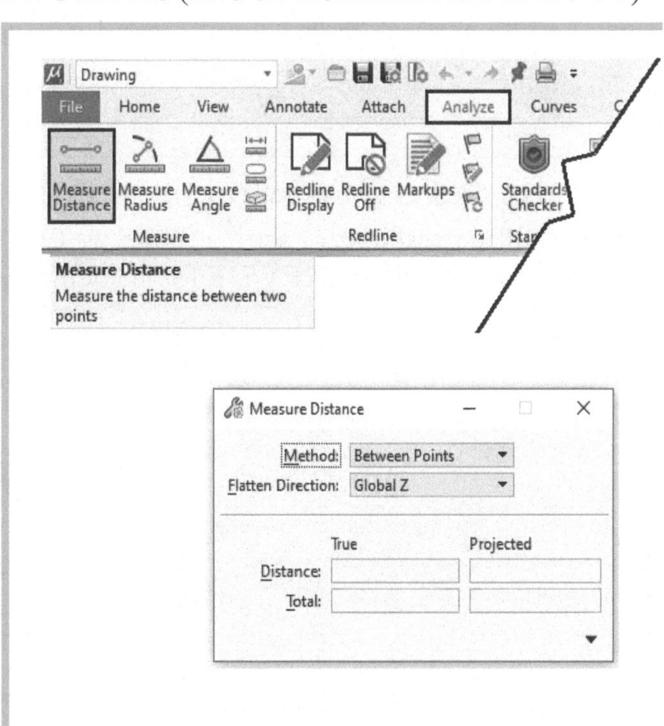

Module 3 – Tools

3. From the **Drawing Panel Task**, Dimension Toolbar:
   - **DIMENSION ANGLE BETWEEN TWO LINES** (Used on HOME PLATE LAYOUT)

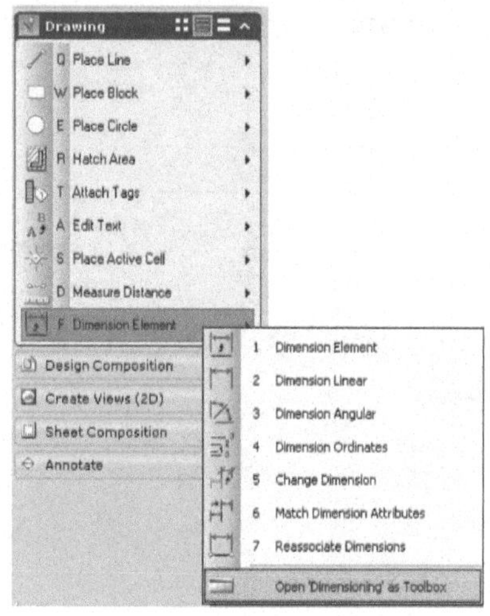

DIMENSION ANGULAR

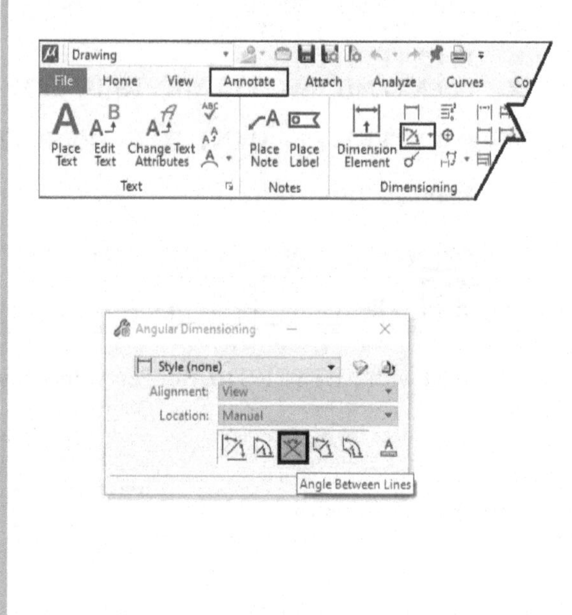

4. Using the **Attributes** Toolbar: (usually docked at the upper left part of the screen)

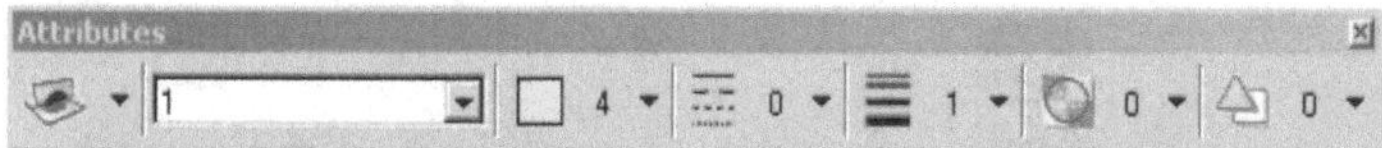

Can be used to set the active LEVEL, COLOR, LINE STYLE and LINE WEIGHT.

We will show setting or setting the active COLOR, LINE STYLE and LINE WEIGHT for now. We will discuss LEVELs for elements in a later module.

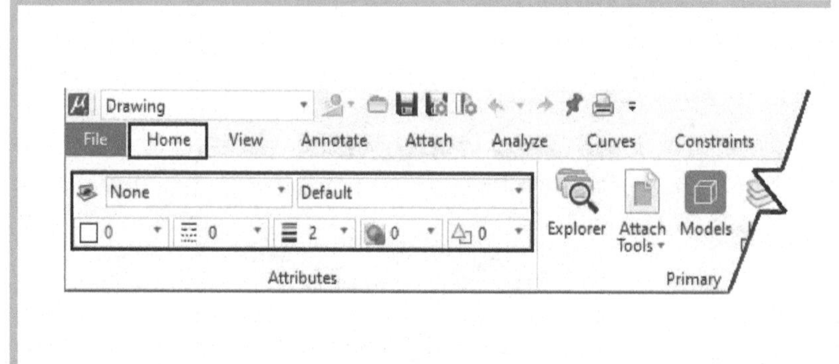

Module 3 – Tools

a. Selecting an active COLOR: (changing from color 0-white, to color 2-green)

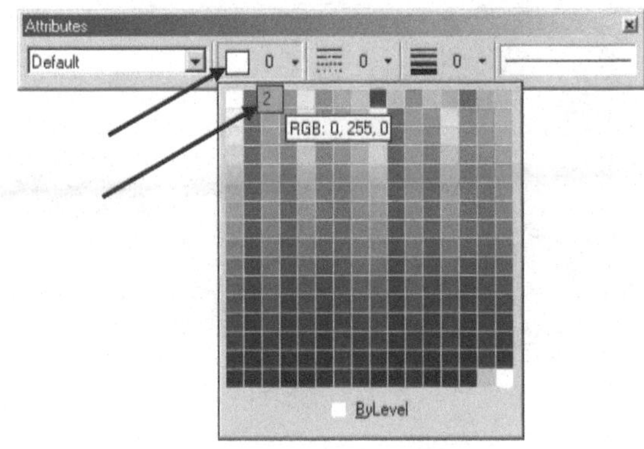

b. Selecting an active Line Style: (changing from style 0-solid, to style 2-dashed)

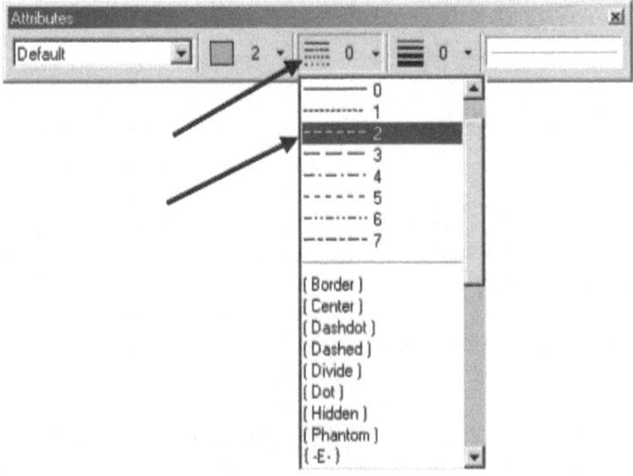

c. Selecting and active LINE WEIGHT: (changing from weight 0, to weight 3)

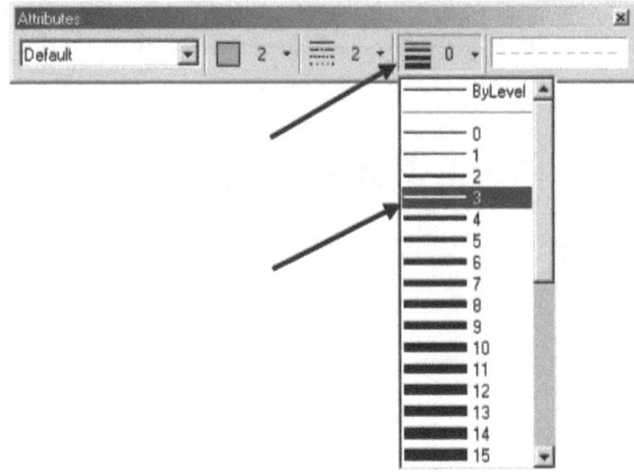

Symbology/Snaps/Locks

MicroStation V8*i*

MicroStation
CONNECT Edition

AUTOCAD

and

Introduction to Civil Engineering

Michael D. Jue, P.E.

© JJFarq/Shutterstock.com. Adapted by Michael D. Jue.

CAD Companion Workbook 3.1

Module 3 Objectives

1. LEARN LEVEL CONCEPTS, COLORS AND OTHER OBJECT ATTRIBUTES
2. LEARN HOW TO CHANGE EXISTING OBJECTS
3. USING SNAPS (TENTATIVE SNAPS IN MICROSTATION)
4. ADDITIONAL COMMANDS RELATED TO GROUPING, EDITING, ALIGNMENTS, ETC.

CAD Companion Workbook 3.2

Examples of controlling Level Display in the THEATER drawing

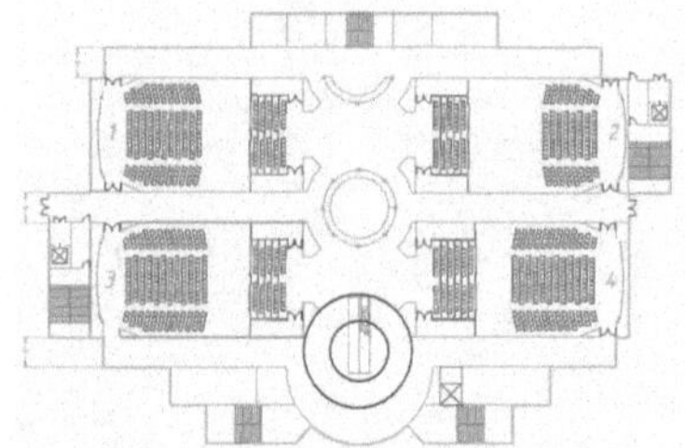

All Levels ON

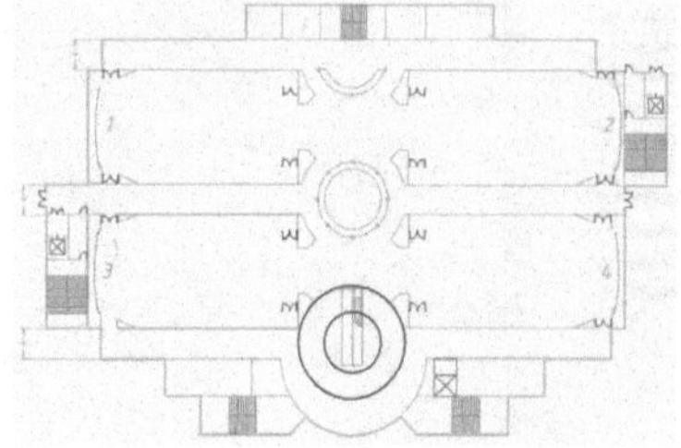

Seats Level OFF

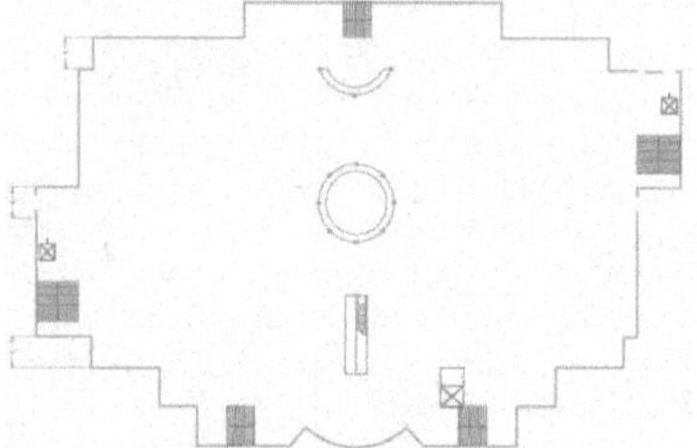

Additional Levels OFF

Level Concepts

- Levels: like Transparencies
  - Can be Displayed ON or OFF
  - µStn <u>used</u> to have a limit of 63 maximum levels/file
  - Now, virtually unlimited, at approx. 4 billion maximum!
    The number of levels that can be created is practically limitless as long as the level name is unique compared to other level names.

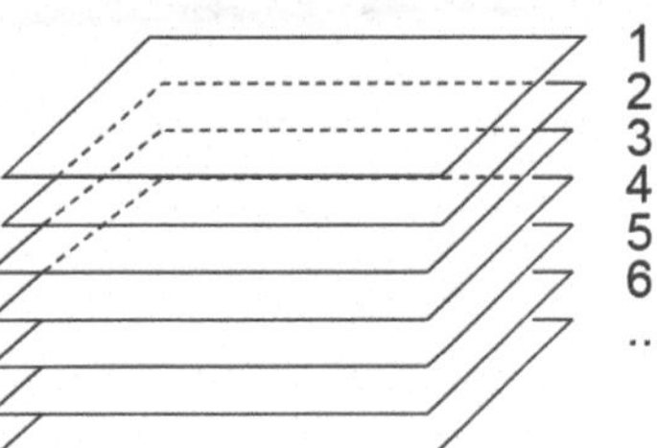

Level Concepts

- Levels/Layers: like Transparencies

	ACAD:	µ-Stn:
■	**Layers**	**Levels**
■	Named or Numbered	Named or Numbered
■	Command: LAYER	Levels Display <Ctrl> E short-cut

Level Concepts

- **LEVEL Commands**
- **µ-Stn: Also See Change Palette**
  - LV= value (1-63) SETS ACTIVE
  - ON = value (1-63) .. or .. range
  - OF = value (1-63) .. or .. range

Level Concepts

- **Purpose is for graphic Organization**
  - Each layer/level should be distinct types of info
    - Outlines
    - Type of item
    - Text - Descriptions
    - Text - Notes
    - Etc.

Note: AutoCAD uses the term "Layer"
MicroStation uses the term "Level"

Settings > Level > Display

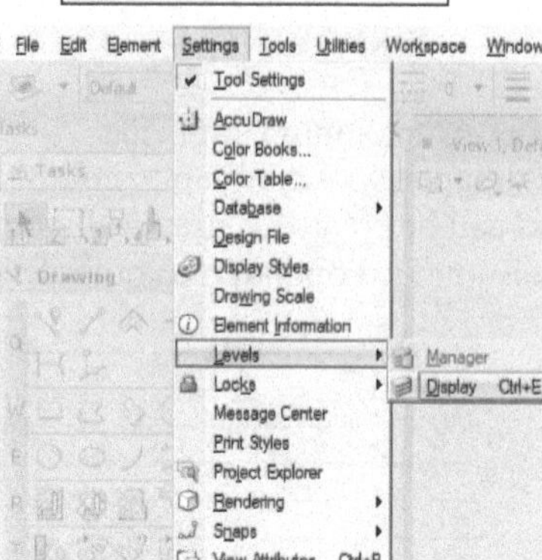

<Ctrl> E is a short-cut!

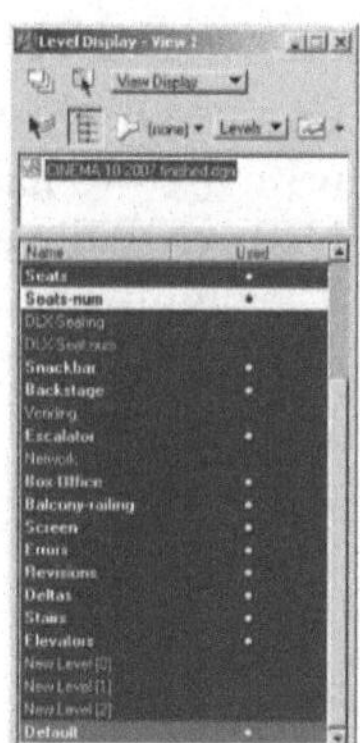

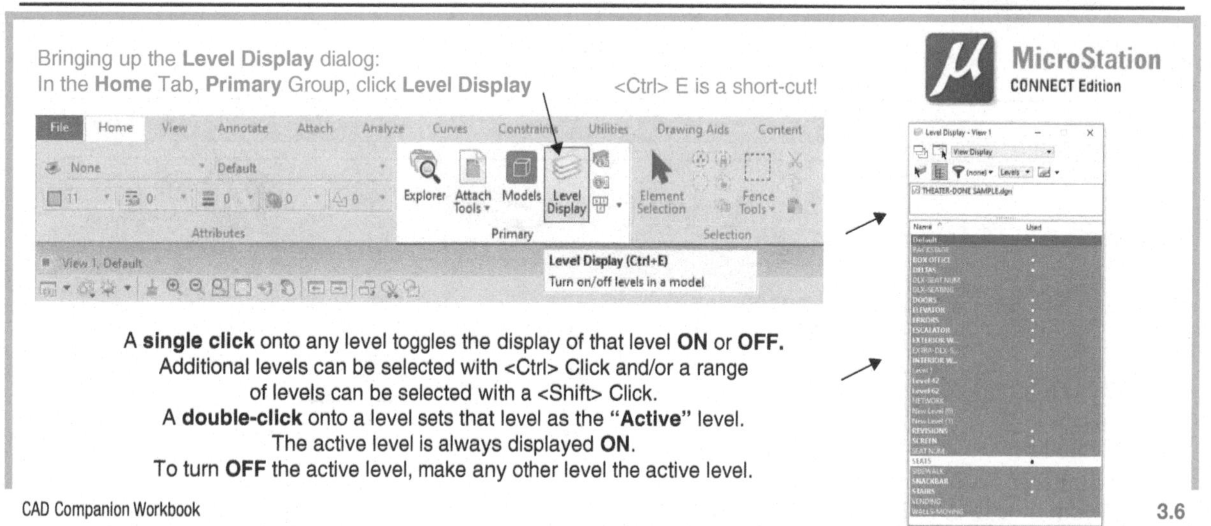

Bringing up the **Level Display** dialog:
In the **Home** Tab, **Primary** Group, click **Level Display**

<Ctrl> E is a short-cut!

A **single click** onto any level toggles the display of that level **ON** or **OFF.**
Additional levels can be selected with <Ctrl> Click and/or a range
of levels can be selected with a <Shift> Click.
A **double-click** onto a level sets that level as the **"Active"** level.
The active level is always displayed **ON**.
To turn **OFF** the active level, make any other level the active level.

CAD Companion Workbook 3.6

MicroStation V8i

Level Concepts

MicroStation CONNECT Edition

- **Drawings with lots of levels!**

  Use of levels improves communications!

Settings > Level > Manager

Elements can be created "ByLevel"

For attributes:

Color, Style, Weight

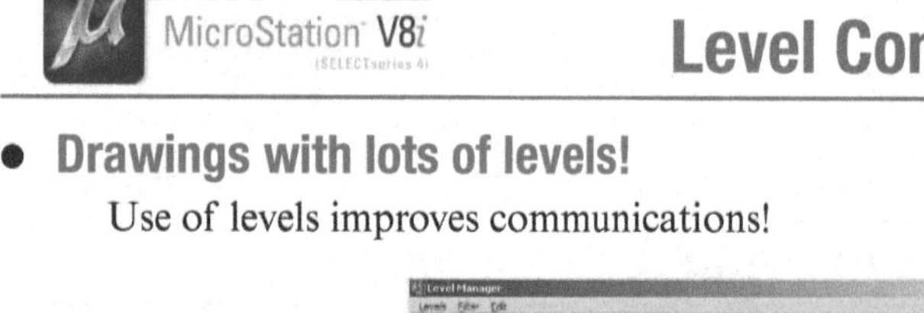

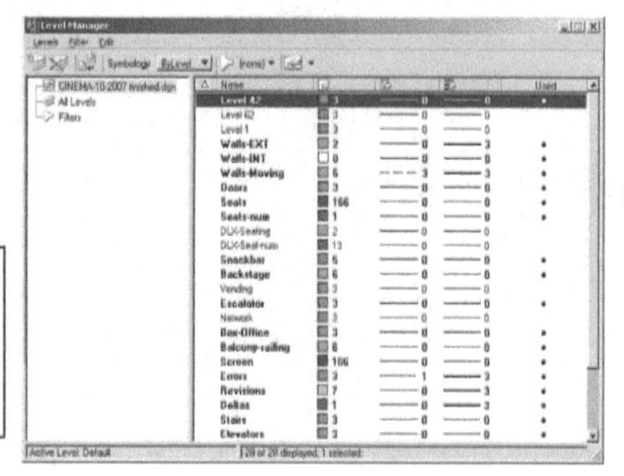

Bringing up the **Level Manager** dialog:
In the **Primary** Group, click **Level Manager**

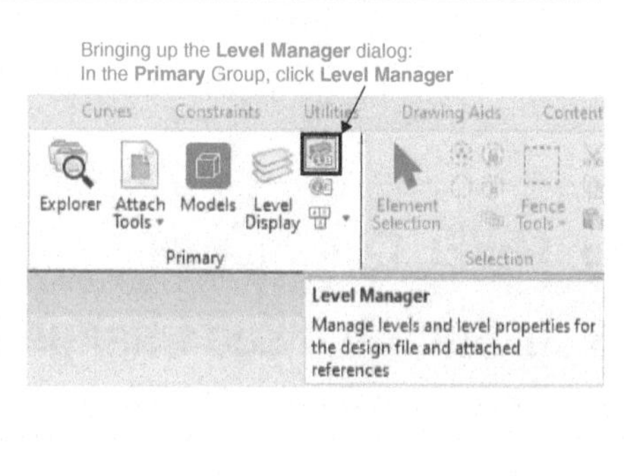

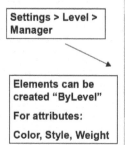

CAD Companion Workbook 3.7

Level Concepts

- **Level Display On/Off can be manipulated individually, too**

Controlling the level display via the Attributes toolbar

Level display ON/OFF control is no longer available in Attributes in the CONNECT Edition

One can also change the level of an element using the Attributes Toolbar in conjunction with the Element Selection Tool, similar to the way one can change color, style or weight, as was done in the Travel exercise.

In the Home Tab, in the Attributes Group, the Active level is displayed here. Clicking the arrow shows more.

Bold levels indicate that the level is displayed **ON**

A **single Click** on a level makes that level the **active level**.

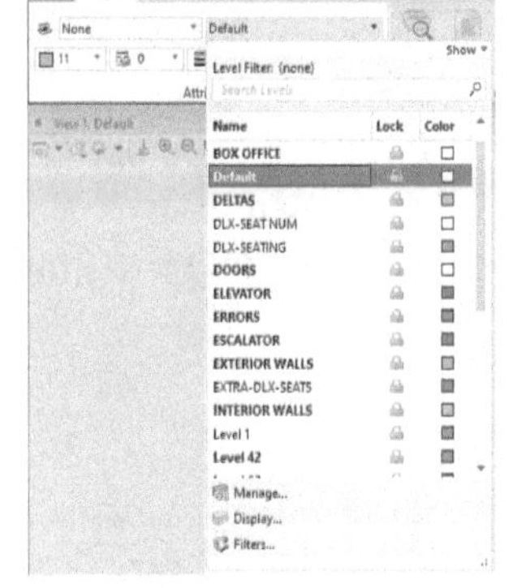

Change Element Attributes

- **A tool that's useful when working with Attributes and Levels is the Change Element Attributes tool.**

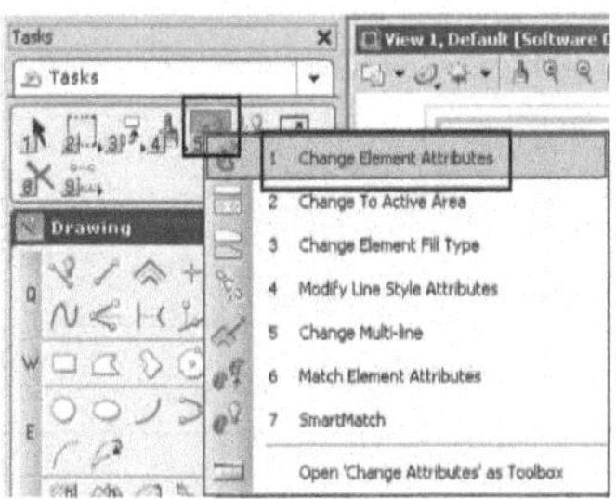

Tool Settings for Change Attributes

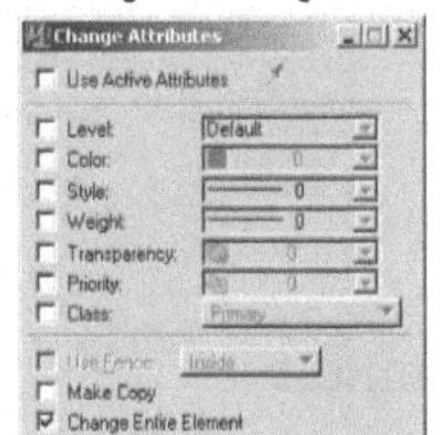

This is particularly effective when used along with a fence!

(covered in mod 4)

MicroStation CONNECT Edition the Change Attributes tool is in the **Home** Tab, **Modify** Group.Click here

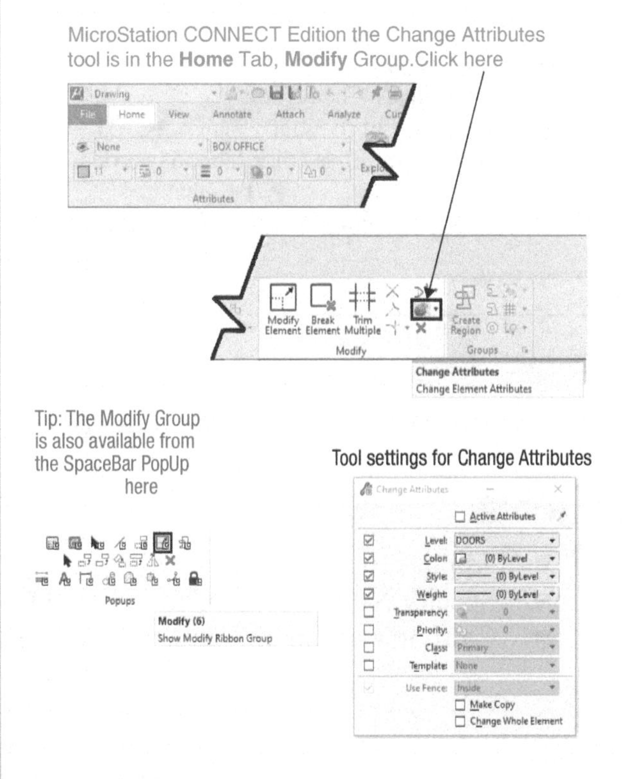

Tip: The Modify Group is also available from the SpaceBar PopUp here

Tool settings for Change Attributes

Color

- Purpose is for Organization
- Speeds up user input / finding elements
- Customizable windows/highlites in µStn
- Color can be set BYLEVEL
  - µStn
    - **CO=** value or Colorname

CAD Companion Workbook 3.10

Color

- Default color scheme:

ACAD	µStn
N/A	0=WHITE
1=RED	1=BLUE
2=YELLOW	2=GREEN
3=GREEN	3=RED
4=CYAN	4=YELLOW
5=BLUE	5=VIOLET
6=MAGENTA	6=ORANGE
7=WHITE	7=CYAN

CAD Companion Workbook 3.11

Other adjustments in µStn:

- Background, Highlight, Pointer & Custom
  - PULLDOWN:
    Workspace - Preferences - View Options
- Color Tables
  - PULLDOWN:
    Settings - Color Table
  - Can easily set to exactly match ACAD
  - Can have multiple color tables if needed
    CT = filename
  - Typical Highlight: Cyan, Pointer: Magenta

- Background, Highlight, Pointer & Custom
  File - Settings - User - View Options
- Color Tables
  File - Settings - File - Color Table

CAD Companion Workbook 3.12

Line Weights (Thickness)

- µ-Stn
  - Applies to any Element
  - Specify Number 0-31 Can display ON or OFF
  - Cannot Vary on an Element **WT= value** (0-31) 0 is thinnest

0
3
6
..

CAD Companion Workbook 3.13

MicroStation V8i (SELECTseries 4)

Filled Shapes

MicroStation CONNECT Edition

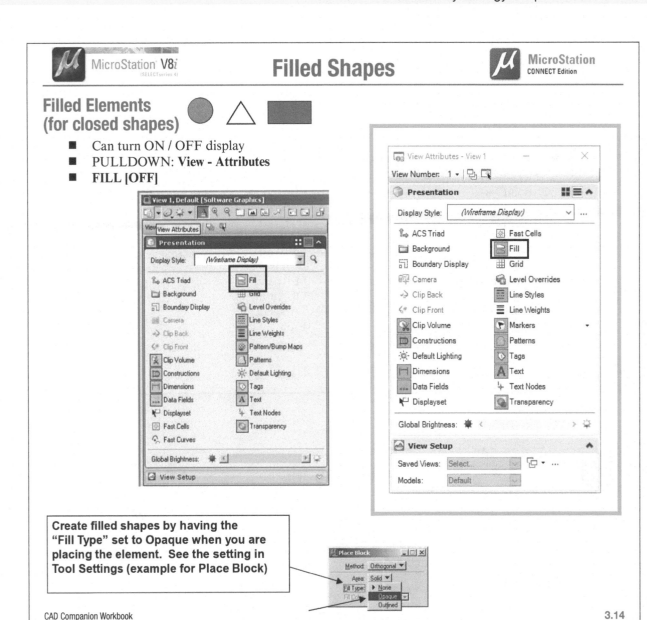

Filled Elements (for closed shapes)

- Can turn ON / OFF display
- PULLDOWN: **View - Attributes**
- **FILL [OFF]**

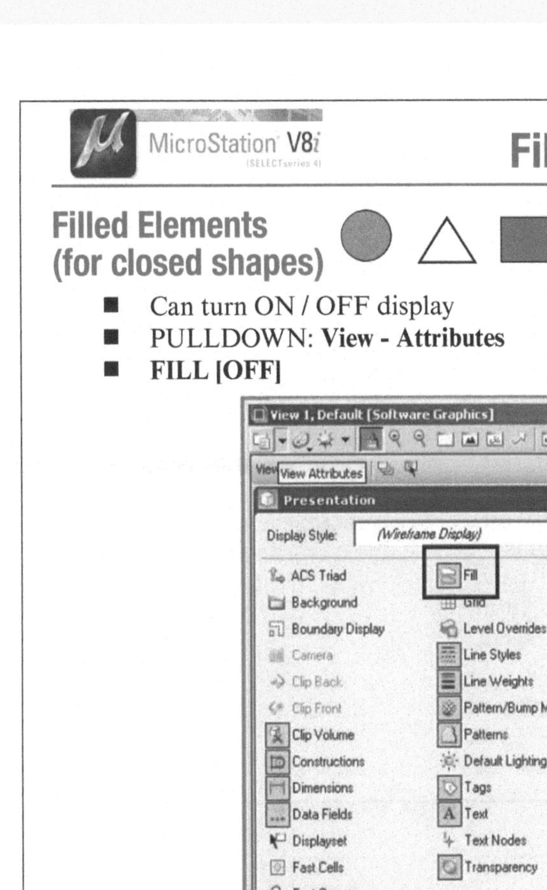

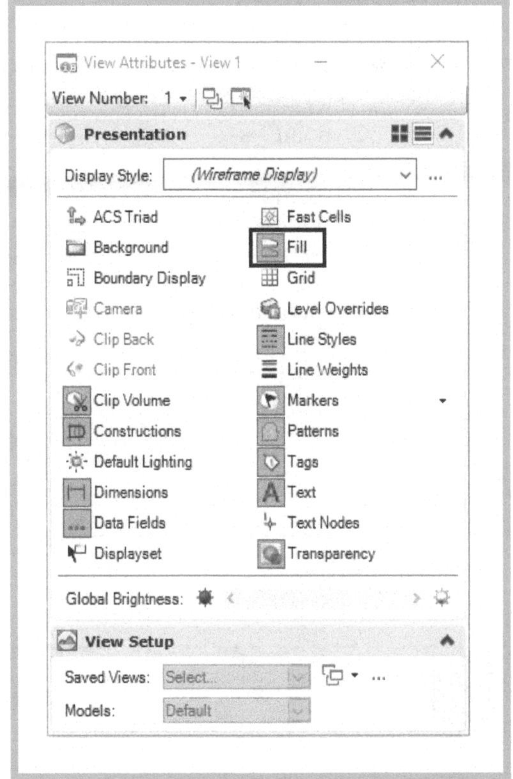

Create filled shapes by having the "Fill Type" set to Opaque when you are placing the element. See the setting in Tool Settings (example for Place Block)

LineStyles/Codes

- µ-Stn
  - Line Style or Code
  - Specify Number 0-7
  - **LC=** value (0-7) or name
  - Can make custom Styles

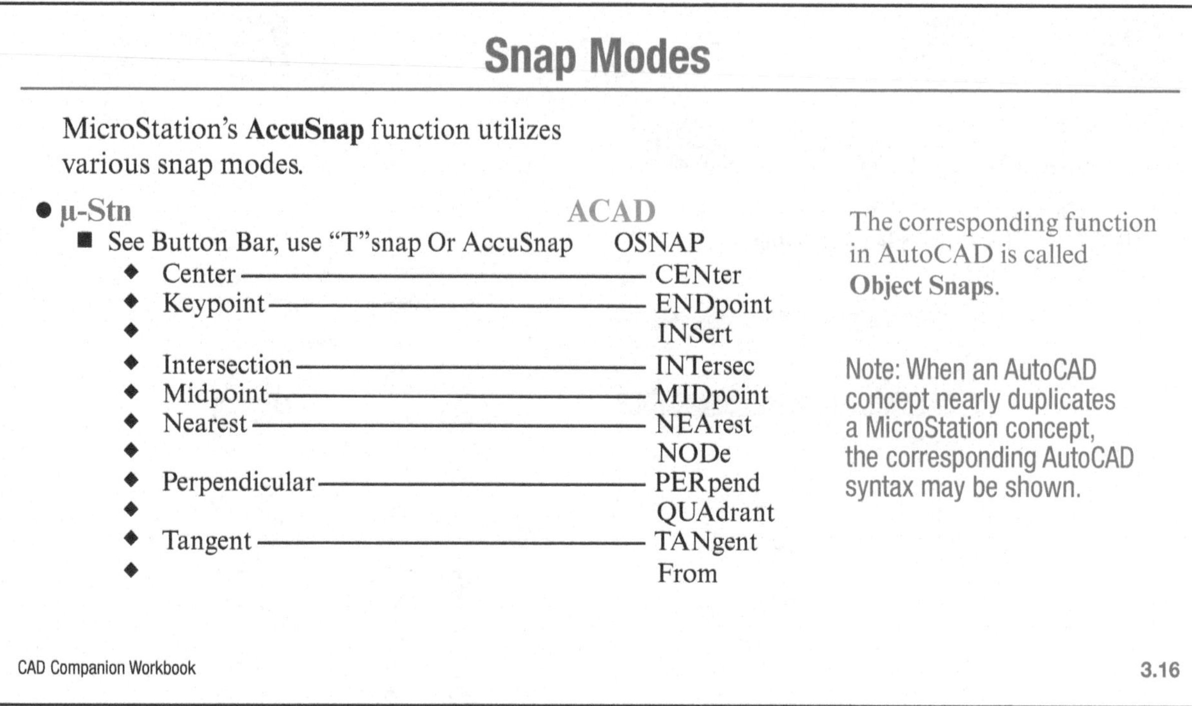
Snap Modes
MicroStation's **AccuSnap** function utilizes various snap modes.
µ-Stn
ACAD
See Button Bar, use "T"snap Or AccuSnap
OSNAP
Center — CENter
Keypoint — ENDpoint
INSert
Intersection — INTersec
Midpoint — MIDpoint
Nearest — NEArest
NODe
Perpendicular — PERpend
QUAdrant
Tangent — TANgent
From
The corresponding function in AutoCAD is called **Object Snaps**.
Note: When an AutoCAD concept nearly duplicates a MicroStation concept, the corresponding AutoCAD syntax may be shown.
CAD Companion Workbook
3.16

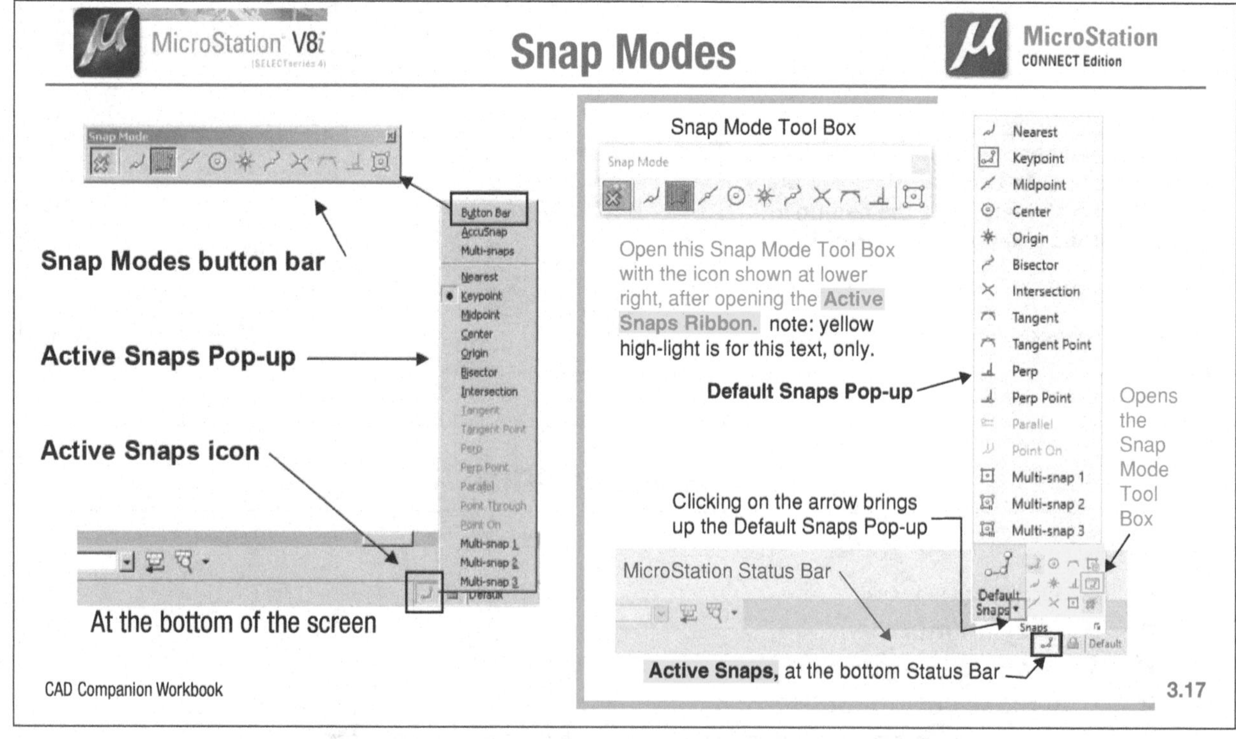
MicroStation V8i
Snap Modes
MicroStation
CONNECT Edition
Snap Mode
Snap Modes button bar
Active Snaps Pop-up
Active Snaps icon
At the bottom of the screen
Button Bar
AccuSnap
Multi-snaps
Nearest
Keypoint
Midpoint
Center
Origin
Bisector
Intersection
Tangent
Tangent Point
Perp
Perp Point
Parallel
Point Through
Point On
Multi-snap 1
Multi-snap 2
Multi-snap 3
Snap Mode Tool Box
Open this Snap Mode Tool Box with the icon shown at lower right, after opening the Active Snaps Ribbon. note: yellow high-light is for this text, only.
Default Snaps Pop-up
Clicking on the arrow brings up the Default Snaps Pop-up
MicroStation Status Bar
Active Snaps, at the bottom Status Bar
Nearest
Keypoint
Midpoint
Center
Origin
Bisector
Intersection
Tangent
Tangent Point
Perp
Perp Point
Parallel
Point On
Multi-snap 1
Multi-snap 2
Multi-snap 3
Opens the Snap Mode Tool Box
Default Snaps
Snaps
Default
CAD Companion Workbook
3.17

MicroStation V8i (SELECTseries 4)

Snap Modes

MicroStation CONNECT Edition

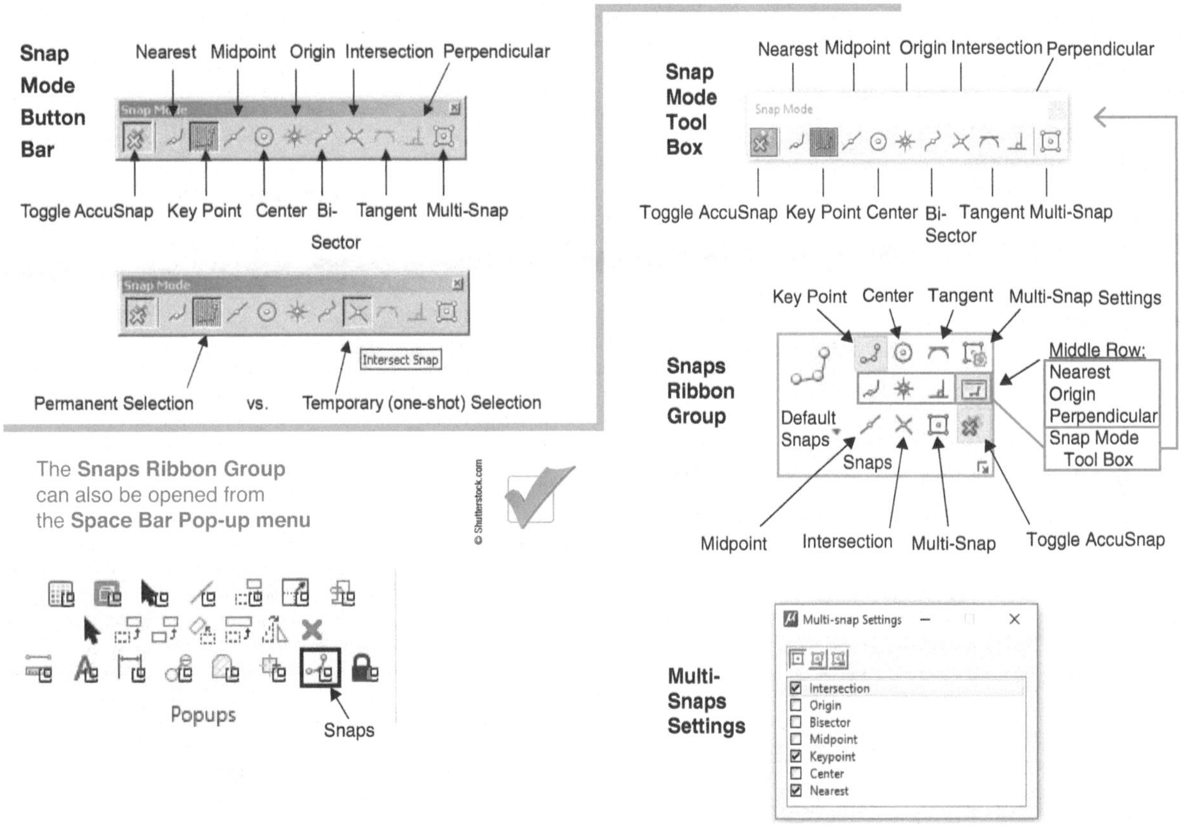

Snap Mode Button Bar

Nearest Midpoint Origin Intersection Perpendicular

Snap Mode

Toggle AccuSnap Key Point Center Bi-Sector Tangent Multi-Snap

Snap Mode

Intersect Snap

Permanent Selection vs. Temporary (one-shot) Selection

Snap Mode Tool Box

Nearest Midpoint Origin Intersection Perpendicular

Snap Mode

Toggle AccuSnap Key Point Center Bi-Sector Tangent Multi-Snap

Snaps Ribbon Group

Key Point Center Tangent Multi-Snap Settings

Middle Row:
Nearest
Origin
Perpendicular

Snap Mode Tool Box

Default Snaps

Snaps

Midpoint Intersection Multi-Snap Toggle AccuSnap

The **Snaps Ribbon Group** can also be opened from the **Space Bar Pop-up menu**

© Shutterstock.com

Popups

Snaps

Multi-Snaps Settings

Multi-snap Settings

- [x] Intersection
- [ ] Origin
- [ ] Bisector
- [ ] Midpoint
- [x] Keypoint
- [ ] Center
- [x] Nearest

CAD Companion Workbook 3.18

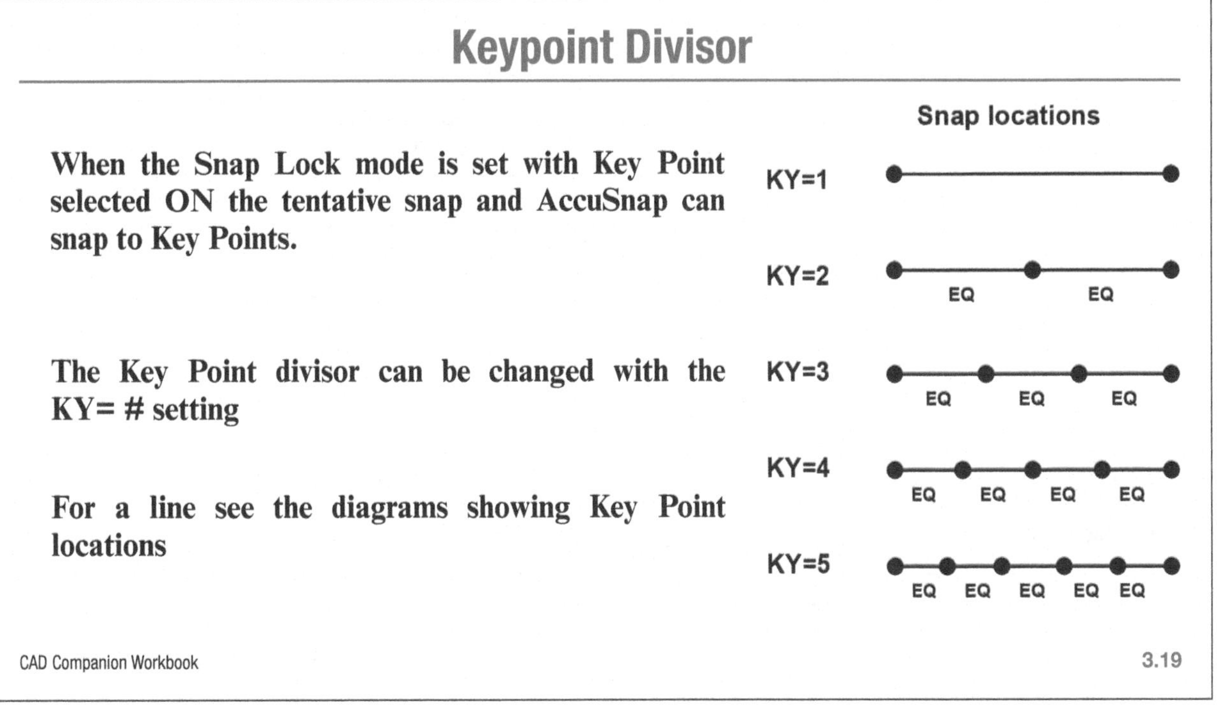

Keypoint Divisor
When the Snap Lock mode is set with Key Point selected ON the tentative snap and AccuSnap can snap to Key Points.
The Key Point divisor can be changed with the KY= # setting
For a line see the diagrams showing Key Point locations
Snap locations
KY=1
KY=2
EQ EQ
KY=3
EQ EQ EQ
KY=4
EQ EQ EQ EQ
KY=5
EQ EQ EQ EQ EQ
CAD Companion Workbook
3.19

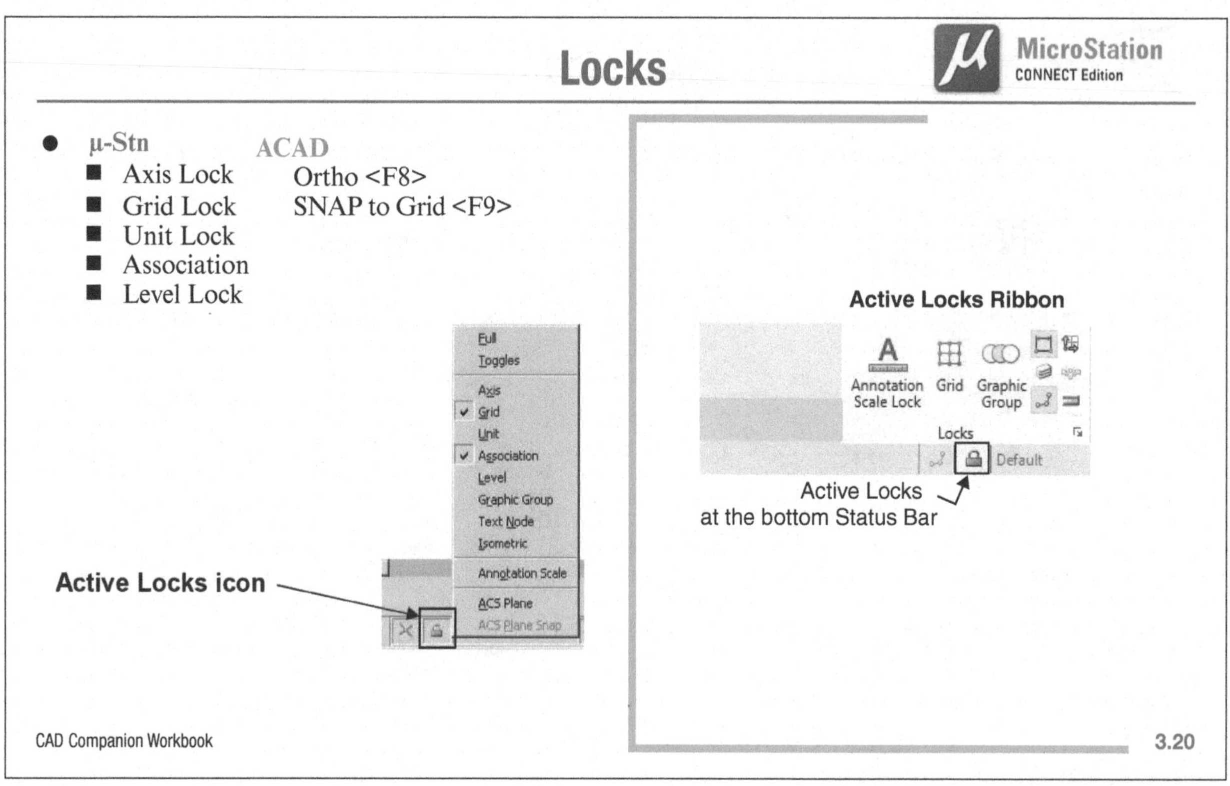
Locks
MicroStation
CONNECT Edition
μ-Stn
ACAD
Axis Lock
Ortho <F8>
Grid Lock
SNAP to Grid <F9>
Unit Lock
Association
Level Lock
Full
Toggles
Axis
Grid
Unit
Association
Level
Graphic Group
Text Node
Isometric
Annotation Scale
ACS Plane
ACS Plane Snap
Active Locks icon
Active Locks Ribbon
Annotation Scale Lock
Grid
Graphic Group
Locks
Default
Active Locks
at the bottom Status Bar
CAD Companion Workbook
3.20

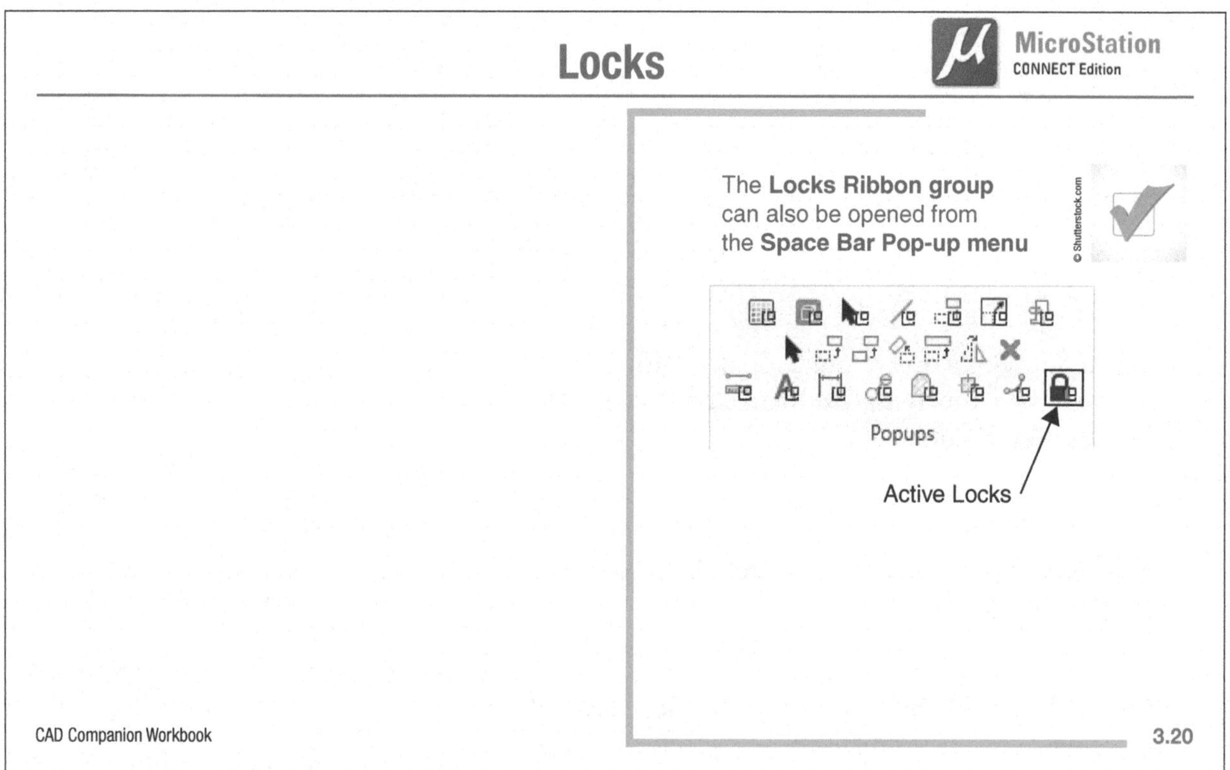
Locks
MicroStation
CONNECT Edition
The Locks Ribbon group
can also be opened from
the Space Bar Pop-up menu
© Shutterstock.com
Popups
Active Locks
CAD Companion Workbook
3.20

Wait! Before you Draw anything …

See these Additional tips, tidbits and Challenge Questions

© Shutterstock.com

TIPS & TIDBITS

1. When beginning to create lines or other elements, **after you enter the first data-point to start the element, make sure you roll the mouse slightly**, (being careful not to hit an accidental data-point) **and observe the result**, before proceeding on.

   *This way, **you'll get immediate visual FEEDBACK** that you have correctly started the first point of your element. If the screen doesn't show what you think is supposed to be happening, perhaps you have made a simple mistake in your entry. It's much better to see and observe the action that you are performing after every few steps, and stop right away after an error, rather than realizing that you've made a mistake after dozens of entries.*

2. Draw with some **COLORS**! Generally, you should use the first 7 or 8 main colors in the palette, before selecting other more exotic colors. Colors help improve efficiency!

   *You can easily change the color (or weight or style also) of previously placed elements using the **Selection Tool**. Select the element(s) you want to change using the **Selection Tool**, then select the color you want in the **Attributes Toolbar** (usually docked at the top), **then data-point in the view** to see the element(s) change to your selected new color.*

3. **Are your data-points jumping from point to point on your screen** and you don't want it to do that? You most likely have the **Grid Lock** function on. Turn it OFF at the Active Locks Settings at the bottom of the screen.

   *Note: **Grid Lock** will function even if you can't see the grid dots (when you are zoomed in too far or zoomed out too far). Also, Grid Lock (if ON) will still function even if the "display" of the grid dots is turned OFF via View Attributes. Verify this, by going to your ORGCHART drawing and checking it out.*

4. **Don't Go Fishing in Uncharted Territories**! If you are looking for a particular tool to do a certain function that we have done in class, DON'T GO LOOKING IN TOOLBARS THAT WE'VE NEVER USED BEFORE. It will NOT be in a toolbar that we have never used before--**GUARANTEED**! DUH!!! You would be surprised at how many students attempt FISHING in completely unknown toolbars and it's done mostly on EXAMS!!
5. **Pay very close attention to your typing accuracy** while keying-in Precision Inputs. Precision Input can also refer to the **precision of the Human Input**!

   A comma is not the same as a period! Also, the letter O is not the same as the numeral 0. And precision Input Key-ins in MicroStation DO NOT CONTAIN SPACES.

   In the early days of the Computer Revolution of the '60s and '70s a catchy phrase coined was G.I.G.O., which stands for GARBAGE IN, GARBAGE OUT. This is still applicable to most all modern software, as well.

6. **Avoid creating "lines on top of lines".** This may not look any different than a single line on the screen to anyone, but it will eventually confuse many users. It also is a sloppy CAD drafting practice that can lead to severe errors, especially in "machine-part drawings" that are used to directly control machine tools.

7. **The Axis Lock**, which restricts input points to align with the axes **can be set to lock input points to something *other* than the primary X and Y axes.** In Settings > Locks > Full see the setting called "Increment" in the Axis section. Instead of the default 90 degree setting, it can be set to 45 degrees or 15 degrees, which are commonly quite useful. A setting of a 10 degree increment may also be quite useful. Try it! Why would a setting of a 1 degree increment not be useful, for most applications?

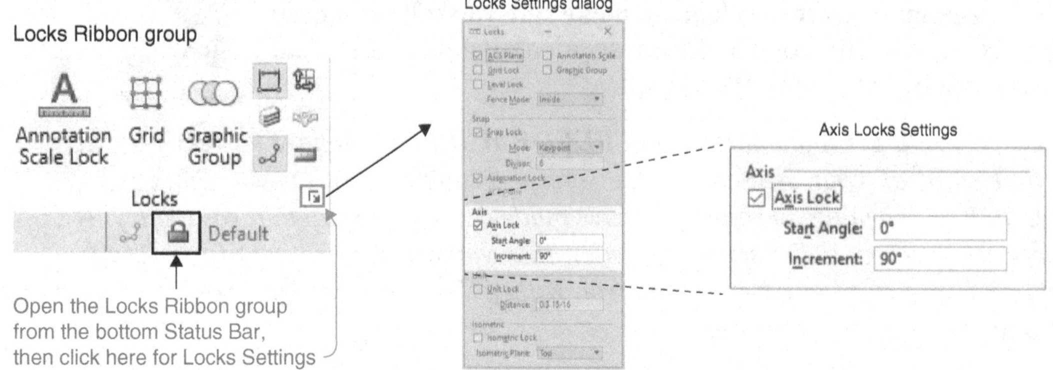

8. When using MicroStation's **Keypoint snap mode**, the snap points are governed by the **keypoint divisor** setting. It is set with a **key-in KY=divisor factor**. KY=2 is the typical default setting in version V8.0 (KY=1 was default for earlier versions.) It allows snapping to keypoints with the element divided into an imaginary 2 segments for lines or arcs. This yields snap points at the ends and at the midpoint. Circles and ellipses divide into 8 imaginary segments and a snap point at the center. For rectangular block shapes, each edge is treated as a line segment. Change the divisor to other settings such as KY=3 to snap at the 1/3 points or KY=4 to snap at ¼ points along an element. The highest practical KY setting is usually not over 10. Why would a setting of KY=25 be impractical?

Element keypoints (with Snap Lock Divisor set to 2 (KY=2) and the text element left top justified). Clockwise from the upper left: Arc, arc, line, line string, text, ellipse, and shape.

Keypoint snap locations for KY=2

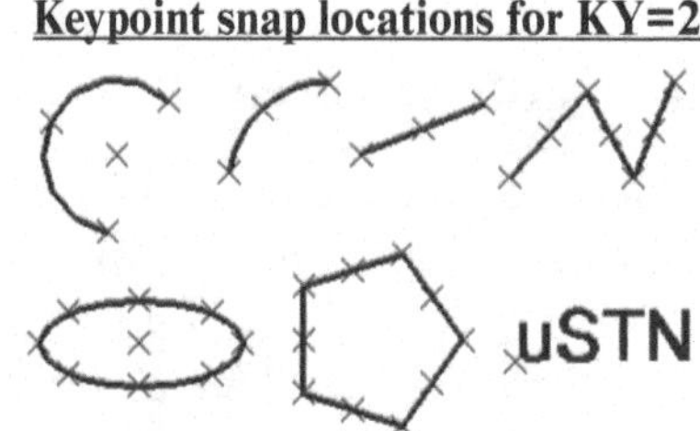

CHALLENGE QUESTIONS *Answers in Answer Section*

1? Find the tools that do these and name them correctly. Now try them out!

2? Name any two of MicroStation's snap modes.

3? Can you measure the distance between two points? This is very useful for determining the spacing between elements already placed on your screen.

4? What does it mean if you measure the distance between two points and instead of the distance reading something like 4.95' MicroStation gives the reading as 1.5087 mu?

5? Symbology is another term meaning the Attributes of an element. What are the three common attributes of an element?

6? What is the short-cut key-in to set each of the three common element attributes?

Module 4

Fences, Text, Levels

Key CAD exercise concepts for Week 4/5

Additional skills are required for completion of the following exercises. The student will be learning to complete some exercises without specific directions being provided by the instructor. The instructor will show additional techniques utilizing snaps and creating graphics from previously drawn elements.

The student will gain expertise with previously introduced tools. The student will be using some of the earlier tools for the fifth and sixth repetition by this time, although applied differently in the new exercises.

The instructor will provide an introduction to the powerful usage of "Fences" and "Levels".

General/All

Fence modes
Fence Operations
- Delete, Copy, Stretch

Change Element Attributes
Levels
- Purpose
- Creation
- Level Manager
- Level Display

Intro to Text
- Text Height & Width setting
- Place text (by origin)
- Edit Text
- Copy and increment text

Phone to "E"

The student will gain expertise thru additional practice with placement and manipulation tools. Student to work on this drawing without specific directions provided. Various precision input/placement and manipulations as needed

Exercise	Concepts / Tools / Lessons	For MODULE 4

Fence Selection Modes.dgn
&
Stretch Limo.dgn

Introduction to the usage of the **Fence** Tool to select multiple elements in a design file for subsequent manipulations. **Fence** placement, fence type and mode are shown. The Stretch-Limo exercise utilizes concepts from earlier modules together with the use of the **Fence** Tool and **Stretch** and briefly touches on additional new concepts: **Line-string, Drop element, AccuDraw, Properties, Locked elements** and more.

Companion Video

Instructon semi-guided warm-up exercises used to introduce the student to use of Fences and additional CAD concepts:

Stretch, Locked elements, Properties, Line-strings and more.

Fence Selection Modes, pg299, Appendix A section

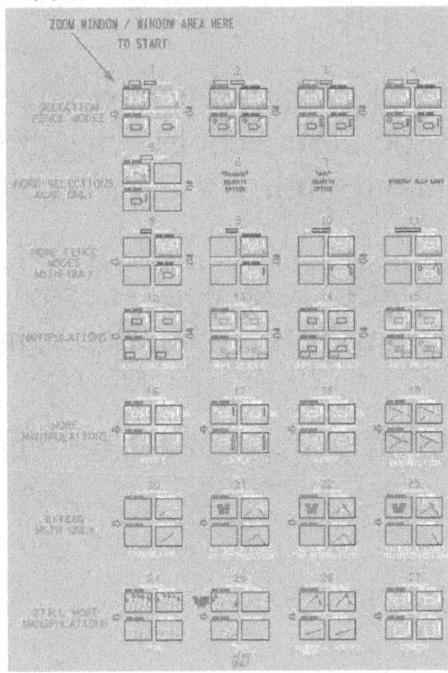
ZOOM WINDOW / WINDOW AREA HERE
TO START

Stretch-Limo, pg142

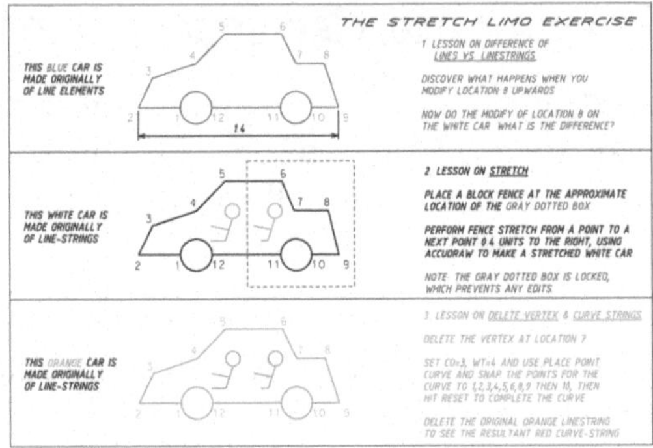
THE STRETCH LIMO EXERCISE
THIS BLUE CAR IS MADE ORIGINALLY OF LINE ELEMENTS
1 LESSON ON DIFFERENCE OF LINES VS LINESTRINGS
DISCOVER WHAT HAPPENS WHEN YOU MODIFY LOCATION 8 UPWARDS
NOW DO THE MODIFY OF LOCATION 8 ON THE WHITE CAR WHAT IS THE DIFFERENCE?
THIS WHITE CAR IS MADE ORIGINALLY OF LINE-STRINGS
2 LESSON ON STRETCH
PLACE A BLOCK FENCE AT THE APPROXIMATE LOCATION OF THE GRAY DOTTED BOX
PERFORM FENCE STRETCH FROM A POINT TO A NEXT POINT 0.4 UNITS TO THE RIGHT, USING ACCUDRAW TO MAKE A STRETCHED WHITE CAR
NOTE THE GRAY DOTTED BOX IS LOCKED, WHICH PREVENTS ANY EDITS
THIS ORANGE CAR IS MADE ORIGINALLY OF LINE-STRINGS
3 LESSON ON DELETE VERTEX & CURVE STRINGS
DELETE THE VERTEX AT LOCATION 7
SET CO=3, WT=4 AND USE PLACE POINT CURVE AND SNAP THE POINTS FOR THE CURVE TO 1,2,3,4,5,6,8,9 THEN 10, THEN HIT RESET TO COMPLETE THE CURVE
DELETE THE ORIGINAL ORANGE LINESTRING TO SEE THE RESULTANT RED CURVE-STRING

note: These are pre-drawn exercise files, that the student will need to have copies of provided to them by your instructor or downloaded from the Great River Learning website. See inside of front cover and pg x in the front material.

Theater.dgn

Instructor to show new techniques demonstrating powerful features of "Fences" and "Levels".

Companion Video

Instructor semi-guided exercise, utilizing a pre-drawn drawing.

See pg298 in the Appendix A section.

Place Fence (Precision usage)
- (for multiple element selection)
  - Types: By Block & Shape
  - Fence Modes:
    - Inside
    - Overlap
    - Clip
    - Void
    - Void-Overlap
    - Void-Clip

Fence Operations
- Delete, Copy, Stretch
- Tool setting "use fence"

Application of Levels
Change Element Attributes
Text usage

Theater (Pre-drawn), to edit, pg298

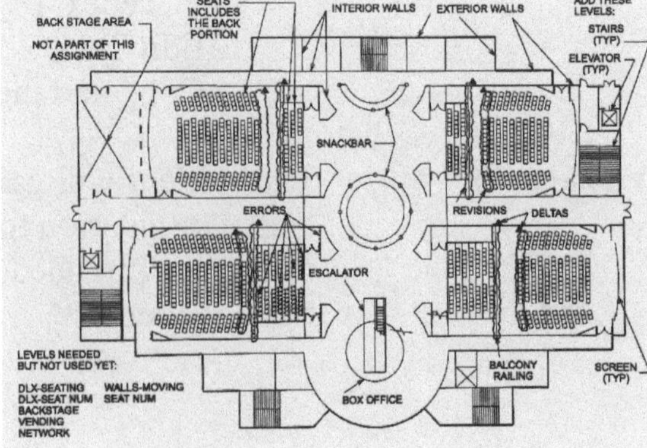
BACK STAGE AREA
NOT A PART OF THIS ASSIGNMENT
SEATS INCLUDES THE BACK PORTION
INTERIOR WALLS
EXTERIOR WALLS
ADD THESE LEVELS:
STAIRS (TYP)
ELEVATOR (TYP)
SNACKBAR
ERRORS
REVISIONS
DELTAS
ESCALATOR
BALCONY RAILING
SCREEN (TYP)
BOX OFFICE
LEVELS NEEDED BUT NOT USED YET:
DLX-SEATING
DLX-SEAT NUM
BACKSTAGE
VENDING
NETWORK
WALLS-MOVING
SEAT NUM

Module 4 – Fences, Text, Levels

The following new tools will be introduced for editing the THEATER drawing:

1. <u>From the **Main Task #2**, **Fence** Toolbar:</u>

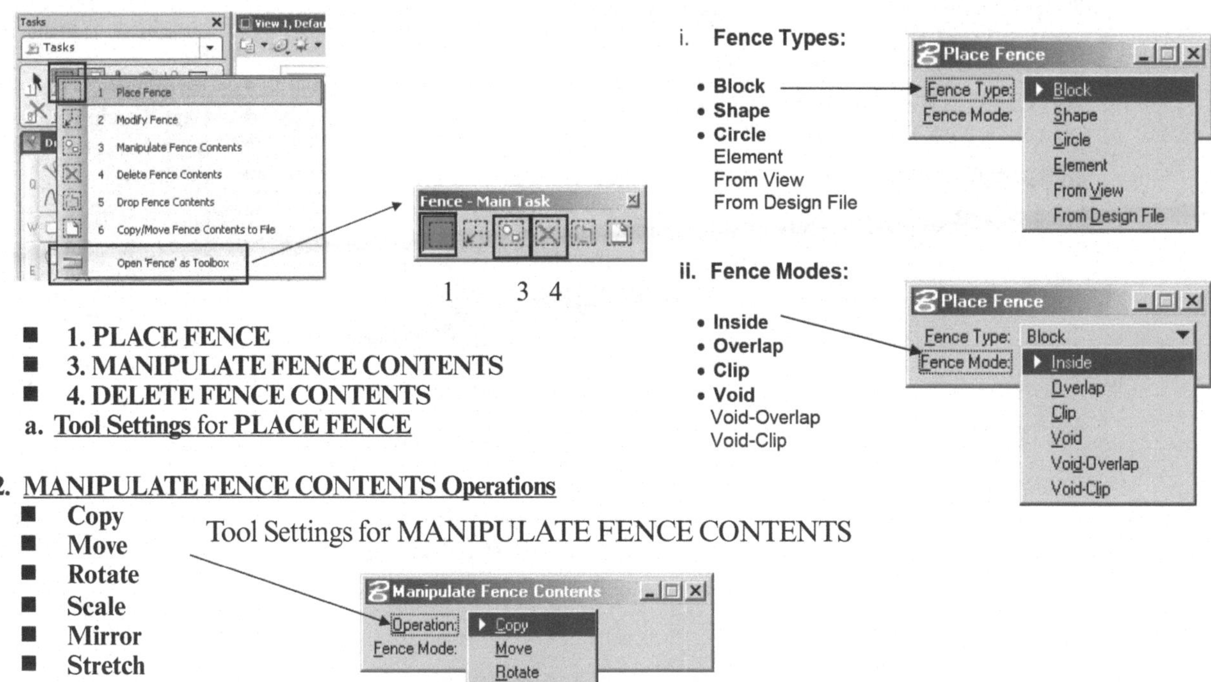

- **1. PLACE FENCE**
- **3. MANIPULATE FENCE CONTENTS**
- **4. DELETE FENCE CONTENTS**

a. <u>**Tool Settings** for **PLACE FENCE**</u>

2. <u>**MANIPULATE FENCE CONTENTS Operations**</u>
   - **Copy**
   - **Move**
   - **Rotate**
   - **Scale**
   - **Mirror**
   - **Stretch**

Tool Settings for MANIPULATE FENCE CONTENTS

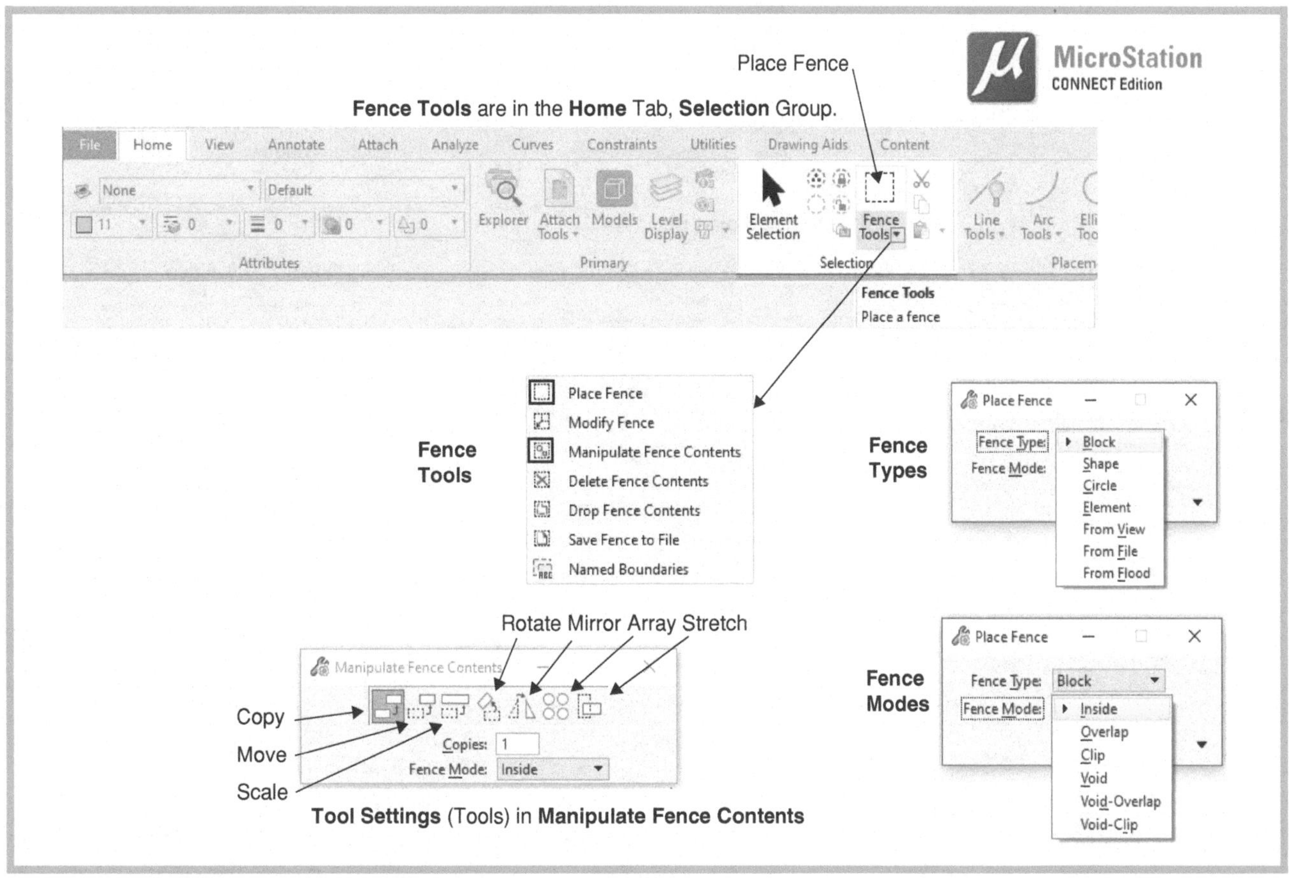

Module 4 – Fences, Text, Levels

The following new tools will be introduced for editing the THEATER drawing:

3. **Additional TEXT Tools**
   a. **PLACE TEXT & New placement Methods**
   b. **MATCH TEXT ATTRIBUTES**
   c. **CHANGE TEXT ATTRIBUTES**

- **Height & Width**
- **Font**
- **Justification**
- **Line Spacing**
- **Intercharacter Spacing**
- **Fractions**

V8

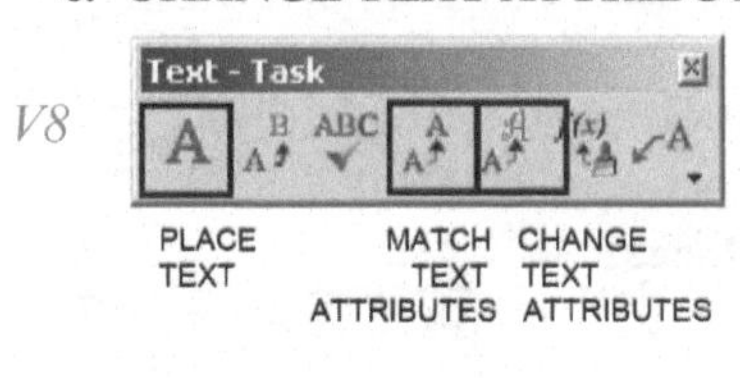

Place Text Methods in Tool Settings for PLACE TEXT

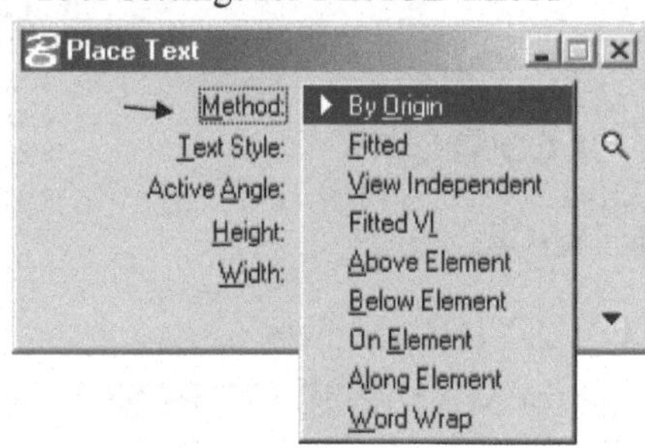

d. **Element > Text Styles**

V8i

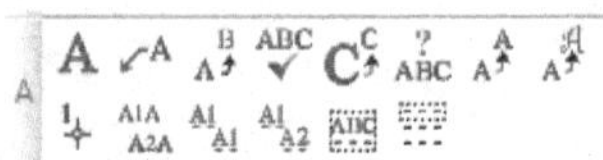

Place Text

Text Tools are in the Annotate Tab

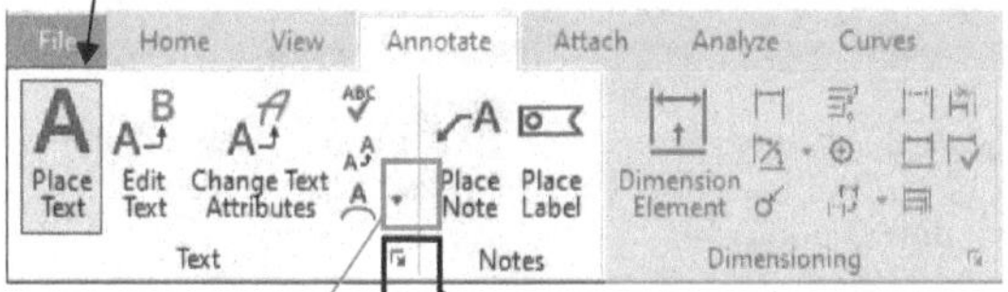

MicroStation CONNECT Edition

File Home View Annotate Attach Analyze Curves

Place Text | Edit Text | Change Text Attributes | Place Note | Place Label | Dimension Element

Text | Notes | Dimensioning

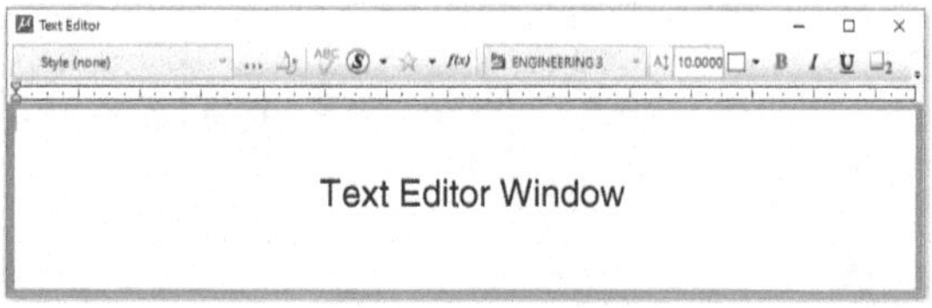

More Text Tools

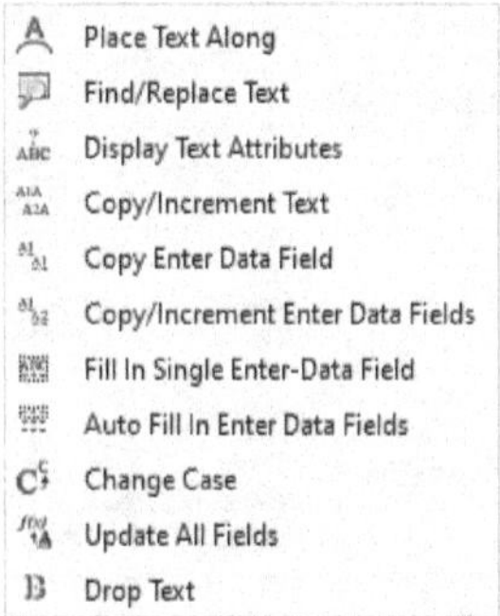

- Place Text Along
- Find/Replace Text
- Display Text Attributes
- Copy/Increment Text
- Copy Enter Data Field
- Copy/Increment Enter Data Fields
- Fill In Single Enter-Data Field
- Auto Fill In Enter Data Fields
- Change Case
- Update All Fields
- Drop Text

Text Editor Window

Text Styles Dialog Box

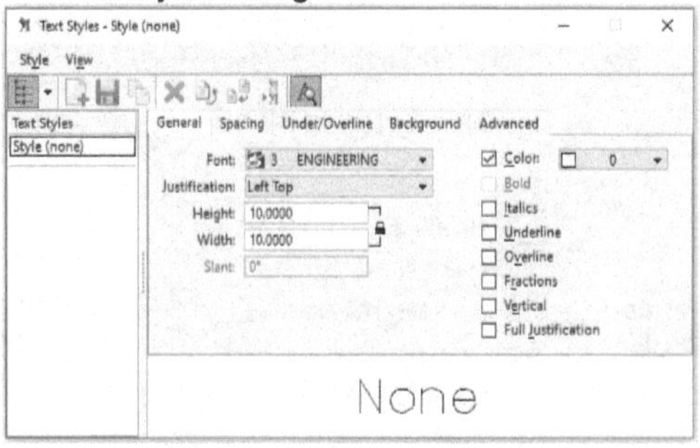

Text Styles - Style (none)

General | Spacing | Under/Overline | Background | Advanced

Font: 3 ENGINEERING
Justification: Left Top
Height: 10.0000
Width: 10.0000
Slant: 0°

Color, Bold, Italics, Underline, Overline, Fractions, Vertical, Full Justification

None

By Origin   Fitted

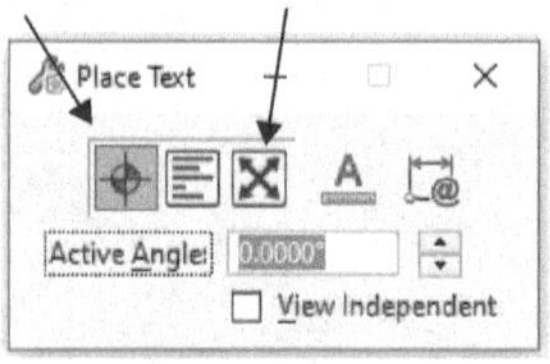

Place Text

Active Angle: 0.0000°

View Independent

Tool Settings for Place Text

Some **Text Tools** are in **Home** Tab, **Placement** Group

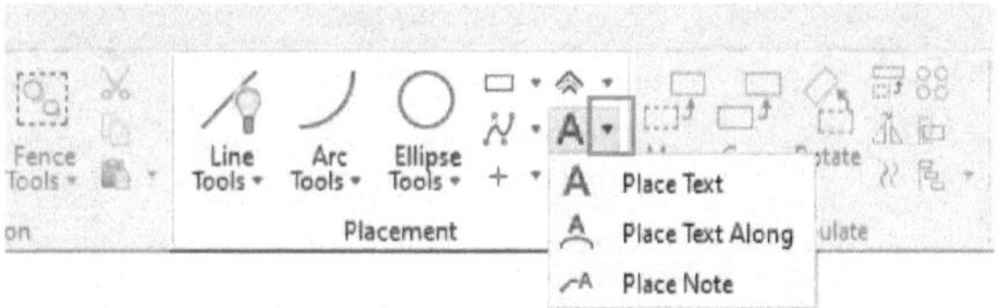

Fence Tools | Line Tools | Arc Tools | Ellipse Tools

Placement

- Place Text
- Place Text Along
- Place Note

Change Text Attributes   Match Text Attributes

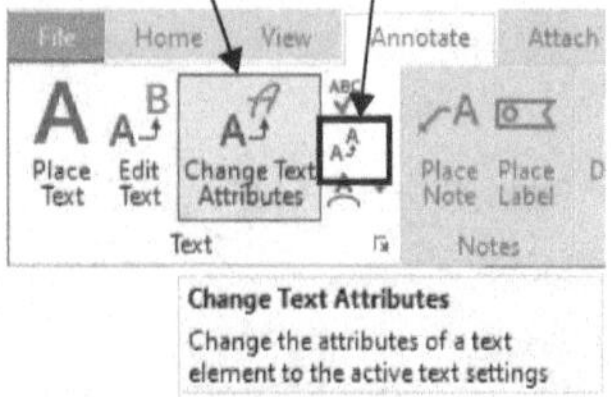

File Home View Annotate Attach

Place Text | Edit Text | Change Text Attributes | Place Note | Place Label

Text | Notes

Change Text Attributes
Change the attributes of a text element to the active text settings

Module 4 – Fences, Text, Levels

4. **ARCS** Toolbar open from **Drawing Task, Circle Toolbar**

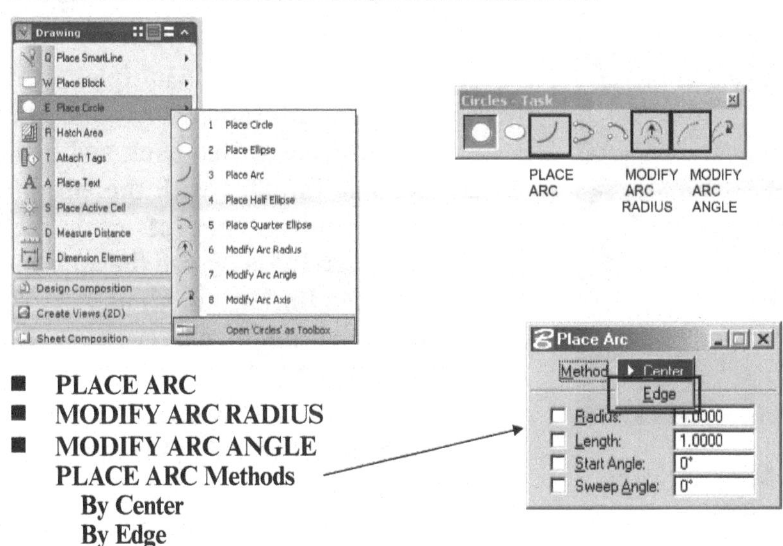

- PLACE ARC
- MODIFY ARC RADIUS
- MODIFY ARC ANGLE

PLACE ARC Methods
By Center
By Edge

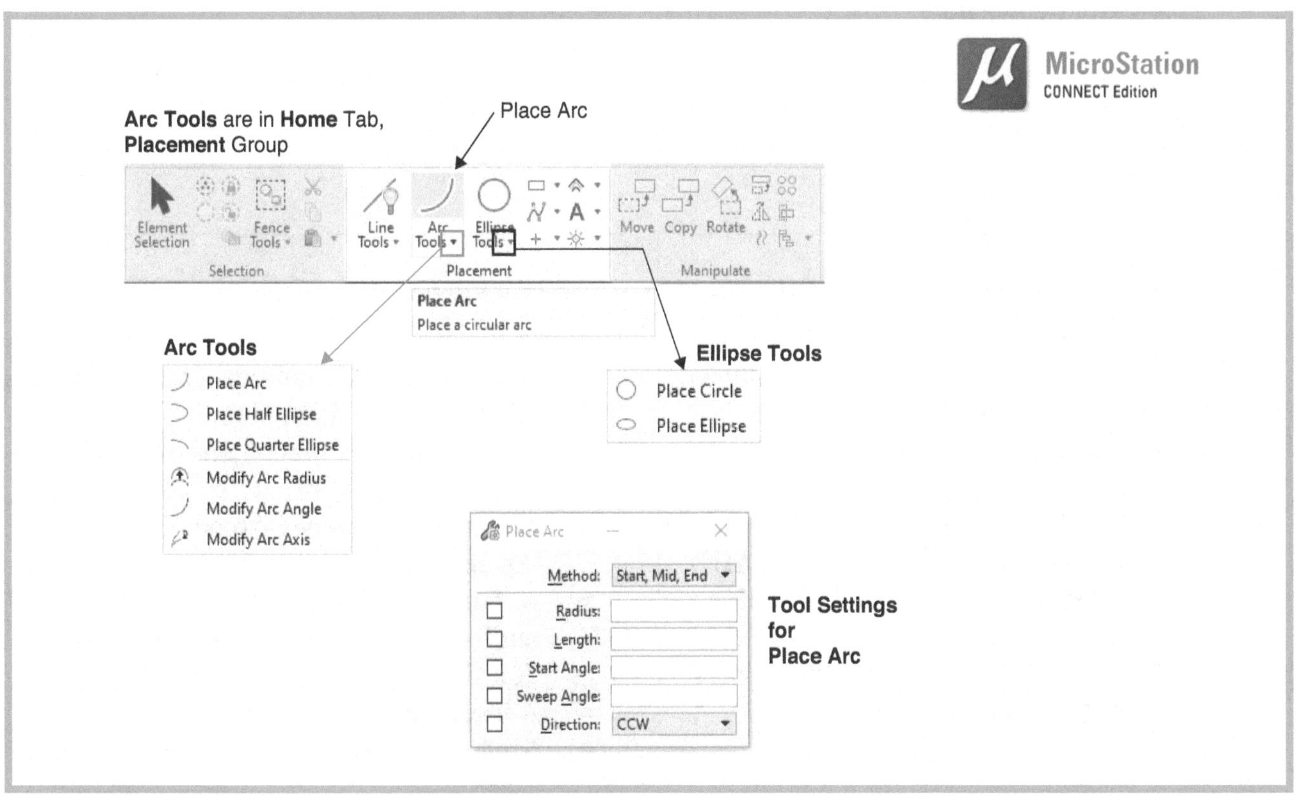

Fence Selection

Module 4 – Fences

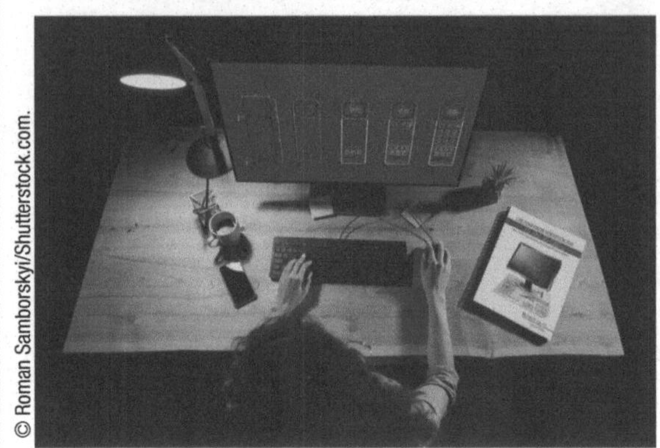

MicroStation V8*i*

MicroStation
CONNECT Edition

and
Introduction to Civil Engineering

Michael D. Jue, P.E.

Module 4 Objectives

1. Learn about Multiple Object Selection Methods & Modes. How to activate and switch back and forth.
2. Become familiar with the advantages and disadvantages of each method and learn to recognize the appropriate situation for each method.
3. Work through exercises with the Selection Modes.
4. Continue drawing exercises already in progress, start using the new selection methods.
5. Start additional exercises as time permits.

MicroStation Fence Modes

- MicroStation has 3 distinct methods of selecting objects
- Using the datapoint is similar to AutoCAD's "picking" objects
- Using MicroStation's FENCE tool is similar to many of AutoCAD's WINDOW selections but also offers "VOID" modes
- Using MicroStation's "SELECT TOOL" was covered in session 1

MicroStation Fence Modes

- MicroStation's default mode of selection is the datapoint
- If a FENCE is placed and the "Use Fence" option of a command is activated, the fence "mode" defines the operation
- A fenced region can be rectangular, multisided or circular (only one fence at a time)
- A fence remains active until deactivated
- Modes remain until changed by the user

Fence Modes

- Modes govern the Fence Operations
  - INSIDE — Selects those Fully inside the Fence
  - OVERLAP — Selects Inside & those Touching Fence
  - CLIP — Selects Inside & Cuts the objects @ boundary
  - VOID — Selects those Fully outside
  - VOID-OVERLAP — Selects Outside and Touching
  - VOID-CLIP — Selects Outside and cuts them @ boundary

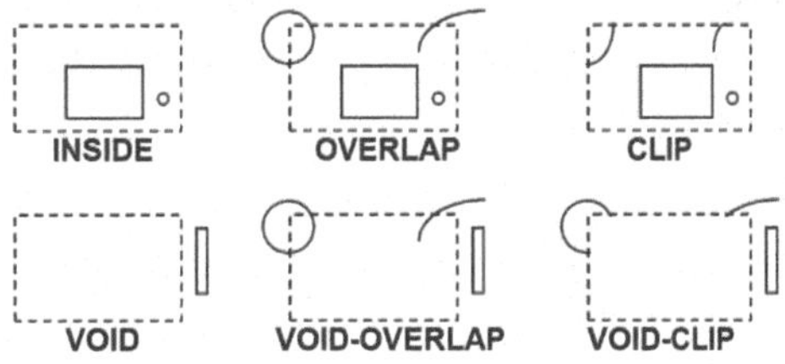

Inside Mode

- Inside Mode - Fully inside the Fence
- Always set mode back to <u>Inside Mode</u>

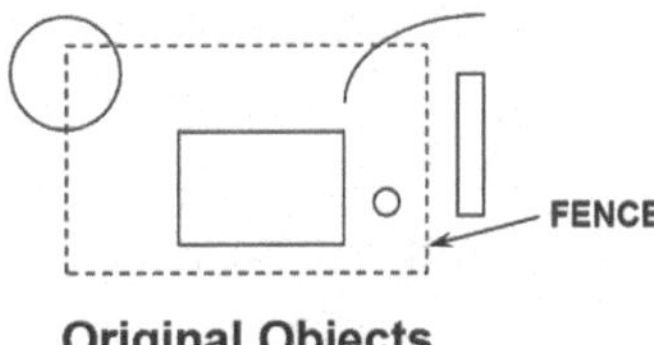

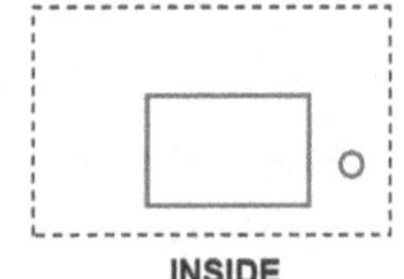

AutoCAD calls this "Window"

Using INSIDE mode, these objects would be <u>selected</u> to be operated on by the command

OVERLAP Mode

- Overlap Mode - "Inside" & Also Touching the Fence

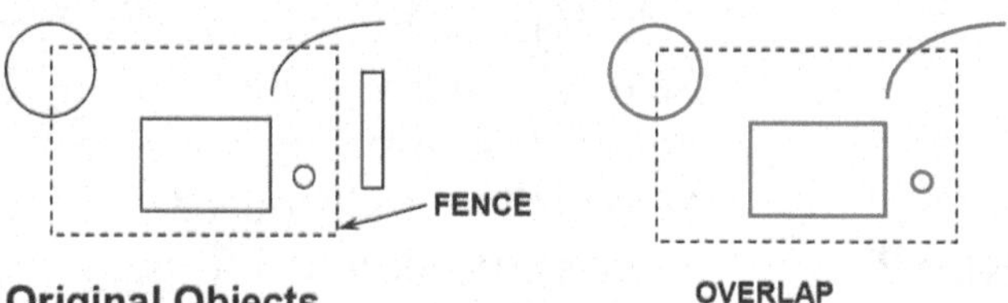

AutoCAD calls this "CROSSING"

Using OVERLAP mode, these objects would be <u>selected</u> to be operated on by the command

CAD Companion Workbook 4.7

CLIP Mode

- Clip Mode - Inside & Touching are CUT Acts like a "cookie cutter"

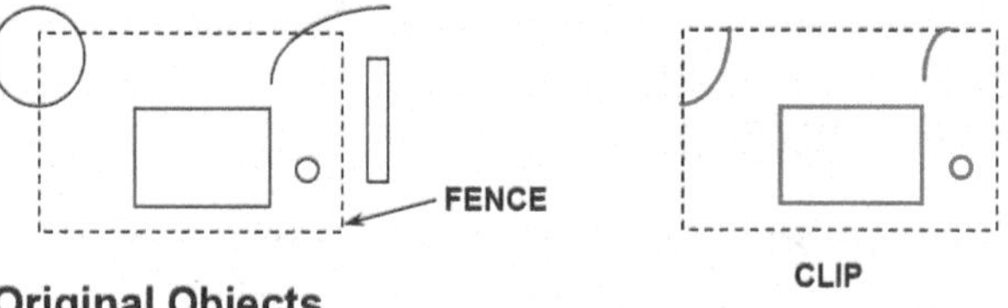

See Special Notes on Clip Mode, slide 4-14

Using CLIP mode, these objects would be <u>selected</u> to be operated on by the command

CAD Companion Workbook 4.8

Inside Mode

- Inside Mode with a multi-sided Fence placed (shape fence)

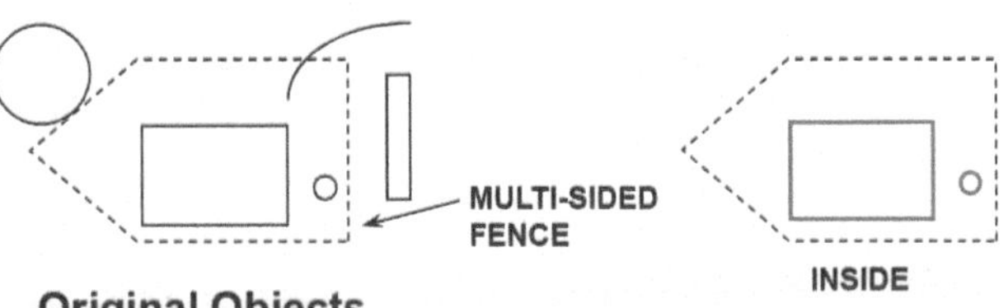

AutoCAD calls this "WPolygon"

Using INSIDE mode, these objects would be <u>selected</u> to be operated on by the command

CAD Companion Workbook 4.9

OVERLAP Mode

- Overlap Mode with a multi-sided fence Placed

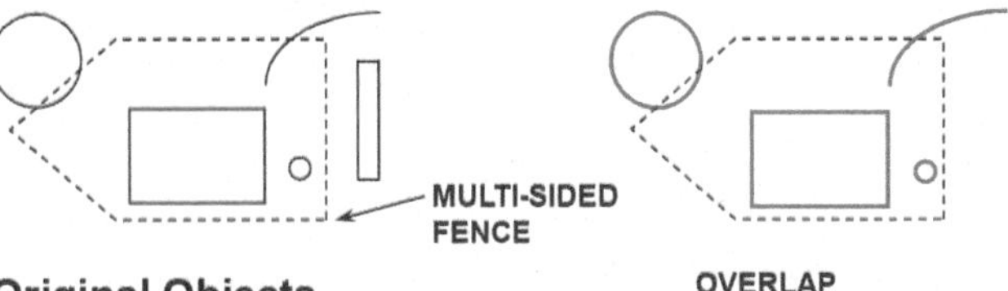

AutoCAD calls this "CPolygon"

Using OVERLAP mode, these objects would be <u>selected</u> to be operated on by the command

CAD Companion Workbook 4.10

VOID Mode

- VOID - Objects Fully "outside" selected Also unofficially called "outside" mode

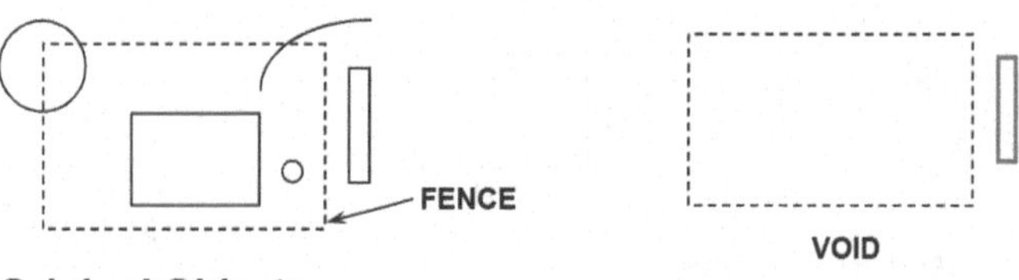

Original Objects

See Special Notes on Void Mode, slide 4-14

Using VOID mode, these objects would be <u>selected</u> to be operated on by the command

CAD Companion Workbook 4.11

Fence Selection Modes

- VOID OVERLAP - Objects Fully "outside" and overlapping are selected

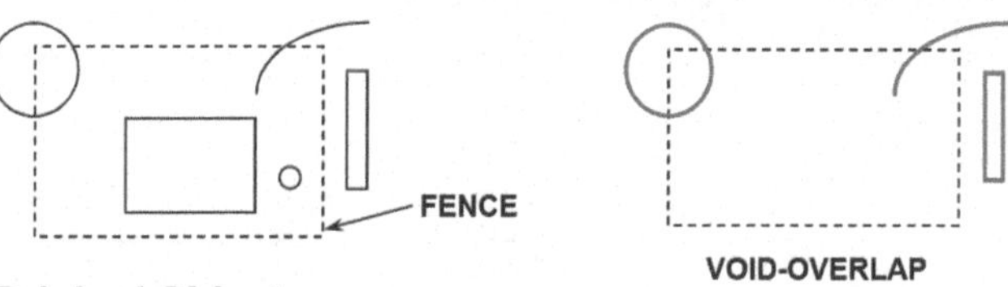

Original Objects

See Special Notes on Void Mode, slide 4-14

Using VOID-OVERLAP mode, these objects would be <u>selected</u> to be operated on by the command

CAD Companion Workbook 4.12

Fence Selection Modes

- VOID CLIP - Objects Fully "outside" and overlapping are CUT

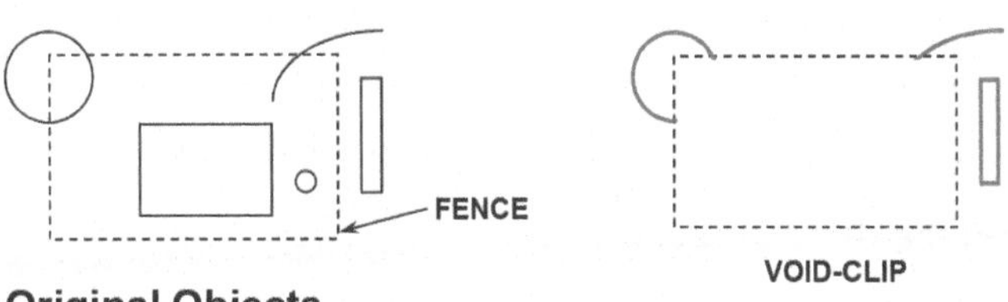

Original Objects

See Special Notes on Void Mode, slide 4-14

Using VOID-CLIP mode, these objects would be <u>selected</u> to be operated on by the command

Special Notes: Void & Clip

- **Many users <u>mistakenly</u> associate Void modes with DELETE. Void mode <u>SELECTS elements</u> outside of the fence for WHATEVER operation you desire, such as move, copy, rotate, scale, change attributes, or delete, etc.**
- **The word Void is used as a NOUN (meaning "outside"). Think of it as meaning the Void of Outer Space!**
- **Void is NOT used as a VERB (meaning "to strike out")**

- **Clip mode will function as shown in this packet if the setting "Optimized Fence Clipping" is turned OFF.**
- **Turn it off in Workspaces > Preferences > Operation, uncheck Optimized Fence Clipping, then hit OK.**

  If using **CONNECT Edition**:
  File - Settings - User - Preferences - Operation
  (then uncheck Optimized Fence Clipping)

- **Optimized Fence Clipping affects clipping of closed elements. A closing segment is added, preserving the element as closed, if it is ON (this is not usually desired)**

Wait! Before you Draw anything . . .

See these Additional tips, tidbits and Challenge Questions

TIPS & TIDBITS

© Shutterstock.com

1. **Don't be "Stingy" when placing a Fence.** Also, **don't try to be "Green" by saving electrons when placing a Fence.** When a user needlessly places a fence very tightly about a set of elements, very often the user "misses" elements, forcing a **second effort** to try to "fence" in the elements.

   In both examples, here, the user is using INSIDE mode to try to select the shape and the two circles, only.

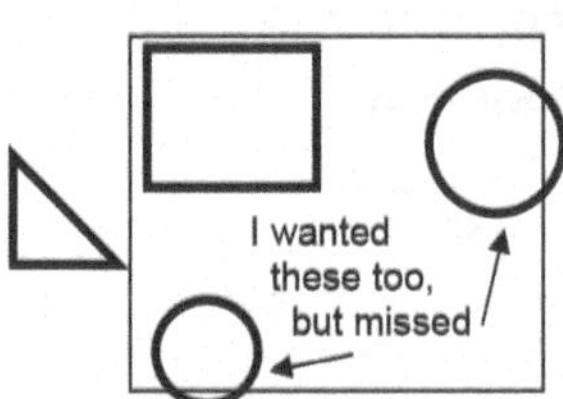

STINGY FENCE PLACEMENT THAT MISSES YOUR INTENDED CHOICES, FORCING REPEATED ATTEMPTS. I SPENT EXTRA EFFORT TO MISS THE THE TRIANGLE ON THE LEFT. DID I NEED TO DO THAT? NO!

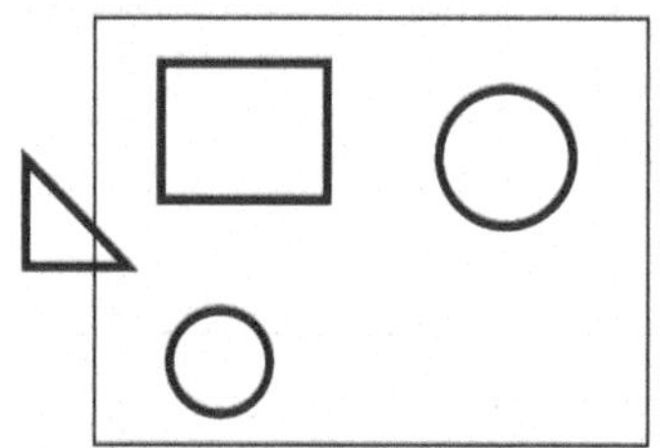

HERE IS A **GENEROUS** FENCE! AND I DON'T MISS ANYTHING! WHY DIDN'T I HAVE TO AVOID TRIANGLE LIKE IN THE DIAGRAM ON THE LEFT? ANSWER: INSIDE MODE WILL NOT SELECT THE TRIANGLE IF THE FENCE GOES THRU THE TRIANGLE.

2. After using a **fence mode** other than INSIDE, return the setting back to INSIDE mode. INSIDE mode is the default and most users will expect that the mode is set to INSIDE. This is "sort of like" expecting the gears in a car to be set to DRIVE and FORWARD, rather than REVERSE when getting into a running car.
3. Get into the habit of doing a **File > Save Settings** (short-cut key-in is <Ctrl> F) immediately after setting the Working Units. This simple habit will prevent lots of lost time and improve your efficiency.
4. The **VOID fence selection mode** is quite useful when you find that there is "some unknown space garbage" somewhere way out there on your drawing. Eventually, when you do a Fit View, the screen will return a very large region and you may eventually find that your drawing is a little spec on the side of the view and that there is some "other stuff" out there somewhere that the Fit View is finding and Fitting into View.

   Get rid of "Space Garbage" like this: Find the stuff you want to keep on your drawing and then place a fence around it. Set the fence selection mode to VOID, then use ***Delete Fence Contents*** *to delete everything that is "outside" of the fence. Voila, the next time you do a Fit View, you should now only see the stuff you kept. The space garbage has been deleted. Now remember to return the fence selection mode back to INSIDE as mentioned in #2 above.*

CHALLENGE QUESTIONS

Answers in Answer Section

Note: Some of these **challenge questions** may come from material shown by your instructor in class and may not be mentioned in this CAD Companion Workbook.

1. What are the short-cut key-ins that set:
   a. Text Height and Text Width to the same value?
   b. Font selection
   c. Text height only
   d. Text width only
   e. Line Spacing
2. What level are your elements drawn on, if you neglected to create or set any levels?
3. Name the first four (and most commonly used) Fence selection modes. Hint: INSIDE is one of them.
4. Do level names have to be set only to numbers?
5. What is the short-cut key-in to do each of the following:
   a. Turn ON all the levels
   b. Turn OFF all the levels
   c. Set the active level to a certain level
6. What is the procedure to create a new level? Describe. Then use it to create several new levels in a sample drawing.
7. How do you?
   a. Rename a level (change the name of one that already exists)
   b. Delete a level (get rid of one you don't want)
8. How do you get rid of a Fence shape that is on your screen that you are done with? (note: this is not the same as deleting the fence contents—This question asks about the fence shape, itself, not the elements you are trying to select.)
9. Using the Fence tool and the Stretch tool, make a copy of your original TUB drawing and create a version of the TUB that is exactly 18" longer, but with the same width and radii in the corners. You should be able to accomplish this in one operation of the Stretch tool without the need to re-draw any elements. Check your work with the **measure distance between points** tool. You will have to use precision input to specify the needed stretch distance, of course.
10. Estimate the number of CAD practice hours you have worked so far. Check your productivity ratio on the CAD Learning Curve, pg 14. Is the ratio much lower than you expected? That is OK. You have only just begun and will speed up immensely after much more practice. Don't believe you are so slow compared to "by hand"? Do this simple experiment. With a PEN, draw a curved line on a piece of paper. Now, write you name along the top of the curved line in block letters, but gradually increase the size of each letter as you go. Now do that with CAD and print it out. Compare the time. (No – obviously you would take a very long time on CAD, since you don't even know how to do these things that are so SIMPLE by Hand) Don't get discouraged. There's more to learn!

Exercise Concepts / Tools / Lessons for MODULES 4 / 5

Stretch-Limo

Instructor-guided exercise showing Stretch tool, Line-strings, Drop Element, Locked elements, Properties and additional new concepts.

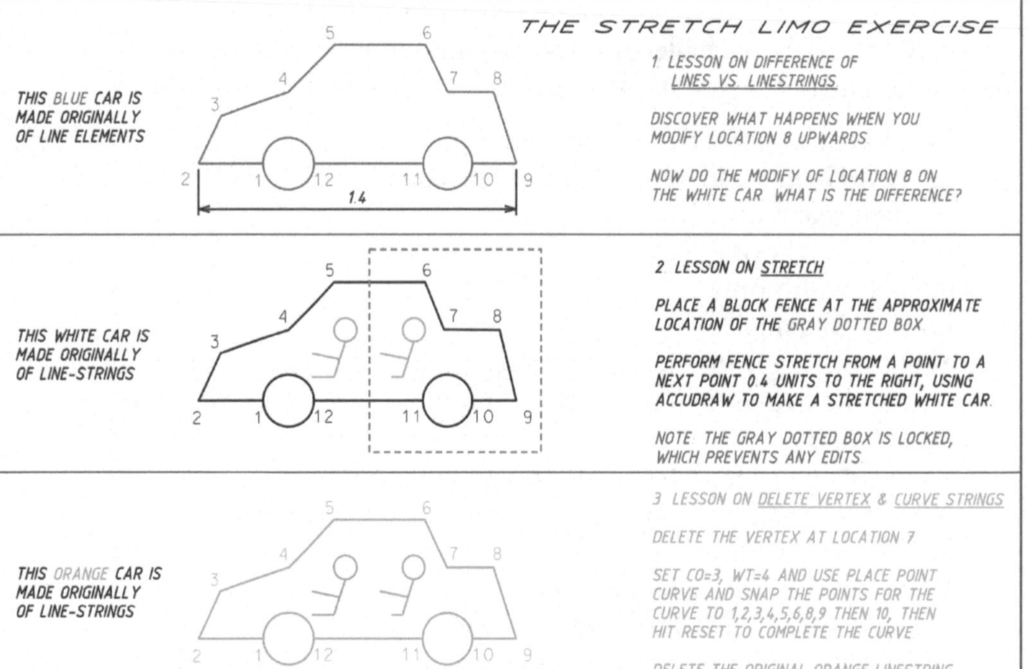

THE STRETCH LIMO EXERCISE
THIS BLUE CAR IS MADE ORIGINALLY OF LINE ELEMENTS
1.4
1. LESSON ON DIFFERENCE OF LINES VS. LINESTRINGS
DISCOVER WHAT HAPPENS WHEN YOU MODIFY LOCATION 8 UPWARDS
NOW DO THE MODIFY OF LOCATION 8 ON THE WHITE CAR. WHAT IS THE DIFFERENCE?
THIS WHITE CAR IS MADE ORIGINALLY OF LINE-STRINGS
2. LESSON ON STRETCH
PLACE A BLOCK FENCE AT THE APPROXIMATE LOCATION OF THE GRAY DOTTED BOX
PERFORM FENCE STRETCH FROM A POINT TO A NEXT POINT 0.4 UNITS TO THE RIGHT, USING ACCUDRAW TO MAKE A STRETCHED WHITE CAR.
NOTE: THE GRAY DOTTED BOX IS LOCKED, WHICH PREVENTS ANY EDITS.
THIS ORANGE CAR IS MADE ORIGINALLY OF LINE-STRINGS
3. LESSON ON DELETE VERTEX & CURVE STRINGS
DELETE THE VERTEX AT LOCATION 7
SET CO=3, WT=4 AND USE PLACE POINT CURVE AND SNAP THE POINTS FOR THE CURVE TO 1,2,3,4,5,6,8,9 THEN 10, THEN HIT RESET TO COMPLETE THE CURVE.
DELETE THE ORIGINAL ORANGE LINESTRING TO SEE THE RESULTANT RED CURVE-STRING

Parking-Lot

Instructor-partial guided exercise that shows new techniques for increased efficiency with basic precision input and edits. Introduces measurements, dimensions and some advanced text tools. p292

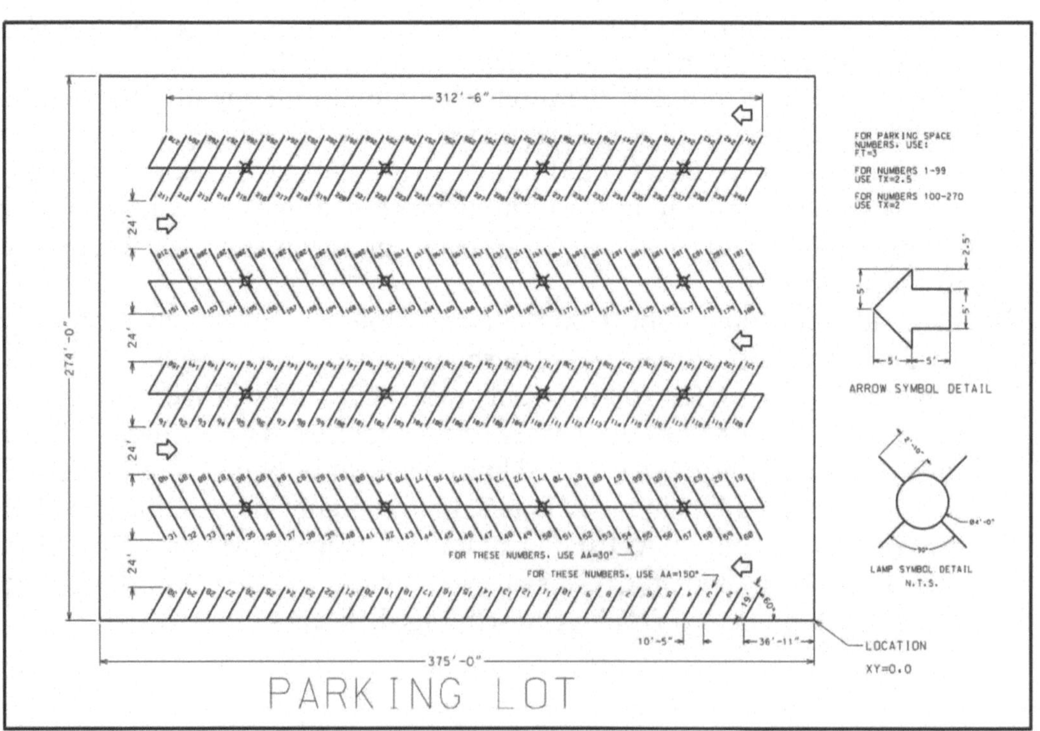

Module 5

Data Fields/Measurements/Dimensions

Key CAD exercise concepts for Week 5/6:

The student is introduced to more specifics of using measurement tools to get location and spacing information off of a drawing and how annotate elements using dimension tools. More text options are also explored.

General/All

- Measurement Tools
  - Between points
  - Length
  - Area (by:)
    - Element
    - Intersection
    - Union
    - Difference
    - Flood
    - Points
- Dimensioning Tools
  - Dimension settings
    - Units, labels, text size, placement
  - Dimension components
    - Dimension Line, Extension Lines, Terminators
  - True & View settings
  - Dimension Element, Dimension Size with Arrows
  - Modify element to adjust dimension placements
- Data Enter Fields
  - Creating
  - Fill in Single Enter Data Field
  - Fill in Automatic
  - Editing Enter Data Fields
- Using View Attributes to Display ON/OFF
  - Enter Data Fields

Phone to "F" The student will gain expertise thru additional practice with placement/manipulation tools.
Student to work on this drawing without specific directions provided
Various precision input/placement and manipulations as needed

Dimensioned Versions of previous Drawings
The student applies dimensioning to drawings previously assigned
Develop familiarity with Dimension settings and placement

Place Block Shape, precision input,Rotate, copy
Measure Area
Measure by Flood, points

Dimension setting & placement
View alignment, True alignment
Modification of dimension placement

Data Enter Fields: Creation, Filling in, Editing

Draw in Full Scale

A basic Fundamental that users must get used to is the notion of drawing everything in CAD in "Full Scale". What this simply means is that the objects in your drawing are to be drawn at their actual sizes, i.e. if a door is 3 ft. wide in real-life, draw it 3 ft. wide in the CAD.

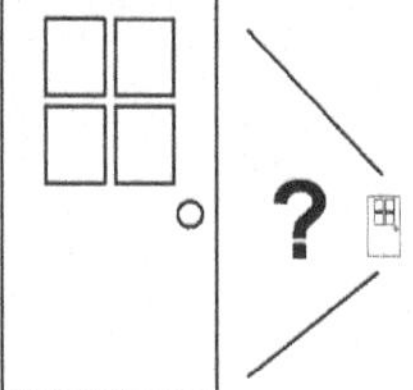

DON'T DO THIS: Figure out with a calculator what the door is in 1/4 inch scale and attempt to "scale" it before you draw it. Like this, architects know that a 3 ft. wide door in 1/4 inch scale is 3/4 inch when plotted. Therefore, draw the door at 3/4 inch wide.

DO THIS: CAD is like a model of the real world. Draw everything full scale. Then, you can plot it out at whatever scale you wish!

Quotes to Ponder:

"The brain is a wonderful organ. It starts the moment you get up and doesn't stop until you get into the office"

-ROBERT FROST

Another automatic function; Brain-Lock or Brain-OFF:

"The brain is a wonderful organ. It starts the moment you get up and doesn't stop until you get **in front of the computer**."

-anonymous CAD user

Data Fields/Measurements/Dimensions

© mofaez/Shutterstock.com

MicroStation V8*i*

MicroStation CONNECT Edition

AUTOCAD

and

Introduction to Civil Engineering

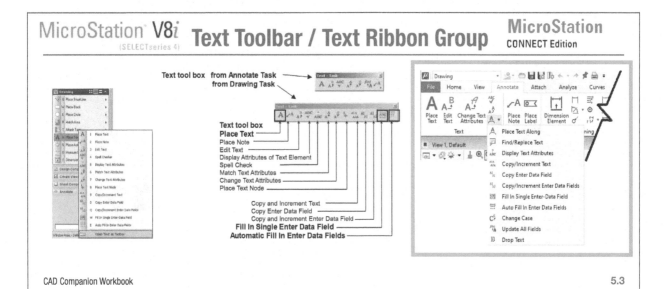

Michael D. Jue, P.E.

CAD Companion Workbook 5.1

Module 5 Objectives

1. Usage of some specific tools related to Text, called Enter Data Fields.
2. Usage of Measurement tools to quickly measure the properties of length, angle and area for 2D elements or regions.
3. Set-up usage and of the tremendously flexible Dimensioning tools.

CAD Companion Workbook 5.2

MicroStation V8*i* (SELECTseries 4) Text Toolbar / Text Ribbon Group MicroStation CONNECT Edition

Text tool box from Annotate Task
from Drawing Task

Text tool box
Place Text
Place Note
Edit Text
Display Attributes of Text Element
Spell Check
Match Text Attributes
Change Text Attributes
Place Text Node

Copy and Increment Text
Copy Enter Data Field
Copy and Increment Enter Data Field
Fill In Single Enter Data Field
Automatic Fill In Enter Data Fields

Drawing
File Home View Annotate Attach Analyze Curves
Place Text | Edit Text | Change Text Attributes | Place Note | Place Label | Dimension Element
Text
View 1, Default

Place Text Along
Find/Replace Text
Display Text Attributes
Copy/Increment Text
Copy Enter Data Field
Copy/Increment Enter Data Fields
Fill In Single Enter-Data Field
Auto Fill In Enter Data Fields
Change Case
Update All Fields
Drop Text

CAD Companion Workbook 5.3

Creating Enter Data Fields

- Enter Data Fields are a special type of text.
- They can be thought of basically as "blank" text fields that are placeholders for future text.
- Enter Data Fields (ED) are created with the regular **Place Text tool** and you simply enter underscore characters.
- Note: These are NOT underlines or dashes, but underscores created with this key with the shift.

<Shift> <_>

© Michael D. Jue

Magnified version of upper right keyboard

CAD Companion Workbook 5.4

Filling in the ED Fields

- Enter Data Fields might look like this when placed onto your HOTEL drawing shapes.
- And like this, when filled in.

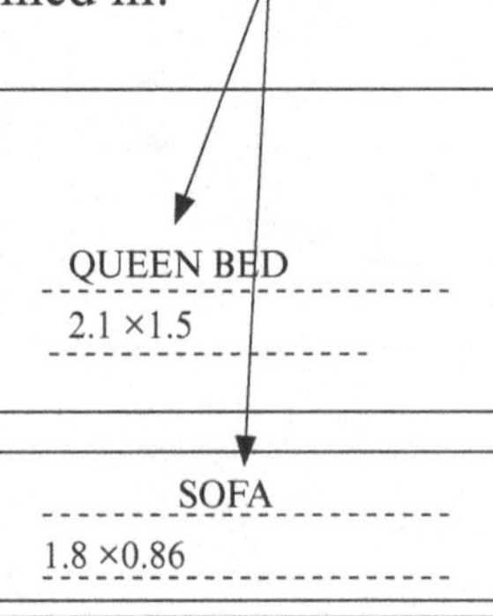

- Fill them in one at a time with the **Fill In Single Data Field Tool**

- Fill them in one after the other with the **Automatic Fill In Enter Data Fields**

- Choose the **view** in which there are blank ED then uSTN will hi-lite the field, you just type and hit <Enter>.

*Note: Your instructor will advise you of the updated procedure to create and fill Enter Data Fields in the CONNECT Edition.

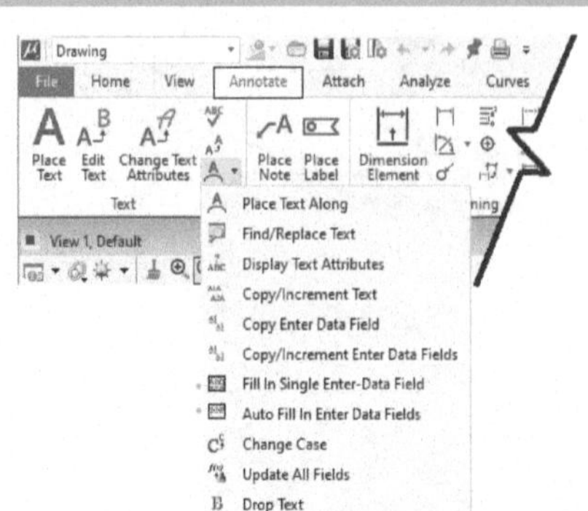

CAD Companion Workbook 5.5

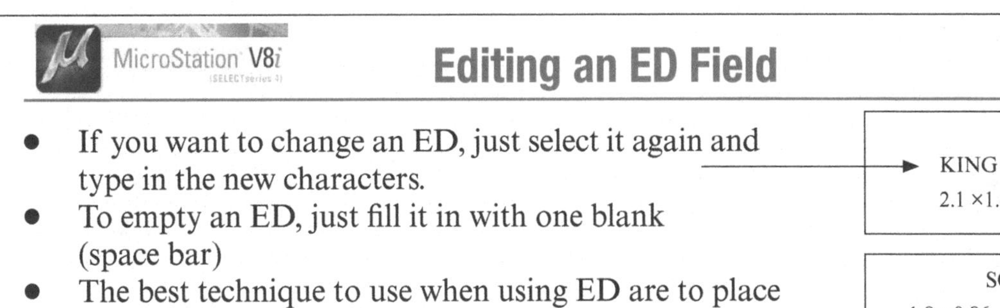

Editing an ED Field

- If you want to change an ED, just select it again and type in the new characters.
- To empty an ED, just fill it in with one blank (space bar)
- The best technique to use when using ED are to place them ALL where you want, then fill them in afterwards.

KING BED
2.1 ×1.5

SOFA
1.8 ×0.86

CAD Companion Workbook 5.6

Displaying OFF the ED fields

- Use View Attributes **<Ctrl> B** to turn off the display of the ED underscores after you have filled them in.

QUEEN BED
2.1 ×1.5

SOFA
1.8 ×0.86

- We will explore a good application of ED when getting to the PHONE F drawing.

CAD Companion Workbook 5.7

Add'l Place Text Methods:

To place fitted text

+

1. **Select the** *Place Text* tool.
   The Text Editor window opens if it is not already open.
2. Set Method to Fitted or Fitted V(iew) I(ndependent).
3. In the Text Editor window, type the text. See Entering and Editing Text.
4. Enter a data point to define the left end of the fitted text.
5. Enter a data point to position the right end of the text and define the height, width, and rotation angle.
6. Return to step 4 to place another instance of the same text. or Return to step 3 to place other text.

Place Text with Method set to Fitted or Fitted VI

1 Text 2

Multi-line text can be placed when Method is set to Fitted or Fitted VI only if the Text Editor Style preference is set to its default, Word Processor.

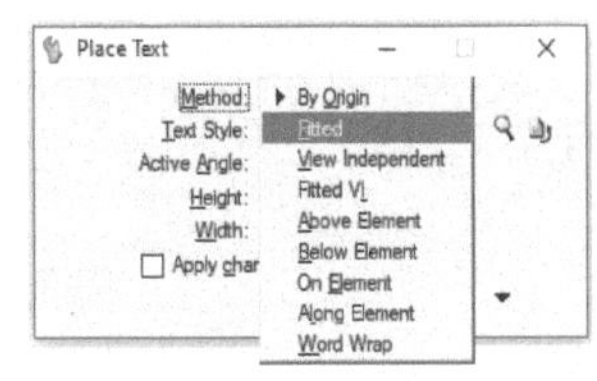

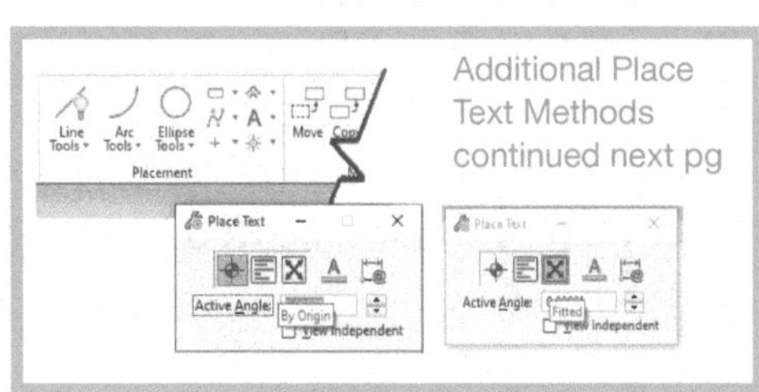

CAD Companion Workbook 5.8

Add'l Place Text Methods:

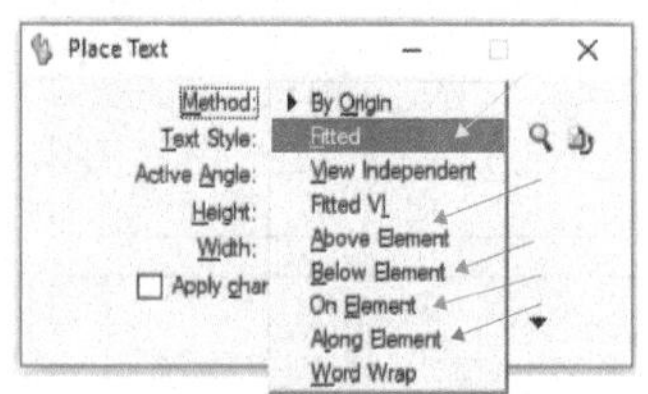

The word DANGER placed as an example of FITTED TEXT

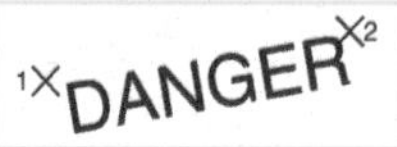

Note, the text size is set by the Place Text tool, depending on where the user selects the datapoint #1 and #2.

This example uses font ARIAL.

TEXT ABOVE EXAMPLE

TEXT BELOW EXAMPLE

GAS GAS GAS GAS ON ELEMENT EXAMPLE

ALONG ELEMENT EXAMPLE

Using these other methods, the text size can be set with: TX=__, TH=__ or TW=__

Spacing above or below is set with LS=__

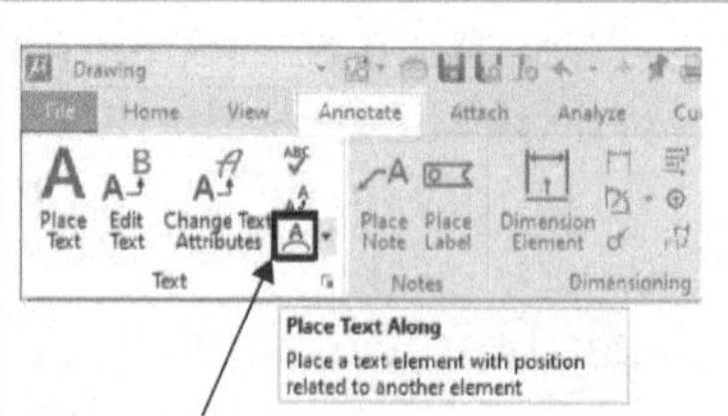

Selecting Place Text Along opens this dialog window, allowing additional choices of placement.

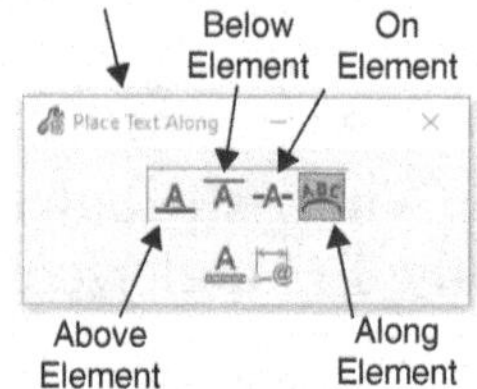

Reminder, the default Place Text method is BY Orgin (in Place Text). See page 147

Copy / Increment Text

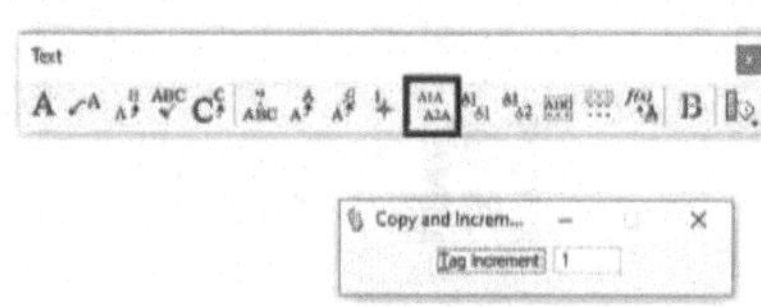

The copy / Increment Text tool can be used to create additional text elements starting off with a text element that is already in your file.

Example with the tag increment set to 1:

Making three new texts using the Copy / Increment tool. Select the existing text "LOT #10435", then data point at the locations 1, 2 and 3. LOT #10435 is copied and incremented

LOT #10435	1 LOT #10436
2 LOT #10437	3 LOT #10438

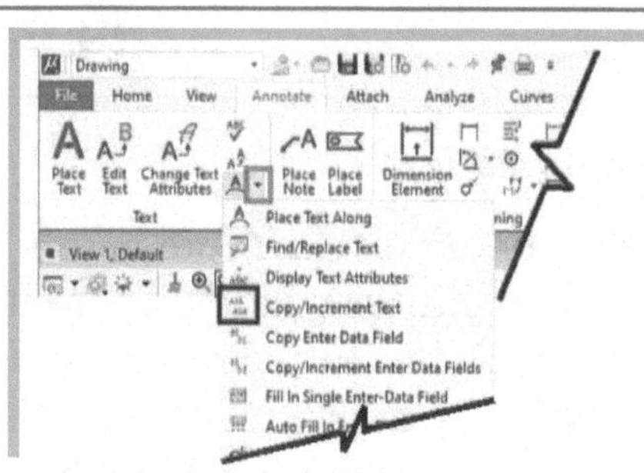

The Copy / Increment tool is especially useful in drawing exercise PARKING LOT. Pg 142 & 192. The parking space numbers are copy / incremented a precision distance each time with this key-in: DI=10:5,180|30 (first 30 numbers)(Please refer to the video lesson)

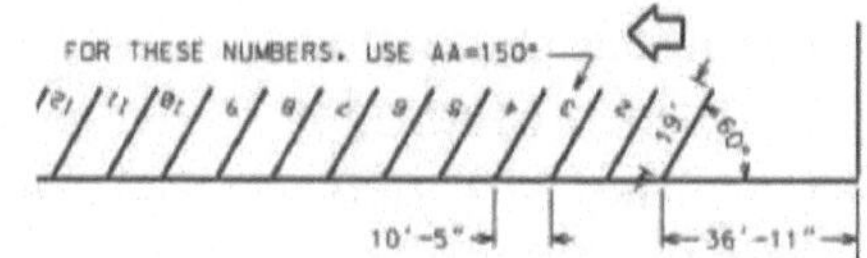

Portion of the PARKING LOT drawing exercise

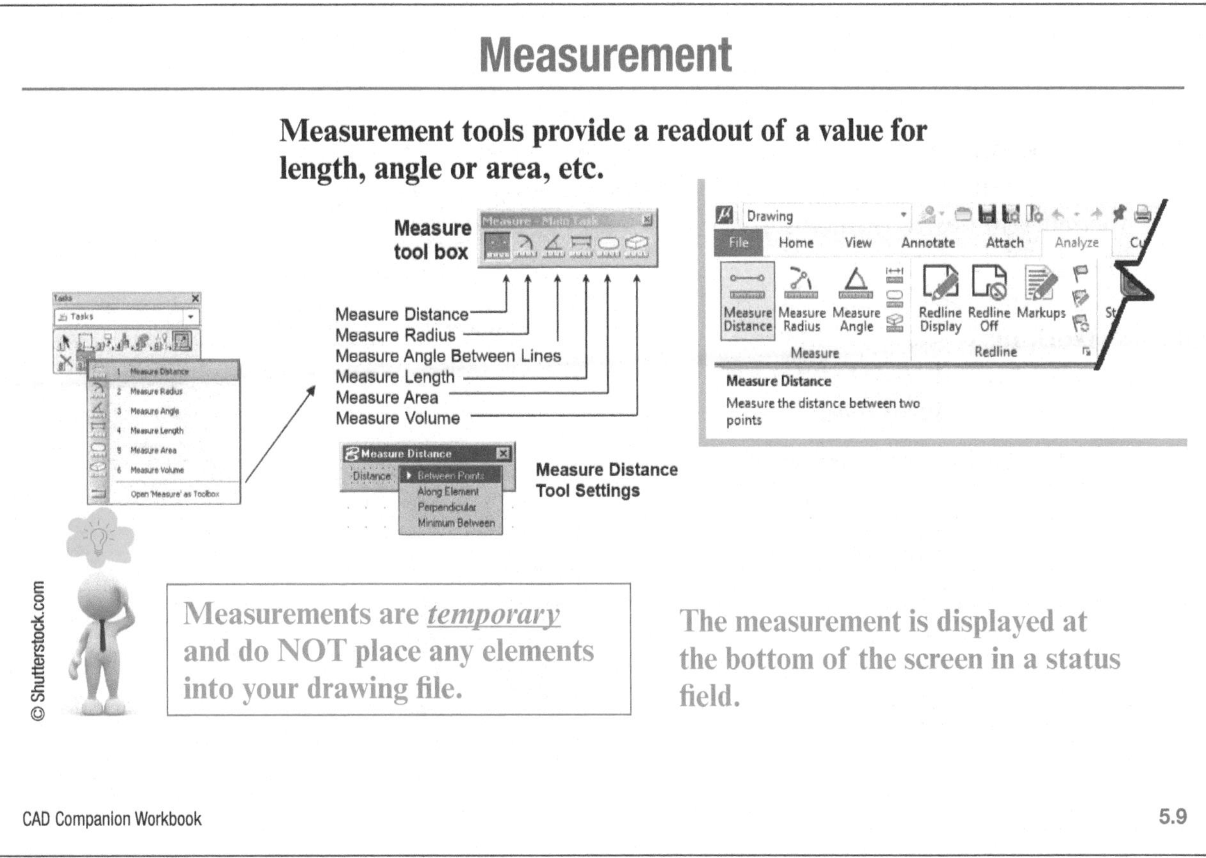
Measurement
Measurement tools provide a readout of a value for length, angle or area, etc.
Measure tool box
Measure Distance
Measure Radius
Measure Angle Between Lines
Measure Length
Measure Area
Measure Volume
Measure Distance Tool Settings
Drawing
File
Home
View
Annotate
Attach
Analyze
Measure Distance
Measure Radius
Measure Angle
Redline Display
Redline Off
Markups
Measure
Redline
Measure Distance
Measure the distance between two points
Measurements are *temporary* and do NOT place any elements into your drawing file.
The measurement is displayed at the bottom of the screen in a status field.
© Shutterstock.com
CAD Companion Workbook
5.9

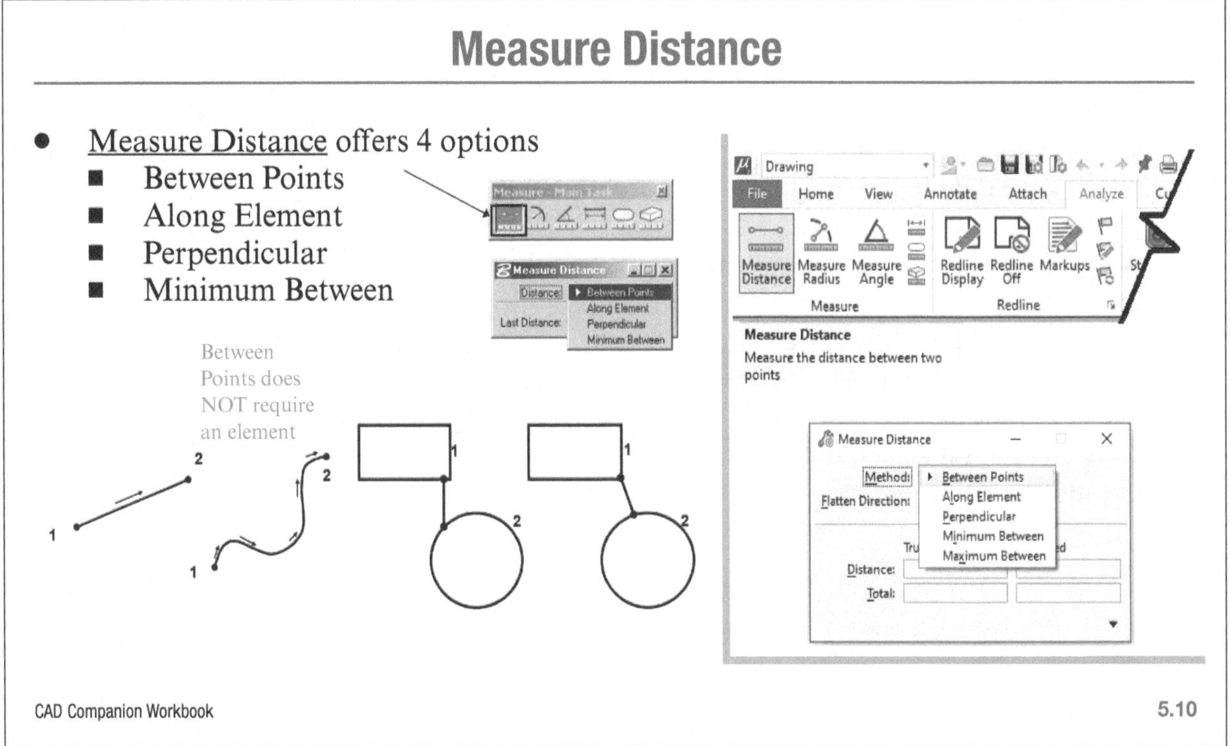
Measure Distance
Measure Distance offers 4 options
Between Points
Along Element
Perpendicular
Minimum Between
Between Points does NOT require an element
Drawing
File
Home
View
Annotate
Attach
Analyze
Measure Distance
Measure Radius
Measure Angle
Redline Display
Redline Off
Markups
Measure
Redline
Measure Distance
Measure the distance between two points
Measure Distance
Method:
Flatten Direction:
Between Points
Along Element
Perpendicular
Minimum Between
Maximum Between
Distance:
Total:
CAD Companion Workbook
5.10

Coordinate Readout

- If the readout at the bottom to the screen is not in the unit format you desire, you can change it.
- Use Settings > Design File > Working Units > Format
- Change format to **MU : SU** for a more meaningful readout.

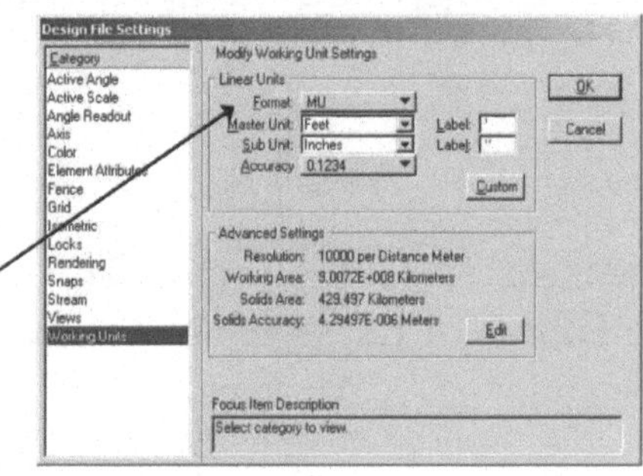

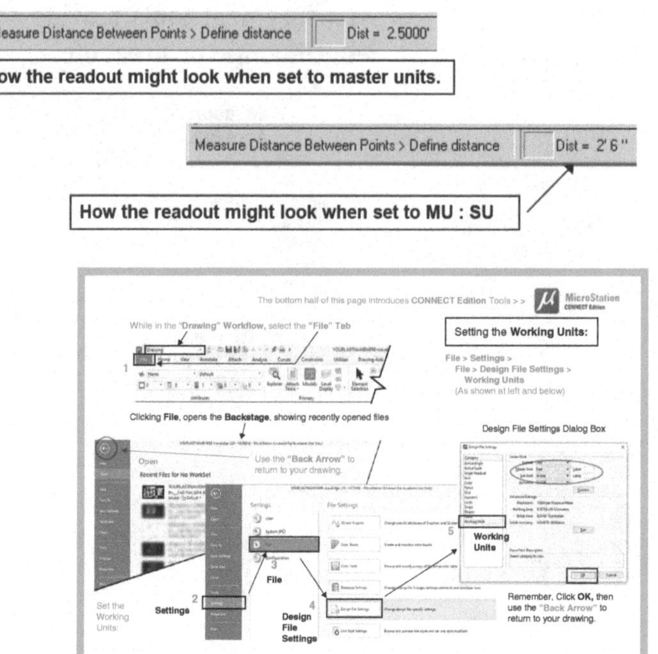

Measure Radius, Angle Betw & Length

- Measure Radius returns both radial and diameter measurements
  - select arcs or circles
- Measure Angle Between Lines
  - select 2 separate lines
- Measure Length returns both the length of a line and its angle
  - Select a line to measure
- Measure Area has many modes, shown on the next slide
- Measure Volume requires a 3D drawing containing solid shapes

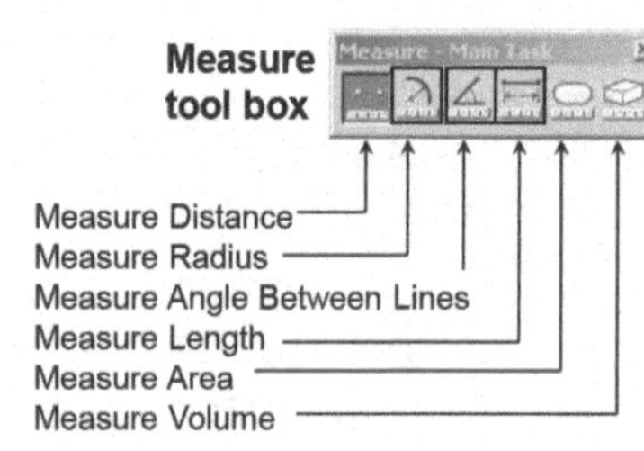

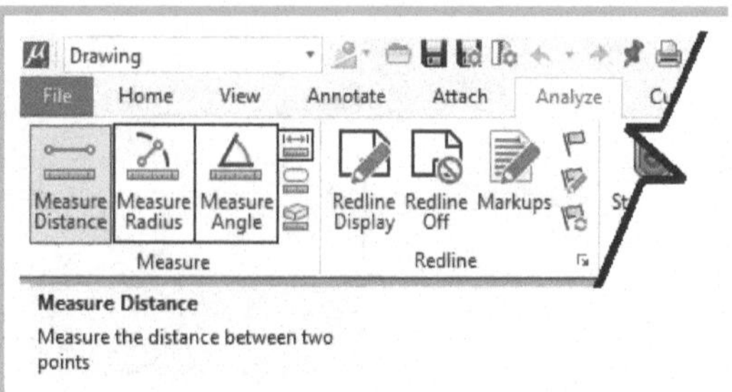

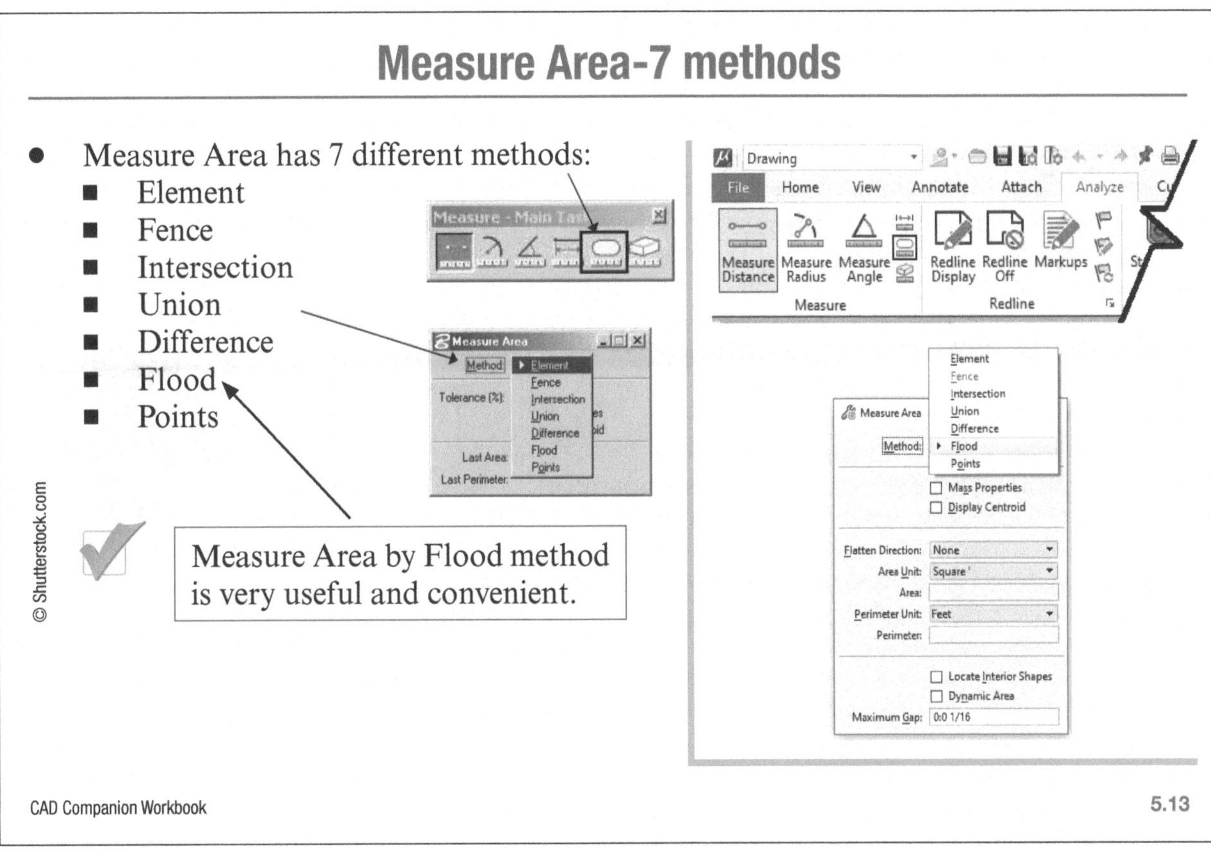
Measure Area-7 methods
Measure Area has 7 different methods:
Element
Fence
Intersection
Union
Difference
Flood
Points
Measure Area by Flood method is very useful and convenient.
© Shutterstock.com
Drawing
File
Home
View
Annotate
Attach
Analyze
Measure Distance
Measure Radius
Measure Angle
Redline Display
Redline Off
Markups
Measure
Redline
Measure Area
Method:
Element
Fence
Intersection
Union
Difference
Flood
Points
Mass Properties
Display Centroid
Flatten Direction:
None
Area Unit:
Square
Area:
Perimeter Unit:
Feet
Perimeter:
Locate Interior Shapes
Dynamic Area
Maximum Gap:
0:0 1/16
CAD Companion Workbook
5.13

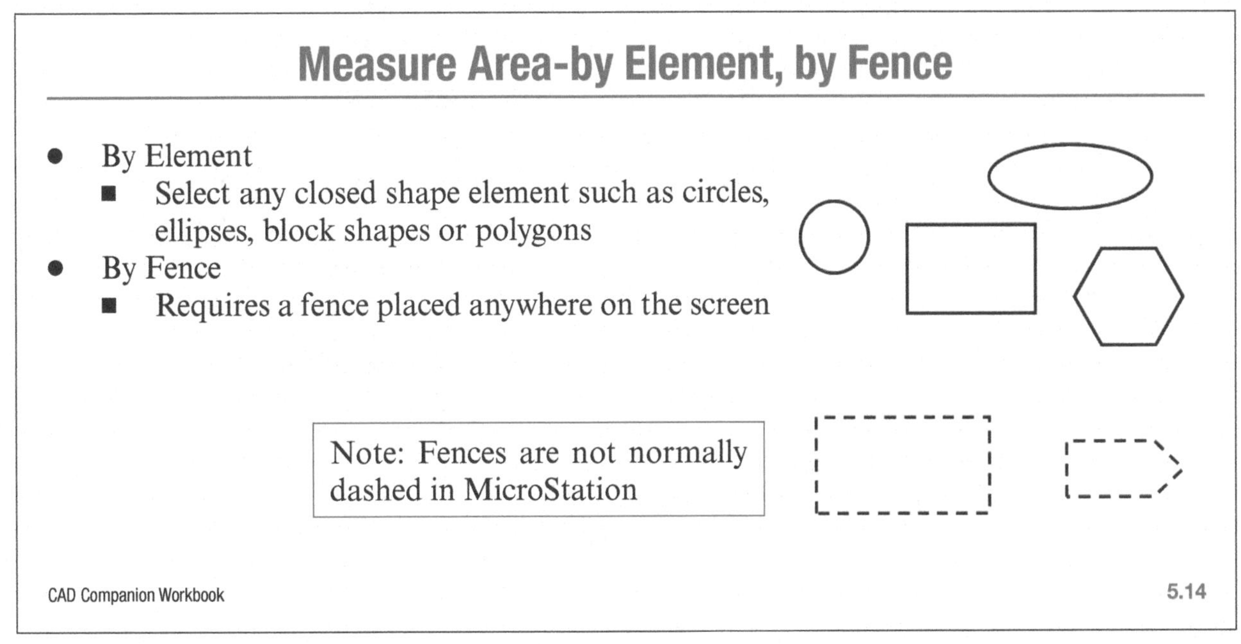
Measure Area-by Element, by Fence
By Element
Select any closed shape element such as circles, ellipses, block shapes or polygons
By Fence
Requires a fence placed anywhere on the screen
Note: Fences are not normally dashed in MicroStation
CAD Companion Workbook
5.14

Measure Area-Intersection, Union

- Intersection
  - Select more than one element: the common, intersecting area is measured
  - Reset to complete
- Union
  - Select more than one element: the union of the elements is measured
  - Reset to complete

Note: These are called Boolean operators

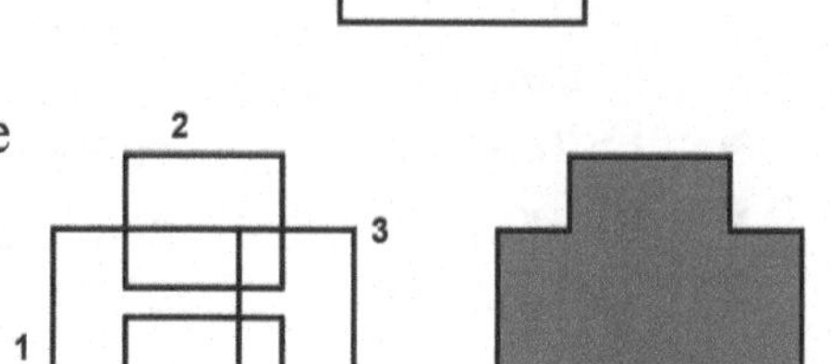

CAD Companion Workbook 5.15

Measure Area-Difference, Flood

- Difference
  - The first element "subtracting" the common area of the other elements is measured
  - Reset to complete
- Flood
  - The area of any enclosed region is measured
  - Data point within the region, then accept to initiate measurement

Any hole in your region will result in the error message: No enclosing region found

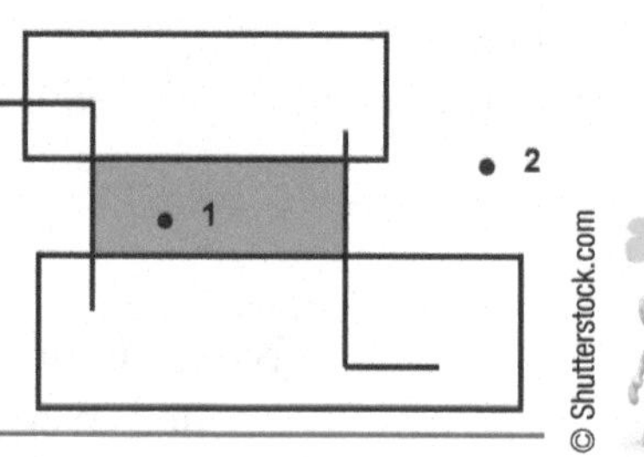

CAD Companion Workbook 5.16

Measure Area-by Points

- Points
  - Use Data Points to define your region
  - Reset to complete
  - Use when a quick measurement is needed
  - Use when there are no elements bounding your region
  - Snap to exact points if accuracy is desired

Example: Area of the Courtyard is needed roughly

Notes/Questions:

Dimensions

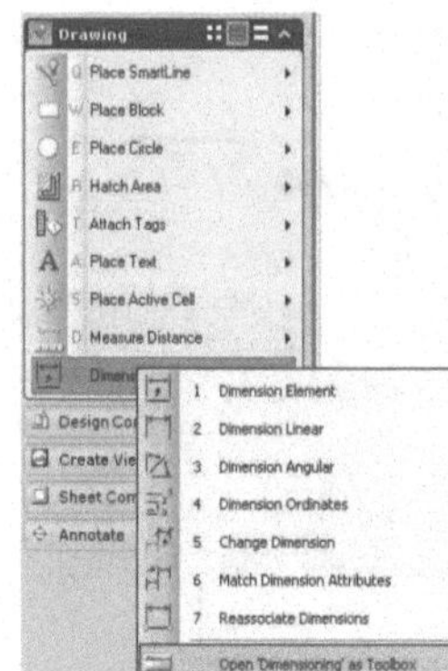

Dimension tools place a special type of element called a dimension element onto your drawing.

The Dimension toolbar resized as a horizontal bar. A preferred configuration

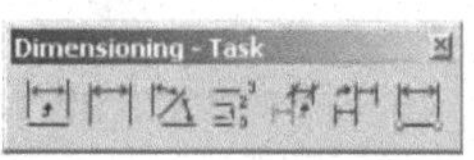

Dimensions are not the same as measurements. Dimensions are a type of element placed onto your drawing file.

Remember:

Measurements are Temporary, but, Dimensions are Permanent placements.

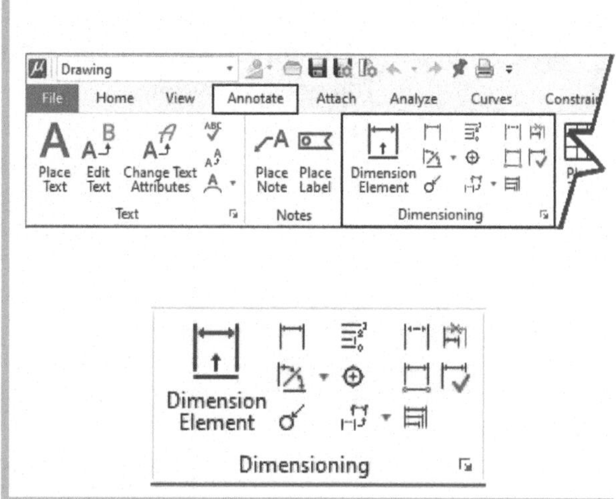

Example Dimensions-general

Dimensions can show length, angle, radius, diameter, center-marks, etc.

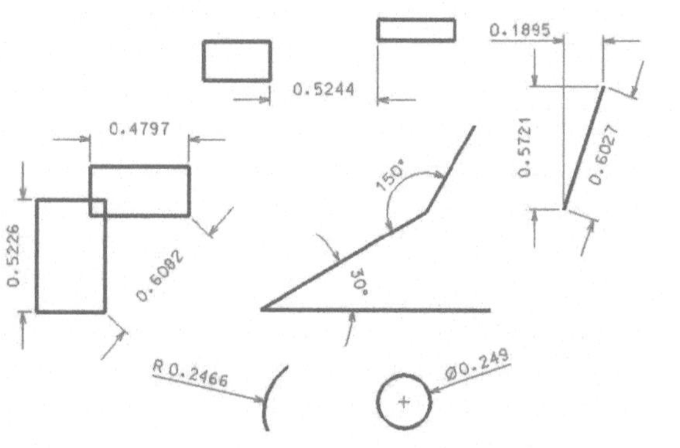

Dimension Element Components

- Basic components:
  - Dimension Text
  - Dimension Line
  - Terminators
  - Extension Lines (also called witness lines)
- Dimensions are complex elements

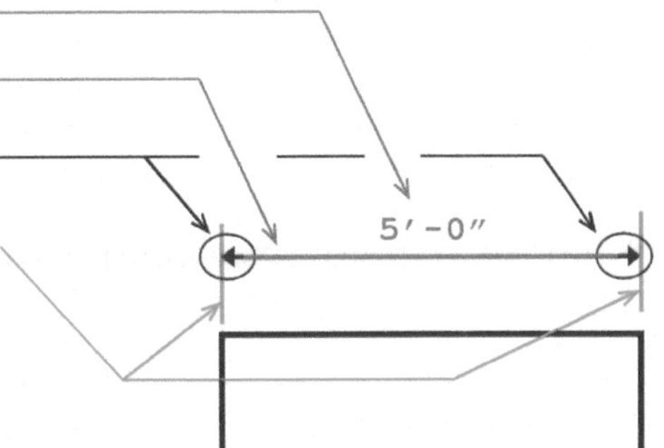

CAD Companion Workbook 5.21

Dimension Styles

- Before we place any dimensions, we must learn about dimension element styles
- Use the pull-down: **Element > Dimension Styles**
- Some specific dimension setting examples are shown on the following slides.

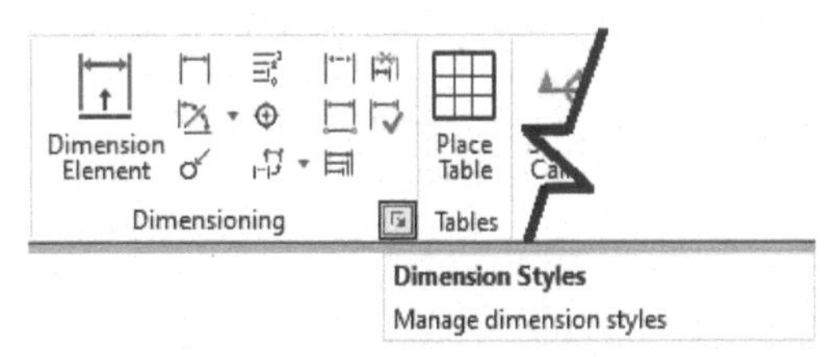

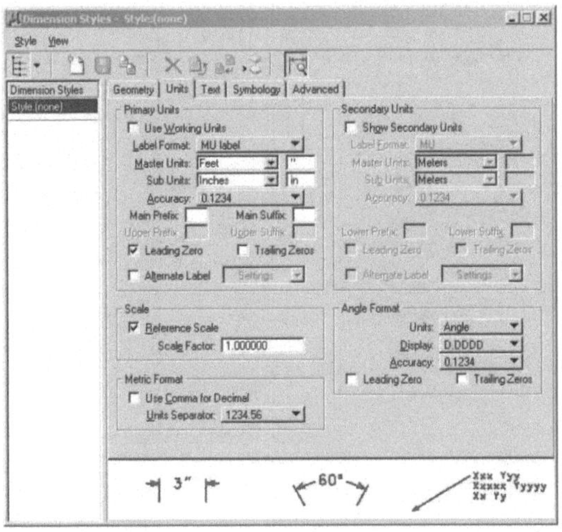

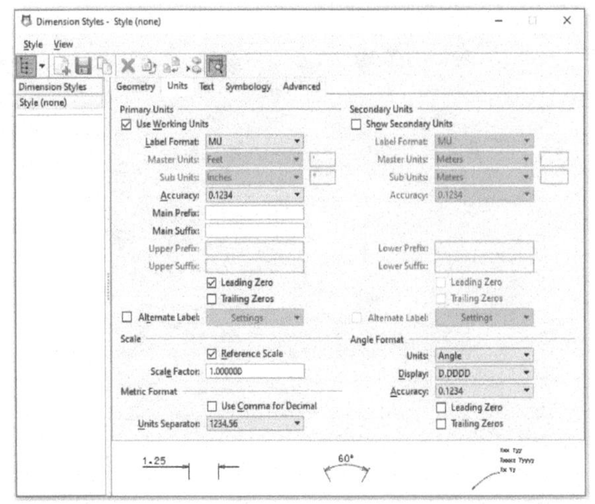

CAD Companion Workbook 5.22

Example: MU (no label)

- **Units can show:**
  - master units only
  - both the master units and sub-units with labels
  - sub-units with labels

  Note: These other settings that are greyed out are shown on the other pages

2.5
1.333
1
2.333
0.666
0.582

Master units, decimal feet, no label

Units > Label Format: > MU

- **Units can show:**
  - master units only

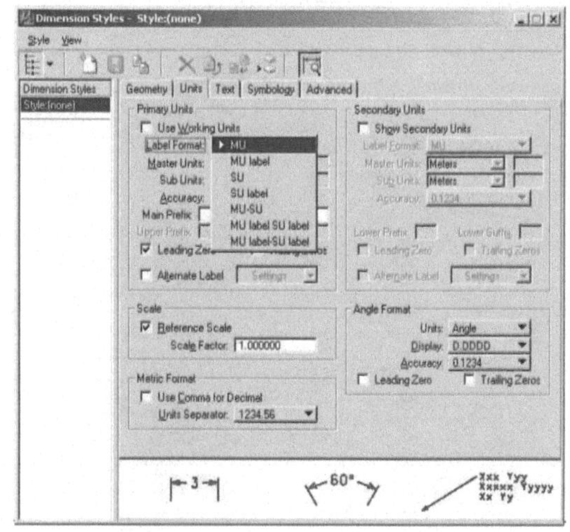

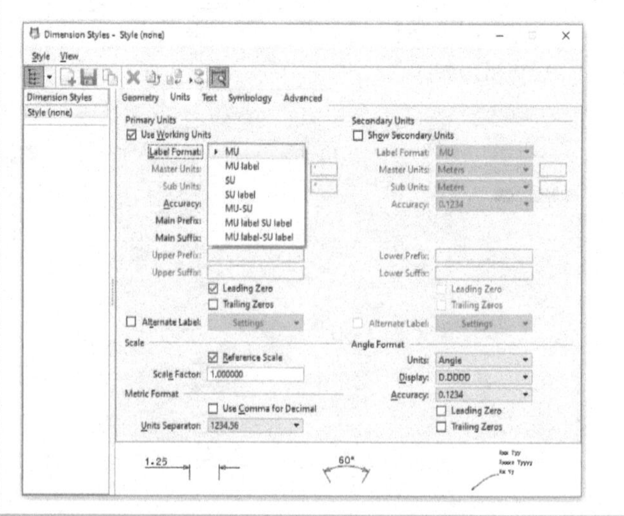

Example: MU label – SU label

- **Units can show:**
  - master units only
  - both the master units and sub-units with labels
  - sub-units with labels

    Note: These other settings that are greyed out are shown on the other pages

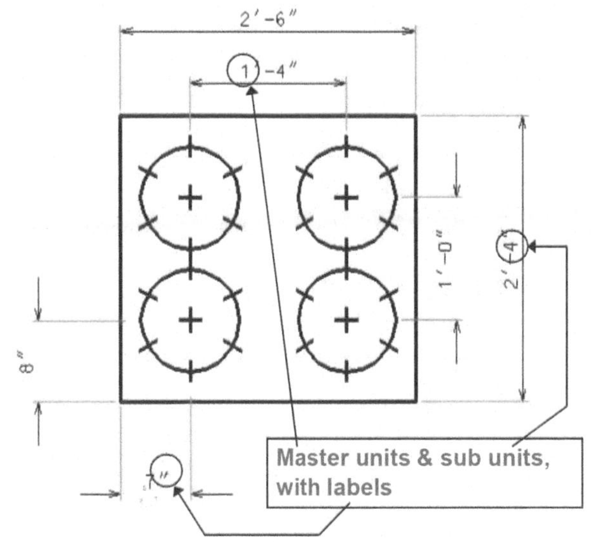

CAD Companion Workbook

5.25

Units > Label Format: > MU label - SU Label

- **Units can show:**
  - both the master units and sub-units with labels

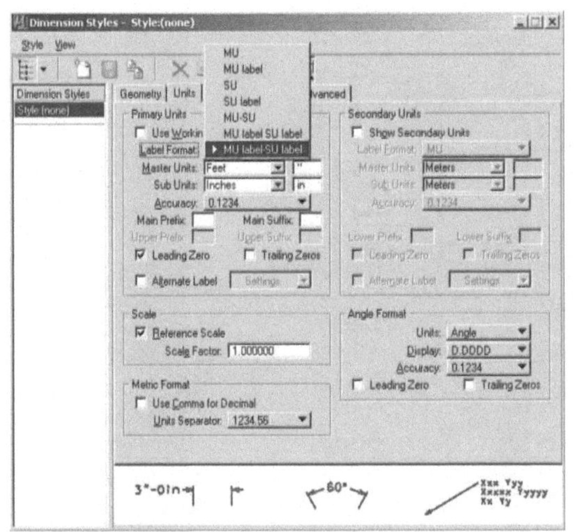

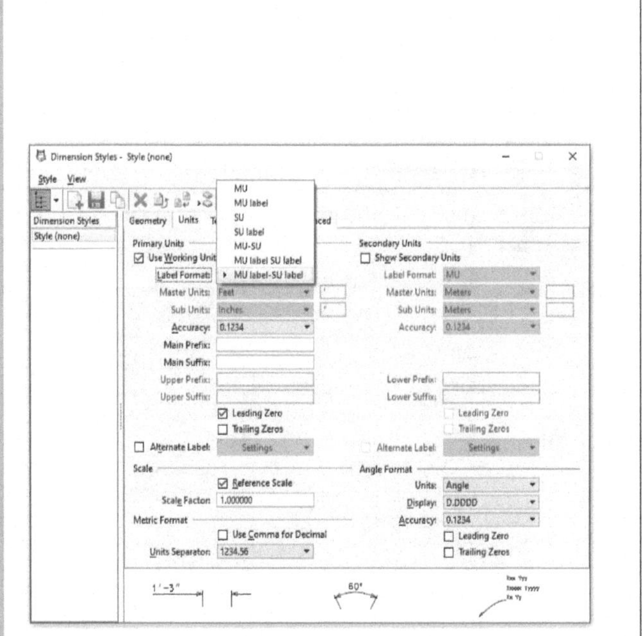

CAD Companion Workbook

5.26

Example: SU - label

- **Units can show:**
  - master units only
  - both the master units and sub-units with labels or
  - sub-units with labels

Note: These other settings that are greyed out are shown on the other pages

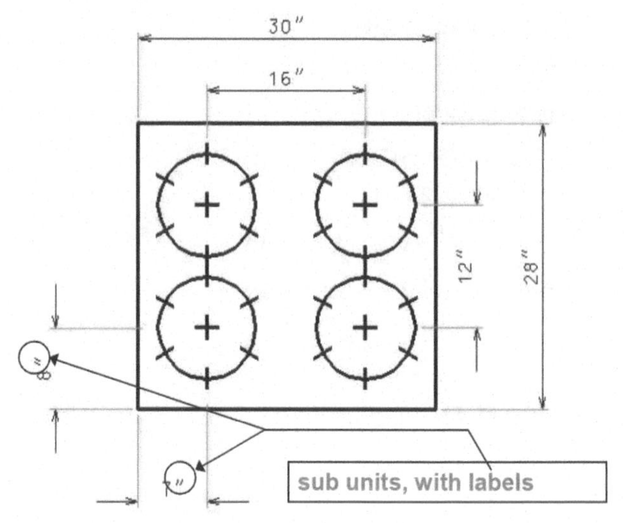

CAD Companion Workbook 5.27

Units > Label Format: SU label

- **Units can show:**
  - sub-units with labels

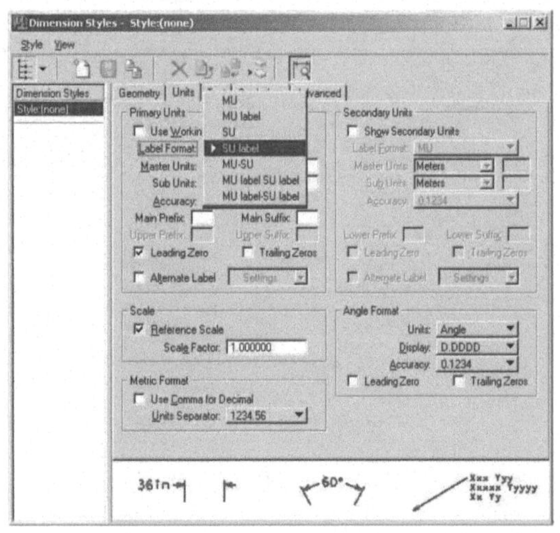

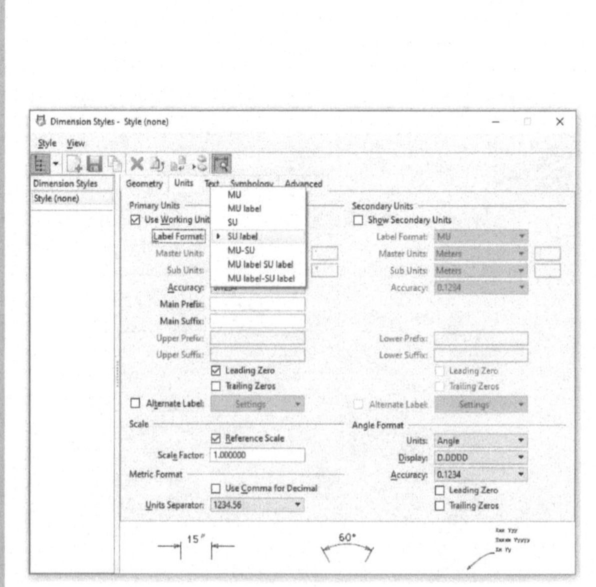

CAD Companion Workbook 5.28

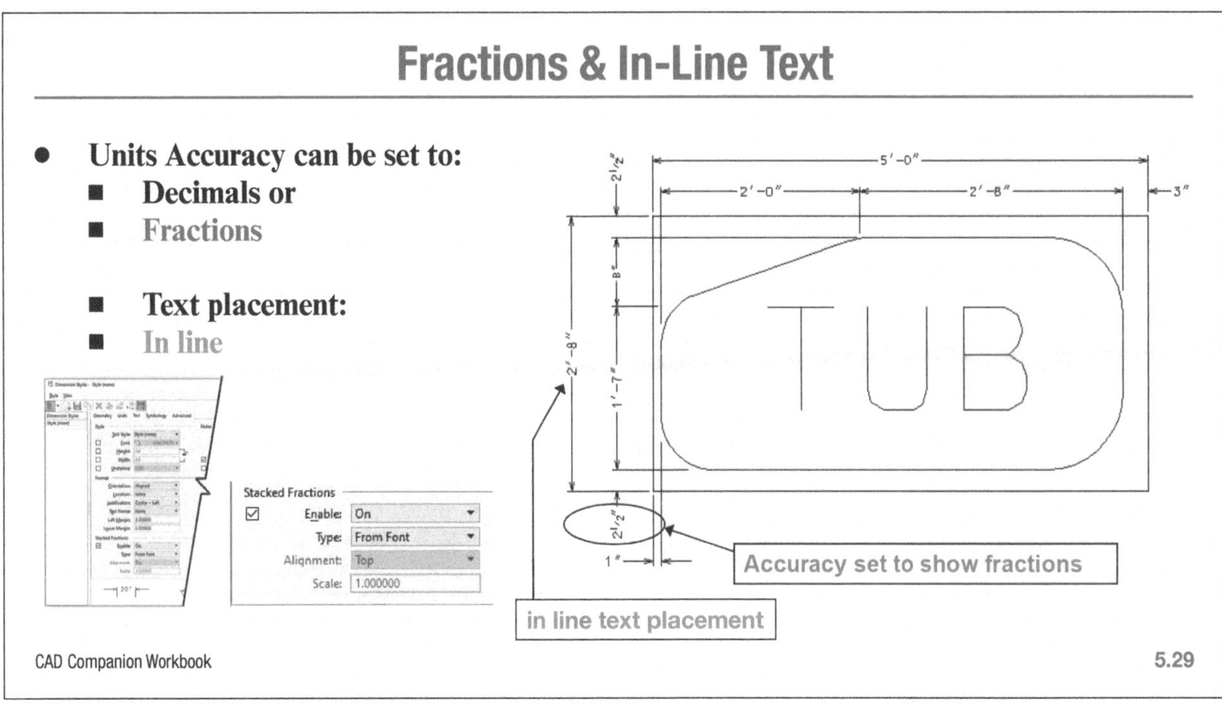

Units > Accuracy

Text Location

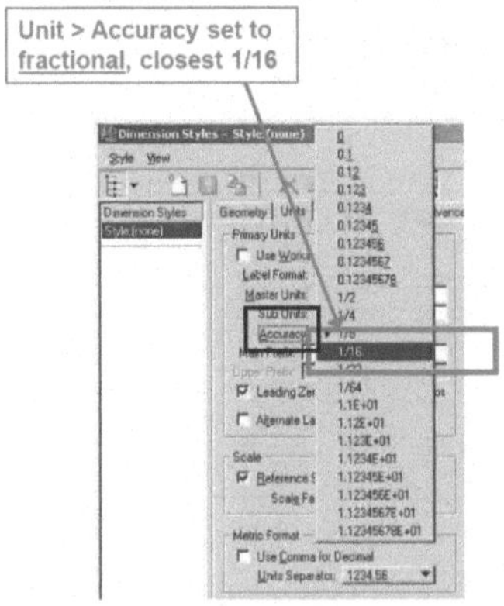

Unit > Accuracy set to fractional, closest 1/16

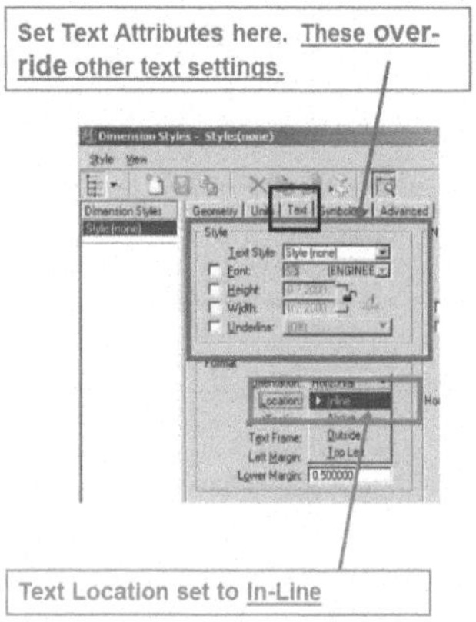

Set Text Attributes here. These over-ride other text settings.

Text Location set to In-Line

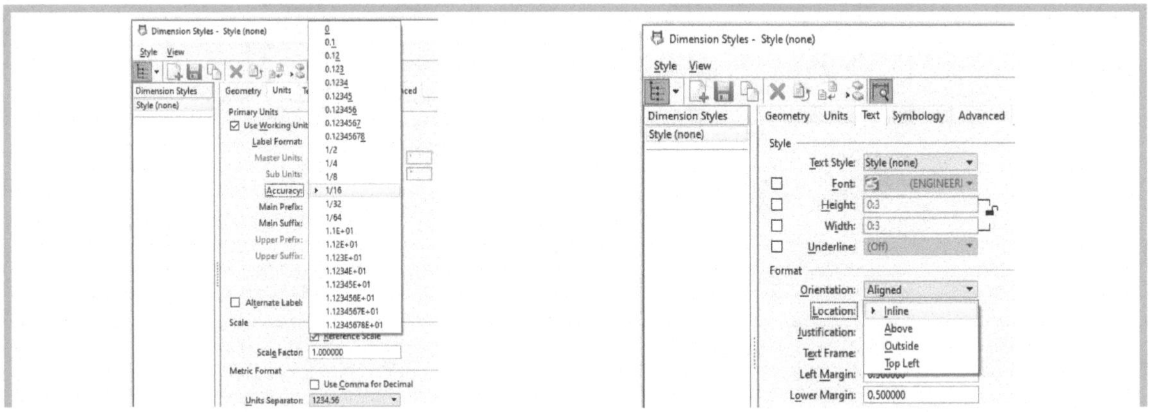

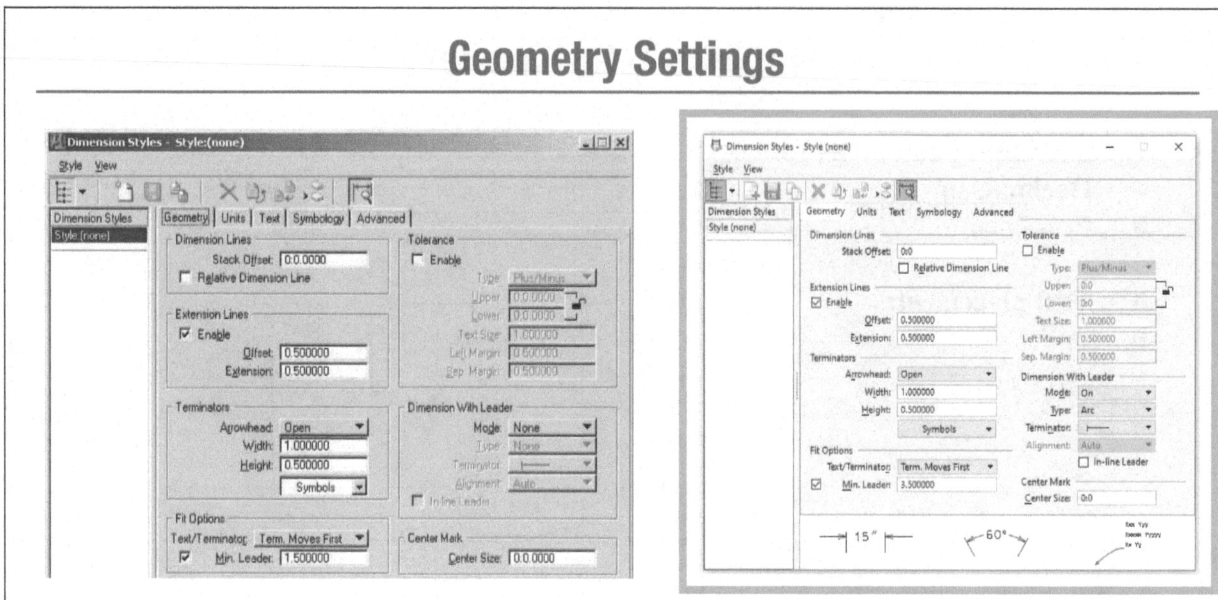

CAD Companion Workbook 5.33

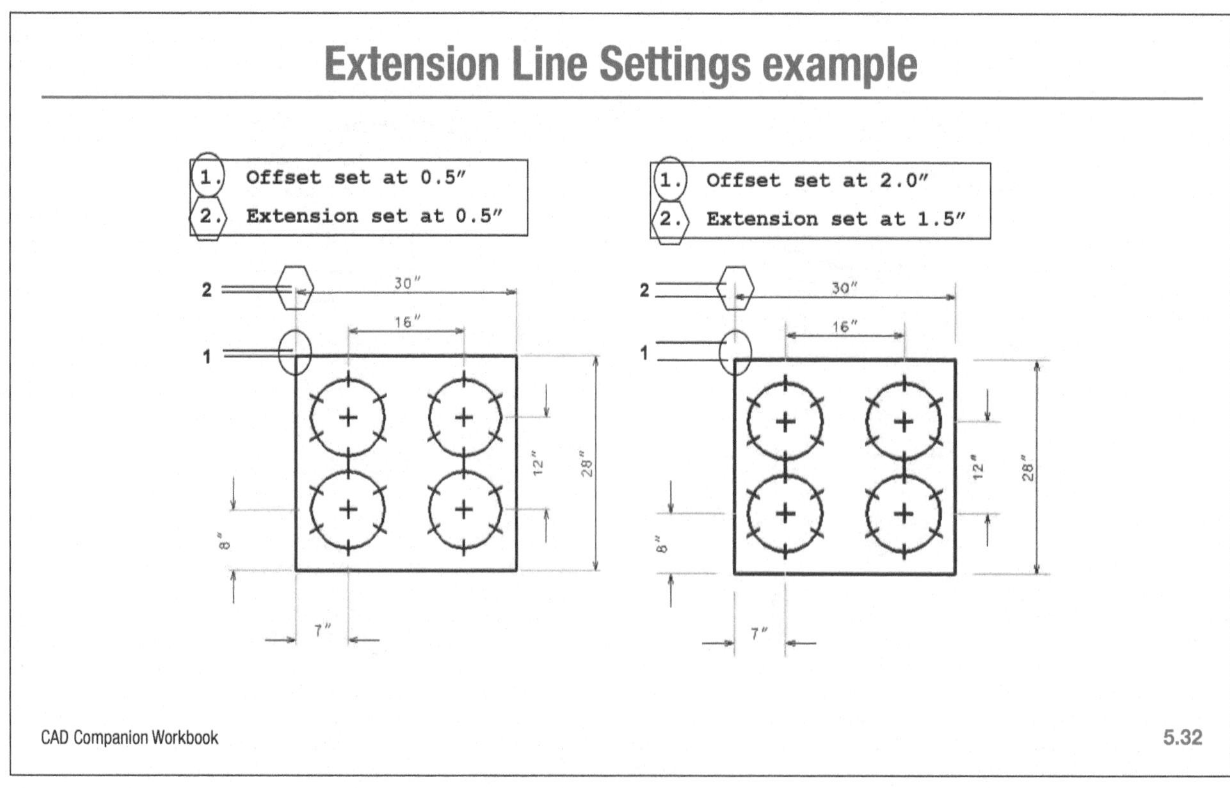

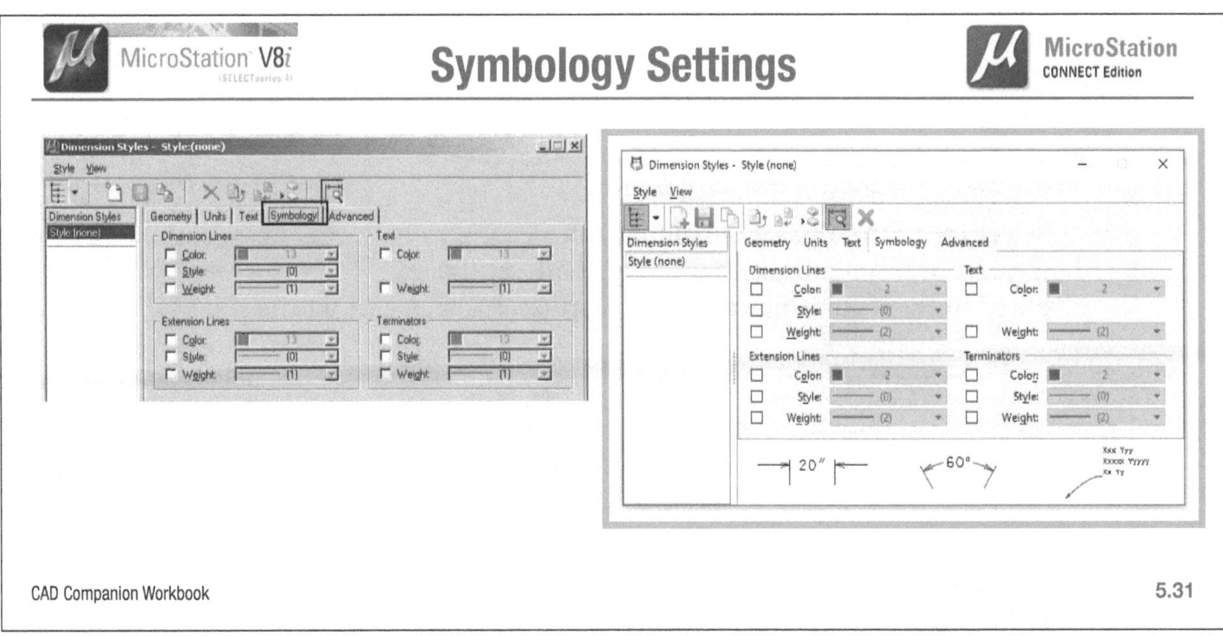

Leader Lines with Place Note

- **This tool is actually on the Text Toolbar, but is used quite often with dimensions.**

PLACE NOTE

Tip:
The Dimension text size can be adjusted as desired with the TX=_____ key-in.

The size of the terminating arrow will also be adjusted by changing the text size.

In **CONNECT Edition**, go to the **Annotate** Tab, **Notes** Group, for the **Place Note** tool

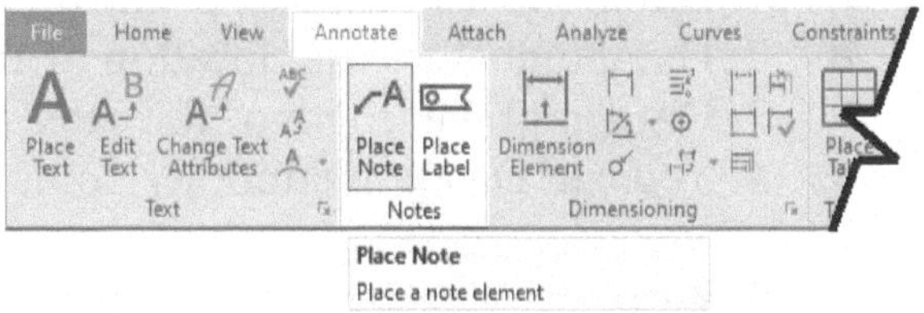

File | Home | View | Annotate | Attach | Analyze | Curves | Constraints

Place Text | Edit Text | Change Text Attributes | Place Note | Place Label | Dimension Element

Text | Notes | Dimensioning

Place Note
Place a note element

The first half of the PLACE NOTE tool can be used to create a leader line. Or extra ones

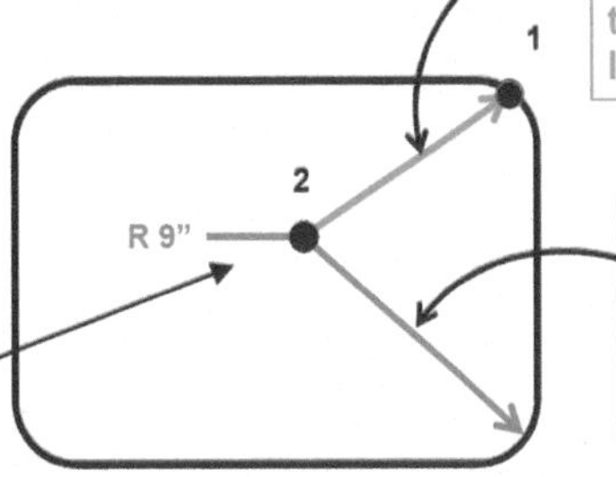

1

2

R 9"

Make sure to set your text orientation to horizontal to get this!

The Dimension Radius tool was used to make the bottom half of this dimension.

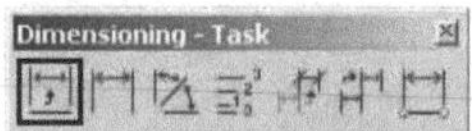

Dimension Element

Dimension Element

Place a dimension on an element

- Simplest of the dimension tools
  - 1. Select an element to dimension
  - 2. Select location to place the dimension
  - If the text or terminators are too big/small, set the text size within the regular place text tool or use TX = ___ to set the size

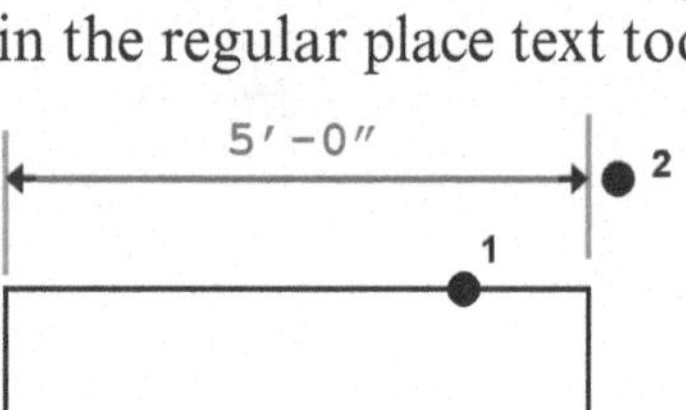

In this example, the dimension text size was set to 4" tall, with the key-in tx=:4

If the user wanted larger text and terminator arrows, then they could use tx=:5

You may also use the Dimension Styles Dialog Box to set text size, but TX= __ is simpler.

CAD Companion Workbook 5.35

Dimensioning - Task

Dimension Linear

Dimension Linear

Place a linear dimension between two points

- Used to dimension a "gap"
  - 1. Datapoint a start point of the dimension
  - 2. Datapoint at the end location of the dimension
  - 3. Datapoint the length of the extension line
  - 4. You can Datapoint another point or Reset if done.

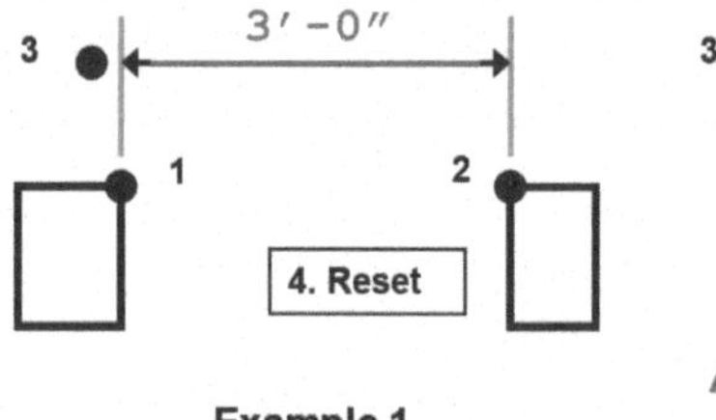

Example 1

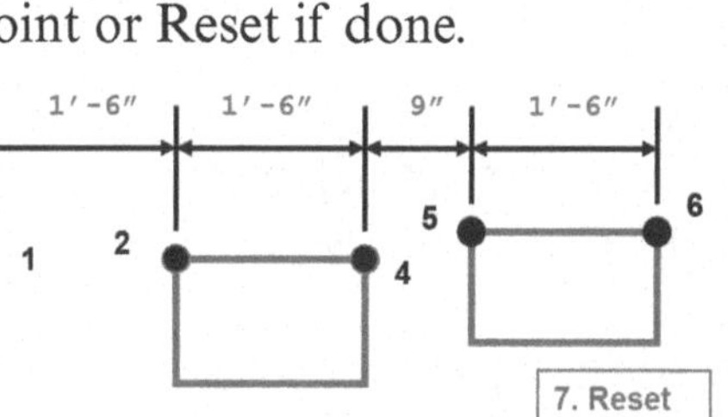

Example 2

Note: Earlier versions interchanged the order of points 2 and 3

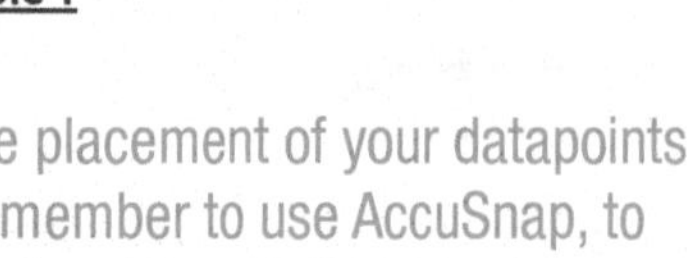

Note: For accurate placement of your datapoints onto elements, remember to use AccuSnap, to "snap" then "click" on the points desired

Hit a few <Reset>'s if you get out of order!

© Shutterstock.com

CAD Companion Workbook 5.36

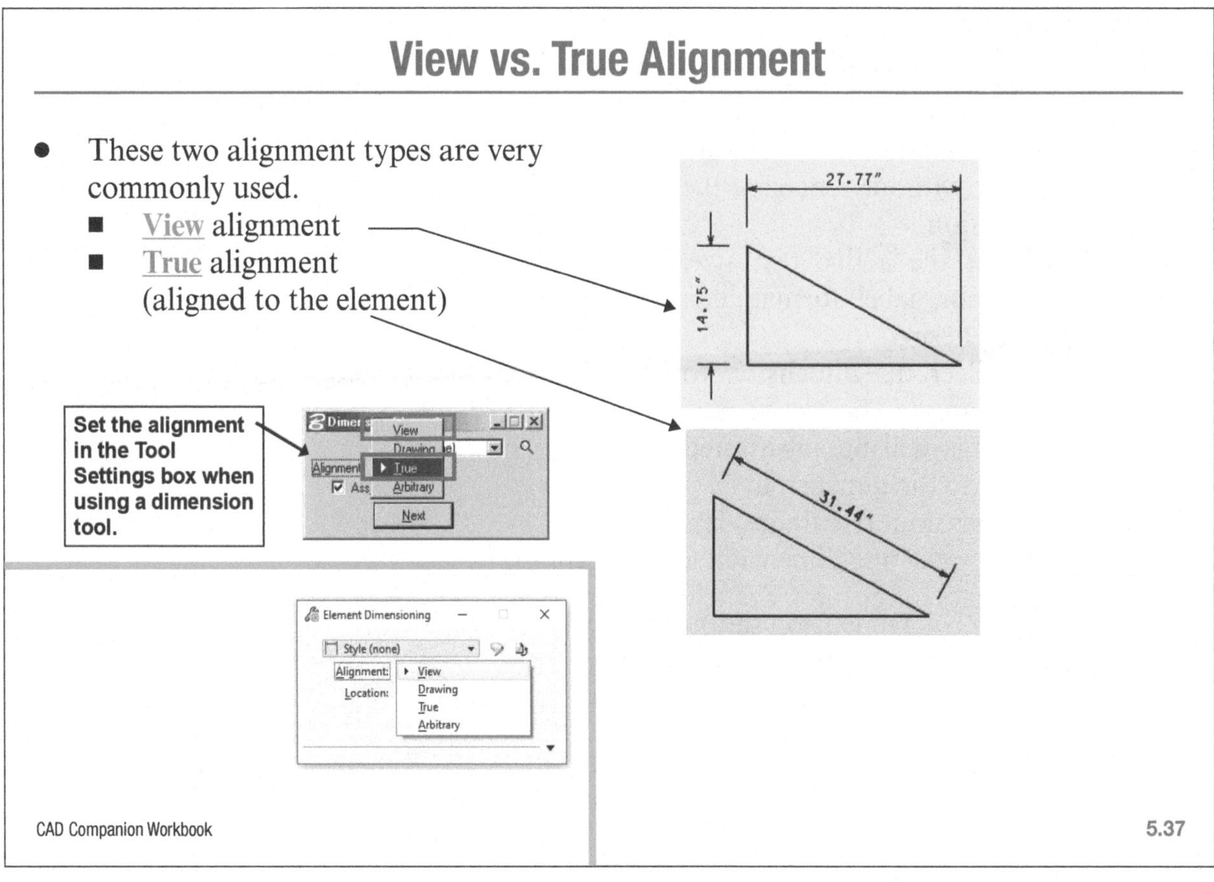
View vs. True Alignment
These two alignment types are very commonly used.
View alignment
True alignment
(aligned to the element)
27.77"
14.75"
31.44"
Set the alignment in the Tool Settings box when using a dimension tool.
View
Drawing
True
Arbitrary
Next
Element Dimensioning
Style (none)
Alignment:
Location:
View
Drawing
True
Arbitrary
CAD Companion Workbook
5.37

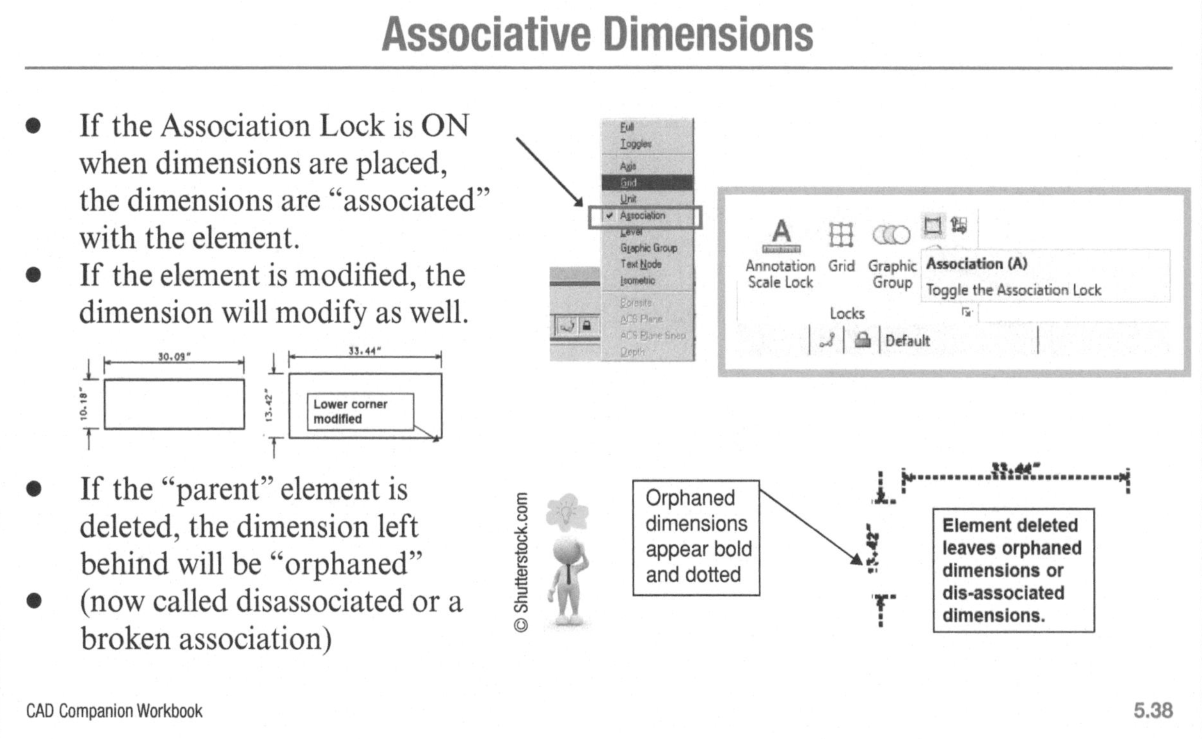
Associative Dimensions
If the Association Lock is ON when dimensions are placed, the dimensions are "associated" with the element.
If the element is modified, the dimension will modify as well.
30.09"
10.18"
33.44"
13.42"
Lower corner modified
If the "parent" element is deleted, the dimension left behind will be "orphaned"
(now called disassociated or a broken association)
Association
Annotation Scale Lock
Grid
Graphic Group
Association (A)
Toggle the Association Lock
Locks
Default
© Shutterstock.com
Orphaned dimensions appear bold and dotted
Element deleted leaves orphaned dimensions or dis-associated dimensions.
CAD Companion Workbook
5.38

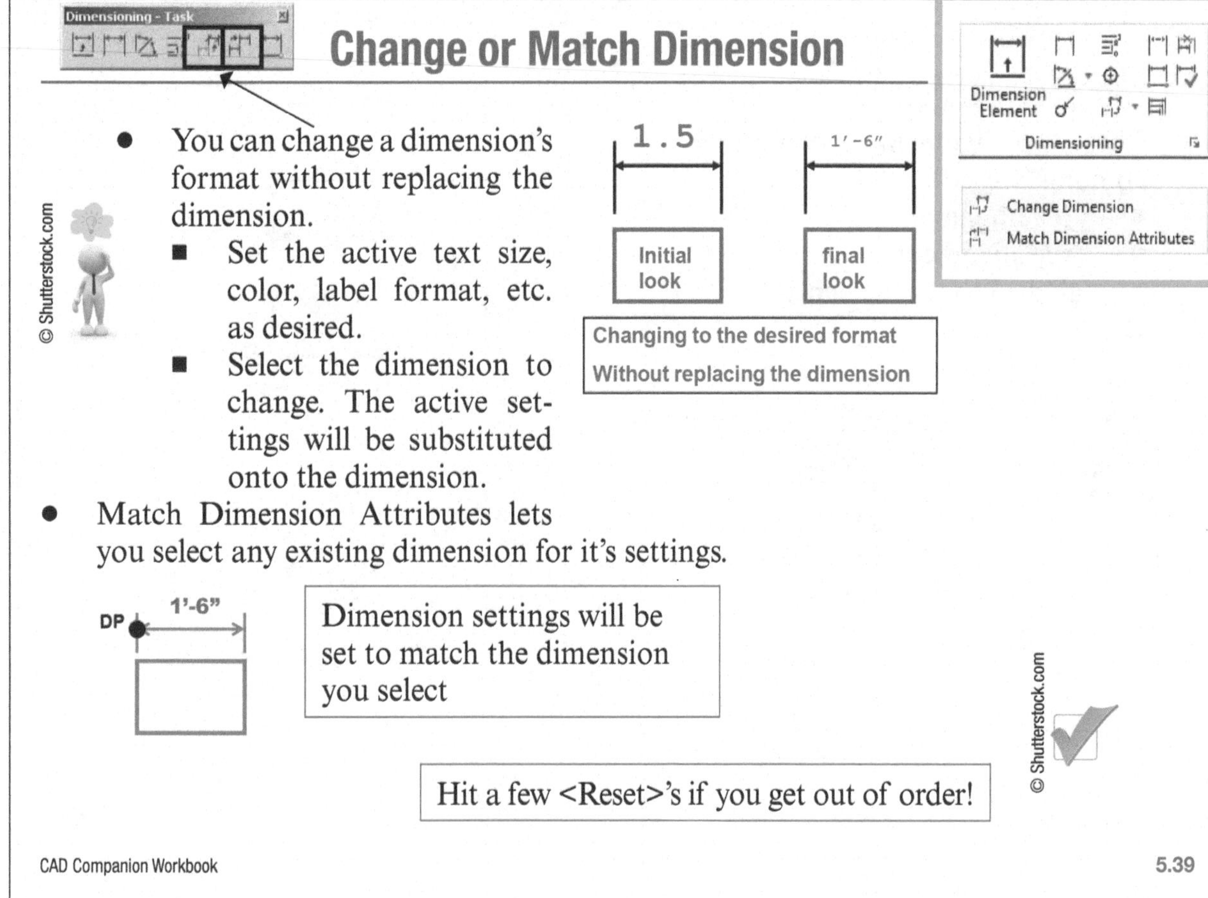

Dimensioning - Task
Change or Match Dimension
You can change a dimension's format without replacing the dimension.
Set the active text size, color, label format, etc. as desired.
Select the dimension to change. The active settings will be substituted onto the dimension.
Match Dimension Attributes lets you select any existing dimension for it's settings.
1.5
1'-6"
Initial look
final look
Changing to the desired format
Without replacing the dimension
Dimension Element
Dimensioning
Change Dimension
Match Dimension Attributes
DP
1'-6"
Dimension settings will be set to match the dimension you select
Hit a few <Reset>'s if you get out of order!
© Shutterstock.com
© Shutterstock.com
CAD Companion Workbook
5.39

Match Dimension – Special Note

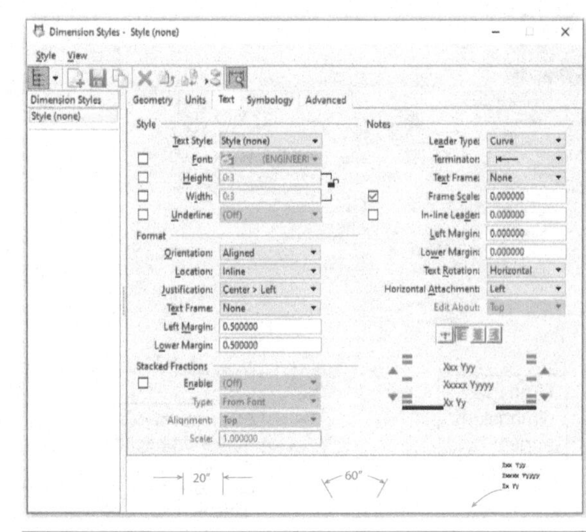

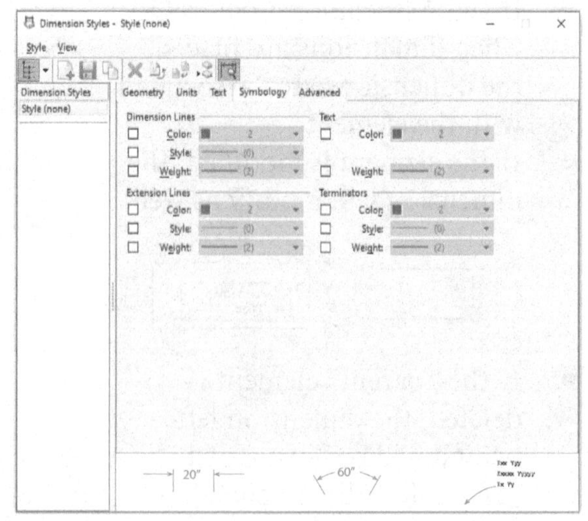

After using Text Match, Text Style and Symbology overrides get turned on. Un-check to end the overrides.

CAD Companion Workbook

Wait! Before you Draw anything . . .

See these Additional tips, tidbits and Challenge Questions

TIPS & TIDBITS

1. Remember to perform a <Ctrl> F immediately after setting the Working Units Format.
2. The easiest way to set the Dimension Text size is thru the regular method of setting the normal Text size. Just make sure that in the Dimension Settings dialog box (from Element > Dimensions) that the Text size settings there are turned OFF.

   The short-cut key-in to set both text height & width to the same value is TX = value; the key-in to set text height is TH=value; the key to set text width is TW = value.

3. Text Match and Text change and the very similar tools for Dimension Text Match and Dimension Text Change are very useful for Text (or dimensions) already on your drawing. It saves you from having to re-DO text and dimensions already placed!
4. After using a Text Match operation, be aware that it will turn ON many settings such as Text Size in the Dimension Settings dialog box. To begin setting Dimension Text size the easy way as mentioned in #2 above, be sure to turn OFF the Text size settings in the Dimension Settings dialog box.
5. Remember that the Modify tool can be used to adjust Dimensions that have already been placed. This is easiest to learn from watching the instructor use this in class.
6. Getting the feet and inches to show up in a dimension is as simple as remembering the very odd sounding "MU label – SU label". Mumble this to yourself as you are walking down the hallway and you'll have other students looking at you strangely, unless you are in the Engineering laboratory building. Then they'll just wink and know that you are in the MicroStation class!
7. The center-mark is a special type of dimension element. Select dimension radial from the Dimension Toolbar and set the mode to Center Mark. Remember to select the circle to place the center mark in by selecting onto the circle's arc edge itself (not the center of the circle). Setting the text size will affect the size of the center mark. Alternatively, you can set the Center Size in the Tool Settings box.

Notes/Questions:

____

____

____

____

____

____

____

CHALLENGE QUESTIONS

Answers in Answer Section

1? Are measurements and dimensions the same thing in MicroStation? Describe.
2? Do you have to have elements that completely enclose an area in order to measure the area?
3? What are the four basic components of a Dimension Element?
4? Describe the difference between a dimension placed with True alignment vs. one place with View alignment.
5? What does your dimension look like if you inadvertently delete the original element that was dimensioned? What Lock has to be on for this to happen?
6? Which Dimension tool should you use if you need to dimension the "gap" between two elements?
7? When using Measure Area by method Flood, what is the meaning of the error message: Error – No enclosing region found?

Exercise — Concepts / Tools / Lessons — for MODULE 5 / 6

CULDESAC

Pranch/Shutterstock.com

(Module 6)
Bearing Angle Expression
AccuDraw

(Module 5)
Measuring Area and Length
Place Text
Place Dimensions
Drop Element
Create Complex Chain

Full-size diagram – pg291

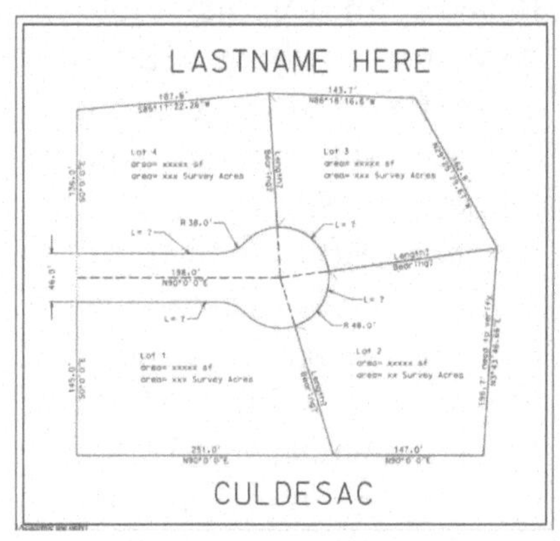

LAYOUT

Pranch/Shutterstock.com

(Module 6)
Multi-lines
AccuDraw

(Module 5)
Place Dimensions

Full-size diagram – pg179

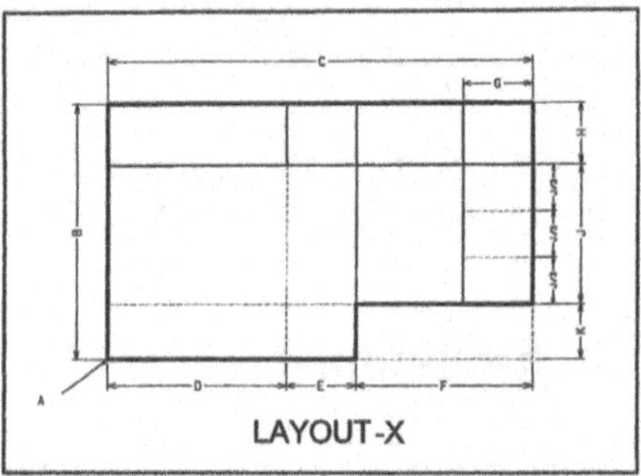

ABC-SITE

Pranch/Shutterstock.com

(Module 6)
Bearing Angle Expression
AccuDraw

(Module 5)
Measurements
Place Dimensions

Full-size diagram – pg178

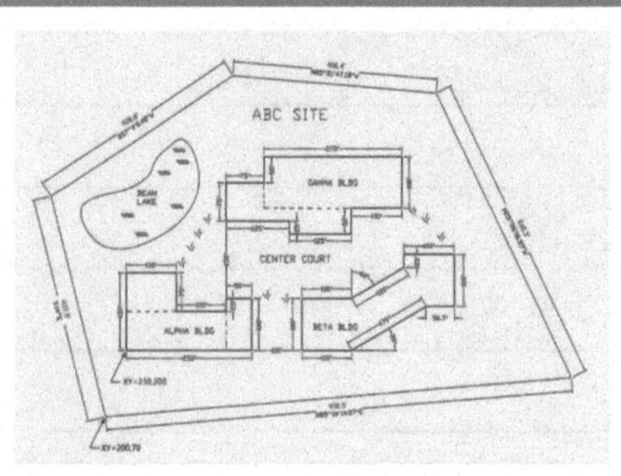

Module 6

Bearing Angles, Multi-Lines, AccuDraw

Bearing Angles, Multi-Lines, AccuDraw

MicroStation V8*i*

MicroStation
CONNECT Edition

AUTOCAD

and

Introduction to Civil Engineering

Michael D. Jue, P.E.

Monkey Business Images/Shutterstock.com. Adapted by Michael D. Jue.

CAD Companion Workbook 6.1

Module 6 Objectives

1. Applying a common method of expressing angles used by Civil Engineers called Bearing Angle Expression vs. Conventional and Azimuth expression methods
2. Introduction to line-strings, curve-strings, complex elements and dropping elements
3. Exposure to setting up and using Multi-Lines
4. Using AccuDraw to enhance the CAD user's productivity.

CAD Companion Workbook 6.2

Angular Expression - Conventional

- Your should be quite familiar with the **Conventional** method of angular expression, by now. For review, see the diagram.
- Key features:
  - 0 degrees is towards the positive X axis
  - Positive angles increment in a counter clock-wise direction
  - Angle values may be pos. or neg.

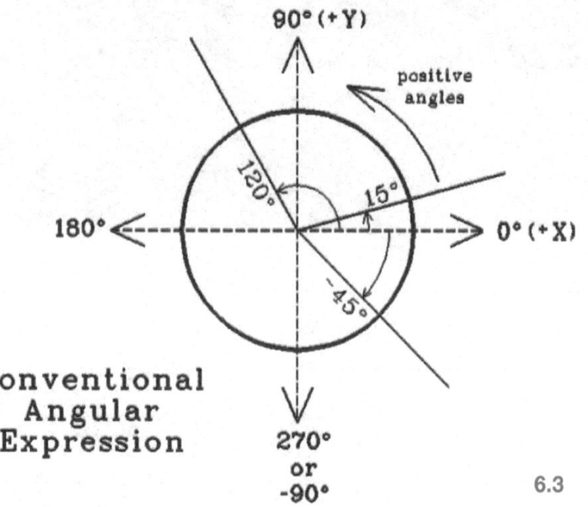

Angular Expression - Azimuths

- **Azimuths** are similar, but the 0° angle is UP and the positive angles are **Clockwise**
- Key features:
  - 0 degrees is towards the positive Y
  - Positive angles increment in a clockwise direction
  - Angle values can ONLY be POSITIVE, no negative angles are allowed.

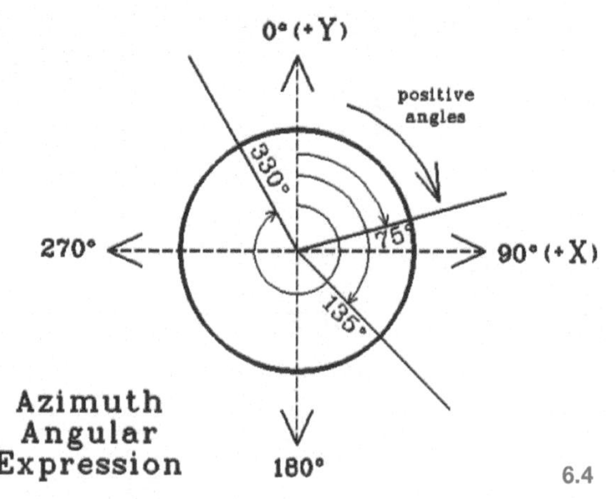

Angular Expression - Bearing

- **Bearing** is unlike the other methods
- Key features:
  - Always start with **North** or **South**
  - Angle values are **positive** in degrees, minutes and seconds
    - DD-MM-SS
  - Then add towards **East** or **West**
  - Angle value maximum is 90°

© Shutterstock.com

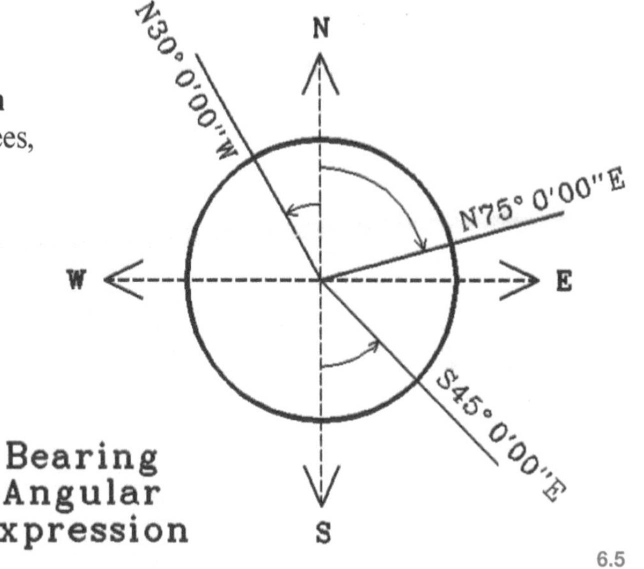

Also called: Surveyor's, Civil Engineering

Example Angle: S27 ° 30' 00"W

CAD Companion Workbook 6.5

Coordinate Readout-Angles

- If a measured angle is not in the format you desire, you can change it.

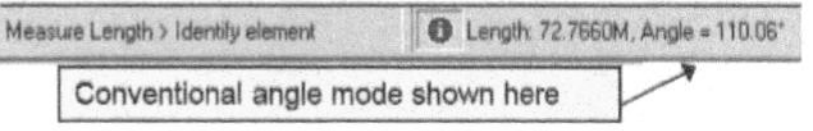

- Use **Settings > Design File > Coordinate Readout**

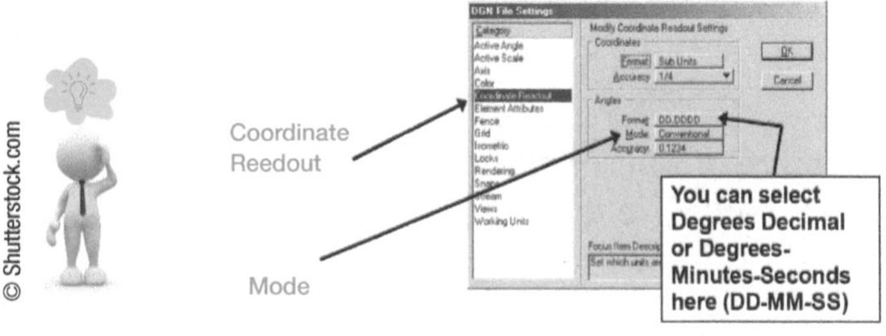

- Change mode from Conventional to Azimuth or Bearing

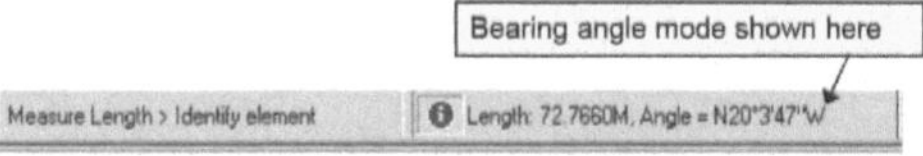

Using the **CONNECT Edition**, to get to **Angle Readout** dialog box shown below, Click **File** (taking you to the Back Stage), **Settings, File, Design File Settings**, then click **Angle Readout**.

(Similar to getting to the following Units dialog box, See pg 77 for review)

Tip: use Search at upper right of screen!

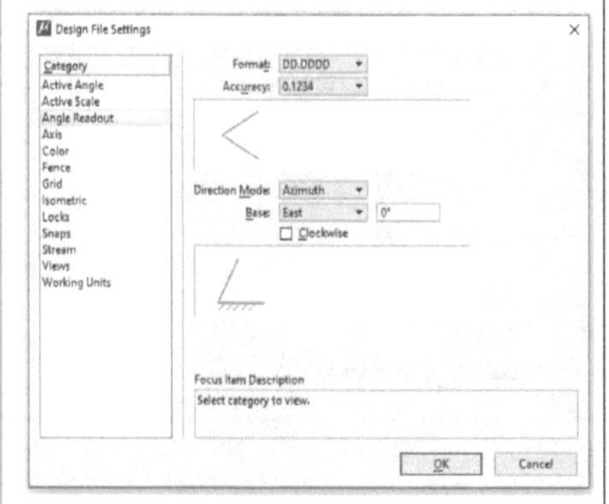

CAD Companion Workbook 6.6

A Note about DD-MM-SS

- DD-MM-SS means:
  - Degrees – minutes –seconds
- A full circle is divided into:
    - 360 degrees of arc or 1/360 of a circle = 1° (1 degree)
  - Each single degree (°) can be divided into:
    - 60 minutes of arc (') or 1/60° = 1' (1 minute)
  - Each single minute (') can be divided into
    - 60 seconds of arc (") or 1/60' = 1" (1 second)

CAD Companion Workbook 6.7

Practice conversions

- Bearing angle N17°00'00"W = ________________Conventional angle
- Bearing angle S31°30'00"W = ________________Conventional angle
- Bearing angle N89°15'00"E = ________________Conventional angle
- Conventional angle 29° = ________________Bearing angle

Answers in Answer Section

Enter a degree symbol in MicroStation with a shift 6. It looks like this ^
This symbol is called "Caret"

CAD Companion Workbook 6.8

Multi – lines

From the **MicroStation V8i** Help files:

Defining Multi-Lines

The active multi-line definition specifies the form of multi-lines placed with the **Place Multi-line** tool.

The component lines can be varying distance apart. Each component line can have its own level, color, line style, and line weight.

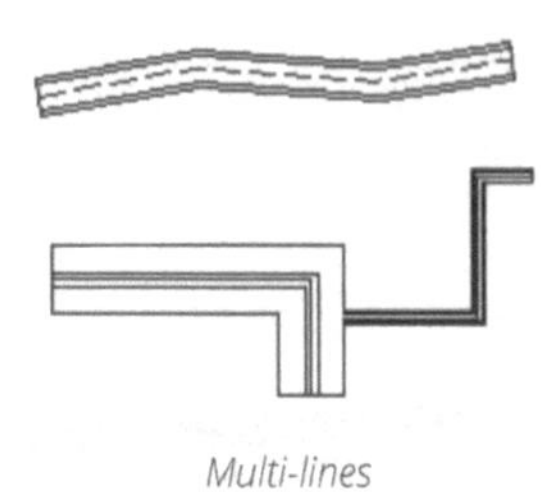

Multi-lines

You can easily "clean up" intersections in multi-lines and modify individual multi-line components using the rools in the Multi-lines toolbox.

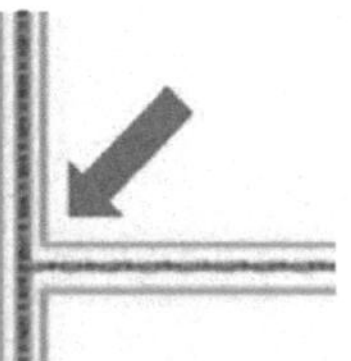

Working with Multi – lines

Tips for working with Multi-lines

Open the Multi-lines Styles dialog box with **Element > Multi-Line Styles,**

Open up the Multi-lines (joints) with **Tools > Multi-lines > Open as Toolbox**

Make sure you have the Working Units set with Format on **MU:SU**
(so you can see the feet and inches in the **Multi-lines Style dialog box**)

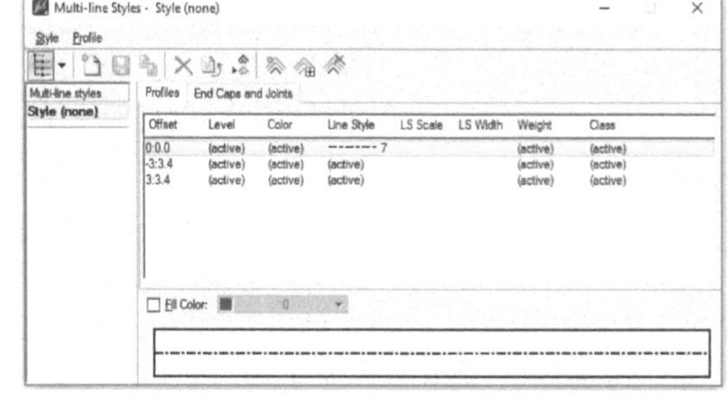

Note:
The Multi - line toolbars from **V8i** and the **CONNECT Edition** are virtually identical!

They work the same in both versions.
The only difference is the method used to open the toolbars and dialog boxes.

The method for opening the **CONNECT Edition** versions will be shown on the following page.

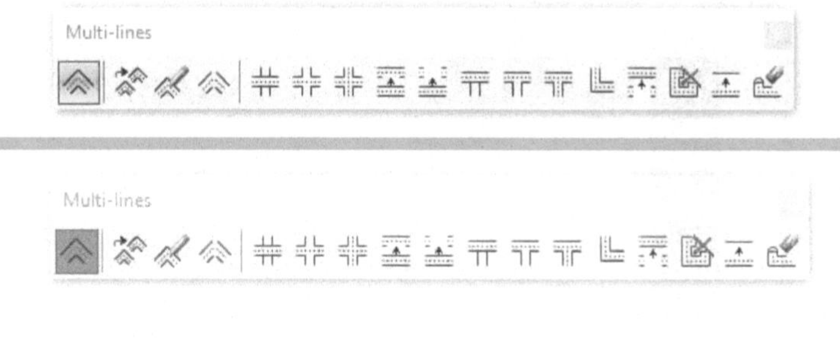

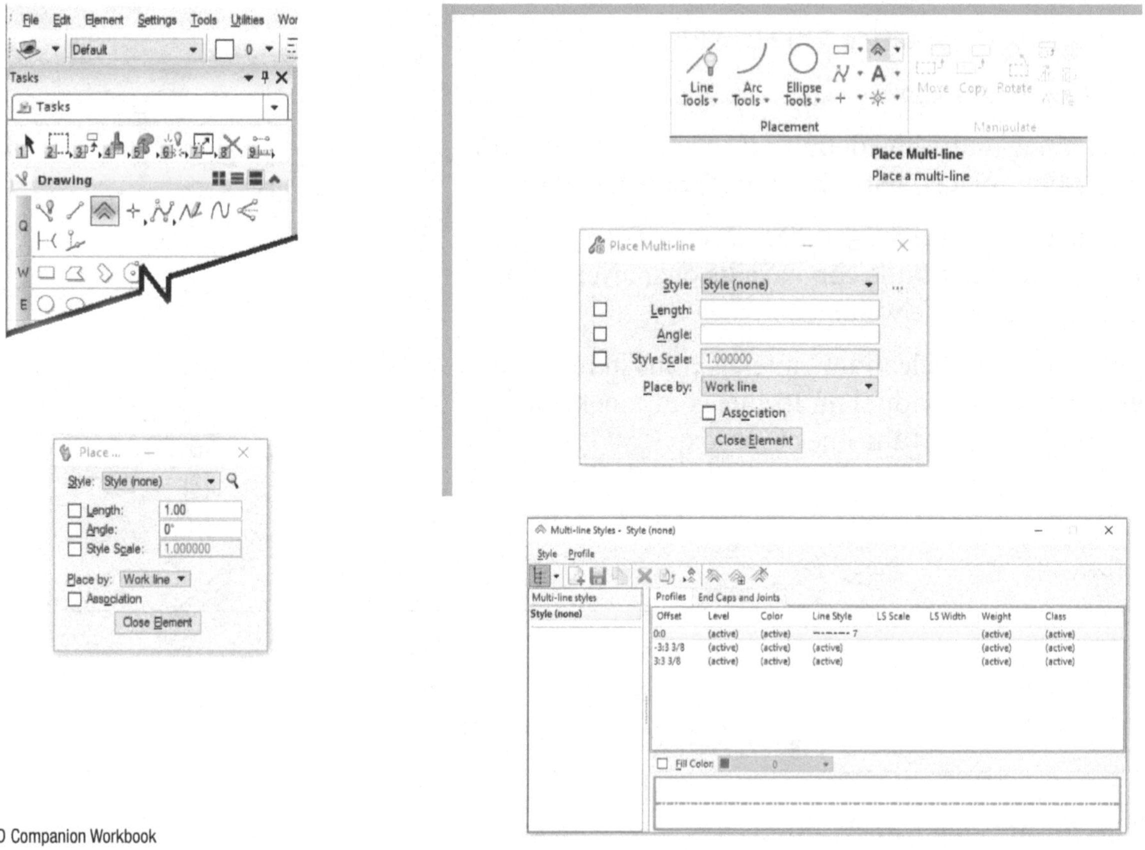

MicroStation V8i (SELECTseries 4)

Working with Multi – lines

MicroStation CONNECT Edition

File Edit Element Settings Tools Utilities Wor

Default

Tasks

Drawing

Line Tools | Arc Tools | Ellipse Tools

Placement

Manipulate

Place Multi-line

Place a multi-line

Place Multi-line

Style: Style (none)

Length:

Angle:

Style Scale: 1.000000

Place by: Work line

Association

Close Element

Place ...

Style: Style (none)

Length: 1.00

Angle: 0°

Style Scale: 1.000000

Place by: Work line

Association

Close Element

Multi-line Styles - Style (none)

Style Profile

Multi-line styles

Style (none)

Profiles | End Caps and Joints

Offset	Level	Color	Line Style	LS Scale	LS Width	Weight	Class
0.0	(active)	(active)	7			(active)	(active)
-3:3 3/8	(active)	(active)	(active)			(active)	(active)
3:3 3/8	(active)	(active)	(active)			(active)	(active)

Fill Color: 0

CAD Companion Workbook

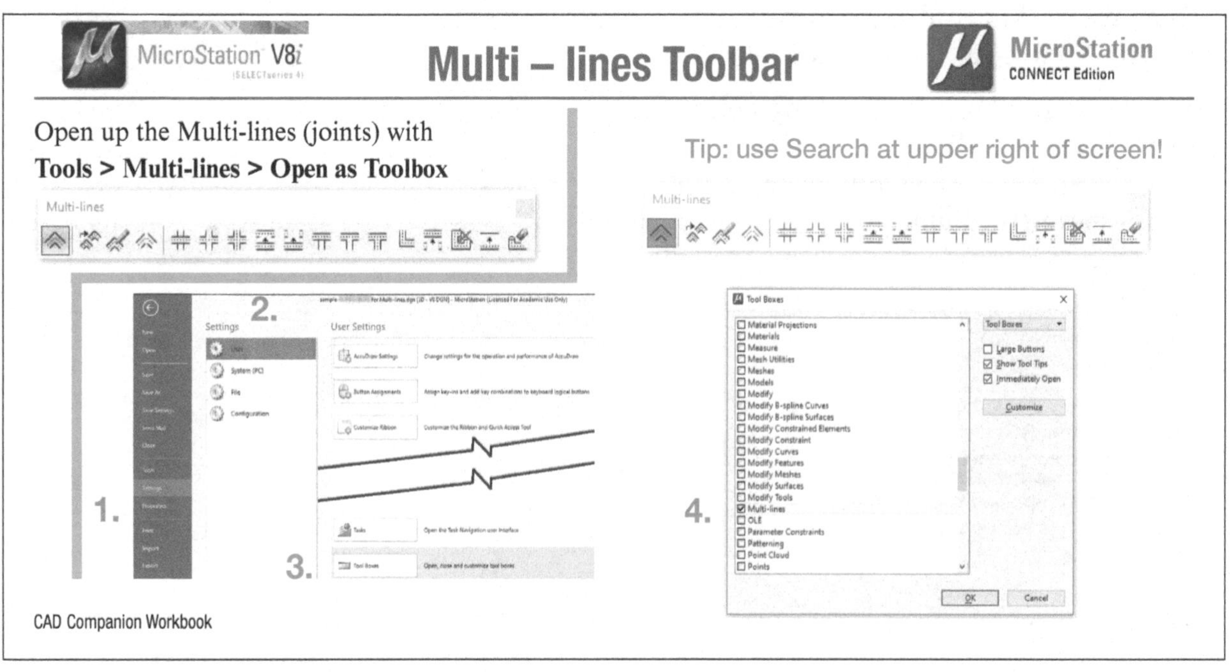

Multi – lines Tools

- Place Multi-line
- Match Multi-line Attributes
- Change Multi-line
- Drop Multi-line
- Construct Closed Cross Joint
- Construct Open Cross Joint
- Construct Merged Cross Joint
- Cut Single Component Line
- Cut All Component Line
- Construct Closed Tee Joint
- Construct Open Tee Joint
- Construct Merged Tee Joint
- Construct Corner Joint
- Uncut Component Lines
- Multi-line Partial Delete
- Move Multi-line Profile
- Edit Multi-line Cap

CAD Companion Workbook

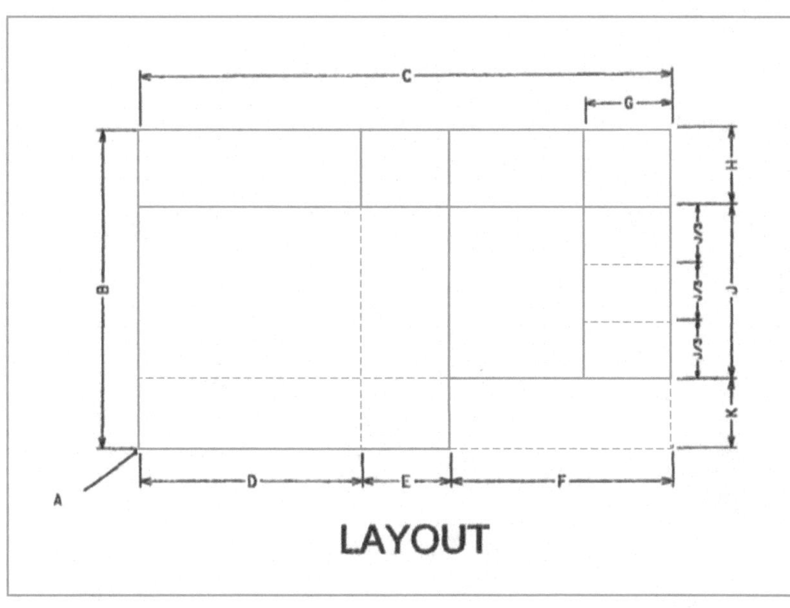

Using Multi-lines is shown on the next pages 174-175.

New Multi-lines will be snapped on top of the regular line elements of the Layout drawing.

The LAYOUT drawing must be drawn first, before the Multi-lines exercise can be performed.

See the detailed diagram of the LAYOUT drawing exercise, in simple lines, on page 179.

Your instructor will let you know which model of layout will be assigned to you or to your class.

CAD Companion Workbook

A MULTI - LINES EXERCISE page 1 of 2

Open the Multi-lines Styles dialog box with Elemant > Multi-line Styles, Open up the Multi-lines (joints) with Tools > Multi-lines > Open as Toolbox

Make sure you have the Working Unit set with Format on MU:SU (so you can see the feet and inches in the Multi-lines Styles dialog box)

The default spacing of the Multi-lines that may come up is line #1 at 0 ft spacing ftom the centerline (that will come out as the centerline), line #2 at -3:3.4 spacing (to one side of the centerline) and line #3 at 3:3.4 spacing (to the other side of the centerline). This default would give you Multi-lines that are 6 ft 6.8 in wide when drawn (quite a bit too wide for our "walls". We want to draw walls10" wide) Change the -3:3.4 to -0:5, and change the 3:3.4 to 0:5. Then you can draw 10" wide walls. See next page for an example of what Multi-lines snapped to the existing lines of LAYOUT look like after their inertsections are fixed with the various Joint tools.

Draw Multi-lines with the Q3 tool. It's just to the right of the Place Line tool! Fix the Multi-line intersections with the Cross Joint, Tee Joint or Corner Joint as needed.

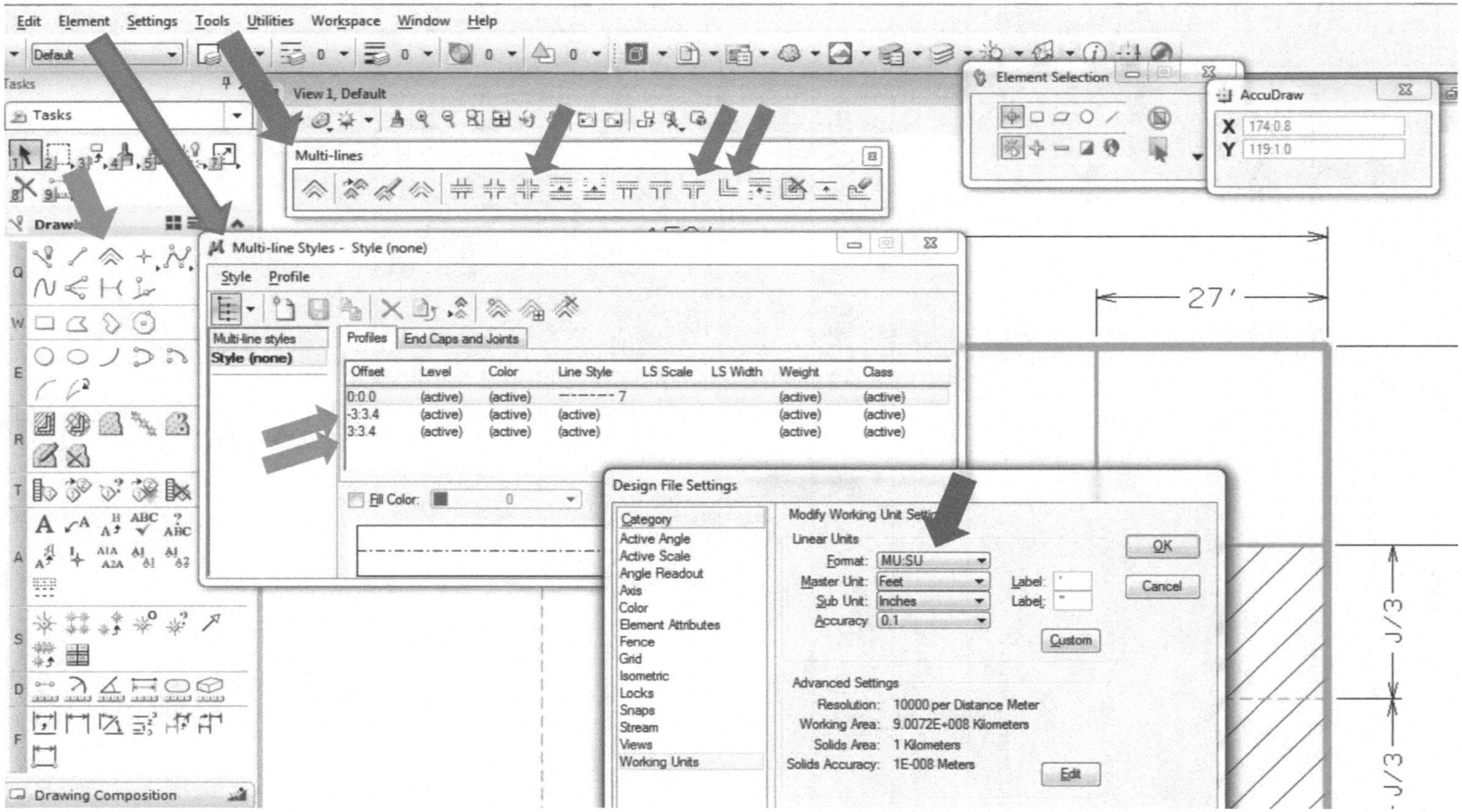

A MULTI - LINES EXERCISE page 2 of 2

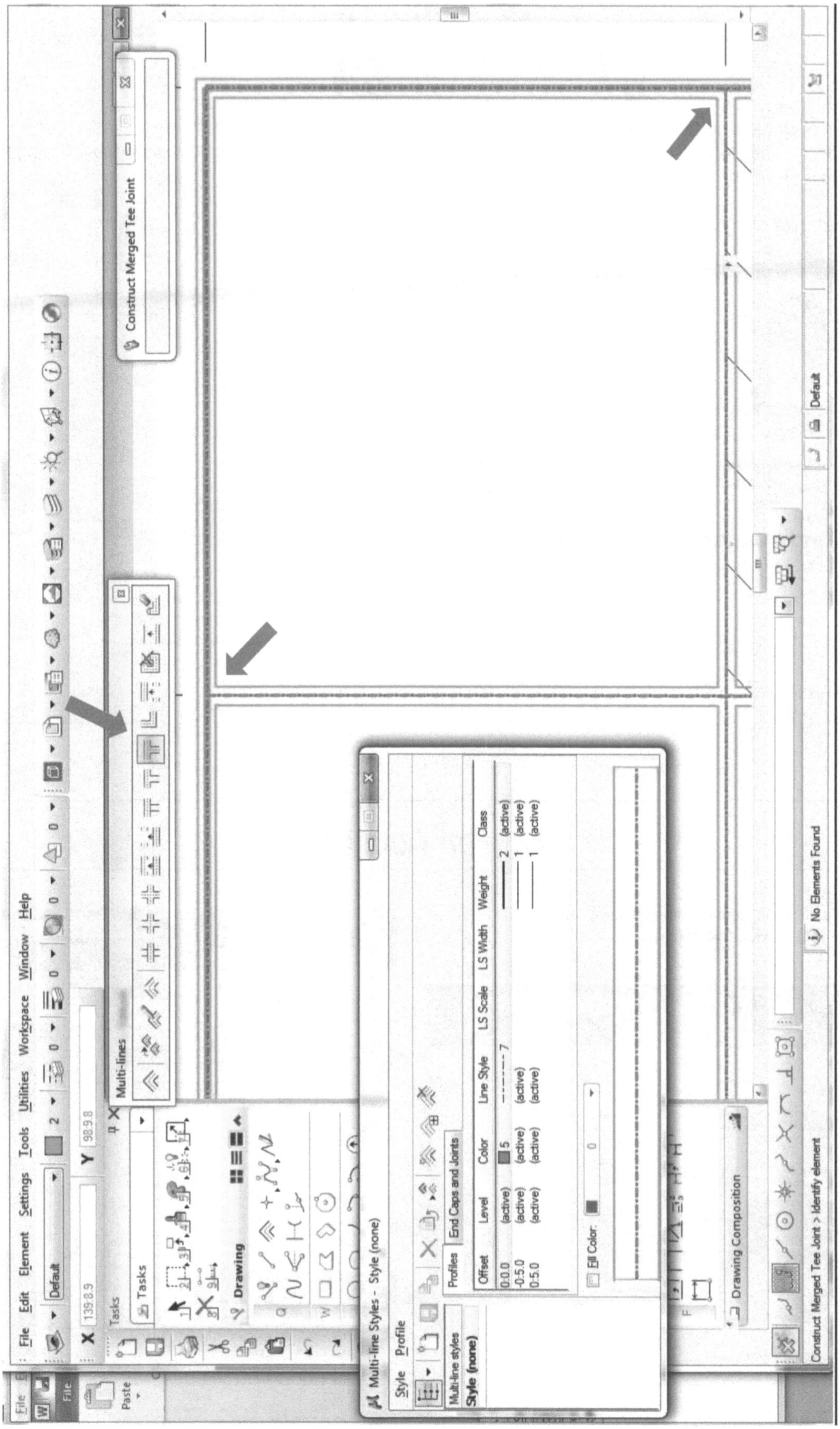

Sample of Multi-lines snapped on top of original lines and Joins Fixed up on the LAYOUT drawing! (Upper right corner shown)

AccuDraw

MicroStation V8i (SELECTseries 4) + MicroStation CONNECT Edition

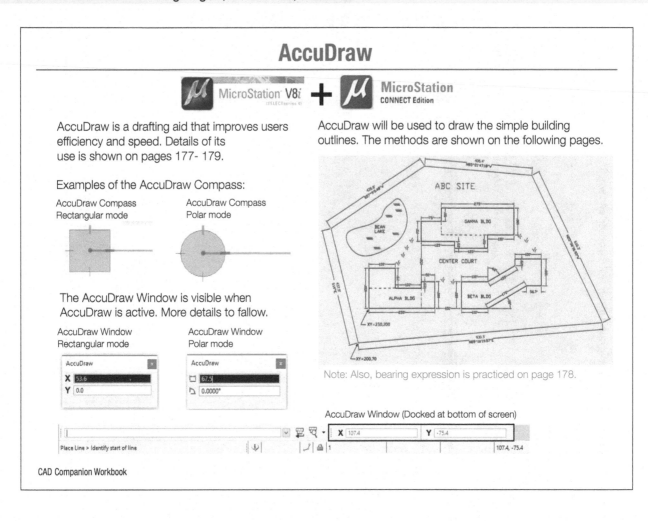

AccuDraw is a drafting aid that improves users efficiency and speed. Details of its use is shown on pages 177- 179.

Examples of the AccuDraw Compass:

AccuDraw Compass Rectangular mode

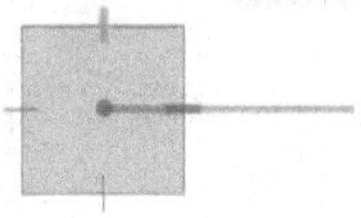

AccuDraw Compass Polar mode

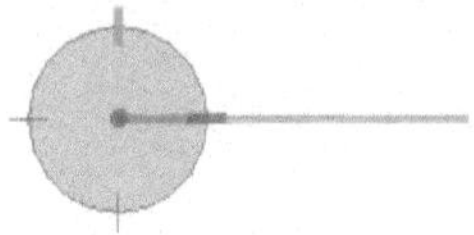

The AccuDraw Window is visible when AccuDraw is active. More details to fallow.

AccuDraw Window Rectangular mode

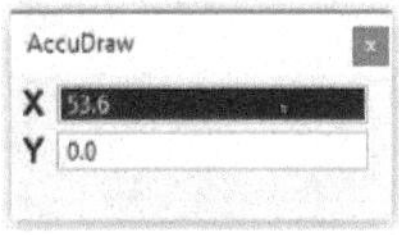

AccuDraw Window Polar mode

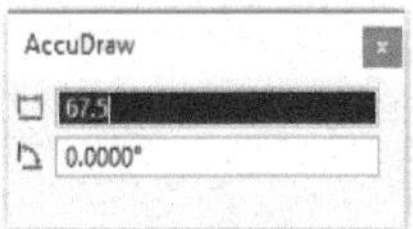

AccuDraw
X 53.6
Y 0.0

AccuDraw
67.5
0.0000°

AccuDraw will be used to draw the simple building outlines. The methods are shown on the following pages.

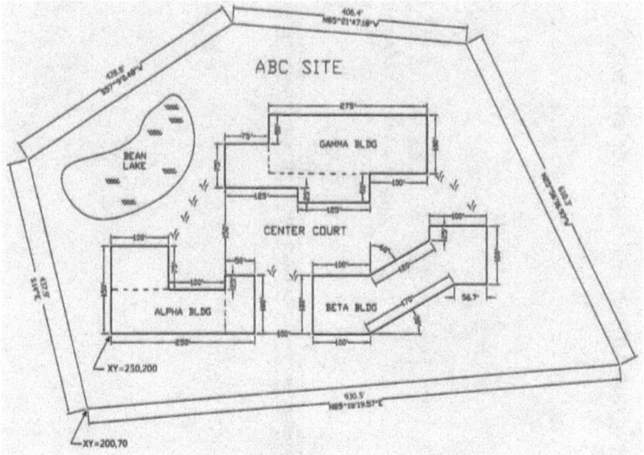

ABC SITE
BEAN LAKE
GAMMA BLDG
CENTER COURT
ALPHA BLDG
BETA BLDG
XY=230,200
XY=200,70

Note: Also, bearing expression is practiced on page 178.

AccuDraw Window (Docked at bottom of screen)

X 107.4 Y -75.4

Place Line > Identify start of line

107.4, -75.4

CAD Companion Workbook

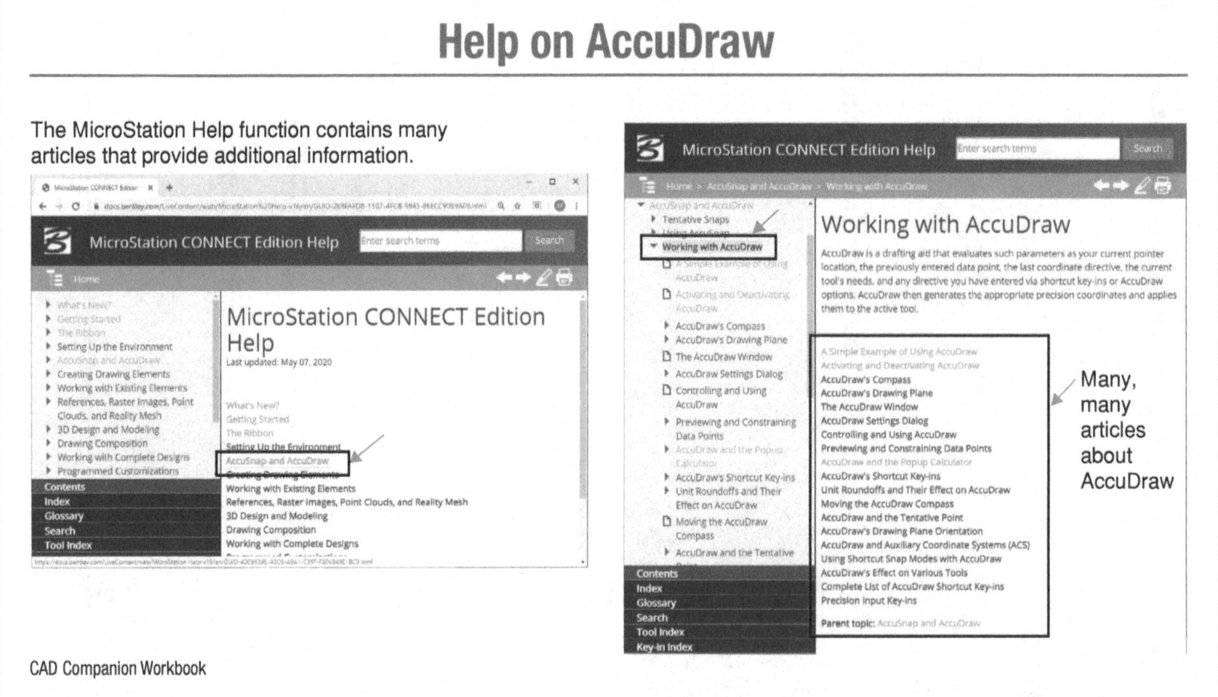
Help on AccuDraw
The MicroStation Help function contains many articles that provide additional information.
MicroStation CONNECT Edition Help
MicroStation CONNECT Edition Help
Last updated: May 07, 2020
AccuSnap and AccuDraw
Working with AccuDraw
Many, many articles about AccuDraw
CAD Companion Workbook

Using AccuDraw

MicroStation V8i

To use **AccuDraw,** it must be activated (ON)

MicroStation CONNECT Edition

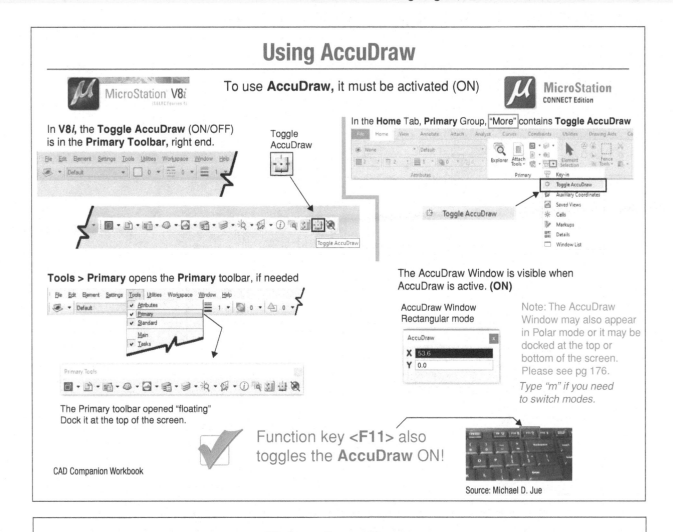

In **V8*i***, the **Toggle AccuDraw** (ON/OFF) is in the **Primary Toolbar,** right end.

Toggle AccuDraw

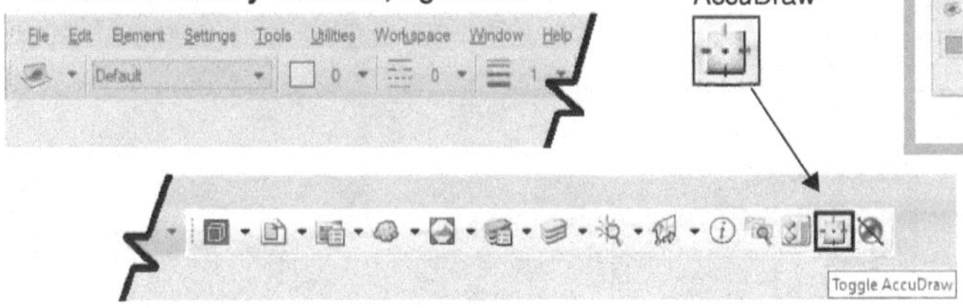

In the **Home** Tab, **Primary** Group, "More" contains **Toggle AccuDraw**

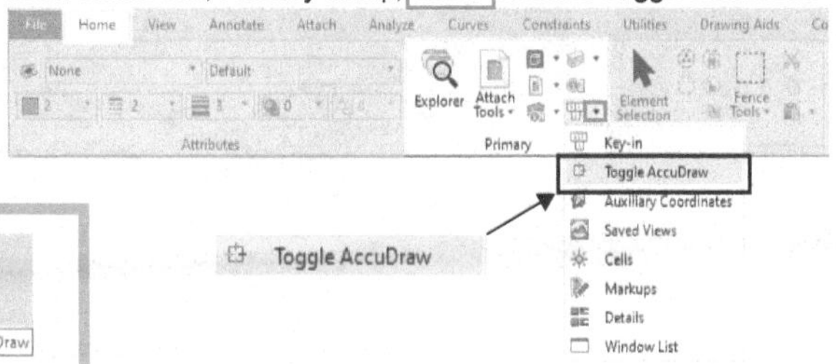

Toggle AccuDraw

Tools > Primary opens the **Primary** toolbar, if needed

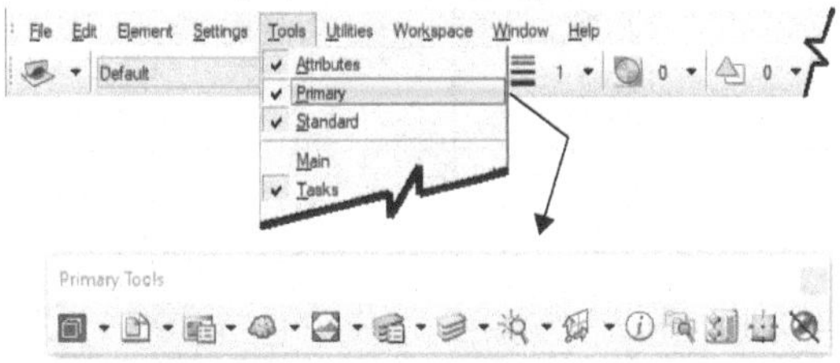

The Primary toolbar opened "floating" Dock it at the top of the screen.

The AccuDraw Window is visible when AccuDraw is active. **(ON)**

AccuDraw Window Rectangular mode

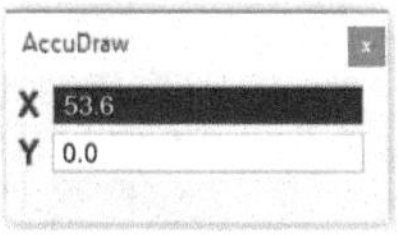

Note: The AccuDraw Window may also appear in Polar mode or it may be docked at the top or bottom of the screen. Please see pg 176.

Type "m" if you need to switch modes.

Function key **<F11>** also toggles the **AccuDraw** ON!

CAD Companion Workbook

Source: Michael D. Jue

Using AccuDraw

This example shows how to draw the boundaries of the Alpha Building using AccuDraw in rectangular mode. It will be compared to the typical steps that may be used if using Precision Input by keying in DI = Polar coordinates. The student will see that the method using AccuDraw is faster requiring less steps.

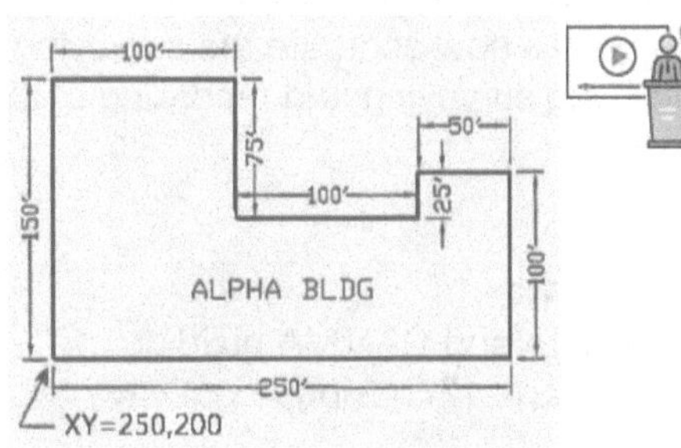

1st four lines by key-ins method:
Activate Place Line
xy=250,200 <Enter>

di=250,0 <Enter> (9 keystrokes)
di=100,90 <Enter> (10 keystrokes)
di=50,180 <Enter> (10 keystrokes)
di=25,-90 <Enter> (10 keystrokes)
Total keystrokes = 39

Total steps after 1st point = 39

1st four lines by AccuDraw method:
Activate Place Line
xy=250,200 <Enter>

Roll mouse right (1 mousemove)
250 Click (3 keystrokes + 1 Click)
Roll mouse up (1 mousemove)
100 Click (3 keystrokes + 1 Click)
Roll mouse left (1 mousemove)
50 Click (2 keystrokes + 1 Click)
Roll mouse down (1 mousemove)
25 Click (2 keystrokes + 1 Click)

Total mousemoves = 4
Total Clicks 4
Total Keystorkes 10
Total steps after 1st point = 18

The steps needed to draw the lines is roughly HALF of the steps needed by precision key-in input! **AccuDraw** eliminates key-in of the angular values. It reads the position of your mouse!

After the first point is placed, the AccuDraw Compass appears

AccuDraw Compass Rectangular mode

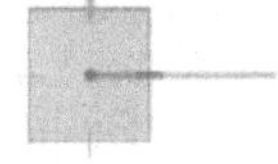

Then **roll the mouse** to the right to line up with the X-axis, then type **250** (the 250 *automatically* goes into the X field in the AccuDraw Window!) Then **Click**

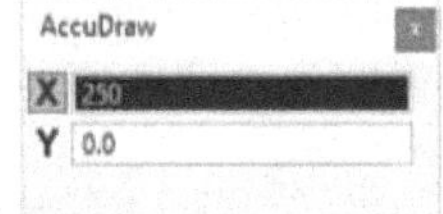

(The AccuDraw Compass moves to the end of the new line)
Roll mouse up, type **100 Click,** repeat steps for remaining lines.

ABC SITE Exercise Drawing, Abbreviated Steps

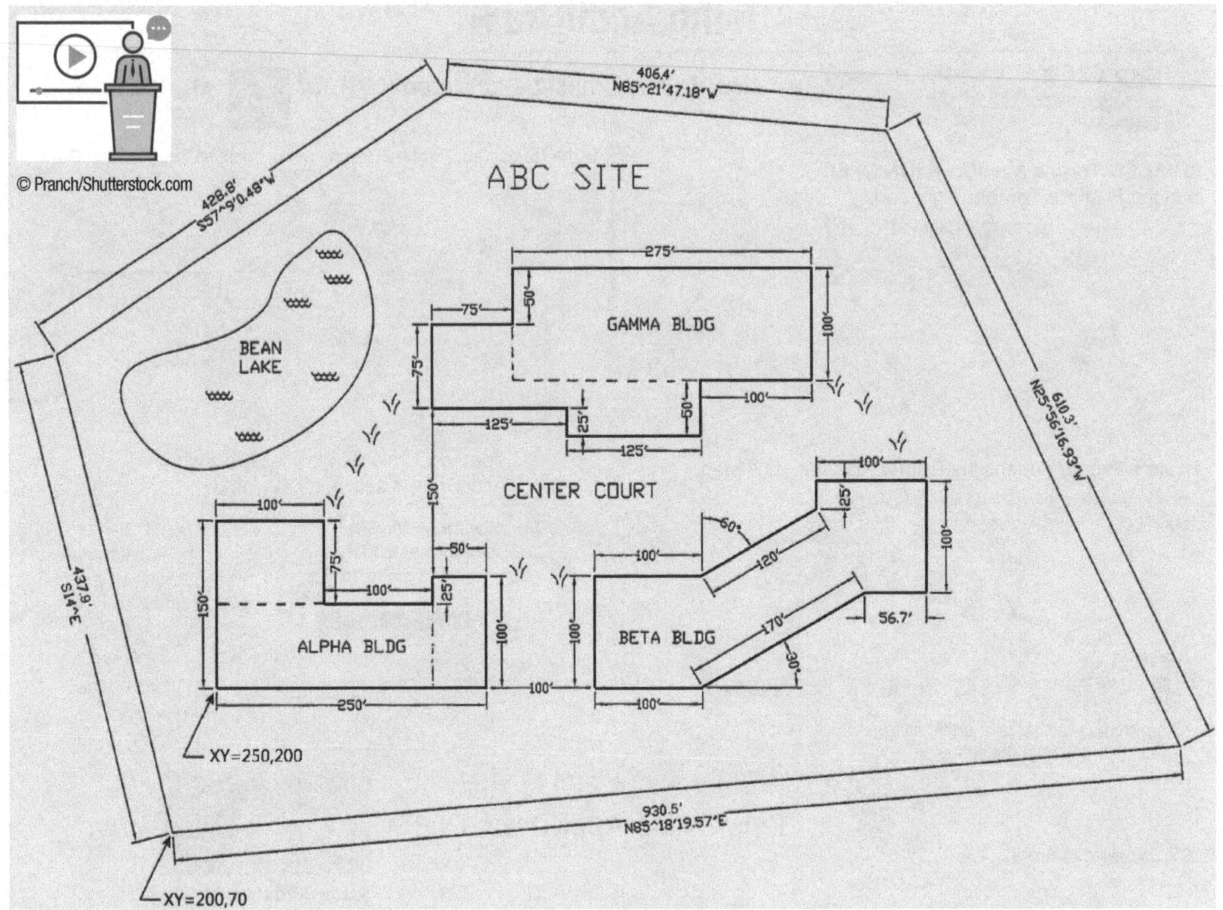

This drawing is used to learn about using Bearing Angle Expression (pages 167-170), and AccuDraw (pages 176-178), previously covered. It can also be used for learning about using cells (pages 197-200) and about drawing in 3D (pages 211-218), coming up

Exercise for Bearing Angle Expression

Create a new drawing called ABC-SITE

Set the following:
W.U. (Working Units) to Feet and inches
Format in the W.U. to MU (master units only)
Accuracy to 0.1 (tenths of a ft)
Set Angle Readout to:
Direction Mode: Bearing, Format: DD.MM.SS
Accuracy: 0.12 (hundredths of a second)

Create a new level: Property Lines
Set CO=2, WT=2, LC=0

Draw the following lines on the Property Lined level: Start Place Line, then,
xy=200,70<Enter>
di=930.5,n85^18'19.57"e<Enter>
di=610.3,n25^56'16.93"w<Enter>
di=406.4,n85^21'47.18"w<Enter>
di=428.8,s57^9'0.48"w<Enter>
di=437.9,s14^e<Enter>

Note: the last line may not "Close" exactly to the beginning point, this is referred to as a "closing error" or "misclosure". It indicates how accurate the surveying team was in performing surveying and recording of their measurements.

Exercise for AccuDraw

Create the ALPHA, BETA and GAMMA building outlines as begun on page 177, using AccuDraw.

Part II: Bearing Angle Expression & AccuDraw

Turn off the property Lines level.
Create a new level: Boundary Lines, set its colour CO=5

Using the Boundary Lines level as your new active level, now create the Boundaries Lines using Bearing Expression and AccuDraw to make the lines, rather than by the di= key-in method shown at left.

LAYOUT Exercies Drawing, Abbreviated Steps

© Pranch/Shutterstock.com

This drawing is used to learn about using Multi-lines (pages 171-175), and AccuDraw (paged 176- 178), previously covered. It can also be used for learning about using Cells (pages 197-200), coming up)

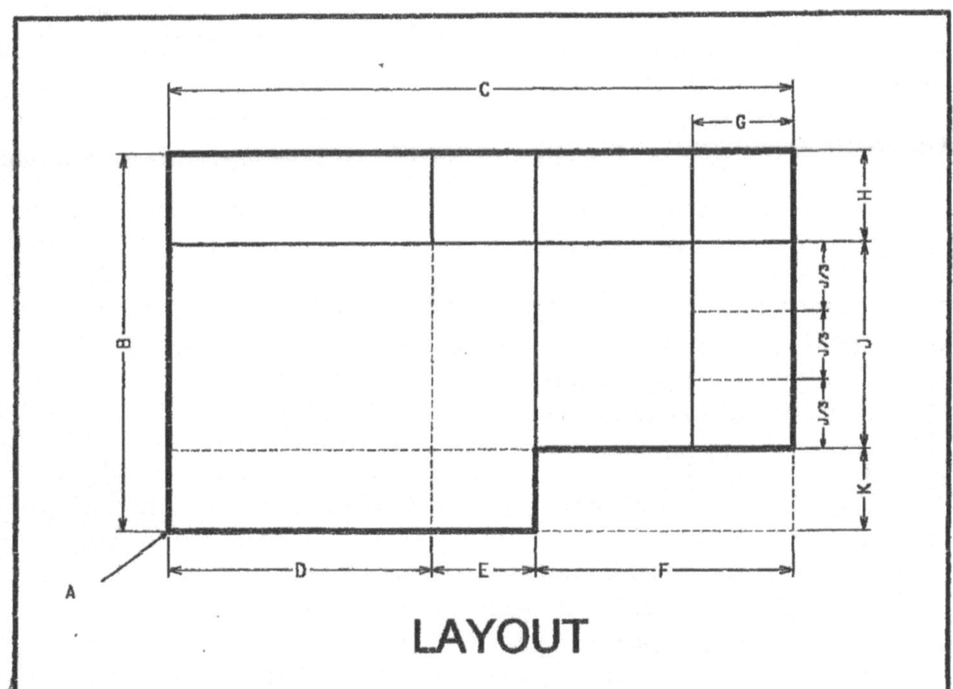

		Value for each X Variation (feet)									
Description		-0	-1	-2	-3	-4	-5	-6	-7	-8	-9
A	Start coordinates	0,0	0,0	10,-6	0,8	2,2	5,-10	10,5	0,5	10,3	0,10
B	Length	92	102	102	98	110	114	96	100	104	94
C	Length	158	168	158	168	152	152	155	150	156	162
D	Length	66	66	62	70	62	60	75	63	60	58
E	Length	26	28	24	24	22	25	18	23	26	21
F	Length	66	74	72	74	68	67	62	64	70	83
G	Length	26	28	25	30	26	27	24	35	33	24
H	Length	22	27	28	24	26	24	28	22	18	22
J	Length	50	53	48	48	50	56	48	50	55	50
K	Length	20	22	26	26	34	34	20	28	31	22

ADDITIONAL NOTES

LINES DESCRIPTION	LINECODE	LINEWEIGHT	COLOR
OUTER LINE	0-SOLID	6	2-GREEN
INTERIOR SOLID	0-SOLID	2	2-GREEN
INTERIOR DASHED	3-LONG DASH	0	2-GREEN

note: Draw one model of LAYOUT assigned to you. ie. LAYOUT-3 dimensions are highlighted above. Other students may be assigned other LAYOUT-#.

DRAWING BORDER	0-SOLID	3	3-RED

DIMENSIONS	NOT NEEDED

TEXT	LINECODE	LINEWEIGHT	COLOR	FONT	SIXE
DRAWING TITLE	0-SOLID	0	0-WHITE	ARIAL	8 X 8

OTHER SETTINGS	
WORKING UNITS	FEET : INCHES
GRID DISPLAY	OFF
FILL	ON

Exercise	Concepts / Tools / Lessons	for MODULE 7

Alpha Bldg.dgn

pg 206

Creation and usage Cells, Hatch, Cross-Hatch and Paaerning.

Additional practice with Multi-lines, AccuDraw, Area measurements and Text placements.

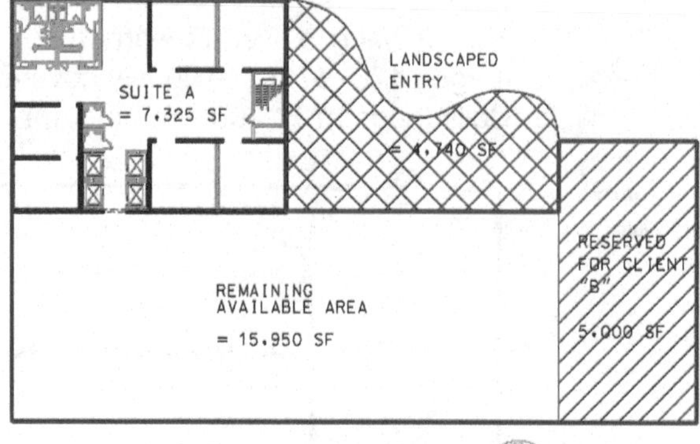

ALPHA BLDG

ABC SITE.DGN

pg 300–302

Working in 3D, View Control in 3D, creation of 3d surfaces and solids. Manipulation and Modifications in 3D. Visualization techniques. Image capture. Section and Elevation concepts.

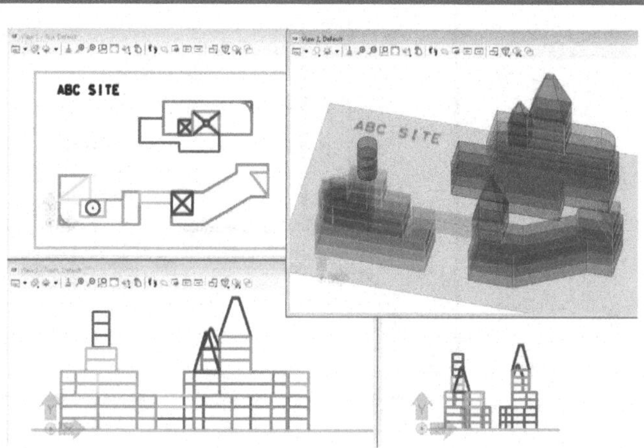

SKYPORT.dgn

pg 294-296

Working with Reference Files. Attaching and manipulating the Parking Lot dgn file created in previous sessions. 2D & 3D ref. files.

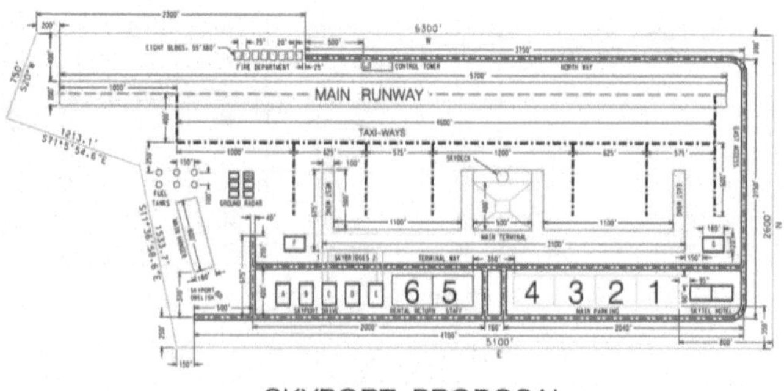

SKYPORT PROPOSAL

Additional file for practice for the advanced student in 3D. pg 294-296

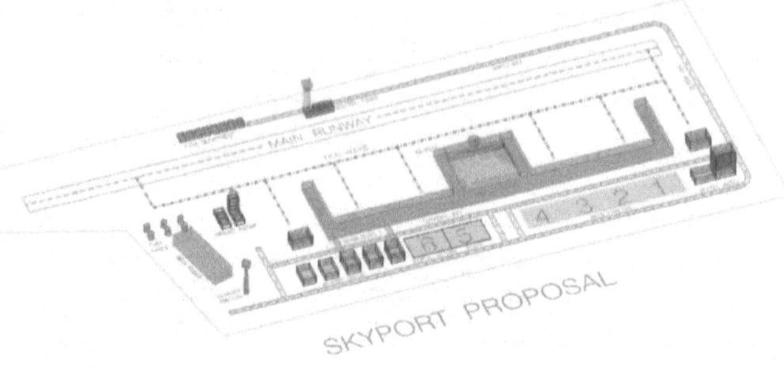

Module 7

Reference Files, Cells & 3D

Key CAD exercise concepts REVIEW up to Week 7

* indicates concepts that were not thoroughly covered yet, but will be shown in class, depending on time

1. **Text Placement and Manipulation**
   a. Settings (in Tool Settings Dialog box)
      i. KEY-IN short-cuts (as listed) *
      ii. Height, TH = value
      iii. Width, TW = value
      iv. Font, FT = number
      v. Line Spacing *, LS = value (Element > Text Styles)
      vi. Justification *
   b. Placement Method
      i. By Origin
      ii. Fitted
      iii. Above Element
      iv. Below Element
      v. On Element
      vi. Along Element
   c. Place Note *
   d. Edit Text *
   e. Spell Checker *
   f. Match Text Attributes *
   g. Change Text Attributes *
   h. Place Text Node *
   i. Copy/Increment Text *
   j. Enter Data Fields
      i. Fill In Single Enter Data Field
      ii. Auto Fill In Enter Data Fields
      iii. Copy Enter Data Field *
      iv. Copy/Increment Enter Data Field *

Text Styles

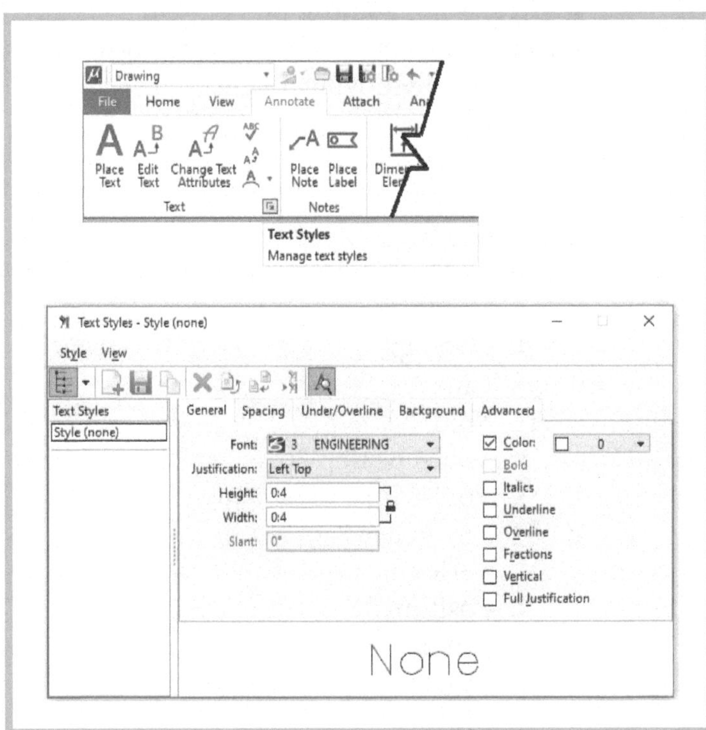

- **k.** Additional Text Related
    - **i.** Importing Text from external files
        - **1.** File > Import > Text
        - **2.** Include command (INCL)
    - **ii.** Fractions *
    - **iii.** Drop Text *
    - **iv.** View Attributes **<Ctrl>** b (affects visibility of Fill, Text, Nodes & Enter Data Fields)

Importing Text from External Files

Simplest! For the CONNECT Edition: File (Takes you to the Backstage), Import, Common File Types, Text (*.txt)

2. AccuDraw and AccuSnap

- **a.** Turning ON/OFF
- **b.** Utilize as a time-saver
- **c.** AccuDraw Compass
    - **i.** Rectangular entry mode
    - **ii.** Polar entry mode
    - **iii.** Locking to axes
- **d.** AccuSnap audio sound On/Off

3. Fence Manipulation (Multiple Element Selection)

- **a.** Placing/Removing a Fence
- **b.** Fence Type
    - **i.** Block
    - **ii.** Shape
    - **iii.** Circle *
- **c.** Fence Mode (Defines the Fence Contents)
    - **i.** Inside
    - **ii.** Overlap
    - **iii.** Clip
    - **iv.** Void
    - **v.** Void-Overlap
    - **vi.** Void-Clip
- **d.** Modify Fence *
    - **i.** Vertex *
    - **ii.** Position *
- **e.** Manipulate Fence Contents
    - **i.** Copy
    - **ii.** Move
    - **iii.** Rotate
    - **iv.** Scale
    - **v.** Mirror
    - **vi.** Stretch
    - **vii.** NOTE: Additional commands also have the option to "Use Fence" such as when using Change Element Attributes, Copy or Move or Construct Array, etc. *
- **f.** Similar Command: *Element Selection Tool*
    - **i.** NOTE: This is NOT a fence, but does some similar functions
    - **ii.** Single Selection

- iii. Multiple Element Selection
  1. Adding elements to the set (hold down shift, then select more)
  2. Removing elements from the set (hold down shift, select to remove)
- iv. Canceling the selection set when done

4. **Measurement Tools**
   - a. Related Settings:
     - i. Settings > Design File > Coordinate Readout (See pg 150 for CONNECT Edition)
   - b. Distance
     - i. Between Points
     - ii. Along Element *
     - iii. Perpendicular *
     - iv. Minimum Between *
   - c. Radius
   - d. Angle (between lines)
   - e. Length (gives length and *bearing* if readout is set right)
   - f. Area

     Method:
     - i. Element
     - ii. Fence
     - iii. Intersection
     - iv. Union
     - v. Difference
     - vi. Flood
     - vii. Points
5. **Dimensioning**
   - a. General Terminology
     - i. Dimension Line
     - ii. Extension Lines
     - iii. Arrow or Terminators
   - b. Settings, use Element > Dimensions (See pg 155 for CONNECT Edition)
     - i. Text (turn on items and set as needed)
       1. Color
       2. Weight
       3. Font
       4. Height
       5. Width
     - ii. Units
       1. Label (MU label – SU label, for xx'-xx" if using English units)
       2. Accuracy (decimal places or fractional accuracy, ¼" , ½" , etc.)
     - iii. Unit Format
       1. Length
       2. Degrees
          - a. Decimal … or …
          - b. Degrees, Minutes, Seconds (Bearings)

c. Distance (between points)
d. Radius (Radius, Diameter, Center Mark)
e. Length (of element)
f. Angle (between lines & by defined points)

6. **Multi-Lines**
   a. Creating new lines and offsets
      i. Startcaps & Endcaps
      ii. Symbologies
   b. Multi-Line Joints
7. **Other Misc. Commands**
   a. Place Point Curve
   b. Place Stream Curve
   c. Modification (more)
      i. Modifying curves *
      ii. Insert/Delete Vertices *

NOTES

Reference Files

Module 7

MicroStation V8*i*

MicroStation
CONNECT Edition

 AUTOCAD

and

Introduction to Civil Engineering

Michael D. Jue, P.E.

Module Objectives

7. **Familiarization with concept of Cells, Patterning & Reference Files**
8. **Exposure to Plotting Concepts & Methods - View many samples provided by the instructor**
9. **Intro to 3D drawing Concepts, view 3D files, images, show creation of simple models, introduce rendering concepts**
10. **Closing thoughts / Class Evaluation**

Reference File Concepts

- Lets you view external files
- External files cannot be altered by you
- Very similar to more levels (μ-stn) or like inserting a block (ACAD)
- Others can be working on the External File, even though you have it attached!
- Extremely useful for sharing drawings!
- ACAD Xref's can be nested, μStn can, also

Reference File Concepts

- Attachments can be Coincident .. or ..
- Moved, Scaled, Rotated, Mirrored, etc
- Selected Layers/blocks/etc can be attached (ACAD) XBind
- Selected Levels can be displayed on or off (mStn) REF LEV ON/OFF
- Portions by fence can be displayed or masked (mStn) "Clip Boundary/Mask"

CAD Companion Workbook 7.4

Reference File Concepts

- You can use Snaps to locate specific points in reference files
- µStn allows you to copy items from reference files into the active file
- µStn allows you to override the symbology display of reference files
- µStn allows you to decide whether the reference file should be printed or not

CAD Companion Workbook 7.5

Reference File Example

Two Separate Files:

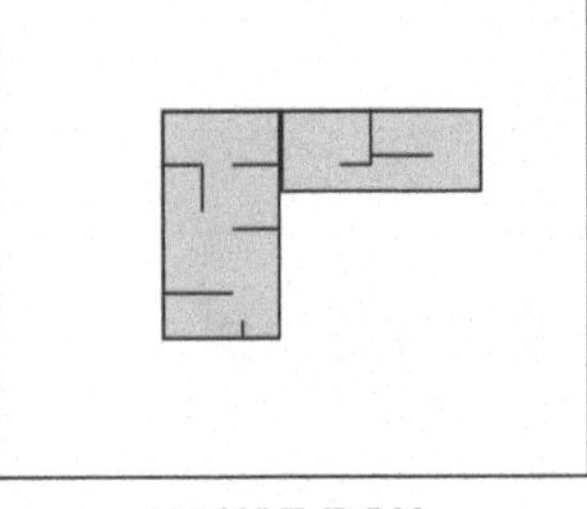

HOUSE.DGN

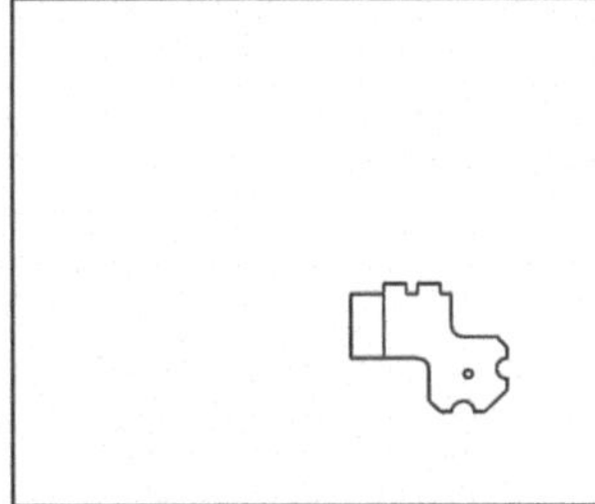

POOL.DGN

CAD Companion Workbook 7.6

Reference File Example

HOUSE.DGN, with POOL.DGN file attached:

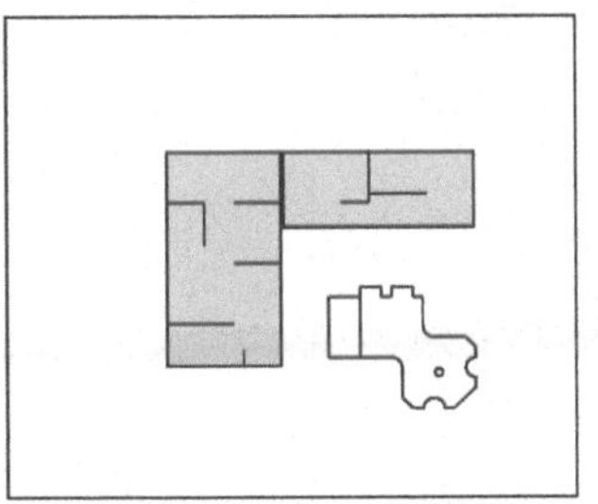

This is Coincident Attachment

Reference File attachments are like having additional files stuck onto the bottom of a clear dining room table.

You can see the files, but you cannot change them.

Reference File Example

Another Separate File:

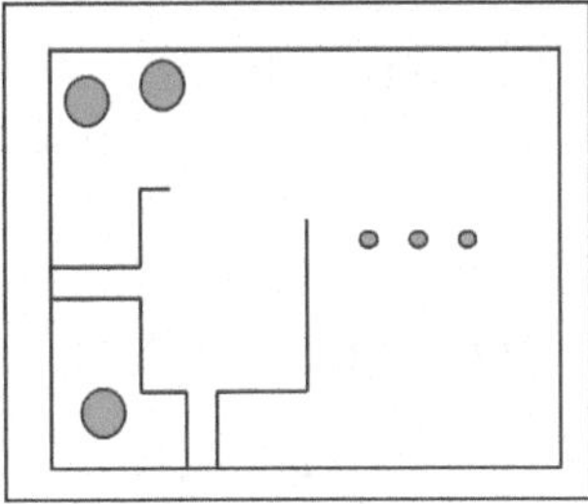

YARD.DGN

HOUSE.DGN after YARD.DGN is also attached.

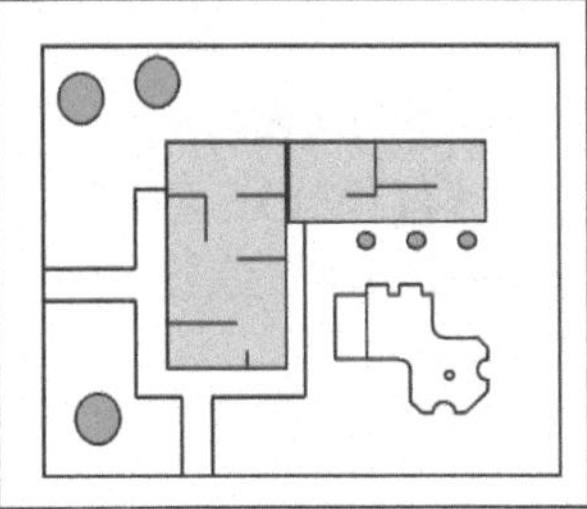

Files Attached Coincidentally "Aligned"

Reference File Example

This is what YARD. DGN looks like with HOUSE.DGN attached

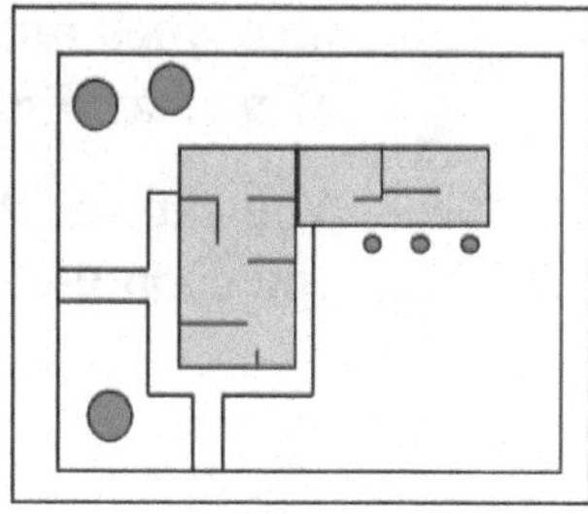

YARD.DGN

YARD.DGN also with POOL.DGN attached, moved and rotated -90°

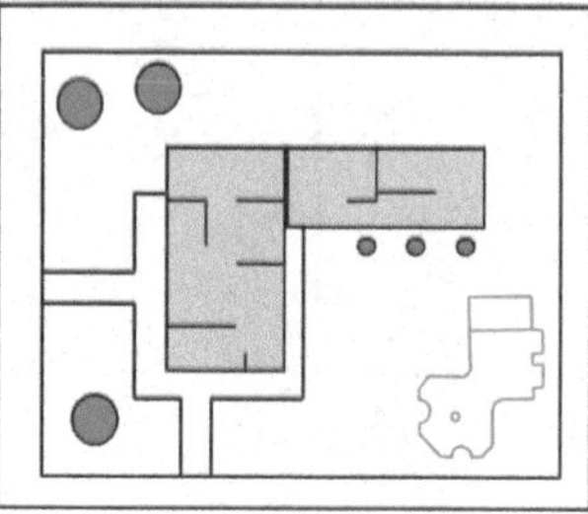

YARD.DGN POOL.DGN is NOT Attached Coincidentally

Pool.dgn won't actually change to red

Reference File Example

FINAL CHANGES, ADDITION OF PATIO TO THE YARD.DGN DRAWING

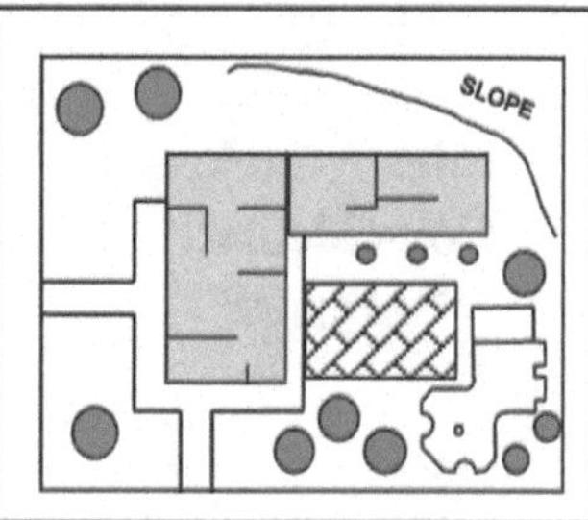

YARD.DGN

THIS IS HOW POOL.DGN STILL LOOKS!

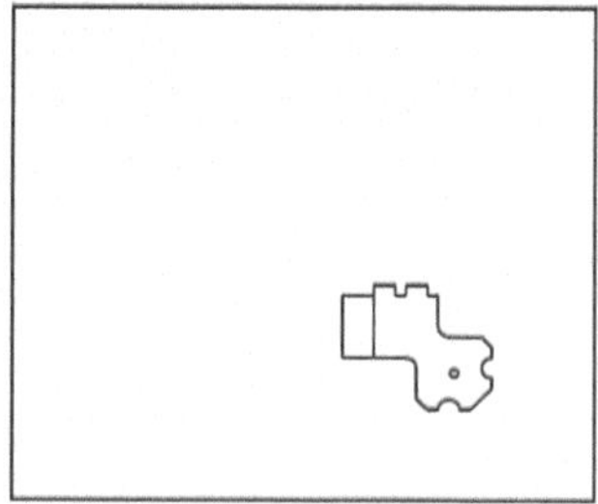

POOL.DGN

Reference File Example

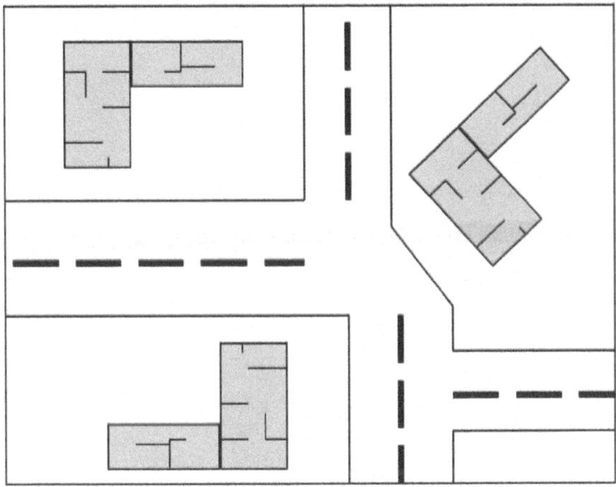

Yet Another File with HOUSE. DGN Attached three times. Note the different locations and the Rotations.

µStn Reference Files

- SHO REF Displays dialog box
- RF = filename, logical name, description (key-in for Attaching reference files)
- a Logical name is like a nickname for a file instead "newpool.dgn", use "pool"
- RF = by itself shows the Attach dialog box

µStn References Toolbar

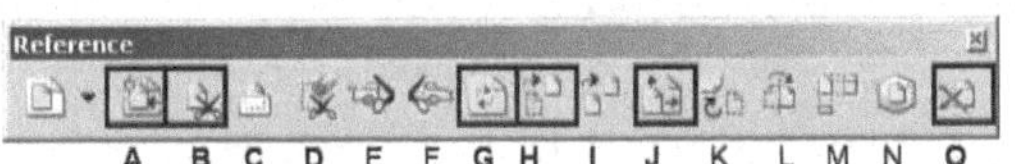

- References Toolbar Menu (major tools hi-lighted)

A. **Attach**
B. **Clip Reference**
C. Mask Reference
D. Delete Clip
E. Clip Front (3D only)
F. Clip Back (3D only)
G. **Reload Reference**
H. **Move Reference**
I. Copy Reference
J. **Scale Reference**
K. Rotate Reference
L. Mirror Reference
M. Copy/Fold Reference
N. Set Reference Presentation
O. **Detach Reference**

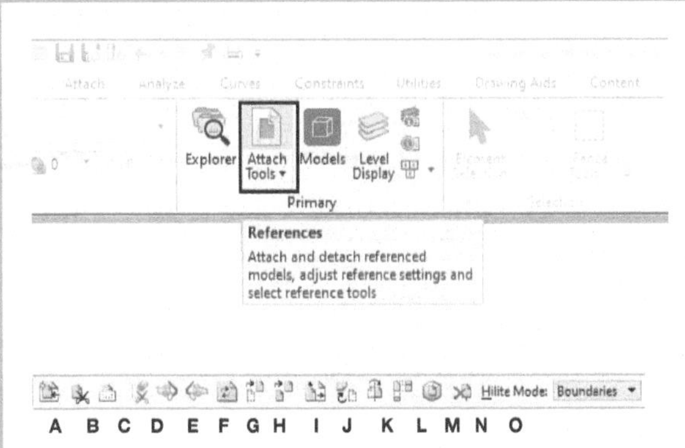

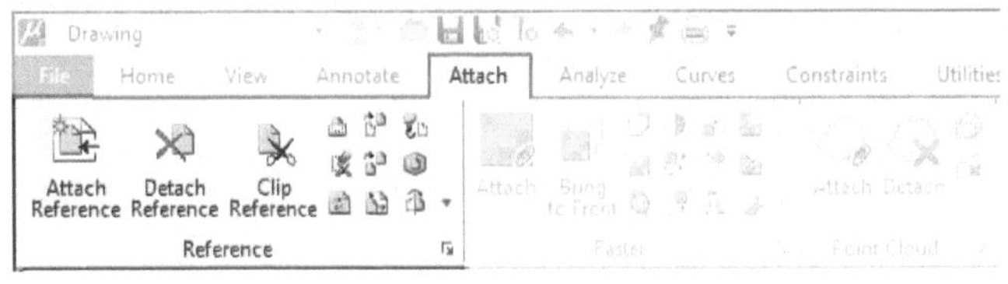

µStn Reference Files Dialog

- Settings Menu
  - Attachment On/Off for:
    - Display
    - Snap
    - Locate
  - Levels On/Off
  - Level Symbology Overrides
    - Controls: Color, Line Style, Weight Display

CAD Companion Workbook 7.13

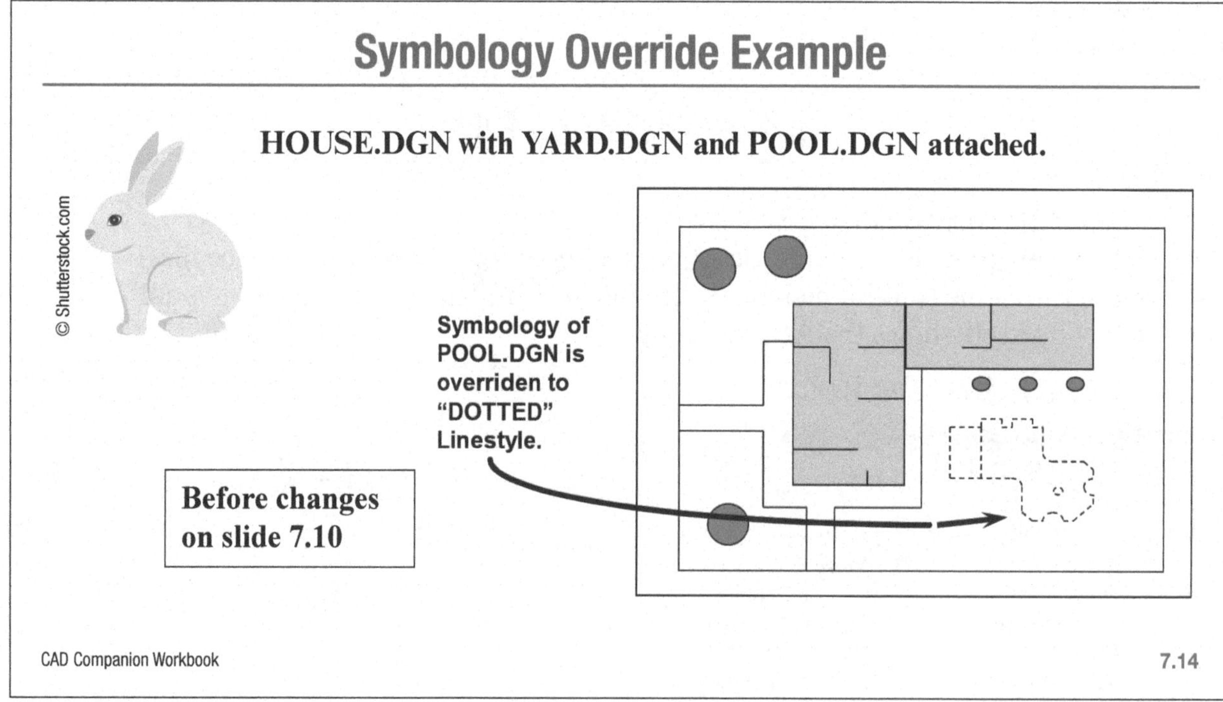

Symbology Override Example
HOUSE.DGN with YARD.DGN and POOL.DGN attached.
© Shutterstock.com
Symbology of POOL.DGN is overriden to "DOTTED" Linestyle.
Before changes on slide 7.10
CAD Companion Workbook
7.14

Symbology Override Example

THIS IS HOW POOL.DGN STILL LOOKS!

POOL.DGN

CAD Companion Workbook 7.15

µStn Reference Files Dialog

- **Additional Key-ins**
  - REF ATT [Name]
  - REF DET [Name/ALL]
  - REF DISP ON/OFF [Name/ALL]
  - REF LEV ON/OFF [Name] (levels)
  - REF SNAP ON/OFF [Name/ALL]
  - REF LOC [ON/OFF] [Name/ALL]
  - REF CLIP BOUND [Name/ALL]
  - REF CLIP MASK [Name/ALL]

CAD Companion Workbook 7.16

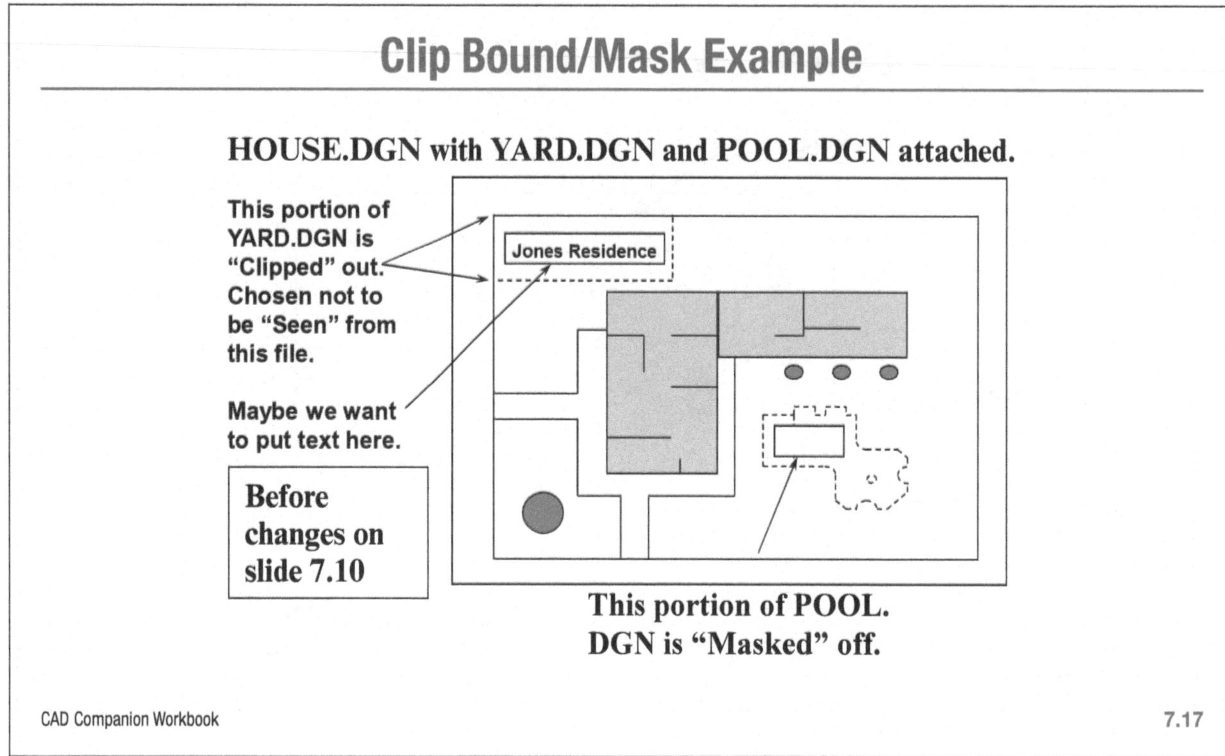
Clip Bound/Mask Example
HOUSE.DGN with YARD.DGN and POOL.DGN attached.
This portion of YARD.DGN is "Clipped" out. Chosen not to be "Seen" from this file.
Jones Residence
Maybe we want to put text here.
Before changes on slide 7.10
This portion of POOL. DGN is "Masked" off.
CAD Companion Workbook
7.17

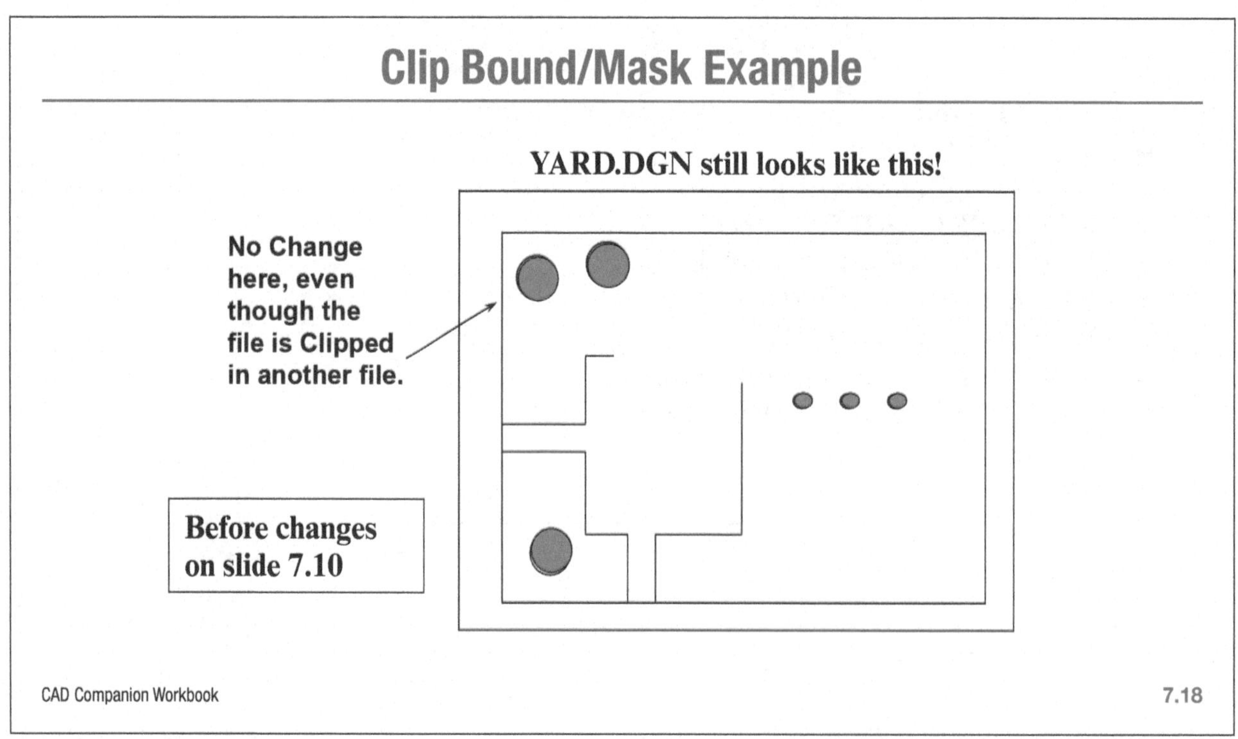
Clip Bound/Mask Example
YARD.DGN still looks like this!
No Change here, even though the file is Clipped in another file.
Before changes on slide 7.10
CAD Companion Workbook
7.18

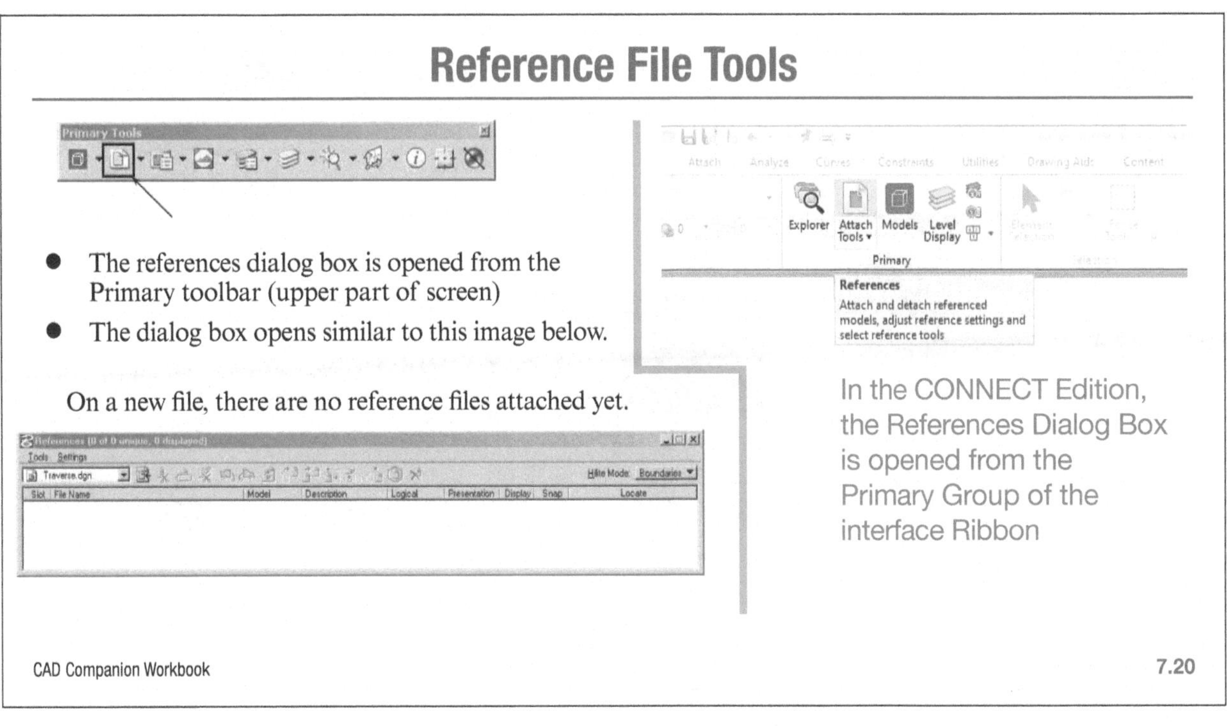

Reference File Tools
- The references dialog box is opened from the Primary toolbar (upper part of screen)
- The dialog box opens similar to this image below.
On a new file, there are no reference files attached yet.
In the CONNECT Edition, the References Dialog Box is opened from the Primary Group of the interface Ribbon
CAD Companion Workbook
7.20

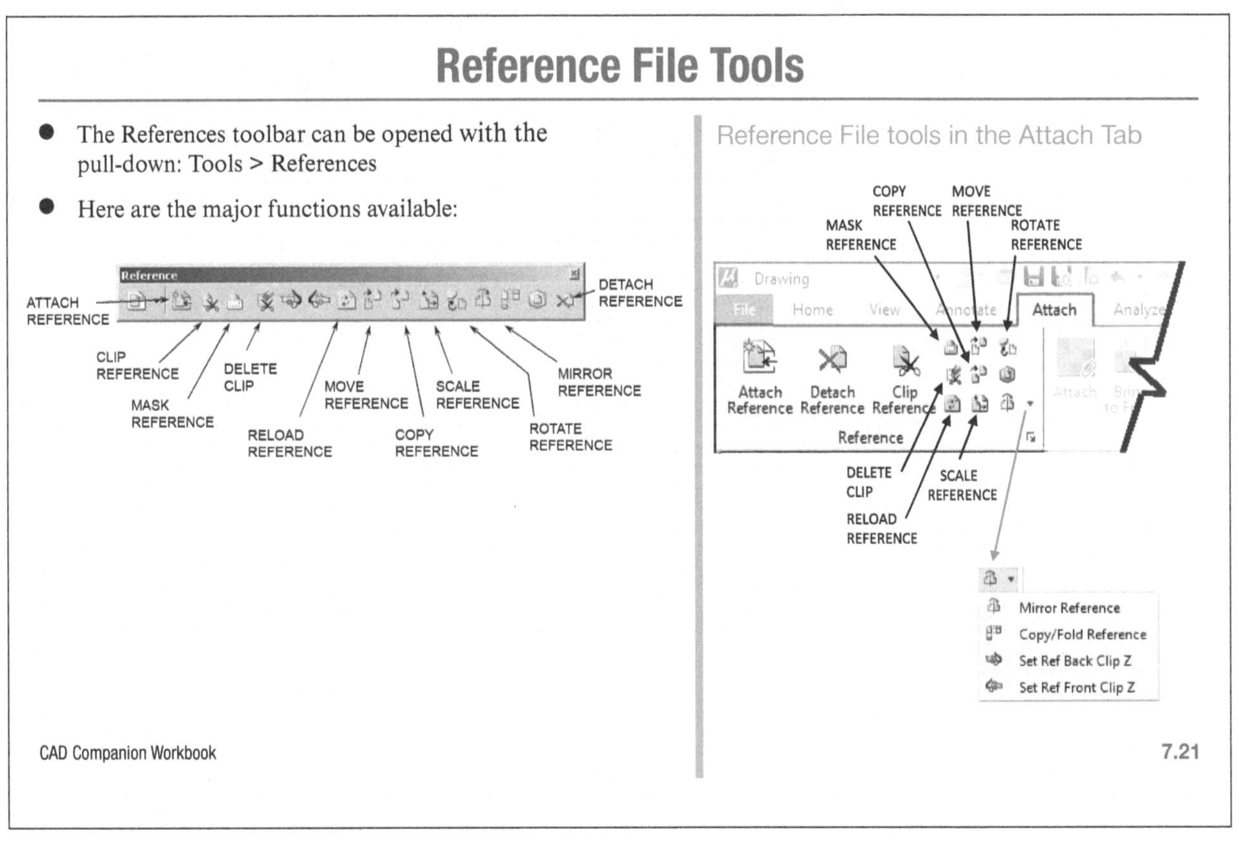

Reference File Tools
- The References toolbar can be opened with the pull-down: Tools > References
- Here are the major functions available:
ATTACH REFERENCE
CLIP REFERENCE
MASK REFERENCE
DELETE CLIP
RELOAD REFERENCE
MOVE REFERENCE
COPY REFERENCE
SCALE REFERENCE
ROTATE REFERENCE
MIRROR REFERENCE
DETACH REFERENCE
Reference File tools in the Attach Tab
COPY REFERENCE
MOVE REFERENCE
MASK REFERENCE
ROTATE REFERENCE
Attach
Attach Reference
Detach Reference
Clip Reference
Reference
DELETE CLIP
SCALE REFERENCE
RELOAD REFERENCE
Mirror Reference
Copy/Fold Reference
Set Ref Back Clip Z
Set Ref Front Clip Z
CAD Companion Workbook
7.21

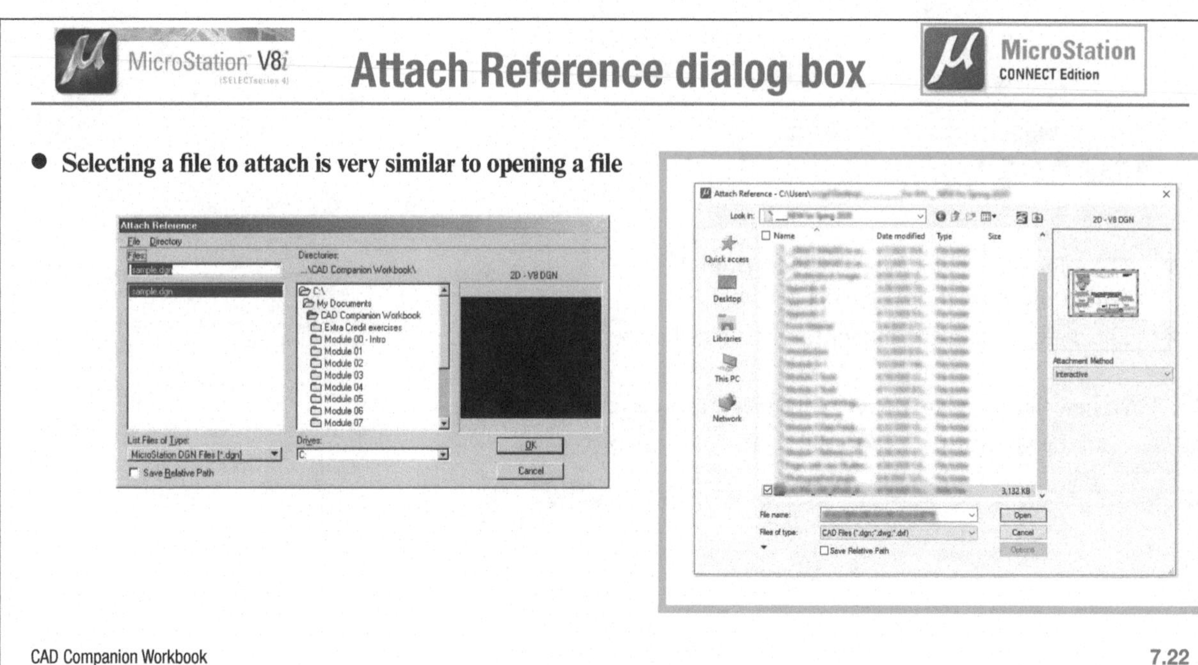
MicroStation V8i
Attach Reference dialog box
MicroStation CONNECT Edition
Selecting a file to attach is very similar to opening a file
CAD Companion Workbook
7.22

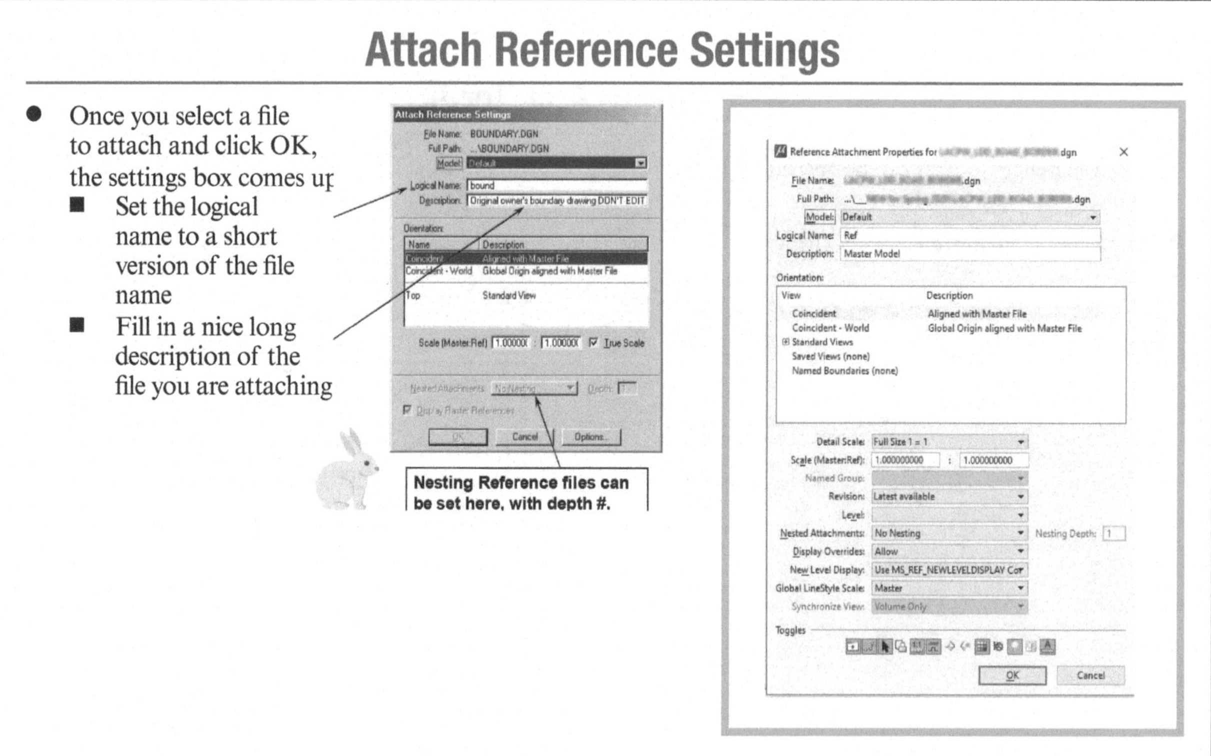
Attach Reference Settings
Once you select a file to attach and click OK, the settings box comes up
Set the logical name to a short version of the file name
Fill in a nice long description of the file you are attaching
Nesting Reference files can be set here, with depth #.
CAD Companion Workbook
7.23

EXAMPLE OF FINISHED DRAWING

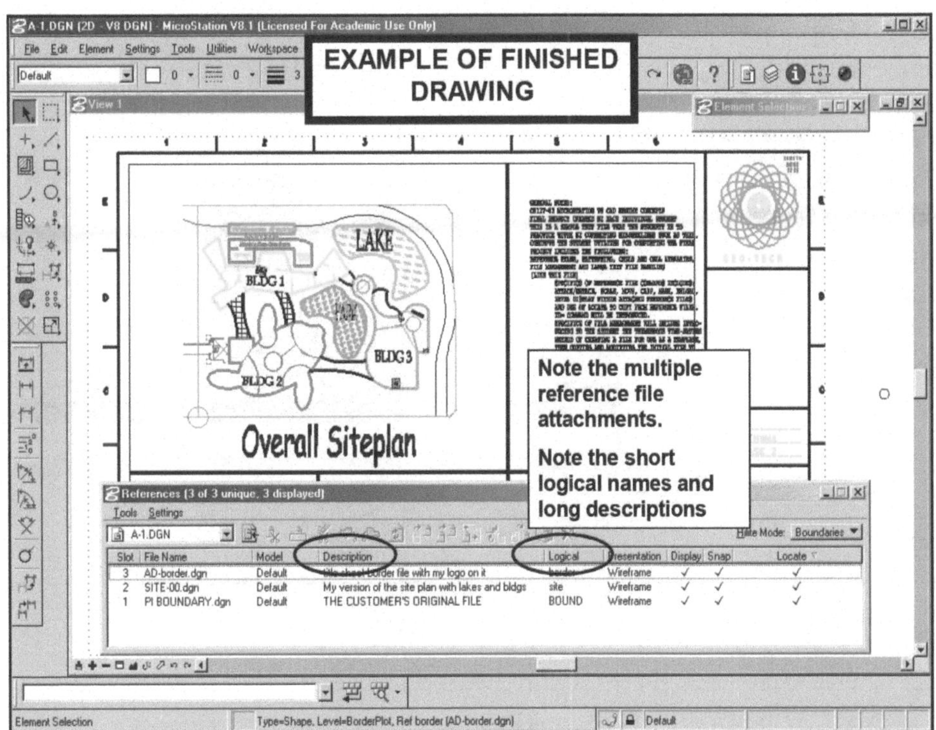

CAD Companion Workbook 7.24

Preparing to Clip References

- Select files to clip
- Place a fence around area that you want to show
- Then select Clip Reference and set method "by fence"
- Results on next slide

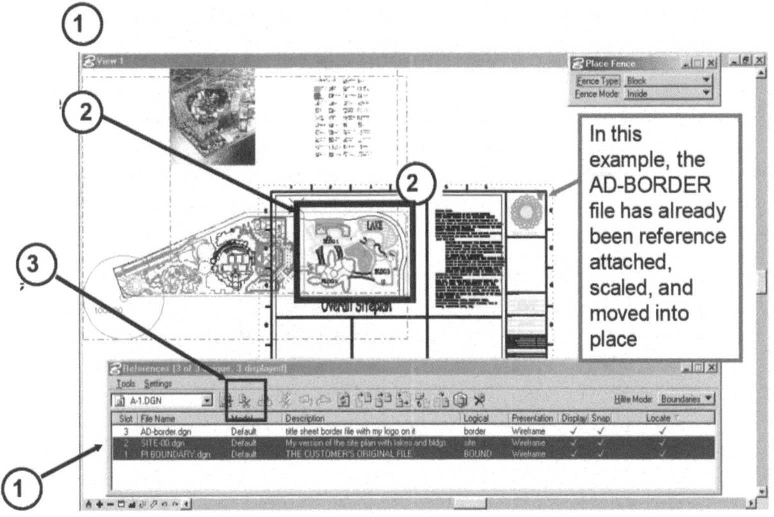

CAD Companion Workbook 7.25

Result of Clip Reference

- Notice the Clip Reference method was set to Fence
- The 2 files selected were reference clipped to the fence boundary placed by the user
- The 2 original files are unaffected!

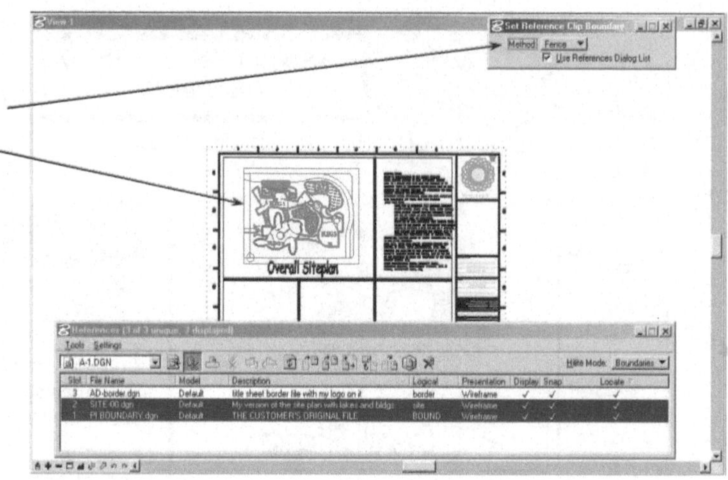

Notes:

Here's a better way to understand the last statement:

The 2 original files are unaffected.

It's like when a video camera operator crops the view closer to a movie star on a television show to show only the face. On the television screen, we now only see the actor's face, but in reality, the person's body, his arms and legs were NOT cut OFF!!! The clipping by the camera did not affect them in the least. Aren't we glad! Aren't they glad?!!

Cells & Patterning

Cells are a group of graphics that the user can place over and over again on a drawing. They are like grouped elements, but are named. Examples Of Cells: North Arrow, Delta symbol.

Cells are stored in cell libraries. Cell libraries are a special type of file and are not drawing files. Cell libraries can be shared with other users allowing them to use cells that others have created.

Cells can be used for patterning, also. Using cells can save CAD users lots and lots of drawing time!

MicroStation V8i
Cells Toolbox
Cells - Task
Place Active Cell
Cell Origin
The Cells dialog box: Element > Cells
Drawing
Place SmartLine
Place Block
Place Circle
Hatch Area
Attach Tags
Place Text
Place Active Cell
Measure Distance
Dimension Element
Design Composition
Create Views (2D)
Sheet Composition
Annotate
1 Place Active Cell
2 Place Active Cell Matrix
3 Select And Place Cell
4 Define Cell Origin
5 Identify Cell
6 Place Active Line Terminator
7 Replace Cells
8 Place Cell Index
Open 'Cells' as Toolbox
File
Use Shared Cells
Display All Cells In Path
Display: Wireframe
Name Description Type Where
AREAINFO Table to record names and... Grph Lbry
elevator small elevator-Dover brand Grph Lbry
Lav Single Lavatory Grph Lbry
North North Arrow Symbol Grph Lbry
Restroom Mens and Womens RR core Grph Lbry
stair stair typical Grph Lbry
stair2 stair typical new code Grph Lbry
Active Cells
Placement Restroom
Point Restroom
Terminator NONE
Pattern NONE
Edit...
Delete
Create...
Share

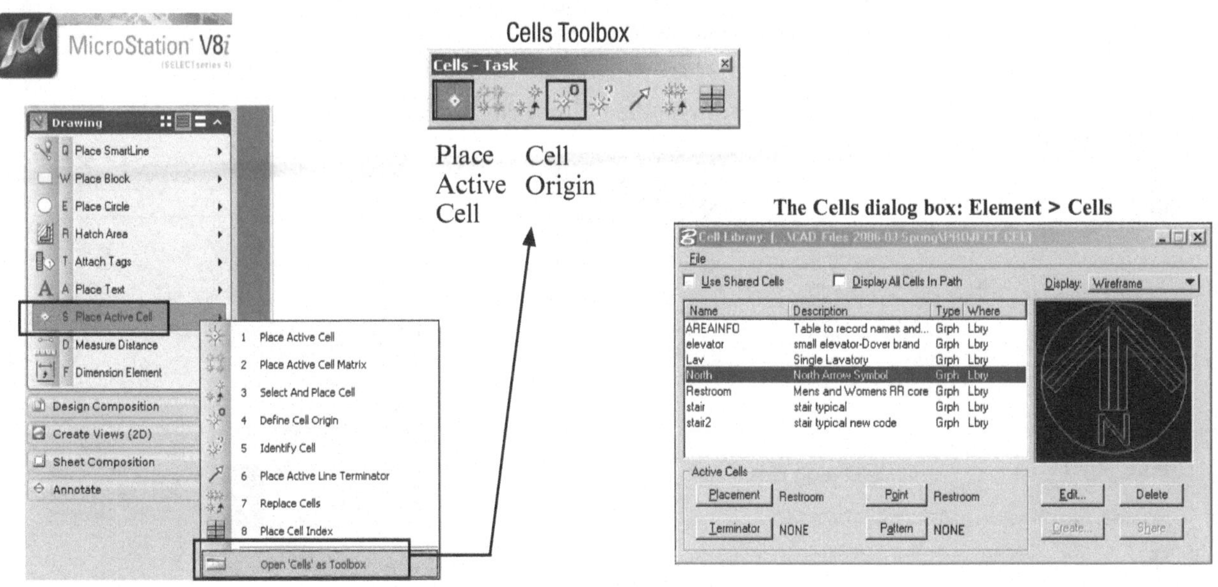

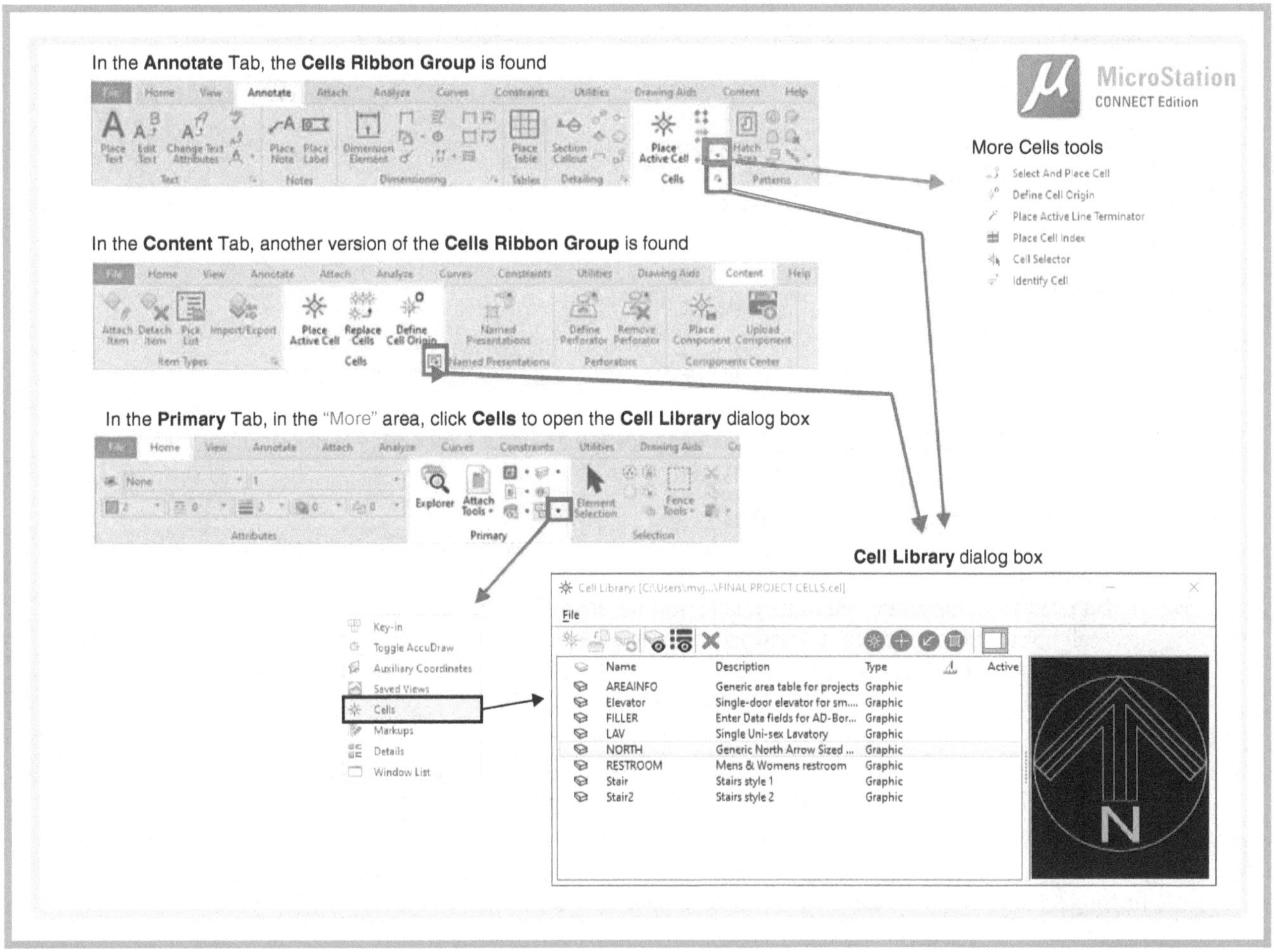

In the **Annotate** Tab, the **Cells Ribbon Group** is found
MicroStation CONNECT Edition
More Cells tools
Select And Place Cell
Define Cell Origin
Place Active Line Terminator
Place Cell Index
Cell Selector
Identify Cell
In the **Content** Tab, another version of the **Cells Ribbon Group** is found
In the **Primary** Tab, in the "More" area, click **Cells** to open the **Cell Library** dialog box
Cell Library dialog box
Key-in
Toggle AccuDraw
Auxiliary Coordinates
Saved Views
Cells
Markups
Details
Window List
File
Name Description Type Active
AREAINFO Generic area table for projects Graphic
Elevator Single-door elevator for sm.... Graphic
FILLER Enter Data fields for AD-Bor... Graphic
LAV Single Uni-sex Lavatory Graphic
NORTH Generic North Arrow Sized ... Graphic
RESTROOM Mens & Womens restroom Graphic
Stair Stairs style 1 Graphic
Stair2 Stairs style 2 Graphic

Place Active Cell is the main tool for placing existing cells onto your drawing file. Upon placement, the user can select the active angle and scale of the placement. Dropping a cell returns it to its original components.

Cell Origin is a tool used in the creation of new cells. See description below.

Creating New Cells- Four requirements **must be satisfied in order to create a new cell in a cell library.**

1. A **cell library** must be attached (see notes on Attaching Existing or New cell libraries below)
2. You must have some **graphics drawn** on the screen that will be used for the cell.
3. The graphics must be **selected by a fence contents or selection set**.
4. You must place a **cell origin** somewhere on the screen (see notes on selecting cell origins, below)

Once all four of these occur, the **Create** button on the Cells dialog box becomes available. See below.

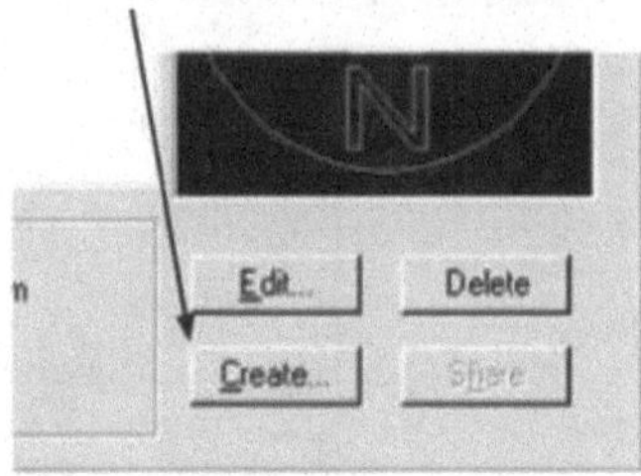

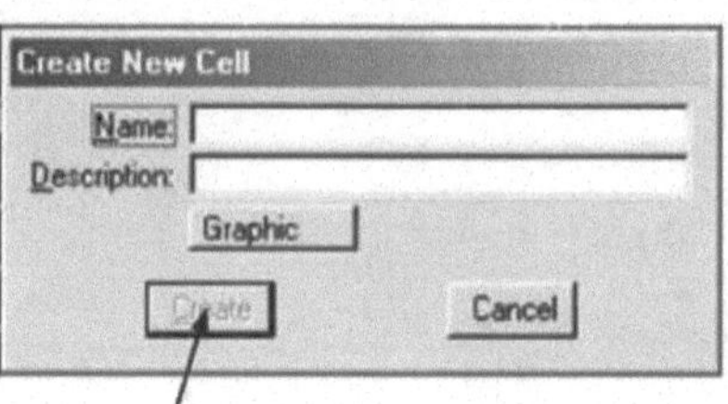

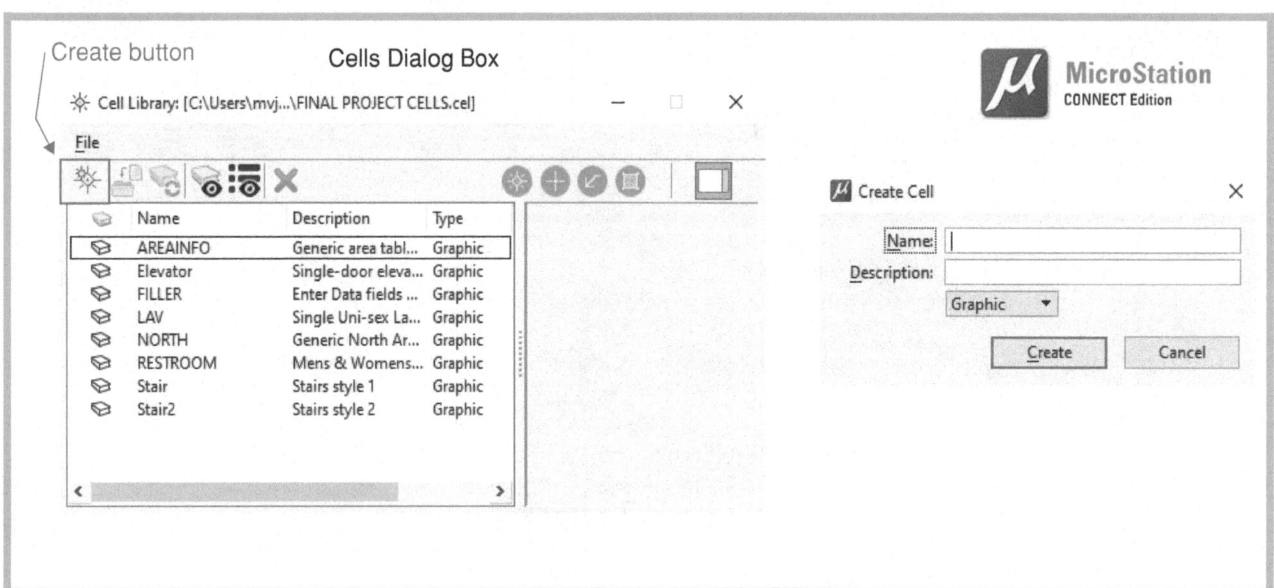

Next, fill in the desired cell name and a description of the cell, then select Create. The new cell should then appear in the Cells dialog box and can be previewed if desired.

Attaching Existing or Creating New Cell Libraries

A. Attach an **existing cell library** with a pull-down on the Cells dialog box: **File > Attach**, then select the existing cell library file. ...or...

B. If you need to **create a new cell library,** use this pull down: **File > New,** then select the location to store the new cell library file at and select a new name for it. Note: Take note of the location and name given. Since the user selects these, the instructor would have no idea where you select to store the file or what you may have named the file, in case you lose track of these at a later date.

Cell Origins

A. Cell origins are generally **placed at the center of cells**, if there is a center. For rectangular shaped cells, users may generally select the **lower left corner** or other convenient corner for the cell origin.

B. The **Cell Origin** tool places a **bold plus sign** at the selected origin location. It stays on the screen until the user reselects the **Cell Origin** tool, again. (That is how a cell origin mark is removed from the screen, similar to removing a fence from the screen by reselecting Place Fence.

Placing Cells

A. Select Place Active Cell or use the Cell Selector. **Utilities > Cell Selector**

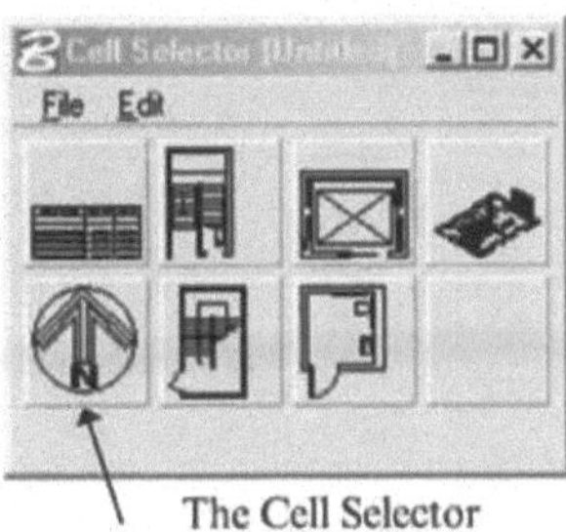

The Cell Selector

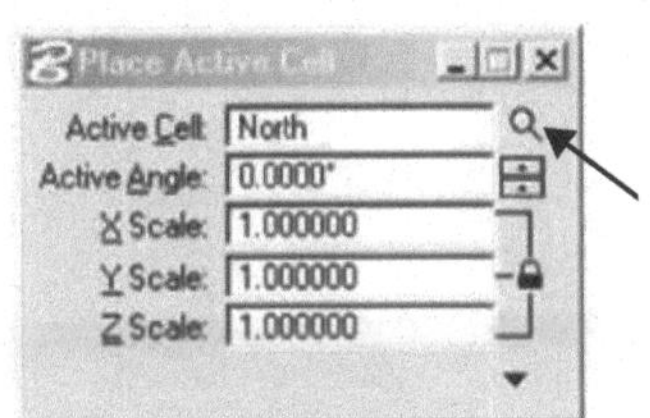

Tool Settings box for Place Active Cell

One can select the cell from its picture on the Cell Selector or by typing its name in the Tool Settings box.

© Pranch/Shutterstock.com

Alternatively, selecting the magnifying tool, will bring up the Cells Dialog box.

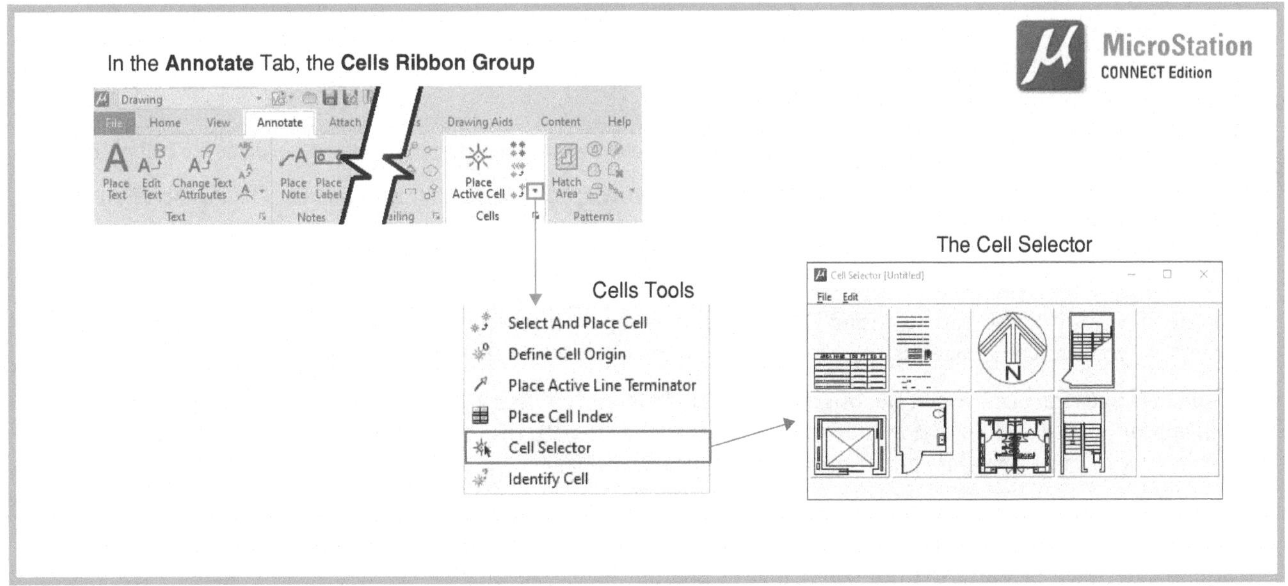

Pre-made Cell Libraries

Many pre-made cell libraries are supplied with MicroStation. Some are area patterns, others are linear. See the location, within the MicroStation product: C:\Program Files\Bentley\Workspace\System\cell

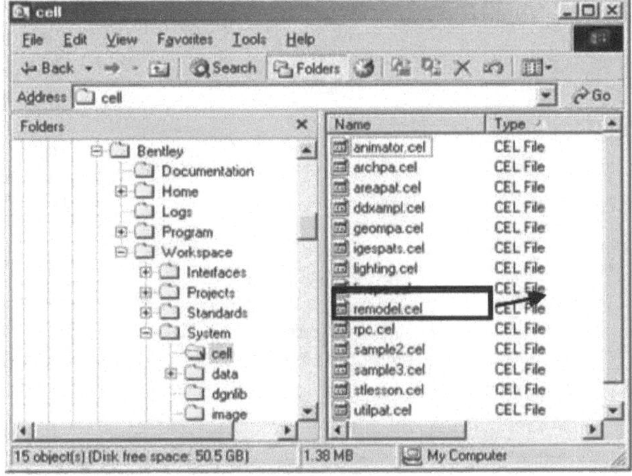

Patterning with Cells

One can select a cell to be used as a pattern. From the **Patterns toolbar**, select **Pattern Area**

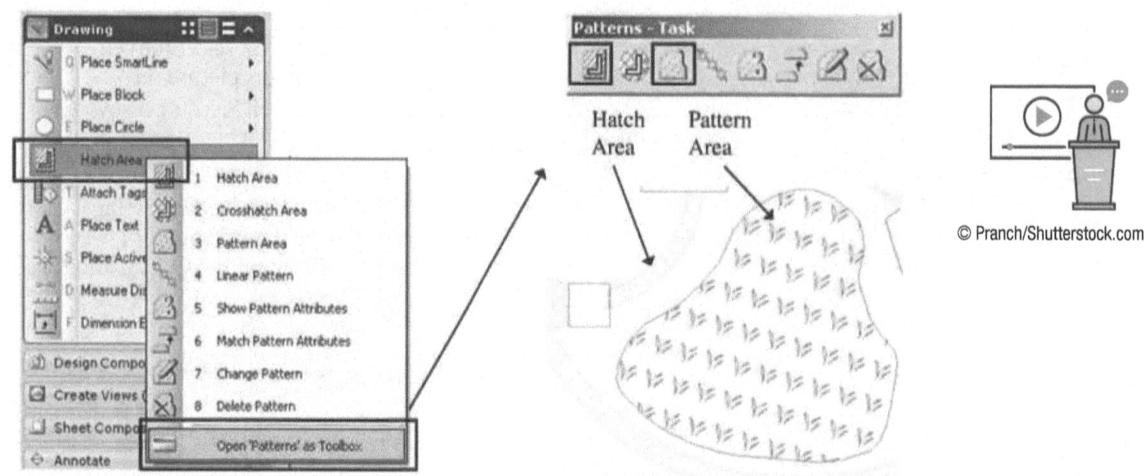

On the Tool Settings box, type in the cell name to use, or use the magnifying tool method to select the cell pattern.

When patterning with a cell, you may set: Scale, Angle, row spacing and column spacing. The Association lock may be set on or off.

The example at right shows a Pattern Area with a cell by the method Flood.

Delete previously placed patterns using Delete Pattern. Note: if you delete lots of patterns you may want to compress your design to save disk space. Select the pull-down: **File > Compress Design**.

Orphaned patterns occur when the original associated region boundary outline is deleted. Then the pattern will appear dashed and bold. It is not proper to leave orphaned patterns on your file. Delete the orphaned pattern, recreate the original boundary and then pattern the area once again.

MicroStation can ignore a gp in the boundary if you set the Max gap setting to a higher value; typically it starts out at zero. A gap in your boundary is indicated by the error message: **No enclosing region found,** when you attempt to hatch or pattern a boundary that hs a gap.

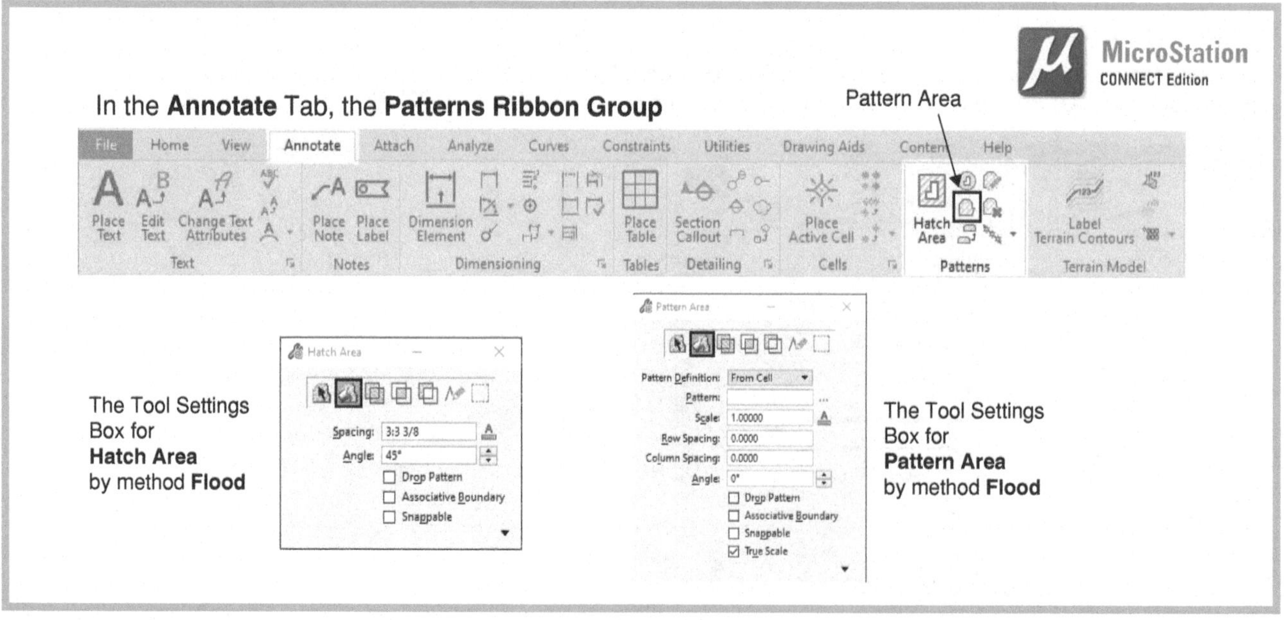

The Tool Settings Box for **Hatch Area** by method **Flood**

The Tool Settings Box for **Pattern Area** by method **Flood**

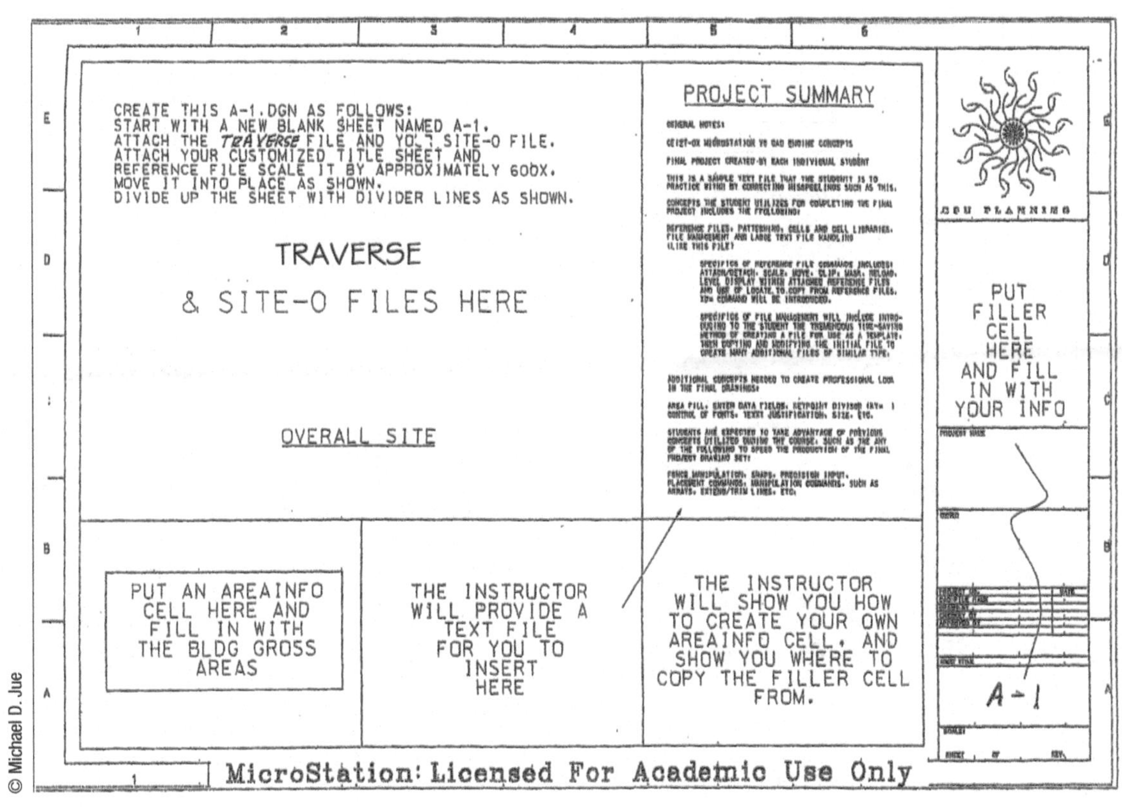
CREATE THIS A-1.DGN AS FOLLOWS:
START WITH A NEW BLANK SHEET NAMED A-1.
ATTACH THE TRAVERSE FILE AND YOUR SITE-O FILE.
ATTACH YOUR CUSTOMIZED TITLE SHEET AND
REFERENCE FILE SCALE IT BY APPROXIMATELY 600X.
MOVE IT INTO PLACE AS SHOWN.
DIVIDE UP THE SHEET WITH DIVIDER LINES AS SHOWN.
TRAVERSE
& SITE-O FILES HERE
OVERALL SITE
PROJECT SUMMARY
PUT FILLER CELL HERE AND FILL IN WITH YOUR INFO
PUT AN AREAINFO CELL HERE AND FILL IN WITH THE BLDG GROSS AREAS
THE INSTRUCTOR WILL PROVIDE A TEXT FILE FOR YOU TO INSERT HERE
THE INSTRUCTOR WILL SHOW YOU HOW TO CREATE YOUR OWN AREAINFO CELL, AND SHOW YOU WHERE TO COPY THE FILLER CELL FROM.
A-1
MicroStation: Licensed For Academic Use Only

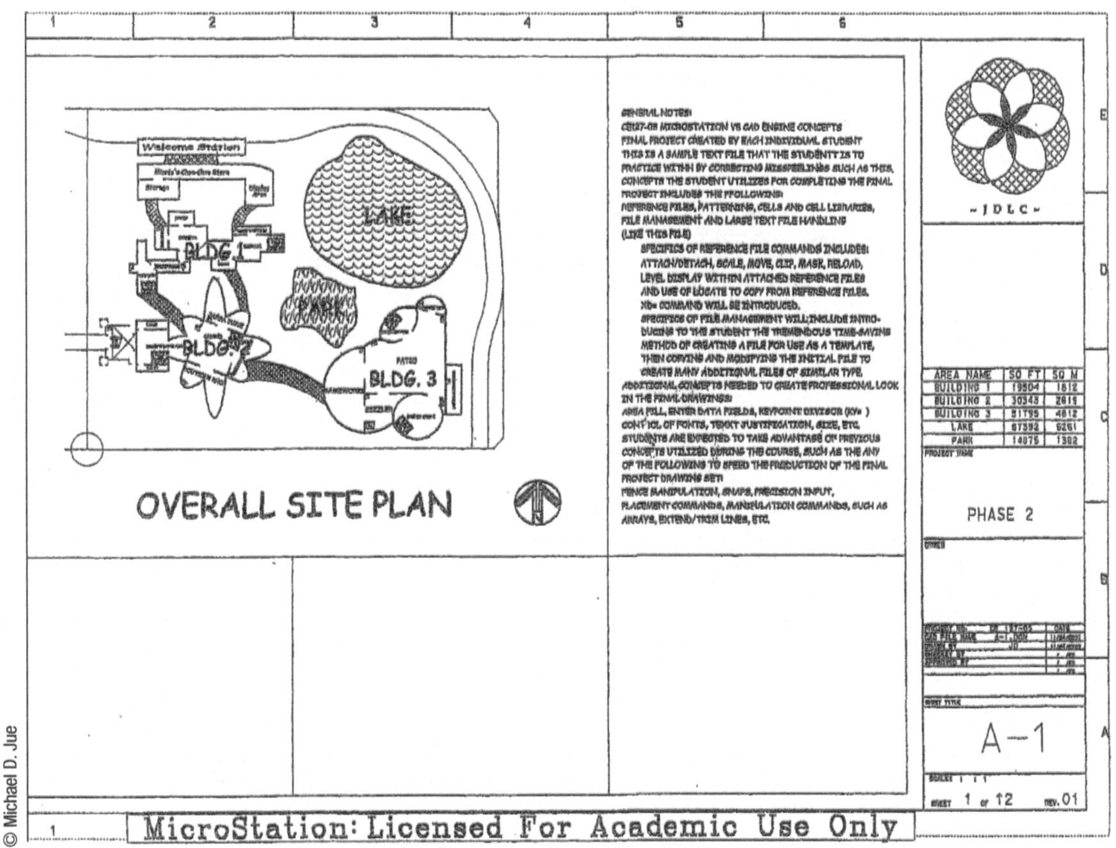
LAKE
PARK
BLDG. 1
BLDG. 2
BLDG. 3
OVERALL SITE PLAN
GENERAL NOTES:
FINAL PROJECT CREATED BY EACH INDIVIDUAL STUDENT
~JDLC~
AREA NAME
SQ FT
SQ M
BUILDING 1
BUILDING 2
BUILDING 3
LAKE
PARK
PHASE 2
A-1
MicroStation: Licensed For Academic Use Only

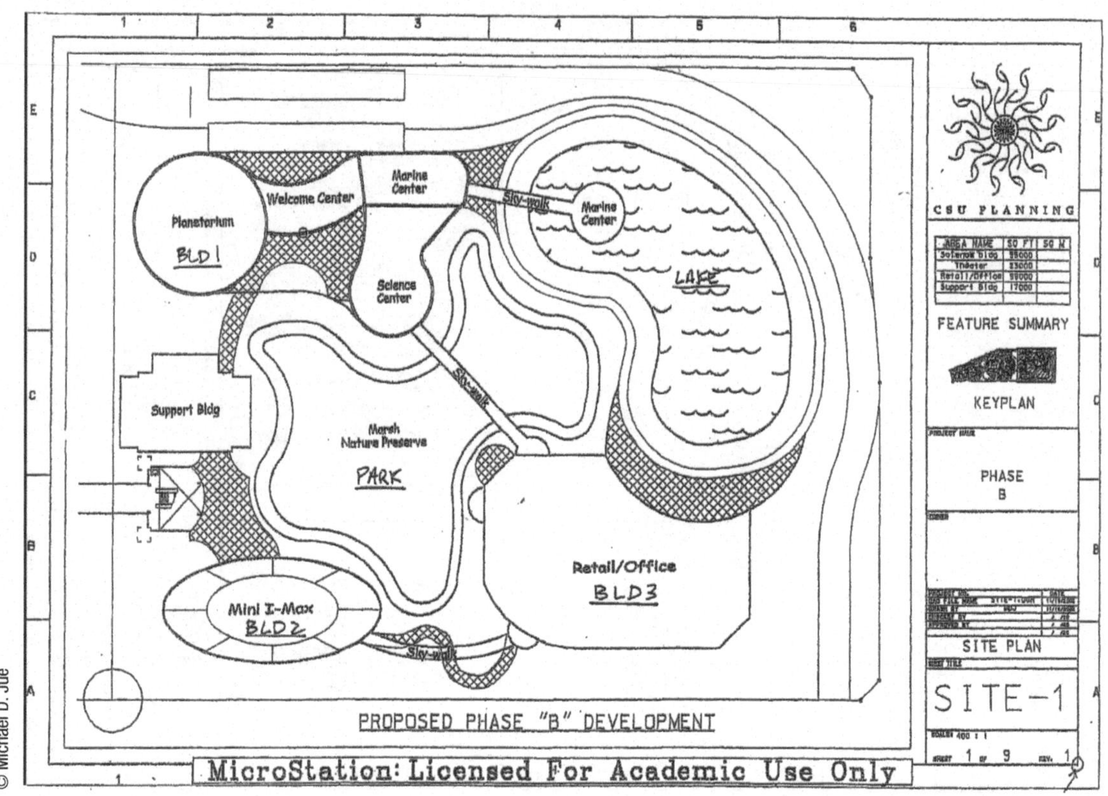
Planetarium
BLD 1
Welcome Center
Marine Center
Sky-walk
Marine Center
Science Center
LAKE
Support Bldg
Marsh Nature Preserve
PARK
Retail/Office
BLD3
Mini I-Max
BLD2
Sky-walk
CSU PLANNING
FEATURE SUMMARY
KEYPLAN
PHASE B
SITE PLAN
SITE-1
PROPOSED PHASE "B" DEVELOPMENT
MicroStation: Licensed For Academic Use Only

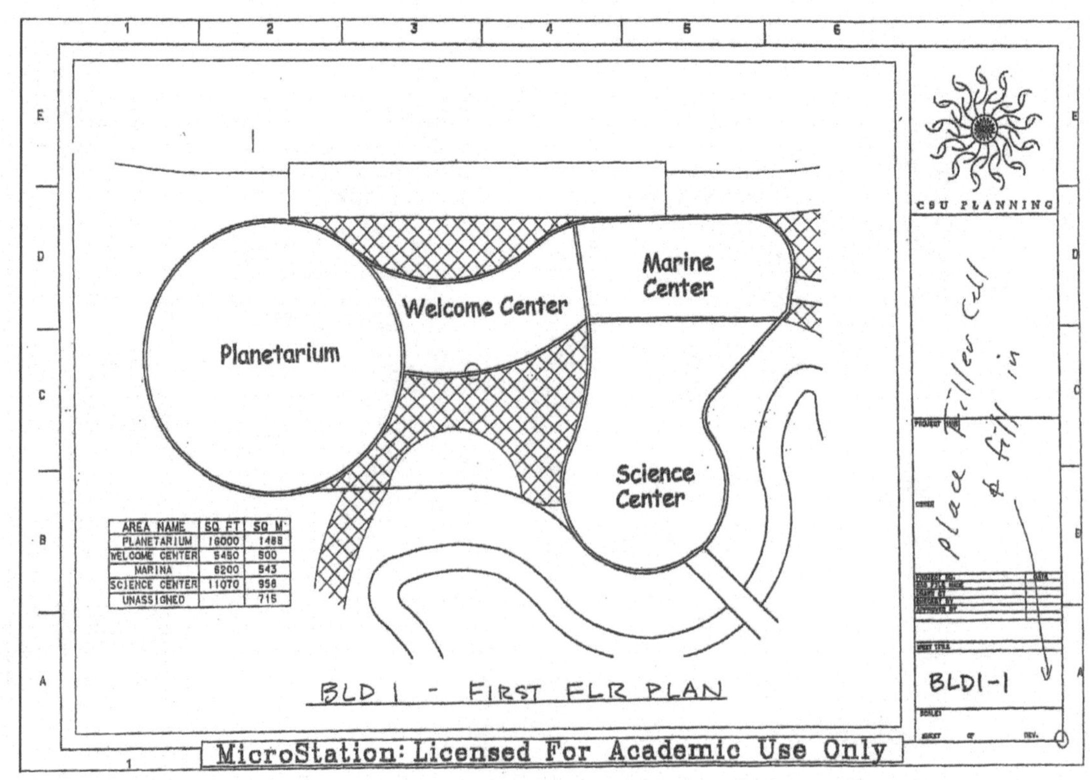
Marine Center
Welcome Center
Planetarium
Science Center
AREA NAME | SQ FT | SQ M
PLANETARIUM | 16000 | 1488
WELCOME CENTER | 5450 | 500
MARINA | 6200 | 543
SCIENCE CENTER | 11070 | 958
UNASSIGNED | | 715
CSU PLANNING
BLD1-1
BLD 1 - FIRST FLR PLAN
MicroStation: Licensed For Academic Use Only

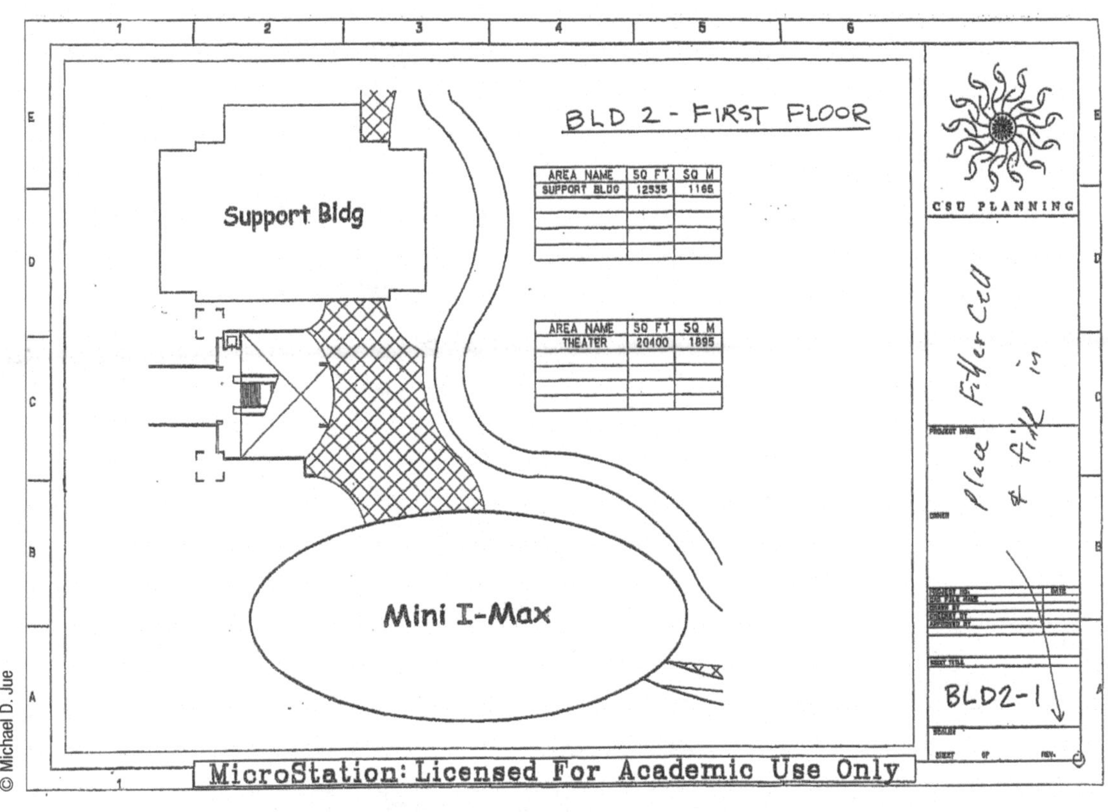
BLD 2 - FIRST FLOOR
Support Bldg
AREA NAME | SQ FT | SQ M
SUPPORT BLDG | 12555 | 1166
AREA NAME | SQ FT | SQ M
THEATER | 20400 | 1895
Mini I-Max
CSU PLANNING
Place Filler Cell & fill in
BLD2-1
MicroStation: Licensed For Academic Use Only
© Michael D. Jue

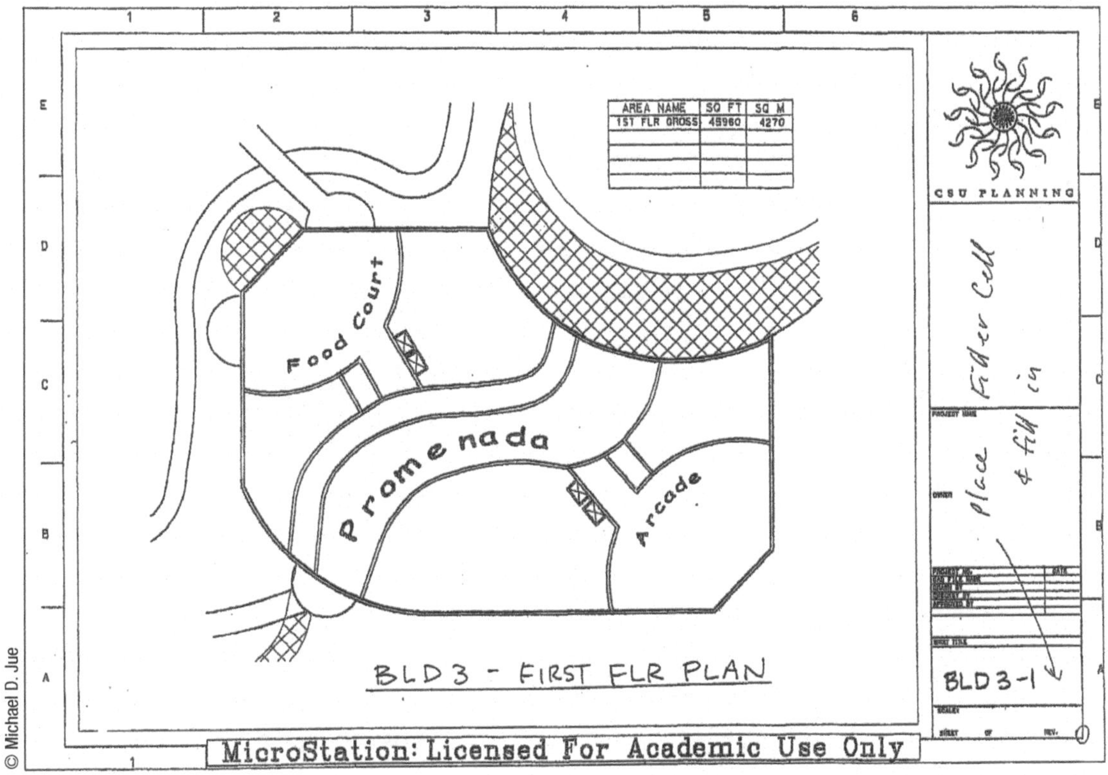
AREA NAME | SQ FT | SQ M
1ST FLR GROSS | 45960 | 4270
Food Court
Promenada
Arcade
BLD3 - FIRST FLR PLAN
CSU PLANNING
Place Filler Cell & fill in
BLD3-1
MicroStation: Licensed For Academic Use Only
© Michael D. Jue

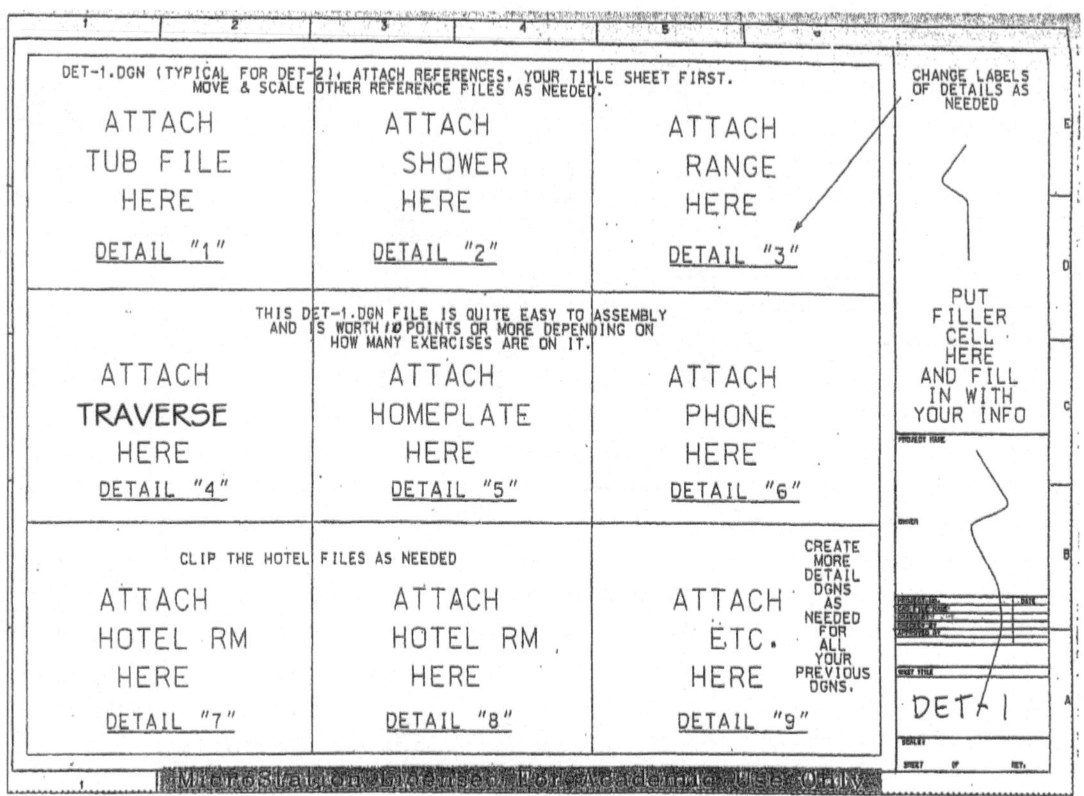
DET-1.DGN (TYPICAL FOR DET-2). ATTACH REFERENCES. YOUR TITLE SHEET FIRST.
MOVE & SCALE OTHER REFERENCE FILES AS NEEDED.
CHANGE LABELS OF DETAILS AS NEEDED
ATTACH TUB FILE HERE
DETAIL "1"
ATTACH SHOWER HERE
DETAIL "2"
ATTACH RANGE HERE
DETAIL "3"
THIS DET-1.DGN FILE IS QUITE EASY TO ASSEMBLY AND IS WORTH 10 POINTS OR MORE DEPENDING ON HOW MANY EXERCISES ARE ON IT.
PUT FILLER CELL HERE AND FILL IN WITH YOUR INFO
ATTACH TRAVERSE HERE
DETAIL "4"
ATTACH HOMEPLATE HERE
DETAIL "5"
ATTACH PHONE HERE
DETAIL "6"
CLIP THE HOTEL FILES AS NEEDED
CREATE MORE DETAIL DGNS AS NEEDED FOR ALL YOUR PREVIOUS DGNS.
ATTACH HOTEL RM HERE
DETAIL "7"
ATTACH HOTEL RM HERE
DETAIL "8"
ATTACH ETC. HERE
DETAIL "9"
DET-1
MicroStation: Licensed For Academic Use Only

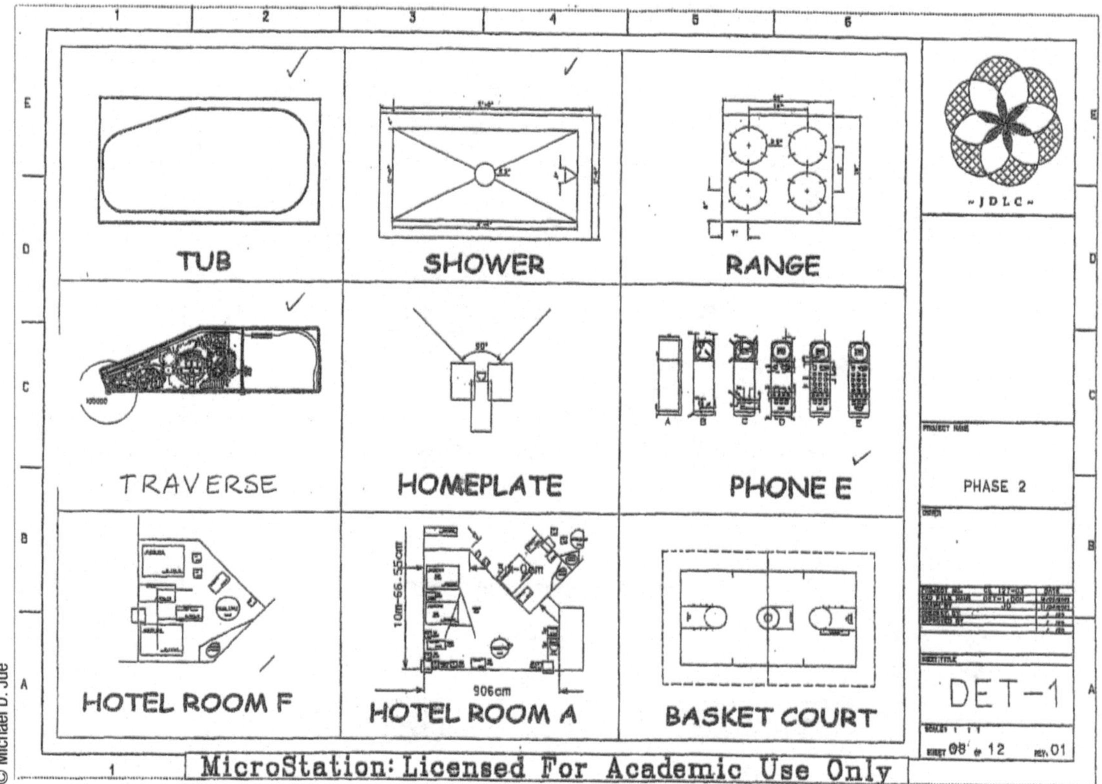
TUB
SHOWER
RANGE
-JDLC-
TRAVERSE
HOMEPLATE
PHONE E
PHASE 2
HOTEL ROOM F
HOTEL ROOM A
906cm
BASKET COURT
DET-1
MicroStation: Licensed For Academic Use Only

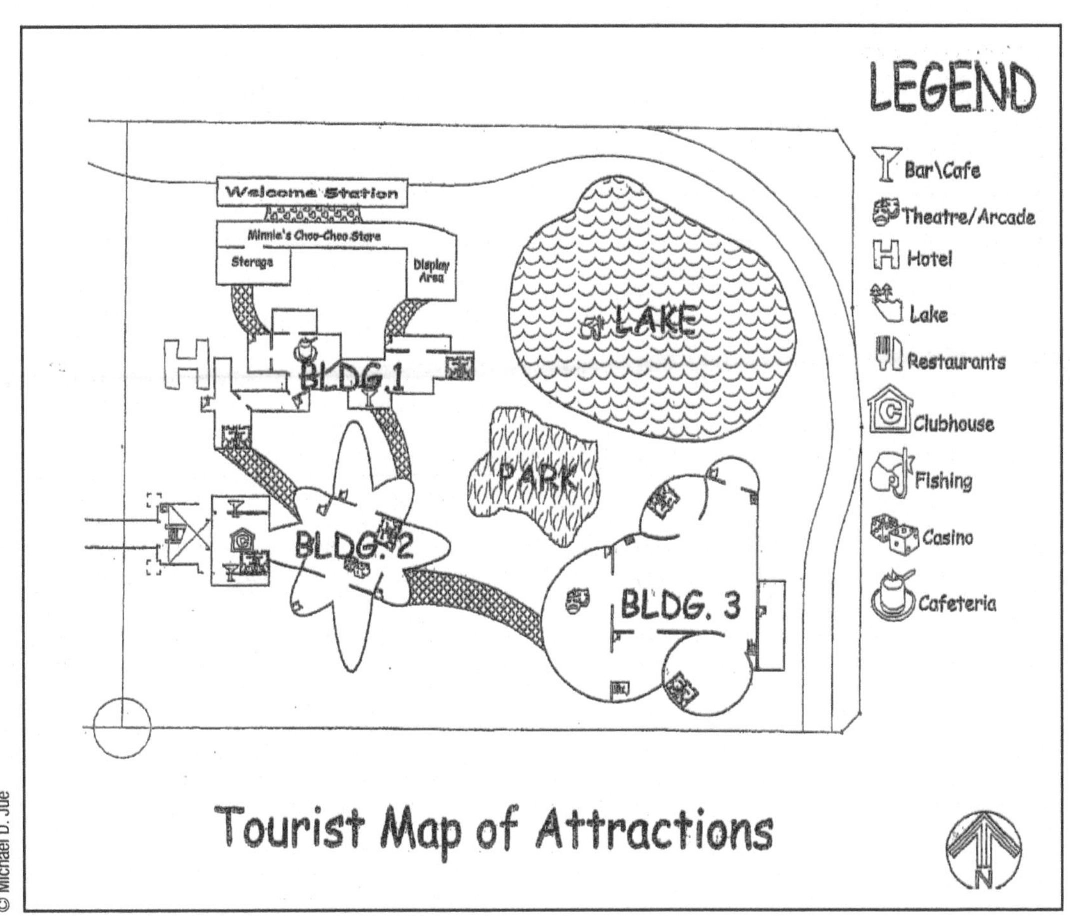
LEGEND
Bar\Cafe
Theatre/Arcade
Hotel
Lake
Restaurants
Clubhouse
Fishing
Casino
Cafeteria
Welcome Station
Minnie's Choo-Choo Store
Storage
Display Area
BLDG.1
LAKE
PARK
BLDG. 2
BLDG. 3
Tourist Map of Attractions
N

Cells and Patterning Exercise

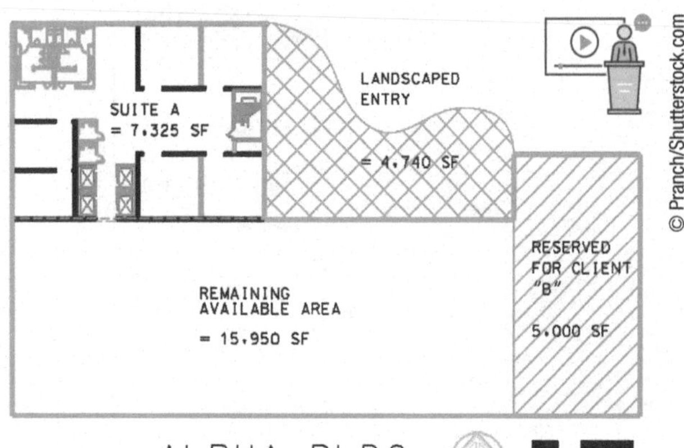

Concepts and Skills:

- Using a CELL LIBRARY
- Placing Active CELL
- CELL Origin, Creation of new CELLS
- Filled Shapes
- Using Hatch and Cross-Hatch Area
- Measure Area tool

Please review and refer to the Module 7 pages: Cells and Patterning, 197 – 200.

Note: The completion of the LAYOUT drawing exercise (see pages 173-175) and basic outline of the ALPHA BLDG, (see bottom of page 177) are required to progress to the lessons in this Cells and Patterning Exercise.

The cell library file, COMPANION.cel is included with this text. Please download the file to your active CAD working files folder. Go to Home tab, Primary group, Cells as shown. Once the Cell Library is attached (Use **File, Attach** on the Cell Library Dialog Box) select and place the pre-drawn cells: RESTROOM, LAV, Elevator and Stair into your LAYOUT drawing as shown, at AS=1, using Place Active Cell. Place NORTH, scale as needed.

Draw the graphics for the 0 – 40' Graphic Scale, (Filled Block Shapes and Lines) then use the steps below to create it as a cell in the cell library.

You will need to place a cell origin onto the graphics of the cell in a typical standard location (lower left corner of the cell graphics)

0' 10' 20' 40'

Figure 1.

Figure 2. shows selecting the **Define Cell Origin** tool. After you place the cell origin (looks like a big plus sign) place a fence around the graphics (see Figure 3.) Then, select the **Create icon** (looks like a cell with a fireball), the Create Cell dialog box opens. Fill it with a short **Name** for the cell and a longer **Description**. Select Create, to place the cell into the library. Then place cell at AS=1.

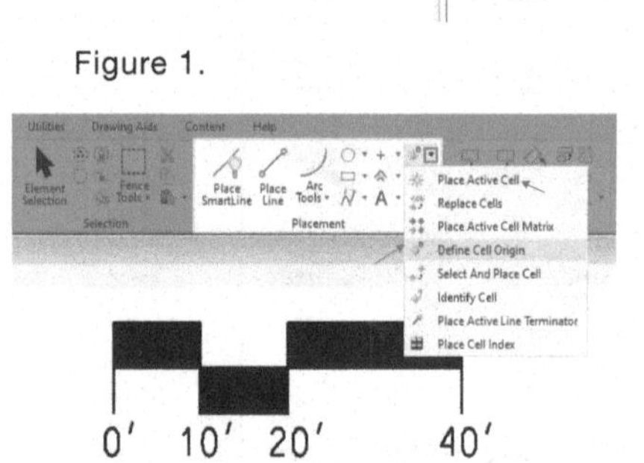

Figure 2.

0' 10' 20' 40'

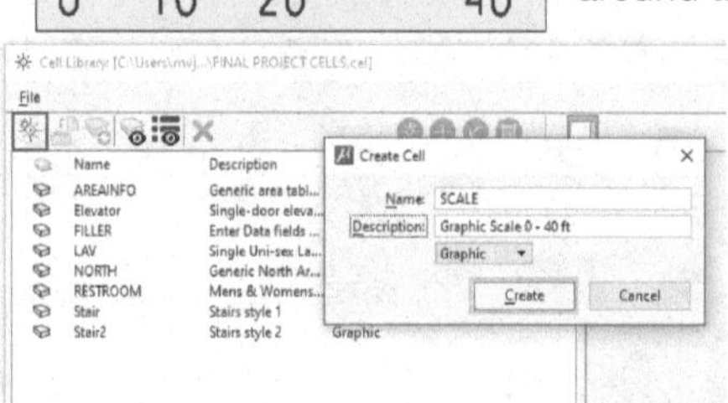

Figure 3. ->

Make the curved portion of the land-caped entry area as shown. Then using Hatch Area and Crosshatch Area using method Flood, create the patterns shown.

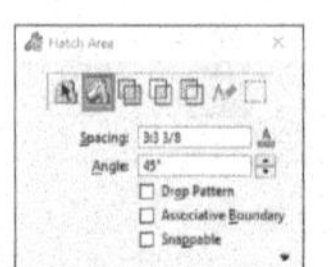

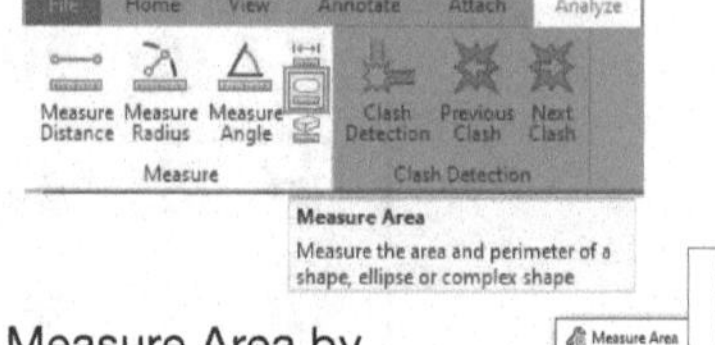

Measure Area by method Flood, then add text to the drawing

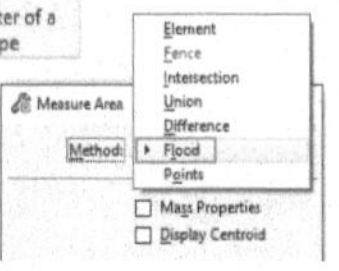

Orthographic Projection

Orthographic Projection is a method of generating 2D drawings that describe a 3D object. The 2D images are created by projecting each side of the object, outwards to *imaginary drawing planes* that are positioned out away from the object. See Figure 1, below.

A minimum of three of the standard 2D images are required to describe a simple shape. The three standard projected views are named: **Top, Front** and **Right** view. The 3D representation may often be referred to as an **Isometric View** (similar to what is seen if the object is on a table in front of you).

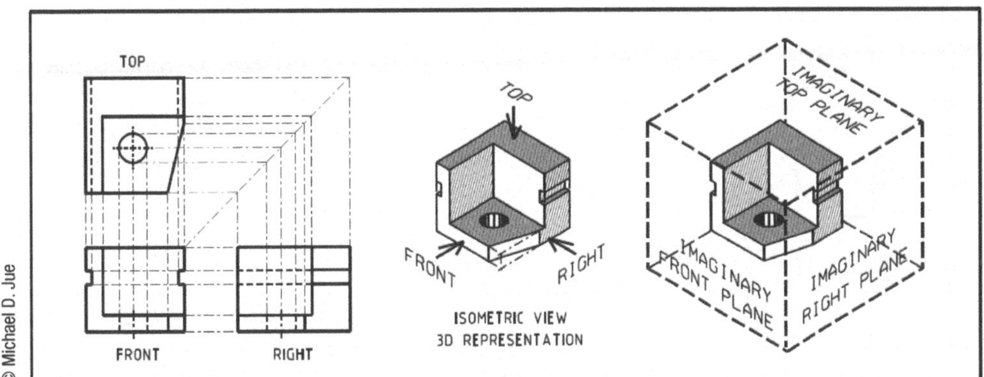

Figure 1. Orthographic Projection Example of three 2D views, the Isometric View and Imaginary Drawing Planes

A typical application:

A component may exist only in an engineer's mind or in rudimentary sketches at first. Using standard drawing methods, the engineer can draw his exact design graphically and communicate it to others. Others can then review the design drawings and eventually approve the design.

The component, may then need to be manufactured and installed in place on a building, bridge or other structure. If the engineer is not the one that actually makes the new component himself, others will be manufacturing the component. The final drawing may also include dimensions and other information.

Understanding the principles of Orthographic Projection helps the engineer create drawings that correctly convey designs that were previously just abstract thoughts, not yet recorded onto paper or yet created digitally as CAD documents.

Standards / Guidelines

U.S. based engineering firms typically use the **Third-Angle Projection** method for the arrangement of the three primary views. The *symbol* designating Third-Angle Projection is shown below. The alternative method, **First-Angle Projection**, typically used by most European and other engineering firms, is shown for comparison.

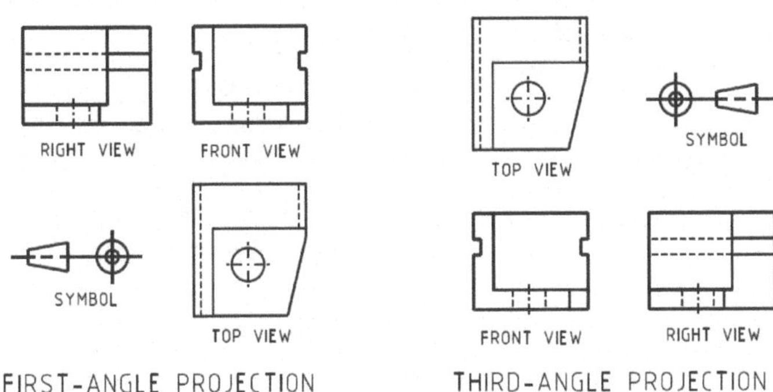

For more details on Orthographic Projection, please see:

Engineering Graphics Essentials

https://static.sdcpublications.com/pdfsample/978-1-58503-610-3-1.pdf

Orthographic Projection — Example #1, Answer provided

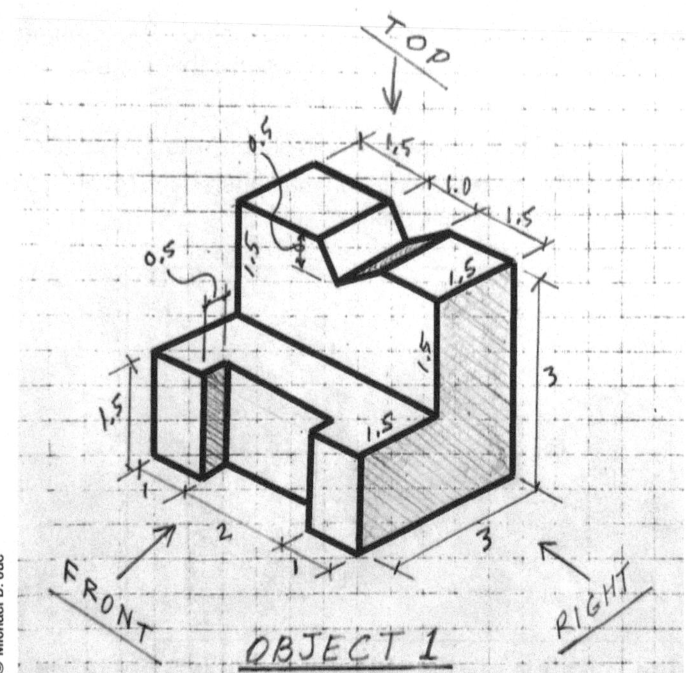

Typical image provided to you

Orthographic Projection
(also called 3-View Projection)

Learn about standard Line-weights and Line-styles and image positioning.

GIVEN: OBJECT 1 Isometric image at left, with dimensions shown and scale is 1 Grid = 0.5 units.

PROBLEM: Complete the assignment on graph paper, MAKING the drawing by HAND, using PENCIL (you may use ruler and an eraser as needed):

1. Create the **TOP, FRONT** and **RIGHT** views. Third-Angle Projection

2. The ***visible edges*** shall be in ***solid, thick lines***.

3. ***Non-visible edges*** shall be drawn with ***dashed*** Hidden lines, medium lines (not as thick)

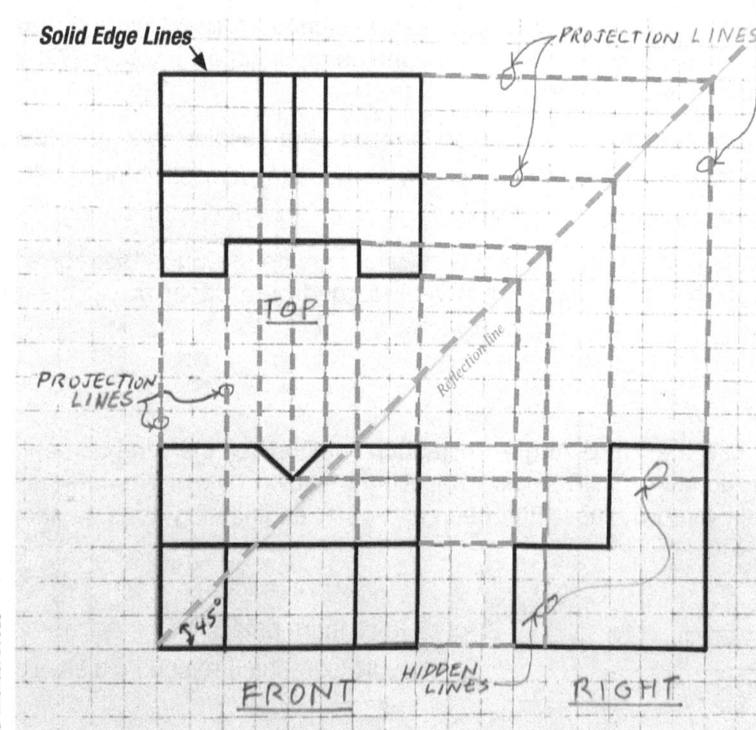

The Answer is provided above with some tips noted for you. The colors are added for learning, only.

4. Include ***thin dashed*** Projection Lines from: TOP image to the FRONT image,

FRONT image to the RIGHT image and,

TOP image to the RIGHT image reflected across the *45-degree reflection line.*

5. Label the views with bold text, large, underlined.

TIPS:
The TOP view is what you see from a Drone directly over the shape, looking straight down.

Hidden lines are the edges that you would see if you had *Super-Hero X-Ray vision!* You would be able to see thru the solid matter! — If standing at the right side of the shape, you would "see' the hidden edge of the "Slot" at the front and of the bottom vertex of the "Vee" shape at the top.

Plans, Elevations, Sections

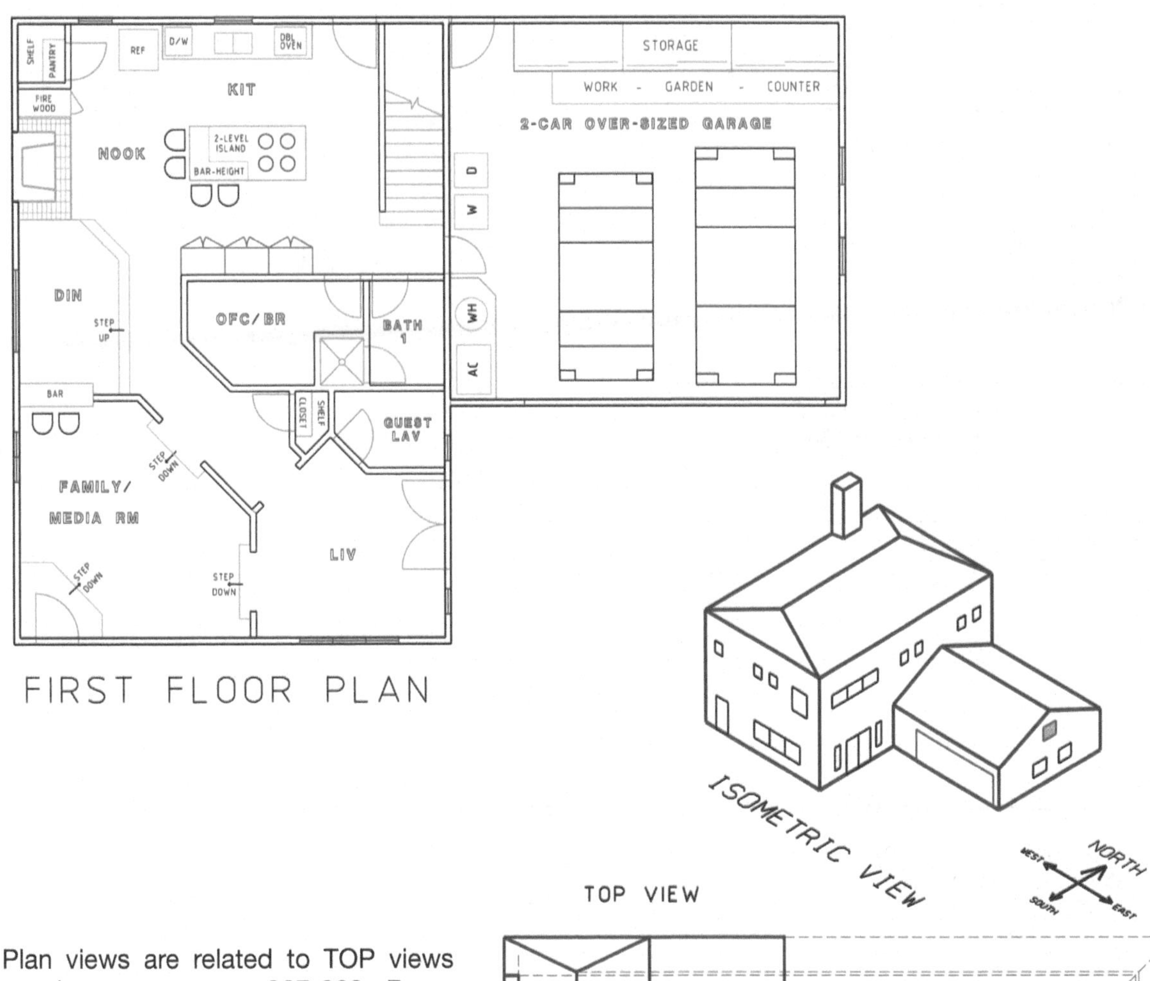

FIRST FLOOR PLAN

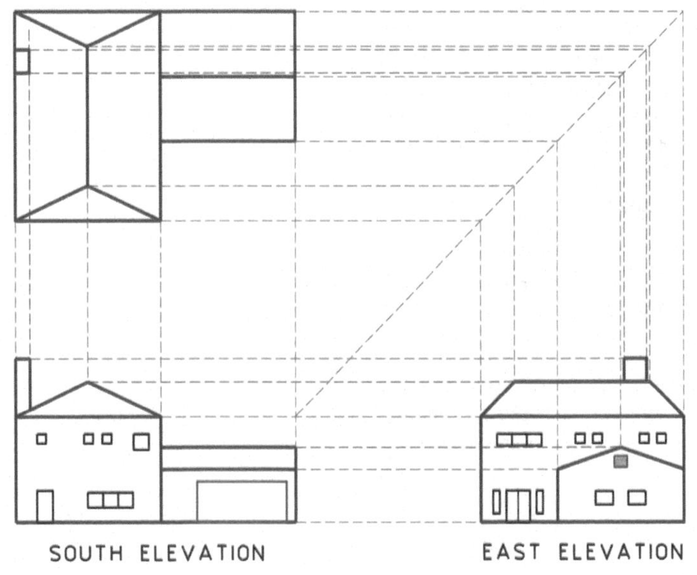

Plan views are related to TOP views as shown on pages 207-208. For a "Plan" such as the FIRST FLOOR PLAN shown above, the imaginary plane cuts thru the object at the level of the ceiling of the first floor. The view is in the direction of the object.

It is as if the roof and the 2nd floor are missing entirely, and the viewer is looking into the first floor from above; *another example of X-Ray Vision*!

Again, a TOP view is like the view from a drone over the object. A SOUTH Elevation is a view of the object from the south side. An EAST Elevation is a view of the object from the East side.

Plans, Elevations, Sections

Section views imagine a "CUT" thru a Plan view or other view. For the Section A-A of the FIRST FLOOR PLAN, the Figure 1. at right shows how it is constructed.

Utilizing projection lines out to the left, the drafter determines the location of all pertinent items; exterior walls, BAR, FIREPLACE, PANTRY, etc.

After the side projection image is made, the SECTION A-A (also referred to as an INTERIOR ELEVATION) can be rotated and located elsewhere on the page. See Figure 2.

Additional detail can be added and the image can be larger if desired.

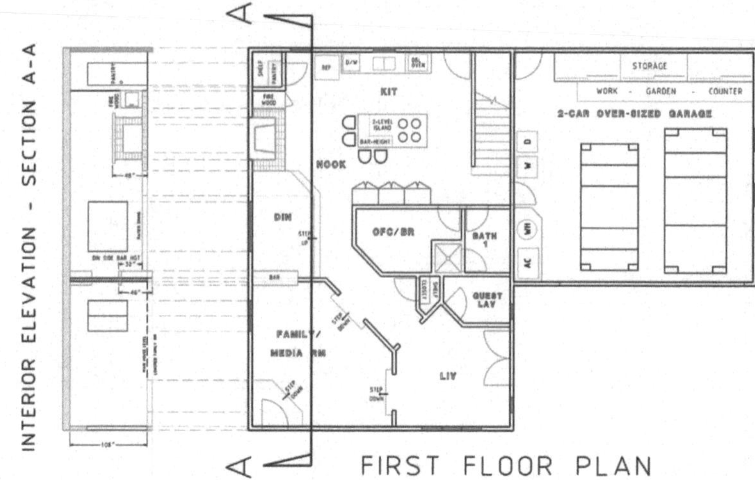

Figure 1.

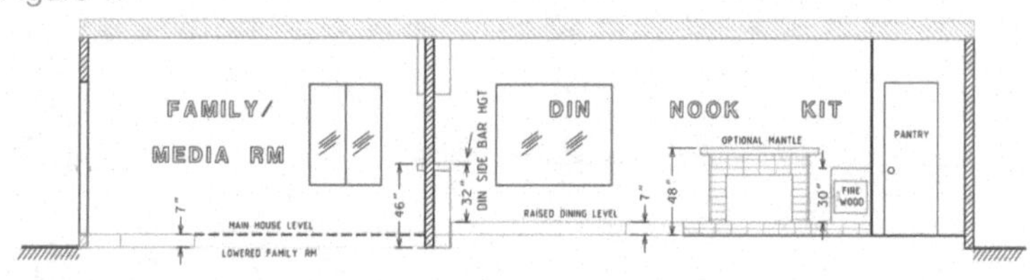

INTERIOR ELEVATION - SECTION A-A

Figure 2.

The Figures 3. and 4. illustrate how an OFFSET section cut B-B can be made thru the FIRST FLOOR PLAN

Notice that the section line B-B in Figure 3. does not travel in a perfectly straight line, but contains a jog or "offset" around the washer and stairs. Also notice that the section line, when it passes thru the kitchen/nook, jogs around the island with the four seats.

The resulting INTERIOR ELEVATION - SECTION B-B illustration, Figure 4. fully shows the washer and the stairs, but does not show the island.

Placement of section lines and offsets can be chosen to illustrate features that the engineer wish to show.

INTERIOR ELEVATION - SECTION B-B

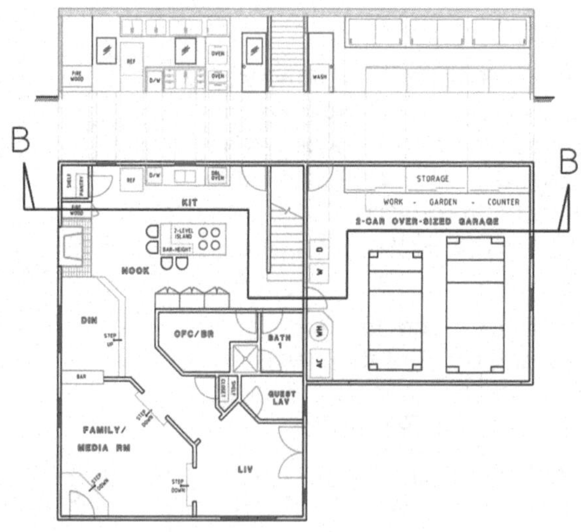

Figure 3.

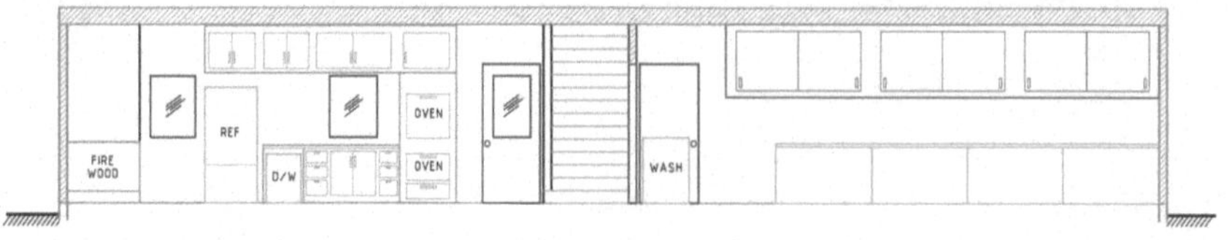

INTERIOR ELEVATION - SECTION B-B

Figure 4.

Basic 3D notes

© Michael D. Jue

Outline

1. Concepts
   a. 2D vs. 3D & Seed Files
   b. 3D Coordinate Systems & the Z-Axis
   c. Precision Input
2. Working in 3D
   a. Visualization
      i. Display modes
         ➤ Wire Frame thru Rendered Images
      ii. View Orientation
         ➤ Standard & Isometric Views
         ➤ Right-hand rule
         ➤ Controlling Active Z-depth
   b. Creating and Modifying Elements
      i. Solids vs. Surfaces
      ii. Creating Basic Elements
         ➤ Placement and Movement
         ➤ Manipulations
      iii. Creating More Complex Elements
         ➤ Boundary Representation (B-rep)
         ➤ Constructive Solid Geometry (CSG)
   c. Basic Animation
3. Advanced Topics List (optional)
   a. Photo realistic Imaging Techniques
      i. Perspective and Camera Control
      ii. Surface Materials Rendering
      iii. Solar and Manual Lighting Control

© Michael D. Jue

3D Concepts

2D vs. 3D Seed Files

To draw in 3D, new dgn files must be created with a 3D dgn seed file rather than the regular 2D seed file.

© Michael D. Jue

After selecting **File > New** or the New icon, this dialog box pops up. See the choice at the bottom in the section titled Seed File. Notice the seed file may show the 2D seed file selection named seed2d.dgn. Click onto the Select… button at the right.

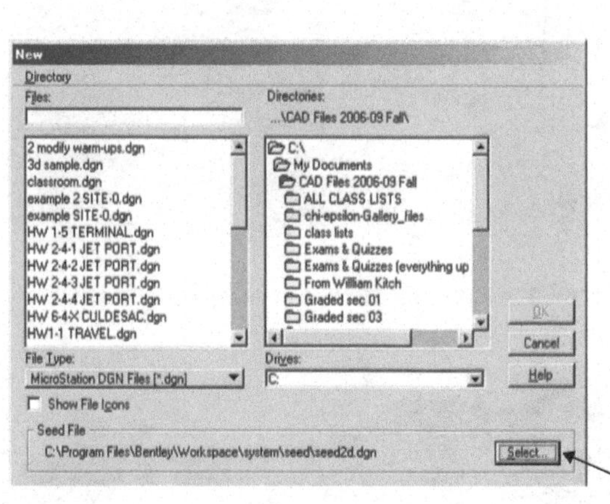

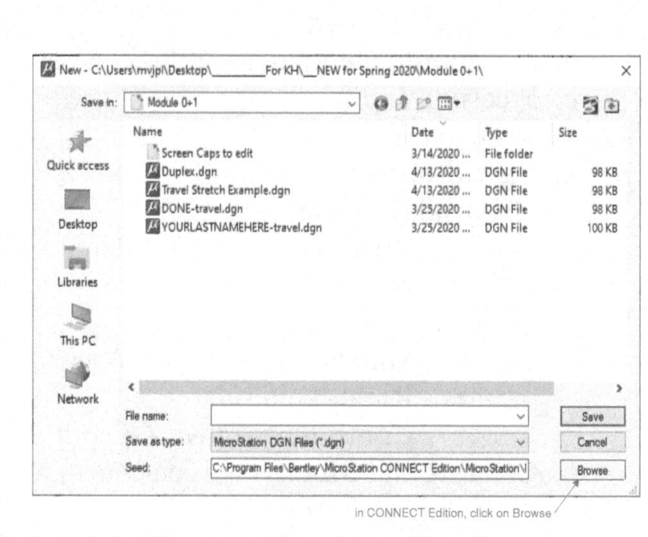
in CONNECT Edition, click on Browse

On the Select Seed File dialog box, select seed3d.dgn from the list and then click OK. Then proceed and your new drawing will be created using the 3D seed file, rather than the 2D file.

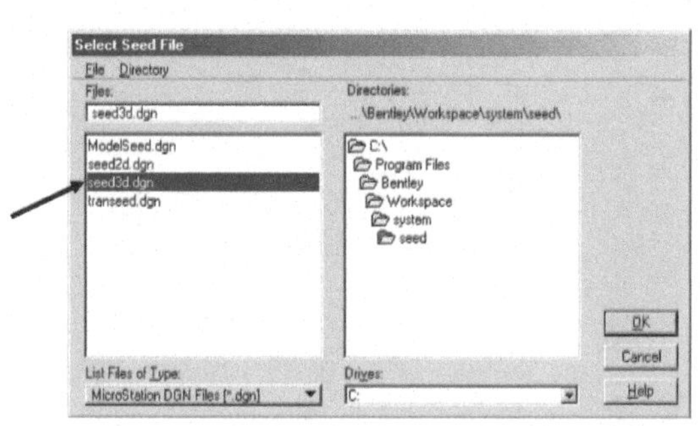

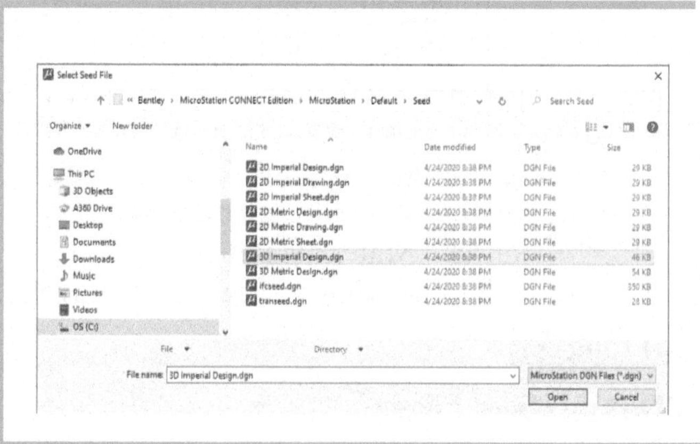

3D adds the "Z" axis to the original x & y axes.

Major concepts involve creating and modifying geometry & display of the file (or imaging)

Viewing 3D files

Concepts:

Display modes:

Wireframe
Wiremesh
Hidden-Line
Constant Shaded
Smooth Shaded
Phong Shaded
Ray-traced

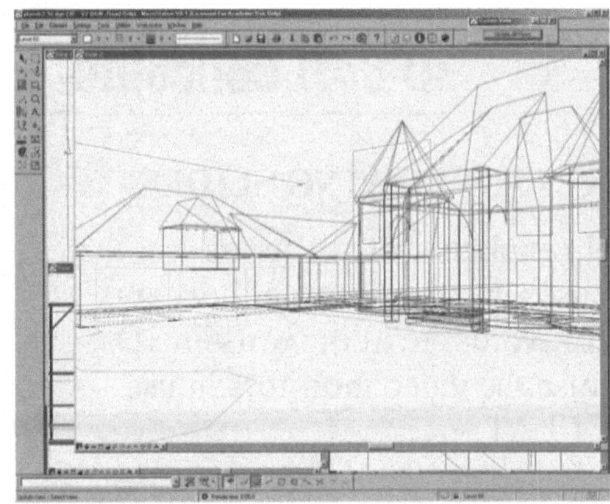

View orientation-the 3D drawing can be viewed from any angle.

There are several standard Viewing angles:

Top, Bottom, Left, Right, Front, Back, Isometric with many variations.

The normal 2D drawing can be thought of as the "plan" or "top" view of a 3D drawing.

Use Of multiple views helps the user in understanding the drawing.

Other factors such as perspective (lens focal length), Surface properties, lighting and shadows affect the appearance of the image.

Creating & Modifying elements in 3D

Tools work the same. Such as move. Copy, delete, scale, etc.

Most are sensitive to the active view.

Precision key-ins for 3D:

DX=
DL=
DI=
AZ=

Setting the Display depth aids the User in selecting elements properly

3D toolbars

3D view control

Solids vs. Surfaces
Box vs. Brick

Boundary Representation (b-rep)
Start with a profile
Surfaces & solids of revolutions
Extrusions

CSG Constructive solid geometry
Boolean ops to create shapes/solids

3D CAD Concepts

CONCEPTS

VISUAL EXAMPLES ON FOLLOWING SLIDES

- Visual Examples help explain abstract terms
- 3D CAD programs use a particular set of concepts and related syntax (or words) to allow work in 3D
- This is difficult because the video monitors in use today are all 2D (ie. FLAT)

VISUAL EXAMPLES ON FOLLOWING SLIDES

3D CONCEPTS 1

3D Concepts

CONCEPTS

- Here is an example of a simple model.
- It is displayed as a "wireframe"
- This **VIEWING ANGLE** is called a "right isometric" or "S.E. isometric" in AutoCAD
- The "labels" match std Mstation view names, but are universal

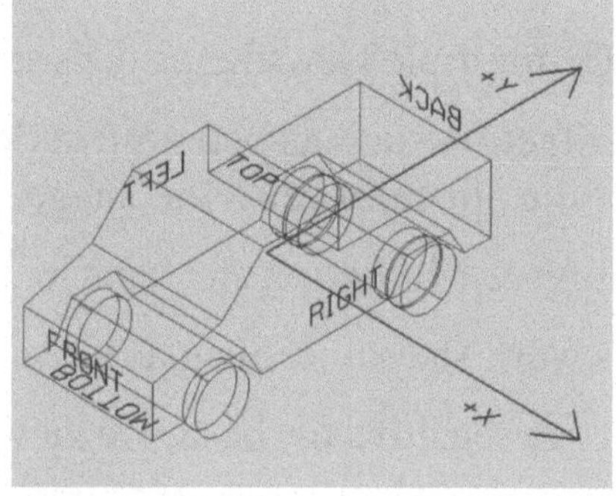

Figure 1

3D CONCEPTS 2

3D Concepts

CONCEPTS

- About the LABELS:
  - FRONT - front grille
  - BACK - above tailgate
  - TOP - above cab
  - BOTTOM - under the radiator
  - RIGHT - on the driver's side
  - LEFT - on the passenger's window

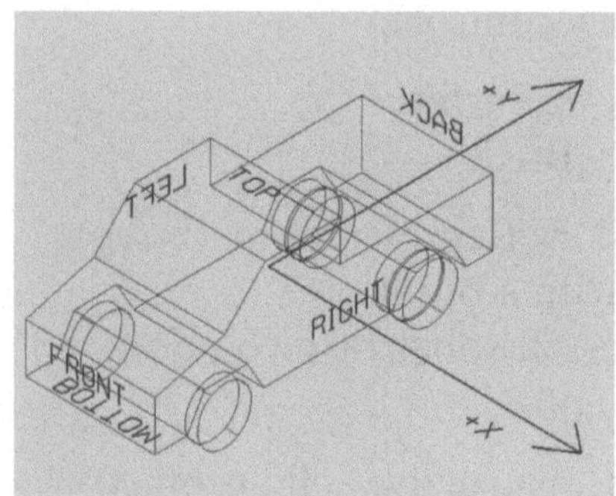

Figure 1

3D CONCEPTS 3

3D Concepts

CONCEPTS

- Here is that same model truck
- It is now displayed as a "shaded hidden-line" rendering
- The angle of view is still called a right isometric
- Reference notes about the "toy" truck drawing:
  - There are 4 rear tires

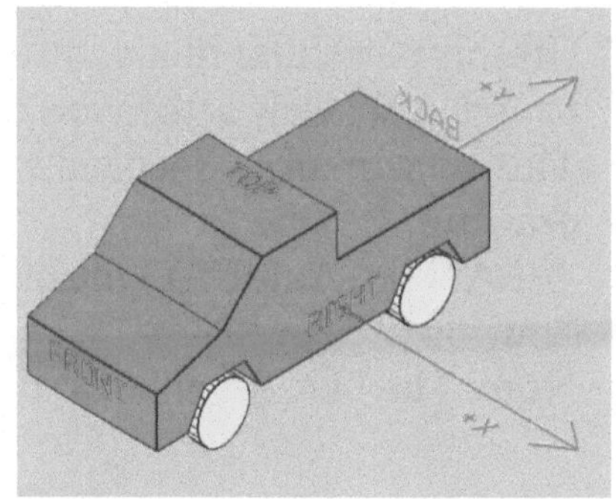

Figure 1A

3D CONCEPTS 4

3D Concepts

CONCEPTS

- More About the LABELS:
  - Labels on 3D models are typically arranged so that they "READ CORRECTLY" when the viewing angle changes.
  - For example, "TOP" reads correctly when we go to a "TOP" or "PLAN" view.

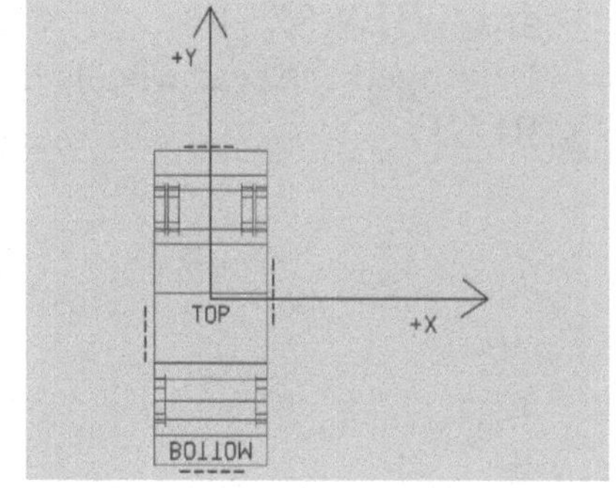

Figure 2

3D CONCEPTS 5

3D Concepts

CONCEPTS

- On this particular model of the truck, the "TOP" or "PLAN" view is the view of the X-Y plane.
- This is normally associated with typical 2D drawing
- "PLAN" in AutoCAD means normal to the XY drawing axes or "UCS"
- Note: The "UCS" will be repositioned often

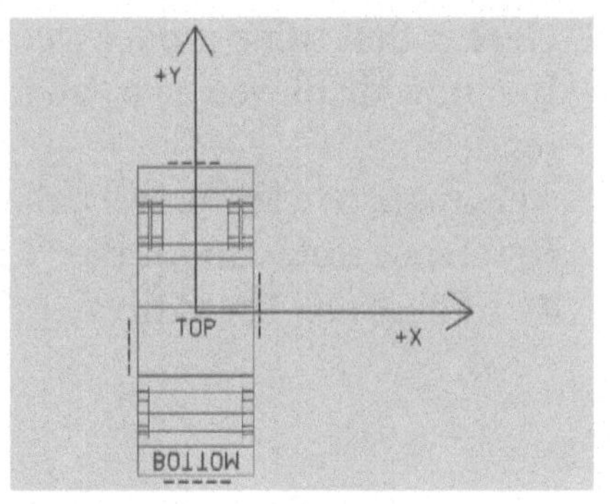

Figure 2

3D CONCEPTS 6

3D Concepts

CONCEPTS

- Here are some of the other standard "VIEWS"
- I changed the rear wheels to BLUE

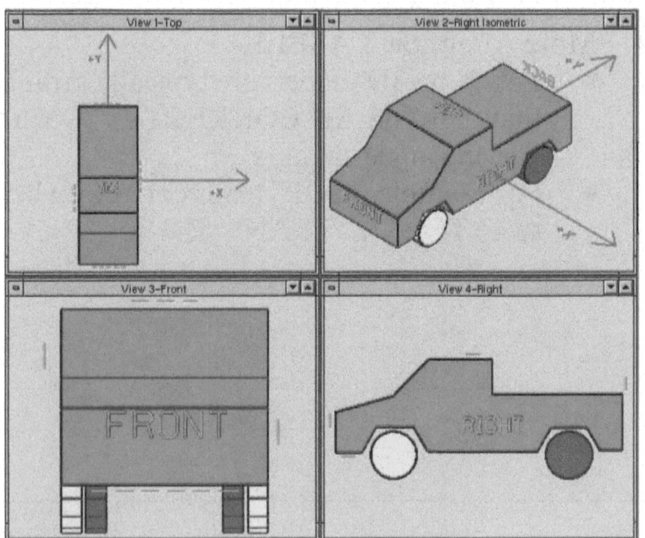

Figure 3

3D CONCEPTS 7

3D Concepts

CONCEPTS

- Additional standard "VIEWS"
- Note: there is not any particular order to these views.

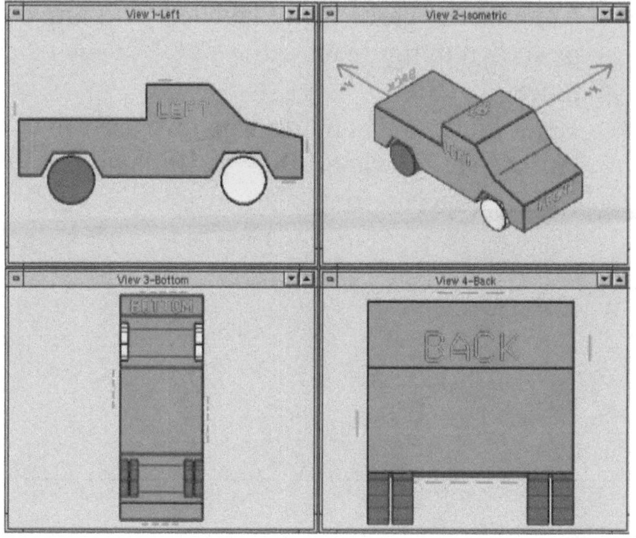

Figure 4

3D CONCEPTS 8

3D Concepts

CONCEPTS

- Think of the drawing as a 3 dimensional model sitting at the center of a sphere or globe.
- This concept is the basis of the AutoCAD method for defining **View Points**
- Imagine a camera on the surface of the globe pointing to the model at the center.

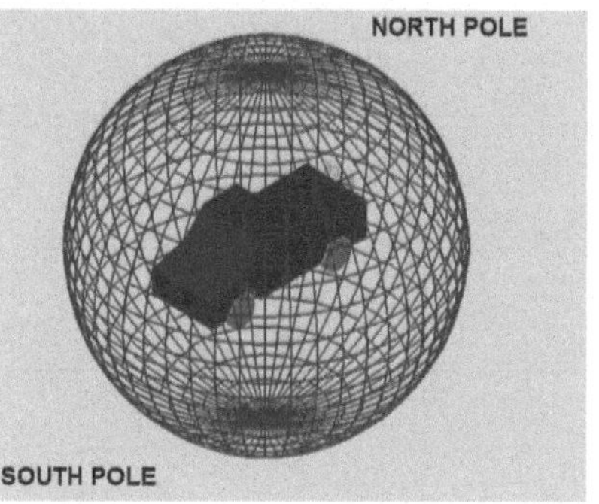

Figure 5

3D CONCEPTS 9

3D Concepts

CONCEPTS

- Imagine the globe being labelled with angle values as shown in figure 6 for the "TOP" view of the globe
- Refer back to this figure when we use the AutoCAD Viewpoint Presets Dialogue box for the From: X Axis setting

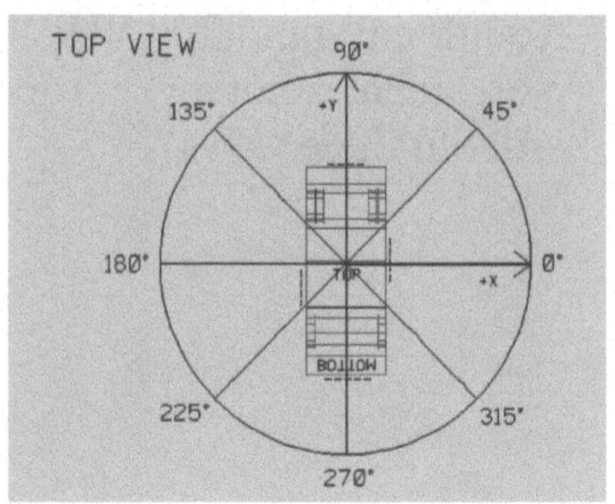

Figure 6

3D CONCEPTS 10

3D Concepts

CONCEPTS

- Imagine the globe being labelled with angle values asshown in figure 7 for the "FRONT" view of the globe
- Refer back to this figure when we use the AutoCAD Viewpoint Presets Dialogue box for the From: XY Plane setting.

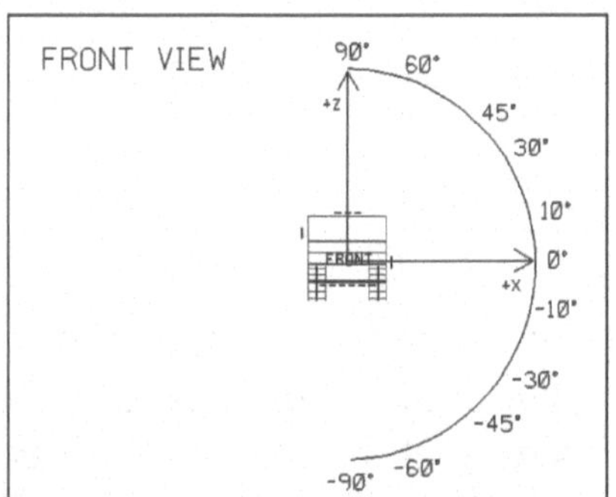

Figure 7

3D CONCEPTS 11

3D Concepts

CONCEPTS

- This is the AutoCAD Viewpoint Presets Dialogue box
- It can be used to control the viewing angle of the model
- To open the dialogue box:
  - Type DDVPOINT ↲

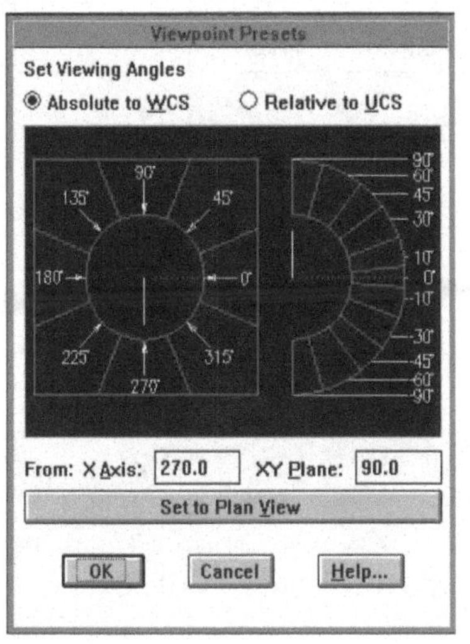

Figure 8

3D CONCEPTS 12

Stonehenge (meters)

	Approximate Actual	1/8 scale Mini Version
Diameter of Sarcen Circle	33M	4.125M
Number of Stones	30	30
Stone Height	4	0.5
Stone Width	2	0.25
Stone depth	1	0.125

Sarcen Lintels (optional, atop the 30 stones to form a circle)

Length	3.2	0.4
Lintel cross-section HxW	0.8 x 1	0.1 x 0.125
Location of Circle Center	n/a	

The Pentagon	feet	meters	1/8 scale
Length of side	92.1	280.7	35.1
Height	77.3	23.6	2.9

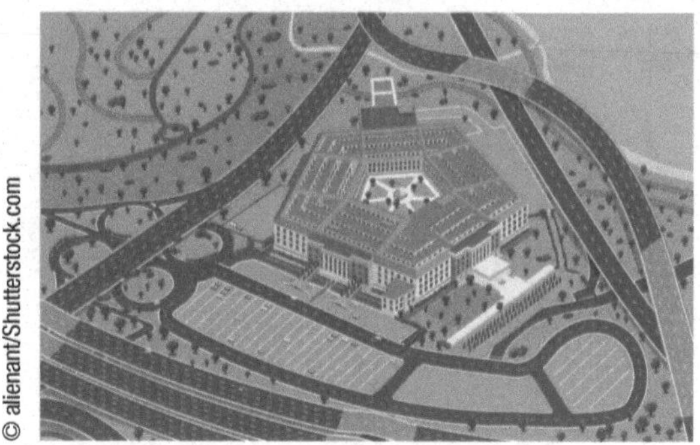

Transamerica Pyramid (S.F.)	feet	meters	1/8 scale
Length of side	150	45.7	5.7
Height	853	260.0	32.5

The Coliseum (Rome, Italy)	feet	meters	1/8 scale
Length	617	188	23.5
Width (Diam. of end)	512	156	19.5
Height	177	54	6.8

Appendix A

SHOWER Exercise Drawing, ABBREVIATED STEP-BY-STEP INSTRUCTIONS

Instruction type: Step-by-step, abbreviated **Level:** Beginner (module 2) **Duration:** 30–40 minutes

Use MicroStation V8*i* or the CONNECT Edition

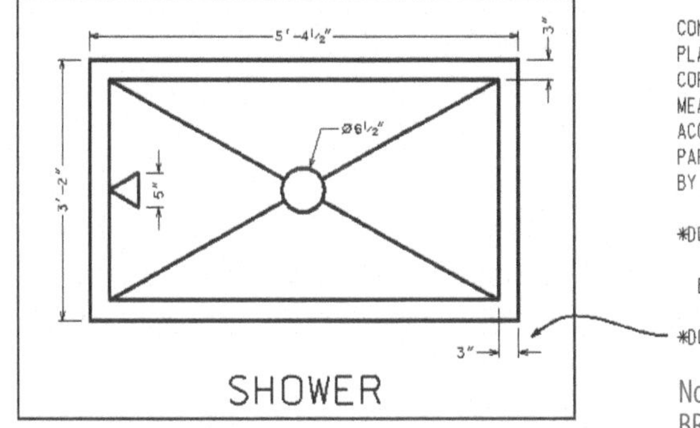

CONCEPTS: WORKING UNITS, KEY-IN FIELD, PLACE BLOCK SHAPE BY PRECISION INPUT, COPY PARALLEL A SHAPE VS. LINES, MEASURE DISTANCE & RADIUS, TOOL SETTINGS, ACCUSNAP WITH KEYPOINT AND INTERSECT MODES, PARTIAL DELETE AND TRIM, REGULAR POLYGON BY METHOD EDGE, SELECTING A NEW TEXT FONT.

DO NOT DRAW THE INSTRUCTIONS

BUT, DO THE INSTRUCTIONS!

DO NOT DRAW THE DIMENSIONS Add dimensions after covering module 5.

Note: PARTIAL DELETE, in MicroStation V8i, is now named BREAK ELEMENT in MicroStation CONNECT Edition.

File Creation and Preparation portion

1. Read all instructions first! Start MicroStation and create a new drawing in your H: directory. Name it **SHOWER-LASTNAME,** Use a seedfile if provided for your class**.**
2. In the drawing, close the **AccuDraw** function. Place text **"student name here"** as needed. Scale the text as required for an appropriate size.
3. Turn off the grid display. Use **<Ctrl>b, Settings> View Attributes**, or **choose the icon** at upper left of view, uncheck **Grid,** apply to open views**,** Turn **OFF Grid Lock.** Use the **Lock symbol** on the lower right. Uncheck **Grid**
4. Set the Working Units. Use **Settings > Design File > Working Units**, click the word **Meters** in the **Master Unit** section, to see the selections. Then select **Feet,** change **Format**: to **MU:SU**, change **Accuracy**: to **1/16**, click **OK** (if using **CONNECT Edition**, please refer to pg 77)
   The steps are: **File** > **Settings** > **File** > **Design File Settings** > **Working Units**
5. Open up the **Key-in Field**, using **Utilities > Key-in**, then re-size and dock the **Key-in Field** onto the lower portion of the screen. (if using **CONNECT Edition**, please refer to pg 39)
6. Save these settings using **<Ctrl>f,** or **File > Save Settings**

Drawing portion **XY will be given in class!**

7. Select the **Place Block Shape** icon and draw a block shape, sized 5'–4½ "W x 3'-2"H, starting at the lower left corner per the location specified by your instructor. Fill in the following values before drawing: Use XY= ______, ______ for the first corner, and **DL=** ______, ______ for the opposite corner.

(Continuation on next page)

© Pranch/Shutterstock.com

(SHOWER exercise continued)

Use MicroStation V8*i* or the CONNECT Edition

8. Check the lengths of the block shape sides with the Measure Distance point to point tool. **Copy Parallel** the block shape INWARDs by 3”. option “Keep Original”
9. Change color to **Green**. Draw 2 lines criss-crossing diagonally across the inner block shape. Make sure you snap to each opposite corner for the line start and end points.
10. Place a 6–½” diameter circle at the mid-point of one of the diagonal lines. Use the **Measure Radius** tool to check if you created the correct size circle.
11. Open the **button-bar** for snap modes and set the **Snap mode** to Intersection snap by double-clicking onto the appropriate icon.

    If using **CONNECT Edition**, open the **Snaps Ribbon Group** and **Snap Mode toolbox** as shown on pg 124 & 125.
12. Using **Partial Delete**, delete the portion of one of the diagonal lines that is inside the circle. Make sure you use the **intersection-snap** and observe the correct snapping action at the beginning of the partial delete action and at the end of the partial delete action. Repeat for the other diagonal.

    The “**Partial Delete**” tool in **V8*i*** is the “**Break Element**” tool **CONNECT Edition**.
13. Use **Undo** to restore the portions of the diagonal lines in the circle. Repeat #12 above, but now perform it using the simpler **Trim** tool, instead.
14. At a blank space, create a **Red** 3-sided **regular polygon** (triangle) by method edge, with 5” sides. (NOT LINES, you use the 4th tool in Polygons toolbar) Start the polygon at some point, and then specify the next point for the end of the edge, exactly 5” inches away, say directly 90° either up or down, or exactly to the right or to the left.
15. Rotate the triangle as needed to match the orientation shown on the diagram and then use **Move Element** (NOT dragged with Element Selection), to move it precisely to the midpoint of the left inner side of block shape.
16. Add text **SHOWER** below the figure; add a block shape around your whole drawing (both of these sized as you wish for a good look), fit view and <Ctrl>f.

NOTES:

RANGE Exercise Drawing, ABBREVIATED STEP-BY-STEP INSTRUCTIONS

Instruction type: Step-by-step
Level: Beginner (module 2)
Duration: 15–20 minutes

Use MicroStation V8*i* or the CONNECT Edition

File Creation and Preparation portion

1. Read all instructions first! Start MicroStation and create a new drawing in your H: directory. Name it **RANGE-LASTNAME.** This time, use the ***English units*** **seed file.** Instructor to specify.
2. In the drawing, close the **AccuDraw** function. Place text **"student name here"** as needed. Scale the text as required for an appropriate size.
3. **Notice:** by virtue of using the ***English units*** **seed file**, the Grid Settings are already set for you as OFF!
4. CHECK the Working Units. Use **Settings > Design File > Working Units**, Ensure they are **ft:in Notice**: by virtue of using the ***English units*** seed file, the Working Units Settings are already set for you! (if using **CONNECT Edition**, please refer to pg 77)
   The steps are: **File > Settings > File > Design File Settings > Working Units**
5. Open up the **Key-in Field**, using **Utilities > Key-in**, then re-size and dock the **Key-in Field** onto the lower portion of the screen. (If using **CONNECT Edition**, please refer to pg 39)
6. Save these settings using **<Ctrl>f,** or or **File > Save Settings**
7. Stop! Check! Are 1–6 done?

Drawing portion (model # _________) **note: refer to Exercise diagram on page 225**

Your instructor will let you know which model of Range to draw, ie 2–1 or 2–2, etc. Use the table to determine the required length for each letter, ie. in the range model 2–1, length A=45", B=28", diam. C=9", etc. It is suggested to write in the length values at each letter on your diagram at this time.

8. Select the **Place Block Shape** icon and draw a block shape, sized **A"** width **by B"** height, starting at the lower left corner per the location specified by your instructor. Use **XY** = ______, ______ for the first corner, and **DL=** ______, ______ for the opposite corner.
9. Draw a **C"** diameter circle for the lower left burner, out from the lower left corner, **D"** to the right and **E"** up. (many methods will be shown for this, record the ways below)
10. Draw a 2" line going straight down, starting at the 12 o'clock position on the circle just drawn.

(Continuation on next page

NOTES:

Tip: If you are not already doing this, start doing so: Check off each step as you complete it!

This way, if you get interrupted, or need help, you will know exactly where you are at!

Also, this is obvious, but some students do NOT do this: DO THE STEPS IN ORDER!

(RANGE exercise continued)

Use MicroStation V8*i* or the CONNECT Edition

11. Use **Construct Array polar** to array the line just drawn, around the exact center of the circle 8 times, 45 degrees apart. Be sure to select the rotate elements option. Snap to the center of the circle for the center of the polar array.
12. Use the select tool to drag a selection boundary around the burner. Perform **<ctrl> g** to turn the selected elements into a group, also called an orphaned or no-name cell. Note: **<ctrl> u**, performs an un-group if needed.
13. Stop! Check! Are 8–12 done?
14. Use **Construct Array rectangular** to create six burners in a 2 x 3 array with **G"** row spacing and **F"** column spacing. Make sure to have the array **angle set to 0**. can key-in AA=0 Note: columns run up and down, vertically. Rows run side to side, horizontally
15. Place a **centermark** at the center of each burner using the radial dimension tool. If the first centermark is too big, adjust the text size with TX=_____, then try another. **TX=:1** may work well. You can check the existing text height and width setting with TX=<enter>.

    Note: The **Centermark** tool is a part of the **Dimensioning** function. Your instructor will show this.
16. Add the text RANGE, below the figure and place a block shape around your whole drawing.
17. Fit view and then do a File > Save Settings (or <Ctrl> f). Note: <ctrl>f may not successfully enter into the key-in field if the last tool active was a place text or edit text action. A simple way to make it work it to hit any other non-text tool, such as Element Selection, or Copy/Move Element then proceed with **<Enter>**, then **<Ctrl>f.**
18. Stop! Check! Are 14–17 done?

NOTES:

____

____

____

____

____

____

____

(See instructions on pages 223 - 224)

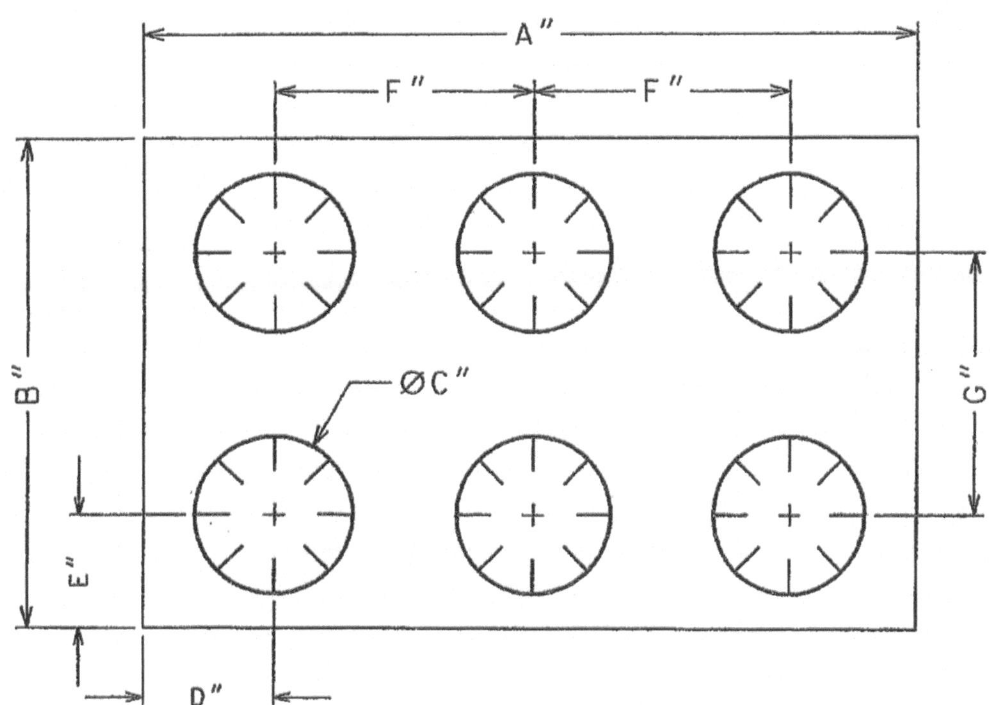

RANGE

Range Variations/Models *note: Draw one model of RANGE assigned to you. ie. Model # 2-2 dimensions are highlighted below. Other students may be assigned other model #s.*

	All Lengths are inches						
	width	height	diameter	dX	dY	col sp.	row sp.
Model #	A	B	C	D	E	F	G
2-1	45	28	9	7.5	8.5	15	11
2-2	48	28	9	8	7	16	14
2-3	51	28	9	8.5	6.5	17	15
2-4	45	30	9.5	7.5	9	15	12
2-5	48	30	9.5	8	8.5	16	13
2-6	51	30	9.5	8.5	7.5	17	15
2-7	45	32	10	7.5	9.5	15	13
2-8	48	32	10	8	9	16	14
2-9	51	32	10	8.5	8	17	16
2-10	54	34	11	9	10	18	14
2-11	54	34	11	9	9.5	18	15

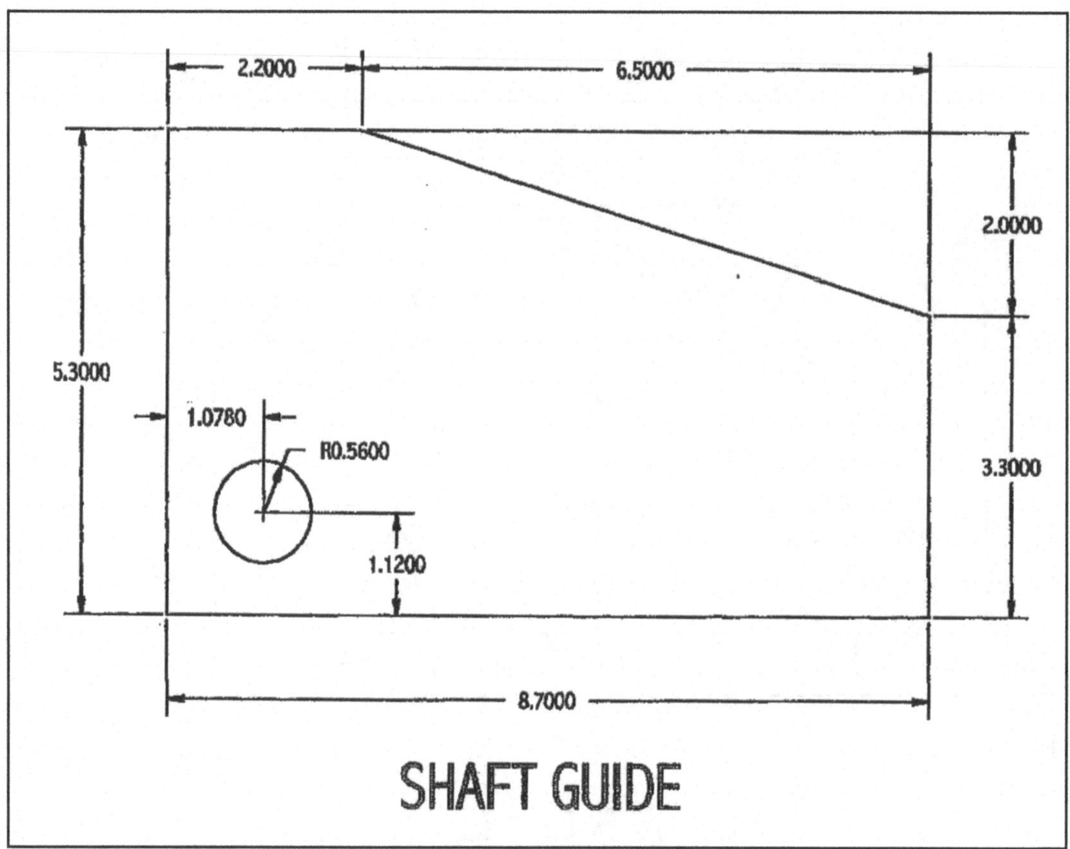

Dimension Elements are not needed on these beginning exercises.

These two are unitless, so the lengths are meters.

Lower left start corner is not specified, so it may be at the user's choice.

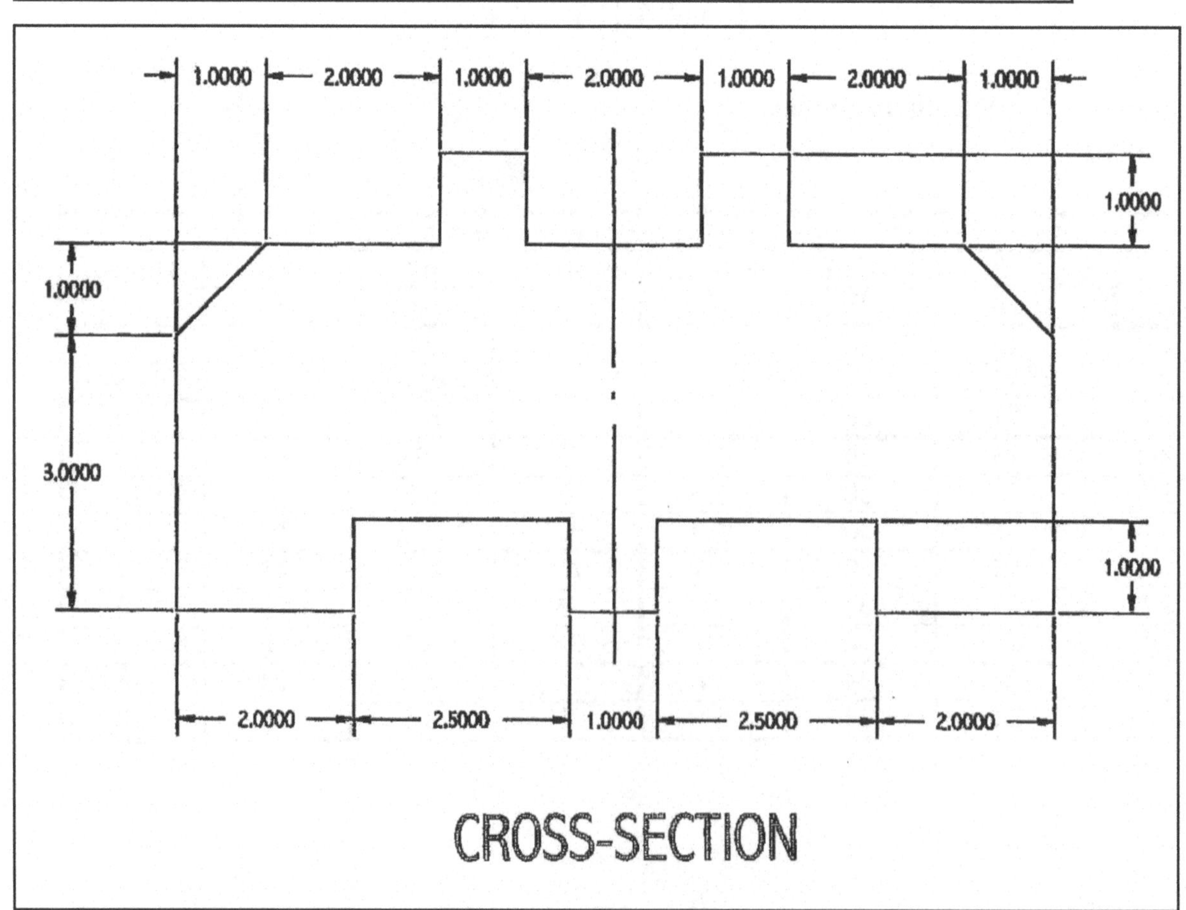

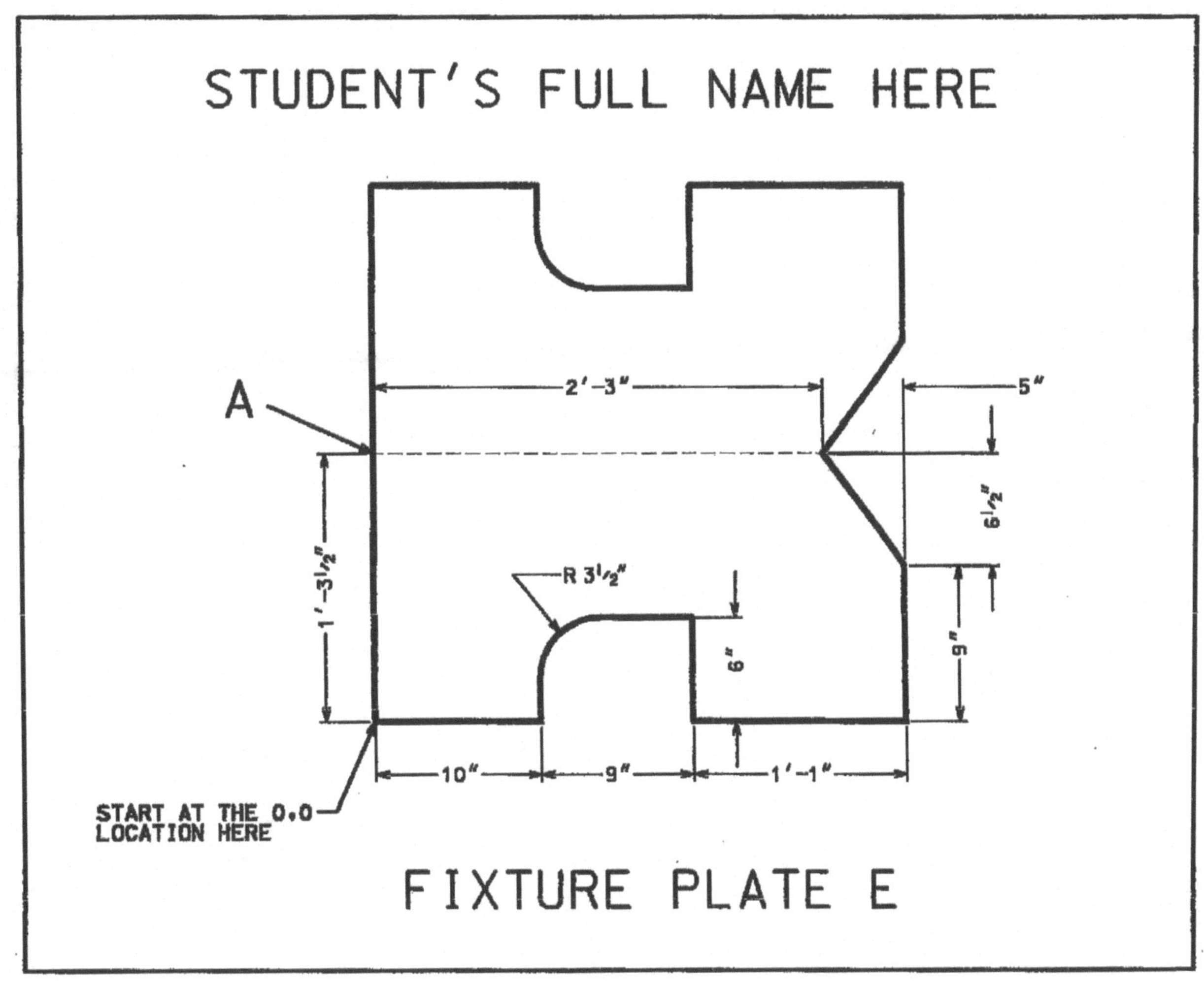

THIS DRAWING IS COMPOSED OF:

17 LINES
2 RADIUSED CORNERS
1 RECTANGULAR BLOCK SHAPE

DRAW THE BOTTOM HALF OF THE FIXTURE ONLY. USE MIRROR TO CREATE THE TOP HALF MIRRORED ABOUT THE HORIZONTAL LINE AT THE LETTER A. DRAW A DASHED LINE WHERE SHOWN AT LETTER A.

USE WEIGHT = 3 FOR ALL LINES. YOU DO NOT NEED TO PLACE THE DIMENSIONS. PUT YOUR NAME AT THE TOP AND THE TITLE AT THE BOTTOM AS SHOWN.

SET WORKING UNITS TO FEET AND INCHES TURN OFF THE GRID DISPLAY

USE FONT 3, ENGINEERING, WEIGHT = 1 FOR ALL TEXTS

WHEN DONE, PLACE A RECTANGULAR BLOCK SHAPE AROUND YOUR DRAWING AS SHOWN.

YOUR FINAL DRAWING SHOULD BE FITTED TO THE VIEW AND YOU SHOULD FILE SAVE SETTINGS BEFORE SAVING YOUR WORK TO YOUR PERSONAL NUMBERED FOLDER AND TO YOUR NAMED SUBMITTAL FOLDER.

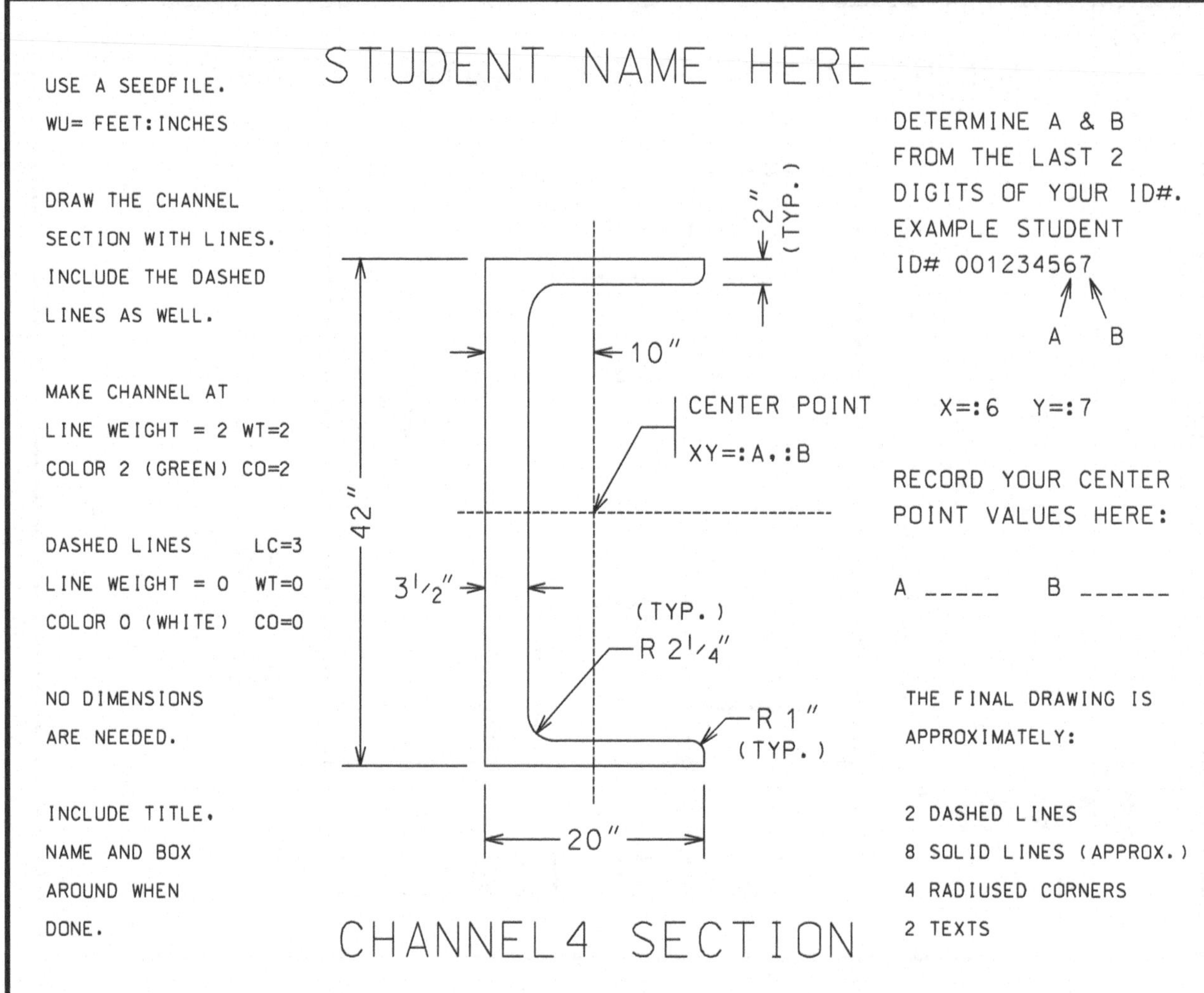
STUDENT NAME HERE
USE A SEEDFILE.
WU= FEET:INCHES
DRAW THE CHANNEL
SECTION WITH LINES.
INCLUDE THE DASHED
LINES AS WELL.
MAKE CHANNEL AT
LINE WEIGHT = 2 WT=2
COLOR 2 (GREEN) CO=2
DASHED LINES LC=3
LINE WEIGHT = 0 WT=0
COLOR 0 (WHITE) CO=0
NO DIMENSIONS
ARE NEEDED.
INCLUDE TITLE,
NAME AND BOX
AROUND WHEN
DONE.
2″
(TYP.)
10″
CENTER POINT
XY=:A,:B
42″
3 1/2″
(TYP.)
R 2 1/4″
R 1″
(TYP.)
20″
DETERMINE A & B
FROM THE LAST 2
DIGITS OF YOUR ID#.
EXAMPLE STUDENT
ID# 001234567
A B
X=:6 Y=:7
RECORD YOUR CENTER
POINT VALUES HERE:
A _____ B ______
THE FINAL DRAWING IS
APPROXIMATELY:
2 DASHED LINES
8 SOLID LINES (APPROX.)
4 RADIUSED CORNERS
2 TEXTS
CHANNEL4 SECTION

NOTES:

Course #_____ Self Assessment #___ Quiz Name:________________Due:________

Fill-in answers during or after Lecture / Lab as directed by your instructor 20 pts

The Precision Exercise guided you thru (gave detailed steps) using three types of precision input to create simple graphics (drawn to precision lengths, locations, directions, etc.). Let's check your understanding and learning retention of these concepts by making three similar drawings. Let's see if you can provide the remainder of the steps to complete the diagrams correctly. All are done with the Place Line tool. Also, Make sure that the GRID LOCK feature is OFF. These diagrams are NOT made using the Grid for precision, but by using the method of Precision Input Key-ins!

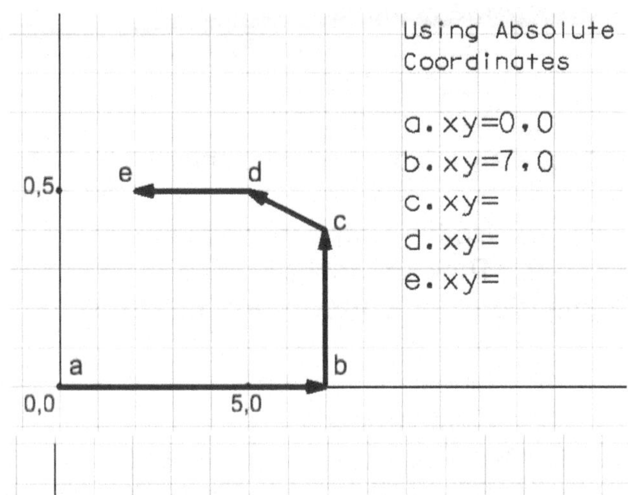

a. xy=0,0

b. xy=7,0

c. xy=______________ 2

d. xy=______________ 2

e. xy=______________ 2

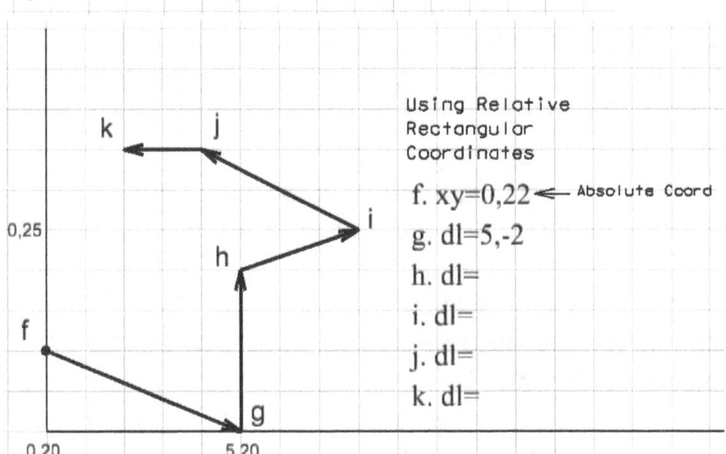

f. xy=0,22

g. dl=5,-2

h. dl=0,4

i. dl=______________ 2

j. dl=______________ 2

k. dl=______________ 2

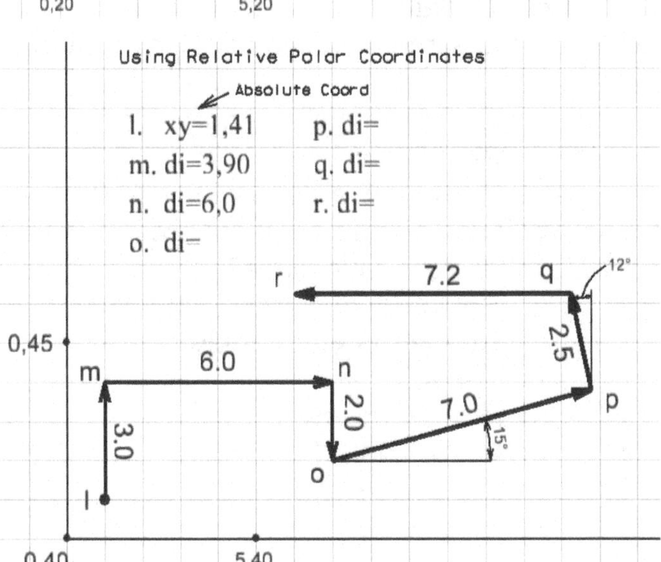

l. xy=1,41

m. di=3,90

n. di=6,0

o. di=______________ 2

p. di=______________ 2

q. di=______________ 2

r. di=______________ 2

Answers in Answer Section

Self-Assessment Exam – Intro to Civil Engineering & CAD Graphics

Modules 4, 5 & 6, Fences, Dimensions, Bearing Angle Expression, etc.

1. Four names of proper Fence Modes are:
   a. Inside, Outside, Add, Delete
   b. Inside, Edit, Rotate, Mirror
   c. inside, Association, Snap, Extend
   d. inside, Overlap, Clip, Void
2. Four major components of a Dimension Element are:
   a. Length, Arrows, Boundaries, Labels
   b. Dimension Text, Terminators, Extension Lines, Dimension Lines
   c. Units, Markers, Limit Lines, Arrows
   d. mu:su, Associated Lines, Measurement, End Lines
3. Which one of the following is a correct Bearing Angle Expression? (only one is correct)
   a. E26^28'30.5"N
   b. N28^W28'30.5"
   c. S26^28'30.5"N
   d. N28^26'30.5"E
4. What happens to the elements that are completely inside the fence during the stretch operation?
   a. They move
   b. They stretch
   c. Nothing happens to them
   d. They are deleted
5. Which of the following are examples of Dimension Elements? (one or more may be correct)
   a. Radial Dimension
   b. Angular Dimension
   c. Linear Dimension
   d. Center mark
6. What is the proper label format within the Element>Dimension Styles dialog box to make the dimension apper as shown: **5' - 11"** (assume working units are alredy set to ft : inches)
   a. mu : su
   b. English
   c. ft : in
   d. mu label - su label
7. In MicroStation, "measurements" and "dimensions" are just different words for the same thing.

   True or False
8. Which ***LOCK***, when on, allows dimensions to automatically update, when the element that is dimensioned is modified by the user?
   a. Automatic
   b. Association
   c. Snap
   d. Update
9. Which of the following phrase(s) can also have the same meaning as "Bearing Angle Expression"?
   a. Surveyor's Angles
   b. Working Units
   c. Civil Engineering Angles
   d. AccuDraw
10. If there is a fence boundary placed on your screen and you a done with it, (it is no longer needed since you are done with the previous editing operation) how do you remove it from the screen and not have any further edits take place?
    a. Hit <delete> key
    b. Hit Fence Delete icon
    c. Select Place Fence icon agin
    d. Use <ctrl> <alt> <del>

Answers here

Answers:

1. d.
2. b.
3. d.
4. a.
5. a,b,c,d
6. d.
7. false
8. b.
9. a. and c.
10. c.

Handy Intergraph/MicroStation Key-ins:

General:

XX=$ or XX=? or XX= <Enter> no value	Show Current Value associated with Key-in
ie. AA= <Enter>	Could show AA=30, in the status field, indicating the current setting

Manipulation Commands:

AA=___	Active Angle, (for rotation, text angle), ie. 0–360^ ie. AA=45, sets the Active Angle to 45 degrees	
AS=___	Active Scale, sets X, Y & Z scale factor to the same value	
XS=___	Active X-axis scale factor	
YS=___	Active Y-axis scale factor	
ZS=___	Active Z-axis scale factor	
KY=___	Snap Mode Divisor	
ROTATE	ROT	Rotate Element
SCALE	SCA	Scale Element
DELETE	DEL	Delete Element
MOVE	MOV	Move Element
COPY	COP	Copy Element
UNDO	<Ctrl>Z	Reverse Last Operation
REDO	<Ctrl>R	Reverse Last Undo Operation
PLACE FENCE	PLA F	Place a Block Fence

Cell Commands:

AC=___	Active Cell, Place cell	AC=cellname
RC=___	Retrieve Cell Library	RC=cell library name
CC=___,___,___	Create Cell	CC=cellname, description,type
CD=___	Delete Cell	CD=cellname
CR=___,___	Cell Rename	CR=oldname, newname
LT=___	Line Terminator	LT=terminator name
TS=___	Terminator Scale	TS=factor

Symbology commands:

CO=___	Color	= number or name of color, ie. 0–255
LC=___	Line Code (Style)	= number (also called line-style), ie. 0–7
WT=___	Weight	= number (line thickness), ie. 0–31
LV=___	Level	= number or name, ie. 1–63

Text commands:

FT=___	Font	= number or name of font
TH=___	Text Height	= dimension in feet:inches or working units
TW=___	Text Width	= dimension in feet:inches or working units
TX=___	Text Hgt&Wth	= sets height & width to the same value
TX=*___	Text Hgt&Wth	multiply current size by factor
LS=___	Line Spacing	= distance between lines in multline text
LL=___	Line Length	= Maximum characters per line before wrap

Precision Input:

XY = X VALUE, Y VALUE	(Absolute Coordinates)
DL = DELTA X, DELTA Y	(Delta Lengths)
DI = DISTANCE, ANGLE	(Distance, Direction)

View Commands:

Name:	Short key-in:	Description:
ON=___		Display on level #, #,# or #-#
OF=___		Display off level #, #,# or #-#
FIT	FIT	Fit ALL elements in the file into view
FIT ALL	FIT A	Fit Design & Reference elements into view
UPDATE	UP	
WINDOW AREA	WI	
ZOOM OUT	ZO O __	Zoom Out [by factor], default factor=2
ZOOM IN	ZO I __	Zoom In [by factor], default factor=2
VIEW ON ___	VI ON ___	Display View #, ie. 1–4 or 5–8 (screen 2)
VIEW OFF ___	VI OF ___	Display Off View #
MOVE LEFT ___	MOV L	Scroll Left by factor, default .5
MOVE RIGHT ___	MOV R	Scroll Right by factor, default .5
MOVE UP ___	MOV U	Scroll Up by factor, default .5
MOVE DOWN ___	MOV D	Scroll Down by factor, default .5
-	<Ctrl> B	View Attributes Dialog, "Better" Viewing
-	<Ctrl> E	Level Control Dialog

File Manipulations:

Name:	Shortest key-in:	Description:
EXIT		End design session, go to DOS
COMPRESS	COM	Removes elements marked for delete
FILE	<Ctrl> F	Save Settings, also File Design
BACKUP	BA [filename]	Create a backup file as named
SHO REF	SH R	Opens Reference Files Settings Box
! Jump out to the operating system, ie DOS or UNIX		
RF=___,___,___	Attach Ref File, RF=filename, logical name, descript.	
RD=___	Retrieve Design, at filed position	
XD=___	Exchange Design, at current position	
CT=___	Attach color table	

Menu Commands:

AM=___,___	Attach Menu, AM=menuname, menutype (cm, mm, sb, fk)
AT=___	Active Tutorial

NOTES

Glossary up to Module 5

A

accept To click the Data button to approve the placement of a data point at the location of a tentative point or to confirm the identification of an element that is highlighted.

AccuDraw Drafting aid used to apply precision to geometry without affecting the flow of drafting or sacrificing the interactivity afforded by dynamic update.

AccuSnap A snapping mode that may be used by itself, or in combination with AccuDraw, to reduce the number of button presses required during a design session. AccuSnap provides graphical assistance — a smart pointer — for snapping to elements.

action string Defines the action MicroStation performs when a tool is selected or a menu item is chosen.

active angle The angle, in degrees, used with cell placement and text placement tools that require an angle specification.

active attributes The setting that determines the color, line style, and line weight of an element upon placement.

active color The setting that determines the color of an element upon placement.

active command The command that has most recently been activated from a tool box, menu, or key-in.

active control indicator The dotted rectangle that indicates the input focus in dialog boxes.

active DGN file The DGN file currently opened for viewing and/or manipulation.

active entity The row in the database table that is linked to a graphic element when a database attachment is executed.

active level The setting that determines the level upon which an element is placed.

active scale factor(s) The setting that determines the amount of scaling applied to a cell when placed, to selected elements, or to the fence contents when using *Scale*. The scale factors in the X-, Y-, or Z-direction can be identical or each can be different.

active line style The setting that determines the line style of an element upon placement.

active line weight The setting that determines the line weight of an element upon placement.

alphanumeric A string of characters that takes the form of letters, numbers, and some symbols (e.g. @, $, and punctuation).

alternate key-in A short cut way to enter a key-in command. For example, AA= is an alternate key-in for ACTIVE ANGLE.

arc A regularly curved open element that has a constant radius around a single center point.

attributes Line color, line style, line weight, and fill color (for closed elements).

B

block A rectangular shape.

buttons Areas in dialog boxes that you click to start, save, or dismiss an operation.

C

cascade The arrangement of stacked views of windows or views in numerical order, with the lowest numbered view entirely visible and the title bars of all other views visible.

check box A square box in a dialog or setting box that can be clicked to toggle the associated setting.

class An element attribute, usually primary or construction.

click To press or tap once on a cursor or mouse button; to press a push button or check button in a dialog box.

closed Elements that completely enclose the area within their boundaries.

color fill An attribute that, when applied to a closed element, indicates the element's enclosed area as a solid shape of color.

color table In a DGN file, the color table determines the correspondence between the 256-color attribute values and display colors. It is displayed in a dialog box.

command An instruction that tells MicroStation what to do. Commands are activated with tools in tool boxes, pull down menus, settings and dialog boxes, key-ins, and function keys. All commands can be activated with a key-in.

controls Parts of a dialog box such as text fields, check boxes, and option menus.

coordinate Location of a point in the design plane along the X (horizontal), Y (vertical), and Z (depth [3D only]) axes relative to the global origin.

coordinate readout Format and precision with which coordinate, measurement, and angle data is displayed in the status bar and in settings and dialog boxes.

D

data button The button on a mouse or digitizing tablet that is pressed to enter data points, identify elements for manipulation, accept a previous action, select tools, and operate dialog box controls.

data point Input entered using the pointing device that designates a point in the design.

delete To remove an element(s) from the DGN file.

DGN file MicroStation document file that contains one or more models. These models may be design models or sheet models.

design plane The area in which elements are created in a 2D design.

design session The period during which a DGN file is active.

dialog box A window displayed on the screen that presents various controls that can be manipulated to set values that MicroStation will use.

digitizing The process of coding graphic information from paper sources (such as a map or other drawing) into a DGN file using a tablet.

double-click To press or tap twice in quick succession on a cursor button or mouse button, or to press on a list box item in a dialog box twice in quick succession.

drawing plane The plane on which data points are previewed with AccuDraw. In 3D, all data points will lie on this plane unless supplied by tentative point snap or by precision input key-in.

drawing plane coordinate system The coordinate system (Rectangular or Polar) that defines the orientation of the drawing plane.

drawing plane origin The origin of the drawing plane coordinate system.

E

element One of the entities that make up a DGN file. See graphic element.

element attributes Color, line style, line weight, class, level, and fill. Other element attributes apply only to certain element types.

element manipulation To delete, copy, move, rotate, mirror, or scale existing graphic elements in the design.

element placement Tools used to place or construct graphic elements in the design.

element symbology The color, line style, and line weight of an element.

entity The fundamental unit of data in a DWG, DXF, IGES, or CGM file. In general, entities are the equivalent of MicroStation elements.

extension — A suffix of characters optionally separated from the main part of a filename by a period (".") character. Traditionally, these have been used to designate the type of the file. For example, ".dgn" is commonly used to represent a DGN file.

F

field — In a dialog box, an area into which a filename or other keyboard input can be entered. In a non-graphical database, a column.

filename — Denotes the string used when calling for a generic file.

filled — Element that is colored within the planar element boundaries, as opposed to being displayed as just an outline.

filter — A filename pattern that limits filenames displayed in a list to those fitting the pattern. For example, "*.dgn."

fit — A viewing operation that expands the area seen within a view to include all elements on all levels turned on in the view.

fitted view — View that shows all elements on the levels turned on in the view.

floating — A dialog box, tool box, or other part of MicroStation's graphical user interface that can be positioned freely on screen.

function keys — Application keys that are programmable; located at the top of the keyboard.

function key menu — A way to assign actions to the function keys on the keyboard.

G

geometry — Type of entity that defines physical shapes, including points, curves, surfaces, solids, and relations (collections of similarly structured entities).

global origin — Location of the origin of the Cartesian coordinate system in design plane coordinates. When design plane positions are specified or reported in working units, they are relative to the global origin.

graphic — A type of cell in which the symbology (color, line style, and line weight) is determined when it is created.

graphic element — A graphic component of the design. Referred to in user documentation as simply an "element."

grid lock — The setting that, when on, forces all graphically entered data points to the grid point nearest to the specified point.

grid — A matrix of grid points (dots) and grid references (crosses) at user-defined intervals, used as a visual aid or in conjunction with the Grid Lock setting for precision input.

grid points Evenly spaced points in the design plane located at integer multiples of the grid units from the global origin.

grid references Reference crosses spaced at user-defined intervals on the grid.

grid units The settings that specify the distance between adjacent grid points and the number of grid points between grid references.

H

handles Small squares drawn on (or sometimes near) elements to indicate that they have been selected. This provides an alternative to highlighting.

help articles Text that displays in the Help window to explain particular concepts, features, and procedures in MicroStation.

help topics A list of the areas covered by help articles that displays in the Help window.

highlight color The color in which an element is displayed upon identification for manipulation.

hypertext The text that appears in color in the online help and allows you to jump from topic to topic by selecting it.

I

identify To enter a data point on an element to distinguish it for manipulation or modification.

input focus The settings or dialog box control upon which the next keystroke will act has the input focus.

item In a dialog box, any control such as a text field, check box, or option menu.

J

K

key-in An instruction entered into the Key-in window to control MicroStation. Most key-ins have GUI control equivalents.

Key-in window A window used to scroll through lists of key-ins, construct key-ins, and submit key-ins to MicroStation. Opens when Key-in is chosen from the Utilities menu.

keypoint Points on an element to which a tentative point will snap when Snap Lock is on activated within Keypoint mode.

keypoint snap mode If active, entering a tentative point close enough to an element causes the tentative point to snap to a keypoint on the element.

L

level In the MicroStation DGN file format, the number of levels is unlimited, and the minimum number of levels is 1. You can delete unused levels. All levels are named and have default colors, line weights, and line styles, providing the foundation for numerous enhancements. An important benefit of the level system is the ability to standardize level structures across DGN files.

level lock The setting that, when turned on, prevents selection or manipulation of any element that is not on the active level.

level structure The hierarchical organization of levels after they are grouped.

level symbology A view setting that, when turned on, causes all elements on a particular level to be displayed with the same element symbology.

line string An open graphic element composed of line segments connected at the vertices.

line style A part of the symbology of an element, for example, whether a line is solid, continuous dashes, dots and dashes, and so on. Each element can have its own line style or each can be defined by separate symbology. You can create custom line styles.

line weight An index in the range 0 to 31 that designates the weight or thickness of the lines used to draw or plot a graphic element. Each element has its own line weight.

list box Rectangular areas in which files, directories, or other items are listed for selection or reference.

locks Settings that you selectively enable or disable. Locks affect the way MicroStation interprets and reacts to your input.

M

manipulate To copy, move, rotate, scale, mirror, or delete an element or group of elements.

master units The largest units in common use in a model.

menu One method for activating a MicroStation command, including pull-down menus, tool boxes, function key menus, and paper menus.

menu item Any of the list of options on a pull-down menu.

mirror A manipulation that reverses the geometry of graphic elements about a horizontal, vertical, or specified arbitrary line.

mnemonic access character The underlined character in each menu name and menu item.

N

noun-verb A manner of operating MicroStation; to select an element in the design before selecting a tool to act upon it.

O

offset In a compound line style component, the value that specifies the distance measured perpendicularly from the working line to where the component is displayed.

opaque A type of fill that is displayed as a solid shape of the active color.

option menu A menu in a dialog box that allows only one value to be selected.

origin See cell origin or global origin.

orthogonal Constructed with right angles or perpendicular lines. An orthogonal shape contains only right angles.

override The mode that allows you to override the Snap Mode.

overwrite mode The mode of text entry in which each new character overwrites an existing character.

P

panning To scroll a view over the design plane.

parameter See settings.

pixel PICture ELement, the smallest dot of light that a monitor can display.

place SmartLine The tool used to place a line, line string, shape, arc, or circle or a combination thereof.

point See data point, tentative point, or active point.

point element A special case of a line element that has no length.

point of intersection The point at which two non-parallel lines intersect, or would intersect if the lines were extended.

pointer The small icon on the screen that moves in response to user inputs and indicates the position where input is supplied to MicroStation.

polar array The set of copies of an element placed in a circular pattern in a design.

polar coordinates The coordinates used in a spherical (auxiliary) coordinate system or in AccuDraw to specify distances and angles.

precision input key-ins A means of entering data points at precise locations either by specifying the coordinates or by specifying the distance from the most recent data point or tentative point.

preferences Settings that customize MicroStation to your particular machine and desired mode of operation.

primary elements Elements whose class attribute is primary (as opposed to construction.)

primitive elements The simplest type of element.

prompt The text in the status bar that tells you what to do next.

properties Element criteria that may be searched, including the area attribute (Solid or Hole), whether an element can be snapped to, whether it is locked, and whether it has been modified.

R

reset A placement action that, with most tools, backs up one step. In some cases a Reset operation completes an action; in other cases, it cancels an action or rejects an identified element.

reset button The button on a mouse or digitizing table cursor that is pressed to enter a Reset.

resetting Entering a Reset.

resize border The frame around each view that permits the view to be resized. When the pointer is placed on the resize border, it becomes a double arrow, and that border can be pulled or pushed to expand or contract the size of the view.

resolution The number of addressable points across a given area. For example, output device resolution is measured in lines per inch, while screen resolution is usually given with two numbers indicating the number of pixels across the width and height of the largest image that can be displayed.

rubberbanding See dynamic update.

S

saved The kinds of settings, such as working units and view configuration, that are kept between sessions.

saved view A named view definition saved in a DGN file for later recall or for attaching to another model file as a reference.

scale To resize an element or elements by the active scale factors. In plotting, the ratio between distance in the DGN file master units and distance represented on the output device.

screen element One of the pieces that make up MicroStation's graphical user interface, such as the desktop, a window border, or a button.

screen menus Pull-down menus, tool frames, dialog boxes, and sidebar menus.

seed DGN file A template file that contains the appropriate default settings and attributes.

select To distinguish an element, identify a list box entry on which to operate, or activate a tool or view control.

select settings window Used to adjust the active settings and select a drawing tool.

selection set A group of selected elements. Selected elements are displayed with handles.

separator bar A horizontal line across a menu that logically subdivides menu items in the same menu.

settings Values that determine how MicroStation displays a design or handles user input.

shape A closed primitive element composed of linear segments.

sidebar menu A menu that displays onscreen and presents commands for selection in a text-based, hierarchical form. Although sidebar menus are still supported, tool boxes have taken their place.

single-shot Selecting a tool for one-time use by double-clicking it.

sink To put a window just below the lowest view.

SmartLine See place SmartLine.

snap lock The setting that, when on, causes MicroStation to try to find an element or element intersection to snap to when a tentative point is entered. See also keypoint snap mode.

snap divisor The setting that determines the positioning of keypoints on linear segments. The number of keypoints per segment is one greater than the snap divisor. If the snap divisor is one, only endpoints of a linear segment are keypoints. If the snap divisor is two or a multiple of two, the center point is also a keypoint.

snap Use of the tentative point to position a data point at an exact point on the target element. Tentative points snap to an element when Snap Lock is on.

snap lock divisor The number of keypoints on each segment of a linear element plus one.

status bar The strip at the bottom of the application window (or screen) that displays messages, prompts, and status information. The area on the screen where messages such as tool prompts, errors, and the current status of MicroStation settings (snaps, levels, element selection, and DGN file disk status) are displayed.

subunits Units that master units are divided into in the working unit definition. For example, if master units are feet, a convenient subunits setting would be inches. The number of subunits per master unit and a one or two character abbreviation for the subunit name is specified in the working unit definition.

suffix See extension.

symbology See element symbology, level symbology, or attributes.

T

tentative button The button that is pressed to enter a tentative data point. The tentative button may also shift the location of the AccuSnap selection.

tentative point A graphic input that is used to preview the location of the next data point, define a point of reference, and/or create an association point. Tentative points may appear with AccuSnap.

tile To arrange views and tool boxes so that they do not overlap.

toggle A type of setting that has only two states, such as off and on. Used as a verb, to change the state of a toggle.

tool A drawing function or the screen icon used to represent that function in a tool box.

tool box Icon-based screen menus from which tools and view controls are selected.

tool frame A tool box that has child tool boxes.

tool settings Special settings that apply to certain tools, such as length and angle settings for the *Place Line* tool.

tool settings window The window that contains controls for adjusting the selected tool's settings.

U

Unit Lock The setting that, when on, forces all graphically entered data points to the nearest point that is an integer multiple of the unit distance from the global origin in the X, Y, and (in 3D files) Z directions.

unit distance The setting that specifies the spacing between points that data points will be restricted to when Unit Lock is turned on.

update To redraw the contents of a view window(s).

user preference See preferences.

V

verb-noun A manner of operating MicroStation: choosing a tool before identifying an element in the design for it to act upon.

vertex The highest point or apex of a figure, the intersection of lines or curves, or the endpoint of an element.

view Collectively, the portion of the active model (and its attached references) and displayed in a view window and the display orientation.

view configuration The arrangement of view windows on the screen and the area of the model displayed in each view.

view control bar The bar at the bottom border of each view window from which commonly used view controls can be selected.

view controls Graphically operated controls that affect the portion of the design or the orientation of the information in a view.

view window A window displaying a view.

W

window A bordered rectangular region on the screen displaying a tool box, dialog box, view, or sidebar menu.

window control menu A menu opened by clicking the window menu button on the left end of a window's title bar.

window origin The position in the design plane of the lower-left corner of a view.

windowing A method of selecting new contents for a view.

working units Real-world units that the design plane is configured to.

working unit settings The settings that designate the working units and working resolution. In the current implementation, MicroStation uses IEEE 64–bit floating point storage, which allows for a high degree of accuracy and a working volume with each axis roughly 2 million times larger than the axes in V7.

workspace A custom MicroStation environment or configuration.

Z

zoom To decrease (zoom in) or increase (zoom out) the portion of the design displayed in a view.

Glossary - Modules 5–End

A

active cell	The cell that is placed with the cell placement tools.
active font	The setting that determines the font of a text element upon placement.
active pattern angle(s)	The setting that determines the angle at which the active pattern cell is placed by *Pattern Area*, the angle of the lines placed using *Hatch Area*, or two settings that determine the angles of the lines placed using *Crosshatch Area*.
active pattern cell	The setting that determines the cell that is used for patterning.
active pattern scale	The setting that determines the scale at which the active pattern cell is placed during area patterning and linear patterning.
active pattern spacing	The distance(s) between adjacent pattern cells placed using *Pattern Area*. The distance(s) between lines placed using *Hatch Area* or *Crosshatch Area*.
active point	The setting that determines whether a cell, symbol, or zero-length line is drawn by the point placement tools.
active text height	The setting that determines the height of text upon placement.
active text width	The setting that determines the width of text upon placement.
area filling	See fill.
area patterning	Placement of the active pattern cell (at the active pattern angle, scale, and spacing) in an area bounded by a shape, ellipse, circle, fence, or complex shape. The cell is repeated in a rectangular array spacing as many times as necessary to fill the area.
associated dimensions	Dimensions that update automatically as the element they dimension is modified.
association lock	The setting that, when turned on, causes element associations to be created when an element is snapped to while using *Place Multi-line*, a dimensioning tool, or a cell placement tool (with Use Shared Cells on).
attach	To activate a (paper, cursor button, or sidebar) menu. To define (a cell library, color table, or reference) for use with a DGN file.

B

C

cell	A complex element composed of a group of primitive or other complex elements that is stored in a cell library for repeated placement.
cell definition	The graphical elements that make up a cell.
cell library	A file that is used to store cells. To access cells in a cell library, the library must be attached to the active DGN file, except if the Cell Selector dialog box is used.
cell origin	The point, specified during cell creation, about which the cell is placed (the origin corresponds to the data point when the cell is placed in the design).
clipping boundary	A boundary (established with a fence or from a named view) that separates the part of a reference that is displayed from the part that is hidden.
clip mask	Used with the Raster Manager or Reference tools, a clip mask allows you lets you clip out a portion of the image. Masking can be used, for example, to clear an area for text display.
coincidentally	Attaching a reference by aligning the coordinates of its design plane with those of the active DGN file, without any rotation, scaling, or offset.
coincident reference attachment	A coincidentally attached reference has a one-to-one correspondence between its design plane and the design plane of the active DGN file. If the working units settings and global origin are identical in the two files, the coordinates in working units are identical as well.
compass	A square or circle used to indicate the AccuDraw drawing plane origin, axes, and coordinate system. Color-coded hash marks indicate the positive X and Y axes.
crosshatch	The process of constructing two sets of evenly spaced lines in a closed area bounded by a complex shape, closed element, or fence at the active pattern angles and spacing.

D

default font	The font used to display a text element in the design when the font with which the element was placed is not found.
dimension	A label in a design owing a linear, angular, or radial distance or angle measurement.
dimension attributes	The settings for all components of dimension elements, including text (color, weight, font, height, and width), lines (color, style, weight, and alternates), and level.

dimension element An element that contains all of the lines, arcs, terminators, and text in a dimension.

dimension line terminators Symbols placed at the end of dimension lines that clarify the meaning of the dimensions.

dimension line The line component of a dimension that is usually parallel to and the same length as the object being dimensioned.

dimension mark Symbols placed with dimension text that clarify the meaning of the dimension text.

drop complex element To return the primitive elements composing a complex element to their primitive element status.

E

element tag Where associated data is stored in the DGN file with the graphical elements. Tags allow you to associate non-graphical data to elements in the DGN file if the data is relatively simple or if you must maintain compatibility with other CAD packages that store data inside their drawing files. The associated tag data may be copied from the tag, loaded into a database and linked back to the tag.

enter data field One or more placeholders representing characters that reserve space in a text element for future input.

extension lines Component of dimensions that consists of lines extending from the dimensioned points to the dimension line.

F

fence A polygonal boundary that designates multiple elements for simultaneous manipulation using fence tools.

fence contents The elements and portions of elements operated on by fence tools determined by the fence selection mode. These elements can be enclosed by, outside of, or overlap the fence.

fence manipulation Tools that operate on the fence contents.

fence selection mode A setting that determines the fence contents.

filled Element that is colored within the planar element boundaries, as opposed to being displayed as just an outline.

fillet An arc constructed between and tangent to two converging lines.

filter A filename pattern that limits filenames displayed in a list to those fitting the pattern. For example, "*.dgn."

font A style of lettering. Fonts are identified by both a number and a font name.

font library A file that contains fonts for use by MicroStation or other applications. These fonts may include TTF and SHX formats.

G

graphic group A permanent grouping of elements (primitive or complex). An element can be a member of only one graphic group at a time.

graphic group lock The setting that, when on, causes all elements in a graphic group to be manipulated whenever one member of the graphic group is manipulated. For example, if an element in a graphic group is deleted with Graphic Group Lock on, all elements in the graphic group are likewise deleted.

group A complex element (actually an unnamed cell) that is not defined in a cell library. Groups can be created to keep elements together, or to be copied for repeated placement in a design.

H

hatch The process of constructing a set of evenly spaced lines in a closed area.

I

insertion point The point, represented by a vertical bar, at which new characters are inserted.

inside Elements completely enclosed in a fence are inside the fence.

J

joints Intersections of multi-lines.

K

L

library See cell library.

line terminator A cell placed at the end of an open element, oriented in the direction of the element. A commonly used line terminator is an arrowhead placed at the end of a line segment.

linear patterning The repetitive placement of the active pattern cell along a line, line string, shape, arc, circle, ellipse, or curve element.

locate To find an element in the DGN file.

M

mark See dimension mark.

mask An area of a reference that is not displayed.

multi-line element A set of two or more parallel lines treated as a single object, commonly used for drawing walls in floor plans. A multi-line element can be defined to include up to 16 separate lines, each with its own symbology, level, and class.

N

nested When part of a cell is used as part of an additional cell.

nested reference attachments MicroStation provides live nested reference attachments as an alternative to flattening all reference attachments in the active model. When this option is enabled, changes to reference attachments in designs that are referenced to other designs are reflected the next time either the active model's views are updated or the file is reopened.

node Shorthand for text node. Also a computer in a network.

non-coincidental reference attachment A non-coincidentally attached reference is offset, rotated, or scaled from the active DGN file.

O

offset In a compound line style component, the value that specifies the distance measured perpendicularly from the working line to where the component is displayed.

opaque A type of fill that is displayed as a solid shape of the active color.

origin See cell origin or global origin.

overlap A fence selection mode that includes only the elements inside or overlapping the fence.

P

pattern element An element with a class attribute of pattern. It can be placed only with a patterning tool.

patterning See area patterning.

place SmartLine The tool used to place a line, line string, shape, arc, or circle or a combination thereof.

point See data point, tentative point, or active point.

point cell A cell with a single, snappable point. Point cells are commonly used for symbols and to establish monument points. The snappable point in a point cell is the cell origin. Point cells are always placed relative to the active level with the active symbology.

point curve A type of curve that has no settings that control the curve's shape.

point element A special case of a line element that has no length.

point of intersection The point at which two non-parallel lines intersect, or would intersect if the lines were extended.

point symbols A type of line style component.

R

reference A model attached to and displayed with the active model for printing or construction purposes. A reference cannot be modified. You can attach, as a reference, a model that resides in either the open DGN file or some other DGN file.

S

SmartLine See place SmartLine.

stacked dimensions A group of dimensions that have at least one witness line in common.

style A multi-line definition or set of dimension attributes that can be saved in a settings file for later recall.

T

tags Non-graphical attributes that may be attached to elements drawn in designs.

tag set Set of associated tags.

tag set definition Information that specifies, for each tag in a tag set, several tag attributes, such as whether the tag is displayed and its default value, if any.

terminator See dimension line terminators or line terminator.

text attributes The color, weight, font, height, and width of text.

text element MicroStation places text in DGN files as a distinct type of element.

text node A group of multiple text elements grouped in a complex element. MicroStation automatically forms a text node when multi-line text is placed.

text node lock A setting that, when turned on, forces subsequently entered text to be attached to empty text nodes. If an empty node is not available, no text is placed.

text style Comprises a group of text attributes such as font type, width, height, and color. Text styles allow you to place text within a model file in a consistent and automated manner. The fonts that are supported natively in MicroStationare True Type and AutoCAD fonts (.shx)

U

V

void A fence selection mode that selects elements or parts of elements outside the fence, rather than within the fence.

void-clip A fence mode in which only the elements that are completely outside the fence and those parts of elements outside or overlapping the fence are included in the fence contents.

void-overlap A fence mode in which only the elements outside or overlapping the fence are included in the fence contents.

W

witness lines See extension lines.

AutoCAD vs. MicroStation Cross-Reference

AUTOCAD: (typed entries)		MICROSTATION: (select by pointer "mouse" or key-in)
OPEN		(PULL-DOWN) FILE-OPEN or use μStn manager dialog or ^O
NEW		(PULL-DOWN) FILE-NEW or ^N
LIMITS		none
GRID or <F7>		(PULL-DOWN) VIEW-ATTRIBUTES (GRID on/off on dialog) or ^B
ORTHO or <F8>		(PULL-DOWN) SETTINGS-LOCKS (AXIS on/off on dialog) or key-in LOCK AX
SNAP or <F9>		(PULL-DOWN) SETTINGS-GRID or key-in LOCK GR
REDRAW or R		(ICON) UPDATE or key-in UPDATE or UP
ZOOM or Z		
Z WINDOW	W	(ICON) WINDOW AREA or key-in WI
Z CENTER	C	(ICON) WINDOW CENTER or key-in WI CE
Z EXTENTS	E	(ICON) FIT or key-in FIT
Z 2X		(ICON) ZOOM IN or key-in ZO I
Z 10X		key-in ZOOM IN 10 or ZO I 10
Z .5X		(ICON) ZOOM OUT or ZOOM IN .5
Z DYNAMIC	D	none
Z PREVIOUS	P	(PULL-DOWN) VIEW-PREVIOUS or <Alt> V P
none		(PULL-DOWN) VIEW-NEXT or <Alt> V N
VIEW		(PULL-DOWN) VIEW-SAVED or key-in SV=, VI= or DV=name
PAN		key-in MOVE LEFT, RIGHT, UP or DOWN [factor], ie MOV L .3 (SHIFT & DRAG MANEUVER) DYNAMIC PAN
LINE or L		(ICON) PLACE LINE or key-in PLA LI
CIRCLE or C		(ICON) PLACE CIRCLE or key-in PLA C
none		(ICON) PLACE BLOCK or key-in PLA B
MOVE	or M	(ICON) MOVE or key-in MOV
COPY	or CP	(ICON) COPY or key-in COP
ERASE	or E	(ICON) DELETE or key-in DEL
MIRROR		(ICON) MIRROR or key-in MIR
QUIT, END		(PULL-DOWN) FILE-EXIT or key-in EXIT
PURGE		(PULL-DOWN) FILE-COMPRESS or key-in COM
none		(PULL-DOWN) FILE-SAVE SETTINGS or key-in FILE or ^F

AutoCAD	MicroStation
"cancel", ^C	<Esc> or <Reset> button (Right Mouse Button)
<Enter>, (Right Mouse Button)	<Enter>
"Flip Text Screen" <F1>	none
UNDO or U	UNDO or ^Z
REDO	REDO
(PULL-DOWN) VIEW-LAYOUT-TILED VIEWPORTS	(PULL-DOWN) VIEW-OPEN/CLOSE or key-in VI ON 1–4 WINDOW TILE key-in WI T or (PULL-DOWN) VIEW-TILE (PULL-DOWN) WINDOW CASCADE
Selection Options:	Fence Modes:
Window or W	"INSIDE" fence contents mode
Crossing or C	"OVERLAP" fence contents mode
WP "Window Polygon"	"INSIDE" fence contents mode with multi-sided fence
CP "Crossing Polygon"	"OVERLAP" fence contents mode with multi-sided fence
Fence	none
ALL	none
Remove (mode)	none
Add (mode)	none
Last	none
none	"CLIP"
none	"VOID" (outside)
none	"VOID-CLIP"
none	"VOID-OVERLAP"
LAYER or LA	LEVELS COMMANDS
SET	LV= (Active Level)
NEW	
COLOR	

NOTES

AutoCAD vs. MicroStation Concepts (Cross-Reference Chart)

Terminology/Concept comparison: Differences and/or Similarities highlighted below

	AutoCAD	MicroStation
Wk#	Drawing set-up:	
1	AutoCAD drawings have **LIMITS** which define the maximum drawing area	MicroStation maximum drawing area is automatically defined by the **Working Units** selected
1	Default AutoCAD **LIMITS** are X-axis 12.0000, Y-axis 9.0000	Default MicroStation maximum drawing area is 10^{32} x 10^{32} of the smallest units of resolution – usually not a setting changed by the user but which are defined as 1/1000 or 1/8000 of the sub-unit length.
1	Default **UNITS** are decimal inches	Default **Working Units** are mu:su (master units:sub units with mu defined as Meters)
1	AutoCAD users must typically set both the **UNITS** and **LIMITS** if drawing precision drawings	MicroStation users must typically set the **Working Units** if creating precision design files

Wk#	Drawing File Save:	
1	AutoCAD users **must manually SAVE** their drawings at the end of the drawing session or when desired.	MicroStation automatically SAVES each and every drawing and editing action **as the user works** (although this feature may be switched off if desired)
1	Default **automatic file save** increment time is 10 minutes (which is user adjustable and may also be switched off if desired)	Continuous (upon each graphic/editing action)
1	The **maximum drawing/editing amount of loss possible** (ie. from power failure or software interruption) = **amount of graphics since time of the last save** (typically 10 minutes).	The **maximum drawing/editing amount of loss possible** (ie. from power failure or software interruption) = **the last single graphic or editing action, only** (virtually no losses)
1	Settings are saved along with the file save action. Zooming actions are also saved.	MicroStation users must perform a "File > Save Settings" if desired. The automatic saving of all drawing and editing features does not save view control activity (zooming/window areas) or settings.

AutoCAD vs. MicroStation Concepts (Cross-Reference Chart)

	AutoCAD	MicroStation
Wk#	**General:**	
1	Objects	Elements
1	Draw something	Place or Create something
1	Drawing files	Design files
1	**Single-shot command action** (the AutoCAD commands end, and the user generally re-enters or re-selects the command if needed to repeat it)	**Locked/continuous tool action** (MicroStation tools are active for re-use until the user selects another tool)
1	Can only abbreviate typed in commands if they are in the "authorized" PGP file (user editable)	Can abbreviate key-ins of tool names to the shortest unique entry, ie UP, UPD = UPDATE
1	Command Line	Key-in Field
1	Pickpoint or pick (hit Left mouse button)	Data, datapoint or click (hit Left mouse button)

	Zoom Control Commands	View Control tools
1	Zoom Extents **Z ↲ E↲**	Fit View
1	Zoom Window **Z↲** (default zoom command)	Window Area
1	Redraw **R↲**	Update
1	Zoom Previous **Z↲ P↲**	View Previous
1	N/A	View Next
1	Regen **RE**	N/A
1	Undo and redo also include all zoom actions.	Undo and redo ignore all view control actions.

1	GRID ON/OFF **F7**	View Attributes Display Grid ON/OFF
1	SNAP ON/OFF **F9**	Grid Lock ON/OFF

1	Right mouse click is **<Enter>** or a **pop-up menu**	Right mouse click is a **reset or reject** action
1	**<Space bar>** is "space" in the TEXT command **<Space bar>** is same as **<Enter>**	**<Space bar>** is "space" in the Text Editor window **<Space bar>** toggles AccuDraw mode when using AccuDraw (V8i) **<Space bar>** opens the **Space Bar Pop-Up** menu in **CONNECT Edition**

AutoCAD vs. MicroStation Concepts (Cross-Reference Chart)

	AutoCAD	MicroStation
1	**<Esc>** Cancels the command or the **Grips** selection	**<Enter>** changes the focus to the key-in field
1	typed in	keyed in or Entered
1	typed in commands automatically enter into the Command Line, unless the user is typing text in the MTEXT editing window	**<Enter>** is needed to change the focus to the key-in field (or click in the key-in field, but this is inefficient)
1	Double-click on a text to edit it	available
1	Command Line options	N/A
1	Erase **E**	Delete
1	Rectangle **REC** RECTANG	Block Shape
1–3	Offset	Copy/Move Parallel
1–3	Break	Partial Delete (**V8i**), Break **CONNECT Ed.**
1–3	Mirror, Move, Copy, Rotate, Scale, Stretch, Extend, Trim, Fillet & Chamfer (all similar!)	Mirror, Move, Copy, Rotate, Scale, Stretch, Extend, Trim, Fillet & Chamfer (all similar!)

Wk#	Precision Input:	
2	$\mathbf{X_{value}, Y_{value}}$	**XY=**$\mathbf{X_{value}, Y_{value}}$
2	**@**$\mathbf{\Delta X_{value}, \Delta Y_{value}}$	**DL=**$\mathbf{\Delta X_{value}, \Delta Y_{value}}$
2	**@L<**α	**DI= L,**α
2	X-Y axis definitions same as Mstn!	X-Y axis definitions same as ACAD!
2	Angular direction definitions same!	Angular direction definitions same!
3	Layer **LA**	Level
3	Object Properties	Element Attributes (or symbology)
4	Object Snaps/O-Snap Settings	AccuSnap/Snap Modes
4	Ortho ON/OFF **F8**	Axis Lock ON/OFF
5	List **LI**	Element Information (V8i), Properties
5	Grips Object Modifications	Element Selection Tool Modifications
6	Multiple Object Selection	Fence Selection (Multiple Elements)

AutoCAD vs. MicroStation Concepts (Cross-Reference Chart)

Wk#	AutoCAD	MicroStation
7	Distance **DI**	Measure distance between points icon
7	Area	Measure area icon
8	Tracking/Polar/Dynamics	AccuDraw
8	Direct Entry	AccuDraw
9	Blocks	Cells
9	Explode **X**	Drop Element
9	External Reference file **XR**	Reference file

AutoCAD	MicroStation	MicroStation
Multiple Object Selection	Fence Selection Tool (Multiple Elements)	Element Selection Tool
Many simultaneous selections allowed	Only one fence allowed at a time	Simultaneous selections allowed
Objects are de-selected at the end of the action, but can be easily re-selected by specifying the previous selection	The fence remains active until removed by the user, allowing additional actions by the user on the fence selection if desired	Elements remain selected until de-selected by the user, allowing additional actions on the same selection set if desired
<Esc> cancels the selection set (this also cancels the active command as well)	Hit Place Fence an additional time to remove the fence from the screen	Select on any blank part of the view to deselect any selected elements
Window selection **W** default	Inside mode w/ block fence	Selection window
Crossing selection **C**	Overlap mode w/ block fence	Drag Right to Left (Overlap) <Shift><Ctrl> click or drag
N/A	Void mode	N/A
N/A	Clip mode	N/A
Window Poly selection **WP**	Inside mode w/ shaped fence	Shape mode
Crossing Poly selection **CP**	Overlap mode w/ shaped fence	Shape mode Right to left
Fence selection **F** (like a crossing selection but specified by a line of points)	N/A	Line mode

AutoCAD vs. MicroStation Concepts (Cross-Reference Chart)

AutoCAD	MicroStation	MicroStation
Multiple Object Selection	**Fence Selection Tool (Multiple Elements)**	**Element Selection Tool**
N/A	Void-Overlap mode	
N/A	Void-Clip mode	
N/A	Fence type: Circular	N/A
N/A	Fence type: from View	N/A
Remove objects from selection **R** or <Shift> pick the objects	N/A	Re-select the element(s) to de-select
Add objects to selection **A**	N/A	<Ctrl> click or drag, or <Shift><Ctrl> click or drag
ALL	Fence type: From design file	Edit > Select All
Previous P	N/A	N/A

Grips Object Selections		Element Selection tool
Active when the Command Line is blank		Activate from the Main Tool bar by icon
Pick objects, pick more for addition to the selection set		Click Elements, <Ctrl> click for addition to the selection set
<Shift> pick on the objects to remove objects from selection set		Remove with <Ctrl> click on the elements to remove elements from selection set

Executive Discussion: *Blueprint for Success*

One CAD Manager's Summary of a Dozen Years of Valuable Experience gained at Rockwell International

Foreword and Acknowledgements

Michael D. Jue, P.E.

Executive Discussion: Blueprint for Success

One CAD Manager's Summary of a Dozen Years of Valuable Experience gained at Rockwell International

Foreword and Acknowledgements

Michael D. Jue, P.E.

Don't be fooled by the above title. If you don't think of yourself as an executive, think again. If you are a one-man shop, your destiny with the CAD rests squarely with you. If you are in a slightly bigger operation, you may be slightly off-the-hook, since management does have a significant impact on your future success with CAD. Here's the bottom line, the executives in charge, whether it's just yourself or the brass up above can drastically affect your prospects for future success in CAD.

This said, I need to acknowledge the source of the many lessons to be revealed, my employer Rockwell International. Without the successes achieved at Rockwell, none of this would have been possible. There was truly a sense of teamwork as we implemented CAD at Rockwell in the Facilities and Industrial Engineering group beginning way back in 1985. The management and engineering staff, all the way down to the CAD operators had a certain focus and vision on what had to be done to be successful.

I sincerely thank the managers and co-workers I've worked with over the years for being pro-active. I especially thank many of the "old-timers" who were quite excited about using this new "star-wars" type technology. Back in 1985, a computer drawing pictures on a computer screen, even in black and white, running on a 12.5 mega-Hertz processor was a big deal. (Yes, that's twelve point five mega-Hertz and not a typo) It has been an exciting time!

Note: Opinions and thoughts contained in this work are exclusively the author's and are not intended to relay policies and procedures or endorsements for or from any of the corporations mentioned, including Rockwell International, Autodesk, Inc., Intergraph, Bentley Systems, Inc., or any other entity.

The following 10 points listed are not necessarily in order of importance and may not seem related to each other at first, but they all do share something in common… They are all points that you might not typically find in a CAD textbook. You may have a better chance at finding them in a CAD Manager's course book. The point of including them here for you is that I believe they could have tremendous importance for you in your CAD learning experience. I know that I came to realize the importance of each tip over the years and found that reinforcing them contributed to our continuing successes. May you be as successful, yourself! CAD is a wonderful toy, erh, I mean *tool.*

February 5, 1998 Michael D. Jue, P.E.

Lesson 1 Management support for your CAD effort

1. This was done many ways at Rockwell. From the beginning, our CAD system had management backing, a big plus! Upper management decided to investigate the performance of several CAD suppliers. Rockwell Corporate Headquarters arranged a CAD benchmark to put many competing systems through their paces. This resulted in a *clear winner* among the CAD vendors that eventually resulted in a rather large contract for equipment, software and ***training***.
2. This was a definite key to the success of the CAD implementation at Rockwell. Without active support and involvement from the department leaders and their mentors in even higher ranks, the individual CAD users would have had little chance to survive, let alone acheive tremendous success.

Side note: The initial CAD Vendor and Software benchmark was crucial to selecting the correct vendor. Now almost 15 years later, the one system vendor we selected, out of 12 tested, is still in business, commanding significant portions of the CAD market. Nearly none of the other competitors, today, sell any viable CAD products, having abandoned their unproductive efforts long ago!

Lesson 2 Training

Training? Yes! This was a novel idea at the time. And who was supposed to get the first training sessions? The managers! The managers?? Yes! Our CAD vendor understood that if management did not have a firm grasp of CAD concepts, the CAD implementation was doomed to fail. They had special courses designed for executives and CAD management staff to expose them to what was involved with successful CAD usage. Our manager in charge of the CAD implementation along with the lead engineers all went to the initial CAD training.

Since the Rockwell CAD managers developed a firm foundation upon which to build, the progression of skills for all users was natural and many pitfalls were avoided. This foundational knowledge about CAD concepts is not something that everyone is automatically born with and is quite often overlooked. When serious CAD management problems develop, very often 20/20 hindsight will offer up some assessment such as "the management (or operator) didn't quite understand what the goal of using the CAD was on this project!! … that's why we got all goofed up!!"

Lesson 3 Observation is a skill to be cultivated

This one is more "nuts-and-bolts" than the other tips, but handy none-the-less. Over the years we found that the most successful CAD users were those that developed keen senses of observation. Being able to observe their own actions as well as those being taken by others enabled them to learn the fastest and also helped during the inevitable trouble-shooting sessions. This also applied to observing the workings of the CAD software and what was happening on the screen.

We also learned why the vendor always encouraged two people to train together; one operating the software and the other *observing*. It is most difficult to observe one's own actions while in the midst of learning a foreign and new skill, such as CAD is for many. The "backseat-driver" on the other hand, has no problem observing every little mistake that the "driver" is making. Learning *self-observation* is a tough, but worthwhile skill to develop.

Lesson 4 Attitude is as Important as Aptitude

Common wisdom would tend to tell us that the young, computer-savvy, CAD student should out-perform the older, "been-around for a million years" long timer CAD student, but this isn't automatically the case. Attitude has tremendous relevance to CAD success.

Many important decisions and actions are required for the successful use of CAD. The one person taking interest in what's going on, will tend to make the better decisions. On the other hand, a person who may actually be very proficient, but is totally flippant about what needs to be done, may not get the job done right. I've seen this personally.

At Rockwell, managers understood that dedicated employees who cared and knew about what they were doing, even if they were slow, were much more highly valued than their counterparts who may have had proficient skills but didn't care to exercise them the right way. You know the ones I'm referring to, they're usually called the goof-offs.

The knowledgeable ones treated their CAD skills as something quite valuable and didn't just fetter away their productive hours with the computer. This leads us right into one of the next points, which is Ownership.

Lesson 5 Ownership, Vision and Focus

Ownership is a term referring to one's sense of responsibility for processes or projects. All too often, is heard the cry from across the cubicles, "It's not my job, man!" Well, ownership is the opposite of that notion. In the world of CAD, often, if something needs to get done, you are the one that can set things in motion or let things die. When one is learning CAD, the ownership of the process of CAD training lies mostly with the student. The trainers and managers really can't force you to learn.

Vision and Focus are required to keep ones goals in mind. These are referred to in the philosophical realm. Vision refers to looking ahead, visualizing what is down the road. Focus refers to the ability to see things clearly with sharply defined boundaries and edges, and elimination of fuzzy, gray areas.

At Rockwell, Ownership, Vision and Focus are routinely emphasized for their importance in achieving personal as well as corporate success.

> Interestingly enough, Vision and Focus are also terms related to working on the CAD but in a more **literal** sense. Imagine trying to view the CAD monitor's screen if you have poor **vision** and cannot **focus**! More said about this in the section on Ergonomics, below.

Lesson 6 Backups, DO THEM OFTEN!!

Well, Lesson 6 gets us back to nuts and bolts. Let's discuss the importance of backups. We all know what they are and how valuable they are … or do we? Why are they needed you say, how often have you heard of disk failures? Well in this, the *real* world, disk crashes and other un-recoverable failures do occasionally occur.

Our first instructors told us about a competitor of ours that lost **six department months** of work due to a head crash and not keeping updated backup copies. When told to load up their backups to recover, at first they didn't know where they were kept. They found them, soon enough. Their system manager kept them in the trunk of his car! Unfortunate for him, it had been over 100 degrees several times in the last few months.

Other failures: I was just reminded today at a CAD conference about another common problem. I was told that someone had deleted an entire project due to an I/O error. This was not the I/O errors that we all know as Input/Output errors, but the dreaded **I/O … Idiot Operator!** Most I/O problems … or I/O problems (the regular ones) can be overcome, assuming that care is religiously taken to make regular, periodic backups!

Lesson 7 Ergonomics

This topic is very well recognized in today's environment, but I was always amazed to see CAD installations at other locations (non-Rockwell) where ergonomics took a backseat to everything else. Many obvious problems, such as putting PC's and workstations right onto regular desks, without any adjusting chairs available and poor lighting were common.

As CAD manager at our installation, I can say that I never heard of a single back or wrist complaint due to CAD usage the entire time I was there from any of the hundreds of CAD users we had. We encouraged regular breaks away from the stations and had even programmed the stations to pop up windows onto the screens announcing break times. All of our stations had fully adjustable digitizing surfaces that could be tilted, raised and lowered easily. The monitors also had tilt and elevation "motorized" controls.

We included in our initial training how to adjust all aspects of the workstations and understandably everybody always readjusted the environment as was needed for their physique. Readjustments were even made throughout the workday as needed. We even had varying light levels in our CAD rooms as we found that some users preferred darker areas and some preferred lighter areas. We couldn't quite get the budget for individually readjustable zoned overhead lighting, although we did spend funds to get very nice adjustable task lights for each workstation.

> Refer to your own Environmental, Safety and Health department for recommendations for maintaining a safe work environment. And then follow their recommendations!

Lesson 8 Goals and Assessment

Make sure you set targets to shoot for. One of the axioms that I've heard over and over again rings true in the CAD arena, "One sure-fire way to miss your target is to not have one in the first place." All CAD training should include clear goals for each course or session.

Periodically examine the progress that you are making (or your department) in achieving that successful CAD implementation or usage. Look back at your drawings and projects and ask yourself how to improve next time. For beginners, it's very useful to think back to the first day of CAD training and reflect on all the skill acquired since that time. This is something few remember to do, but when they do, they realize that **mountains** of skills are usually acquired by them in short periods. Give 'em a pat on the back when needed. This is the next lesson…

Lesson 9 Recognition, Rewards, Career Advancement

When CAD students progress into the stage of working on active projects, the work, hopefully eventually gets out. Engineers and drafters gain skills and the payback of having CAD produced documents slowly starts to filter into the organization. At some point, all the hard work needs to be recognized.

It's true that for many CAD users, enjoyment comes just from the knowledge that they've completed the project with the new software and their new skills, but for others, management recognition of accomplishments is extremely important. Always complement students (or even yourself) for the little and big achievement of goals along the way. After all, and this I've not said before, CAD is not exactly easy to master.

Recognition is one form of deserved reward for jobs well done, but other forms exist also. It's important to have appropriate policies regarding what is deserving of employees who gain significant skills. I consider CAD proficiency in the category of a significant skill in today's Engineering offices. Consider the consequence of not having the skill and you immediately begin to see why students are filling these CAD classes.

> Rockwell has always encouraged learning. One particular mentor suggested that anyone who is not either involved in learning new things himself or involved with teaching others new skills is really missing the boat. Rockwell rewards those either taking classes or **teaching** classes. I find this improves the prospects for success and is helpful for all.

Lesson 10 Patience and Persistence

Learning CAD is likened by some to the craft of carpentry. One does not learn how to build houses and kitchen cabinets overnight. Many varied tools are required and I think most would not settle for something just slapped together by a guy using a screwdriver and hammer for everything.

Have patience with yourself, your CAD users, and with the CAD equipment and software. Over time the performance of all of these components will improve. Persistence is required for little things like laser printers, networks and the like that sometimes don't always work the first time, or the second time or the third … you get the idea.

Patience. Patience. Remember, no matter what you do, the computer always takes too long to boot up. That is a fact I think will never change. Good luck!

NOTES:

CAD System Production Tips

CAD Basics and Beyond

These listing and bits of knowledge may be of help to many individuals in their quest to utilize and learn the ins and outs of CAD production. Much of the advice may sound simplistic and seem obvious at first glance, but it is truly amazing how even seasoned veterans of the CAD environment sometimes waste hours and hours of their own time (not to mention their employer's time also) because they have NOT learned some of the basic "truths" revealed below.

Subject 1: Basic Problem Solving Techniques for Success:

There are many different situations that a CAD user may find himself in, but the most common ones can be found below. Each of the different categories of usage requires different methods for the user to progress and solves his or her individual problems. Please try to determine how you may fit into the categories and choose the appropriate set of procedures. All of the following might be considered typical "problems":

"Something" is NOT working as it is supposed to!

Cannot Log On **Cannot Log Off** **Cannot Plot** **Cannot Open Drawing**

Operation is Slow **Software Won't Run** **Command Doesn't Work**

Cannot Understand the Helper **"I can't get time on the schedule"**

… And Many, Many more, you get the idea!

General Category of Usage "A": Individual User, no assistance available.

This is the person, who has no immediate source of outside assistance, such as an individual-one man firm, someone working alone on the week-end who cannot get hold of any of his regular sources of assistance, or maybe someone, who may have assistance available, but chooses to "tough-it-out" and try to solve the problem on his own. This category would also apply to a student taking a final exam in a CAD class, where no outside assistance is available during the test! There are specific techniques that can help a person in this category of usage.

General Category of Usage "B": CAD User with assistance available.

This is the person who knows that there is someone around or someone he can call for help. Knowing exactly what to ask and how to ask it is the key to getting appropriate assistance.

Problem Solving Techniques: Category "A", No outside assistance available.

1. Observe what you are doing. Can you identify a problem? Are you skipping a step? Do you know what the proper steps are? Does the command require a "click" or a "drag" maneuver? Did you select the right command for the task?
2. Observe everything on the screen. Can you identify a problem. Is there an Error message or Status message on the screen? If you are typing in a command, is it being typed into the right place? Is there a typo?
3. Check your notes. Can you remember if the proper steps are written down someplace?
4. Have you tried a different method to accomplish the task attempted? Does another method give you the same exact error? Does the error only occur with a specific procedure.

Try altering just one parameter at a time. Can the problem be duplicated? After you are sure you can duplicate the problem, go on to a different method. Please do not try the same thing over, and over and over for the next 30-40 minutes. Chances are that the situation will not change, especially if you are performing the exact same steps over and over and over.

5. Is the equipment functioning properly? Are the plotters turned on? Are they ready? Are there any trouble lights, jams? Are you unsure of how to tell? Are there any documents or signs available that you can read immediately? If there are machine faults, do you know the correct procedure for turning on the equipment? or clearing a jam? Make sure you make a note of any "machine" problems and that the system administrator gets a copy of your note describing the situation.
6. Is everything working properly and you are just expecting something else? Did your plot go to the "other" plotter, the one that is shown on the plot dialog box? Did the plot come out of the "bottom" of the plotter, where it was supposed to, instead of on the "top", like you thought it would?
7. Try to get success by using a different ***workstation.*** If you are **successful** at the "other" workstation, there may be a problem with the "original" machine. Make a note of the situation occurring at that "problem" machine. Make sure the system administrator gets a copy of your note describing the situation.
8. Try to get success by trying the same procedure with a different ***drawing***. If you are **successful** with a different drawing, but not the original one, the drawing with the "problem" may have a "corruption" of some sort. These are not easy to fix by novice users, but are not that difficult for those with more experience to take care of. These "problem" drawing do take time to diagnose the problem with them.
9. For future reference, write down any problem very specifically. Make sure you can accurately record all of the steps you are taking. Ensure that the system administrator gets a copy of your note. Note for yourself what areas you are having problems with. Concentrate on getting training on these areas.

Problem Solving Techniques: Category "B", Assistance Available

1. Who are you gonna call? Who are you **supposed** to call? What are their phone numbers? What are their beeper numbers? Do you have their home phone numbers? Do you know who the system administrator is? How about the back-up to the system administrator or the back-up to the back-up
2. Specifically state what you need done or are trying to do. Do you want the helper to just perform the work for you, which is typically the fastest solution? Or do you have enough time to listen to a full explanation and get a tutorial. Does your helper have the time to give you help? Have you tried to solve the situation yourself, first? How many times, for how long? Is the "problem" exactly the same for each attempt?
3. Be prepared to demonstrate the **exact** steps that you are taking in the failed attempt at whatever task you are doing. Try to use proper **terminology** when asking for help and when describing the problem. If you cannot accurately describe the steps or commands used, be sure to tell the one that is helping you. Tell the one helping you whether other users are experiencing the same problem(s). Is the problem restricted to a particular drawing or specific workstation? Is the problem related to just one building?
4. Schedule time with the helper if the task is a special requirement, such as large plot jobs, setting up a new project or drawing, securing training, etc.

HOME PLATE LAYOUT drawing. Suitable for students that have completed warm-up exercises up thru the end of Module 3. Create this drawing without the dimensions. After finishing Module 5, which covers dimensions, the student can add dimensions to this drawing as shown.

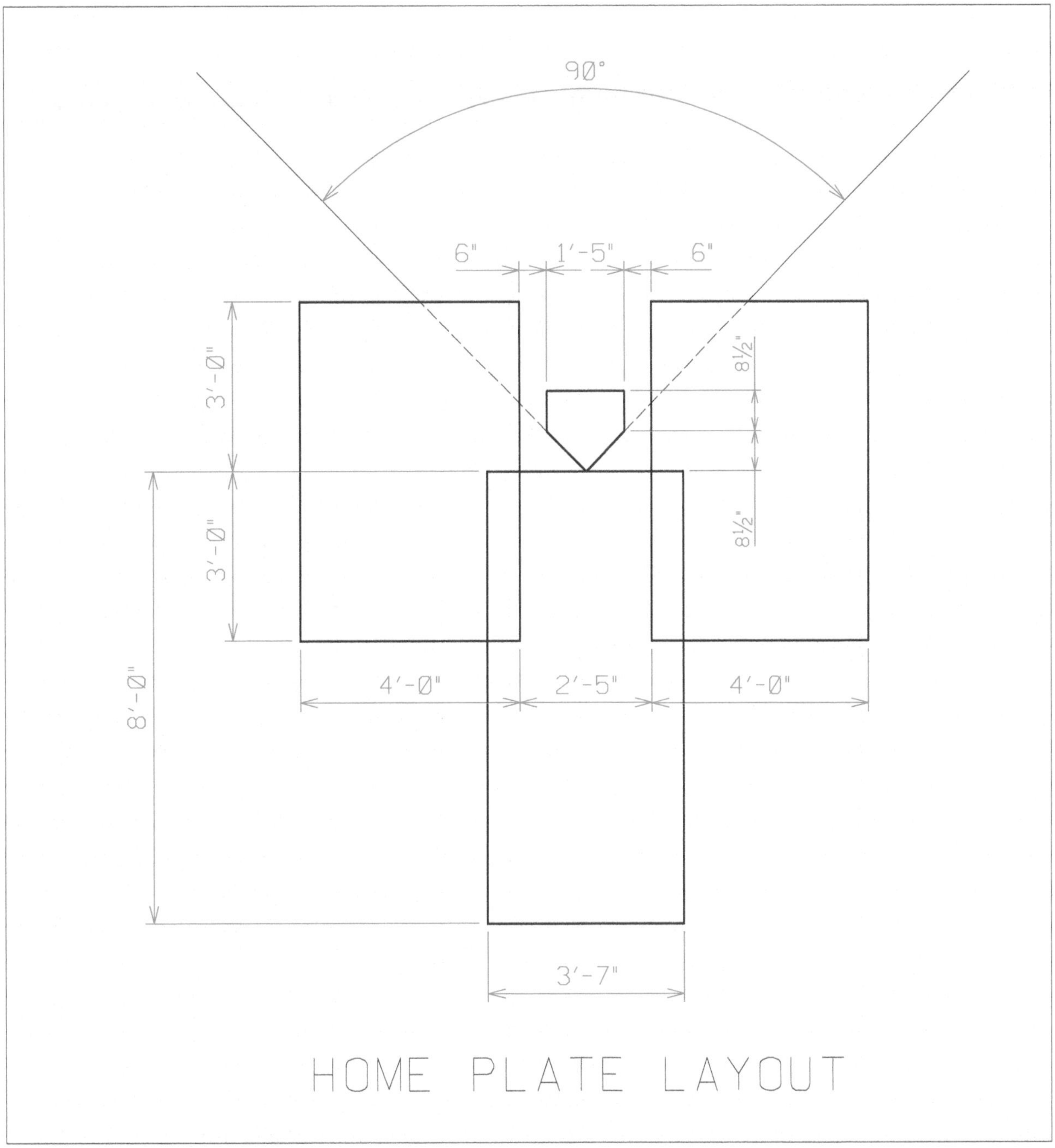

90°

6" 1'-5" 6"

3'-Ø" 3'-Ø" 8'-Ø"

8½" 8½"

4'-Ø" 2'-5" 4'-Ø"

3'-7"

HOME PLATE LAYOUT

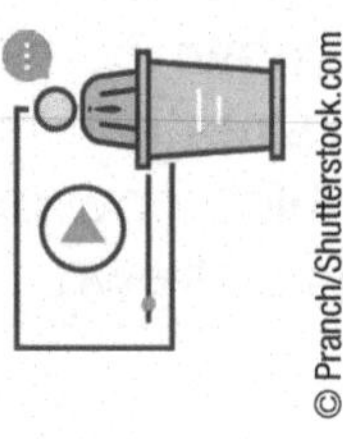

A

B

C

D

E

F

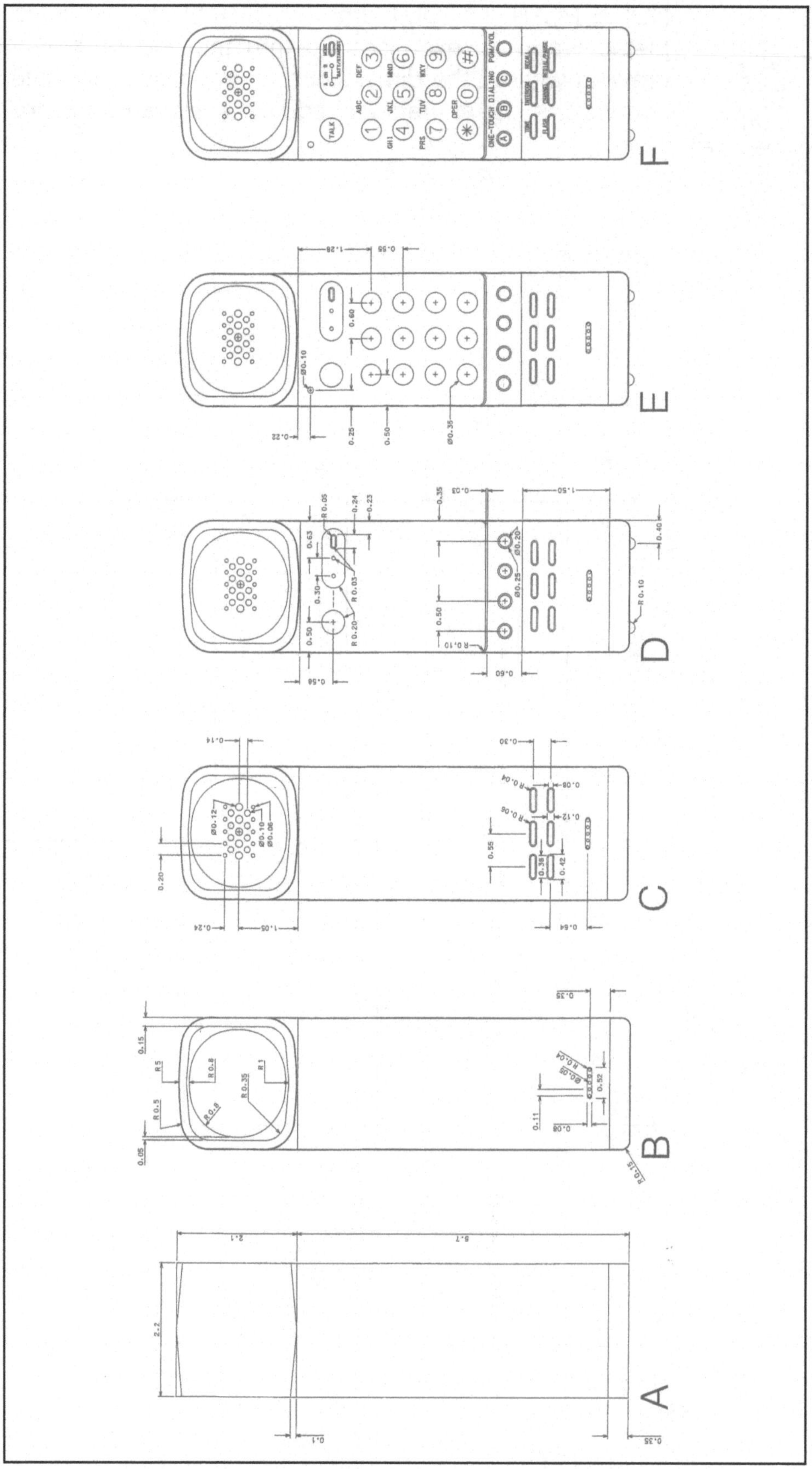

PHONE

© Pranch/Shutterstock.com

THE "PHONE" EXERCISE: (refer to the diagrams on pages 270, 272-277

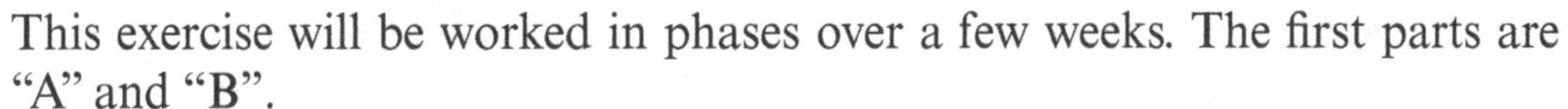

This exercise will be worked in phases over a few weeks. The first parts are "A" and "B".
This will get you started …

1. Remember to **set the working units: Master units** to inches and **Sub-units** to mils. Use a pull-down menu selection.

   Settings > Design File > Working Units, (see pg 77 for CONNECT Ed.)

   Then, Select the choices as shown by your instructor

   (The **sub-units** are mils and is **not** a typo of miles—a mil is 1/1000 of an inch and is a common unit in small machine part dimensions)
2. **Open a key-in field**, required for precision key-in fields to be entered.

   Utilities > Key-in (See pg 30 for CONNECT Edition)

   Then resize the menu and dock it at the bottom of the screen.
3. **Start Place Line** and place the first point of the first line in the lower left corner Exactly at the location 20,20 (or whatever location is specified by your instructor—this varies from quarter to quarter and from class section to class section)

   XY=20, 20 <ENTER>
4. Draw the first line on the left straight up to a length of 5.7 inches.

   DI=5.7, 90 <ENTER>

   Then, without stopping, draw another line segment upwards a distance of 2.1 inches,

   DI=2.1, 90<ENTER>

   then reset to STOP drawing lines. (Yes, this does make two separate lines, but you will see why this is desired, when we draw more)
5. Go back to the start position at the bottom of the first line and SNAP to that location for beginning a new line. Create another line going to the right by 2.2 incehs,

   DI=2.2,0 <ENTER>

   Then, reset to STOP drawing lines.
6. The instructor will then show the very quick techniques using copy to create the rest of the vertical and horizontal lines using a combination of **COPY** with the **SNAP** function.
7. The instructor will show how to create the slanted lines using **SNAP and the DL=key-in** and the **MIRROR** command.
8. The instructor will introduce a very good use of **COLORS** and will show how to quickly construct features of the "B" detail using **Move Parallel (with Make COPY option "ON")** for the top of "B", and several entirely new techniques for constructing the "microphone" (five circles and line work) at the bottom of "B"

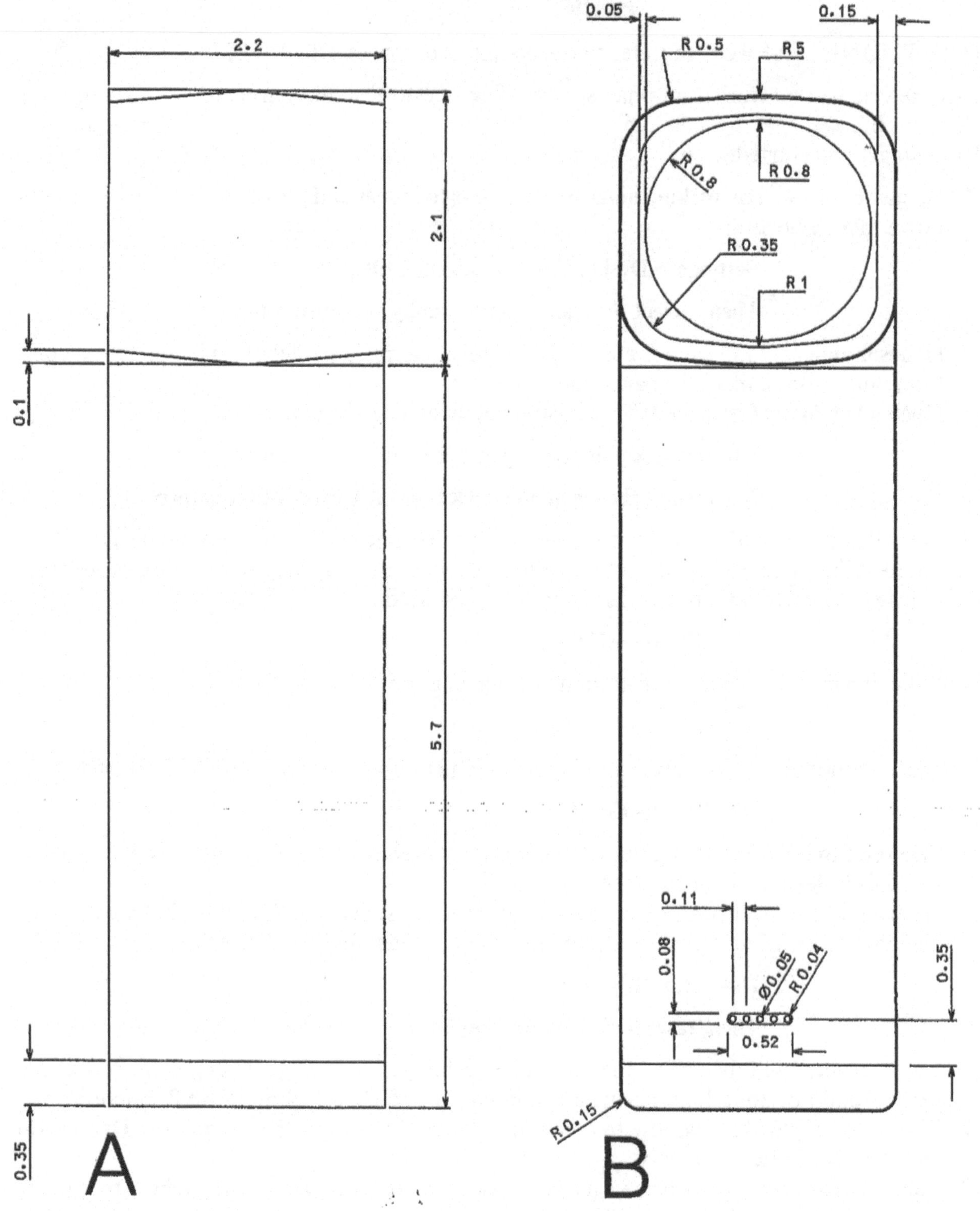
2.2
2.1
0.1
5.7
0.35
A
0.05
0.15
R 0.5
R 5
R 0.8
R 0.8
R 0.35
R 1
0.11
0.08
Ø0.05
R 0.04
0.35
0.52
R 0.15
B

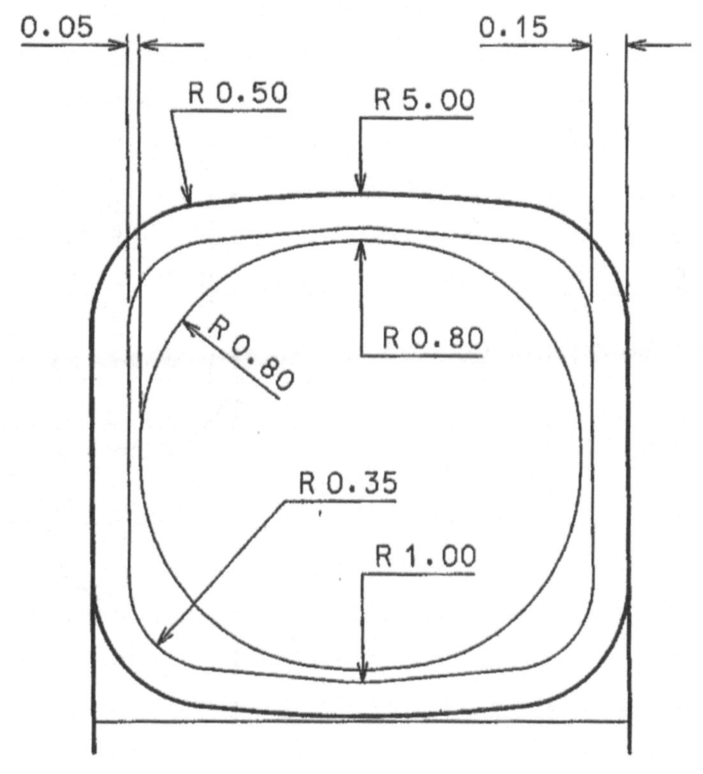
0.05
0.15
R 0.50
R 5.00
R 0.80
R 0.80
R 0.35
R 1.00

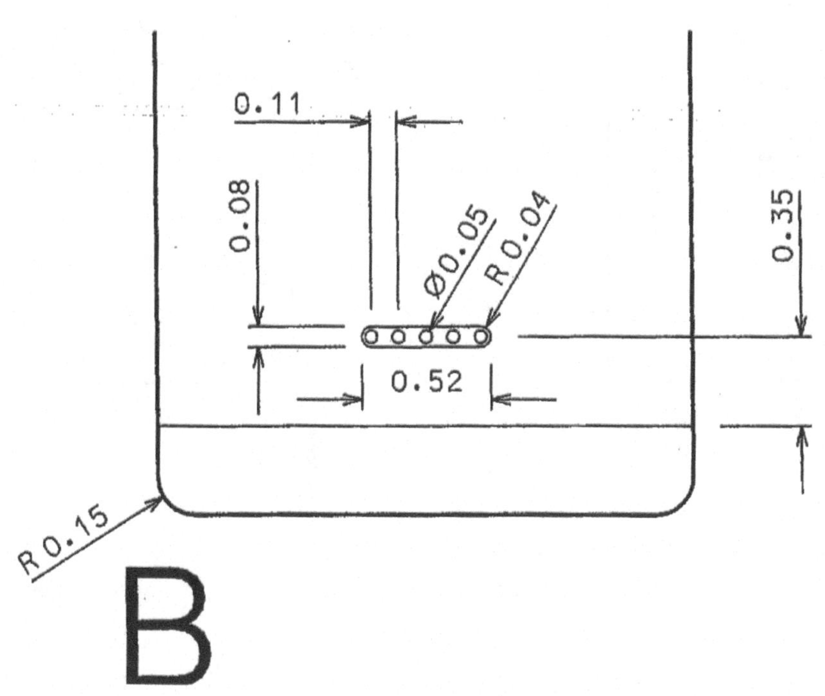
0.11
0.08
Ø0.05
R 0.04
0.35
0.52
R 0.15
B

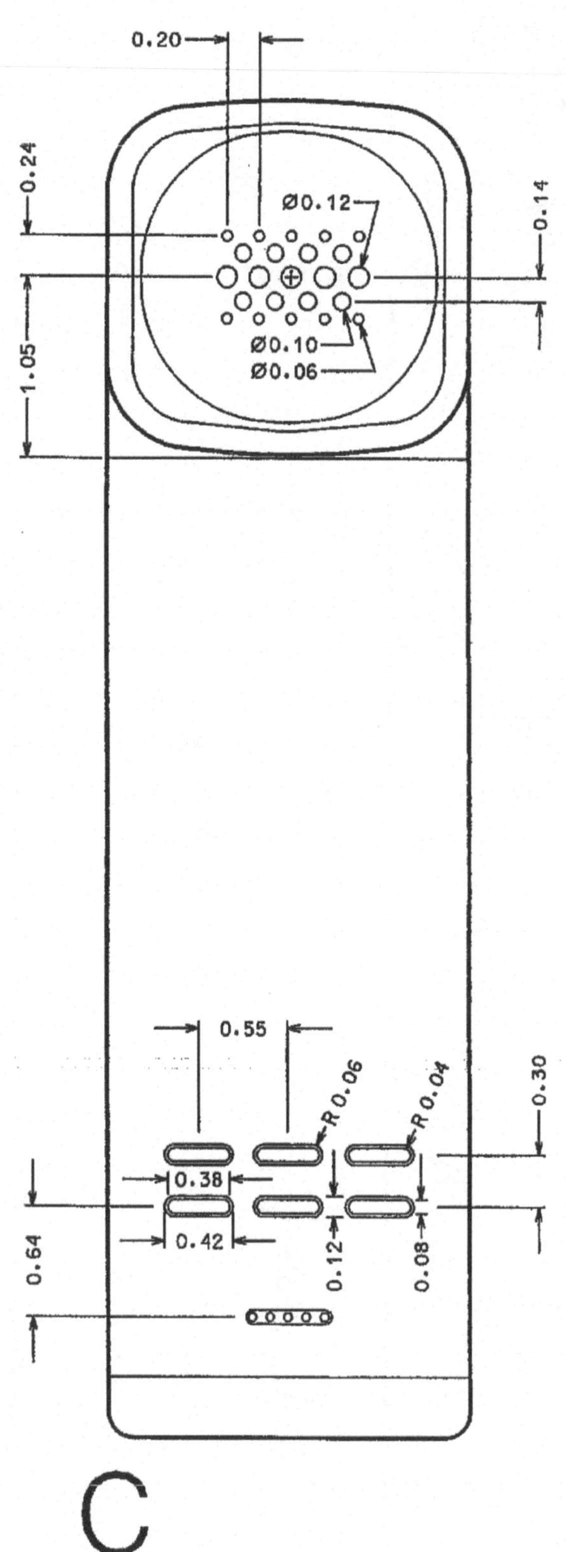
0.20
0.24
Ø0.12
0.14
1.05
Ø0.10
Ø0.06
0.55
R 0.06
R 0.04
0.30
0.38
0.42
0.64
0.12
0.08
C

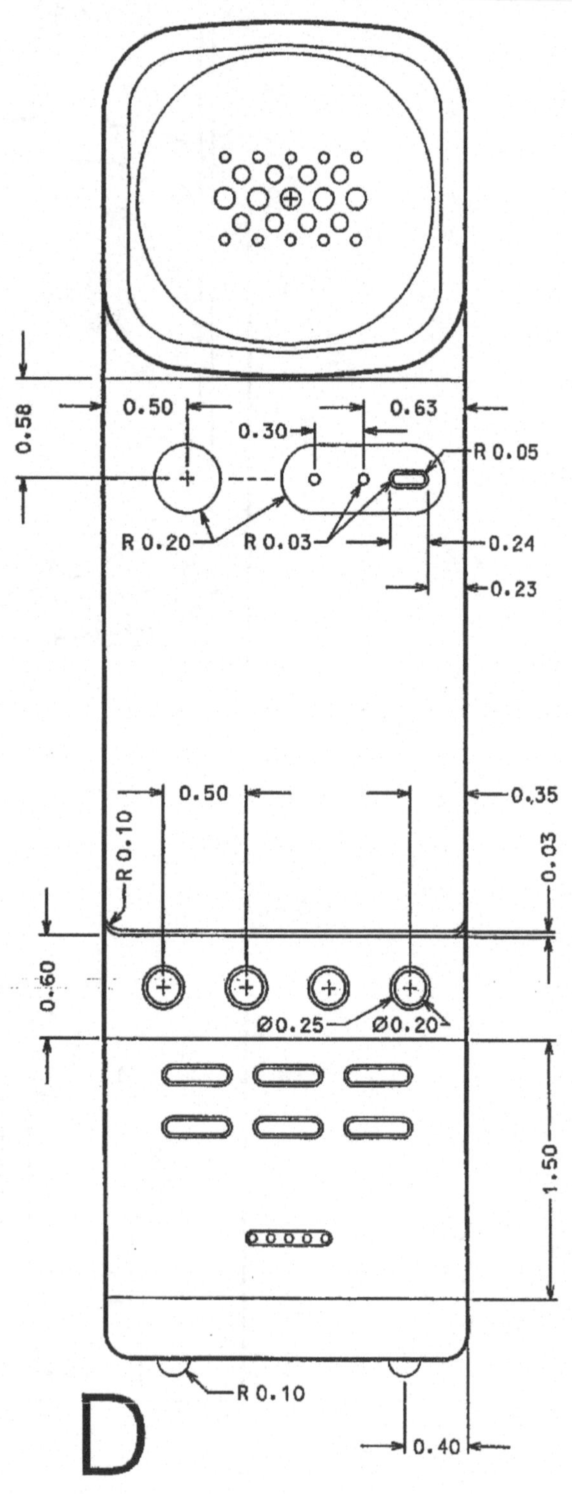
0.58
0.50
0.63
0.30
R 0.05
R 0.20
R 0.03
0.24
0.23
0.50
0.35
R 0.10
0.03
0.60
Ø0.25
Ø0.20
1.50
R 0.10
0.40
D

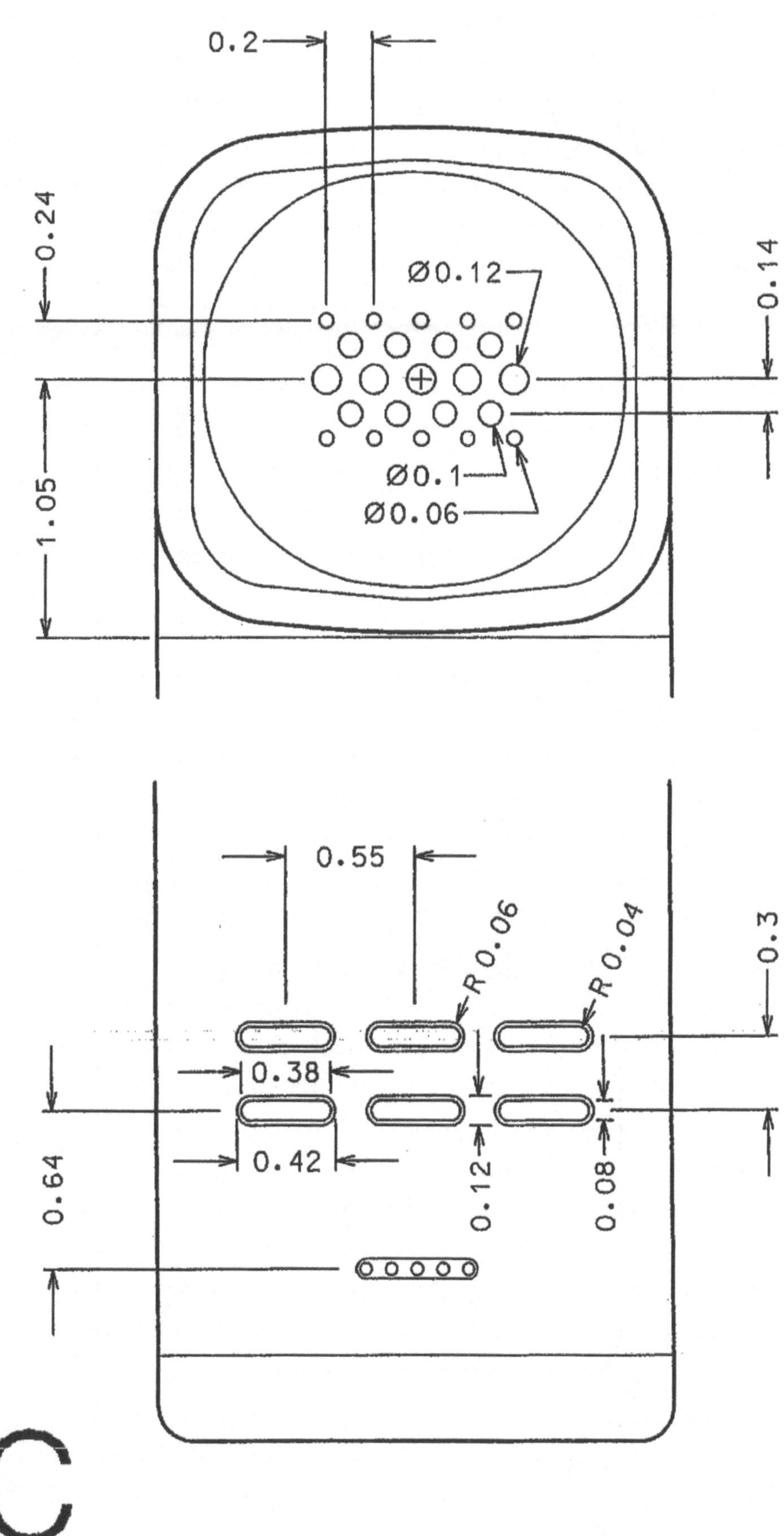
0.2
0.24
0.14
Ø0.12
Ø0.1
Ø0.06
1.05
0.55
R 0.06
R 0.04
0.3
0.38
0.42
0.64
0.12
0.08
C

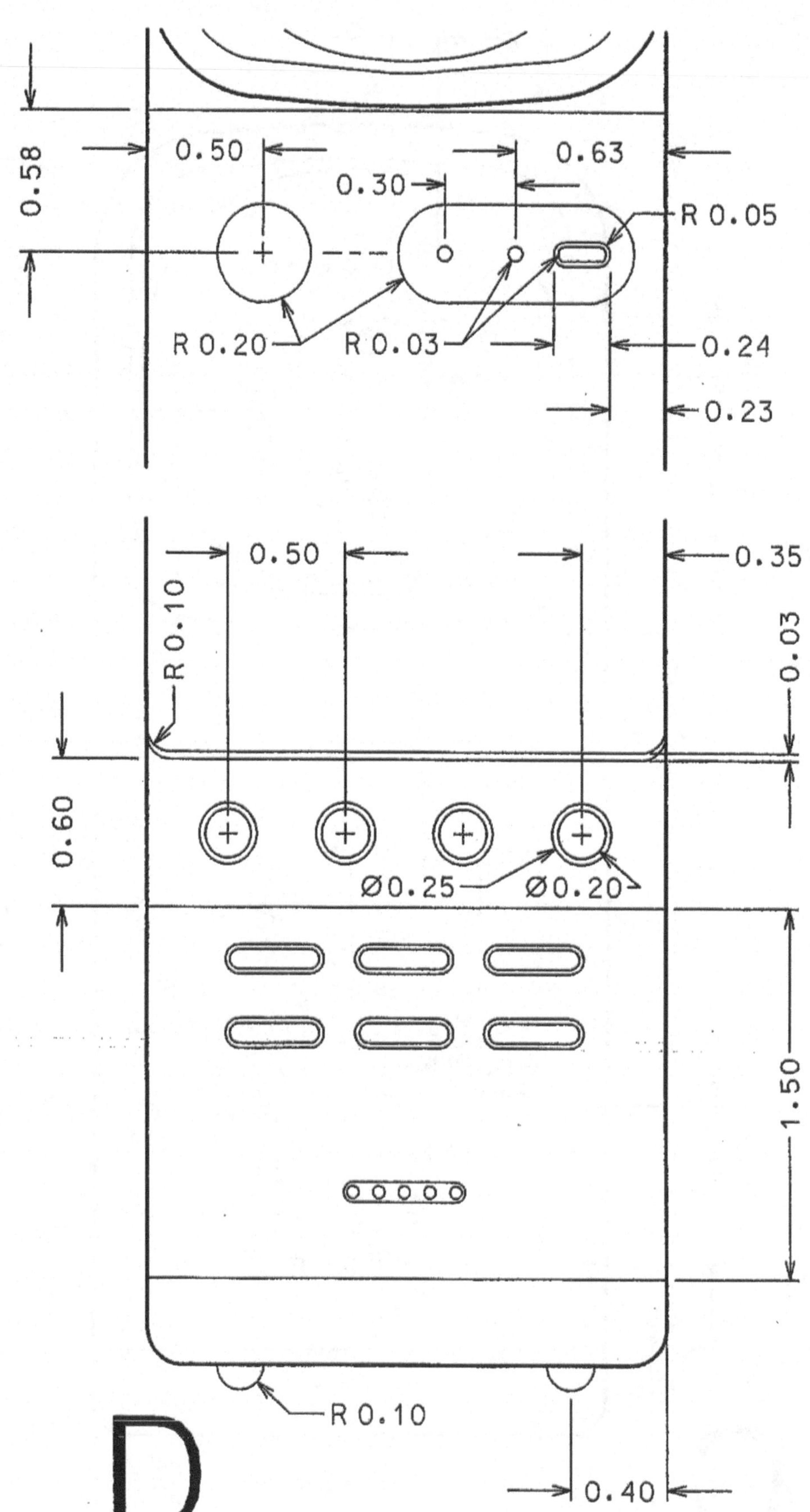
0.58
0.50
0.30
0.63
R 0.05
R 0.20
R 0.03
0.24
0.23
0.50
0.35
R 0.10
0.03
0.60
Ø0.25
Ø0.20
1.50
R 0.10
D
0.40

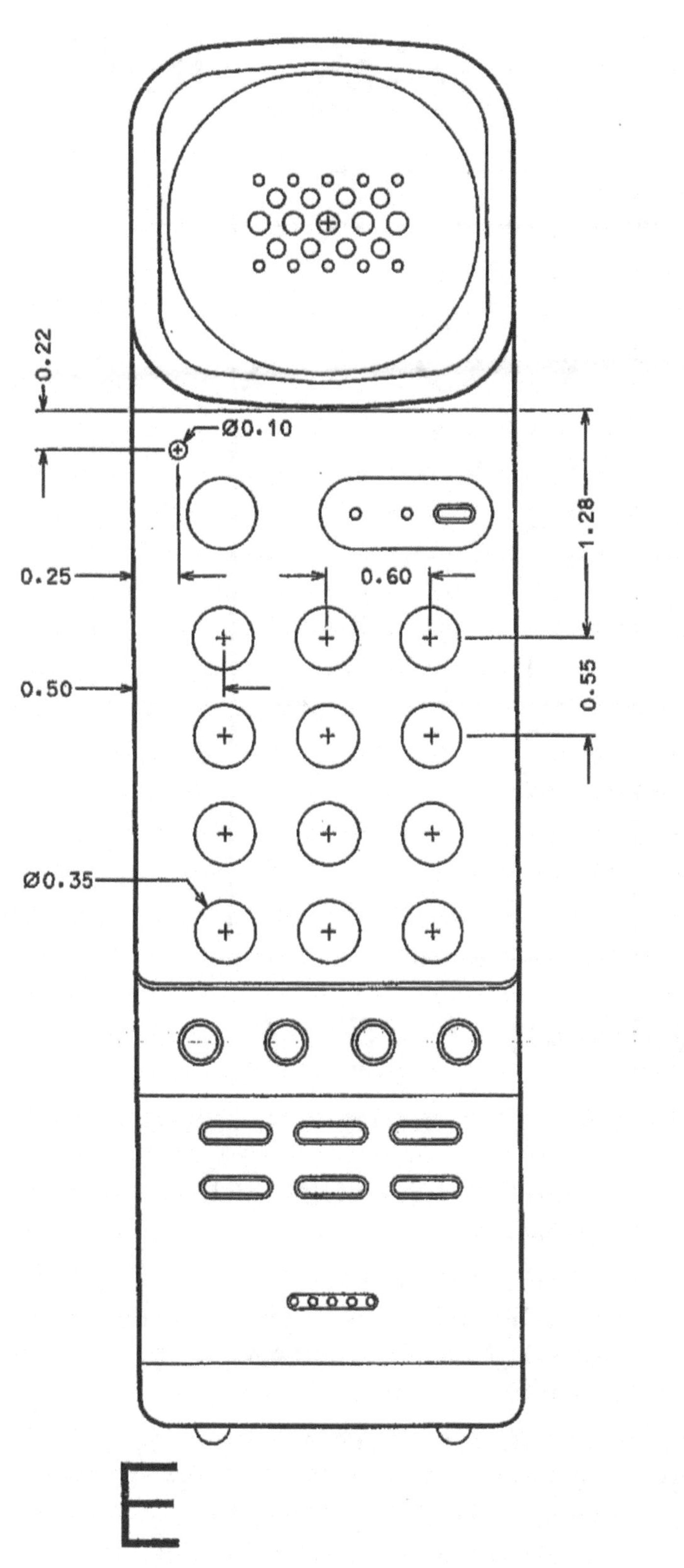
0.22
Ø0.10
1.28
0.25
0.60
0.50
0.55
Ø0.35
E

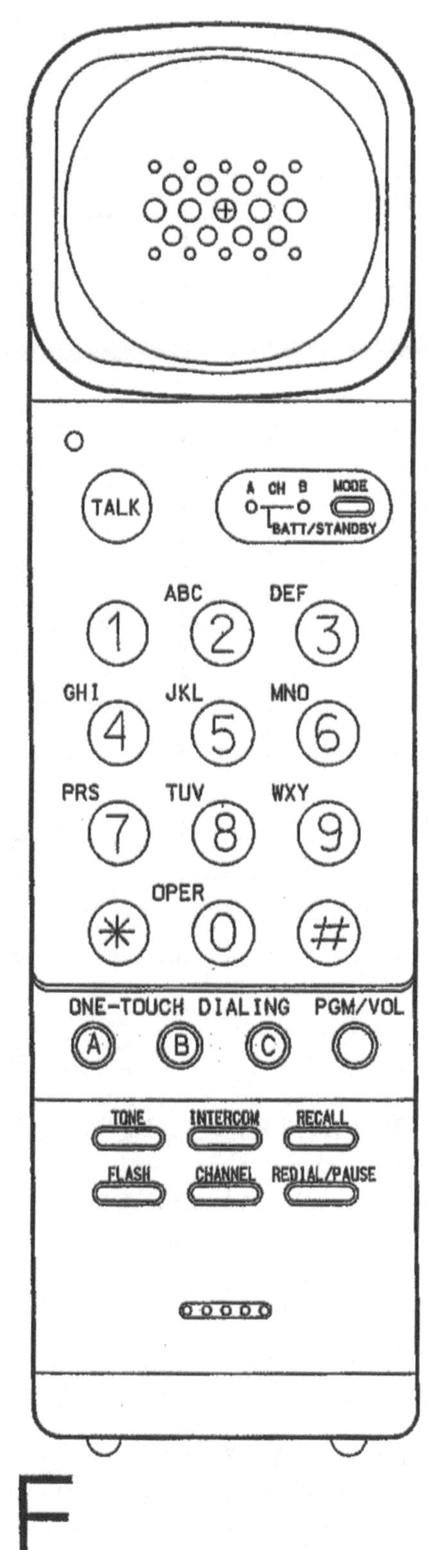
TALK
A CH B
MODE
BATT/STANDBY
ABC
DEF
1
2
3
GHI
JKL
MNO
4
5
6
PRS
TUV
WXY
7
8
9
OPER
*
0
#
ONE-TOUCH DIALING
PGM/VOL
A
B
C
TONE
INTERCOM
RECALL
FLASH
CHANNEL
REDIAL/PAUSE
F

STUDENT'S FULL NAME HERE

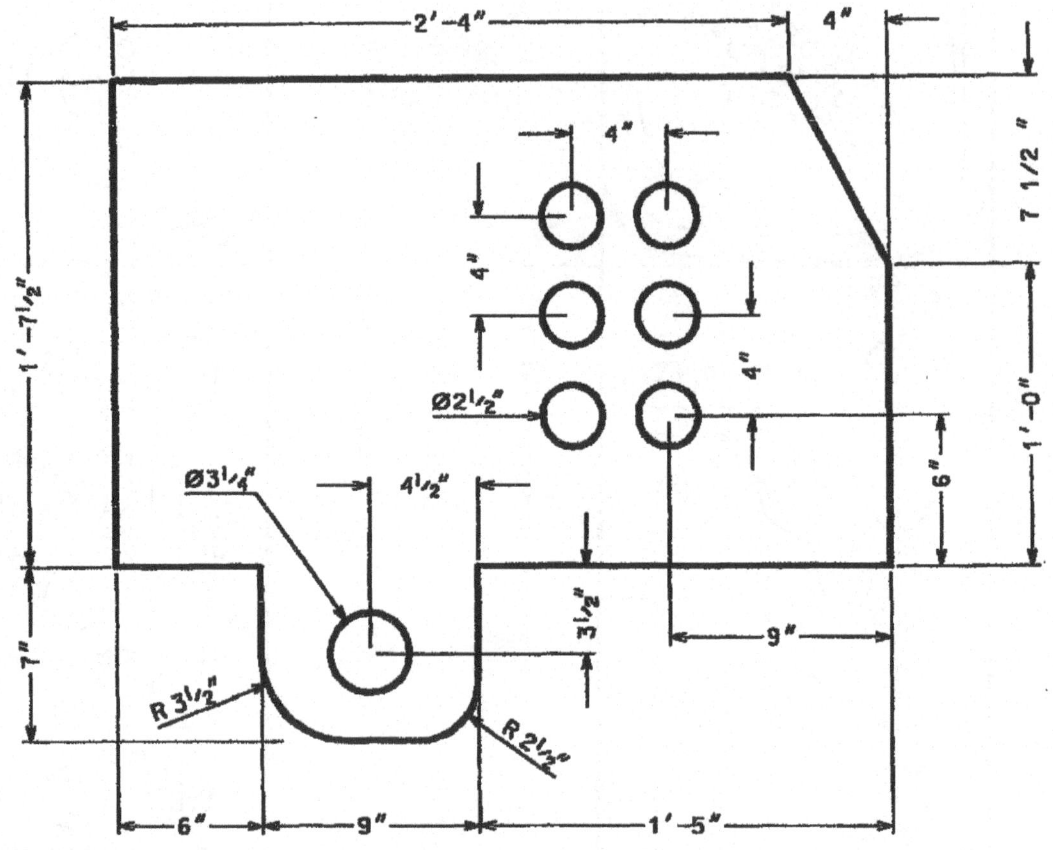

FIXTURE PLATE C

SET WORKING UNITS TO FEET AND INCHES AND TURN OFF THE GRID DISPLAY

THIS DRAWING IS COMPOSED OF:

9 LINES
7 CIRCLES
2 RADIUSED CORNERS
1 RECTANGULAR BLOCK SHAPE

DRAW ALL BOLD ELEMENTS TO EXACT DIMENSIONS AS SHOWN ABOVE. WEIGHT = 3

PLACE TEXTS AS SHOWN:
PUT YOUR NAME AT TOP AND DRAWING TITLE AT BOTTOM AS SHOWN. YOU DO NOT NEED TO PLACE DIMENSIONS!

USE FONT 3, ENGINEERING, WEIGHT = 1

WHEN DONE, PLACE A RECTANGULAR BLOCK SHAPE AROUND YOUR DRAWING AS SHOWN.

YOUR FINAL DRAWING SHOULD BE FITTED TO THE VIEW AND YOU SHOULD FILE SAVE SETTINGS BEFORE SAVING YOUR WORK

TO YOUR PERSONAL NUMBERED FOLDER AND TO YOUR SUBMITTAL FOLDER.

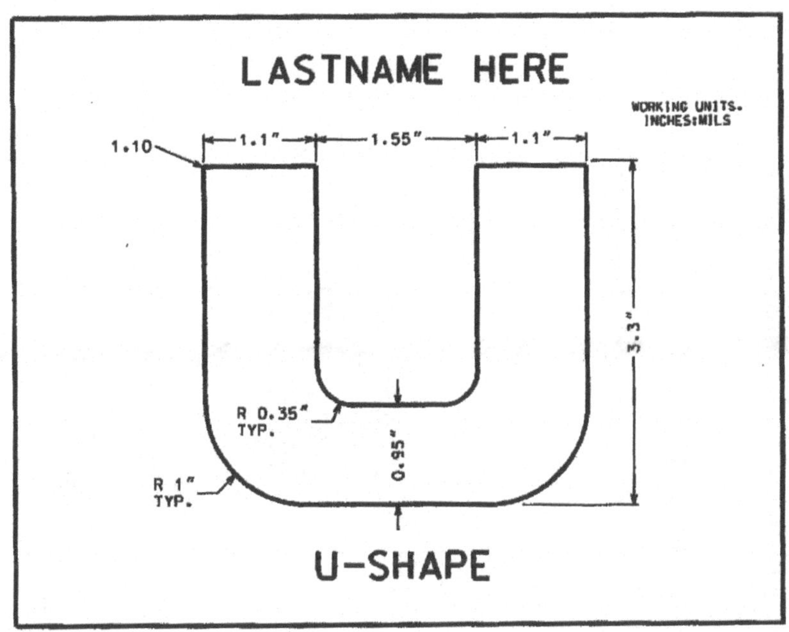

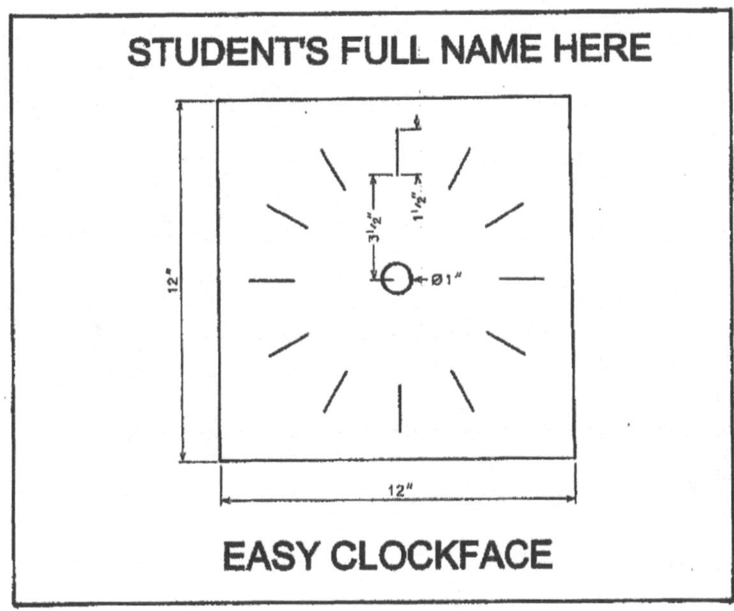

INSTRUCTIONS:

SET WORKING UNITS TO INCHES:MILS. DRAW THIS PERFECTLY SYMMETRICAL CLOCK FACE. WT=2, COLOR, YOUR CHOICE. CENTER OF CIRCLE AT 0,0.

DRAW THE LNE AT THE 12 0'CLOCK POSITION AT THE SIZE AND LOCATION SHOWN. USE THE CONSTRUCT ARRAY COMMAND WITH A SETTING OF −30° TO ARRAY THE REST OF THE HOUR MARKS.

BEFORE SUBMITTING, REMEMEBER TO FIT EVERYTHING TO THE VIEW, TURN OFF THE DISPLAY OF THE GRID & FILE, SAVE SETTINGS.

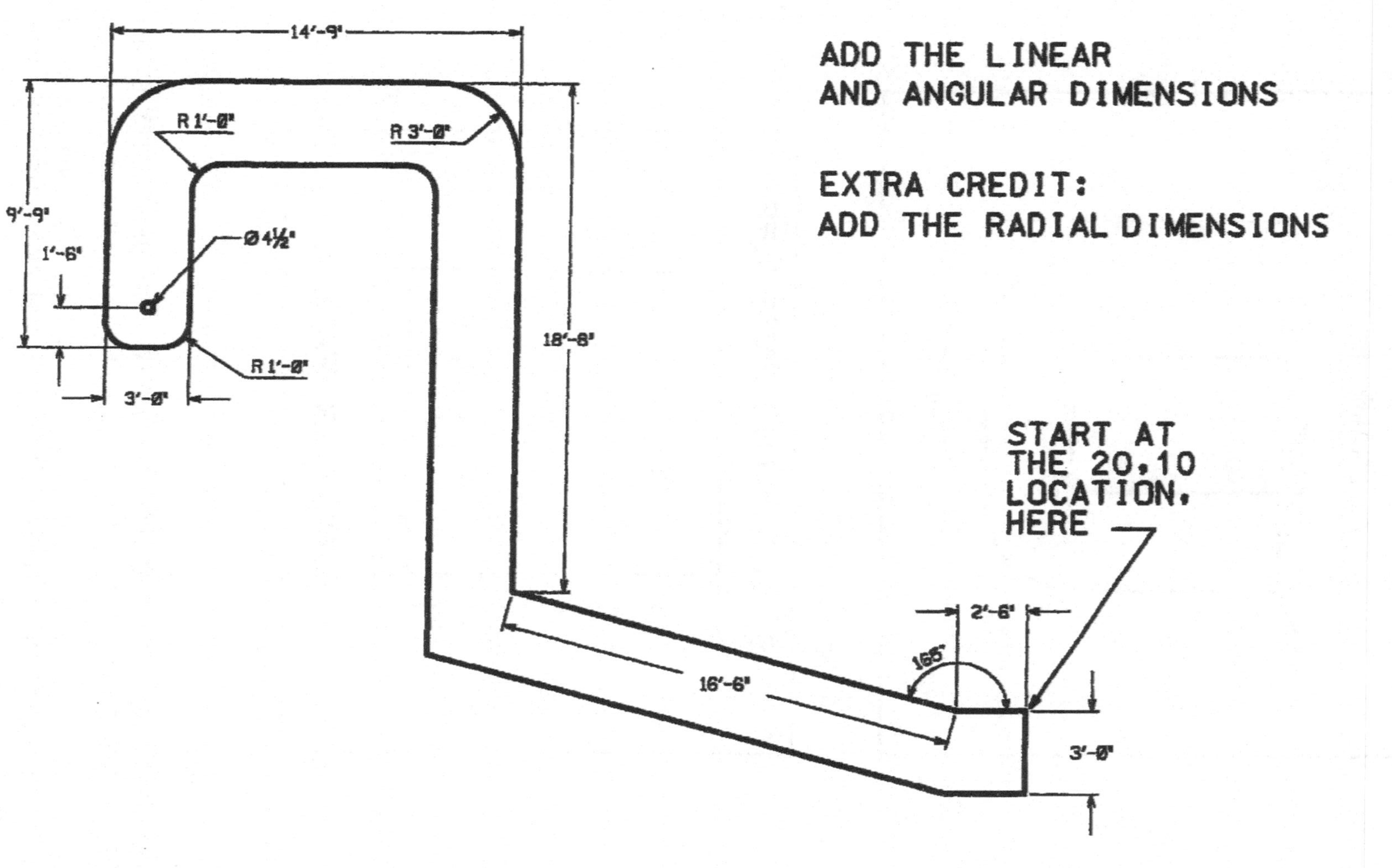
STUDENT'S NAME HERE
14'-9"
ADD THE LINEAR
AND ANGULAR DIMENSIONS
EXTRA CREDIT:
ADD THE RADIAL DIMENSIONS
R 1'-0"
R 3'-0"
9'-9"
1'-6"
Ø 4½"
18'-8"
R 1'-0"
3'-0"
START AT
THE 20,10
LOCATION,
HERE
2'-6"
165°
16'-6"
3'-0"
PUTT-PUTT HOLE 10

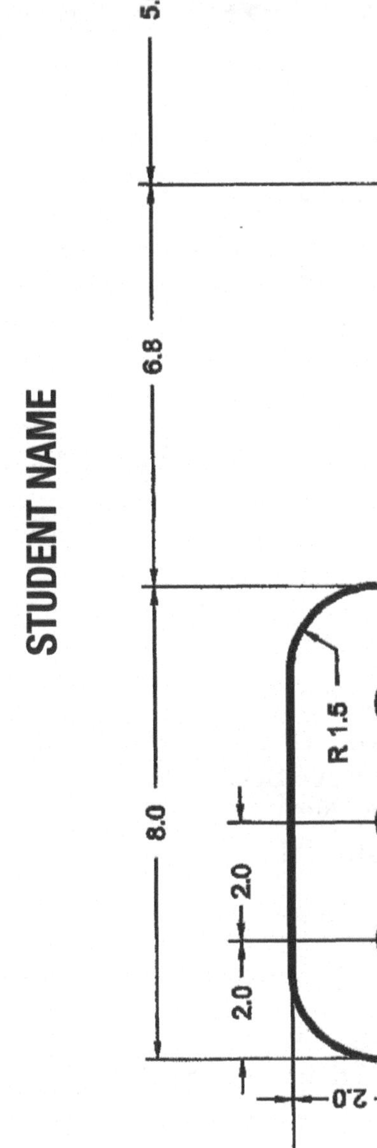
STUDENT NAME
PART-0220
5.0
3.0
2.0
2.3
1.3
2.5
2.5
R 1.0
Ø 1.7
6.8
4.3
12.5
R1.0
R 1.5
8.0
2.0
2.0
Ø 1.0
6.0
2.0
2.3
1.5
5.8
4.3
10,10

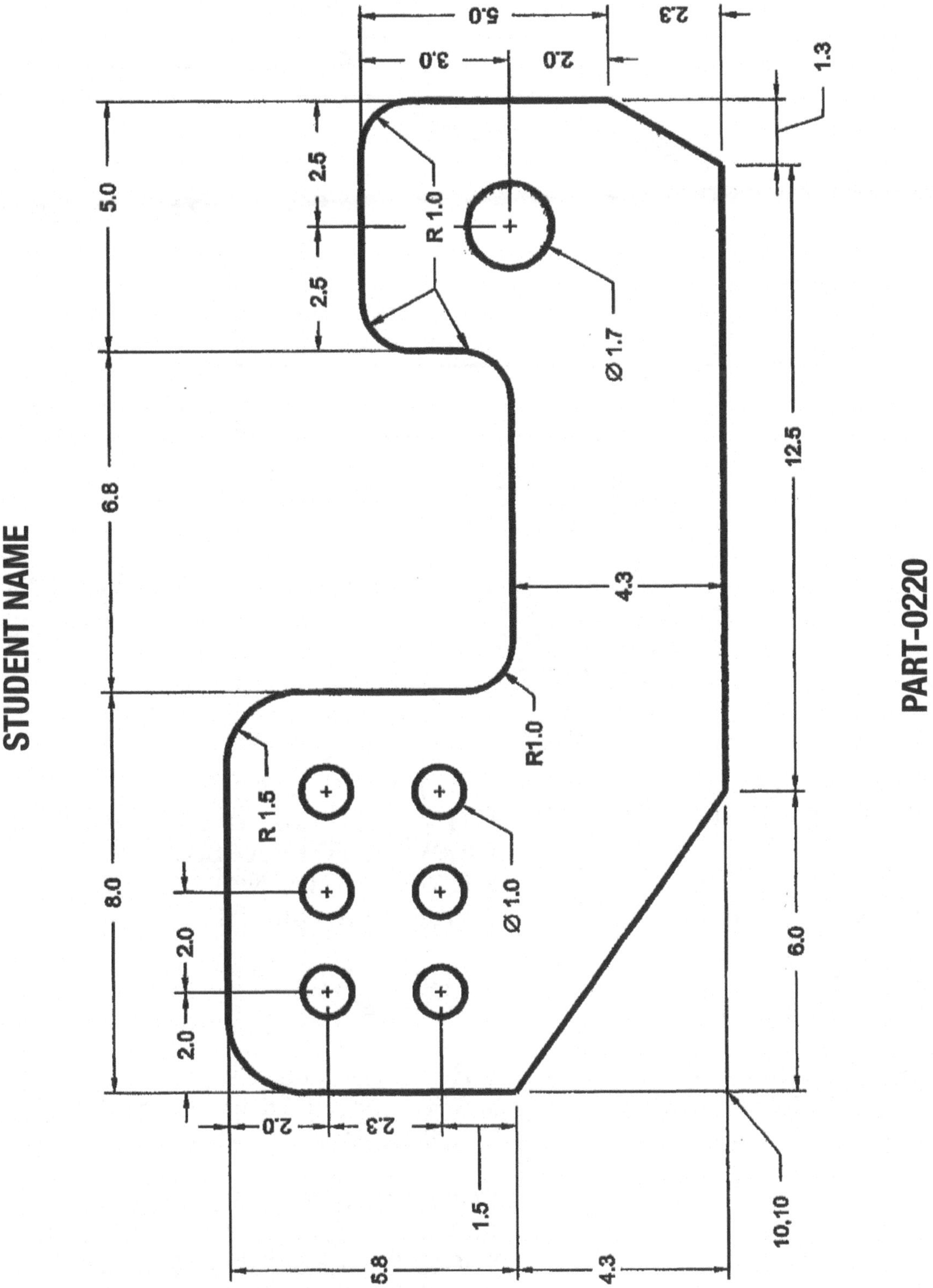

STUDENT'S FULL NAME HERE

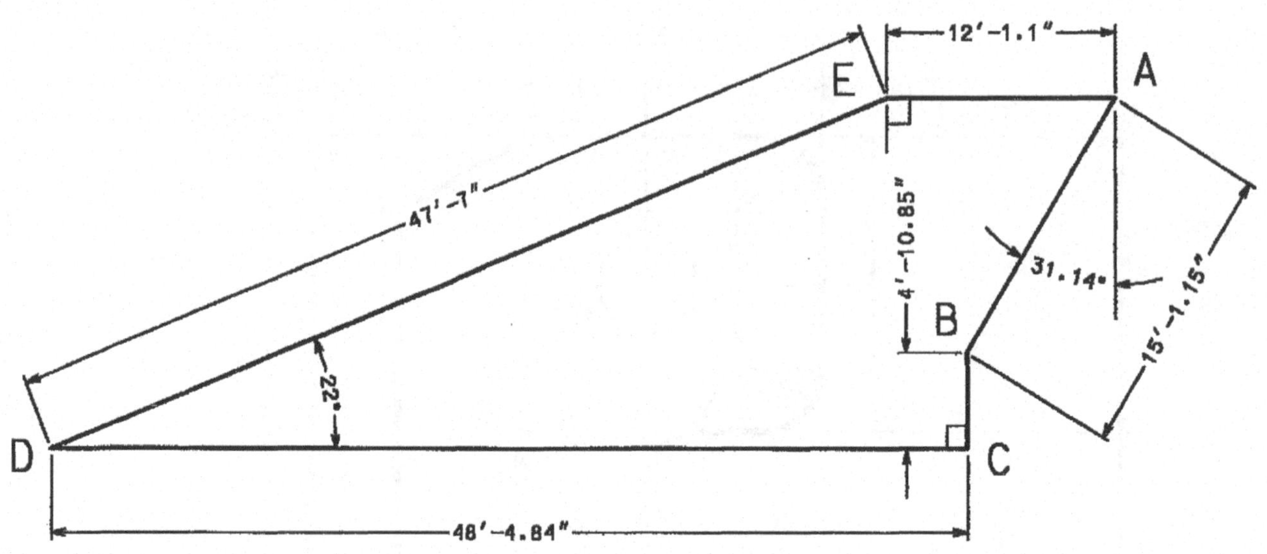

WING SHAPE

LINE SEGMENTS ARE THE FOLLOWING LENGTHS:
AB = 15′1.15″
BC = 4′10.85″
CD = 48′4.84″
DE = 47′7″
EA = 12′1.1″

SET WORKING UNITS TO FEET AND INCHES TURN OFF THE GRID DISPLAY

THIS DRAWING IS COMPOSED OF:
5 LINES
2 TEXT ELEMENTS
1 RECTANGULAR BLOCK SHAPE

DRAW THEM TO THE EXACT DIMENSIONS AS SHOWN ABOVE.
USE WEIGHT=3, COLOR=GREEN

PLACE TEXTS AS SHOWN:
PUT YOUR NAME AT TOP AND DRAWING TITLE AT BOTTOM AS SHOWN. YOU DO NOT NEED TO PLACE DIMENSIONS!

USE FONT 3, ENGINEERING.
WEIGHT = 1

WHEN DONE, PLACE
A RECTANGULAR BLOCK SHAPE
YOUR DRAWING AS SHOWN.

YOUR FINAL DRAWING SHOULD BE FITTED TO THE VIEW AND YOU SHOULD FILE SAVE SETTINGS BEFORE SAVING YOUR WORK TO YOUR PERSONAL NMBERD FOLDER AND TO YOUR NAMED SUBMITTAL FOLDER.

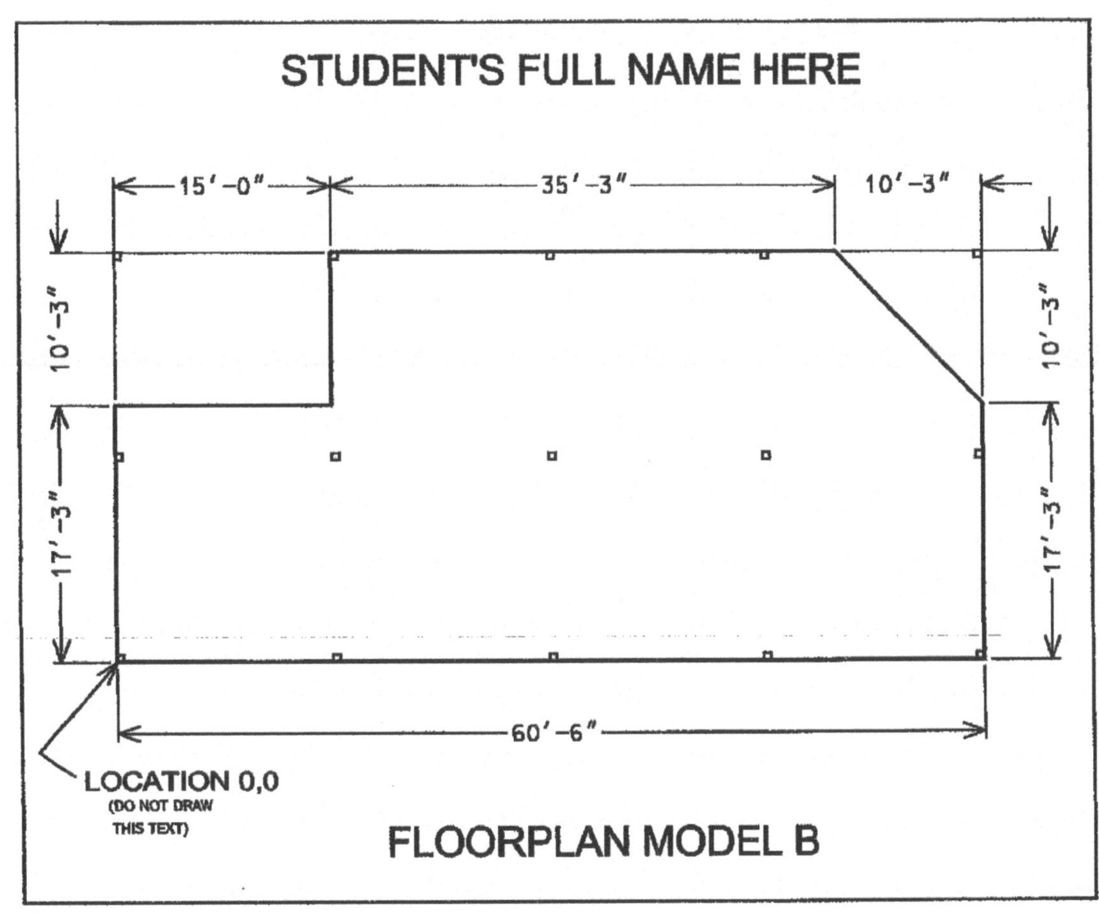

DRAWING THE FLOORPLAN:

OPEN THE FILE "FLOORPLAN BLANK.DGN" FROM THE CLASS FOLDER. USE SAVE-AS, MAKE A COPY: FLOORPLAN MODEL B-YOUR NAME

CREATE 3 NEW LEVELS: OUTERWALLS, COLUMNS & DIMENSIONS

DRAW THE OUTLINE OF THE BUILDING ON THE OUTERWALLS LEVEL AS SHOWN, USE COLOR RED, LINEWEIGHT = 2

MEASURE THE AREA OF THE BUILDING, BEFORE DRAWING IN THE COLUMNS.

MAKE A NOTE OF THE ANSWER HERE ONLY: ________________________ SQ. FT. (DO NOT PUT THE ANSWER ON THE DRAWING):

USE THE COLUMN LEVEL, COLOR WHITE AND LINEWEIGHT = 1 FOR YOUR COLUMNS. DRAW ONE 6″ × 6″ BUILDING COLUMN WITH ITS LOWER LEFT CORNER SNAPPED TO THE LOWER LEFT CORNER OF THE BUILDING OUTLINE. USE CONSTRUCT ARRAY TO MAKE THE REST OF COLUMNS: 3 ROWS, 5 COLUMNS, 15′ BETWEEN COLUMNS, 13.5′ BETWEEN ROWS.

ADD THE DIMENSIONS AS SHOWN ON THE DIMENSIONS LEVEL, COLOR WHITE, LINEWEIGHT = 0. DIMENSION TEXT HEIGHT AND WIDTH = 0.8 FT

© Pranch/Shutterstock.com

The instructor will show techniques to create the diagram at the right, in much less time than one would think possible. This series of four JETPORT proposals is ONE drawing, comprised of four JETPORTS. (See the instructional video) ->

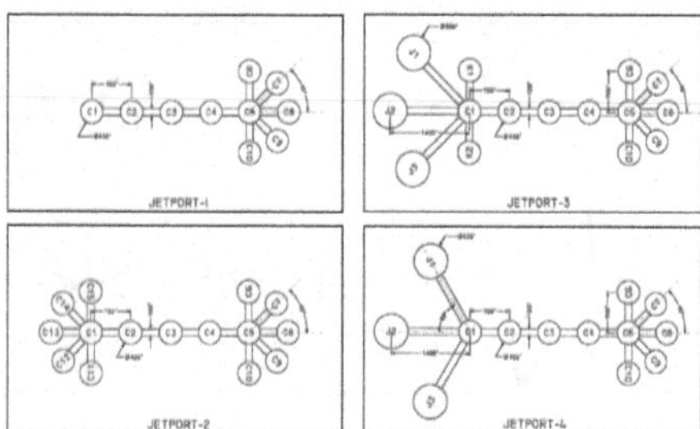

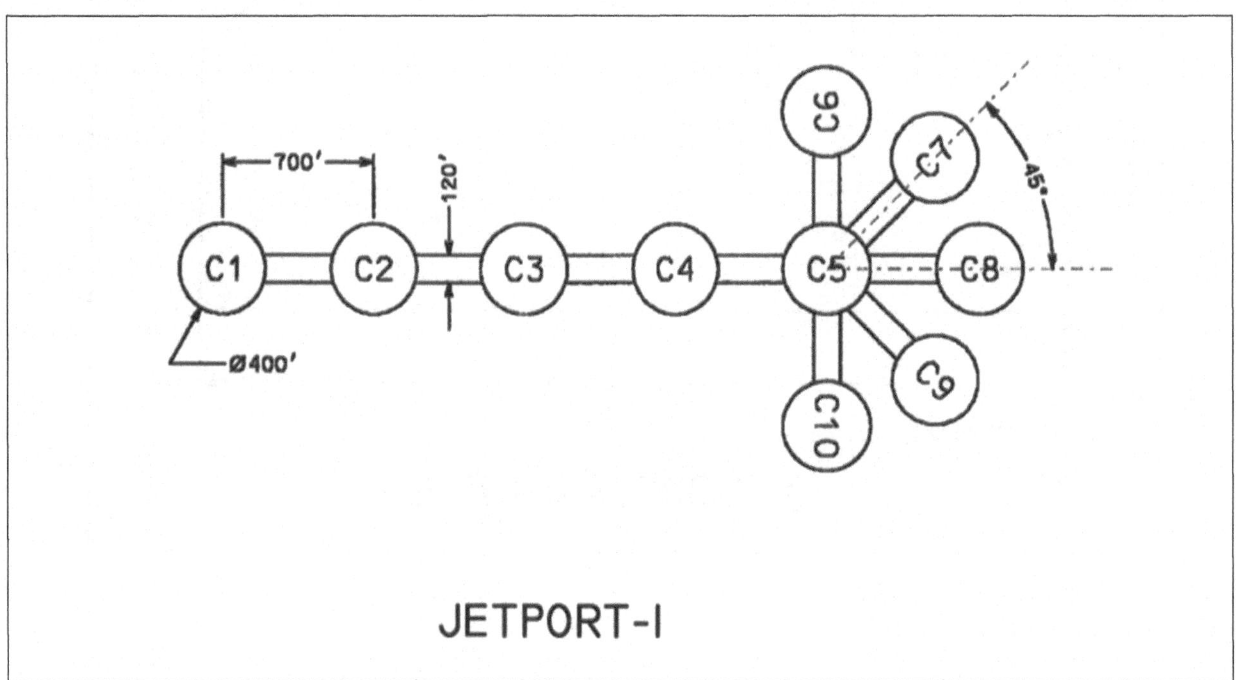

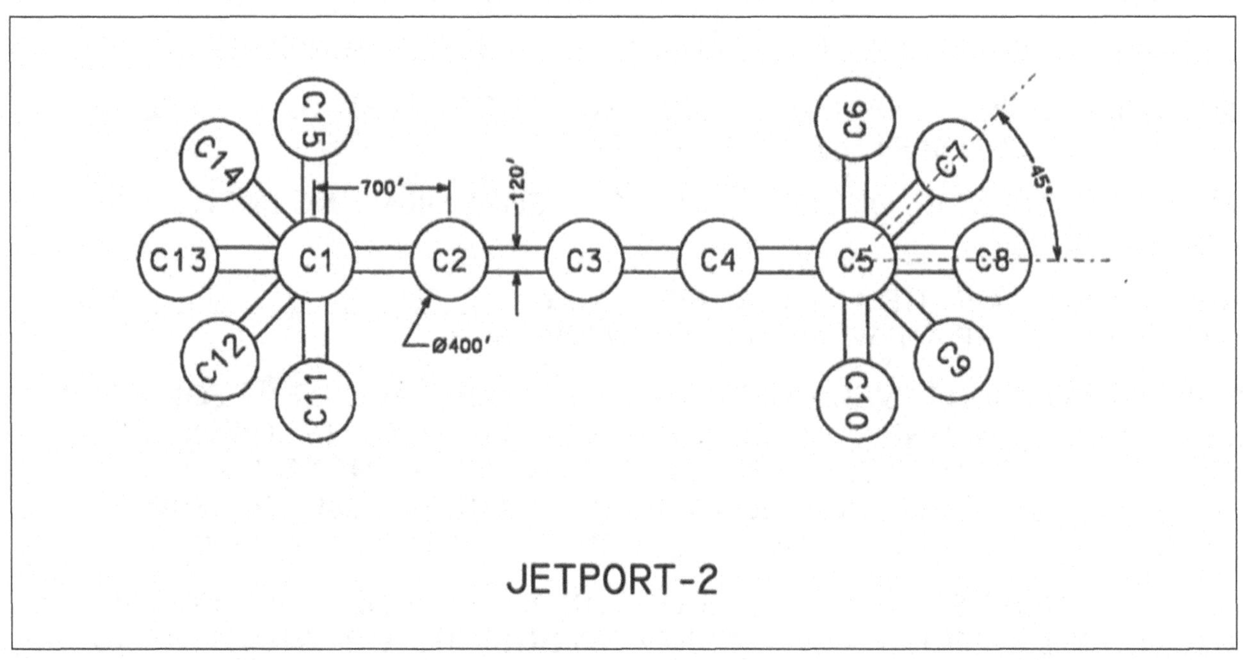

© Pranch/Shutterstock.com

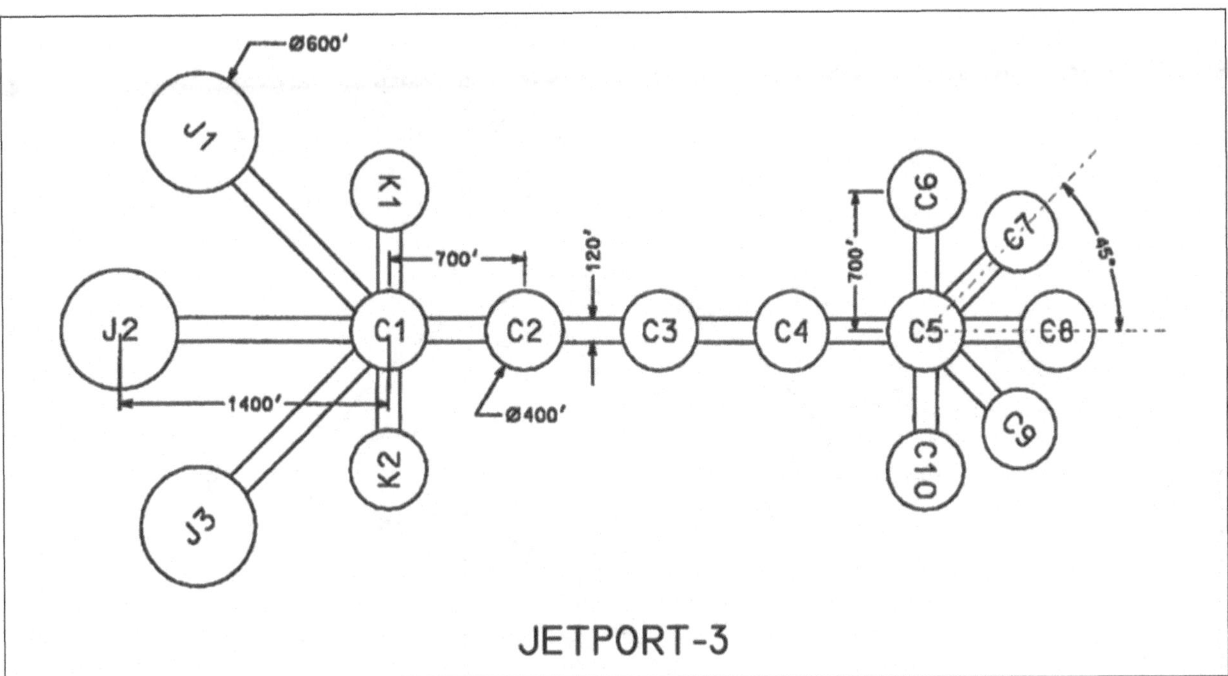

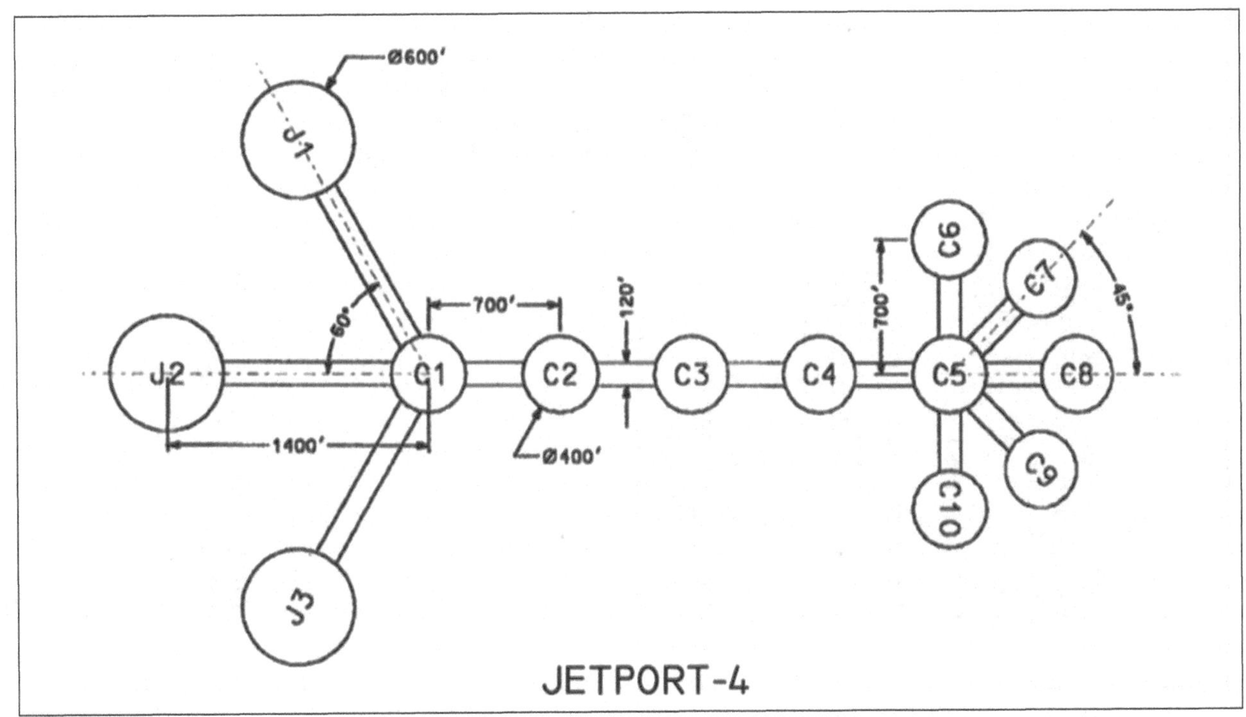

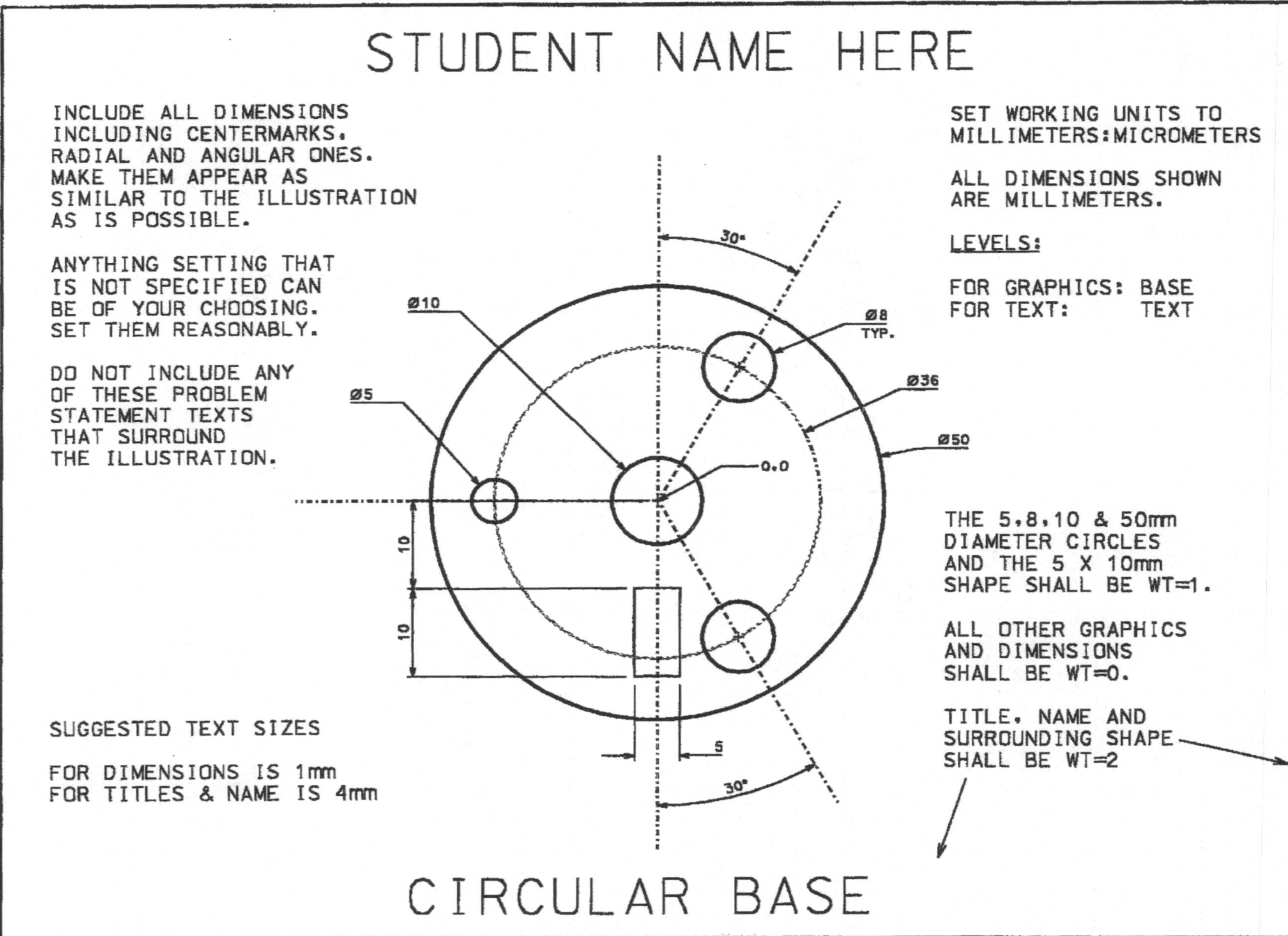
STUDENT NAME HERE
INCLUDE ALL DIMENSIONS
INCLUDING CENTERMARKS,
RADIAL AND ANGULAR ONES.
MAKE THEM APPEAR AS
SIMILAR TO THE ILLUSTRATION
AS IS POSSIBLE.
ANYTHING SETTING THAT
IS NOT SPECIFIED CAN
BE OF YOUR CHOOSING.
SET THEM REASONABLY.
DO NOT INCLUDE ANY
OF THESE PROBLEM
STATEMENT TEXTS
THAT SURROUND
THE ILLUSTRATION.
SET WORKING UNITS TO
MILLIMETERS:MICROMETERS
ALL DIMENSIONS SHOWN
ARE MILLIMETERS.
LEVELS:
FOR GRAPHICS: BASE
FOR TEXT: TEXT
30°
Ø10
Ø8
TYP.
Ø5
Ø36
Ø50
0,0
10
10
THE 5,8,10 & 50mm
DIAMETER CIRCLES
AND THE 5 X 10mm
SHAPE SHALL BE WT=1.
ALL OTHER GRAPHICS
AND DIMENSIONS
SHALL BE WT=0.
SUGGESTED TEXT SIZES
FOR DIMENSIONS IS 1mm
FOR TITLES & NAME IS 4mm
5
30°
TITLE, NAME AND
SURROUNDING SHAPE
SHALL BE WT=2
CIRCULAR BASE

DRAWING FILENAME SHALL BE SPAN-HANGER-LAST NAME

SET WORKING UNTIS TO FEET: INCHES

START POINT IS YOUR CHOICE.

DRAW EVERYTHING SHOWN AT THE RIGHT, BUT LEAVE OFF THE DIMENSIONS.

DRAW THE CENTERMARKS.
DRAW ALL TEXT.
DRAW THE OUTER BOX.

ALL LINEWORK TO BE COLOR YELLOW, CO=4 AND WEIGHT=2, EXCEPT FOR THE CUT-LINES AND THE CENTERMARKS.

THE CUT-LINES AT EACH END OF THE SPAN AND THE CENTERMARKS SHALL BE WEIGHT=0.

MAKE YOUR BEST APPROXIMATION FOR ANYTHING NOT SPECIFIED.

REMINDER. NO GRID DISPLAY.
NO GRID LOCK AND MAKE SURE TO FIT VIEW & SAVE SETTINGS.

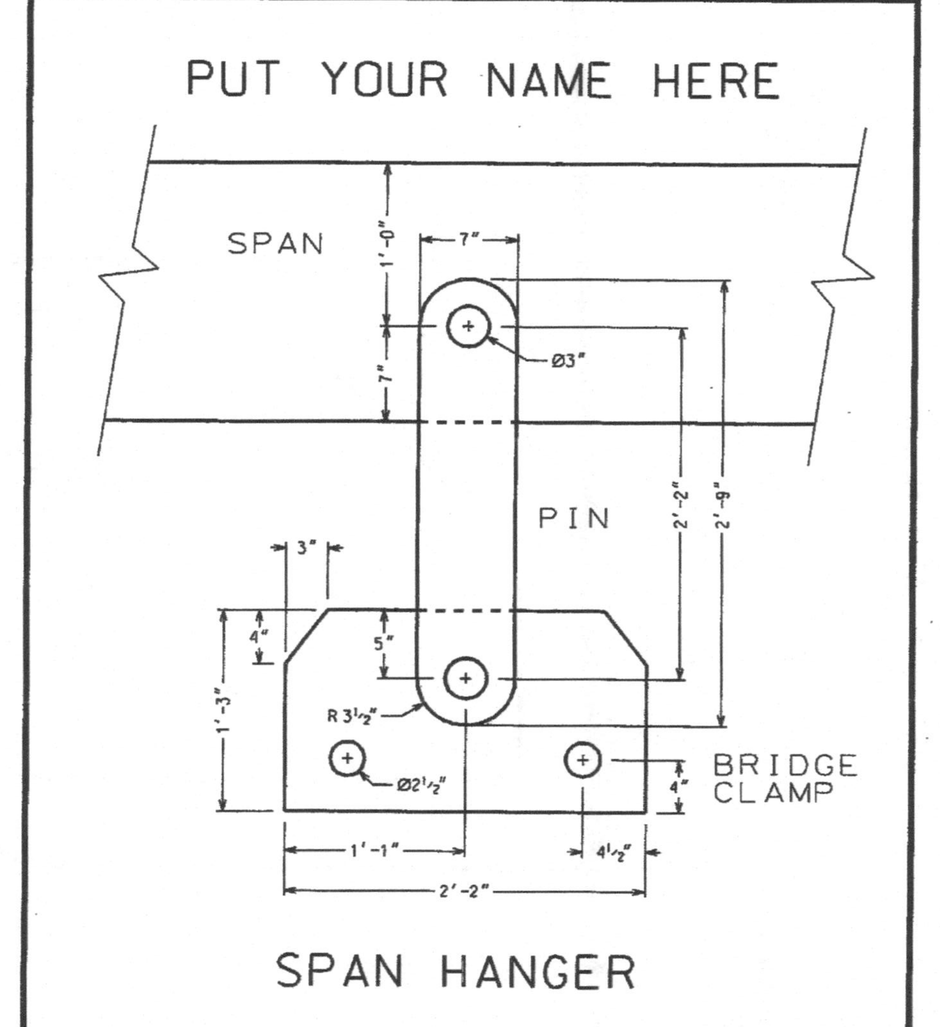

Some examples of similar bridge pin/hanger details are within: http://conf.tac-atc.ca/english/annualconference/tac2014/s-8/banthia.pdf

FULL NAME HERE

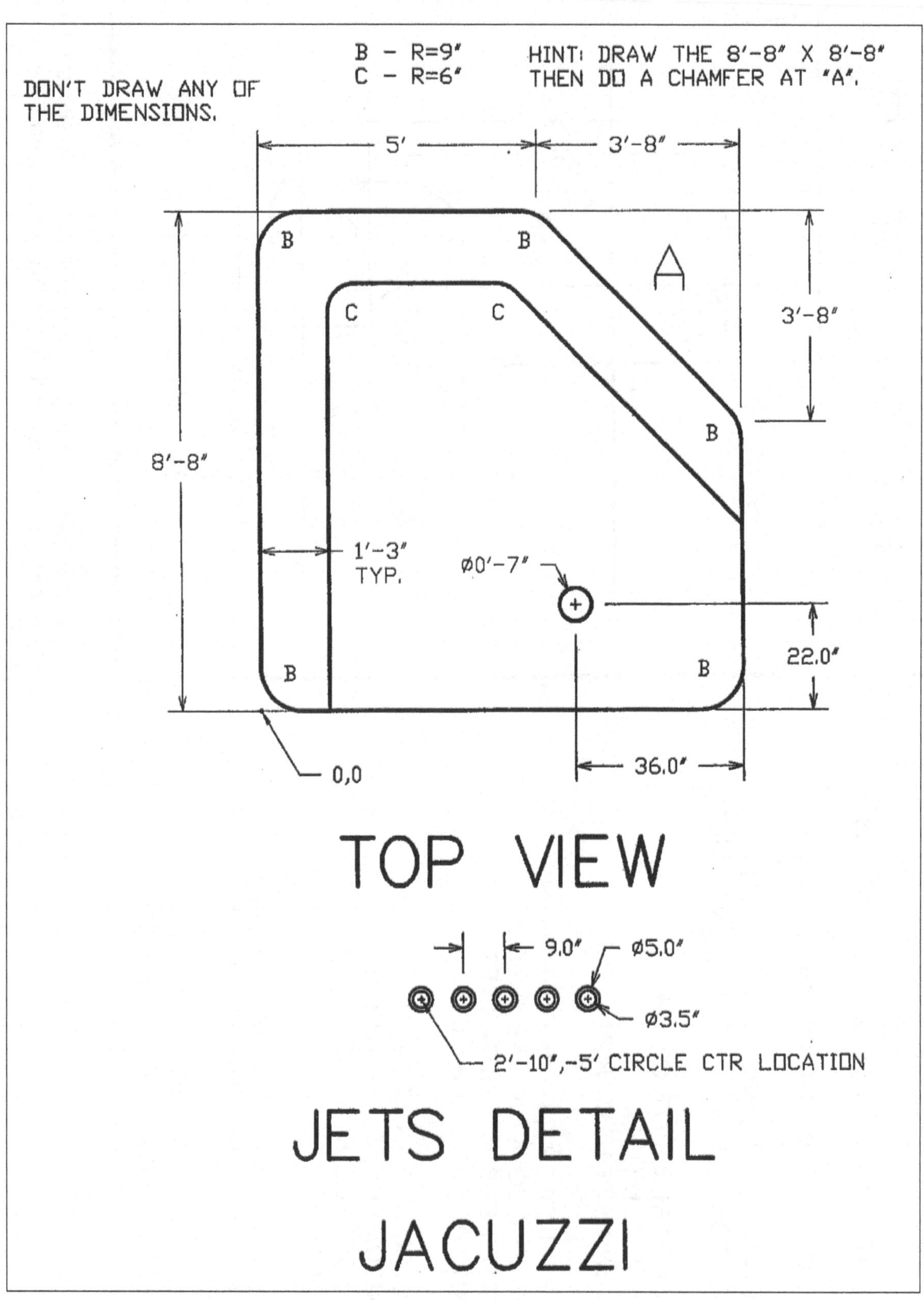

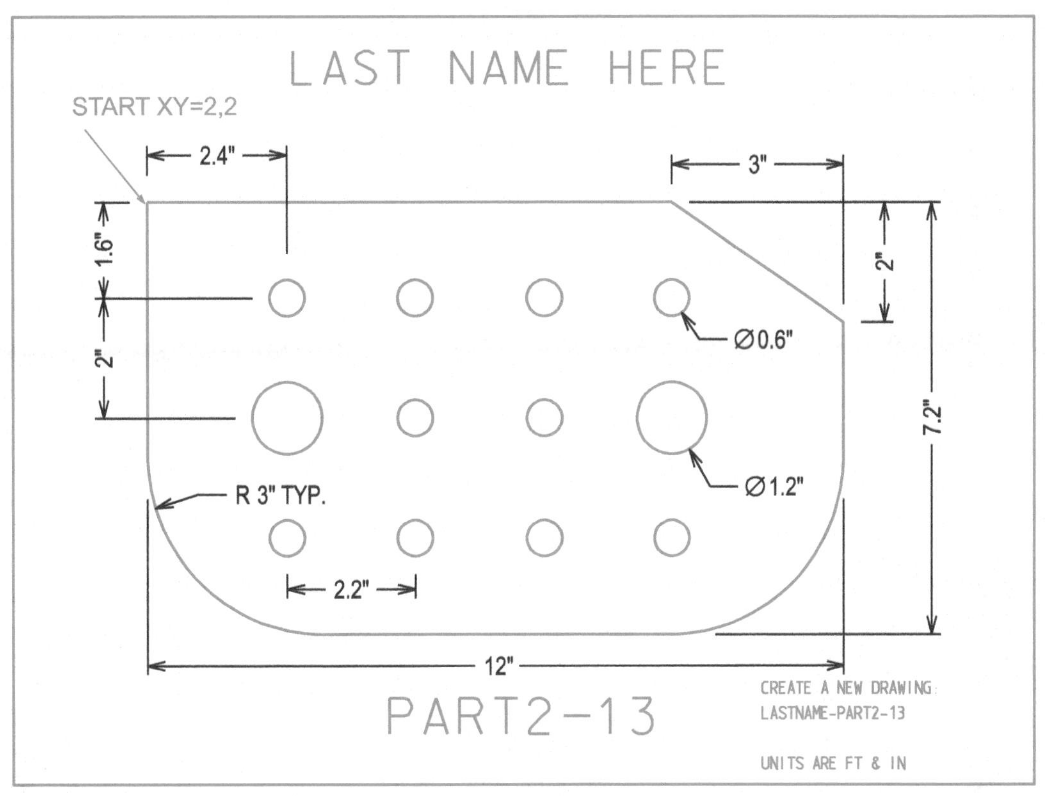
LAST NAME HERE
START XY=2,2
2.4"
3"
1.6"
2"
2"
7.2"
Ø0.6"
Ø1.2"
R 3" TYP.
2.2"
12"
PART2-13
CREATE A NEW DRAWING:
LASTNAME-PART2-13
UNITS ARE FT & IN

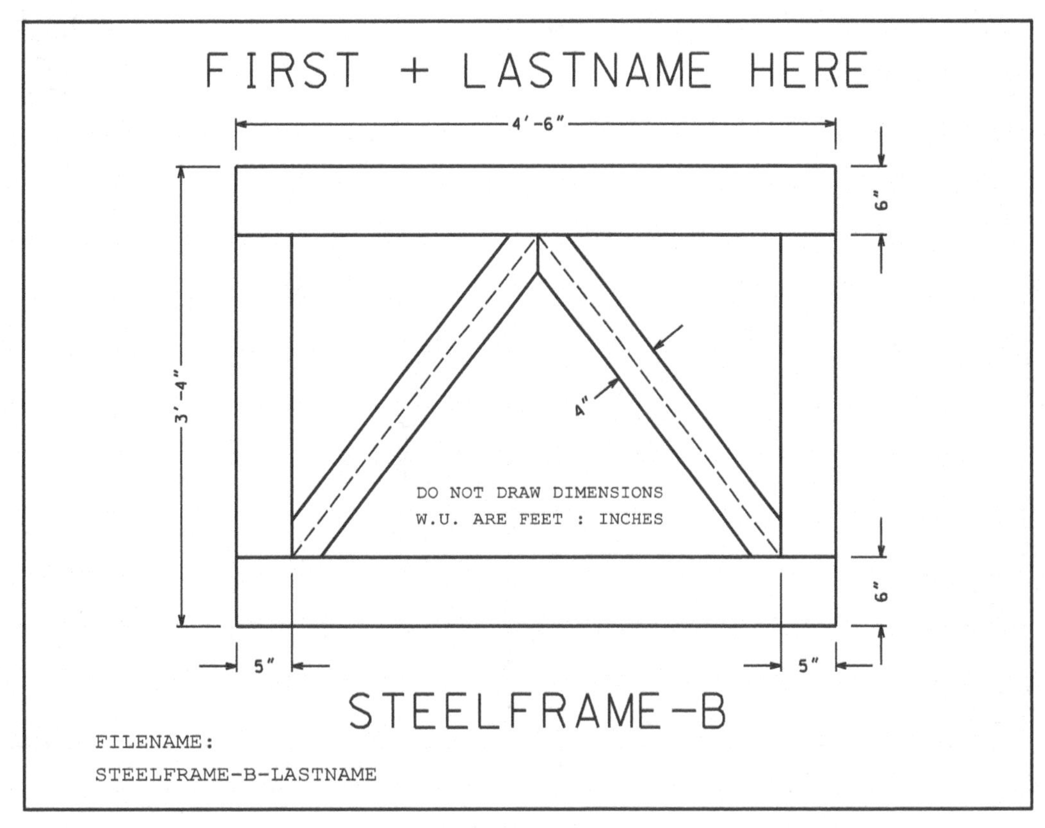
FIRST + LASTNAME HERE
4'-6"
6"
3'-4"
4"
DO NOT DRAW DIMENSIONS
W.U. ARE FEET : INCHES
6"
5"
5"
STEELFRAME-B
FILENAME:
STEELFRAME-B-LASTNAME

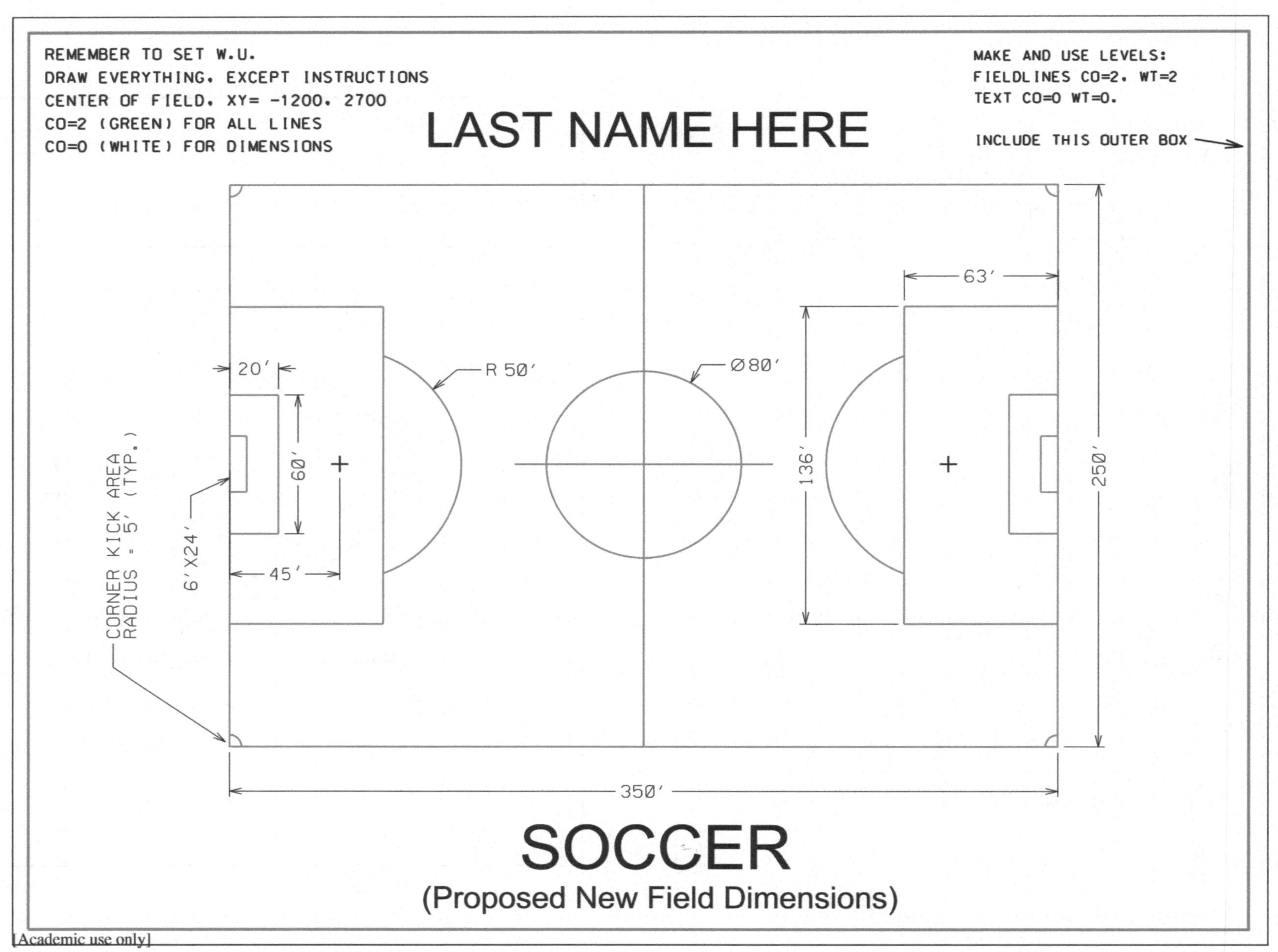

REMEMBER TO SET W.U.
DRAW EVERYTHING. EXCEPT INSTRUCTIONS
CENTER OF FIELD. XY= -1200. 2700
CO=2 (GREEN) FOR ALL LINES
CO=0 (WHITE) FOR DIMENSIONS
LAST NAME HERE
MAKE AND USE LEVELS:
FIELDLINES CO=2. WT=2
TEXT CO=0 WT=0.
INCLUDE THIS OUTER BOX
63'
20'
R 50'
Ø80'
60'
136'
250'
CORNER KICK AREA
RADIUS = 5' (TYP.)
6'X24'
45'
350'
SOCCER
(Proposed New Field Dimensions)
[Academic use only]

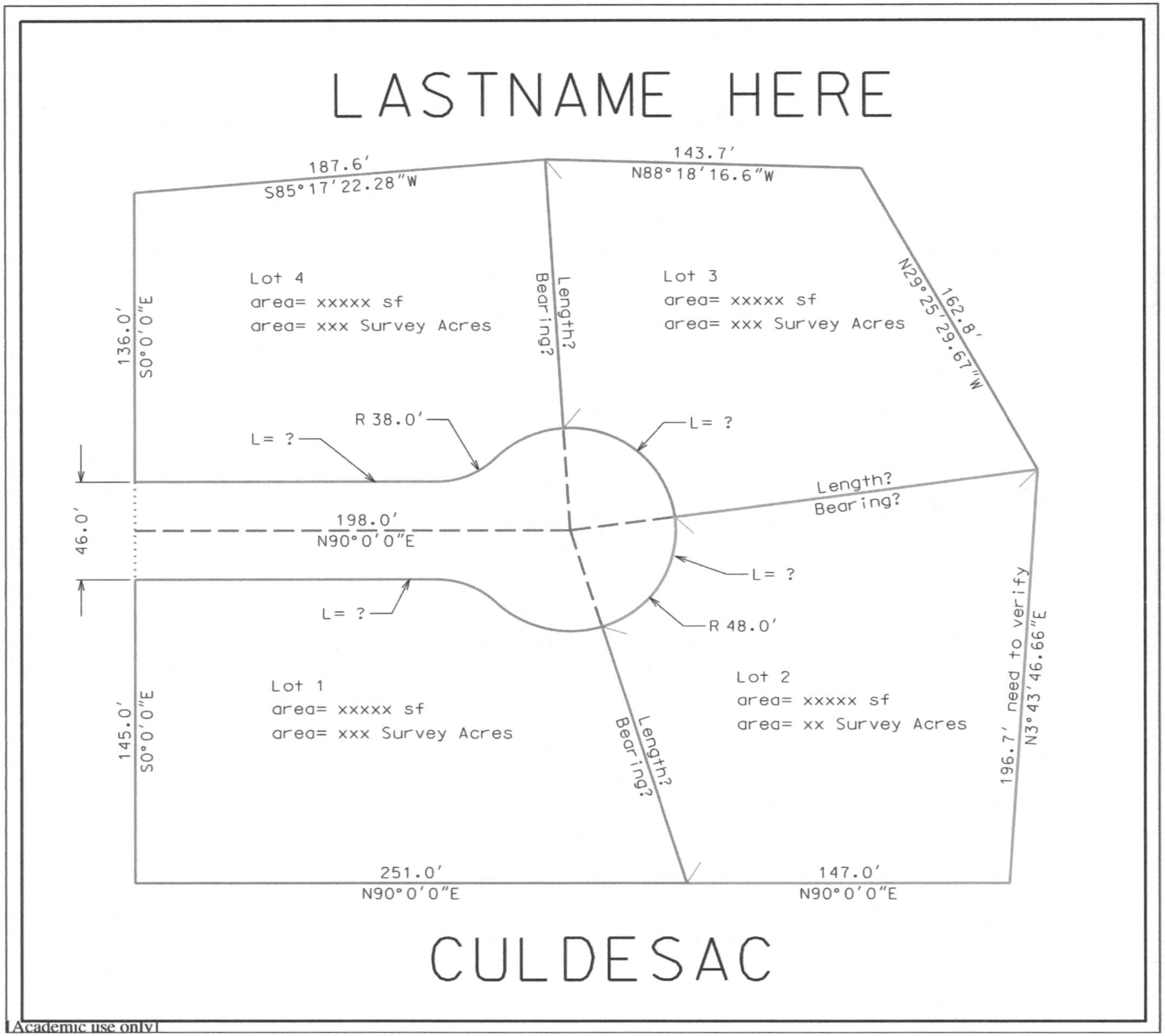

LASTNAME HERE

187.6′
S85°17′22.28″W
143.7′
N88°18′16.6″W
162.8′
N29°25′29.67″W
196.7′ need to verify
N3°43′46.66″E
136.0′
S0°0′0″E
145.0′
S0°0′0″E
251.0′
N90°0′0″E
147.0′
N90°0′0″E
46.0′
198.0′
N90°0′0″E
R 38.0′
R 48.0′
L= ?
L= ?
L= ?
L= ?
Length?
Bearing?
Length?
Bearing?
Length?
Bearing?

Lot 4
area= xxxxx sf
area= xxx Survey Acres

Lot 3
area= xxxxx sf
area= xxx Survey Acres

Lot 1
area= xxxxx sf
area= xxx Survey Acres

Lot 2
area= xxxxx sf
area= xx Survey Acres

CULDESAC

[Academic use only]

Create a new drawing called CULDEAC

Set the following:
W.U. (Working Units)
to Feet and inches

Format in the W.U. to MU
(master units only)
Accuracy to 0.1 (tenths of a ft)

Set Angle Readout to:
Direction Mode: Bearing,
Format: DD.MM.SS
Accuracy: 0.12
(hundredths of a second)

Create a new level
Property Lines
Set CO=2, WT=2, LC=0

Draw the property Lines

You will need to use Place Circle and other editing tools to make the diagram.

Color-code the Lots after drawing each.

Measure the areas in Sq Ft and in Acres.

Measure the dividing lines between each Lot.

Place Texts as shown

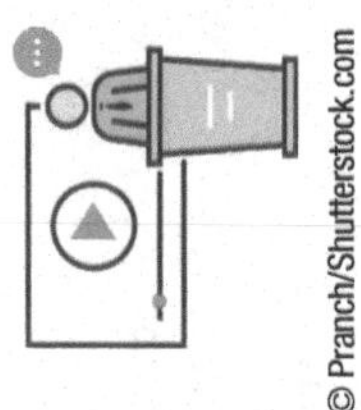

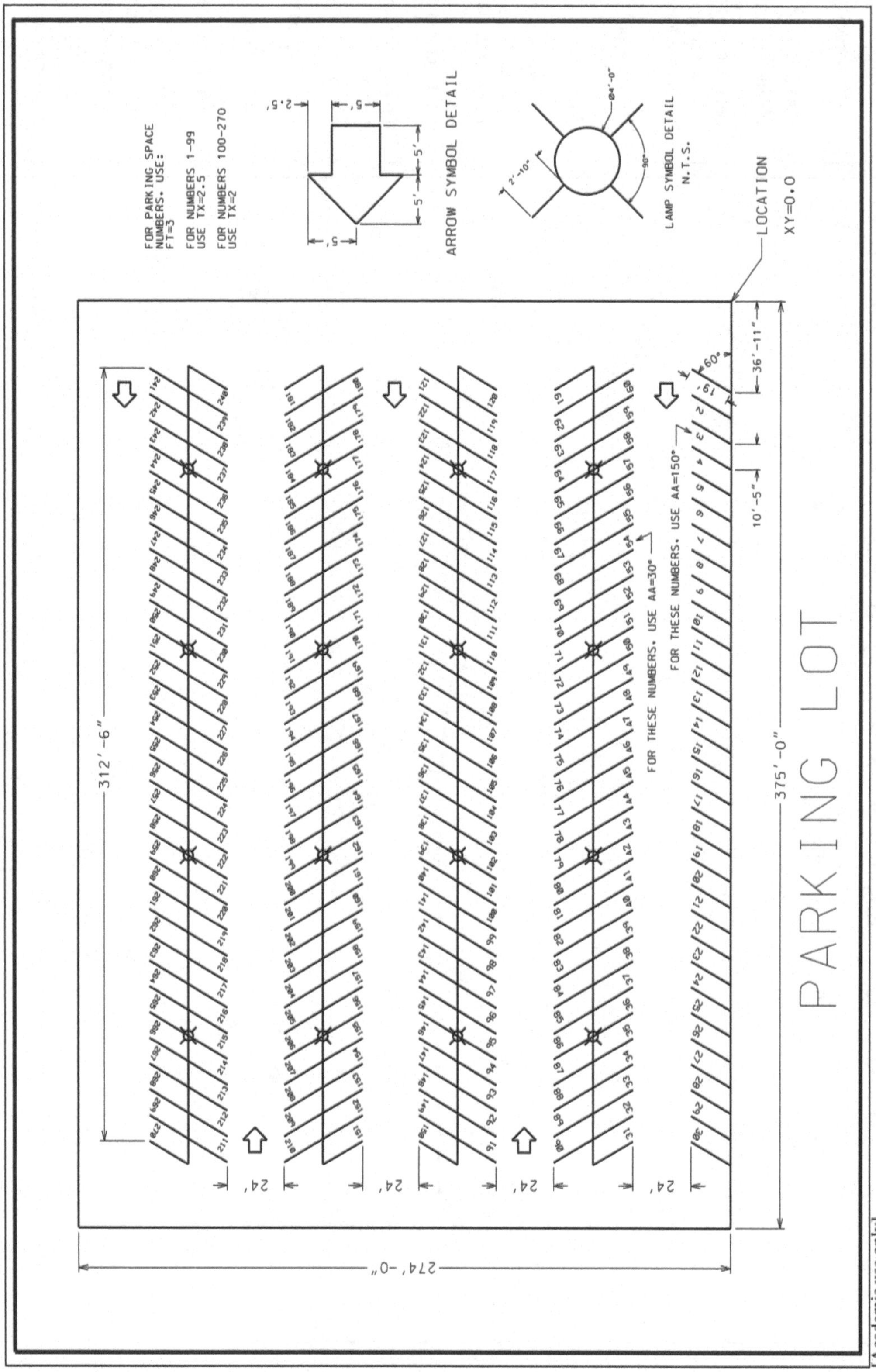

FOR PARKING SPACE NUMBERS, USE: FT=3
FOR NUMBERS 1-99 USE TX=2.5
FOR NUMBERS 100-270 USE TX=2

.5'
.5'
2.5'
5'
5'
ARROW SYMBOL DETAIL

2'-10"
Ø4'-0"
90°
LAMP SYMBOL DETAIL
N.T.S.

LOCATION
XY=0,0

312'-6"
36'-11"
60°
19'
10'-5"
FOR THESE NUMBERS, USE AA=30°
FOR THESE NUMBERS, USE AA=150°
24'
24'
24'
24'
375'-0"
274'-0"

PARKING LOT

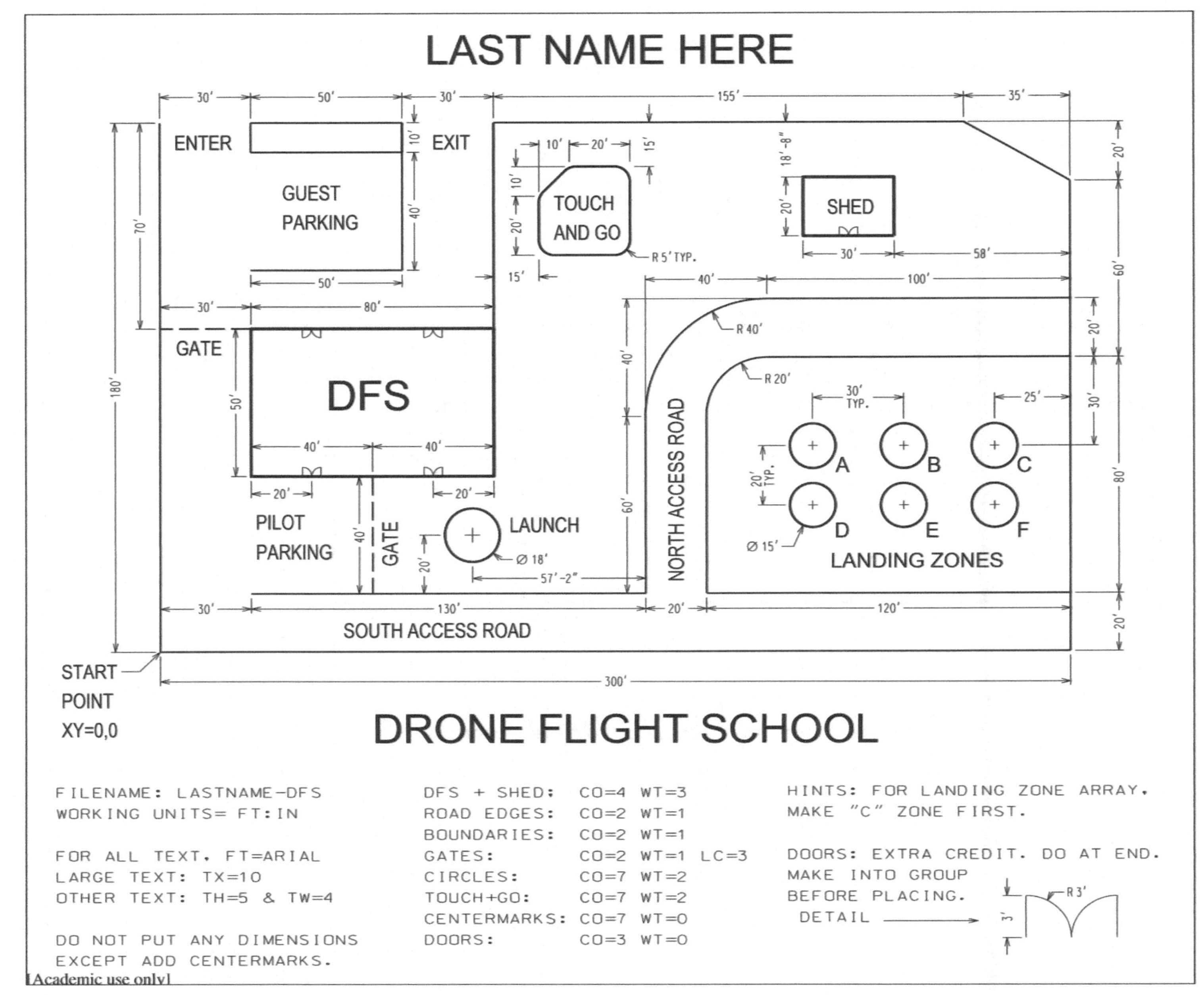
LAST NAME HERE
ENTER
EXIT
GUEST PARKING
TOUCH AND GO
SHED
GATE
DFS
PILOT PARKING
GATE
LAUNCH
NORTH ACCESS ROAD
LANDING ZONES
SOUTH ACCESS ROAD
START POINT XY=0,0
DRONE FLIGHT SCHOOL
FILENAME: LASTNAME-DFS
WORKING UNITS= FT:IN
FOR ALL TEXT, FT=ARIAL
LARGE TEXT: TX=10
OTHER TEXT: TH=5 & TW=4
DO NOT PUT ANY DIMENSIONS
EXCEPT ADD CENTERMARKS.
DFS + SHED: CO=4 WT=3
ROAD EDGES: CO=2 WT=1
BOUNDARIES: CO=2 WT=1
GATES: CO=2 WT=1 LC=3
CIRCLES: CO=7 WT=2
TOUCH+GO: CO=7 WT=2
CENTERMARKS: CO=7 WT=0
DOORS: CO=3 WT=0
HINTS: FOR LANDING ZONE ARRAY,
MAKE "C" ZONE FIRST.
DOORS: EXTRA CREDIT. DO AT END.
MAKE INTO GROUP
BEFORE PLACING.
DETAIL

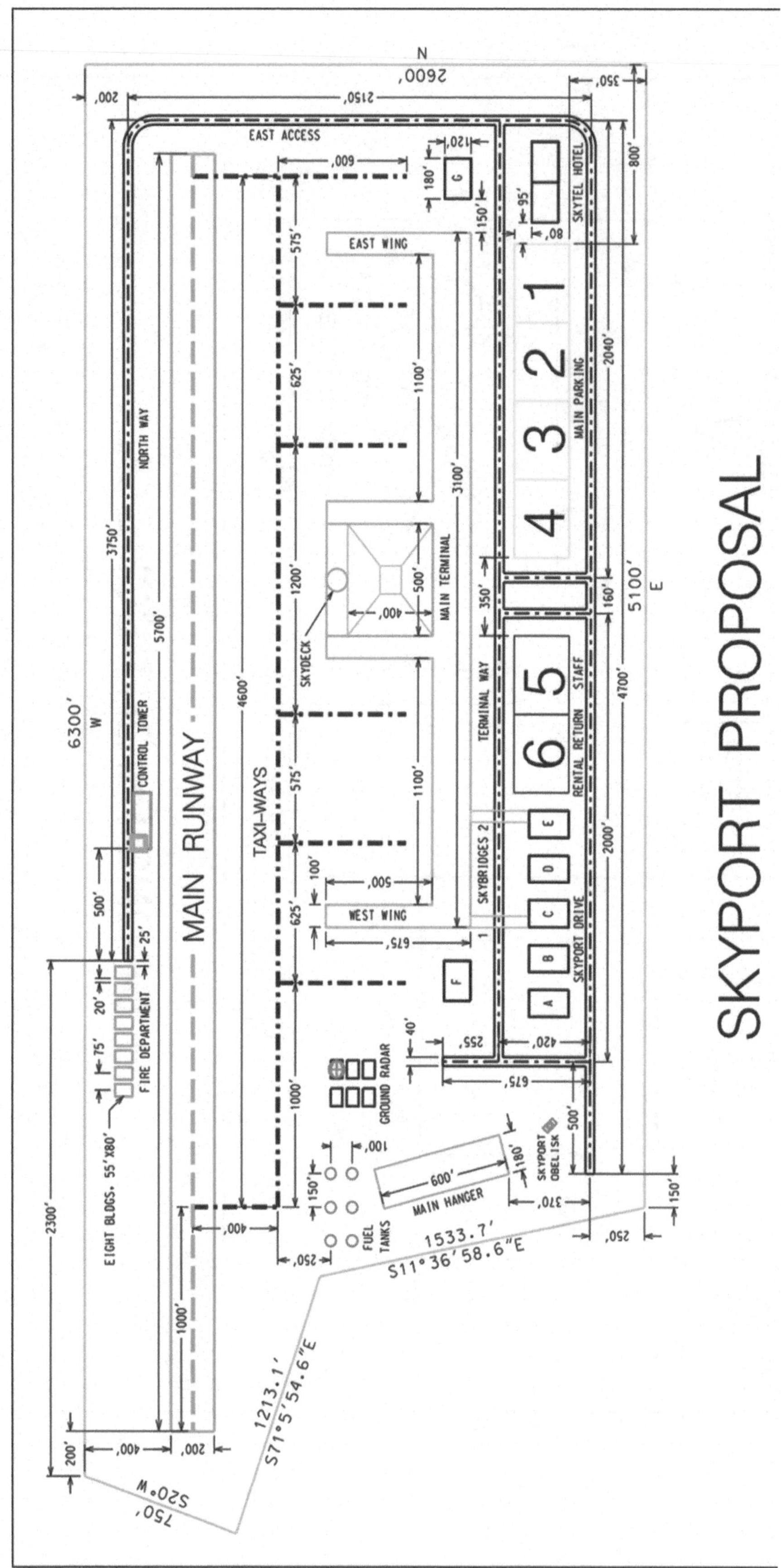
SKYPORT PROPOSAL
N
E
W
2600'
5100'
6300'
MAIN RUNWAY
TAXI-WAYS
NORTH WAY
EAST ACCESS
EAST WING
WEST WING
MAIN TERMINAL
SKYDECK
TERMINAL WAY
SKYBRIDGES 2
SKYPORT DRIVE
RENTAL RETURN
STAFF
MAIN PARKING
SKYTEL HOTEL
CONTROL TOWER
FIRE DEPARTMENT
EIGHT BLDGS. 55'X80'
GROUND RADAR
FUEL TANKS
MAIN HANGER
SKYPORT OBELISK
1533.7'
S11°36'58.6"E
1213.1'
S71°5'54.6"E
750'
S20°W

Notes for SKYPORT PROPOSAL

Please refer to the drawing on the opposite page and 3D image:
(See the SKYPORT 3D file provided by your instructor)

Parts of the SKYPORT Proposal drawing are ALREADY COMPLETED with many elements in the drawing Locked, to prevent accidental deletion or changes. Draw all basic shapes and text in the TOP View! Use any view as needed for working on the 3D extrusions (or copying them) Note: you can COPY Locked elements!

Include All text and notes and dimensions. Choose color, style and weight to best match the handout.

Correctly Add as much of the following as possible. Do any parts you can in any order that you choose. Partial credit is awarded for any partial work done. Note: some portions of the work are MUCH EASIER than other portions!

Finish Property Lines, Taxi-way Lines and Roads.
All Roads are 40' total width each. Centerline to road edge is 20'.

ROADS: Skyport Drive, Terminal Way, East Access, North Way
The fillet radii of the rounded corners of East Access/North Way and East Access/Skyport Drive are:
R of Center line of road = 120' R of Inner edge of road = 100'
R of Outer edge of road = 140'

Create (or copy as needed) all 3D features, such as Fuel Tanks, Buildings (composed of individual floors), etc.

FUEL TANKS 50' diam. X 55' tall

FIRE DEPT Bldgs 55' x 80' x 30' tall

CONTROL TOWER

Bottom FLRs	2 FLRS 80' x 250' x 30' tall
Skinny Tower	50' x 50' shape 200' tall, N.W. corner at the N.W. corner of the top of 2nd flr portion
Control Rm	50' x 50' then Extrude up 75' at the center of the 50' x 50' shape, with X-scale & Y-scale = 1.5

MAIN HANGER 1 FLR
180' x 600' x 110' tall (rotated at 15 degrees about the lower left corner)

BLDGS	120' x 180' x each floor has height 30' (Includes the Skytel Hotel bldg)
C, D, E, F & G	3 FLRS (note: Bldg F is symmetrical to placement of Bldg G)
A & B	2 FLRS
SKYTEL HOTEL	2 FLRS (LOBBY portion at west side of Hotel)
SKYTEL HOTEL	8 FLRS (High-Rise portion at east side of Hotel)

SKYDECK 100' diam. X 50' tall
(Observation Area and Lounge, centered on top of northern, center part of the Main Terminal)

MAIN TERMINAL ROOF 400' x 500' shape, snapped to top inner edge corners of the Main Terminal Bldg
Extrude up 85' at the center of the 400' x 500' shape, with X-scale & Y-scale = 0.25

SKYBRIDGES 50' Wide x 20' Tall x 270' length
(bottom edge aligns to bottom of 3rd floor of Bldg. C and/or Bldg. E)
Skybridge 1 corner aligns to west edge of Bldg. CSkybridge 2 corner aligns to east edge of Bldg. E

PARKING LOTS
Parking Lot #1 is a Reference File attachment of the 375' x 274' Parking Lot file provided for you in the Distribution Folder (or that was assigned earlier). Attach that file and then Reference Move it into the proper location as noted by the rectangle at location 1. The next parking lot 2 can be made by a REFERENCE COPY of the first reference file that you attached (do this a total of 5 times to get to have 6 attachments of the 375' x 274' parking lot file).

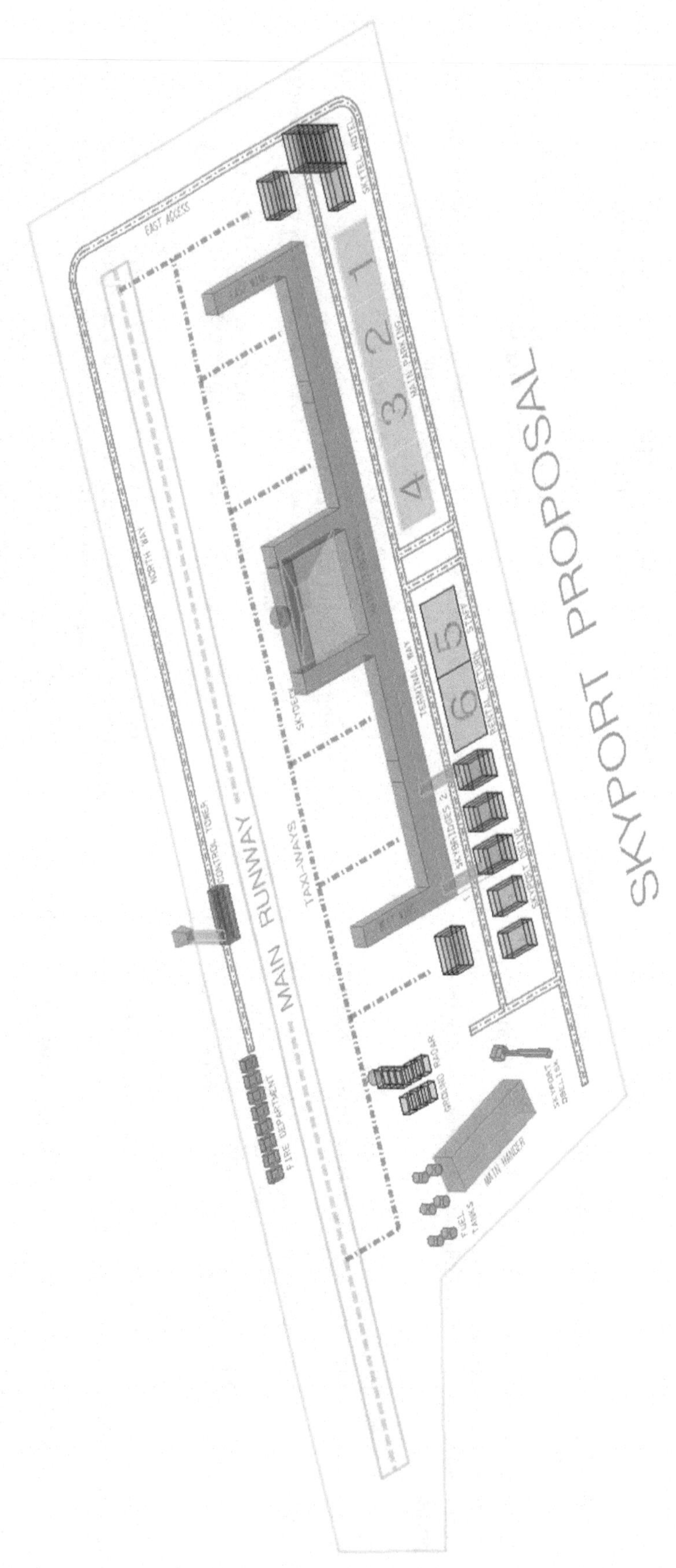
SKYPORT PROPOSAL
MAIN RUNWAY
TAXI-WAYS
EAST ACCESS
NORTH WAY
CONTROL TOWER
FIRE DEPARTMENT
GROUND RADAR
MAIN HANGER
FUEL TANKS
TERMINAL BAY
MAIN PARKING
1
2
3
4
5
6

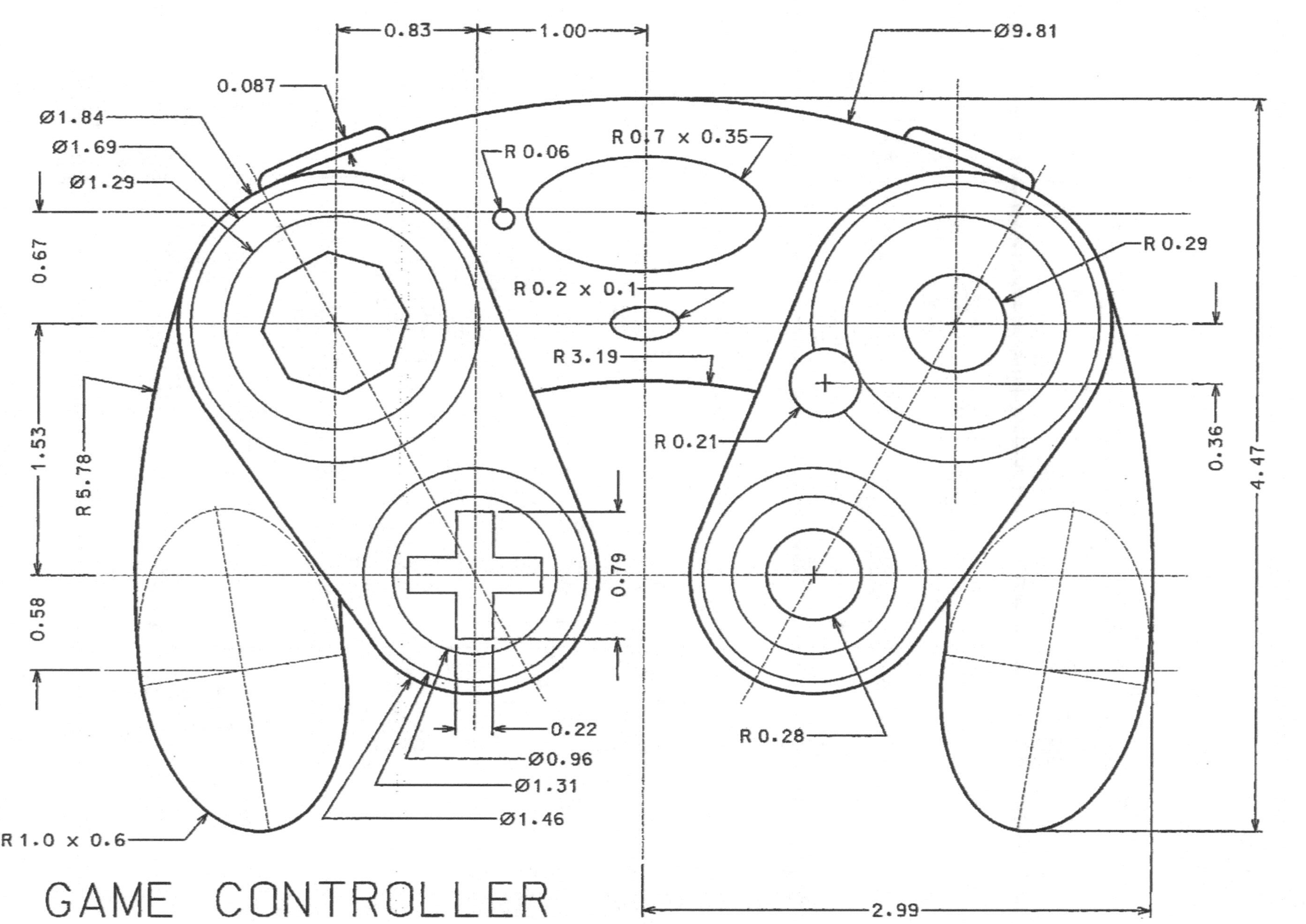
0.83
1.00
Ø9.81
0.087
Ø1.84
Ø1.69
Ø1.29
R 0.06
R 0.7 × 0.35
R 0.29
R 0.2 × 0.1
R 3.19
0.67
1.53
R 5.78
R 0.21
0.36
4.47
0.79
0.58
0.22
Ø0.96
Ø1.31
Ø1.46
R 0.28
R 1.0 × 0.6
GAME CONTROLLER
2.99

THEATER exercise

(Pre-drawn, for Levels practice)

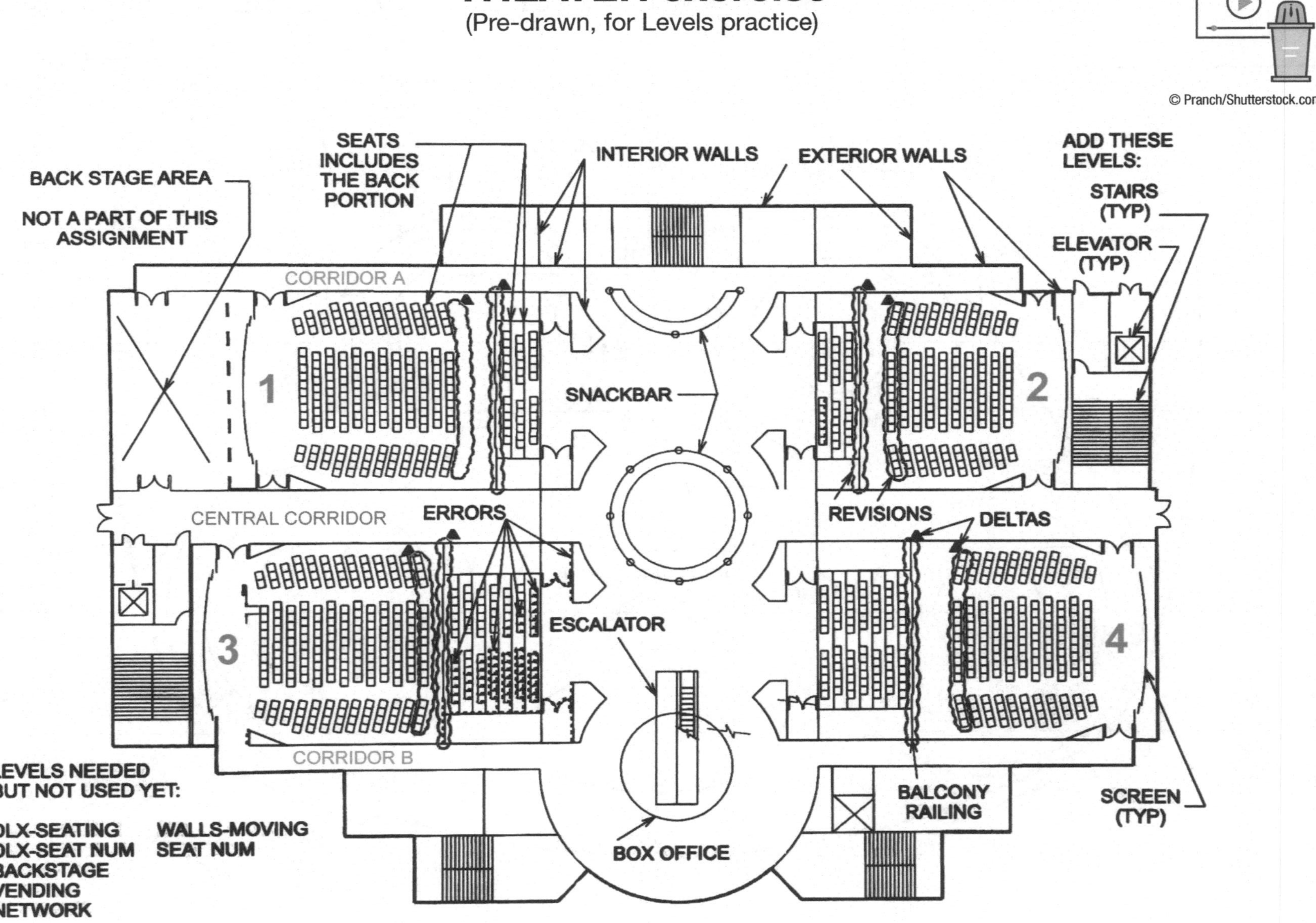

Fence Selection Modes Exercise

© Pranch/Shutterstock.com

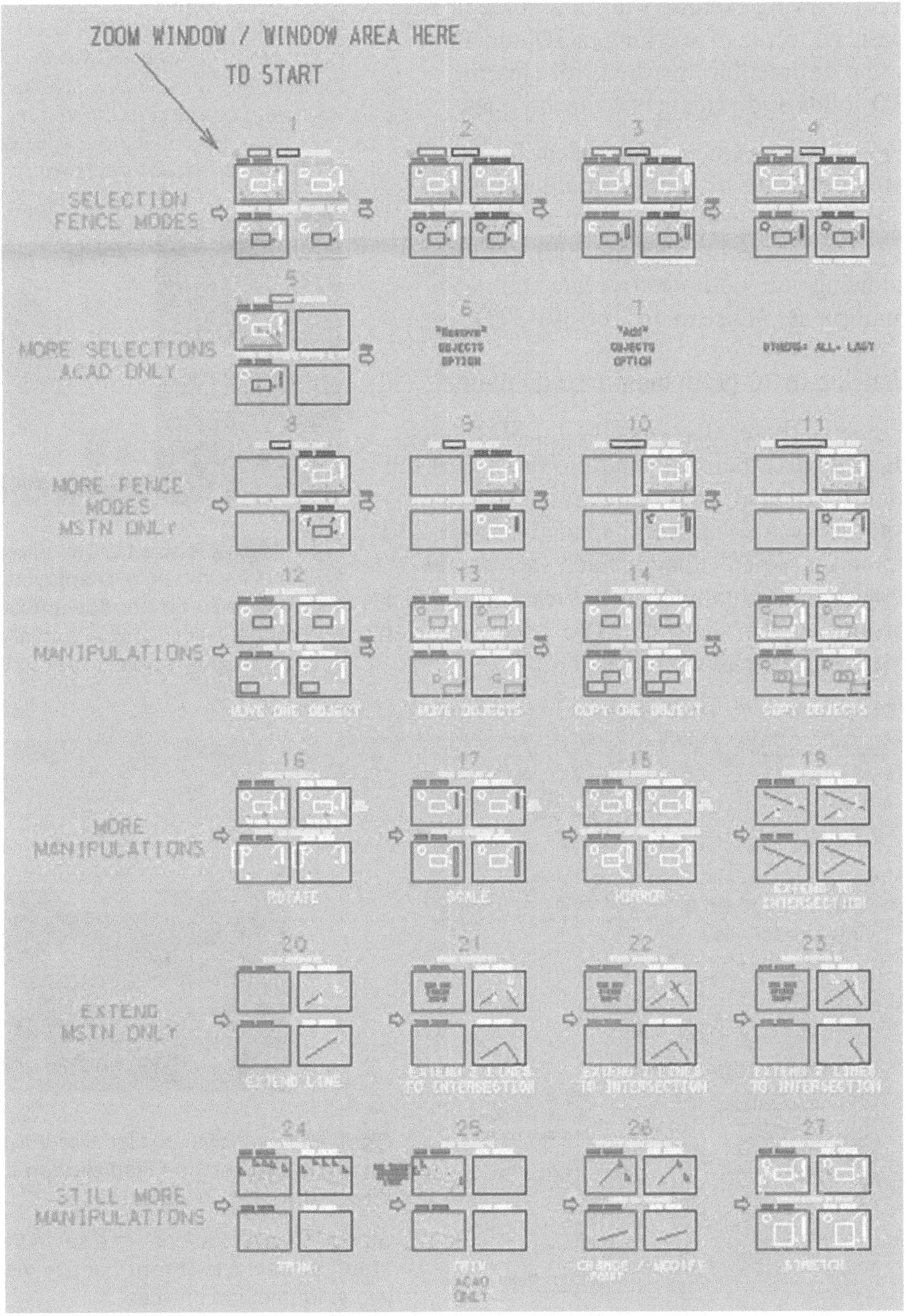

ZOOM WINDOW / WINDOW AREA HERE
TO START

1 2 3 4

SELECTION FENCE MODES

5 6 7

MORE SELECTIONS ACAD ONLY

"Remove" OBJECTS OPTION

"Add" OBJECTS OPTION

OTHERS: ALL, LAST

8 9 10 11

MORE FENCE MODES MSTN ONLY

12 13 14 15

MANIPULATIONS

MOVE ONE OBJECT

MOVE OBJECTS

COPY ONE OBJECT

COPY OBJECTS

16 17 18 19

MORE MANIPULATIONS

ROTATE

SCALE

MIRROR

EXTEND TO INTERSECTION

20 21 22 23

EXTEND MSTN ONLY

EXTEND LINE

EXTEND 2 LINES TO INTERSECTION

EXTEND 2 LINES TO INTERSECTION

EXTEND 2 LINES TO INTERSECTION

24 25 26 27

STILL MORE MANIPULATIONS

TRIM

TRIM ACAD ONLY

CHANGE / MODIFY POINT

STRETCH

3D Site Drawing Exercise

This drawing exercise will show some of the basic concepts of working in 3D and show some rudimentary methods for creating 3D solids and visualization techniques.

Please see the **Companion Videos** for this exercise. Your instructor should step you thru a demonstration of 3D drawing set-up and viewing techniques (pg 300), before showing you methods to create and manipulate 3D elements (pg 301-302).

Viewing in 3D (with instructor guidance)

Please observe, after opening the **3D Sample.dgn** file, that there are multiple views, that the **view rotation** angle is different in each view and that some views are "shaded" images and some are "lined" images. Each view can be resized individually, such as View 2 (*in Fig 1.*) or they can be tiled with "**Tile**" as shown in the **Modeling Workflow** (*in Fig 2 + 5.*)

The **3D Sample.dgn** file is used to learn about standard 3D views, view rotation and view display styles. See your instructor and/or the inside front cover for obtaining the file provided with this text for this exercise.

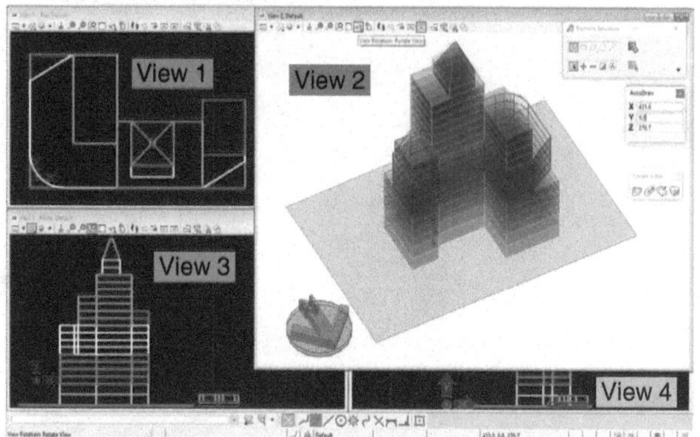

Fig 1. View 2 is sized larger, **View Rotation** is from a different angle, **Display style** is set to **Transparent with Shadows**. View 1 at upper left and View 3 below, View 4 partially covered. Views 1, 3 & 4 **Display style** are set to **Wireframe** mode.

Fig 2. The **"Modeling" Worlflow,** with **"View" Tab** in the Ribbon menu shown. Window, **Tile** is highlighted, below

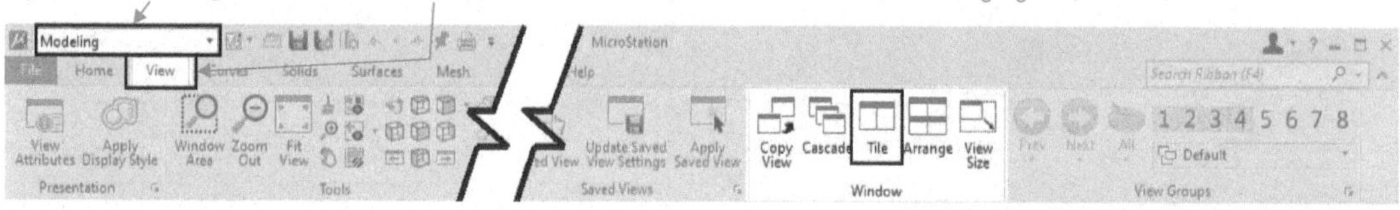

After performing Tile, one may need to do a Fit View in each view.

View Attributes or <Ctrl> b.

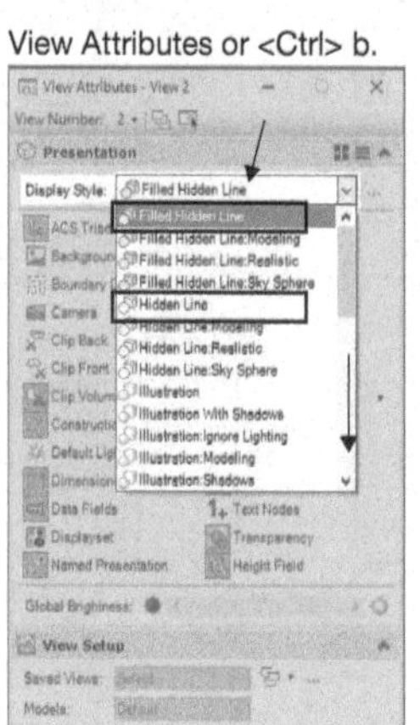

View Controls

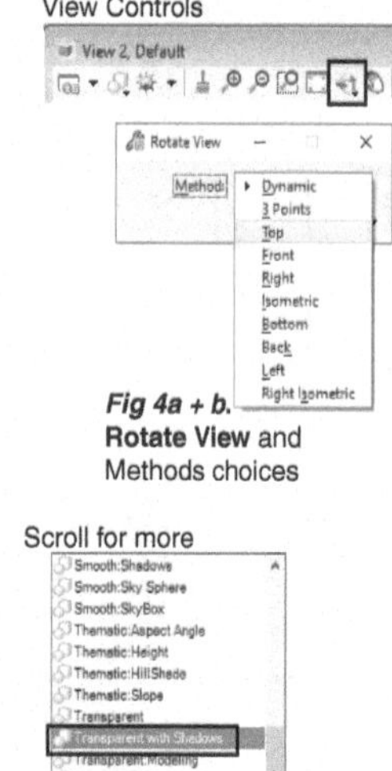

Fig 4a + b. **Rotate View** and Methods choices

Scroll for more

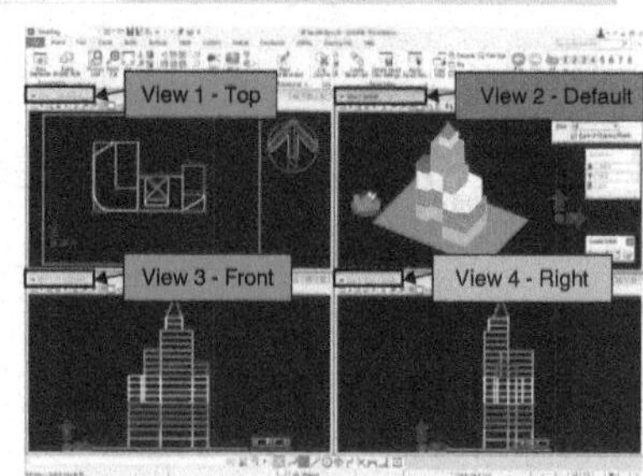

Fig 3a+b. In **View Attributes**, selecting **Display Style: Filled Hidden Line** or **Transparent with Shadows**. Style: **Wireframe** is listed last. Style: **Hidden Line** and **Illustration Ignore Lighting** also yield pleasing displays.

Fig 5. All four views are tiled, the View 2 **Display Style** has been set to **Filled Hidden Line** using **View Attributes** Or **<Ctrl> b.**

Standard view rotations were set in the View 1 to "**Top**", in View 3 to "**Front**", and in View 4 to "**Right**". (*Fig 4*. for method choices)

View 2 rotation was set by the user, with **Rotate View** and the "**Dynamic**" option. The user activates **Rotate View**, positions the mouse In the view and then presses and holds the left mouse button, and drags the pointer resulting In rotation of the view.

Hit right mouse button (reset) to stop rotating the view.

(3D Site Drawing Exercise continued)

2. Creating a New 3D Drawing

Fig 1. 3D-seed file.dgn

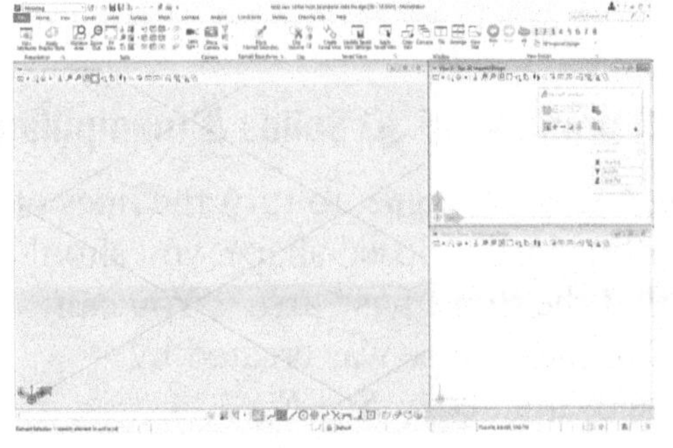

Fig 2. 3D Imperial Design.dgn

Once the student has experience with the basic 3D viewing skills shown on page 300, the next step is to create their own 3D file starting with a 3D seed file. Open the **3D-seed file.dgn** file that is included with this text. It will appear as above in ***Fig 1.***

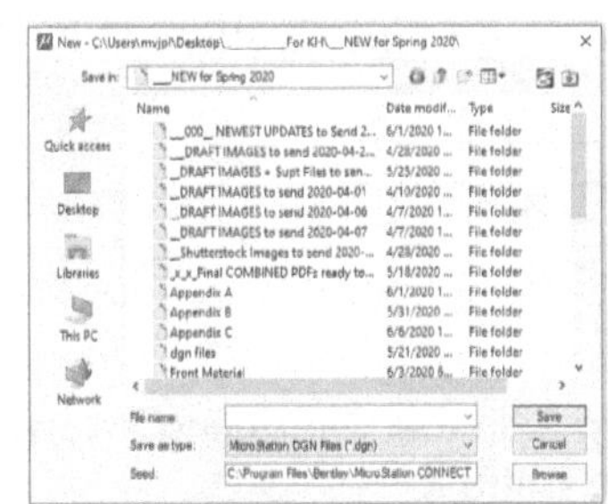

Fig 3. The New file dialog box.

If the **3D-seed file.dgn** is not available, one can create a 3D file as follows: **File > New**, in the New dialog (***Fig 3.***), select **Browse**, in the Select Seed File dialog (***Fig 4.***), select **3D Imperial Design.dgn**. The new file will appear as above in ***Fig 2***.

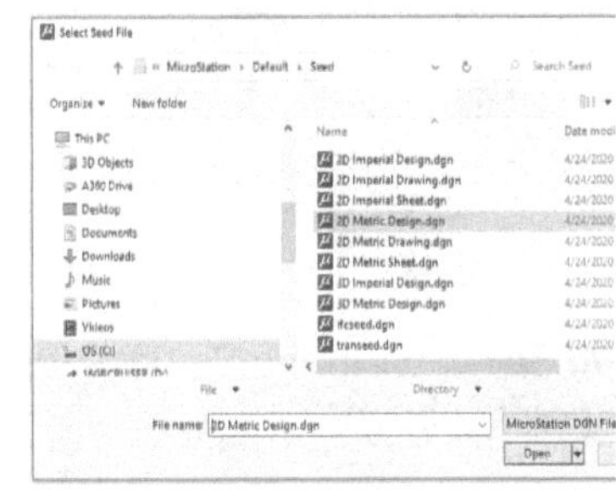

***Fig 4.* Select Seed File** dialog box.

After opening a 3D seed file, use Save - As to call the new file **3D Site.** (*or Lastname-3D Site, or as per your instructor*)

3. Creating the 2D profiles for the 3D solids

A very basic technique for creating 3D solids is to first create 2D profiles, and make them have "area", In the **Top** view, create the ALPHA BLDG outline as was done earlier in the Module 6 exercise (pg 177, 178). Ensure that your View 1 is actually a **Top** view and not accidentally rotated to some other angle. If View 1 is NOT a **Top** view, set it as per ***Fig 4a+b***, pg 300.

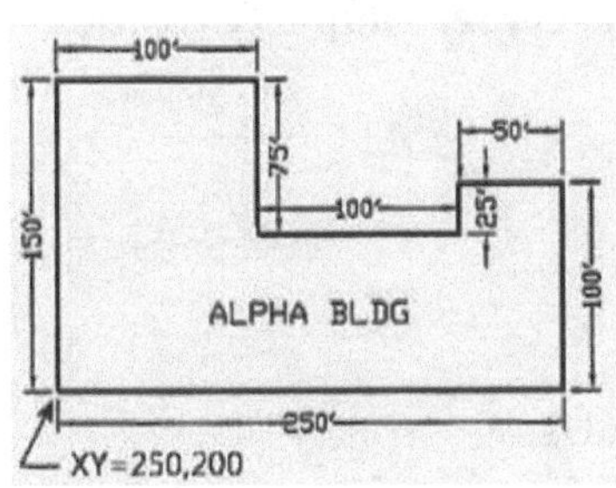

Fig 5. Alpha Bldg outline

Fig 6. Space Bar Pop-up

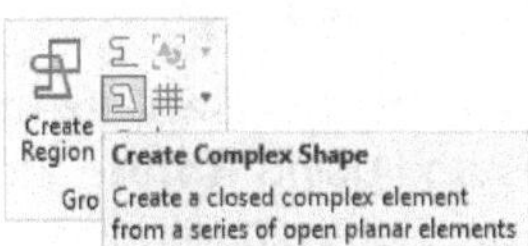

Fig 7. Groups group

After drawing the 8 lines of the Alpha Bldg outline, convert them into a closed shape with area by using the **Create Complex Shape** tool, found in the **Groups** group (***Fig 7.***) in the ***Space Bar Pop-up*** (***Fig 6.***)

Using **Create Complex Shape**, select each line segment of the Alpha Bldg outline one at a time, then click once to "accept", creating a closed shape.

(Continued on next page 302)

(3D Site Drawing Exercise continued)

Please see the **Companion Videos** for this exercise!

4. Extruding the 2D profiles inti 3D Solids & manipulating them

After using **Create Complex Shape**, to turn the lines of the Alpha Bldg outline into a closed shape, you should see in the View 2 that the shape has "area". You can confirm that the Complex Shape was created by hovering the mouse over an edge. See ***Fig 1***.

Also, at this point, if you Fit View, you'll see the initial 3D Seed File "yellow sticky note". It can be deleted.

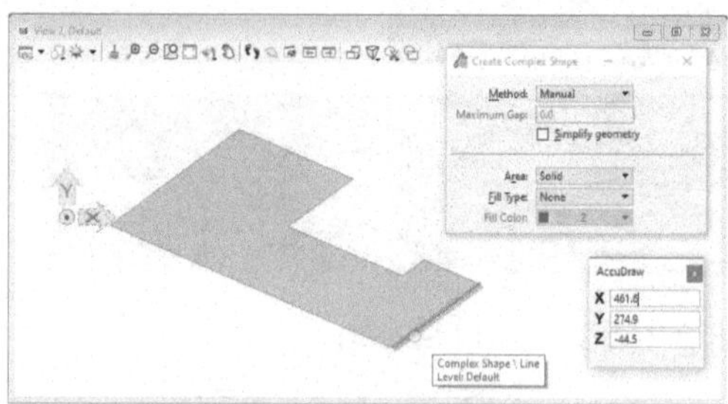

Fig 1. View 2, Complex Shape with area.

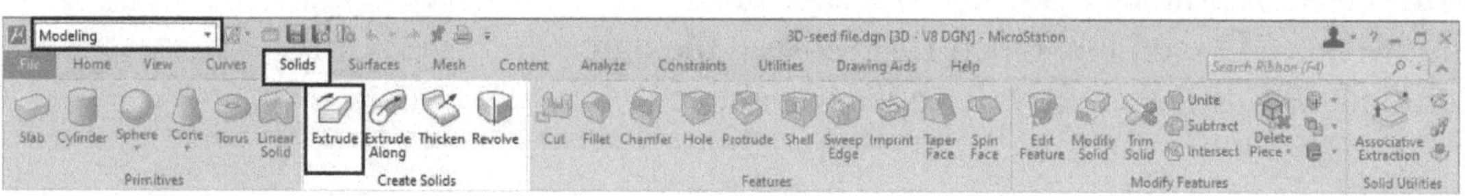

Fig 2. In the **"Modeling" Workflow,** the **Solids** tab contains the **Extrude** tool. Turns 2D shapes into 3D, up in the Z-axis

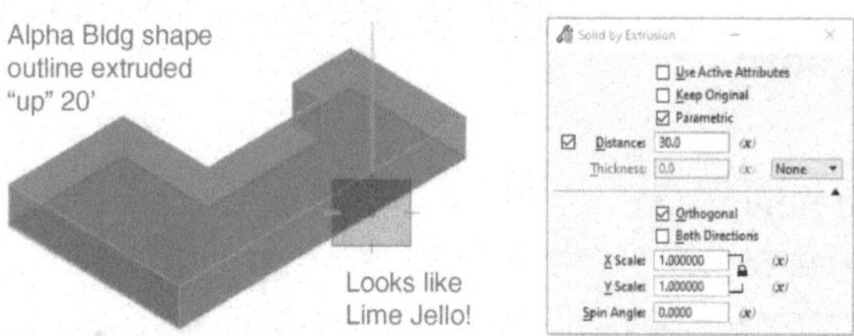

Fig 3a+b. Fill in the Settings for Extrude, click a point "above".

Values to use for the floors: 1st+2nd floors=30' tall, other floors=20' tall. X+Y scale=1.0, Orthogonal. Complete the same steps for the other buildings. Use different colors for each group of floors. You can make other shapes at the extra outlines at left.

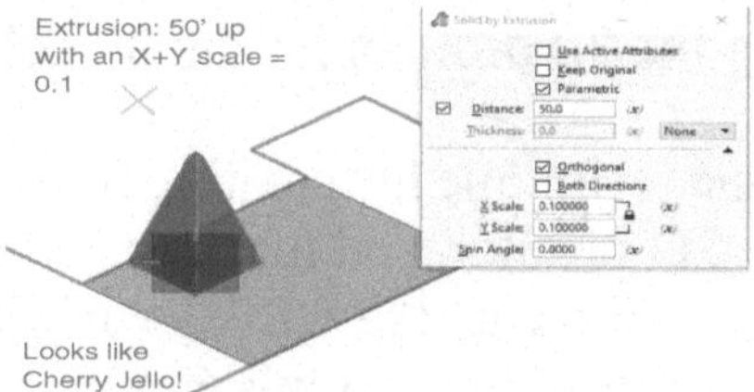

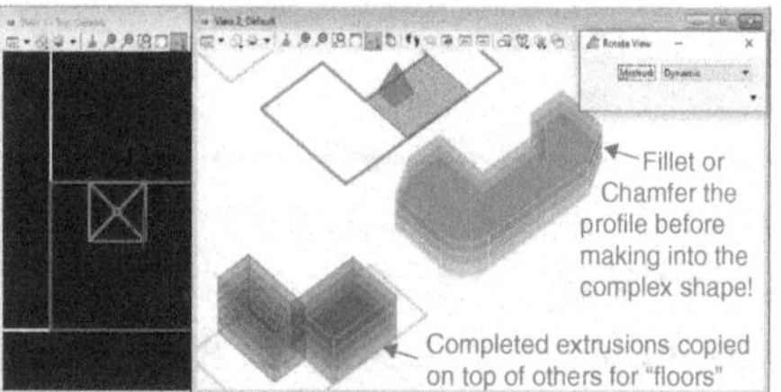

Fig 4. Extra outlines used to create more profiles/floors. Remember, make your 2D profiles in the **Top** view!

Copy or move the additional floors into place with simple move or copy operations (use AccuSnap).

Pyramid specs: Base 30' square, 50' tall. Set the X+Y scale = 0.1, and use **center snap** to extrude.

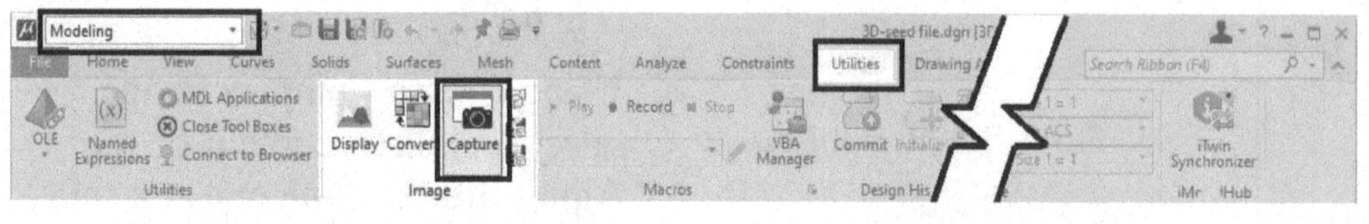

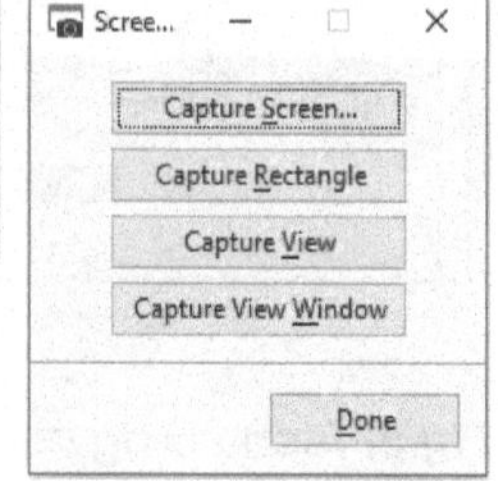

Fig 6a+b. In the "**Modeling" Workflow**, the **Utilities** tab has **Capture** image. Use this after making all of your buildings with features and using **Rotate View** for a pleasing image. Make sure to size your View 2 larger before capturing the image for the best results! See image #8 on page 10 of the Introduction section for a sample captured 3D Buildings image.

Appendix B

Using AutoCAD Help

Recommended Help articles to review and the *approximate* week# of coverage in the class:

Command	wk#
ARC	2-3
AREA	5
ARRAY	2-3
BHATCH	9
BLOCK	9
BREAK	2
CHAMFER	2-3
CHANGE	2-3
CHPROP	5
CIRCLE	1
CLOSE	2-3
COPY	1
DDEDIT	6
DIM or DIM1	7
DIST	2
DIVIDE	2-3
ELEV	8-9
ERASE	1
EXPLODE	9
EXTEND	2-3
EXTRUDE	8-9

Command	wk#
FILLET	2-3
GRID	1
HELP	1
ID	7
INSERT	9
LAYER	3
LEADER	7
LENGTHEN	2-3
LIMITS	1
LINE	1
LINETYPE	3
LIST	3
LTSCALE	3
LWEIGHT	3
MIRROR	2-3
MLINE	9
MLSTYLE	9
MOVE	1
MTEXT	6
NEW	1
OFFSET	2-3
ORTHO	4

Command	wk#
PAN	1
PEDIT	3
PLINE	3
PLOT	10
POINT	2-3
POLYGON	2-3
PROPERTIES	3
PSPACE	10
PURGE	2-3
QDIM	7
QLEADER	7
QNEW	1
QSAVE	1
QUIT	1
RECTANG	1
REDO	1
REDRAW	1
REGEN	1
RENDER	8-9
ROTATE	1
SAVE	1
SAVEAS	1

Command	wk#
SCALE	2-3
SNAP	1
SPELL	6
STRETCH	2-3
STYLE	6
TEXT	6
TIME	3
TRACE	2-3
TRIM	2-3
U	1
UNDO	1
UNITS	1
VPORTS	10
WBLOCK	9
XPLODE	9
XREF	9
ZOOM	1

Recommended Help articles to review and the *approximate* week# of coverage in the class, arranged in week# order of coverage: **(Bold indicates more important topics)**

Command	wk#
CIRCLE	1
CLOSE	1
COPY	1
ERASE	1
GRID	1
HELP	1
LIMITS	1
MOVE	1
NEW	1
PAN	1
QNEW	1
QSAVE	1
QUIT	1
RECTANG	1
REDO	1
REDRAW	1
REGEN	1
ROTATE	1
SAVE	1
SAVEAS	1
SCALE	1
SNAP	1
U	1
UNDO	1
UNITS	1
ZOOM	1

Command	wk#
BREAK	2
DIST	2
ARC	2-3
ARRAY	2-3
CHAMFER	2-3
CHANGE	2-3
DIVIDE	2-3
EXTEND	2-3
FILLET	2-3
LENGTHEN	2-3
MIRROR	2-3
OFFSET	2-3
POINT	2-3
POLYGON	2-3
PURGE	2-3
STRETCH	2-3
TRACE	2-3
TRIM	2-3
LAYER	3
LINETYPE	3
LIST	3
LTSCALE	3
LWEIGHT	3
PEDIT	3
PLINE	3
PROPERTIES	3
TIME	3

Command	wk#
ORTHO	4
AREA	5
CHPROP	5
DDEDIT	6
MTEXT	6
SPELL	6
STYLE	6
TEXT	6
DIM or DIM1	7
ID	7
LEADER	7
QDIM	7
QLEADER	7
ELEV	8-9
EXTRUDE	8-9
RENDER	8-9
BHATCH	9
BLOCK	9
EXPLODE	9
INSERT	9
MLINE	9
MLSTYLE	9
WBLOCK	9
XPLODE	9
XREF	9
PLOT	10
PSPACE	10
VPORTS	10

Work these exercises in the Modify Warm-up AutoCAD file provided

DO THIS: START: END:

Use Command: Copy CO or CP

1 Make 3 more copies of the square as shown

2 Make 3 more copies of the square as shown

Use Command: Move

3 Move the last square to the position shown

4 Move the middle square to the position shown

Use Commands: Move / Copy

5 Move & Copy as needed to change Start to End

Move Rotate Trim Copy Mirror Fillet Stretch Scale Array Modify

Copy CO
Move M

Do the exercise twice. Refer to your handout for the required end result, or see the END: column in the slide at the left.

Modify Commands Warm-up exercises

pg1

DO THIS: START: END:

Use Command: Offset O

6 Offset the line parallel as shown

7 Offset the line parallel exactly 0.26 units

8 Offset Copy the line parallel as shown

This time, left side

9 Offset Copy the line parallel exactly 0.55 units

10 Offset Copy the line parallel exactly 0.4 units, many times

Move Rotate Trim Copy Mirror Fillet Stretch Scale Array Modify

Offset O

Do the exercise twice. Refer to your handout for the required end result, or see the END: column in the slide at the left.

pg2

Work these exercises in the Modify Warm-up AutoCAD file provided

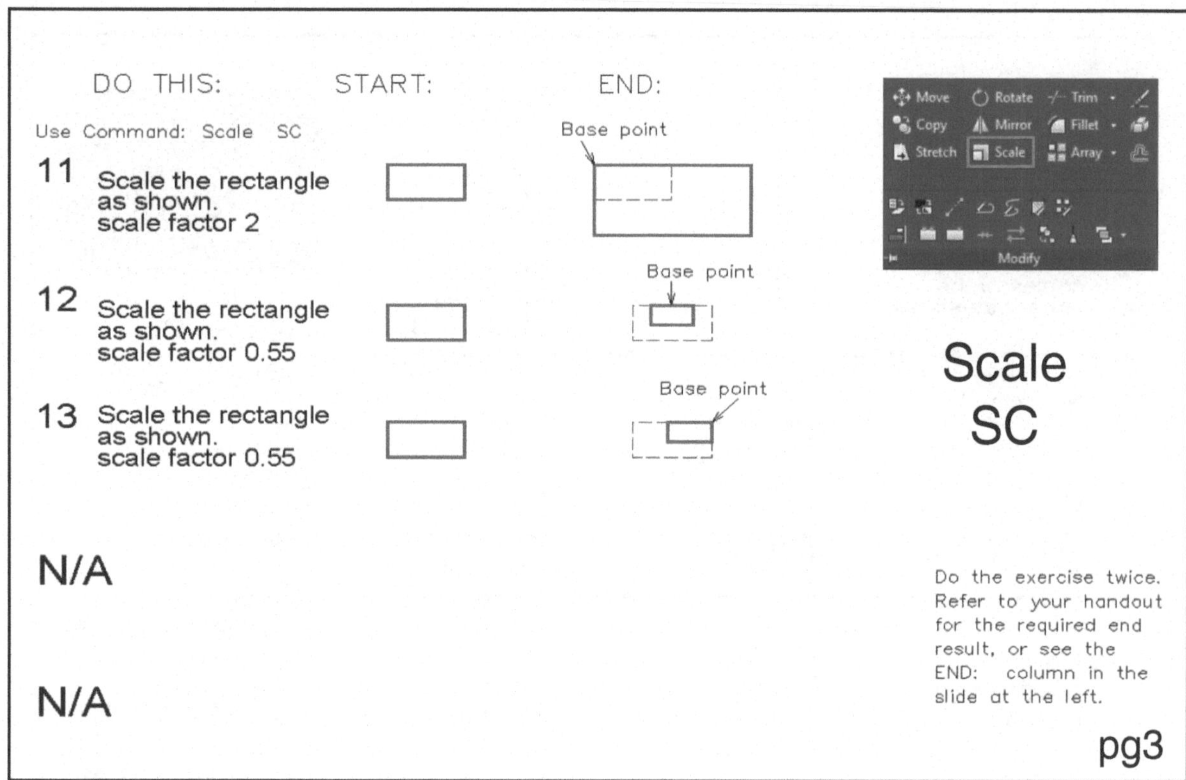

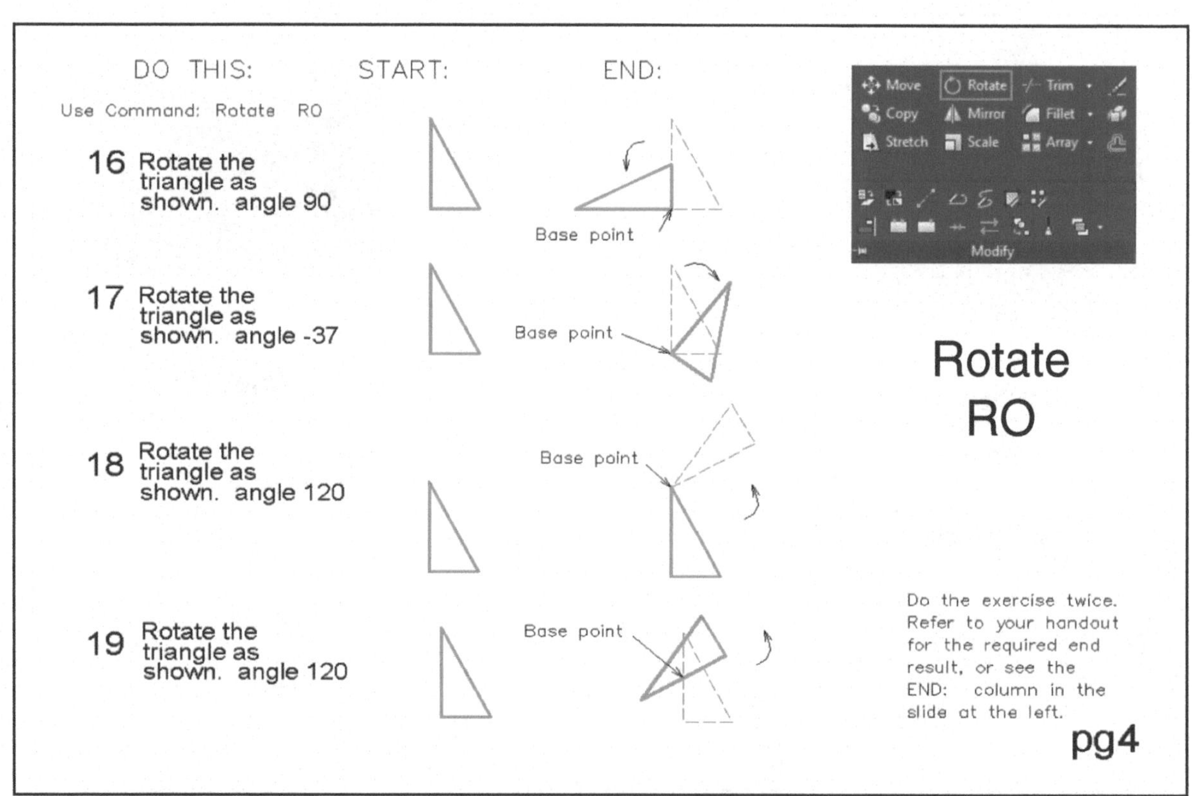

Work these exercises in the Modify Warm-up AutoCAD file provided

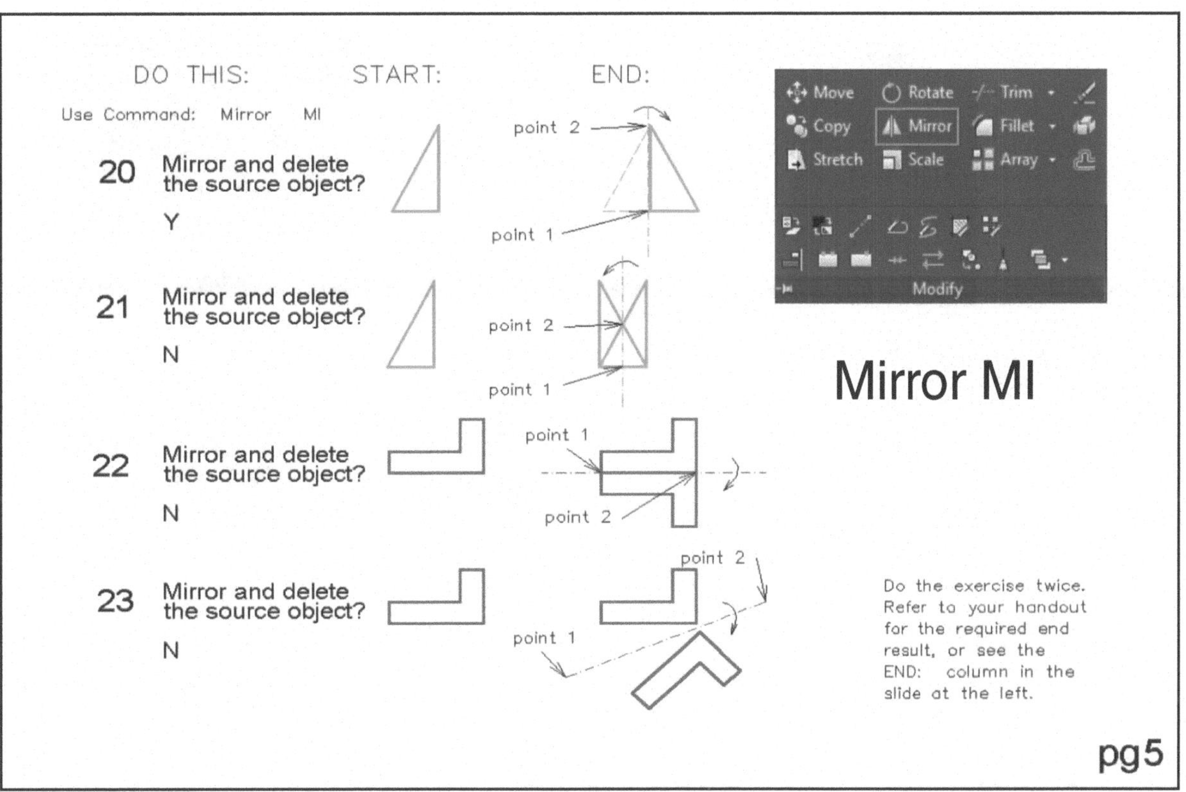

Basic Modifications Exercise

Using a choice of Modificationm commands, create the required Four-plex building plan starting with the basic unit plan on the left.

Use: Mirror, Rotate, Move, Copy, etc. as needed.

Start with the Floorplan A drawing provided.

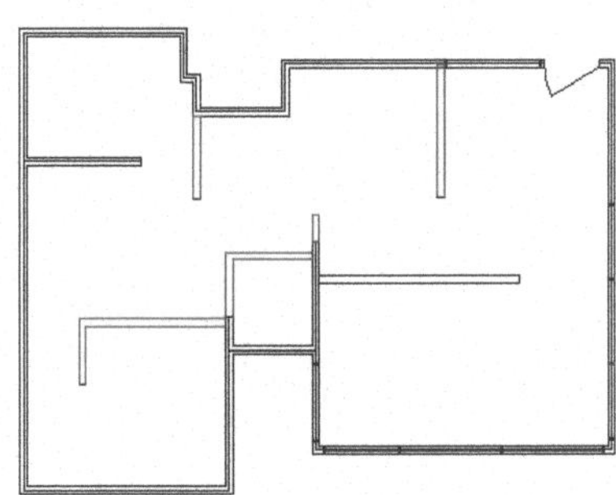

Floorplan A

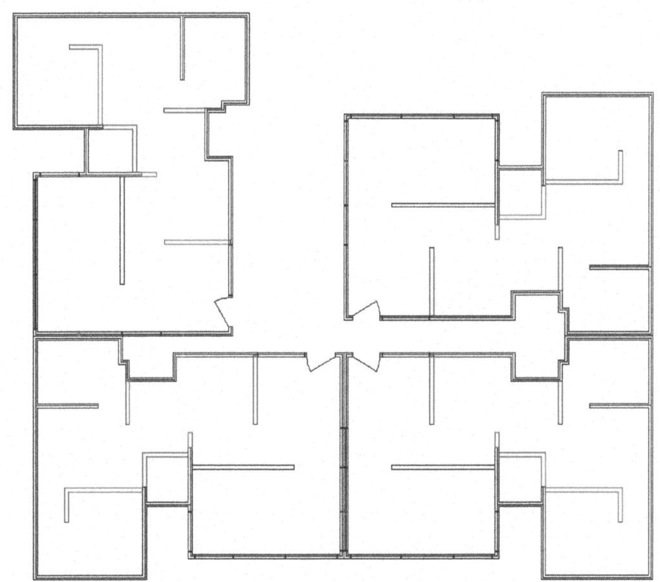

Four-Plex Building Plan

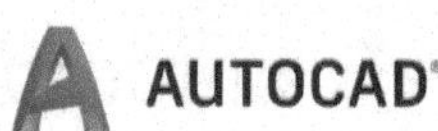

Work these exercises in the Modify Warm-up AutoCAD file provided

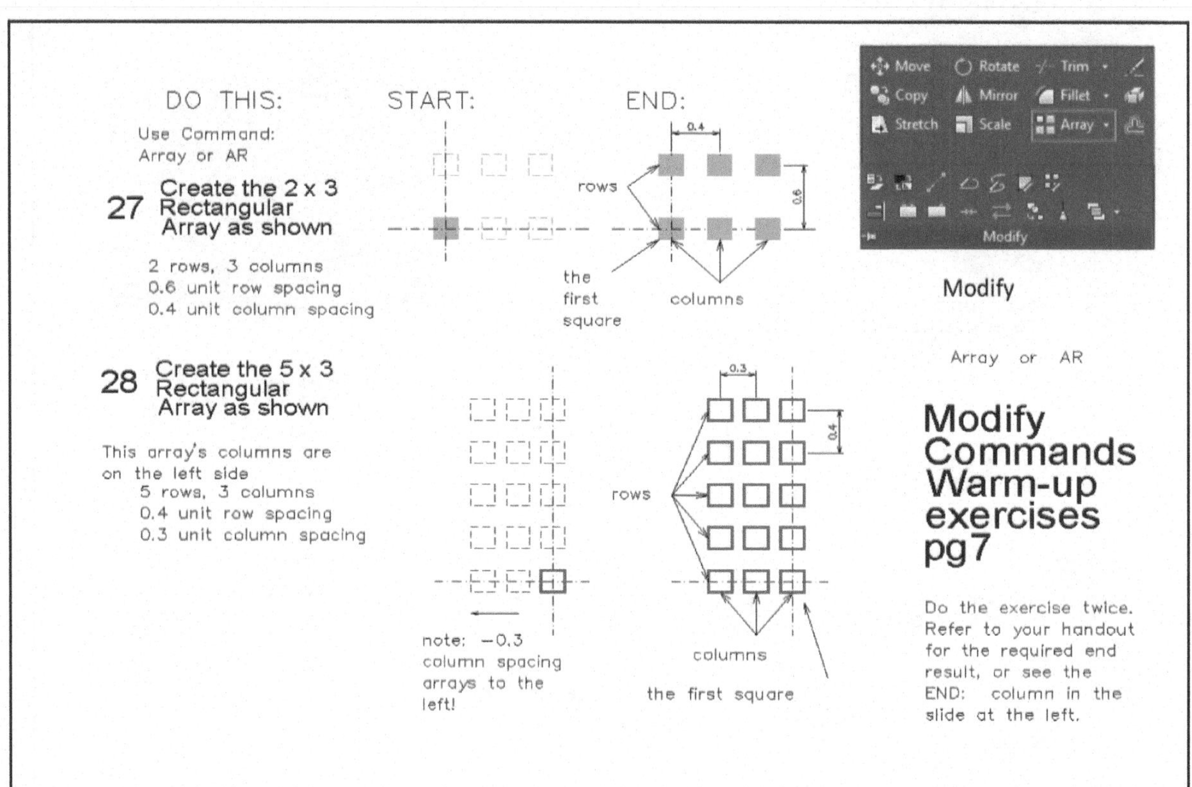

DO THIS:
START:
END:
Use Command:
Array or AR
27 Create the 2 x 3 Rectangular Array as shown
2 rows, 3 columns
0.6 unit row spacing
0.4 unit column spacing
rows
the first square
columns
0.4
0.6
Move
Rotate
Trim
Copy
Mirror
Fillet
Stretch
Scale
Array
Modify
Modify
Array or AR
28 Create the 5 x 3 Rectangular Array as shown
This array's columns are on the left side
5 rows, 3 columns
0.4 unit row spacing
0.3 unit column spacing
note: −0.3 column spacing arrays to the left!
rows
columns
the first square
0.3
0.4
Modify Commands Warm-up exercises pg7
Do the exercise twice. Refer to your handout for the required end result, or see the END: column in the slide at the left.

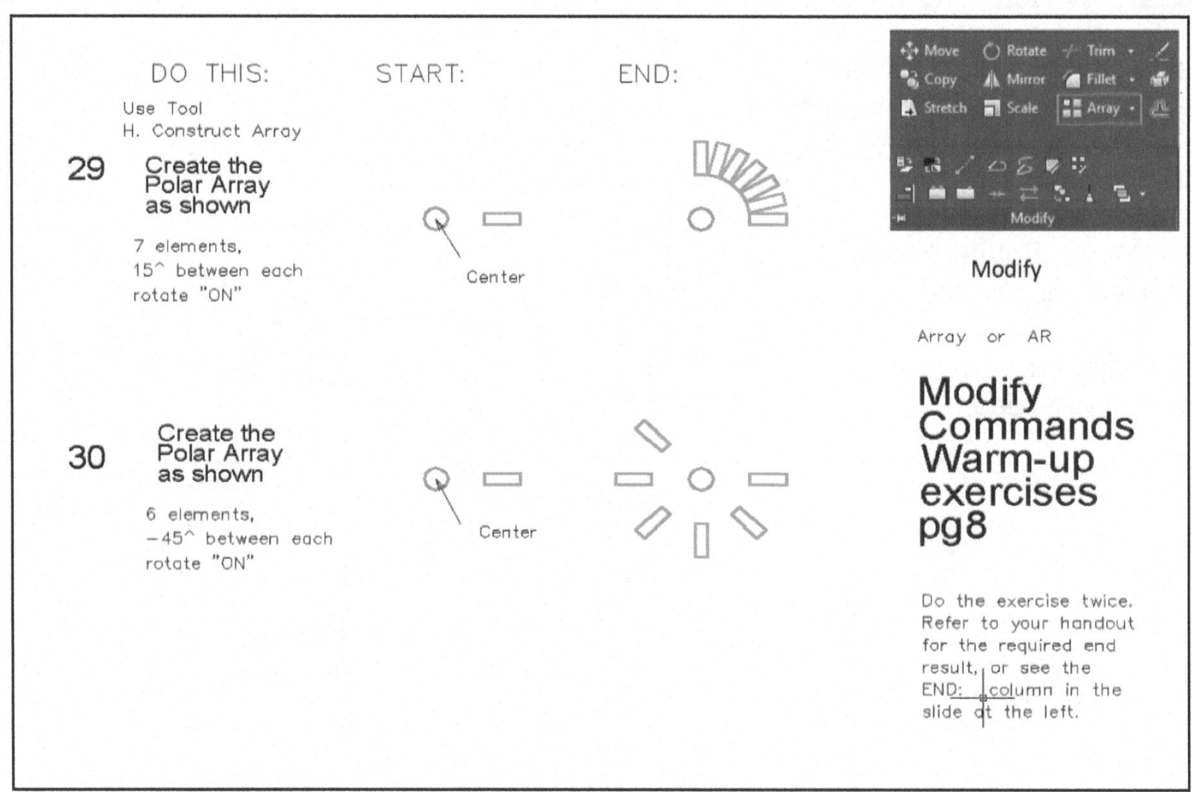

DO THIS:
START:
END:
Use Tool
H. Construct Array
29 Create the Polar Array as shown
7 elements,
15^ between each
rotate "ON"
Center
Move
Rotate
Trim
Copy
Mirror
Fillet
Stretch
Scale
Array
Modify
Modify
Array or AR
Modify Commands Warm-up exercises pg8
30 Create the Polar Array as shown
6 elements,
−45^ between each
rotate "ON"
Center
Do the exercise twice. Refer to your handout for the required end result, or see the END: column in the slide at the left.

Work these exercises in the More Modify Warm-up AutoCAD file provided

Note: Using Grips does not require activating a command. Simply pick onto an object with the cursor to activate Grips.

Break BR

More Modify Commands Warm-up exercises pg1

	TURN THIS:	INTO THIS:	USING TOOL:
1			Grips/stretch
2			Grips/stretch
3			Grips/stretch
4			Break
5			Break

Break BR

Lengthen LEN

More Modify Commands Warm-up exercises pg2

	TURN THIS:	INTO THIS:	USING TOOL:
6			Break
7		Lengthen or LEN option DY	Lengthen DY
8		Lengthen or LEN option DY	Lengthen DY
9		LONGER EXACTLY 0.4 UNITS Lengthen or LEN option T	Lengthen T
10		SHORTER EXACTLY 0.7 UNITS Lengthen or LEN option T	Lengthen T

Work these exercises in the More Modify Warm-up AutoCAD file provided

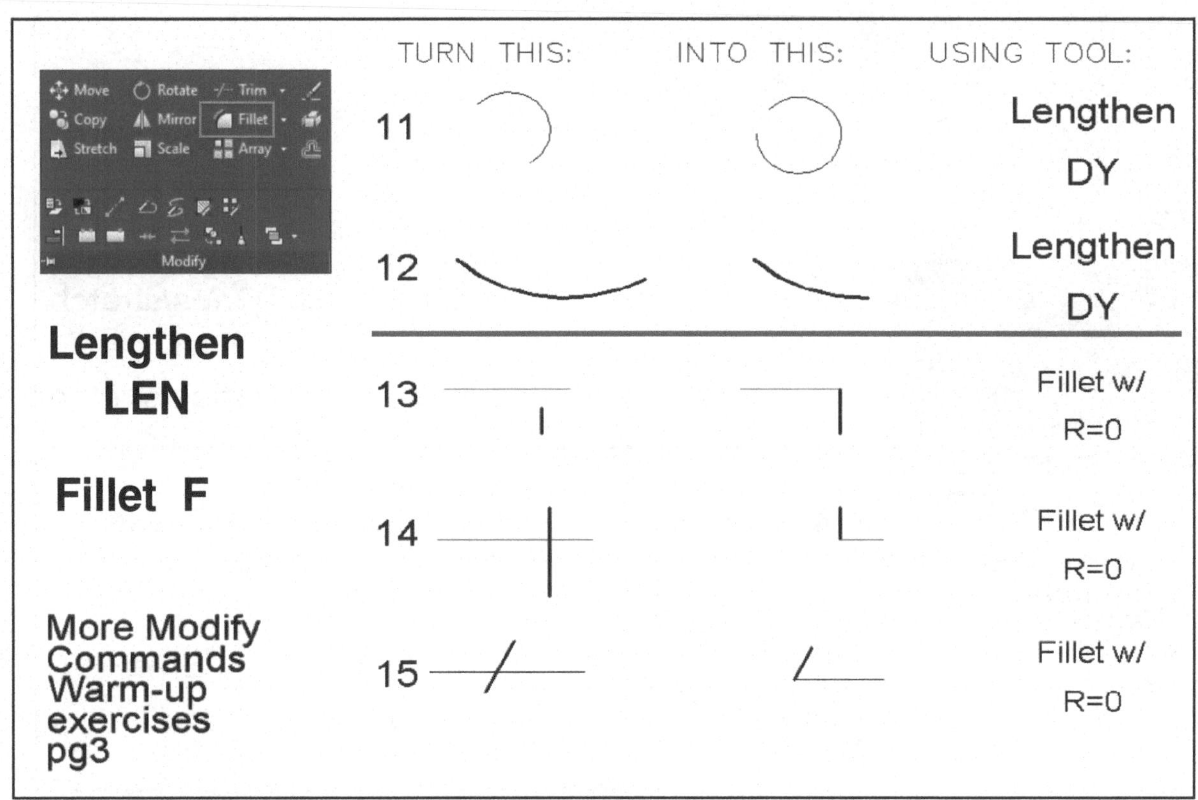

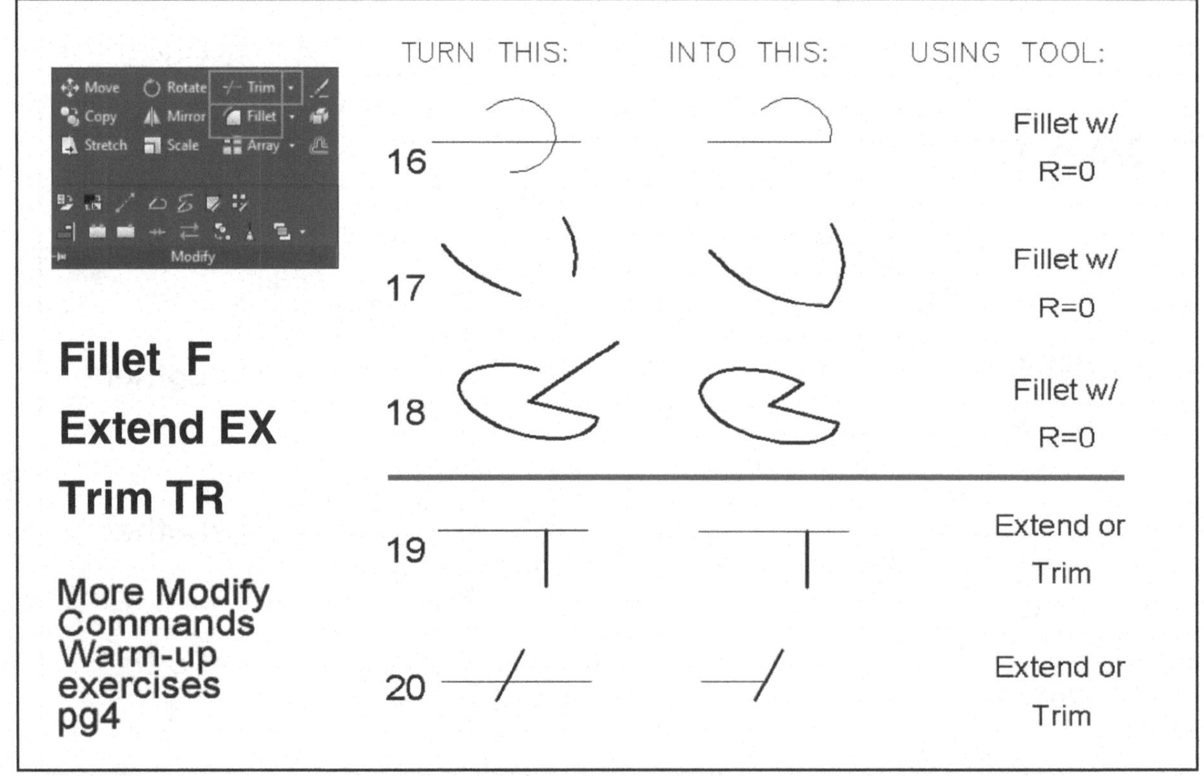

Work these exercises in the More Modify Warm-up AutoCAD file provided

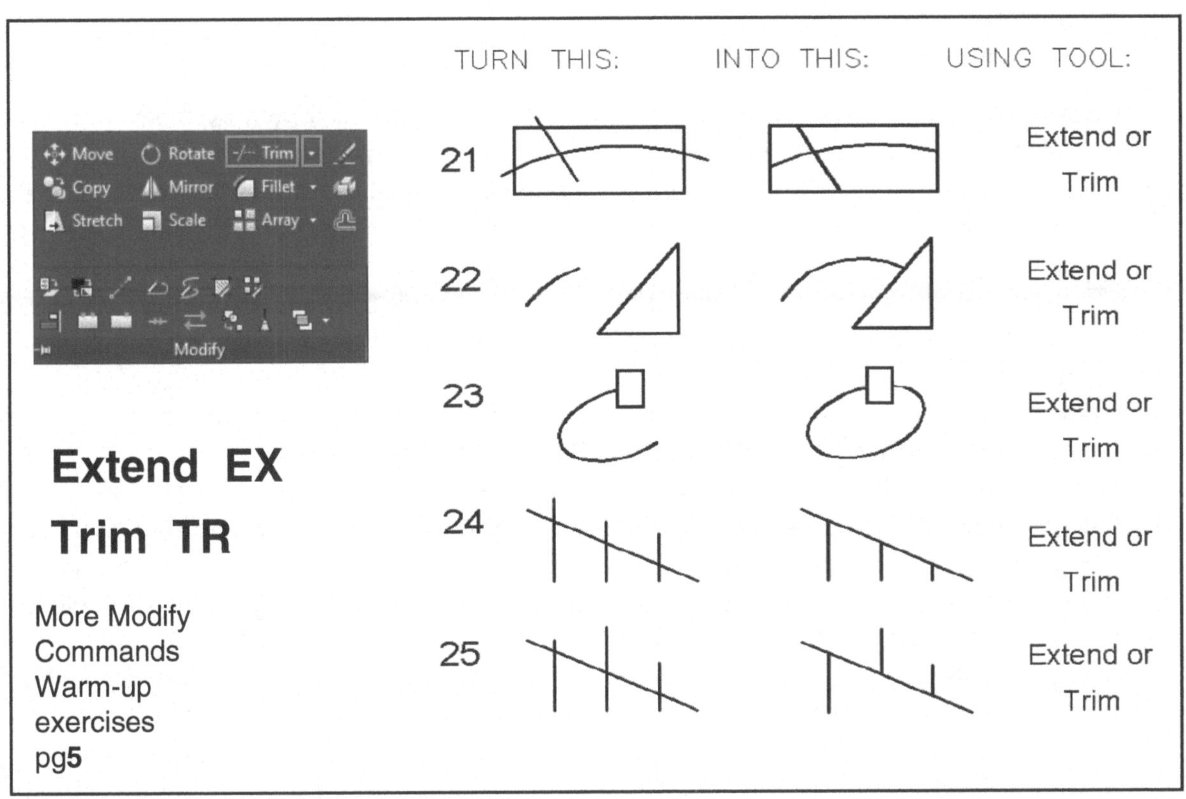

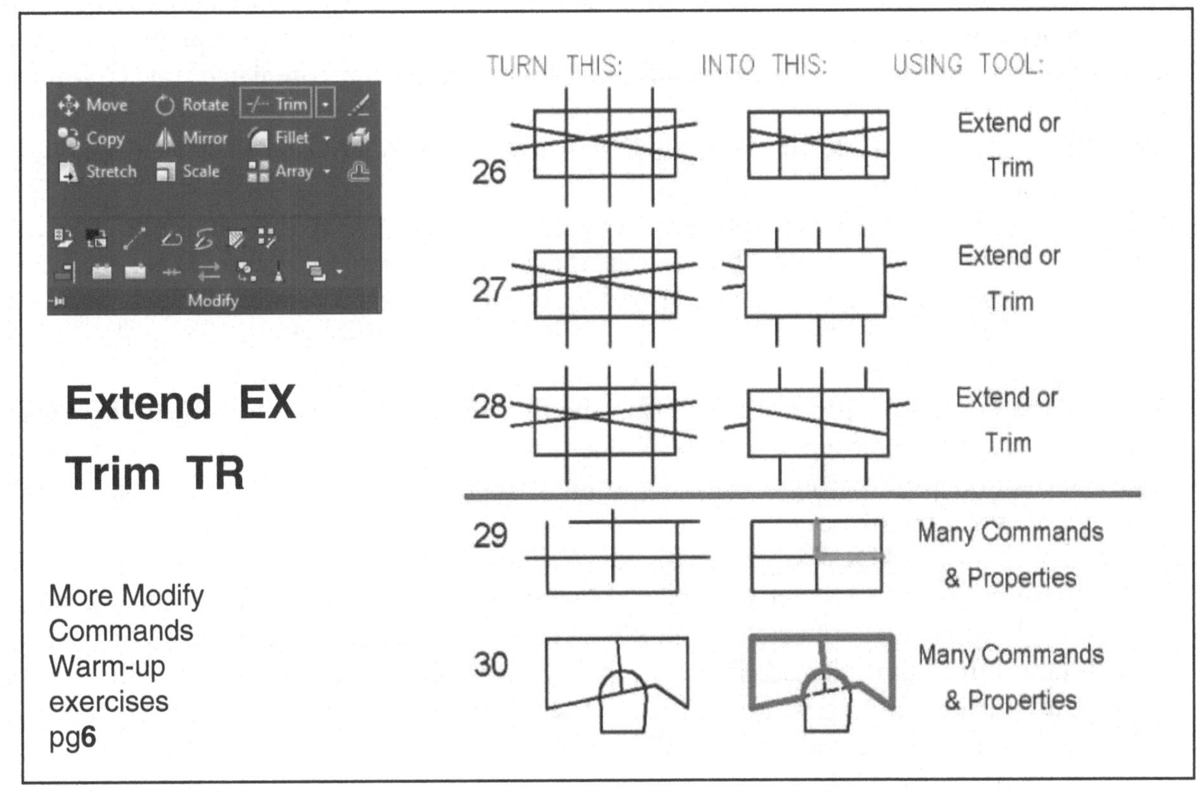

Week 1 AutoCAD Operations Tips

Review Notes, Tips & Misc items
Additional notes from session #1 which may not be specifically written in handouts:

1. Certain keyboard keys are shown as follows: The **Escape Key** is shown as **<Esc>,** The **Enter Key** is shown as **<Enter>,** or as this symbol ↵ (Look closely at the <Enter> key!) The **Shift key** is shown as **<Shift>**, the **F8 function key** as **<F8>**, etc. you get the idea, right?
2. The **<Esc> is used to cancel a command** while you are in the middle of a command-It's very useful to get yourself out of a command that is messing up on you. It never hurts to hit a few Escapes before you start a command. It takes you back to the Command prompt.
3. We used the **middle mouse button (scroll wheel)** to do THREE Viewing or Zooming functions:
   a. **Rolling the mouse scroll wheel performs a ZOOM function**, making the view larger or smaller. ie. We either got closer or farther away from our drawing.
   b. **Pressing and holding down the mouse scroll button turns the cursor arrow into a little "hand"**. With the hand, **we can "push"** the drawing around, called **scrolling or panning** the drawing. This is very similar to what you can do with your real hand to pieces of paper on your desk. You can push them from side to side or away from you to look a particular portion of the page.
   c. **You can "double-click" the middle mouse scroll button to perform an automatic ZOOM EXTENTS** function (showing you everything that is drawn in your drawing)
4. After you have selected an object(s) for a command, AutoCAD may respond again with the prompt **Select Object:** If you are done selecting objects, hit <Enter> and the command will proceed to the next step.
5. Always make sure that you are at the Command prompt when you enter a command. **One of the most common errors of beginning AutoCAD users is to begin to type-in or begin a new command while in the middle of another command that is not completed, yet.** If you are keen while operating CAD, you should always be watching the Command Line prompt area. You will notice ERROR messages that AutoCAD sends out when it receives bogus instructions from the user!
6. **Grips** appear on objects when you select objects while you are at the command prompt. They are the little blue or pink boxes that appear at the corners of an object. In other words, you selected objects without responding to an AutoCAD prompt. To get rid of the grips, hit <Esc> 2 times. We will use grips later. They offer a short-cut way to do lots of basic edits in AutoCAD.
   We used the GRIPS (selection function) in the first session as a way to **"PRE-SELECT"** objects for a subsequent command. ie. While at the command prompt, (hit <Esc> first), Drag a selection window or box around some object or objects. Note: the blue GRIPS should appear on the object(s).
   a. You could hit the <Del> key to erase the object(s).
   b. You could type in CO to activate the COPY command to make copies of the object(s).
   c. You could type in RO to activate the ROTATE command to rotate the object(s).
   d. You could drag the selected object(s) on any NON-GRIP portion of the object(s) to relocate them to a new position. You used the GRIPPED object(s) and are able to move them without even activating the MOVE command!

7. **New! Hit <Enter> to repeat the previous command**. This requires that AutoCAD be set up to do this. This is the way that older versions of AutoCAD operated. The <Space> is the same as <Enter> when you are keying in a command. Hey, and guess what is the handiest?? The Right Mouse Button is ALSO an Enter Key!!
   To set the <Enter> key to repeat a command: From the pull-down menu bar… (typical notation)
   Tools > Options… > User Preferences > Right-click Customization… > (then turn ON the following)
   Default Mode > Repeat Last Command (click the dot to ON, which is darkened)
   Edit Mode > Repeat Last Command (click the dot to ON, which is darkened)
   Command Mode > ENTER (click the dot to ON, which is darkened)
   Then hit <Apply & Close>, then <OK>
   Do the above setting and then test it out with the LINE command (L <Enter>). Draw a few lines then complete the command. Notice that the command line has returned to a **Command:** prompt. Next, repeat the command with a right click of the mouse (which is the same as an <Enter>). You should now be in the LINE command once again!
8. HW & EC (Extra Credit) due dates
   a. Homework due dates will be provided by the instructor. **HW is due at the end of the session**. HW for the majority of the course will be submitted as electronic CAD files. Later in the course, HW files may be turned in as both electronic files and printed hardcopy plots or prints.
   b. Extra Credit will usually not carry any due dates, ie. They can be turned in at any time during the course. However, some of the early offerings of extra credit will expire after about 3-4 weeks, as they will be considered too easy by then. The instructor will let you know which EC assignments these are and when they will expire.
   c. The instructor will inform you of the point value of each HW assignment.
   d. Normal HW is considered LATE if submitted after the due date, ie, submitted at the next class session. HW that is 1 week late will be marked at 50% of the value (half off). You are still encouraged to work the HW anyway, since this is where lots of the CAD learning skill is gained.
9. Drawing Names: Usually set as **EXERCISE-YOUR NAME-DATE**, ie orgchart-kennedy-jf-01-07-2007
   Use your Last Name for the name in the drawing name with your initials. ie: kennedy-jf
   HW that is turned in late shall be noted with LATE at the beginning of the filename,
   ie **LATE-orgchart-kennedy-jf-01-18-2007**
   EC homework shall be noted EC at the beginning of the filename,
   ie **EC-wingshape-kennedy-jf-01-18-2007**
   Do not use special characters or spaces in the drawing name. Special characters not allowed are generally: **< > ? / \ * ( ) ! @ # $ % ^ &**, etc. Don't use these in drawing names!
10. Phones & Pagers, Internet etc.: Keep them off or on silent mode. Do not take calls in class, please!
    Web use is NOT allowed during Class, except at breaks! Same for computer games & e-mail!
11. Lab access: Generally, you may use a lab if it is open or another instructor may open a lab for you if requested. If a class is in session, before you use a station, it is proper to ask for permission at an appropriate break in the class. Instructors, at their discretion, may refuse to let you sit in their class.

Tip # 7 is illustrated below:
Hit <Enter> to repeat a command. The <Space> is the same as "Enter" when you are keying in a command. Another common way to get the "Enter" function is with the right mouse button.
NEW! **Set the right mouse button up to be an "Enter" function**, by the following procedure: Tools > Options > select Tab "User Preferences" > select "Shortcut menus in drawing area" > select "Right-click Customization"> turn on the options "Repeat Last Command", "Repeat Last Command" and "ENTER" > then select "Apply & Close"), then back to OK.

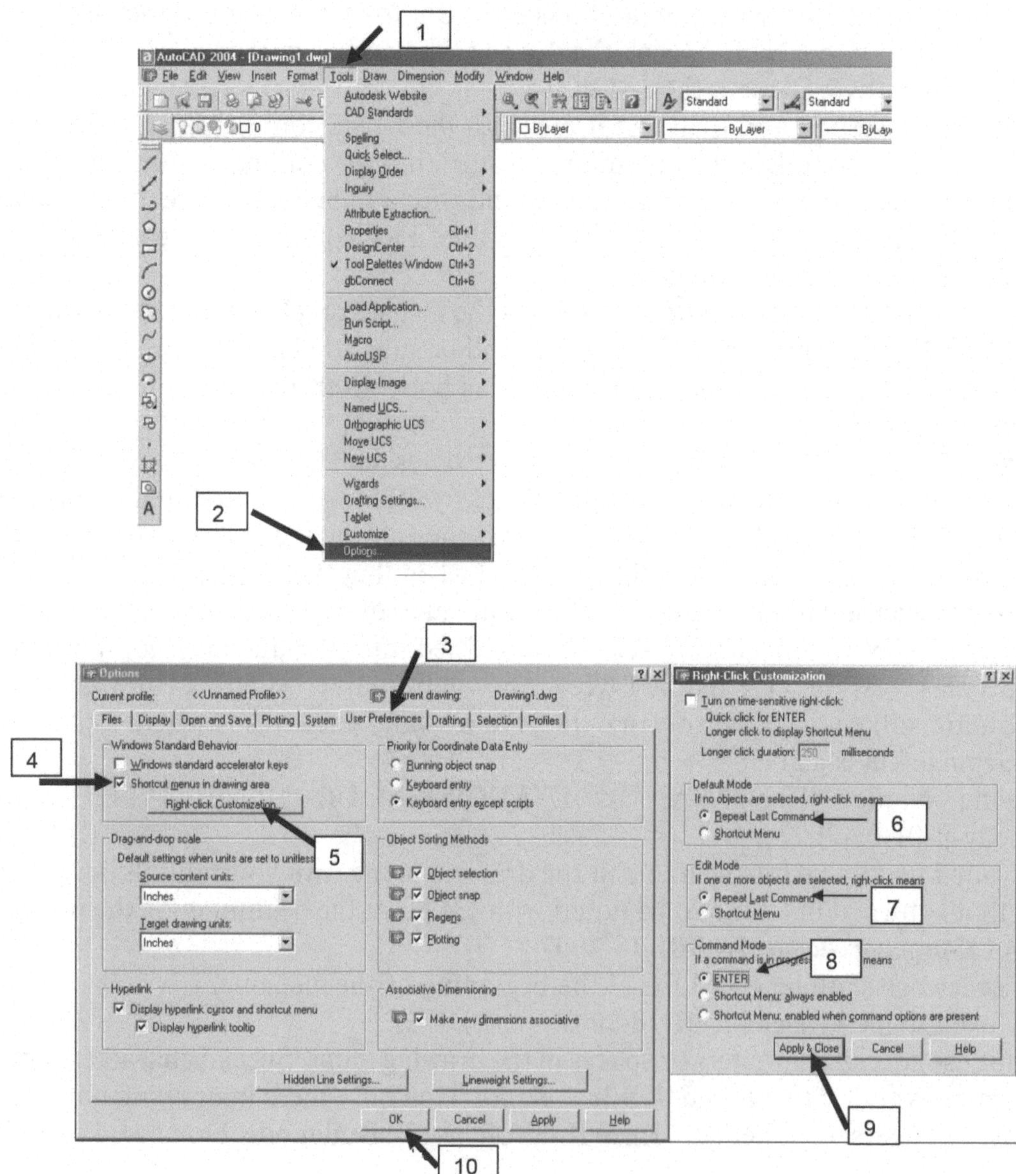

12. List of additional commands shown in week 1:

a. **ZOOM** (note: remember ↵ is the same as <Enter>)

- i. **Z ↵ E ↵** — **Zoom Extents**
  Shows in the view, everything that is drawn in the drawing.
- ii. **Z ↵ A ↵** — **Zoom All**
  Zooms to show the limits of the drawing.
- iii. **Z ↵** — (then window an area you want to view)
  Zoom Window
  Zooms to the area defined by the box you indicate.

b. **LIMITS** — Sets the maximum drawing area and affects the amount of grid dots visible

c. **UNITS** — Set to Architectural for feet & inches. Default is decimal inches.

d. **GRID <F7>** — **<F7>** turns grid display on or off and **GRID** can be used to set the grid spacing.

e. **SNAP <F9>** — **<F9>** turns on or off snapping to the grid and **SNAP** can be used to set the set the snap spacing.

f. Basic Drawing Commands (note: typed in commands are ALL followed by <Enter>)

- i. **LINE** — we activate this command by typing **L** <Enter>
- ii. **RECTANGLE** — activate from the DRAW toolbar or **REC** <Enter>
- iii. **CIRCLE** — we activate this command by typing **C,** we use option **2P**

g. Basic Modify Commands (note: typed in commands are ALL followed by <Enter>)

- i. **MOVE** — we do this with the GRIPS, by selecting objects then dragging
- ii. **COPY** — we activate this command by typing **CO or CP**
- iii. **ROTATE** — we activate this command by typing **RO**
- iv. **MIRROR** — we activate this command by typing **MI**
- v. **ERASE** — we can do this by selecting objects then hitting the <Del> key or by typing **E** then selecting objects

h. File Operations — (from the **menu bar** at the top – the menu bar with words on it)

- i. File > New
- ii. File > Open
- iii. File > Save As

i. **UNDO** or <Ctrl> Z — Undoes the **last action** performed. On the Standard Toolbar.

Examples:

If the last thing you did was **ERASE** a line, an **UNDO** brings it back.

If the last thing you did was a **Zoom Window** to a small part of the drawing, an **UNDO** takes you back to the previous view.

If the last thing you did was **MIRROR** a rectangle, an **UNDO** will restore it back to not being mirrored.

j. **Editing Text** — We can activate this by double-clicking on the text to change.

Shortened version of the AutoCAD PGP file

; Aliases that are recommended for memorizing are in BOLD

; AutoCAD Program Parameters File For AutoCAD 2004
; External Command and Command Alias Definitions

; Each time you open a new or existing drawing, AutoCAD searches
; the support path and reads the first acad.pgp file that it finds.

; — External Commands —
; While AutoCAD is running, you can invoke other programs or utilities
; such Windows system commands, utilities, and applications.
; You define external commands by specifying a command name to be used
; from the AutoCAD command prompt and an executable command string
; that is passed to the operating system.

; — Command Aliases —
; You can abbreviate frequently used AutoCAD commands by defining
; aliases for them in the command alias section of acad.pgp.
; You can create a command alias for any AutoCAD command,
; device driver command, or external command.

; Recommendation: back up this file before editing it.

; External command format:
; <Command name>,[<DOS request>],<Bit flag>,[*]<Prompt>,

; Command alias format:
; <Alias>,*<Full command name>

; The following are guidelines for creating new command aliases.
; 1. An alias should reduce a command by at least two characters.
; Commands with a control key equivalent, status bar button,
; or function key do not require a command alias.
; Examples: Control N, O, P, and S for New, Open, Print, Save.
; 2. Try the first character of the command, then try the first two,
; then the first three.
; 3. Once an alias is defined, add suffixes for related aliases:
; Examples: R for Redraw, RA for Redrawall, L for Line, LT for
; Linetype.
; 4. Use a hyphen to differentiate between command line and dialog
; box commands.
; Example: B for Block, -B for -Block.
;
; Exceptions to the rules include AA for Area, T for Mtext, X for Explode.

```
; — Sample aliases for AutoCAD commands —
; These examples include most frequently used commands.

3A,        *3DARRAY
3DO,       *3DORBIT
3F,        *3DFACE
3P,        *3DPOLY
A,         *ARC
ADC,       *ADCENTER
AA,        *AREA
AL,        *ALIGN
AP,        *APPLOAD
AR,        *ARRAY
-AR,       *-ARRAY
ATT,       *ATTDEF
-ATT,      *-ATTDEF
ATE,       *ATTEDIT
-ATE,      *-ATTEDIT
ATTE,      *-ATTEDIT
B,         *BLOCK
-B,        *-BLOCK
BH,        *BHATCH
BO,        *BOUNDARY
-BO,       *-BOUNDARY
BR,        *BREAK
C,         *CIRCLE
CH,        *PROPERTIES
-CH,       *CHANGE
CHA,       *CHAMFER
CHK,       *CHECKSTANDARDS
COL,       *COLOR
COLOUR,    *COLOR
CO,        *COPY
CP,        *COPY
D,         *DIMSTYLE
DAL,       *DIMALIGNED
DAN,       *DIMANGULAR
DBA,       *DIMBASELINE
DBC,       *DBCONNECT
DC,        *ADCENTER
DCE,       *DIMCENTER
DCENTER,   *ADCENTER
DCO,       *DIMCONTINUE
DDA,       *DIMDISASSOCIATE
DDI,       *DIMDIAMETER
DED,       *DIMEDIT
```

DI, ***DIST**
DIV, *DIVIDE
DLI, *DIMLINEAR
DO, *DONUT
DOR, *DIMORDINATE
DOV, *DIMOVERRIDE
DR, *DRAWORDER
DRA, *DIMRADIUS
DRE, *DIMREASSOCIATE
DS, *DSETTINGS
DST, *DIMSTYLE
DT, *TEXT
DV, *DVIEW
E, ***ERASE**
ED, *DDEDIT
EL, *ELLIPSE
EX, ***EXTEND**
EXIT, *QUIT
EXP, *EXPORT
EXT, *EXTRUDE
F, ***FILLET**
FI, *FILTER
G, *GROUP
-G, *-GROUP
GR, *DDGRIPS
H, ***BHATCH**
-H, *HATCH
HE, *HATCHEDIT
HI, *HIDE
I, ***INSERT**
-I, *-INSERT
IAD, *IMAGEADJUST
IAT, *IMAGEATTACH
ICL, *IMAGECLIP
IM, *IMAGE
-IM, *-IMAGE
IMP, *IMPORT
IN, *INTERSECT
INF, *INTERFERE
IO, *INSERTOBJ
L, ***LINE**
LA, ***LAYER**
-LA, *-LAYER
LE, ***QLEADER**
LEN, ***LENGTHEN**
LI, ***LIST**

LINEWEIGHT, *LWEIGHT
LO, *-LAYOUT
LS, *LIST
LT, *LINETYPE
-LT, *-LINETYPE
LTYPE, *LINETYPE
-LTYPE, *-LINETYPE
LTS, *LTSCALE
LW, *LWEIGHT
M, *MOVE
MA, *MATCHPROP
ME, *MEASURE
MI, *MIRROR
ML, *MLINE
MO, *PROPERTIES
MS, *MSPACE
MT, *MTEXT
MV, *MVIEW
O, *OFFSET
OP, *OPTIONS
ORBIT, *3DORBIT
OS, *OSNAP
-OS, *-OSNAP
P, *PAN
-P, *-PAN
PA, *PASTESPEC
PARTIALOPEN, *-PARTIALOPEN
PE, *PEDIT
PL, *PLINE
PO, *POINT
POL, *POLYGON
PR, *PROPERTIES
PRCLOSE, *PROPERTIESCLOSE
PROPS, *PROPERTIES
PRE, *PREVIEW
PRINT, *PLOT **<Ctrl> P**
PS, *PSPACE
PTW, *PUBLISHTOWEB
PU, *PURGE
-PU, *-PURGE
R, *REDRAW
RA, *REDRAWALL
RE, *REGEN
REA, *REGENALL
REC, *RECTANG
REG, *REGION

REN, *RENAME
-REN, *-RENAME
REV, *REVOLVE
RO, *ROTATE
RPR, *RPREF
RR, *RENDER
S, *STRETCH
SC, *SCALE
SCR, *SCRIPT
SE, *DSETTINGS
SEC, *SECTION
SET, *SETVAR
SHA, *SHADEMODE
SL, *SLICE
SN, *SNAP
SO, *SOLID
SP, *SPELL
SPL, *SPLINE
SPE, *SPLINEDIT
ST, *STYLE
STA, *STANDARDS
SU, *SUBTRACT
T, *MTEXT
-T, *-MTEXT
TA, *TABLET
TH, *THICKNESS
TI, *TILEMODE
TO, *TOOLBAR
TOL, *TOLERANCE
TOR, *TORUS
TP, *TOOLPALETTES
TR, *TRIM
UC, *UCSMAN
UN, *UNITS
-UN, *-UNITS
UNI, *UNION
V, *VIEW
-V, *-VIEW
VP, *DDVPOINT
-VP, *VPOINT
W, *WBLOCK
-W, *-WBLOCK
WE, *WEDGE
X, *EXPLODE
XA, *XATTACH
XB, *XBIND

-XB,	*-XBIND
XC,	*XCLIP
XL,	*XLINE
XR,	***XREF**
-XR,	*-XREF
Z,	***ZOOM**

NOTES:

CONDO, Grid+Snap HW exercise

Follow the directions contained on the following pages to draw the CONDO elevation drawing using these new commands: (Please see the next page for details)

1. NEW
2. UNITS
3. LIMITS
4. GRID
5. SNAP
6. REC
7. ERASE
8. MOVE
9. COPY
10. LINE (Optional)
11. MTEXT

Here is how the screen will look for the first part, drawing the initial rectangles with GRID and SNAP both set to 5'. However, your drawing will not have the dimensions on it.

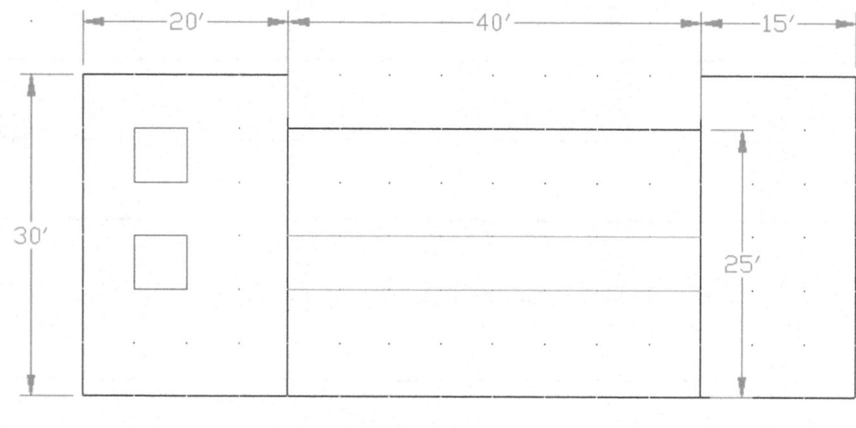

Here is how the screen will look for the second part, after more rectangles are added with GRID and SNAP both set to 1'. Again, your drawing will not have the dimensions on it.

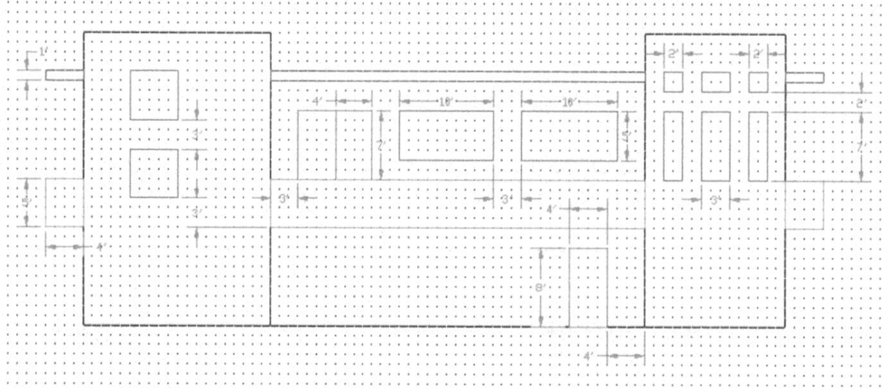

ACAD Command Line Syntax

AutoCAD uses a special "Syntax" on the Command Line:

When there are options to a command, "words" or "lists of words" are shown in square brackets [ ] When there is a list of words for the options, the options are separated by forward slashes / .

For example, the GRID command, looks like this, with the actions or typing the user does in **bold**:

Command: **grid** ↵
GRID
Specify grid spacing (X) or [ON/OFF/Snap/Aspect] <0.5000>: **off** ↵
Command:

In this case, the user has opted to turn off the grid display function. Notice that to select this option, all of the upper case letters of the option were typed in.

For example, the FILLET or F command looks like this, with the actions or typing the user does in **bold**:

Command: **f** ↵
FILLET
Current settings: Mode = TRIM, Radius = 0.5000
Select first object or [Polyline/Radius/Trim]: **r** ↵
Specify fillet radius <0.5000>: **.2** ↵
Select first object or [Polyline/Radius/Trim]: **(user selects first object)**
Select second object: **(user selects second object)**
Command:

In this case, the user wanted to select the Radius option and then change it. Notice only the "r" needed to be typed in to select this option, as it was the only letter that was upper case in the word "Radius".

Here is another example, this time of the command LENGTHEN or LEN:

Command: **len** ↵
LENGTHEN
Select an object or [DElta/Percent/Total/DYnamic]: **dy** ↵
Select an object to change or [Undo]: **(user selects an object)**
Specify new end point: **(user selects a new position of the end point)**
Select an object to change or [Undo]: ↵

Notice that to select the option called DYNAMIC, the user had to type in **dy**, which had its first two letters in upper case. This was to distinguish it from the other option called DELTA. If you wanted the DELTA option, you would have to type in **de.** Also, notice, that options letters that you type in do NOT have to be in upper case. AutoCAD does not care which case the user types his commands in.

Some Commands ask the user to specify a value. Values shown in <angled brackets> are the current settings or values. If the user accepts the value shown in the brackets, simply hit the enter key, ↵. In the following example, the limits values were not changed by the user, but just checked.

```
Command: limits ↵
Reset Model space limits:
Specify lower left corner or [ON/OFF] <0.0000,0.0000>: ↵
Specify upper right corner <12.0000,9.0000>: ↵
```

Week 2 Additional Tips

1. On the Zoom icon from the Pull-down menus, notice that the **most recently used icon will appear**, *not necessarily the default icon.* This is a source of confusion for some new users. Instructor will demonstrate.
2. On beginning drawings, we will turn OFF certain functions from the menubar across the bottom of the screen. Please turn OFF the following: SNAP, GRID, ORTHO, POLAR, OSNAP & OTRACK. We will be turning these on when necessary and when we cover their proper usage. Note, that when the function is OFF, the button appears pushed Out from the screen. When the function is ON, the button appears pushed In.
3. Be aware of the difference between the Model & Layout tabs across the bottom of the AutoCAD drawing area. We will only use the Model tab for the majority of the beginning of the course. We will show the usage of the Layout tab later after about week 9.
4. A quick way to bring up toolbars that are missing is by right-clicking onto any visible toolbar. This brings up a list of toolbars, from which you can select. Try this now. Try activating the Modify II toolbar and then dismiss it.
5. An advanced and easy way to ZOOM & PAN is available from the middle mouse button and wheel in AutoCAD. Watch as the instructor shows this. Roll the wheel up or down to ZOOM In/Out. Press and hold and then drag with the middle button to PAN your drawing view.
6. English units entry. Recall that a **<Space>** is the same as **<Enter>** in AutoCAD typed-in commands, so if you are using Architectural units, be sure to enter mixed fractions as follows WITHOUT SPACES!
   Ten feet and 5 and one-half inch would be:

   10'5-1/2" … or … 10'-5-1/2" (notice, no spaces in either acceptable version)

7. Common short-cut typed-in commands, good to memorize:
   - **a.** E erase
   - **b.** U undo
   - **c.** L line
   - **d.** C circle
   - **e.** CO copy
   - **f.** M move
   - **g.** MI mirror
   - **h.** RO rotate
   - **i.** Z zoom
   - **j.** R redraw
8. Additional Commands we have used:
   - **a.** UNITS
   - **b.** LIMITS
   - **c.** NEW (icon)
   - **d.** SAVE (icon)
   - **e.** GRID
   - **f.** SNAP
   - **g.** CHAMFER
   - **h.** FILLET
   - **i.** EXTEND
   - **j.** TRIM
   - **k.** POLYGON
9. Object Snap Modes:
   - **a.** ENDPOINT
   - **b.** MIDPOINT
   - **c.** CENTER
   - **d.** QUADRANT
   - **e.** NEAREST
   - **f.** INTERSECTION

Week 3 Topics-Layers-Properties

1. <u>**COMMON TIPS:**</u> Before more new topics are covered, a short discussion is needed on some common commands and/or concepts from weeks #1 and #2, <u>which may have been missed or glossed over</u>.
   - **a.** **Type command ALIASES with the LEFT HAND** & start using the **RIGHT MOUSE BUTTON** as the **<enter>** function! ***See how much faster this is than the keyboard <enter> key?*** If you are right-handed, your right hand is usually, already on the mouse and the left hand can be resting on or above the keyboard keys. See handout #1 pg 13 & 14 if your AutoCAD is not set up yet for the **right mouse button** as the **<enter>** function.

   - **b.** Refer to page 23 of week #1 handout **Using AutoCAD Help** and the list of commands with Help Articles and the week # of coverage. **READ ALL THE WEEK #1 & #2 ARTICLES!** Circle, Copy, Erase, Grid, Help, Limits, Move, etc. (See the list, pg 23) Additional tips, here …
     - **i.** **C** (CLOSE option within the LINE command) is automatically used to hit the original point again when you have drawn a series of LINES.
     - **ii.** **Z** (ZOOM), **the default option for the ZOOM command is W**, but you do NOT have to enter it as Z <enter> W <enter>. This is a wasted amount of keystrokes. Just type Z <enter> then select a window (box area) on the screen to Zoom to.

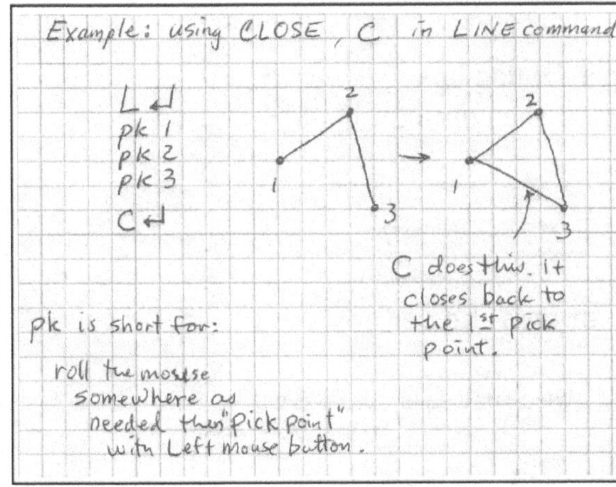

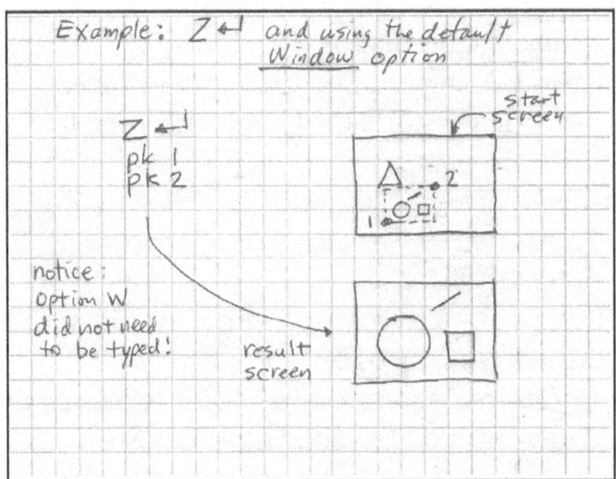

iii. U (UNDO) can be used while Picking points in the LINE command. U will undo the last point you have Picked on the screen.

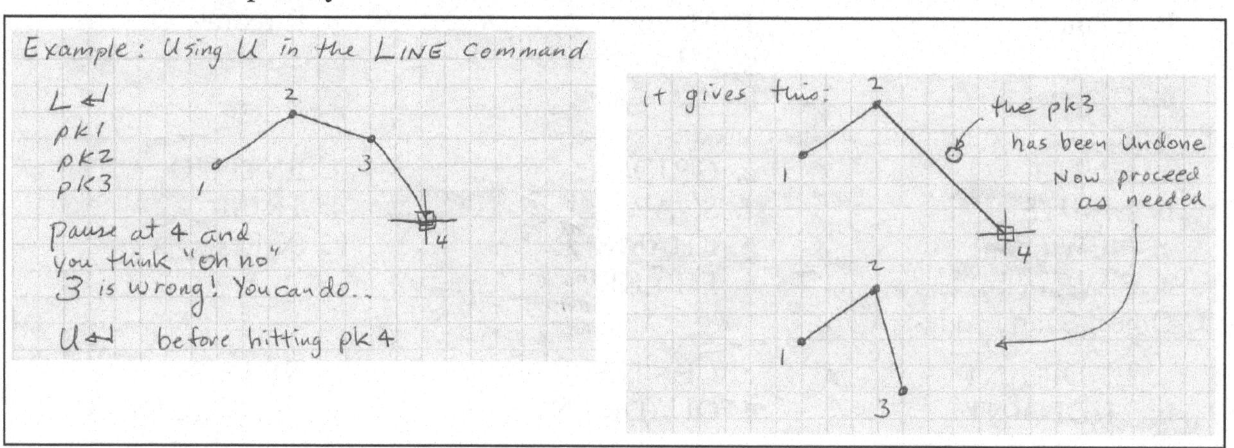

1. b. iv. REGEN from the AutoCAD Help pages. It is used to make your circles look like

Regenerates the entire drawing from the current viewport

View menu: Regen

Command line: regen

REGEN regenerates the entire drawing and recomputes the screen coordinates for all objects in the current viewport. It also reindexes the drawing database for optimum display and object selection performance.

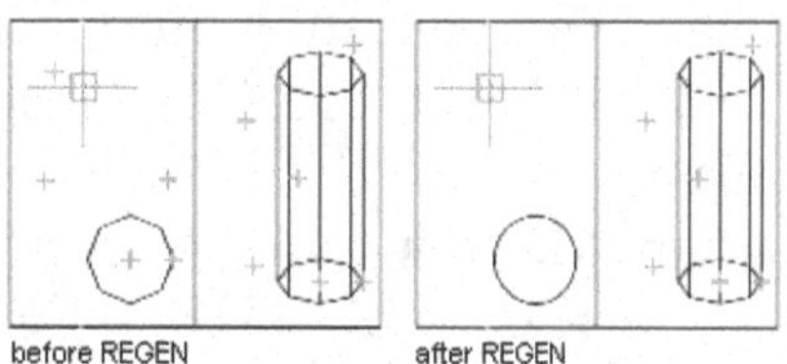
before REGEN after REGEN

circles instead of octagons!

v. CHANGE (These week#2 commands, v. thru viii, will be shown in lab)
vi. DIVIDE
vii. POINT
viii. PURGE
ix. TRACE

← *These may defer to next week, depending on class progress.*

2. <u>LAYERS & PROPERTIES:</u>

Layers Commands

- **LA** Brings up the **Layers Property Manager Dialog box**
- **-LA** Starts the Command Line text version of the command

```
Command: -la ↵
-LAYER
Current layer: "Layer name will be shown here"
Enter an option
[?/Make/Set/New/ON/OFF/Color/Ltype/LWeight/Plot/PStyle/Freeze/
Thaw/LOck/Unlock/stAte]:
```

<u>**Layers Property Manager Dialog box**</u>

Select the command from the icon on the Layers toolbar. ... or ... open it with typed-in command **la**↵

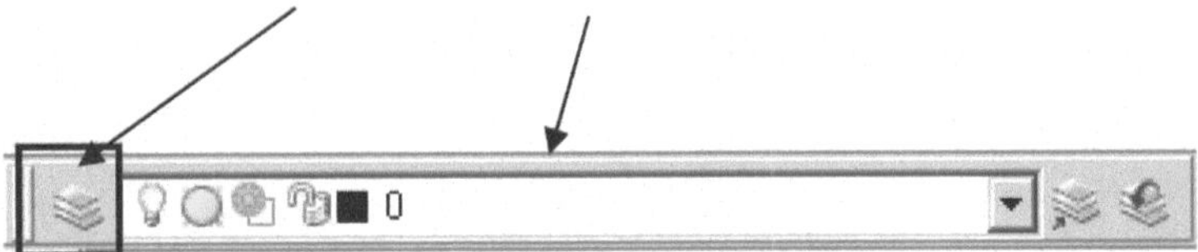

See below for details of each numbered feature of the Layers Properties Manager.

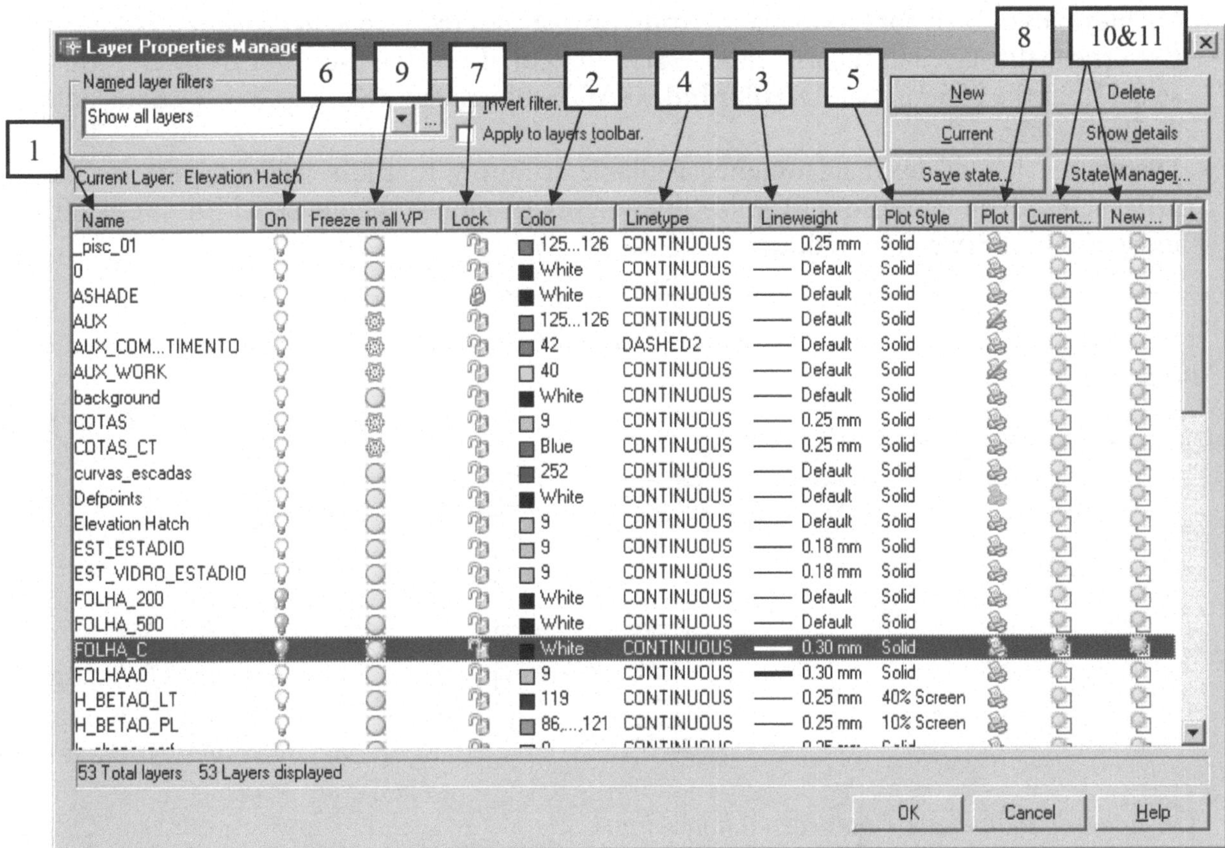

Details of the Layers Properties Manger box <u>from AutoCAD Help</u>, except where ***My Additional Notes:*** are noted:

1. Name

Displays the selected layer name, which can be edited. The name can include letters, numbers, blank spaces*, and any special character not used by Microsoft® Windows® or AutoCAD for other purposes.

******My Additional Notes:*** *Blank Spaces are typically* *<u>NOT recommended</u>* *for use in Layer names, since many users and companies use the <spacebar> as an <enter> key function. Use the "underscore" as a substitute for "blank space". See the example Layer Names in the example above.*

Note the use of "underscore" characters (ie. ***EST_VIDRO_ESTADIO****). Also note, many of the names above are not in English, since this example drawing, that is shipped with AutoCAD, was drawn for a stadium project in Portugal.*

2. Color
Displays a list of colors available to apply to the selected layers. To assign a color other than those displayed in the list, choose Select Color. To define the color of layers, you can select from the 255 AutoCAD Color Index (ACI) colors, true colors, and color book colors.

3. Lineweight
Displays a list of fixed lineweights available to apply to the selected layers including DEFAULT. You can also customize lineweights to plot at whatever width you want by using the Plot Style Table Editor.

My Additional Notes: *Thicker lineweight displays start at 0.30mm. Select your choice on the Properties toolbar*

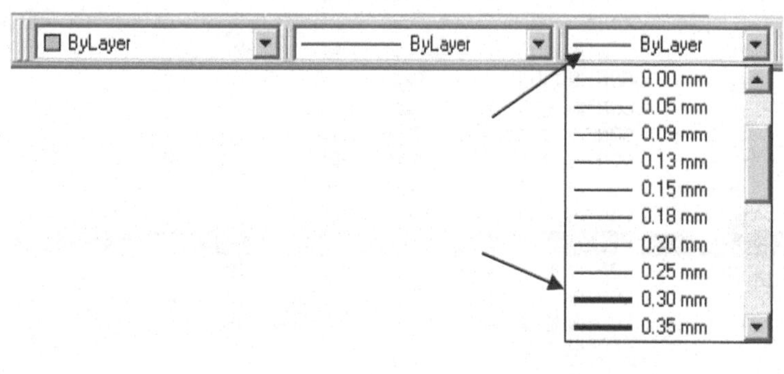

(To view thicker lineweights, turn ON the LWT button in the Status Bar at the bottom of the screen. Lineweight display is a rather newer feature that many older AutoCAD users may not be aware of. Up until recently, AutoCAD never could display thicker lineweights on the screen, even if they were plotted thicker on hardcopy prints.

The lineweights listed are the plotted lineweights.

Portion of the Command Line, Status Bar (bottom of the screen) LWT (lineweight display)

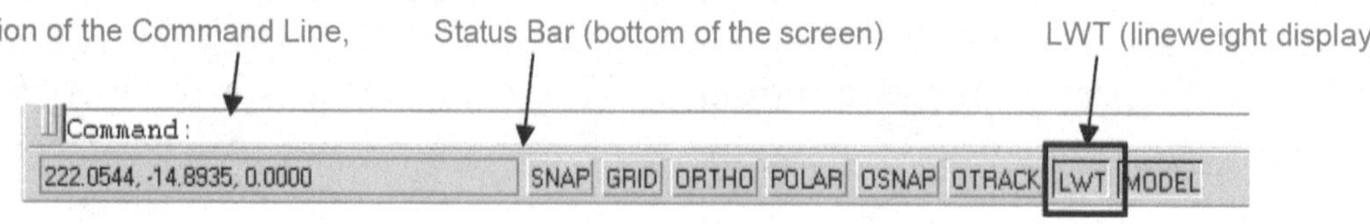

This used to be a major distinction between ***AutoCAD*** *(which had* ***no*** *lineweight displays until recently) and* ***MicroStation*** *(which always had lineweight displays as a standard part of the software)*

4. Linetype

Displays linetypes available to apply to the selected layers. To load additional linetypes, choose a linetype in the list of layers to display the D:\MTSAC + CE128L\CE128\2007-01-18 Handout 03\acr_17.html - 489408 Select Linetype dialog box, and then choose Load.

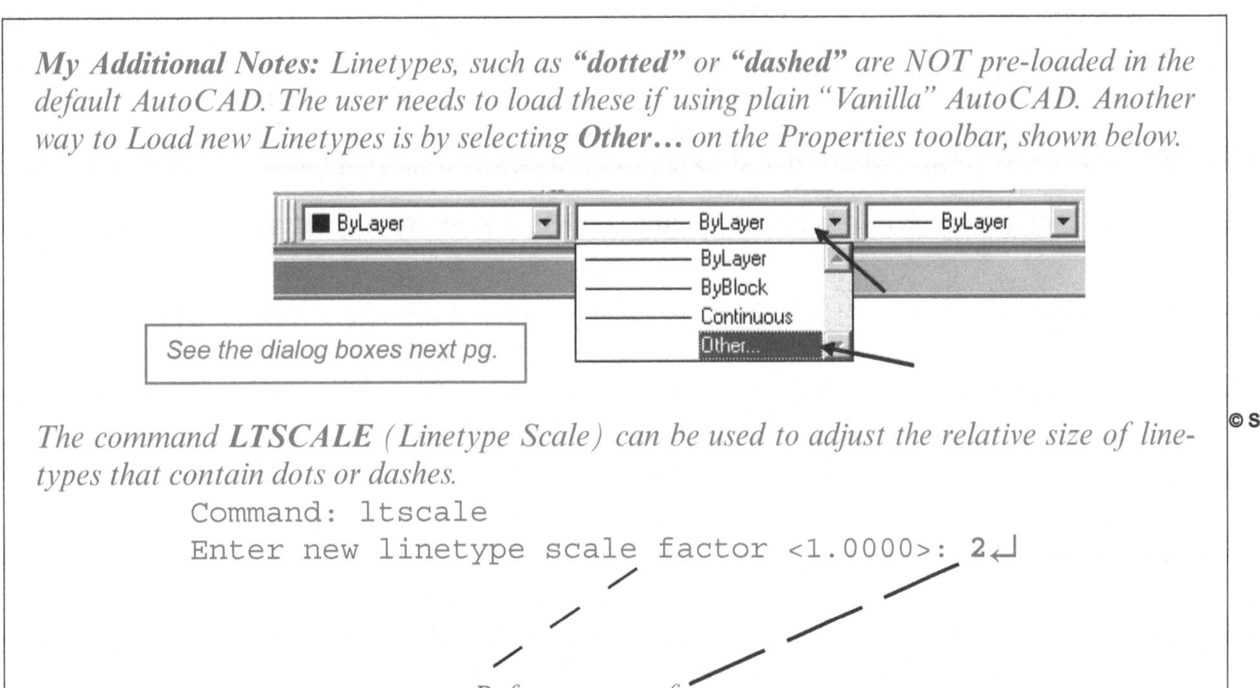

My Additional Notes: *Linetypes, such as* ***"dotted"*** *or* ***"dashed"*** *are NOT pre-loaded in the default AutoCAD. The user needs to load these if using plain "Vanilla" AutoCAD. Another way to Load new Linetypes is by selecting* ***Other…*** *on the Properties toolbar, shown below.*
ByLayer
ByLayer
ByLayer
ByLayer
ByBlock
Continuous
Other...
See the dialog boxes next pg.
The command ***LTSCALE*** *(Linetype Scale) can be used to adjust the relative size of linetypes that contain dots or dashes.*
Command: ltscale
Enter new linetype scale factor <1.0000>: 2↵
Before
after

The **Linetype Manager** with the **Load or Reload Linetypes** dialog box shown after selecting Load….

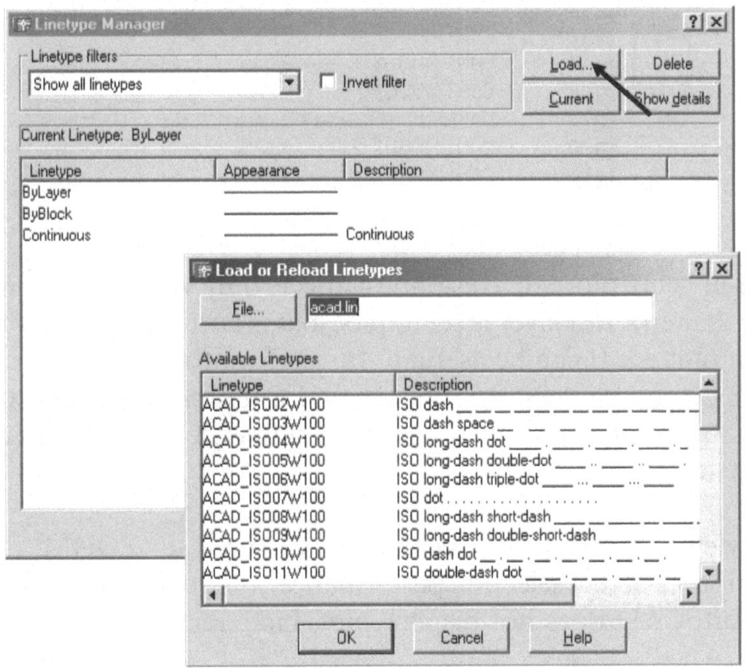

5. Plot Style

Displays a list of plot styles available to apply to the selected layers. If you are working with color-dependent plot styles (the PSTYLEPOLICY system variable is set to 1), you cannot change the plot style associated with a layer. The default plot style is Normal.

6. Off for Display *(Turns layers On or Off)*

Turns selected layers on or off. Turned-off layers regenerate with the drawing but are not displayed or plotted. You can turn layers off rather than freeze layers if you frequently change layers from visible to invisible. By turning layers off to make their objects invisible, you avoid regenerating the drawing every time you restore visibility. When you turn a layer on that has been turned off, the objects are only redrawn on that layer.

Layers that are on, show a yellow light bulb. Layers that are turned off show a blue light bulb.

7. Lock for Editing *(Prevents objects from being changed or copied)*

Prevents objects on selected layers from being edited. Locking layers is useful when you want to edit objects that are associated with particular layers but also want to view objects on other layers. Although you cannot edit objects on a locked layer, they are still visible if the layer is on and thawed. You can make a locked layer current, and you can add objects to it.

Locked and not plotted layers shown below.

Name	On	Freeze in all VP	Lock	Color	Linetype	Lineweight	Plot Style	Plot
_pisc_01				125...126	CONTINUOUS	0.25 mm	Solid	
0				White	CONTINUOUS	Default	Solid	
ASHADE				White	CONTINUOUS	Default	Solid	
AUX				125...126	CONTINUOUS	Default	Solid	
AUX_COM...TIMENTO				42	DASHED2	Default	Solid	
AUX_WORK				40	CONTINUOUS	Default	Solid	
background				White	CONTINUOUS	Default	Solid	

8. Do Not Plot

Prevents the selected layers from being plotted. This option affects only visible layers in the drawing (layers that are on or thawed). If a layer is set to plot, but is currently frozen or off in the drawing, the layer is not plotted. It can be useful to turn off plotting for a layer that contains reference information. You can view the reference information while you work, but you can turn off plotting for that layer to ensure that the reference information does not appear in the plotted drawing.

9. Freeze in All Viewports

Freezes selected layers in all viewports. You can freeze layers to speed up ZOOM, PAN, and many other operations; improve object selection performance; and reduce regeneration time for complex drawings. AutoCAD does not display, plot, hide, render, or regenerate objects on frozen layers.

Freeze the layers you want to be invisible for long periods. When you thaw a frozen layer, AutoCAD regenerates and displays the objects on that layer. If you plan to switch between visible and invisible states frequently, use the On/Off setting. You can freeze layers in all viewports, in the current layout viewport, or in new layout viewports as they are created.

10. **Freeze in Current Viewport**
    Freezes selected layers in the current layout viewport. You can freeze or thaw layers in the current layout viewport without affecting layer visibility in other viewports. Frozen layers are invisible; they are not regenerated or plotted. This feature is useful, for example, if you want to create an annotation layer that is visible only in a particular viewport. Thawing restores the layer's visibility. This option is available only when you are working on a layout.
11. **Freeze in New Viewports**
    Freezes selected layers in new layout viewports. For example, freezing the DIMENSIONS layer in all new viewports restricts the display of dimensions on that layer in any newly created layout viewports but does not affect the DIMENSIONS layer in viewports that already exist. If you then create a viewport that requires dimensions, you can override the default setting by thawing the layer in that viewport. This option is available only when you are working on a layout.

3. <u>MORE ON PROPERTIES:</u>

a. The **Properties Toolbar** and the **Properties Palette** can be used to work with the properties of Objects.

Use the **Properties Toolbar** to <u>set the current properties</u>; *Color, Linetype or Lineweight.*

Example: choosing color red

It can also be used to <u>change an object's properties</u>, if an object or many objects have already been pre-selected with GRIPS.

Select objects then set the new Property as desired. Then hit <Esc> to see the result.

b. The **Properties Palette** shows the complete information set of an object's properties. It can be brought up automatically if a user **double-clicks onto any object**. New settings can also be made on the Properties Palette. Pick onto the value you desire to change and then enter a new value.

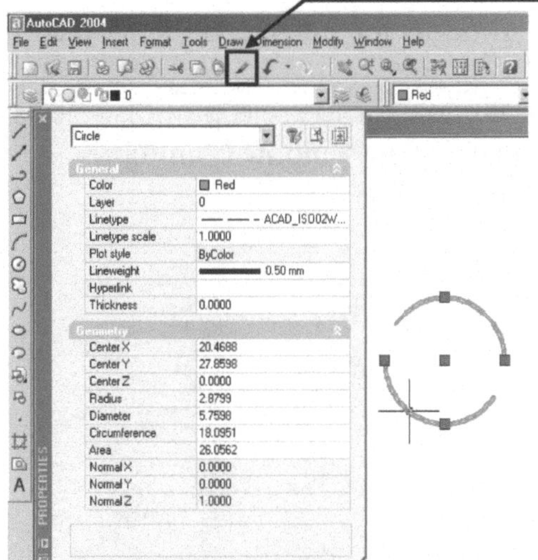

c. **Match Properties** (use the icon)
Used to impose the properties of an existing object on the drawing onto any other object in the drawing.

```
Command: '_matchprop
Select source object:
Current active settings: Color Layer
Ltype Ltscale Lineweight Thickness
PlotStyle Text Dim Hatch Polyline
Viewport
Select destination object(s) or
[Settings]:
```

c. Properties Commands:

Any of these following will bring up the Properties Palette:

CH

MO

<Ctrl> 1

CHPROP — text entry version of (Change Properties)

```
Command: CHPROP ↵
Select objects: 1 found
Select objects: ↵
Enter property to change [Color/LAyer/LType/ltScale/LWeight/
Thickness]:
```

Selected Topics Review Outline

1. Command Options/Operations
   - Choices within [ ]
     - Selecting options by typing the UPPER CASE letters (2 letters if shown)
     - However, the user need NOT type them in as upper case
   - Defaults within < >
   - Activate Toolbars by right click on any open toolbar
2. Object Selection **(NEW)**
   - Modes:
     - Pick – selects objects (turns them dashed and increments selected objects count by 1)
     - Shift Pick – removes objects
     - Automatic mode with Windows
       - Windowing left to right- selects objects inside the window
       - Crossing right to left- selects objects inside the window as well as the objects touching the window boundary
     - W – for window mode, drawing a window around objects selects the objects fully inside the window
     - C – for crossing mode, drawing a window around objects selects objects inside the window as well as the objects touching the window boundary
     - WP – Window Poly, drawing a polygon shaped window for the selection of objects inside
     - CP – Crossing Poly, drawing a polygon shaped window for the selection of objects inside the window as well as the objects touching the window boundary
     - F – Fence selection
     - R – Remove mode
     - A – Add mode
     - P – Previous selection
     - ALL – Selects ALL objects in the drawing
   - With Grips
     - For "pre" selection of objects
3. Object Properties
   - Color
   - Line Weight (turn on the LWT button to see weights)

Linetype

Linetype Scale

CHPROP command

(double-click on an object to call up the Properties Palette and view and/or change the object's properties)

Match Properties

4. Object Snaps
5. Layers

   (use ByLayer, to have the properties follow the Layers Manager Dialog box properties rather than the selected properties in the Properties Palette or toolbar)
6. Misc.

   Divide command

   Format > Point Style

   (use "node" o-snap mode to snap to the points created)
7. Inquiry (from here and below, mostly are NEW topics for future weeks)

   List

   Dist

   Area

   ID
8. Polar Tracking/Direct Distance Entry
9. Dimensions

   Aligned Dimension

   Center Mark

   Quick Dimension

   Quick Leader

   Continue Dimension
10. Blocks

    Wblock

    Insert

    Explode
11. Misc.
    a. Purge
    b. Change
    c. Trace
    d. "up arrow" on keyboard to recall commands

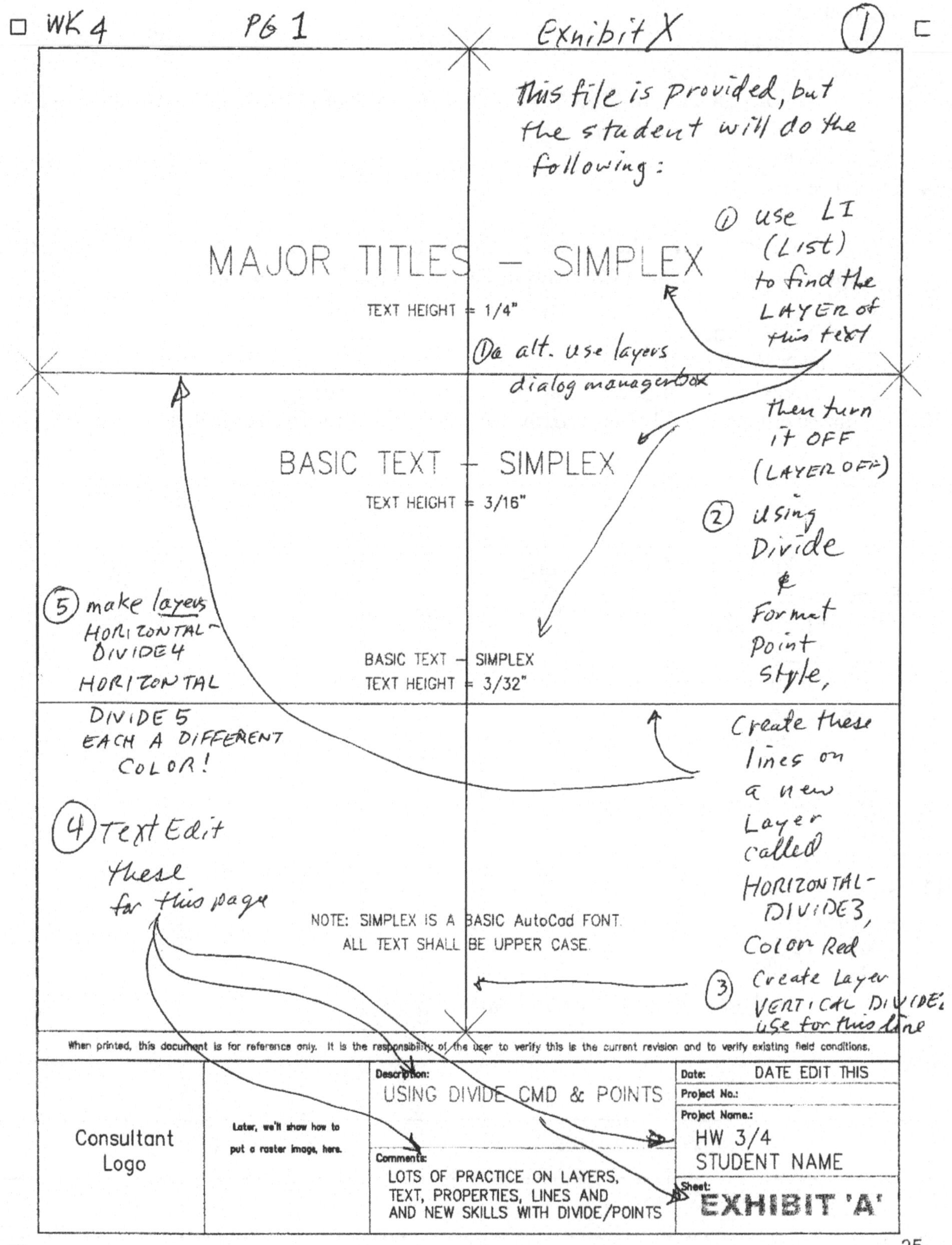
WK 4
PG 1
Exhibit X
1
this file is provided, but the student will do the following:
1 use LI (List) to find the LAYER of this text
1a alt. use layers dialog managerbox
then turn it OFF (LAYER OFF)
2 using Divide & Format Point style,
MAJOR TITLES - SIMPLEX
TEXT HEIGHT = 1/4"
BASIC TEXT - SIMPLEX
TEXT HEIGHT = 3/16"
5 make layers HORIZONTAL-DIVIDE4 HORIZONTAL DIVIDE5 EACH A DIFFERENT COLOR!
BASIC TEXT - SIMPLEX
TEXT HEIGHT = 3/32"
Create these lines on a new Layer called HORIZONTAL-DIVIDE3, Color Red
4 Text Edit these for this page
NOTE: SIMPLEX IS A BASIC AutoCad FONT.
ALL TEXT SHALL BE UPPER CASE.
3 Create Layer VERTICAL DIVIDE, use for this line
When printed, this document is for reference only. It is the responsibility of the user to verify this is the current revision and to verify existing field conditions.
Consultant Logo
Later, we'll show how to put a raster image, here.
Description:
USING DIVIDE CMD & POINTS
Comments:
LOTS OF PRACTICE ON LAYERS, TEXT, PROPERTIES, LINES AND AND NEW SKILLS WITH DIVIDE/POINTS
Date: DATE EDIT THIS
Project No.:
Project Name.:
HW 3/4
STUDENT NAME
Sheet:
EXHIBIT 'A'
25

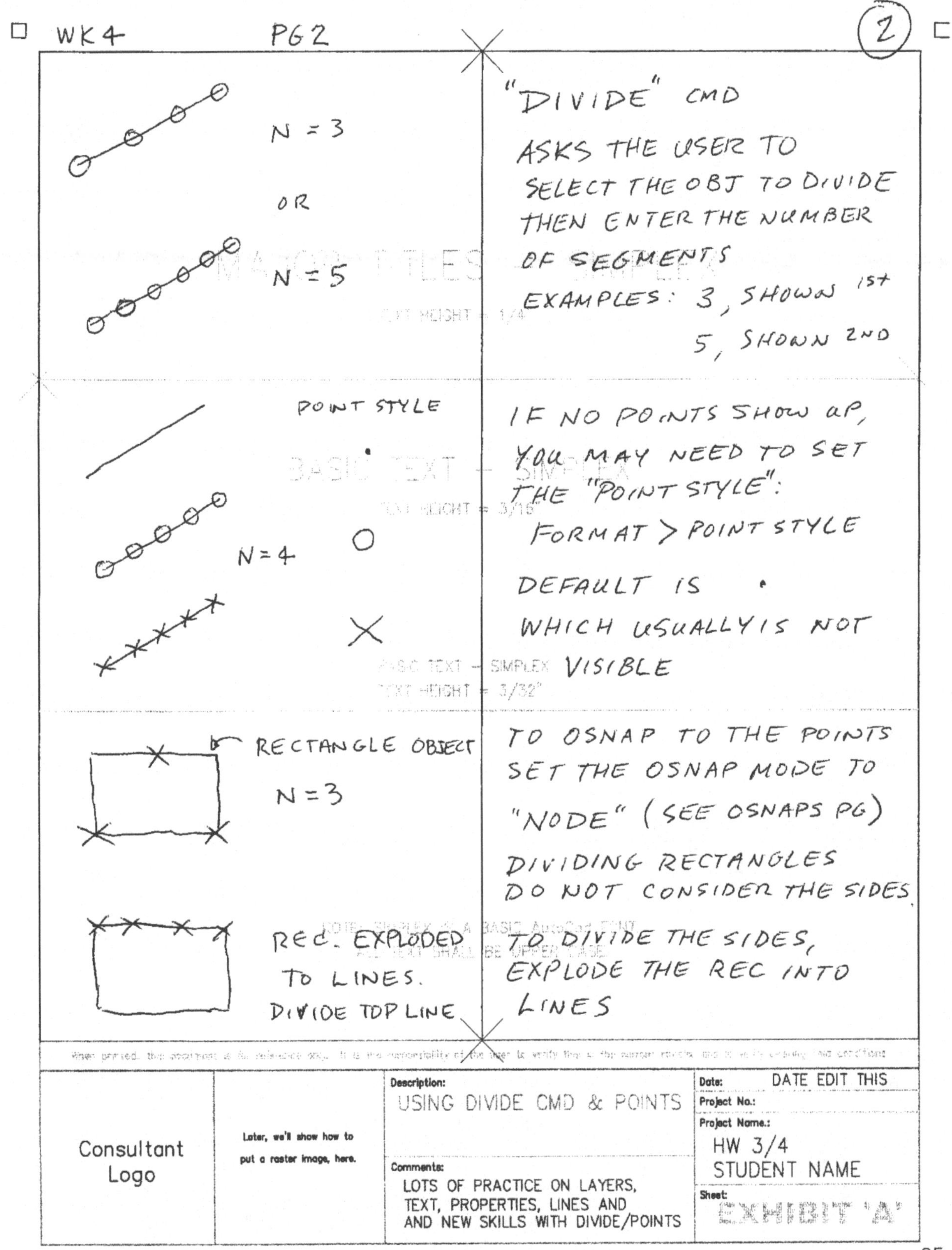
WK4
PG2
2
"DIVIDE" CMD
ASKS THE USER TO SELECT THE OBJ TO DIVIDE THEN ENTER THE NUMBER OF SEGMENTS
EXAMPLES: 3, SHOWN 1ST
5, SHOWN 2ND
N = 3
OR
N = 5
POINT STYLE
IF NO POINTS SHOW UP, YOU MAY NEED TO SET THE "POINT STYLE":
FORMAT > POINT STYLE
DEFAULT IS •
WHICH USUALLY IS NOT VISIBLE
N=4
RECTANGLE OBJECT
N=3
TO OSNAP TO THE POINTS SET THE OSNAP MODE TO "NODE" (SEE OSNAPS PG)
DIVIDING RECTANGLES DO NOT CONSIDER THE SIDES.
REC. EXPLODED TO LINES. DIVIDE TOP LINE
TO DIVIDE THE SIDES, EXPLODE THE REC INTO LINES
Description:
USING DIVIDE CMD & POINTS
Date: DATE EDIT THIS
Project No.:
Project Name:
HW 3/4
STUDENT NAME
Consultant Logo
Later, we'll show how to put a raster image, here.
Comments:
LOTS OF PRACTICE ON LAYERS, TEXT, PROPERTIES, LINES AND AND NEW SKILLS WITH DIVIDE/POINTS
Sheet:
EXHIBIT 'A'

WK 4 PG 3 (3)

OBJECT SNAPS LET THE USER SNAP TO SPECIAL LOCATIONS ON OR ASSOCIATED WITH EXISTING OBJECTS ON YOUR DRAWING	CALL UP OSNAP SETTINGS 1 OF A FEW WAYS... • TOOLS > DraftingSettings (this is slow!) • RT CLICK "OSNAP" BUTTON then settings • (SHIFT) RT CLICK FOR POP-UP
□ ENDPOINT △ MIDPOINT	EXAMPLES OF BASIC OSNAPS Include some discussion here
○ CENTER ◇ Quadrant	
⊗ Node w/ n=3 X Intersection	
INSERTION | Perpendicular | Tangent	Other Less common OSNAPS Nearest | Apperent intersection | Parallel

Consultant Logo	Later, we'll show how to put a raster image, here.	Description: USING OBJECT SNAPS pg 1 Comments: LOTS OF PRACTICE ON OBJECT SNAPS AND CONTINUED PRACTICE WITH LAYERS, PROPERTIES, TEXT, ETC.	Date: DATE EDIT THIS Project No.: Project Name: HW 3/4 STUDENT NAME Sheet: **EXHIBIT 'B'**

WK 4 PG4 (4)

Consultant Logo	Later, we'll show how to put a raster image, here.	Description: USING OBJECT SNAPS pg2 (if needed)	Date: DATE EDIT THIS
			Project No.:
			Project Name.: HW 3/4 STUDENT NAME
		Comments: LOTS OF PRACTICE ON OBJECT SNAPS AND CONTINUED PRACTICE WITH LAYERS, PROPERTIES, TEXT, ETC.	Sheet: EXHIBIT 'B' C

WK 4 PG 5 (5)

Show it here	THE TRACE CMD . . . Student fills in the rest!
Use text . . . show example of part of the "listing" of an object	THE LIST CMD . . .
P_1 P_2 P_3 ⇨	THE CHANGE CMD . . .
Hey, Notice we are using HORIZONTAL-DIVIDE4 on this PG!	THE PURGE CMD . . .

Consultant Logo	Later, we'll show how to put a raster image, here.	Description: CHANGE, TRACE, OTHERS FROM WK 3/4 Comments:	Date: DATE EDIT THIS Project No.: Project Name: HW 3/4 STUDENT NAME Sheet: **EXHIBIT 'D'**

Dimensions, Text & Misc. Tips for Cul-de-Sac & other exercises

Precision Input for Surveyor's Angles:

Type-in syntax

To type in a Polar Precision entry with surveyor's angles, examine the following type-ins creating a line that is **512 feet long at a bearing of N85°15’39”E** (assume that units have already been set to Architectural):

Type letter d in place of the degree symbol.

```
Command: l <enter>
LINE Specify first point: user selects a point on the screen
Specify next point or [Undo]: @512'<n85d15'39"e <enter>
Specify next point or [Undo]: <enter>
Command:
```

Dimensioning notes:

Dimension Text

You can edit a dimension's text by using the **EXPLODE** command.
Alias type in: x <enter>

After using **EXPLODE**, the dimension no longer functions as a dimension, but is just lines and text.
Now you can edit the text as desired.

Turn this: **into this:**

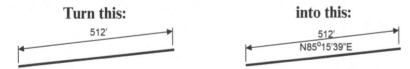

See **Text notes**, below, for making degree symbols

EXPLODE is also used to turn Rectangles into Lines, PLINES into Lines and BLOCKS into original objects. We will cover some of these other types of objects later in the course.

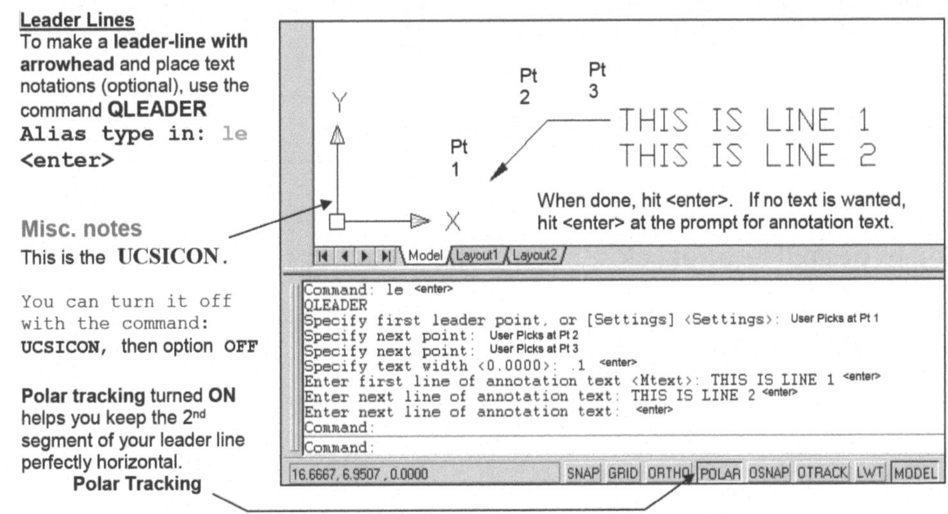

Dimensioning notes: (cont')

Here are the locations of icons to bring up the **dimension style manager** dialog box:

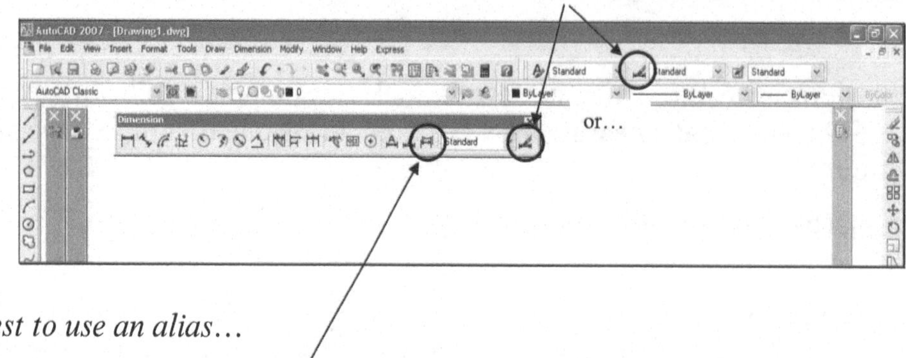

Or it's easiest to use an alias…

Alias type in: d
<enter>

Use the command **Dimension Update** to change an existing dimension to the current style. Select the icon, then select the existing dimension to change it to the current dimension style settings.

Alternatively, you could use **Match Properties** to impose an existing dimension's style onto another dimension. Start Match Properties, select the source dimension, then the destination dimension.

Alias type in: ma <enter>

Adjusting the dimension's location

Use the GRIPS selection to stretch a dimension line to a new location. Select the dimension to modify, and then select the central Grip node, which is at the dimension text, and then reposition the node either closer or farther away from the object as desired.

Dimension placed too far away! Select the dimension, blue GRIP nodes appear.

Drag the node to desired location, closer… or drag it left or right if desired.

Text notes:

Basics

To draw multi-line text,
Alias type in: t **<enter>**

To edit an existing text,
Double-click on the text

Special Characters in Text

To insert these special characters into text, while in the Text command and typing in your characters:

Degree Symbol: example: N63°57'22"E
type %%d

Plus/minus tolerance Symbol: example: 4.5 ± 0.1
type %%p

Circular Diameter Symbol: example: 12"ø
type %%c

Units & List Inquiry:

To check your work, **LIST** is quite helpful (**Alias type in:** li). If your units are set to decimal and angle format set to **decimal degrees**, the "LISTing" of a line might look like the following.

Notice the angle in XY Plane is a decimal 15 degrees.

```
Command: li
LIST
Select objects: 1 found
Select objects:
LIST
Select objects: 1 found
Select objects:
    LINE       Layer: "0"
               Space: Model space
    Color: 6 (magenta) Linetype: "BYLAYER"
    LineWeight: 0.00 mm
    Handle = F2
  from point, X= 8.1533 Y= 9.1542 Z= 0.0000
    to point, X= 15.1260 Y= 11.0410 Z= 0.0000
Length = 7.2234, Angle in XY Plane = 15
  Delta X = 6.9727, Delta Y = 1.8867, Delta Z = 0.0000
```

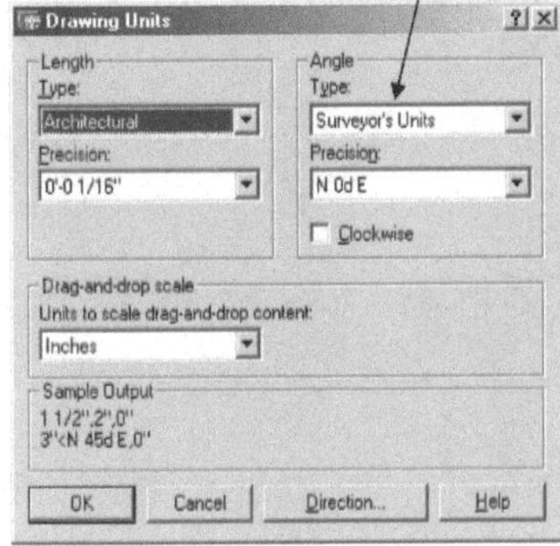

Change the **UNITS** Angle Type to **Surveyor's Units**. Notice the angle in XY Plane is now N 75d E

```
Command: li
LIST
Select objects: 1 found
Select objects:
LINE
Select objects: 1 found
```

```
Select objects:
  LINE Layer: "0"
         Space: Model space
  Color: 6 (magenta) Linetype: "BYLAYER"
  LineWeight: 0.00 mm
  Handle = F2
from point, X= 8.1533 Y= 9.1542 Z= 0.0000
  to point, X= 15.1260 Y= 11.0410 Z= 0.0000
Length = 7.2234, Angle in XY Plane = N 75d E
  Delta X = 6.9727, Delta Y = 1.8867, Delta Z = 0.0000
```

Appendix C

WORKING IN 3D

- A key concept of working in 3D in AutoCAD is the UCS icon.
- Repositioning it allows easier drawing in the 3D model
- First, it must be turned "ON" if it is not already

Moving the UCS icon allows drawing on the "other" SIDES

WORKING IN 3D 1

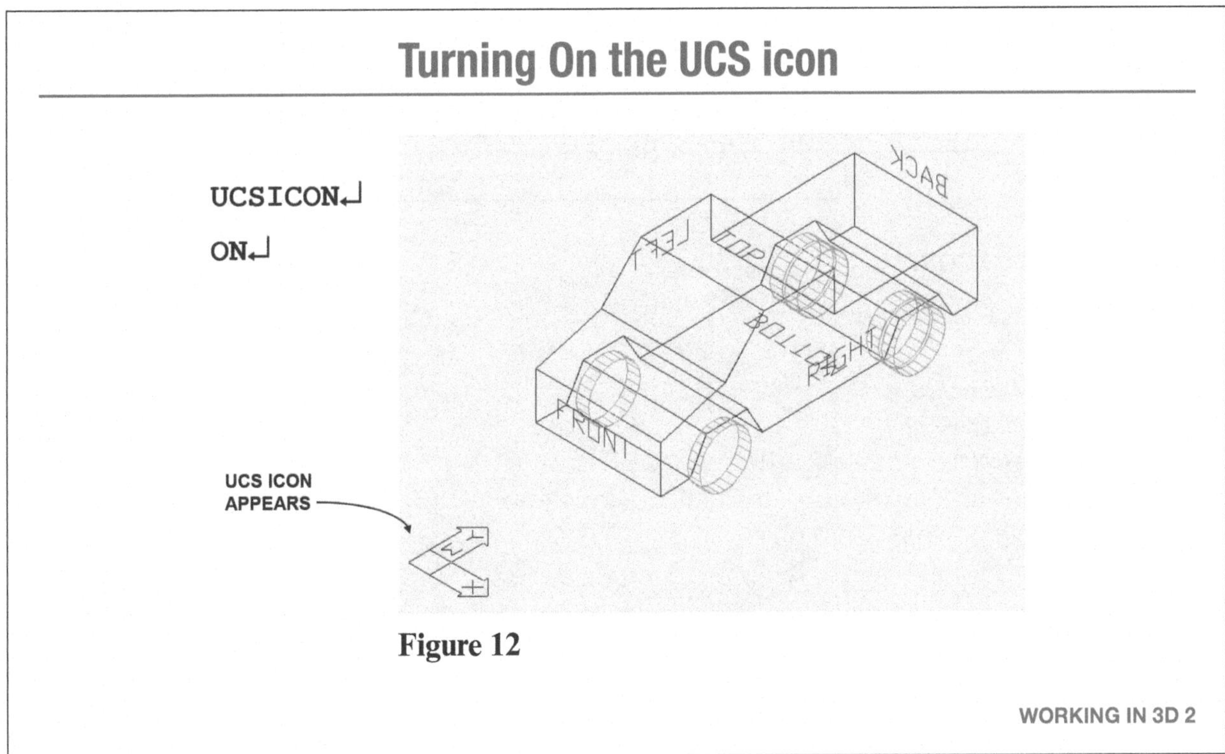

Figure 12

WORKING IN 3D 2

Aligning the UCS to the FRONT

UCS↵

3↵ *for 3point*

INT↵ ***pick at A***
(defines origin)

INT↵ ***pick at B***
(defines X-axis)

INT↵ ***pick at C***
(defines Y-axis)

observe UCS icon ***reorient***

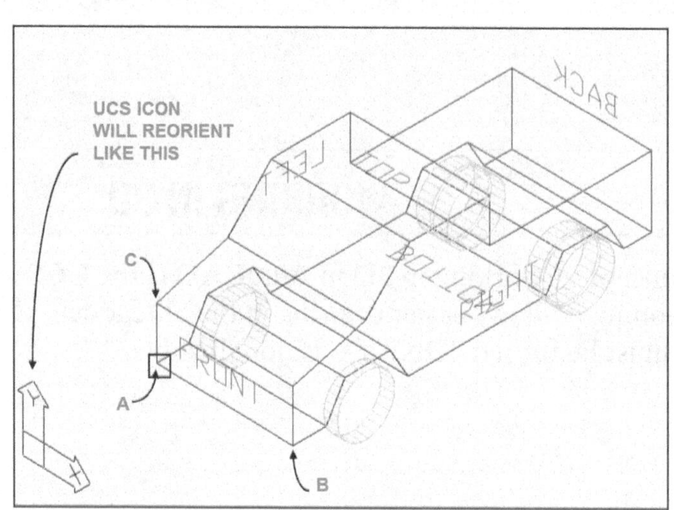

Figure 13

WORKING IN 3D 3

Moving the UCS to the XY Origin

UCSICON↵

OR↵ *for ORIGIN*

observe UCS icon reposition to point A

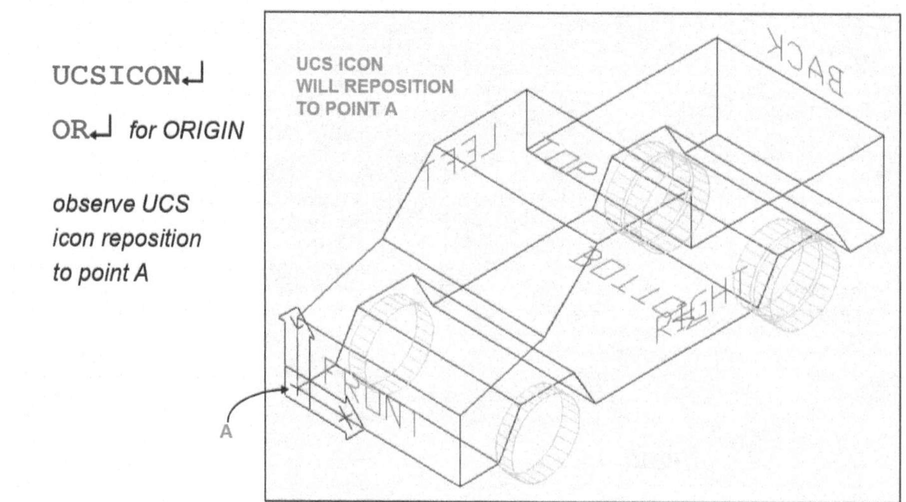

Figure 14

WORKING IN 3D 4

Plan aligns with the XY plane

PLAN ↲

<Current UCS> ↲

Notice that the FRONT view is now displayed.

Note: PLAN no longer aligns to the TOP view. We have re-aligned the UCS!!

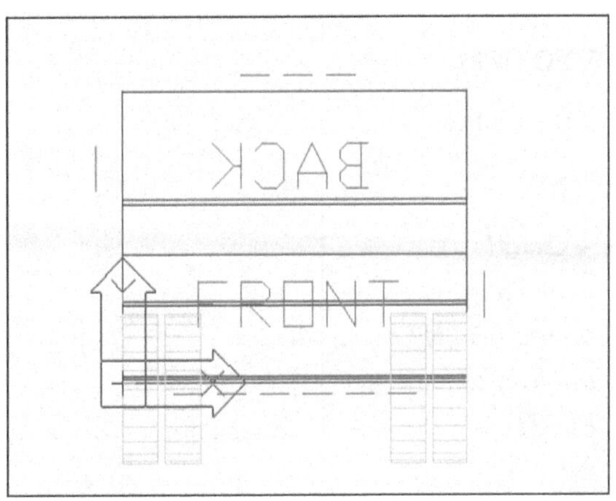

Figure 15

WORKING IN 3D 5

Objects drawn relative to the XY

"headlights"

C↲ *for circle (make one headlight on the left as shown, then copy or mirror one to the right)*

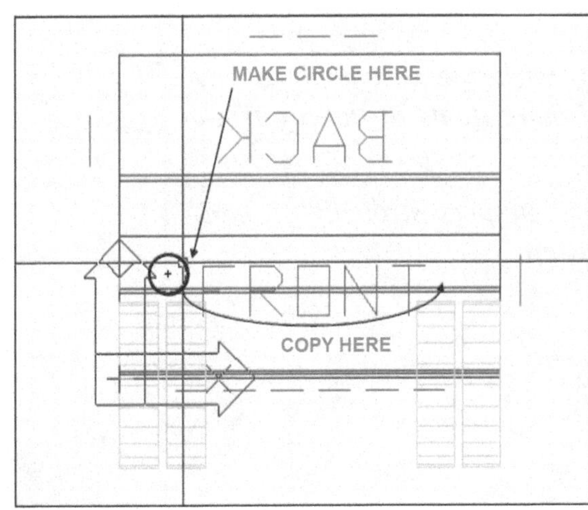

Figure 16

WORKING IN 3D 6

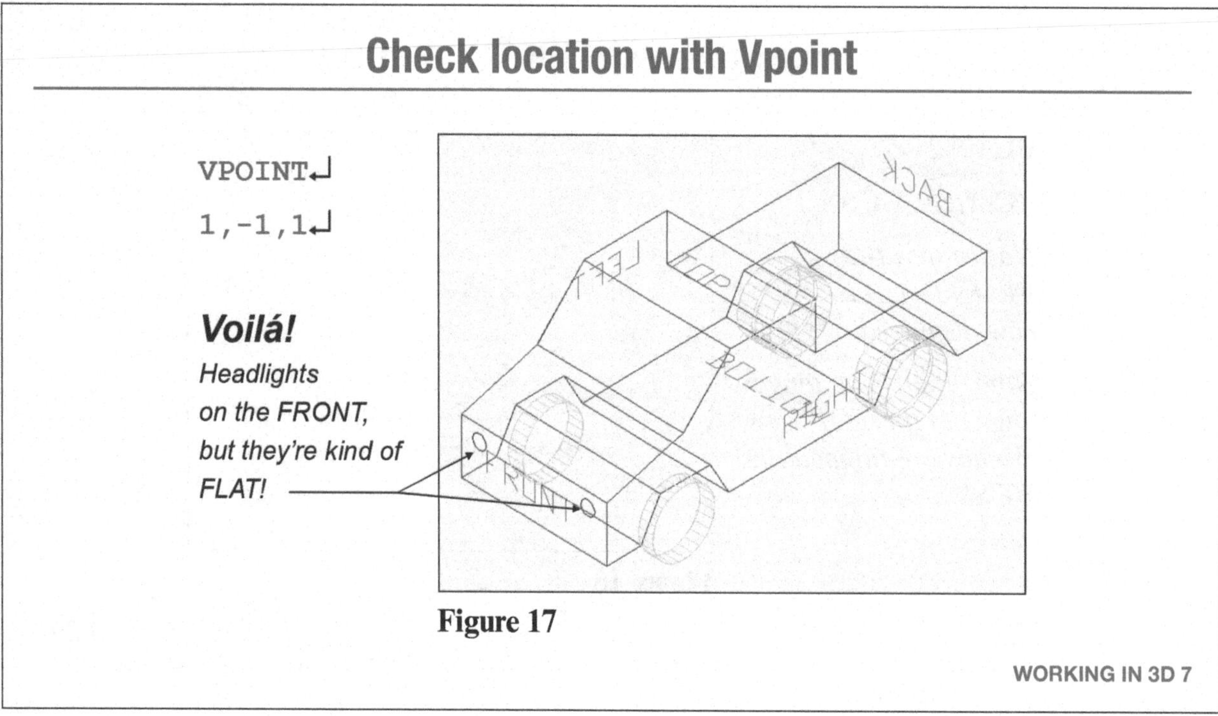

Figure 17

WORKING IN 3D 7

Additional Objects to Add

Follow along with the instructor or by yourself, add more items to the toy truck model.

3D headlights, bumpers, strobelights, handles, roll-cage, etc.

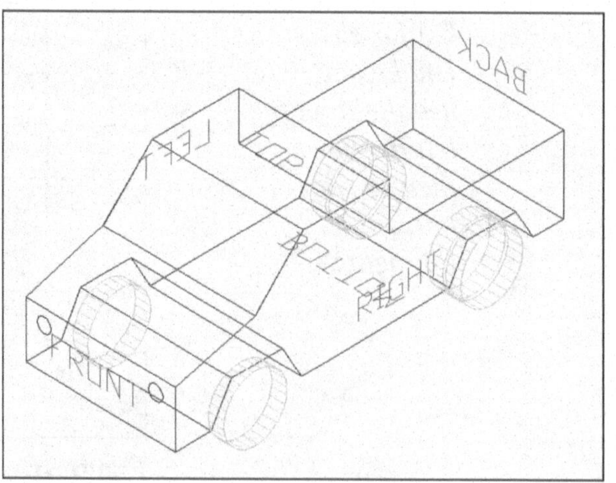

Figure 18

WORKING IN 3D 8

Making a corrugated bumper

Align the UCS to the RIGHT side.

Set thickness to -1. (Toy truck width is 1)

Draw line work.

Change VPOINT to check your work.

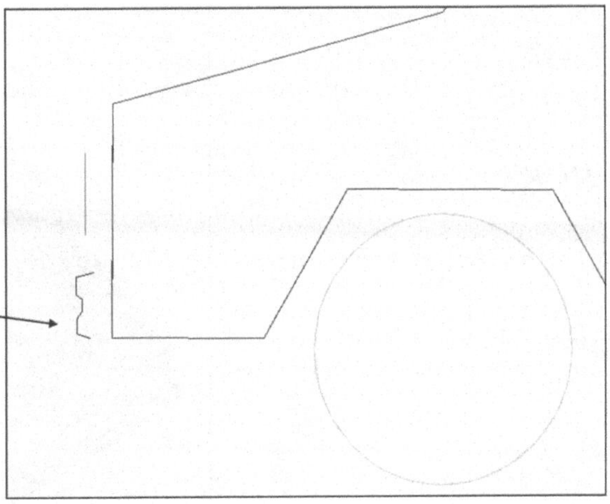

Figure 19

WORKING IN 3D 9

Bumper added, right iso view

SHADE↵

Fills the sides

Remember to reset thickness to 0!

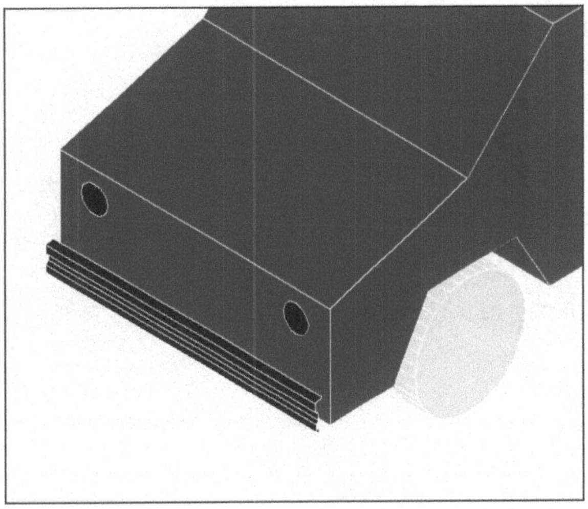

Figure 20

WORKING IN 3D 10

Redo Headlights with depth

- *Move UCS back to the front*
- *Use PLAN*
- *Erase the circles*
- *Set ELEV to -.05*
- *Set THICKNESS to .1*
- *Redraw circles*
- Change VPOINT check your work
- SHADE

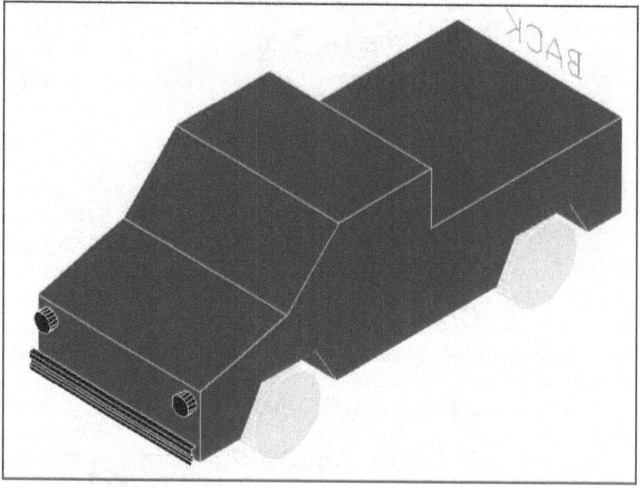

Figure 21

WORKING IN 3D 11

3D Concepts

- Here is that same model truck
- It is now displayed as a "shaded hidden-line" rendering
- The angle of view is still called a right isometric
- Reference notes about the "toy" truck drawing:
  - There are 4 rear tires

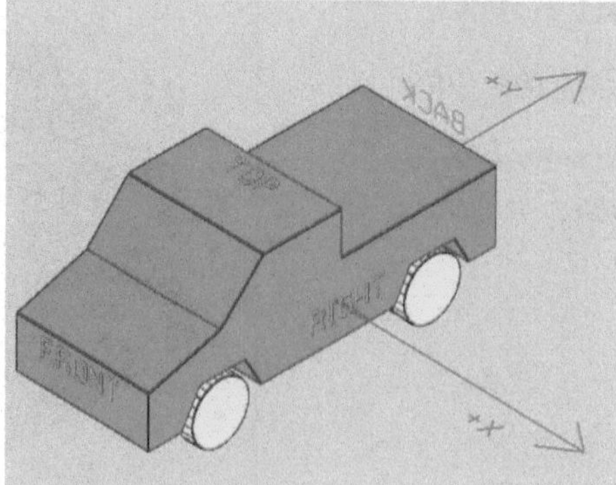

Figure 1A

WORKING IN 3D 12

3D Concepts

- More About the LABELS:
  - Labels on 3D models are typically arranged so that they "READ CORRECTLY" when the viewing angle changes.
  - For example, "TOP" reads correctly when we go to a "TOP" or "PLAN" view.

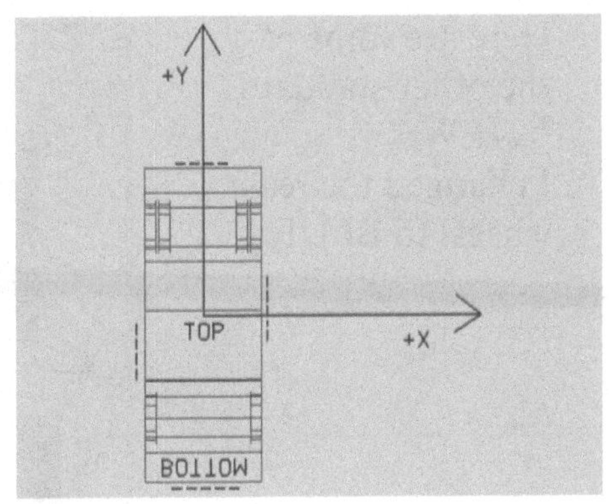

Figure 2

WORKING IN 3D 13

3D Concepts

- On this particular model of the truck, the "TOP" or "PLAN" view is the view of the X-Y plane.
- This is normally associated with typical 2D drawing
- "PLAN" in AutoCAD means normal to the XY drawing axes or "UCS"
- Note: The "UCS" will be repositioned often

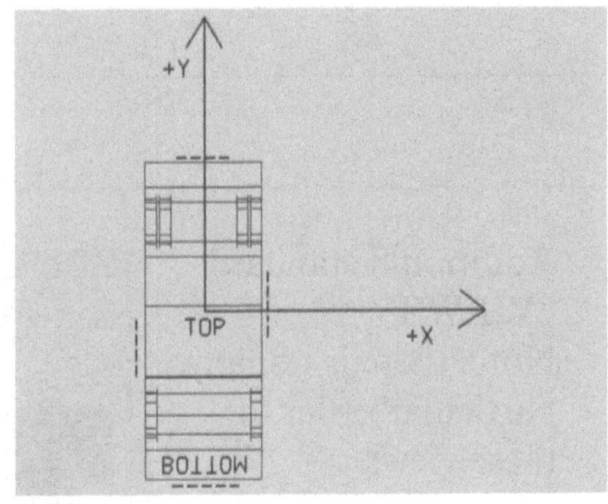

Figure 2

WORKING IN 3D 14

3D Concepts

- Here are some of the other standard "VIEWS"
- I changed the rear wheels to BLUE

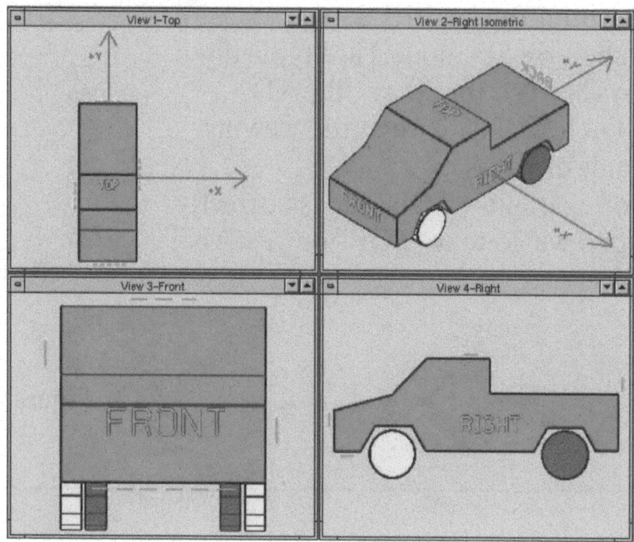

Figure 3

WORKING IN 3D 15

3D Concepts

- Additional standard "VIEWS"
- Note: there is not any particular order to these views.

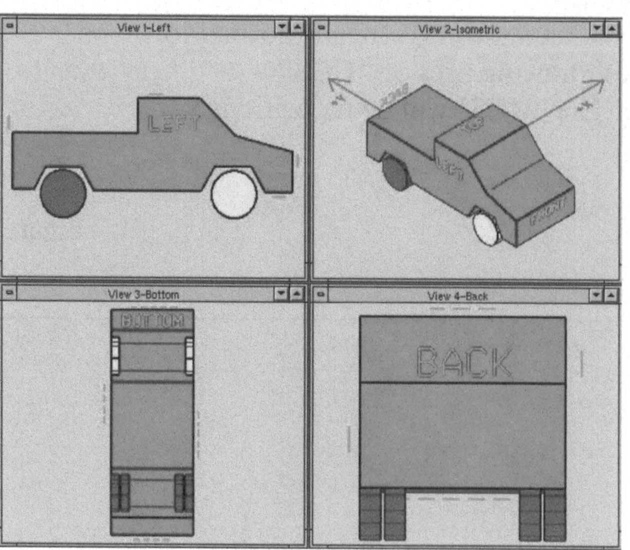

Figure 4

WORKING IN 3D 16

3D Concepts

- Think of the drawing as a 3 dimensional model sitting at the center of a sphere or globe.
- This concept is the basis of the AutoCAD method for defining **View Points**
- Imagine a camera on the surface of the globe pointing to the model at the center

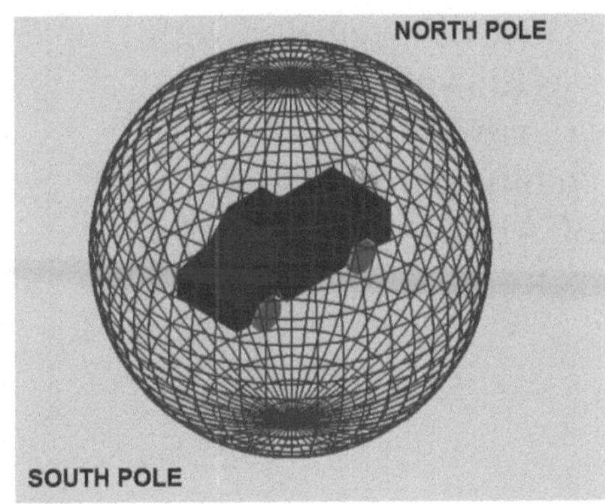

Figure 5

3D Concepts

- Imagine the globe being labelled with angle values as shown in figure 6 for the "TOP" view of the globe
- Refer back to this figure when we use the AutoCAD Viewpoint Presets Dialogue box for the **From: X Axis** setting

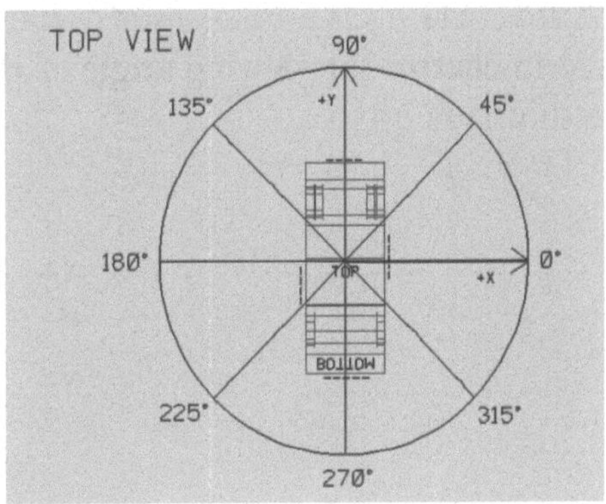

Figure 6

3D Concepts

- Imagine the globe being labelled with angle values as shown in figure 7 for the "FRONT" view of the globe
- Refer back to this figure when we use the AutoCAD Viewpoint Presets Dialogue box for the **From: XY Plane** setting.

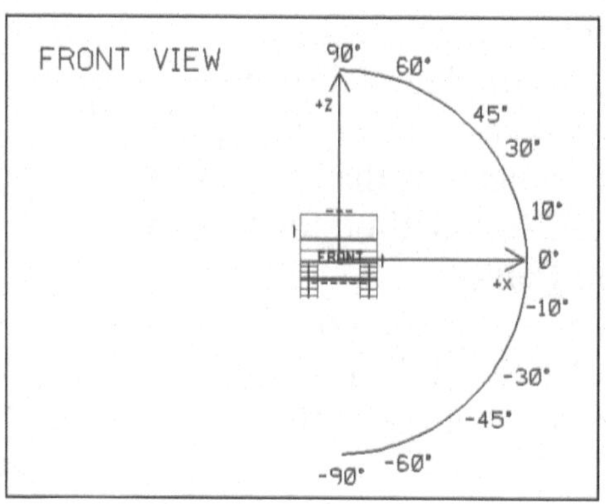

Figure 7

3D Concepts

- This is the AutoCAD Viewpoint Presets Dialogue box
- **It can be used to control the viewing angle of the model**
- To open the dialogue box:
- Type DDVPOINT↲

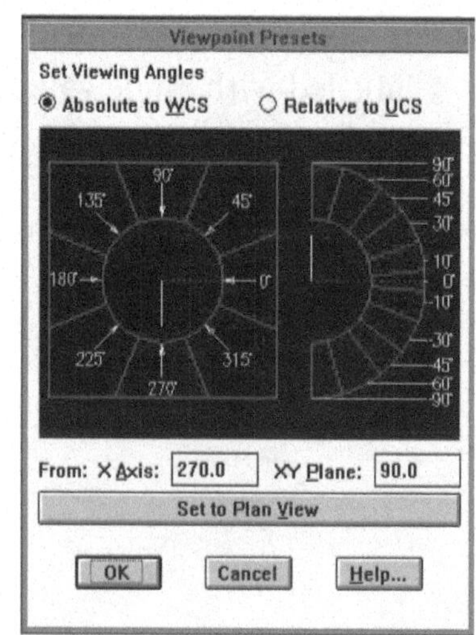

Figure 8

AutoCAD 2021 Menu Reference

Splash screen

Quick Access Toolbar

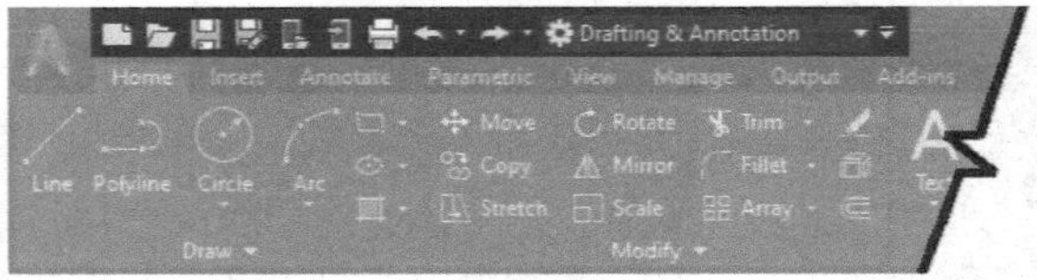

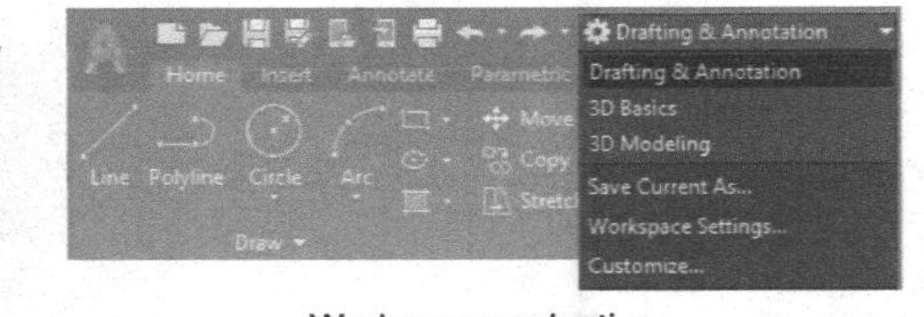

Workspace selection

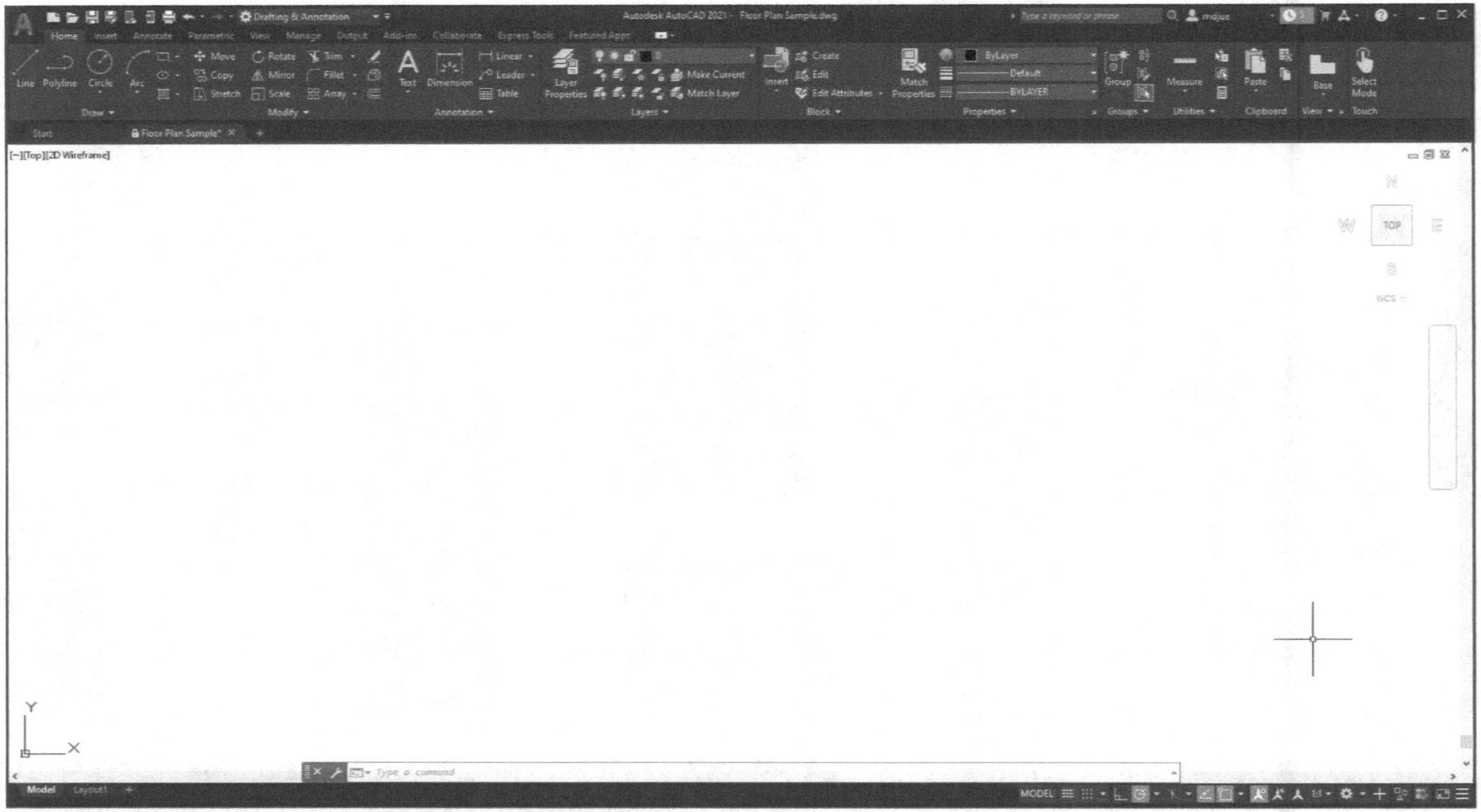

Ribbon Interface at top, central Drawing area and Command line at bottom

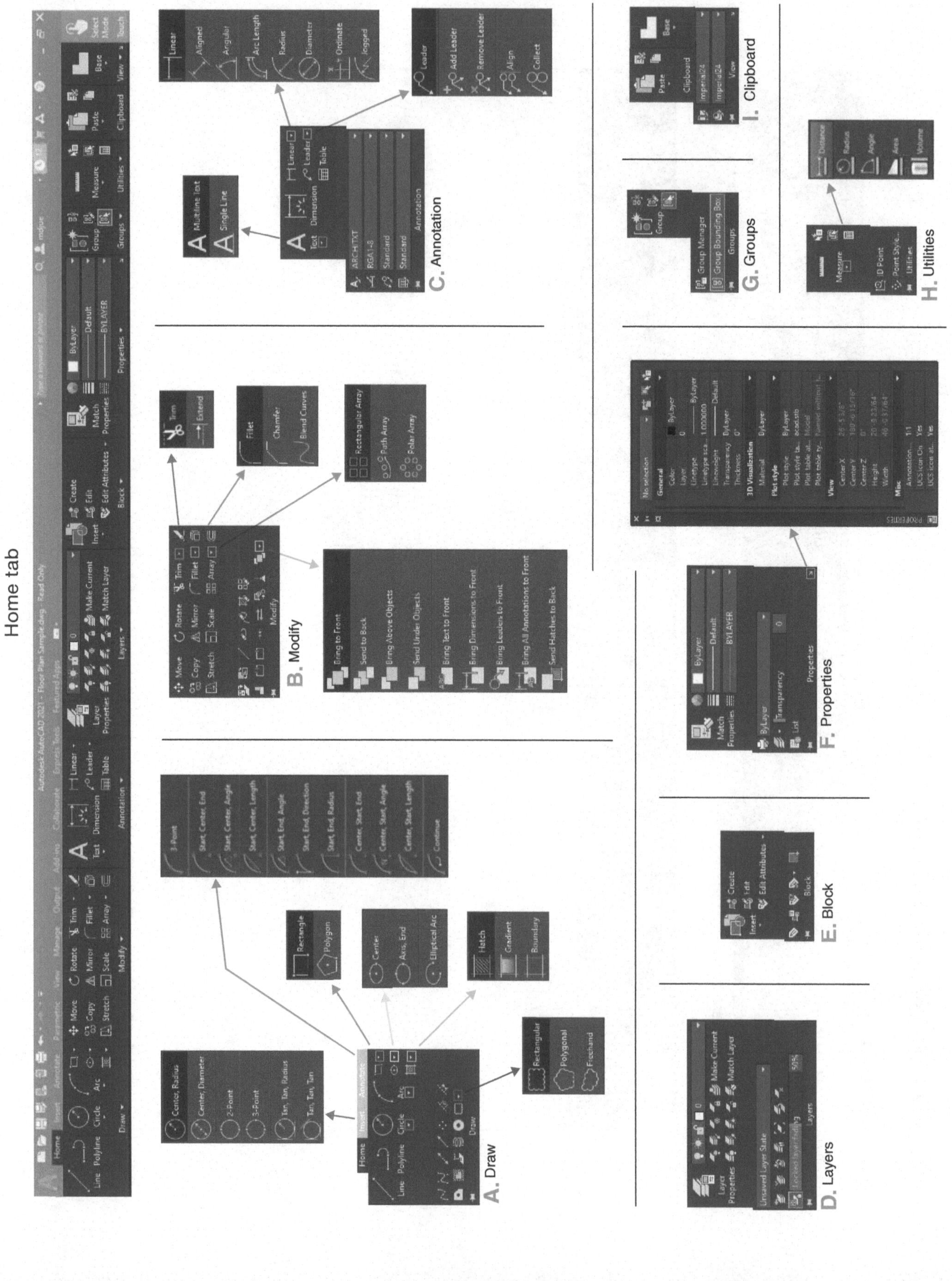

Home tab
A. Draw
B. Modify
C. Annotation
D. Layers
E. Block
F. Properties
G. Groups
H. Utilities
I. Clipboard

Insert tab

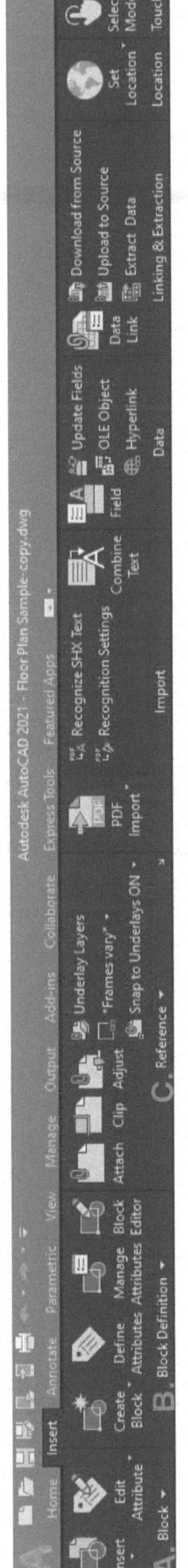

A. Block

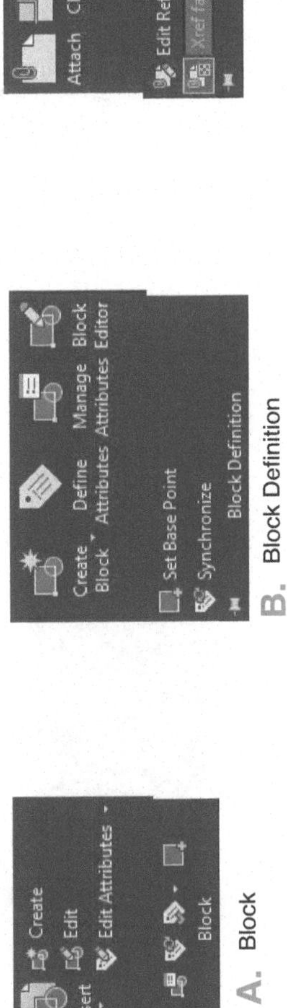

B. Block Definition

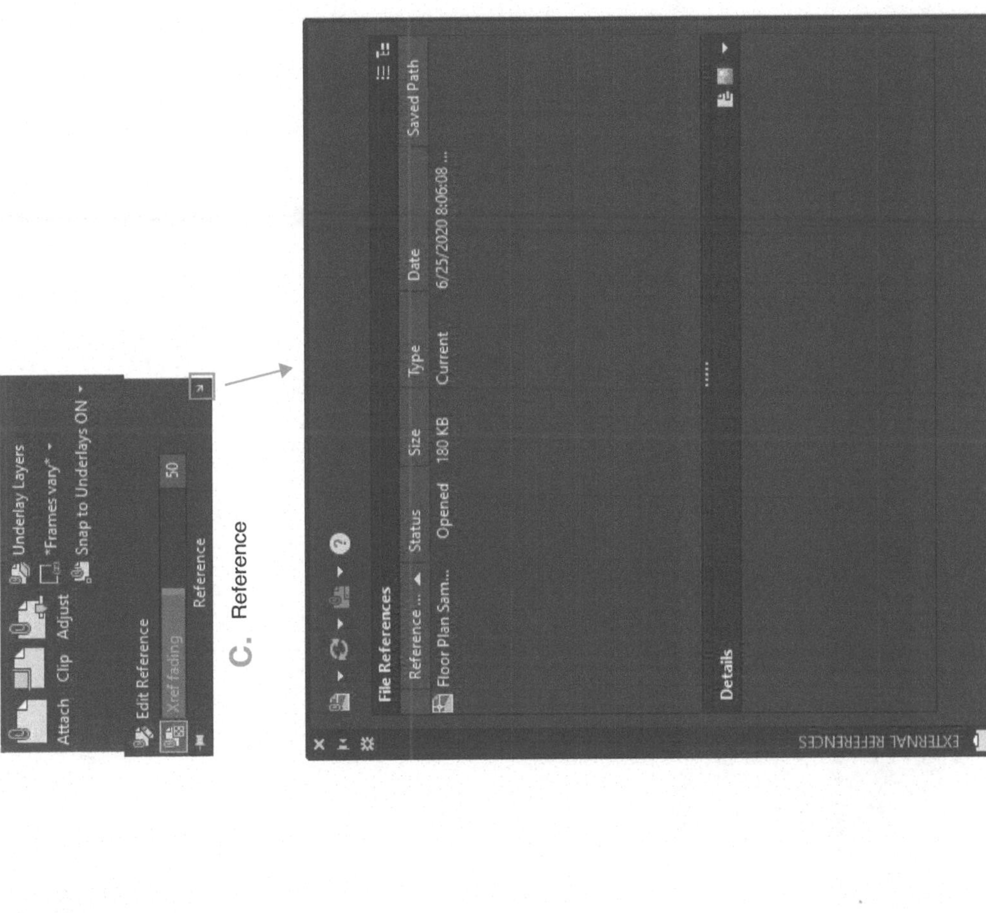

C. Reference

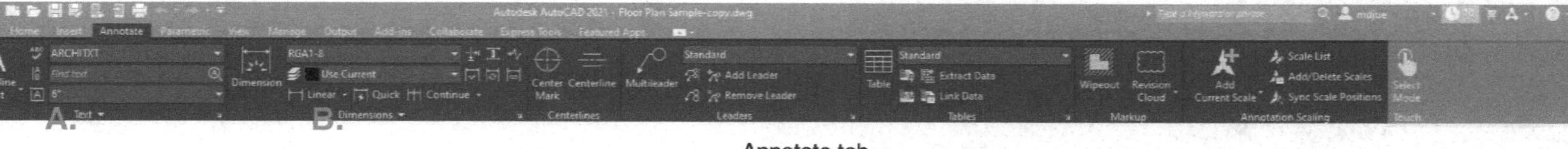

Annotate tab

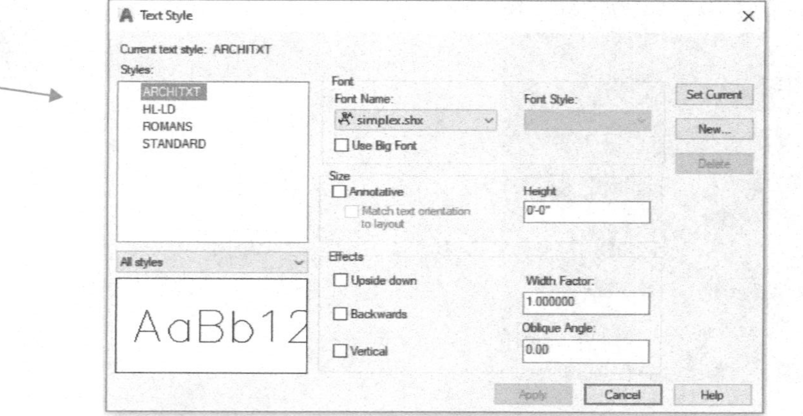

A. Text

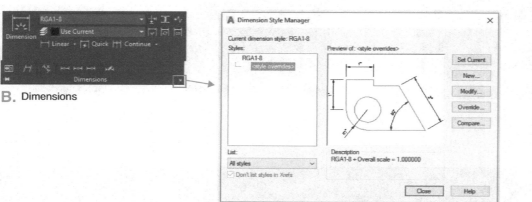

B. Dimensions

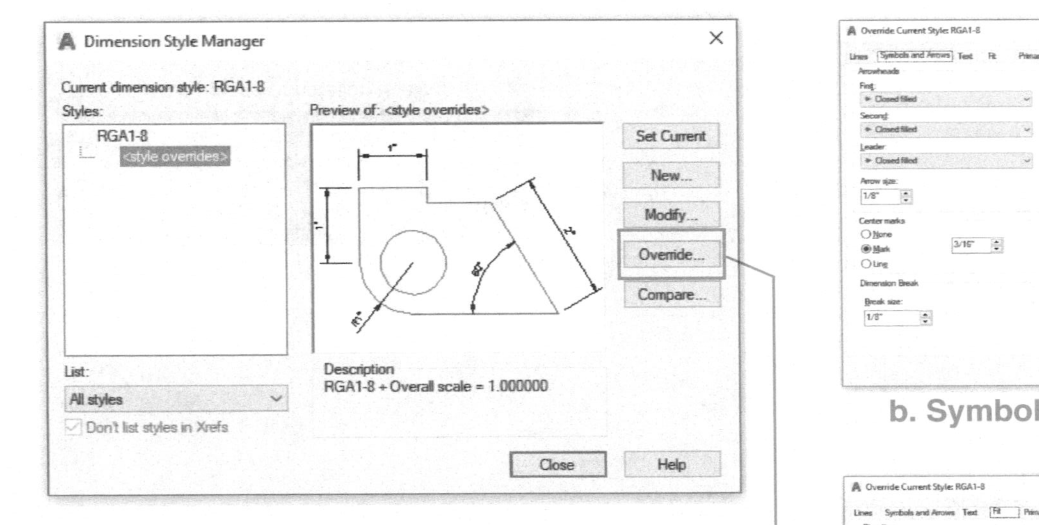

Dimension Style Manager - Override

b. Symbols and Arrows

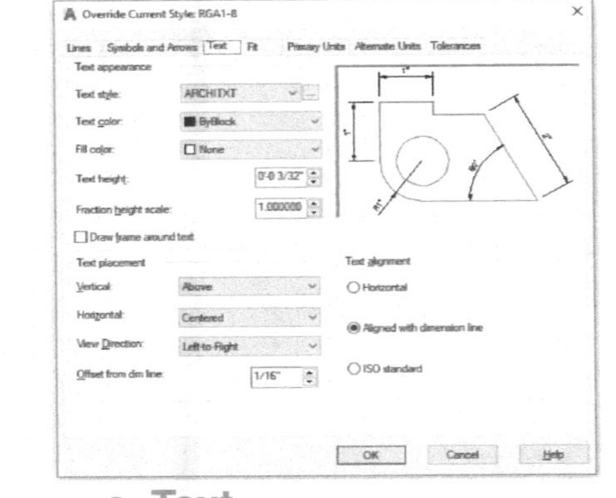

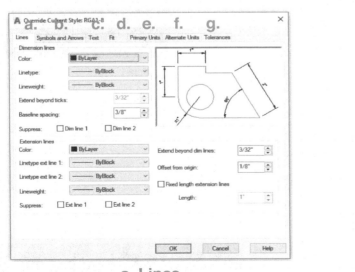

c. Text

a. Lines

Override Current Style

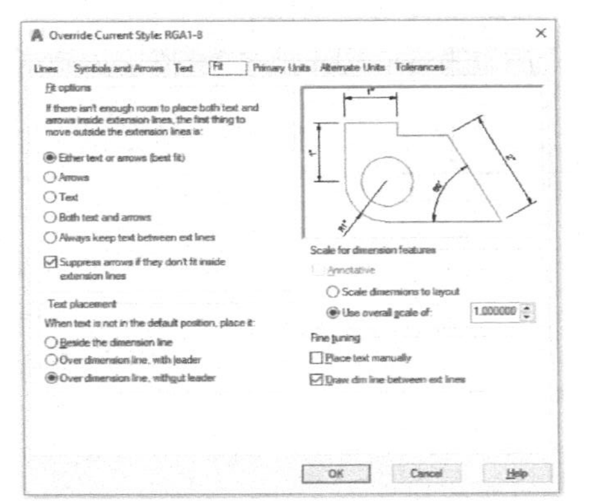

d. Fit

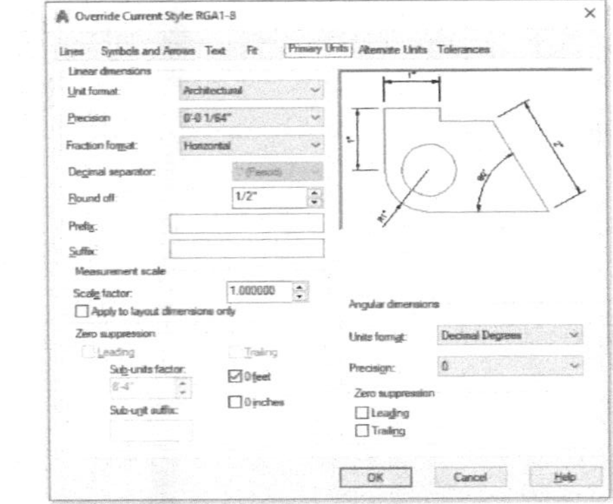

e. Primary Units

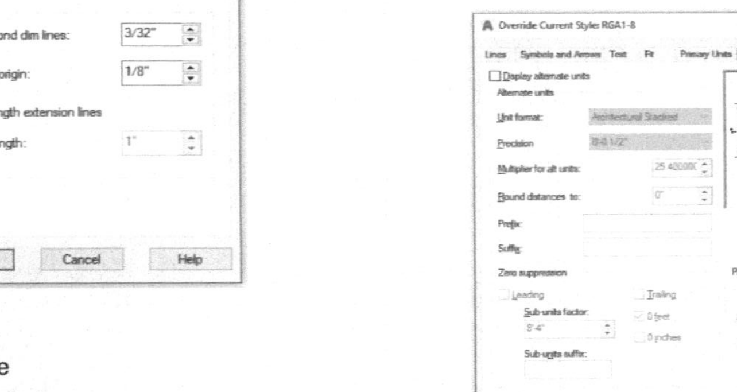

f. Alltternate Units

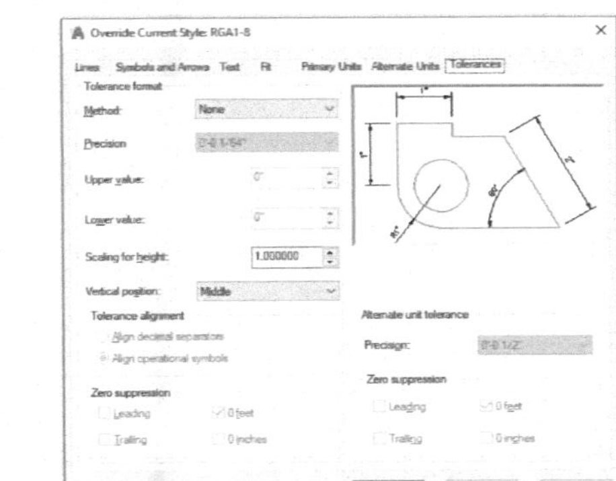

g. Tolerances

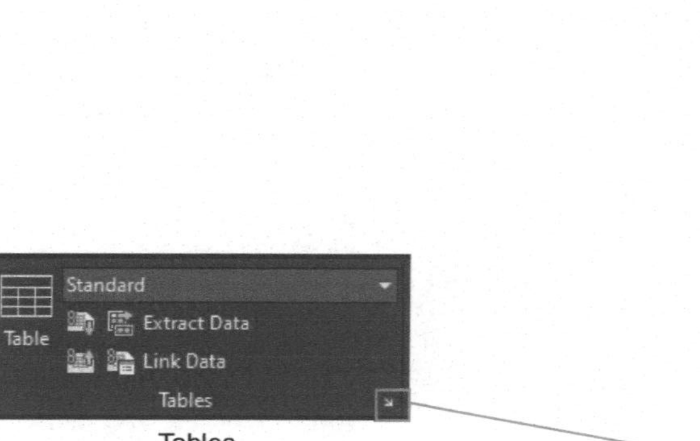

Centerlines and Leaders

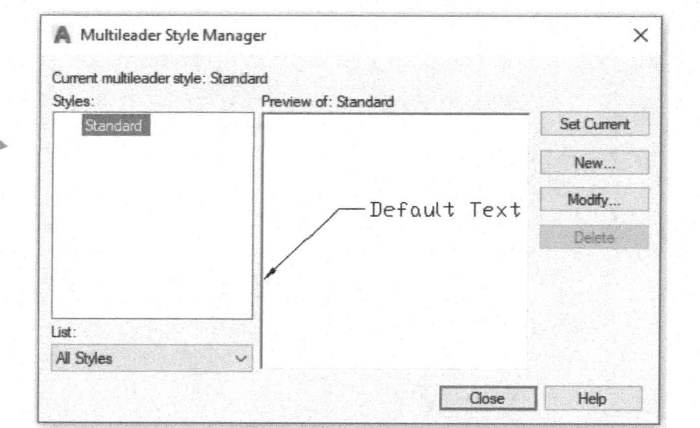

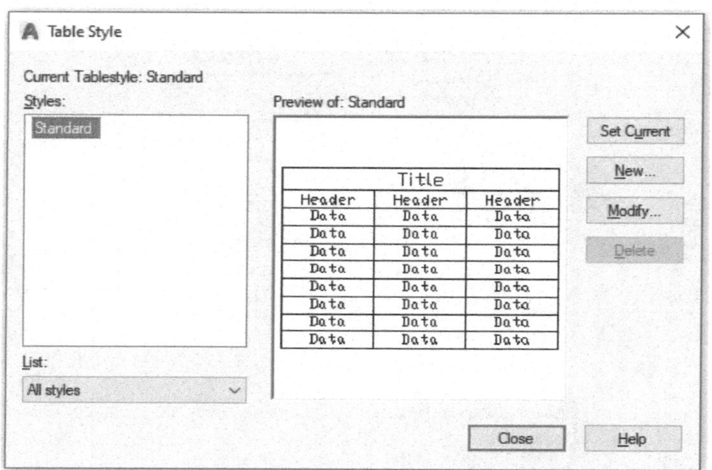

Tables

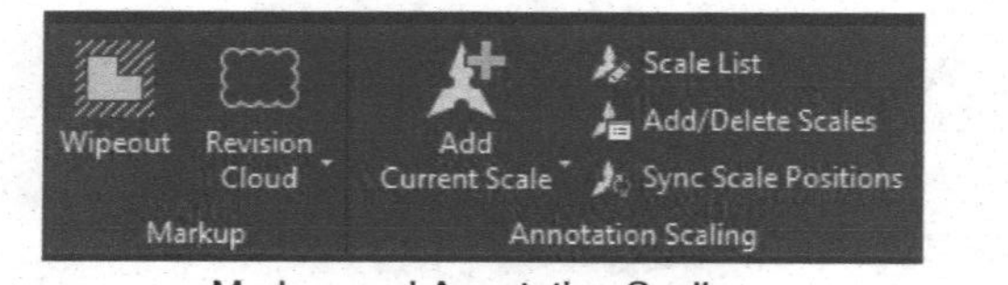

Markup and Annotation Scaling

Parametric tab

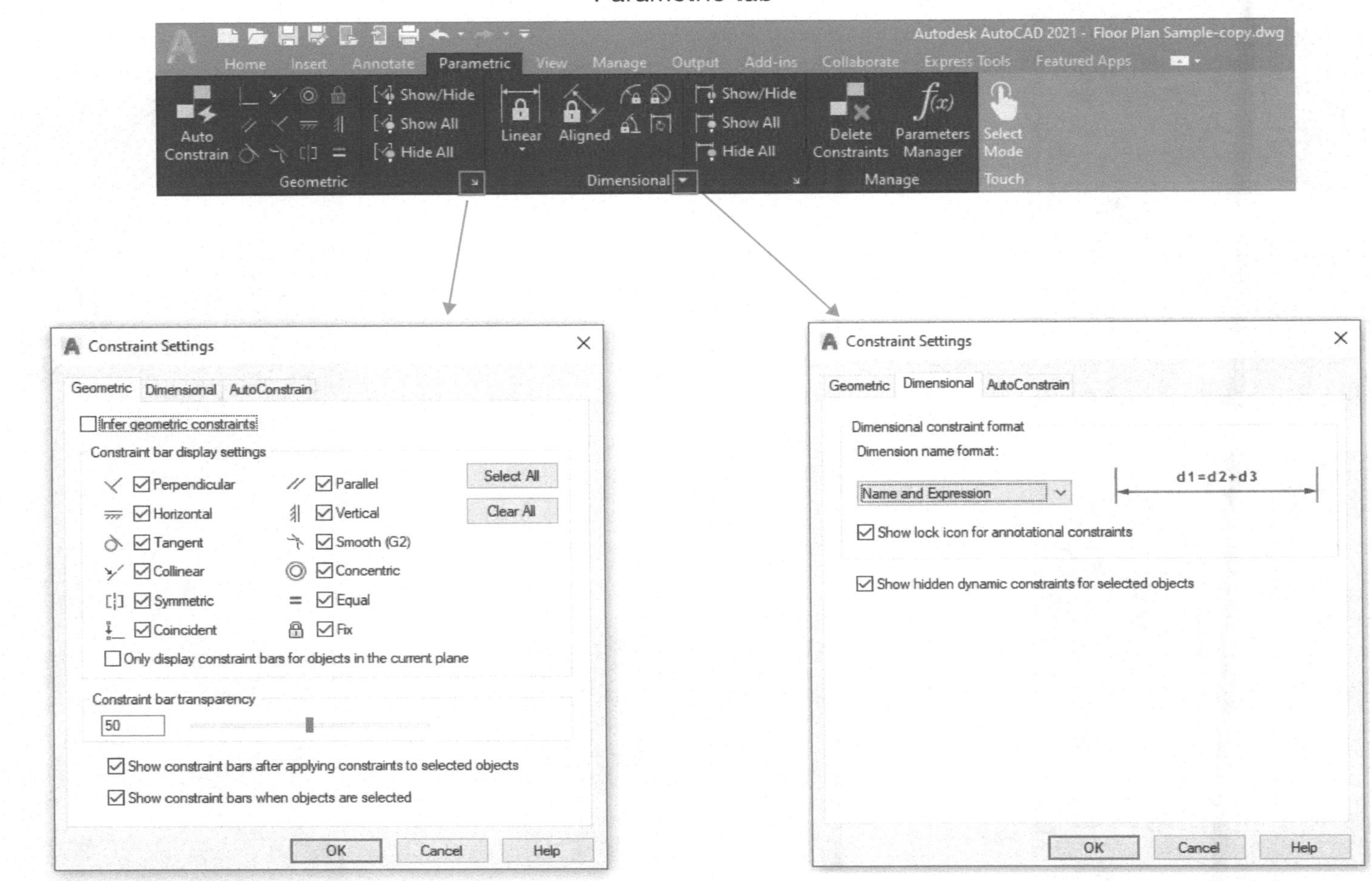

Geometric Constraint Settings

Dimentional Constraint Settings

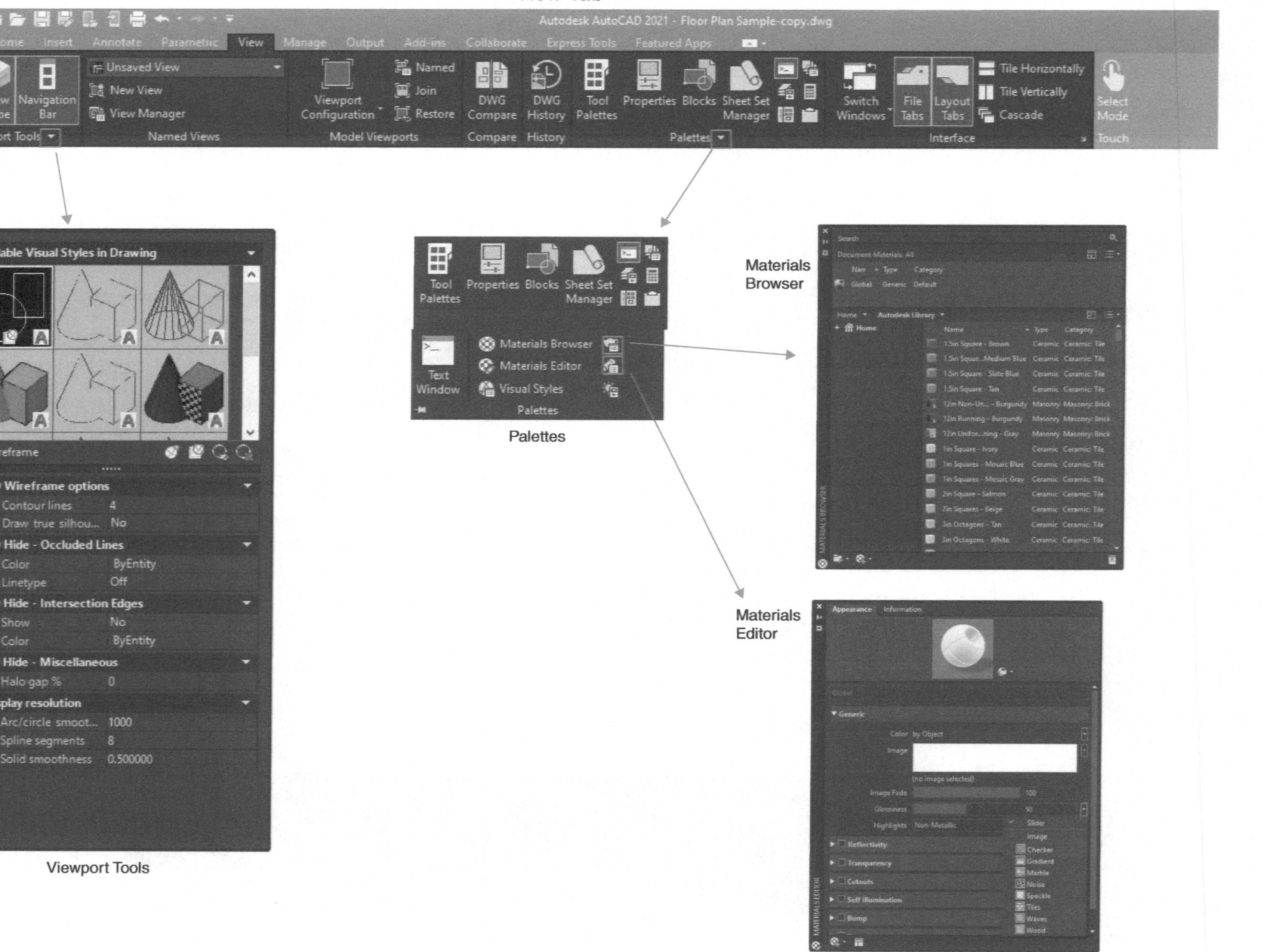
View Tab
Autodesk AutoCAD 2021 - Floor Plan Sample-copy.dwg
Home
Insert
Annotate
Parametric
View
Manage
Output
Add-ins
Collaborate
Express Tools
Featured Apps
UCS Icon
View Cube
Navigation Bar
Viewport Tools
Unsaved View
New View
View Manager
Named Views
Viewport Configuration
Named
Join
Restore
Model Viewports
DWG Compare
Compare
DWG History
History
Tool Palettes
Properties
Blocks
Sheet Set Manager
Palettes
Switch Windows
File Tabs
Layout Tabs
Tile Horizontally
Tile Vertically
Cascade
Interface
Select Mode
Touch
Available Visual Styles in Drawing
2D Wireframe
2D Wireframe options
Contour lines 4
Draw true silhou... No
2D Hide - Occluded Lines
Color ByEntity
Linetype Off
2D Hide - Intersection Edges
Show No
Color ByEntity
2D Hide - Miscellaneous
Halo gap % 0
Display resolution
Arc/circle smoot... 1000
Spline segments 8
Solid smoothness 0.500000
VISUAL STYLES MANAGER
Viewport Tools
Tool Palettes
Properties
Blocks
Sheet Set Manager
Text Window
Materials Browser
Materials Editor
Visual Styles
Palettes
Palettes
Materials Browser
Materials Editor

Interface

Options

Display

Open and Save

Plot and Publish

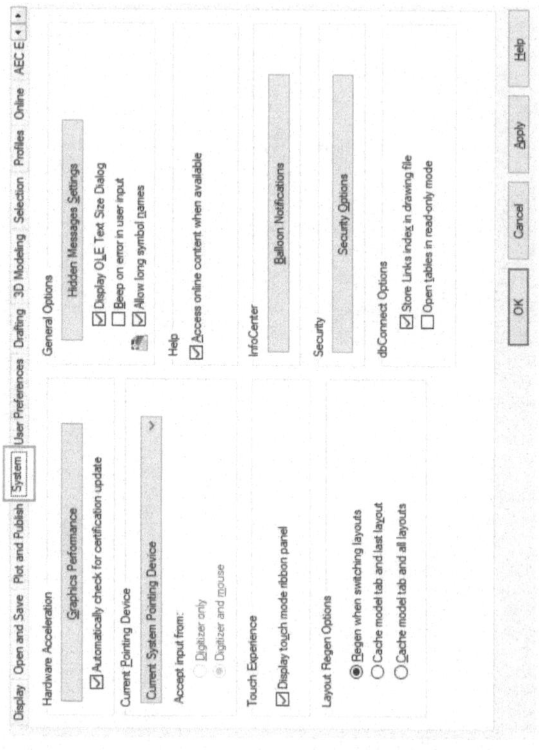

Display | Open and Save | Plot and Publish | System 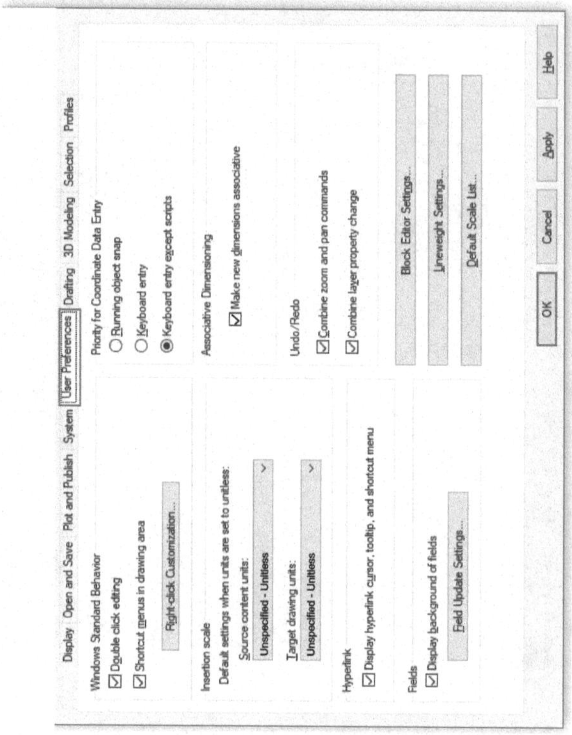 | User Preferences 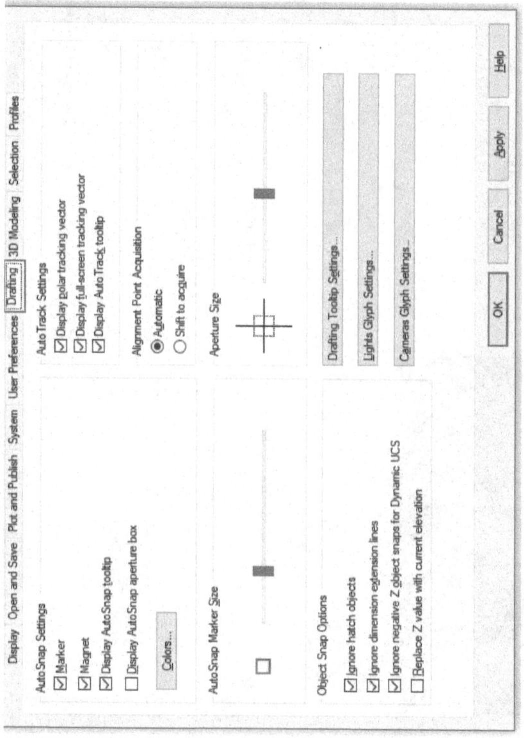 | Drafting | 3D Modeling | Selection | Profiles | Online | AEC E

Hardware Acceleration
Graphics Performance
☑ Automatically check for certification update

Current Pointing Device
Current System Pointing Device
Accept input from:
○ Digitizer only
● Digitizer and mouse

Touch Experience
☑ Display touch mode ribbon panel

Layout Regen Options
● Regen when switching layouts
○ Cache model tab and last layout
○ Cache model tab and all layouts

General Options
Hidden Messages Settings
☑ Display OLE Text Size Dialog
☐ Beep on error in user input
☑ Allow long symbol names

Help
☑ Access online content when available

InfoCenter
Balloon Notifications

Security
Security Options

dbConnect Options
☑ Store Links index in drawing file
☐ Open tables in read-only mode

OK | Cancel | Apply | Help

System

Display | Open and Save | Plot and Publish | System | User Preferences | Drafting | 3D Modeling | Selection | Profiles

Windows Standard Behavior
☑ Double click editing
☑ Shortcut menus in drawing area
Right-click Customization...

Insertion scale
Default settings when units are set to unitless:
Source content units:
Unspecified - Unitless
Target drawing units:
Unspecified - Unitless

Hyperlink
☑ Display hyperlink cursor, tooltip, and shortcut menu

Fields
☑ Display background of fields
Field Update Settings...

Priority for Coordinate Data Entry
○ Running object snap
○ Keyboard entry
● Keyboard entry except scripts

Associative Dimensioning
☑ Make new dimensions associative

Undo/Redo
☑ Combine zoom and pan commands
☑ Combine layer property change

Block Editor Settings...
Lineweight Settings...
Default Scale List...

OK | Cancel | Apply | Help

User Preferences

Display | Open and Save | Plot and Publish | System | User Preferences | Drafting | 3D Modeling | Selection | Profiles

AutoSnap Settings
☑ Marker
☑ Magnet
☑ Display AutoSnap tooltip
☐ Display AutoSnap aperture box
Colors...

AutoSnap Marker Size

Object Snap Options
☑ Ignore hatch objects
☑ Ignore dimension extension lines
☑ Ignore negative Z object snaps for Dynamic UCS
☐ Replace Z value with current elevation

AutoTrack Settings
☑ Display polar tracking vector
☑ Display full-screen tracking vector
☑ Display AutoTrack tooltip

Alignment Point Acquisition
● Automatic
○ Shift to acquire

Aperture Size

Drafting Tooltip Settings...
Lights Glyph Settings...
Cameras Glyph Settings...

OK | Cancel | Apply | Help

Drafting

Display | Open and Save | Plot and Publish | System | User Preferences | Drafting | 3D Modeling | Selection | Profiles

3D Crosshairs
☑ Show Z axis in crosshairs
☐ Label axes in standard crosshairs
☐ Show labels for dynamic UCS
Crosshair labels
● Use X, Y, Z
○ Use N, E, z
○ Use custom labels
X | Y | Z

Display Tools in Viewport
Display the ViewCube
☑ 2D Wireframe visual style
☑ All other visual styles
Display the UCS Icon
☑ 2D Wireframe visual style
☑ All other visual styles
☑ Display the Viewport Controls

3D Objects
Visual Style while creating 3D objects
ByViewport
Deletion control while creating 3D objects
Only delete profile and path curves for solids
Isolines on surfaces
6 in U | 6 in V
Maximum point cloud points per drawing
10000000
Tesselation... | Mesh Primitives...
Surface Analysis...

3D Navigation
☐ Reverse mouse wheel zoom
Walk and Fly ... | ViewCube ...
Animation ... | SteeringWheels ...

Dynamic Input
☐ Show Z field for pointer input

OK | Cancel | Apply | Help

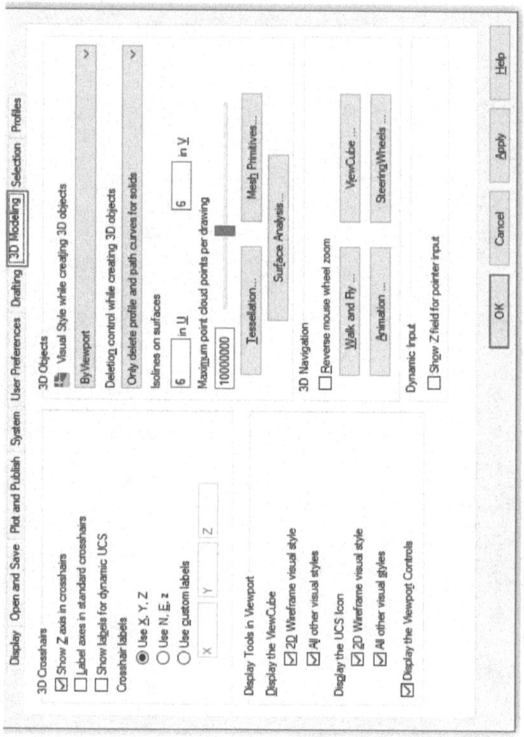

3D Modeling

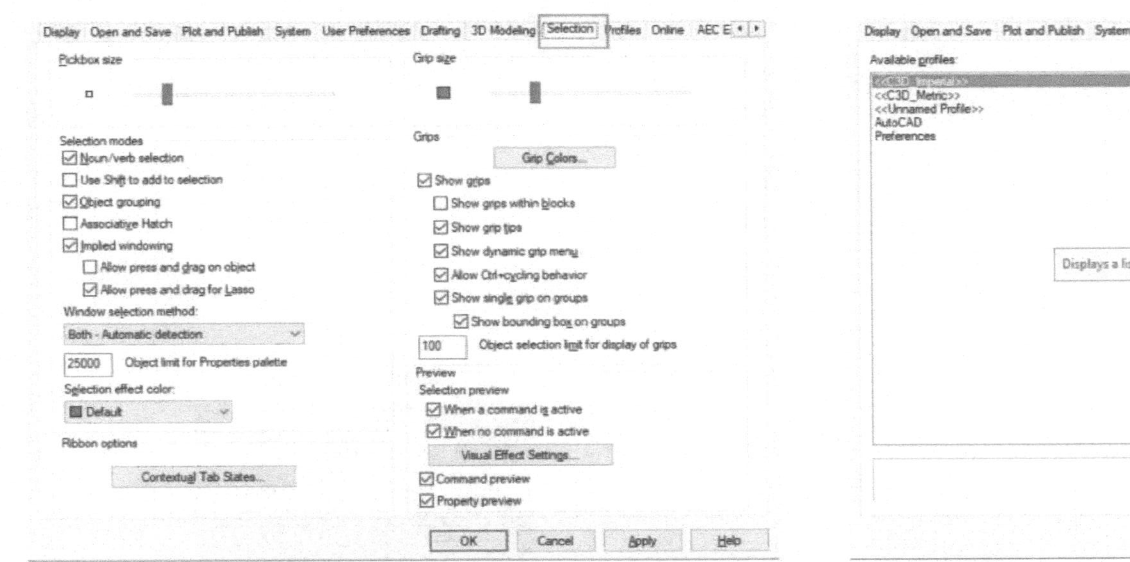
Selection

Profiles

Online

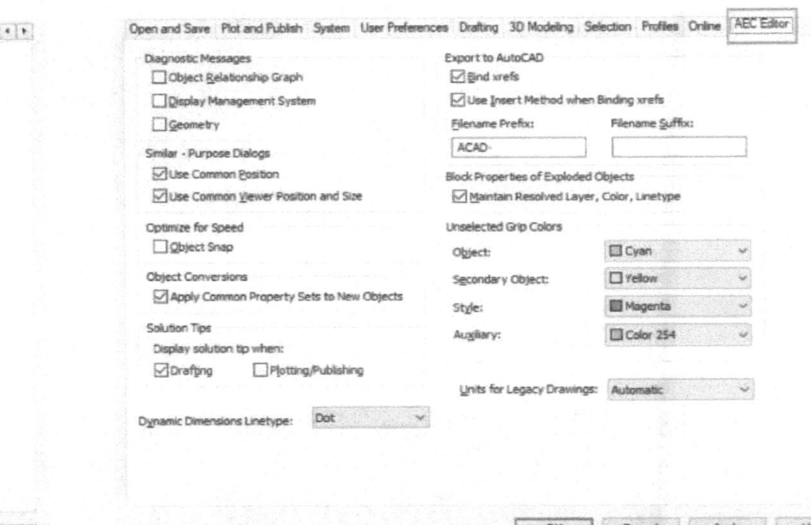
AEC Editor

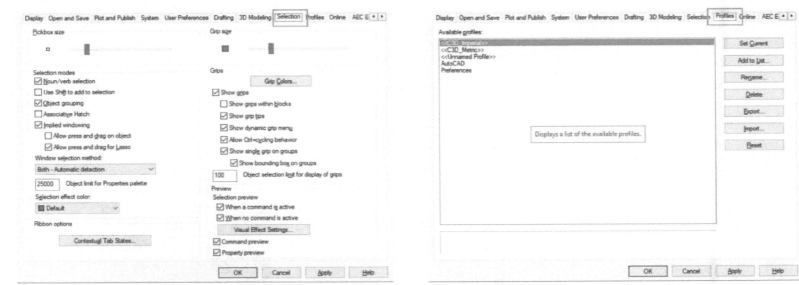

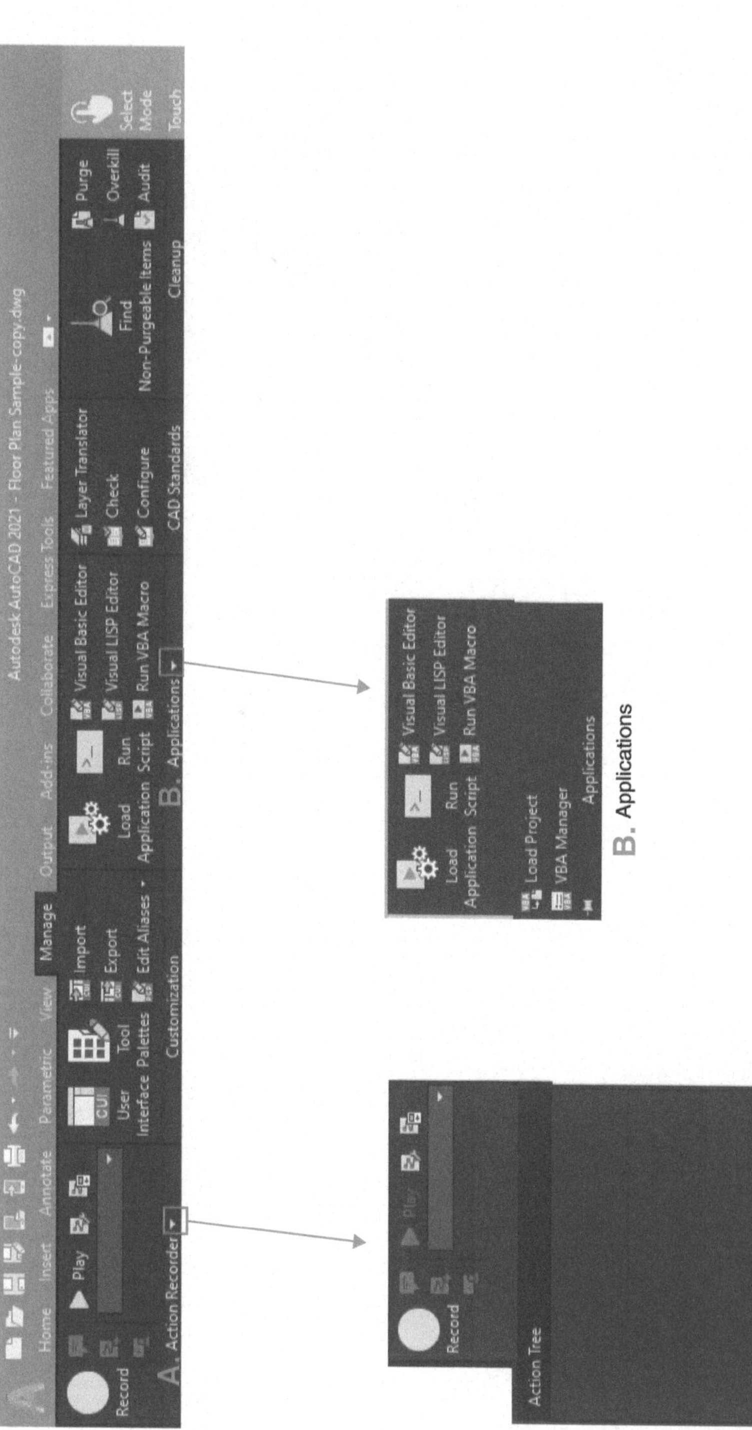

A. Action Recorder

B. Applications

Output tab

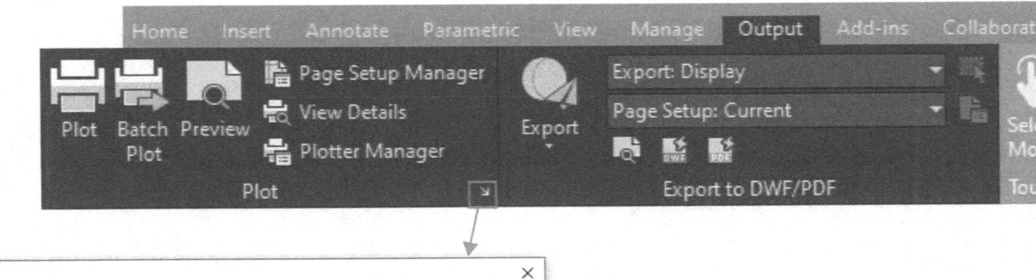

Plot Options

Autodesk 360 tab

Add-ins tab

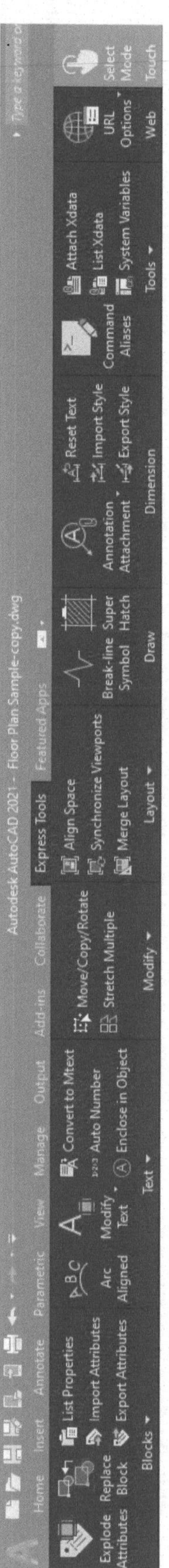

Express Tools tab

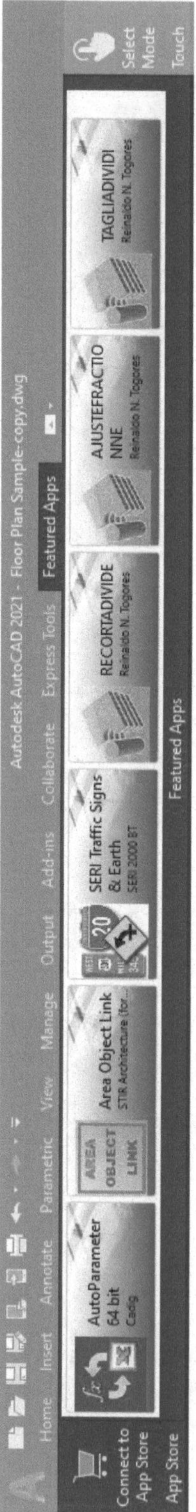

Featured Apps tab

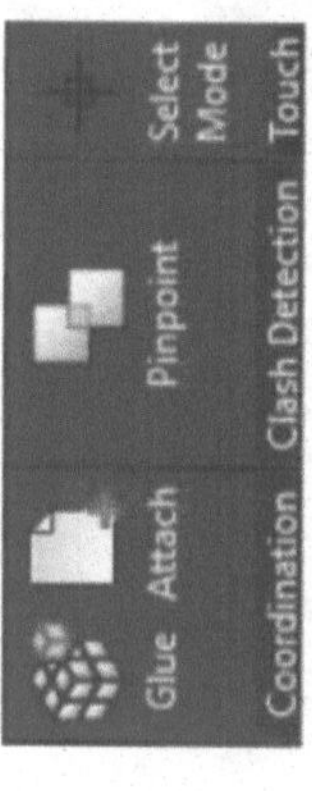

BIM 360 tab

Performance tab

Answers Section (to Selected Questions)

Page 64 CHALLENGE QUESTIONS

1. A little over 1 : 1
2. View Controls, Key-in Field, Drawing Group, Ribbon Interface,
3. Drag
4. Zoom In, Zoom Out, Window Area, Fit View, View Previous, View Next

Page 78 CHALLENGE QUESTIONS

1. 6:7
2. 0:7.356 or :7.356
3. 4.95
4. 129:8.75

Page 99 CHALLENGE QUESTIONS

1. The tool settings box appears when a tool is activated that has settings.
2. At the locks icon at the lower right of the screen.
3. No
4. <Ctrl> b
5. Hit <Enter> for MicroStation V8i or for the CONNECT Edition
6. Metric
7. a. 5.379 b. 5:4 c. No, 10:9 is10 feet, 9 inches, while 10.9 is 10 feet and 0.9 feet
8. Polar Coordinate entry (or relative polar coordinate entry)
9. Absolute Coordinates
10. Relative Cartesian Coordinates, Delta X and Delta Y

Page 128 CHALLENGE QUESTIONS

1. Keypoint Snap, Intersect Snap, Center Snap
2. Yes
3. Perhaps forgot to set the Working Units and they are at default mu (metric)
4. Color, Line-Style, Line Weight
5. CO=, LC=, WT=

Page 141 CHALLENGE QUESTIONS

1. TX=, FT=, TH=, TW=, LS=
2. Default
3. INSIDE, OVERLAP, CLIP, VOID
4. No
5. ON=ALL, OF=ALL
6. Select Place Fence once again.

Page 166 CHALLENGE QUESTIONS

1. No, Dimensions are elements placed onto your drawing, Measurements are temporary readings.
2. No
3. Dimension Line, Dimension Text, Extension or Witness Lines, Terminators
4. Using View Alignment the dimension aligns to X or Y axis, True will align to the element
5. The element goes to a heavy dotted appearance. Association Lock
6. Dimension Linear
7. There is a hole in the shape you are trying to measure by flood

Page 170 Practice conversions

1. 73 degrees
2. 121.5 degrees
3. 0.75 degree
4. N61^00'00"E or N61^E (short-hand expression, when both minutes and seconds are 0)

Page 229 Quiz

c. xy = 7, 4
d. xy = 5, 5
e. xy = 2, 5
h. dL = 3, 1 (or *dl* = 3, 1)
i. dL = −4, 2 (or *dl* = −4, 2)
j. dL = −2, 0 (or *dl* = −2, 0)
o. di = 2, −90 or 2, 270
p. di = 7, 15
q. di = 2.5, 102
r. di = 7.2, 180

INDEX for AutoCAD Material

0–9

A–B

C

I

K

L

M–N

O

P

R

S–T

U–V

WXYZ

Index for MicroStation Material

Note:
*For **AutoCAD** specific entries, please see the **INDEX for AutoCAD Materials** (pg 369)*

Index

M (*continued*) page# slide#

N page# slide#

O page# slide#

P page# slide#

R page# slide#

R (*continued*)	page#	slide#

S	page#	slide#

S (*continued*)	page#	slide#

T	page#	slide#

T (*continued*) page# slide#

U page# slide#

V page# slide#

V (*continued*) page# slide#

W page# slide#

Z page# slide#

LAST NAME - FIRST INITIAL

ASSIGNMENT:

COURSE # - SECTION #

DATE:

NOTES:

SCALE:

FIRST-ANGLE

THIRD-ANGLE